W9-AUD-090

TOMARE!

[STOP!]

You are going the wrong way!

Manga is a completely different type of reading experience.

To start at the *beginning*, go to the *end*!

That's right! Authentic manga is read the traditional Japanese way—from right to left, exactly the *opposite* of how American books are read. It's easy to follow: Just go to the other end of the book, and read each page—and each panel—from the right side to the left side, starting at the top right. Now you're experiencing manga as it was meant to be.

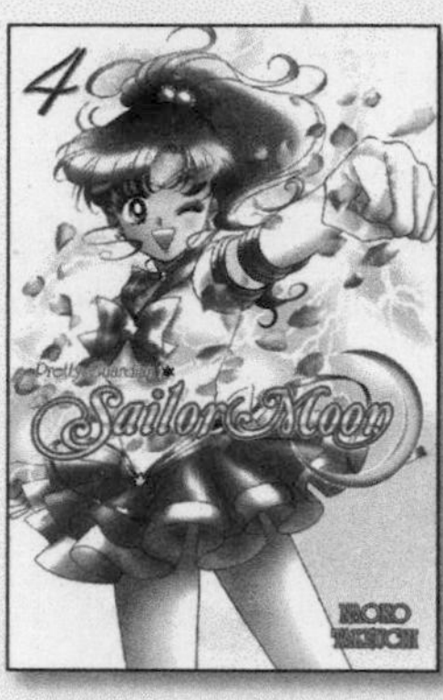
4
Pretty Guardian
Sailor Moon
NAOKO TAKEUCHI

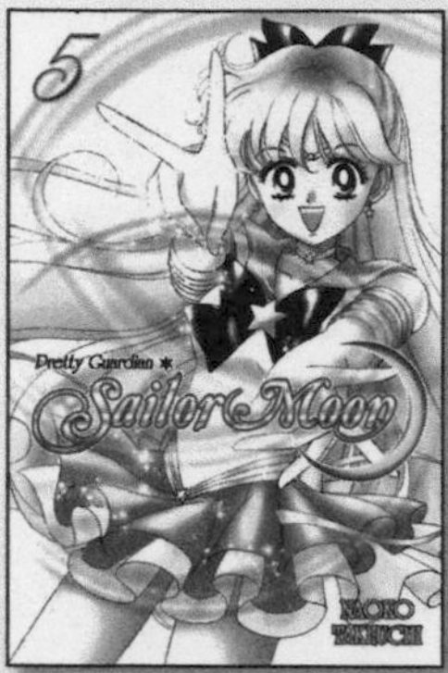
5
Pretty Guardian
Sailor Moon
NAOKO TAKEUCHI

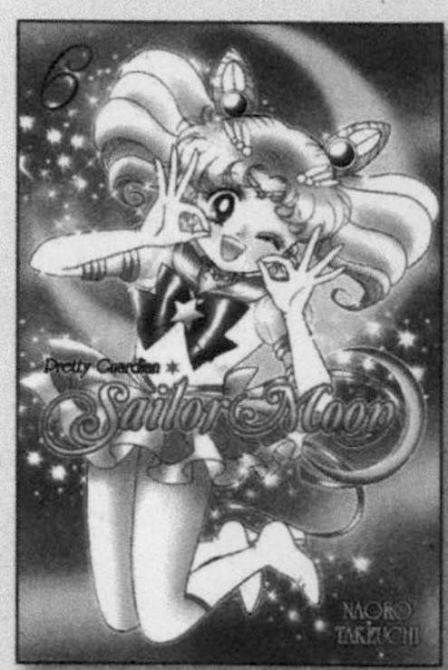
6
Pretty Guardian
Sailor Moon
NAOKO TAKEUCHI

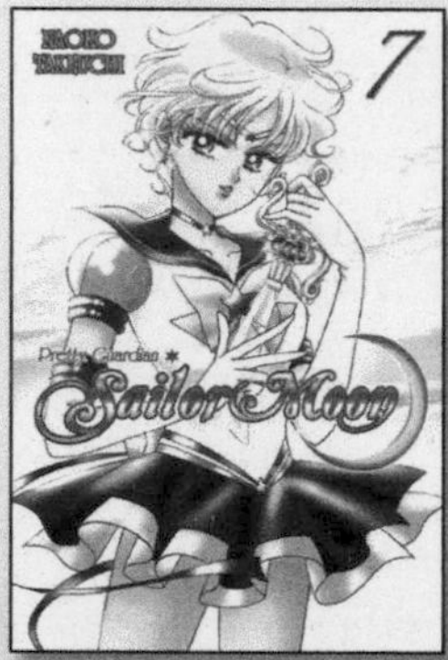
NAOKO TAKEUCHI
7
Pretty Guardian
Sailor Moon

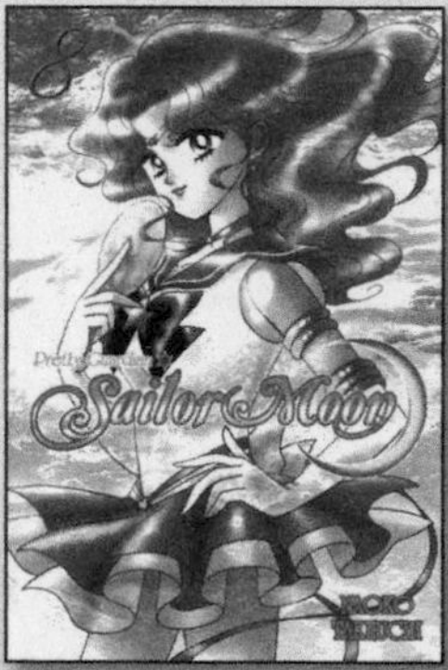
8
Sailor Moon
NAOKO TAKEUCHI

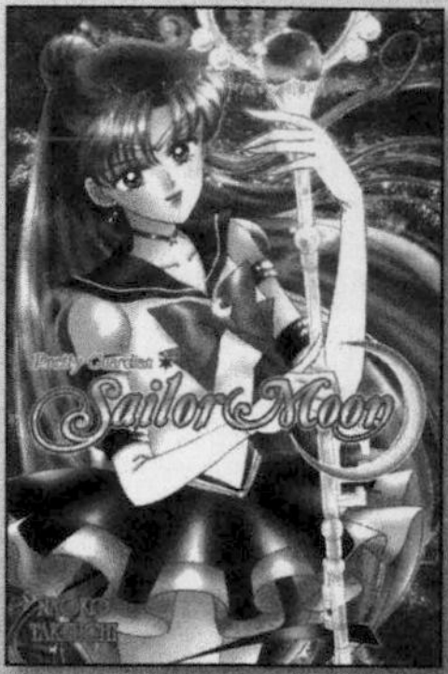
9
Pretty Guardian
Sailor Moon
NAOKO TAKEUCHI

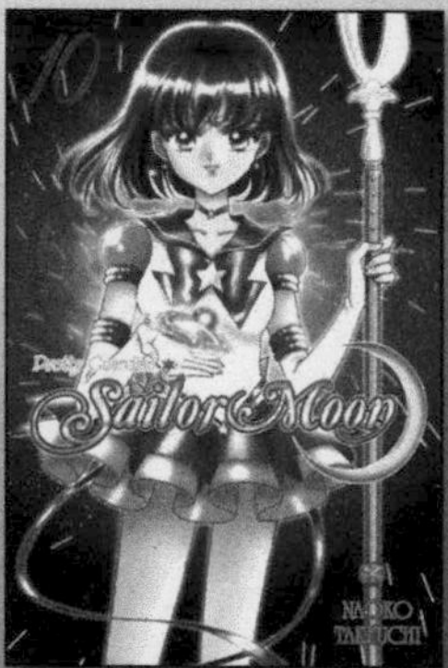
10
Sailor Moon
NAOKO TAKEUCHI

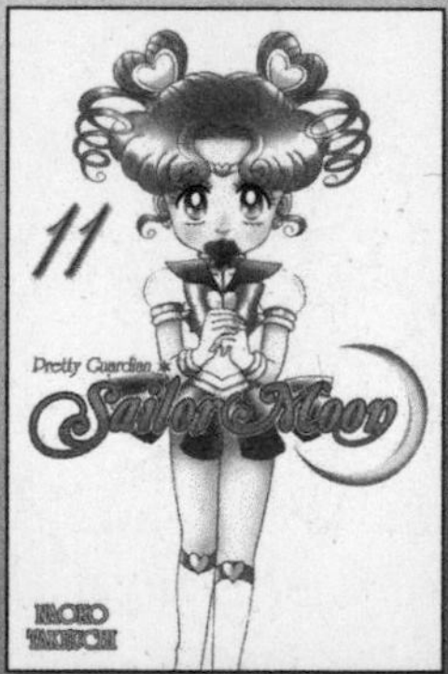
11
Pretty Guardian
Sailor Moon
NAOKO TAKEUCHI

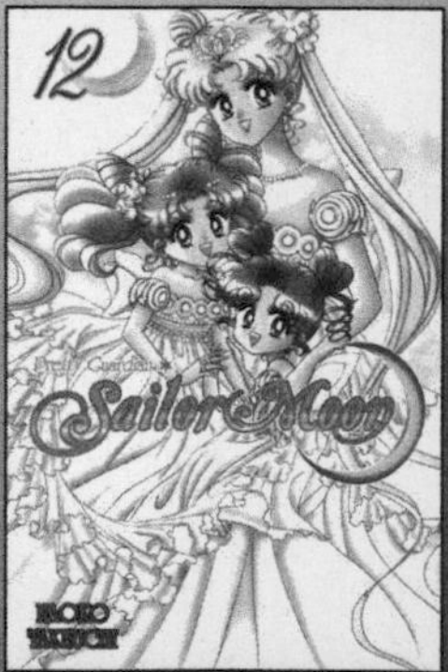
12
Pretty Guardian
Sailor Moon
NAOKO TAKEUCHI

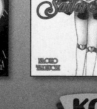

KC
KODANSHA COMICS

I Am Here! volume 1 is a work of fiction. Names, characters, places, and incidents are the products of the author's imagination or are used fictitiously. Any resemblance to actual events, locales, or persons, living or dead, is entirely coincidental.

A Kodansha Comics Trade Paperback Original

Published in the United States by Kodansha Comics, an imprint of Kodansha USA Publishing, LLC., New York.

Publication rights for this English edition arranged through Kodansha Ltd., Tokyo.

First published in Japan in 2007–2008 by Kodansha Ltd., Tokyo, as *Ko Ko Ni Iru Yo* volumes 1, 2, and 3.

ISBN 978-1-61262-336-8

Printed in the United States of America.

www.kodanshacomics.com

9 8 7 6 5 4

Translator/Adapter: Joshua Weeks
Lettering: North Market Street Graphics

I am Here!

Volume 1

Ema Toyama

Translated and adapted by
Joshua Weeks

Lettered by
North Market Street Graphics

KC
KODANSHA
COMICS

CONTENTS

Honorifics Explained

Throughout the Kodansha Comics books, you will find Japanese honorifics left intact in the translations. For those not familiar with how the Japanese use honorifics and, more important, how they differ from American honorifics, we present this brief overview.

Politeness has always been a critical facet of Japanese culture. Ever since the feudal era, when Japan was a highly stratified society, use of honorifics—which can be defined as polite speech that indicates relationship or status—has played an essential role in the Japanese language. When addressing someone in Japanese, an honorific usually takes the form of a suffix attached to one's name (example: "Asuna-san"), is used as a title at the end of one's name, or appears in place of the name itself (example: "Negi-sensei," or simply "Sensei!").

Honorifics can be expressions of respect or endearment. In the context of manga and anime, honorifics give insight into the nature of the relationship between characters. Many English translations leave out these important honorifics and therefore distort the feel of the original Japanese. Because Japanese honorifics contain nuances that English honorifics lack, it is our policy at Kodansha Comics not to translate them. Here, instead, is a guide to some of the honorifics you may encounter in Kodansha Comics books.

-san: This is the most common honorific and is equivalent to Mr., Miss, Ms., or Mrs. It is the all-purpose honorific and can be used in any situation where politeness is required

-sama: This is one level higher than "-san" and is used to confer great respect.

-dono: This comes from the word "tono," which means "lord." It is an even higher level than "-sama" and confers utmost respect.

-kun: This suffix is used at the end of boys' names to express familiarity or endearment. It is also sometimes used by men among friends, or when addressing someone younger or of a lower station.

-chan: This is used to express endearment, mostly toward girls. It is also used for little boys, pets, and even among lovers. It gives a sense of childish cuteness.

Bozu: This is an informal way to refer to a boy, similar to the English terms "kid" and "squirt."

Sempai/ Senpai: This title suggests that the addressee is one's senior in a group or organization. It is most often used in a school setting, where underclassmen refer to their upperclassmen as "sempai." It can also be used in the workplace, such as when a newer employee addresses an employee who has seniority in the company.

Kohai: This is the opposite of "sempai" and is used toward underclassmen in school or newcomers in the workplace. It connotes that the addressee is of a lower station.

Sensei: Literally meaning "one who has come before," this title is used for teachers, doctors, or masters of any profession or art.

-[blank]: This is usually forgotten in these lists, but it is perhaps the most significant difference between Japanese and English. The lack of honorific means that the speaker has permission to address the person in a very intimate way. Usually, only family, spouses, or very close friends have this kind of permission. Known as *yobisute*, it can be gratifying when someone who has earned the intimacy starts to call one by one's name without an honorific. But when that intimacy hasn't been earned, it can be very insulting.

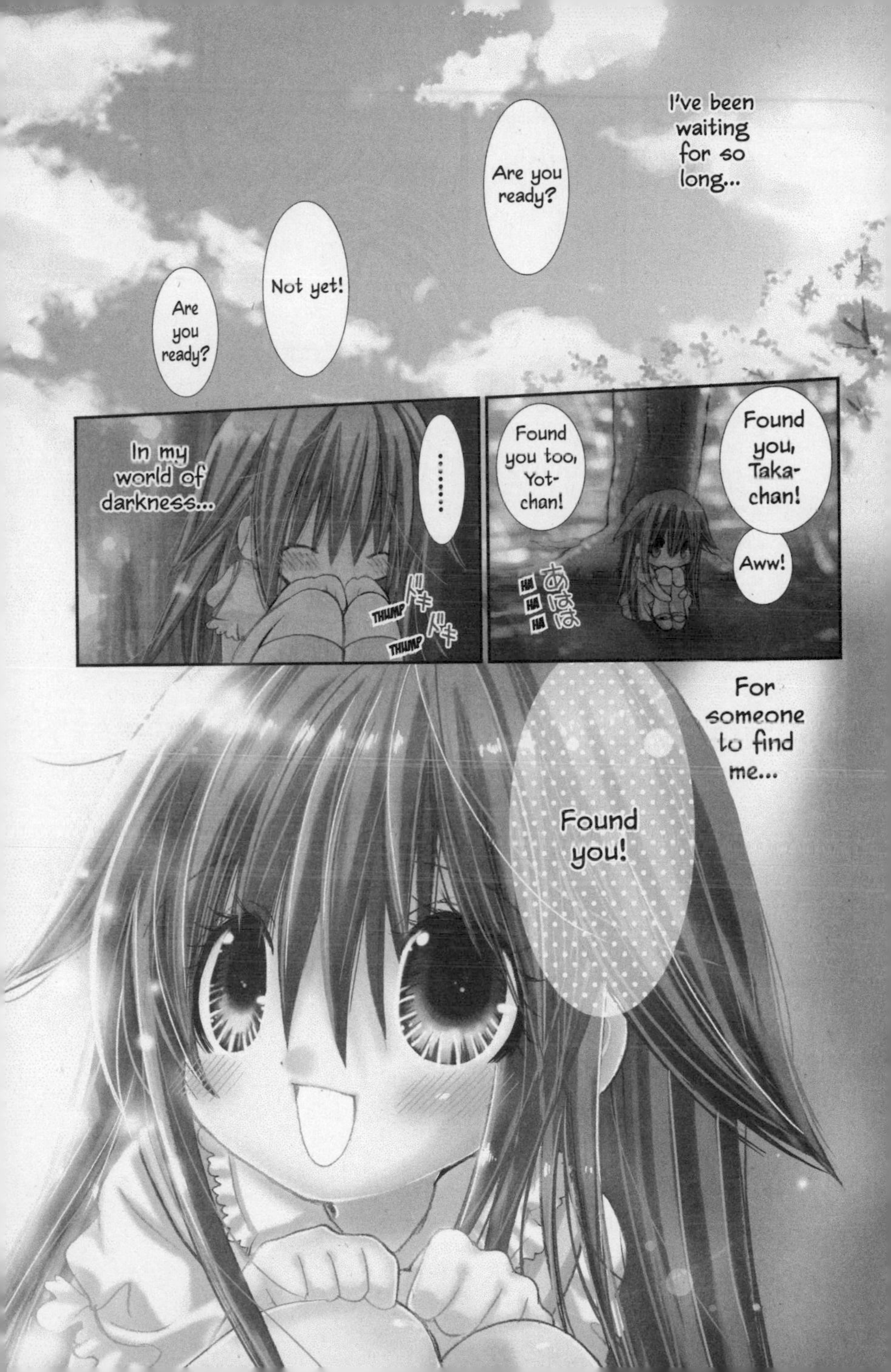
I've been waiting for so long...
Are you ready?
Not yet!
Are you ready?
Found you, Taka-chan!
Found you too, Yot-chan!
Aww!
あはは
HA HA HA
......
In my world of darkness...
ドキドキ
THUMP THUMP
For someone to find me...
Found you!

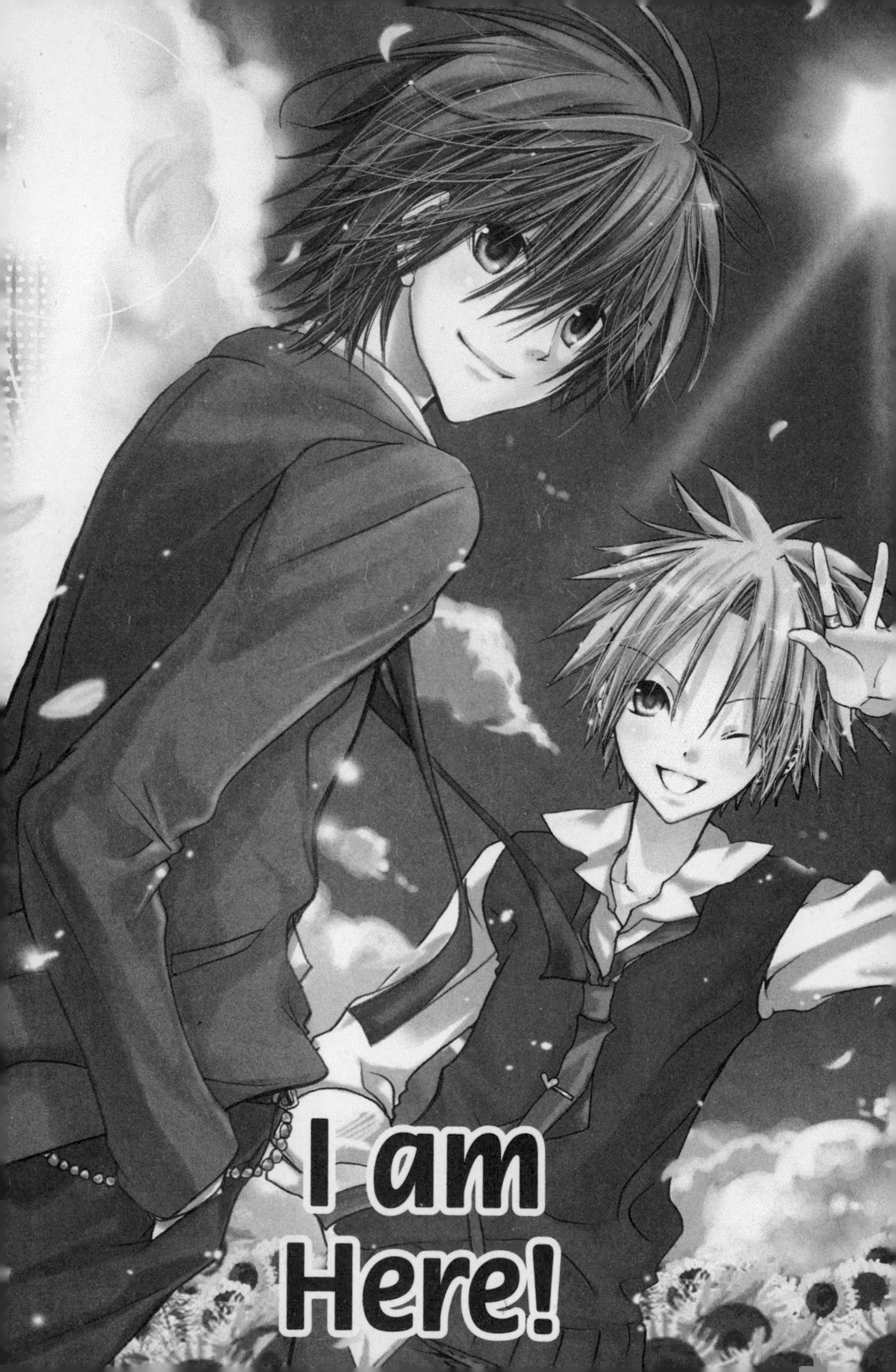
I am
Here!

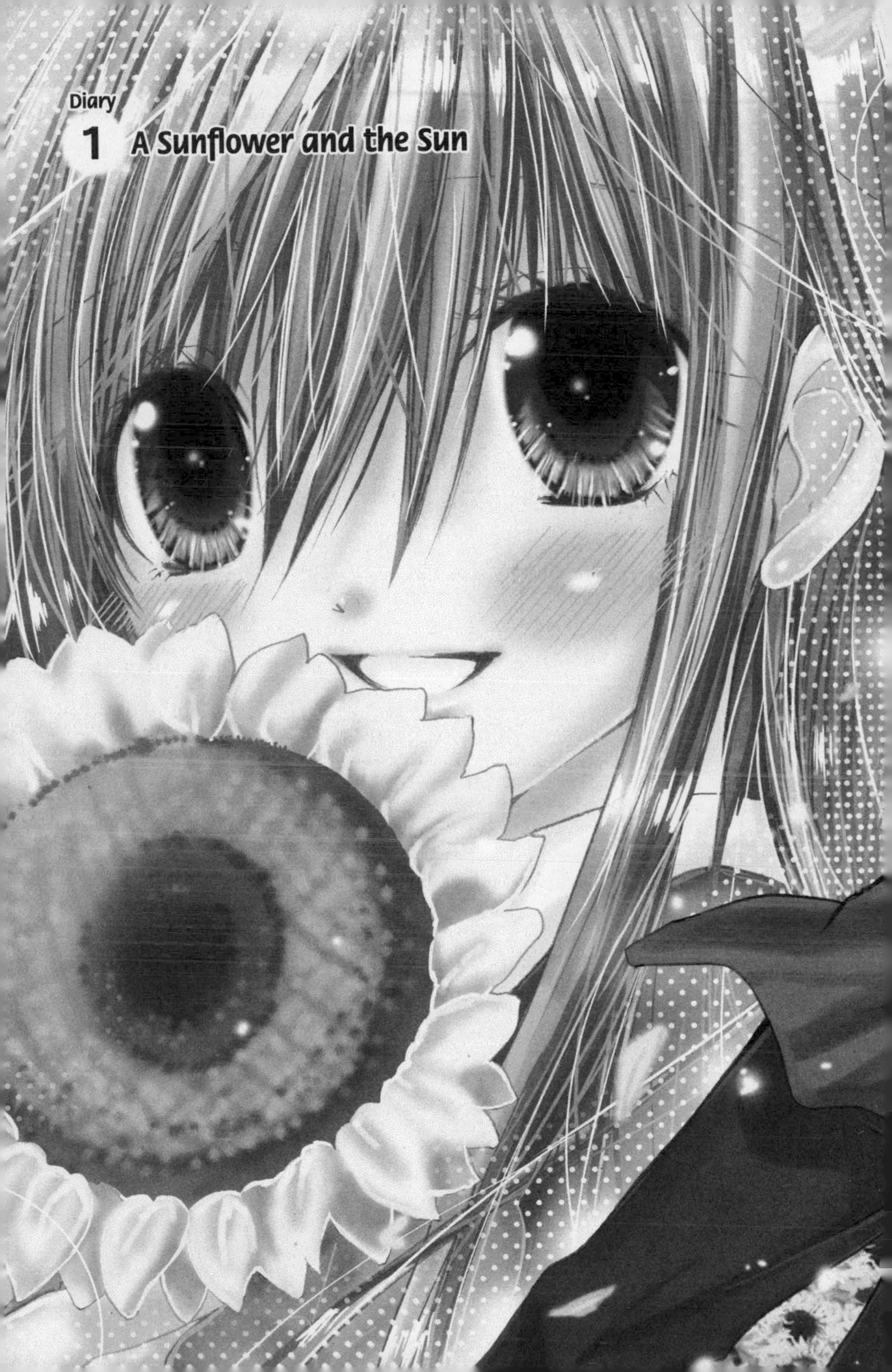
Diary
1 A Sunflower and the Sun

I am Here!

CONTENTS

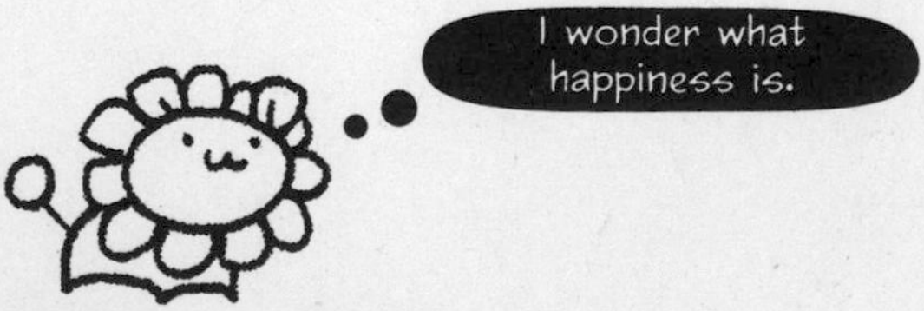

I wonder what happiness is.

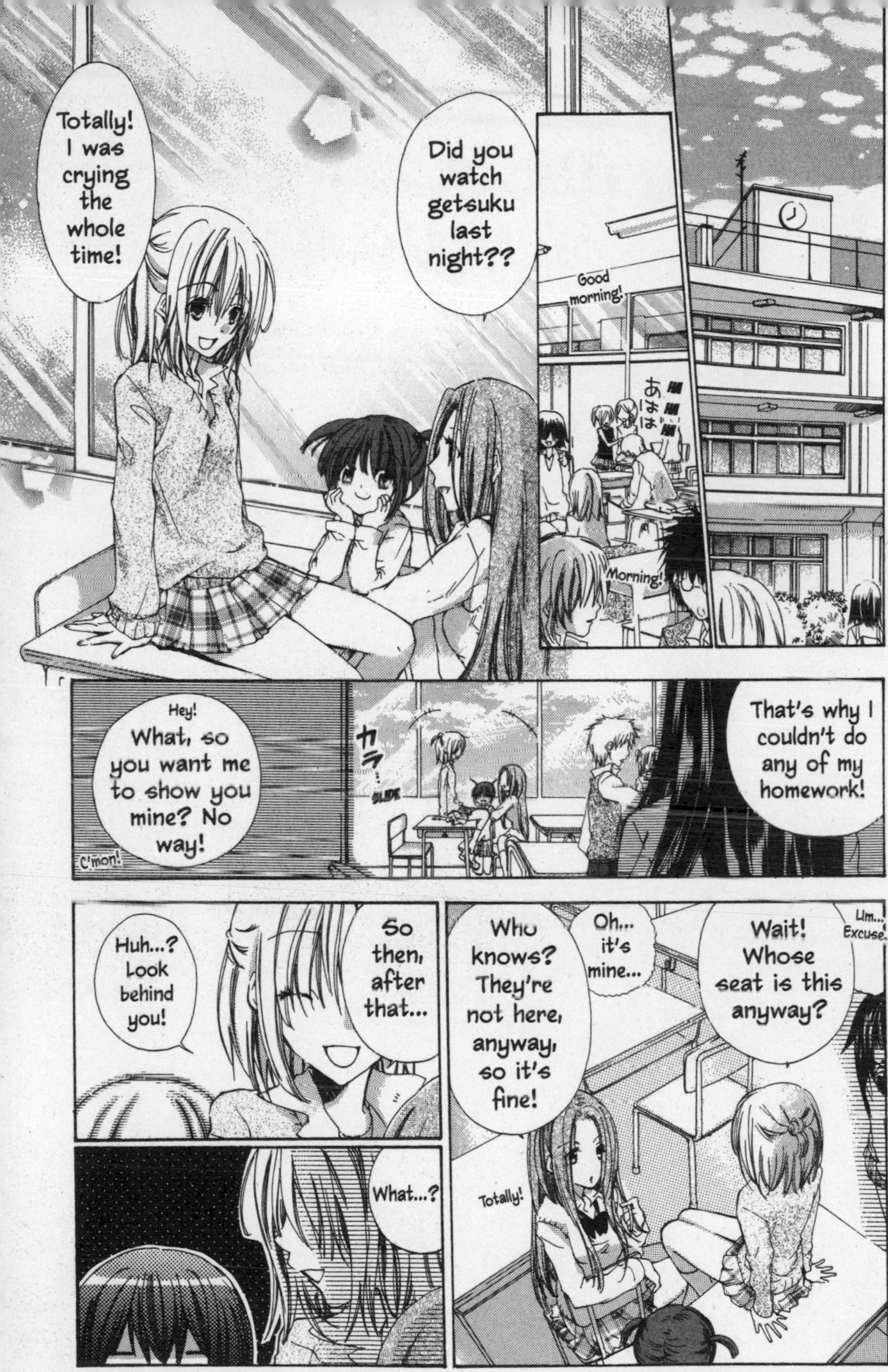

Good morning!
あはは
Morning!
Did you watch getsuku last night??
Totally! I was crying the whole time!
That's why I couldn't do any of my homework!
カラ... SLIDE
Hey!
What, so you want me to show you mine? No way!
C'mon!
Um... Excuse...
Wait! Whose seat is this anyway?
Oh... it's mine...
Who knows? They're not here, anyway, so it's fine!
Totally!
So then, after that...
Huh...? Look behind you!
What...?

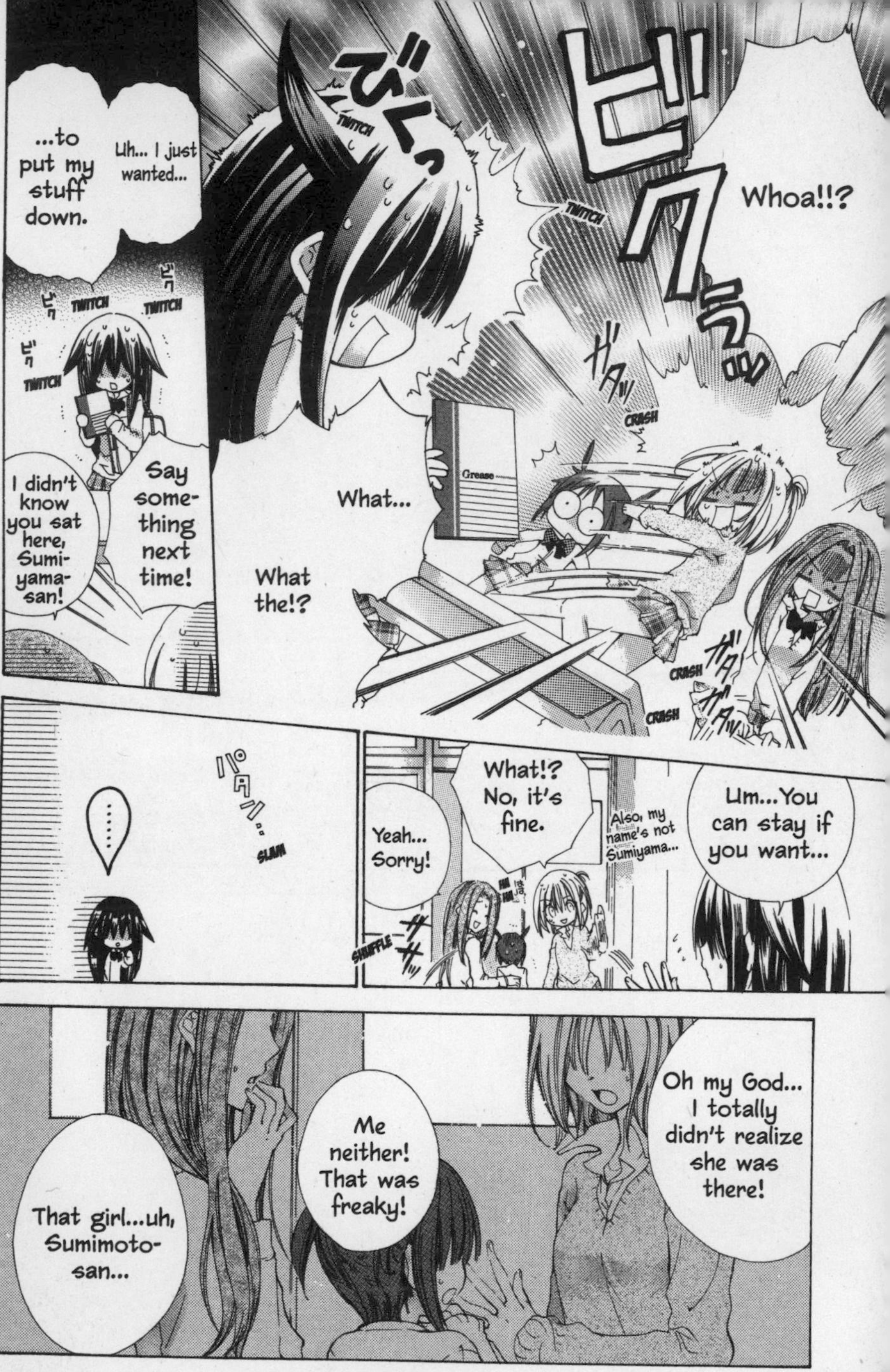
Whoa!!?
TWITCH
TWITCH
CRASH
What...
What the!?
CRASH
CRASH
Uh... I just wanted...
...to put my stuff down.
TWITCH
TWITCH
TWITCH
Say some-thing next time!
I didn't know you sat here, Sumi-yama-san!
Um...You can stay if you want...
Also, my name's not Sumiyama...
What!? No, it's fine.
Yeah... Sorry!
SHUFFLE
SLAM
......
Oh my God... I totally didn't realize she was there!
Me neither! That was freaky!
That girl...uh, Sumimoto-san...

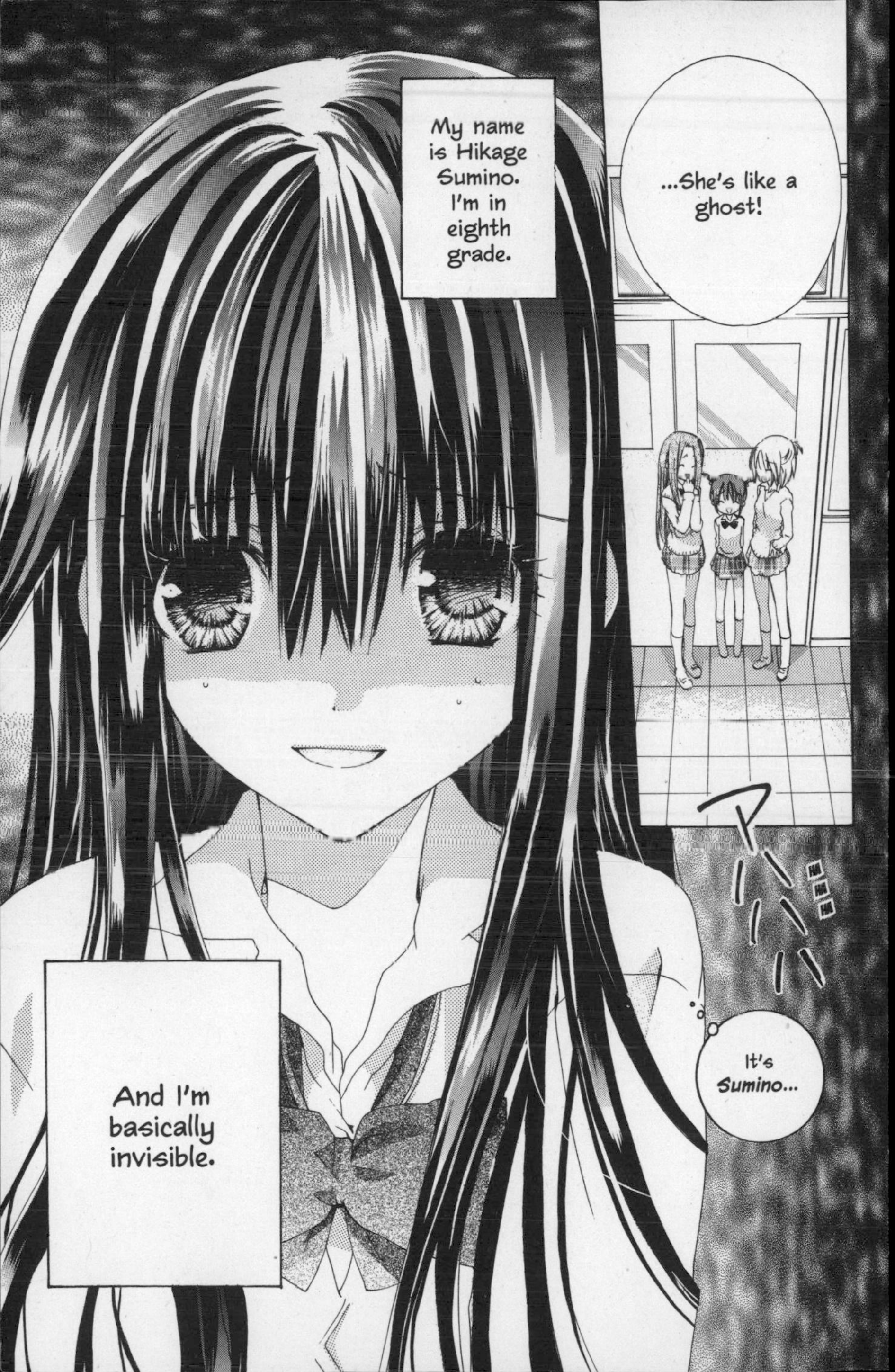
...She's like a ghost!
HA HA HA
It's Sumino...
My name is Hikage Sumino. I'm in eighth grade.
And I'm basically invisible.

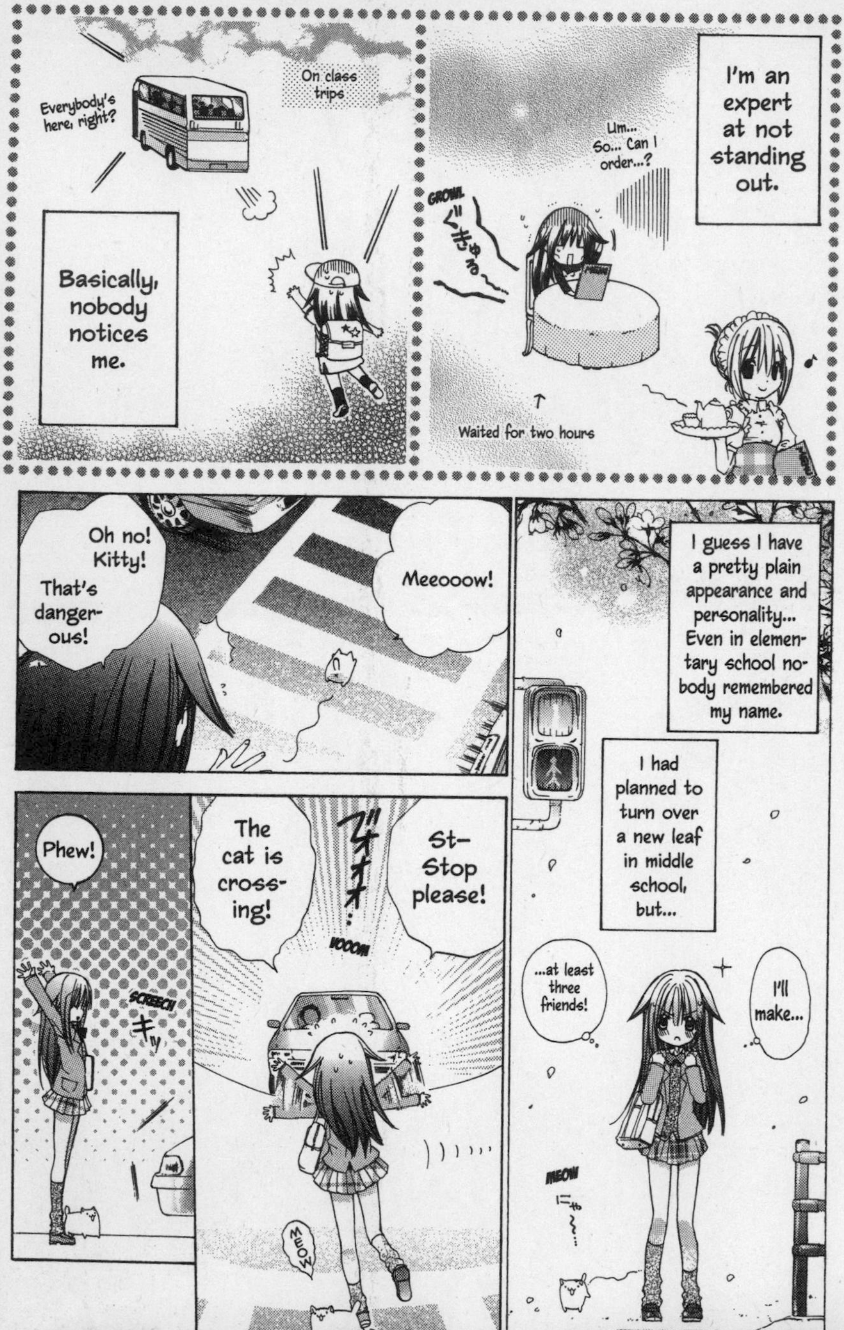
I'm an expert at not standing out.
Um... So... Can I order...?
GROWL
ぐきゅる~
Waited for two hours
On class trips
Everybody's here, right?
Basically, nobody notices me.
I guess I have a pretty plain appearance and personality... Even in elementary school nobody remembered my name.
I had planned to turn over a new leaf in middle school, but...
I'll make...
...at least three friends!
MEOW
にゃ~
Meeooow!
Oh no! Kitty!
That's danger-ous!
St- Stop please!
The cat is cross-ing!
ブオオオ...
VOOOM
MEOW
Phew!
SCREECH
キッ

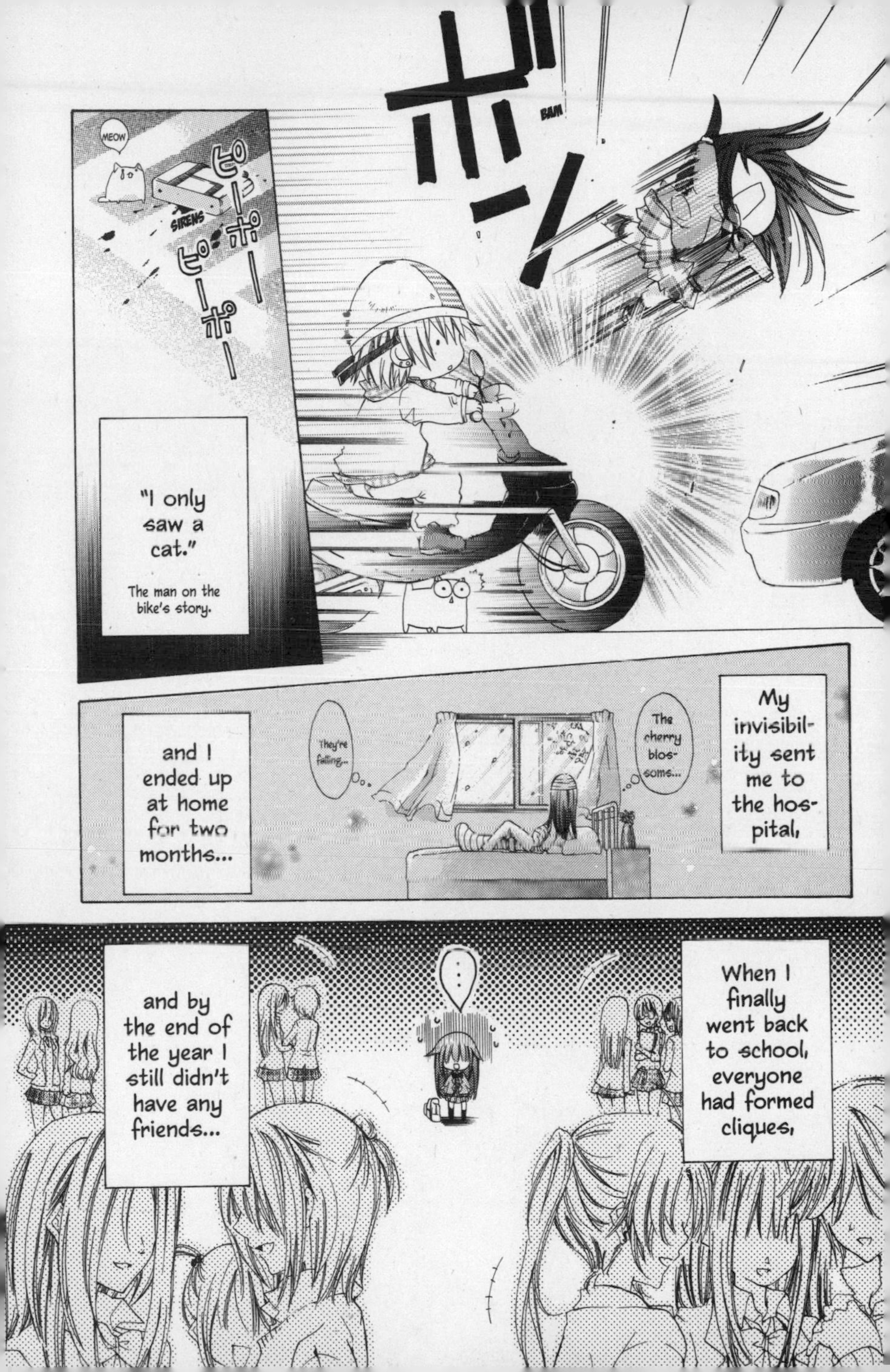

ボーン
BAM
MEOW
ピーポーピーポー
SIRENS
"I only saw a cat."
The man on the bike's story.
My invisibility sent me to the hospital,
The cherry blossoms...
They're falling...
and I ended up at home for two months...
When I finally went back to school, everyone had formed cliques,
...
and by the end of the year I still didn't have any friends...

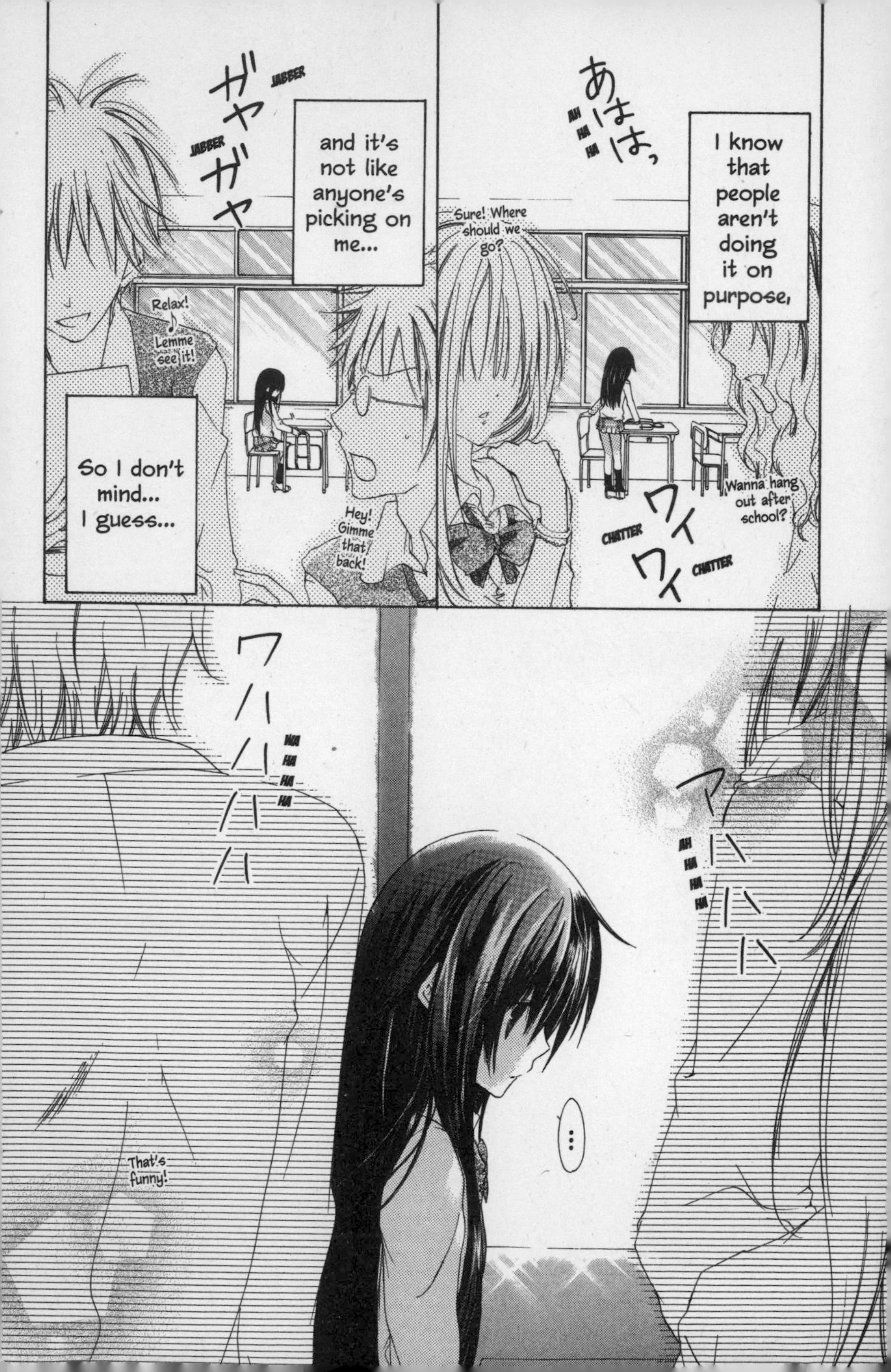

I know that people aren't doing it on purpose,
あはは、
AH HA HA
Sure! Where should we go?
Wanna hang out after school?
ワイワイ
CHATTER
CHATTER
and it's not like anyone's picking on me...
ガヤガヤ
JABBER
JABBER
Relax! ♪ Lemme see it!
Hey! Gimme that back!
So I don't mind... I guess...
アハハハ
AH HA HA HA
ワハハハ
HA HA HA HA
...
That's funny!

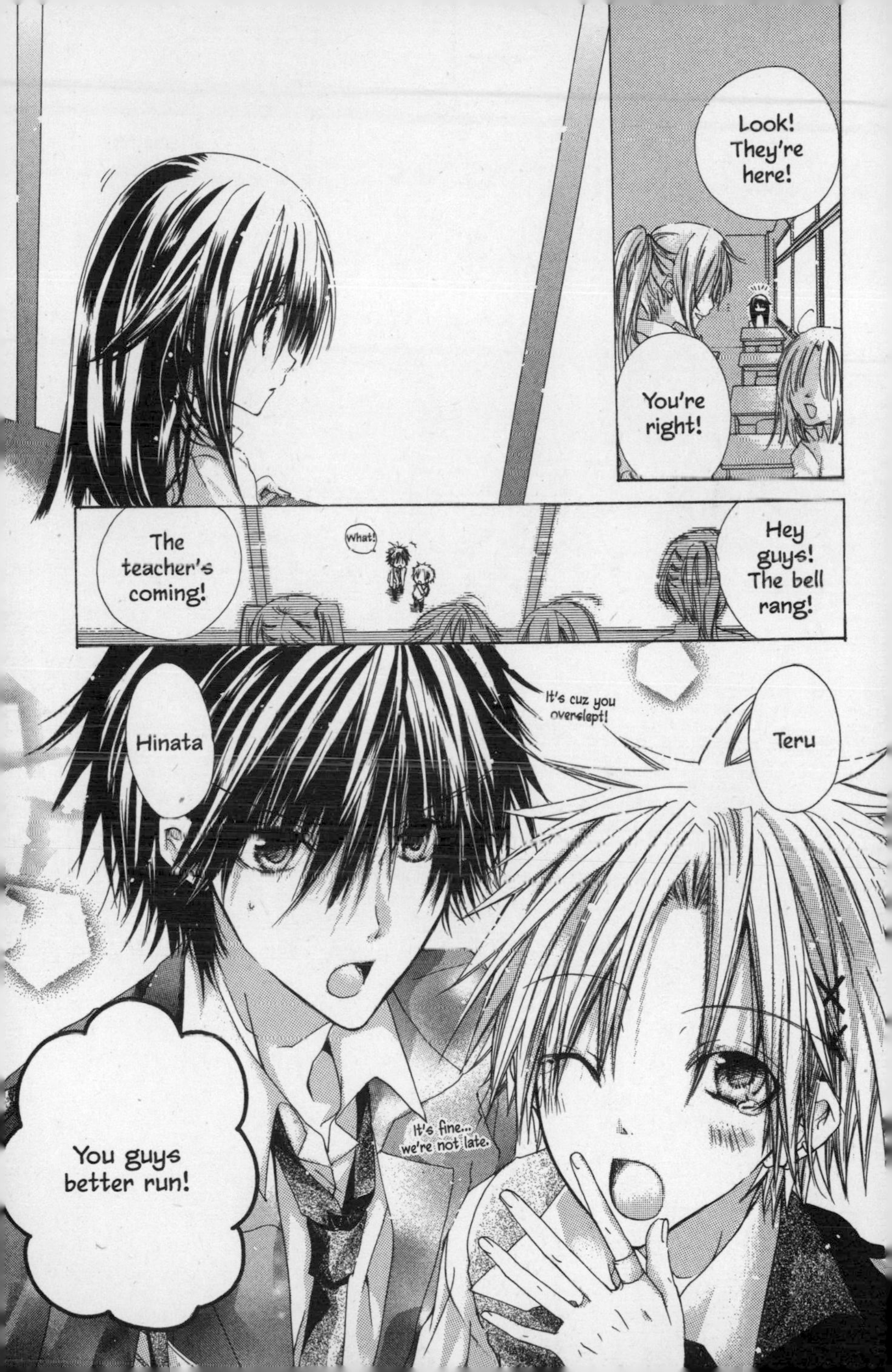
Look! They're here!
You're right!
Hey guys! The bell rang!
What!
The teacher's coming!
Teru
It's cuz you overslept!
Hinata
It's fine... we're not late.
You guys better run!

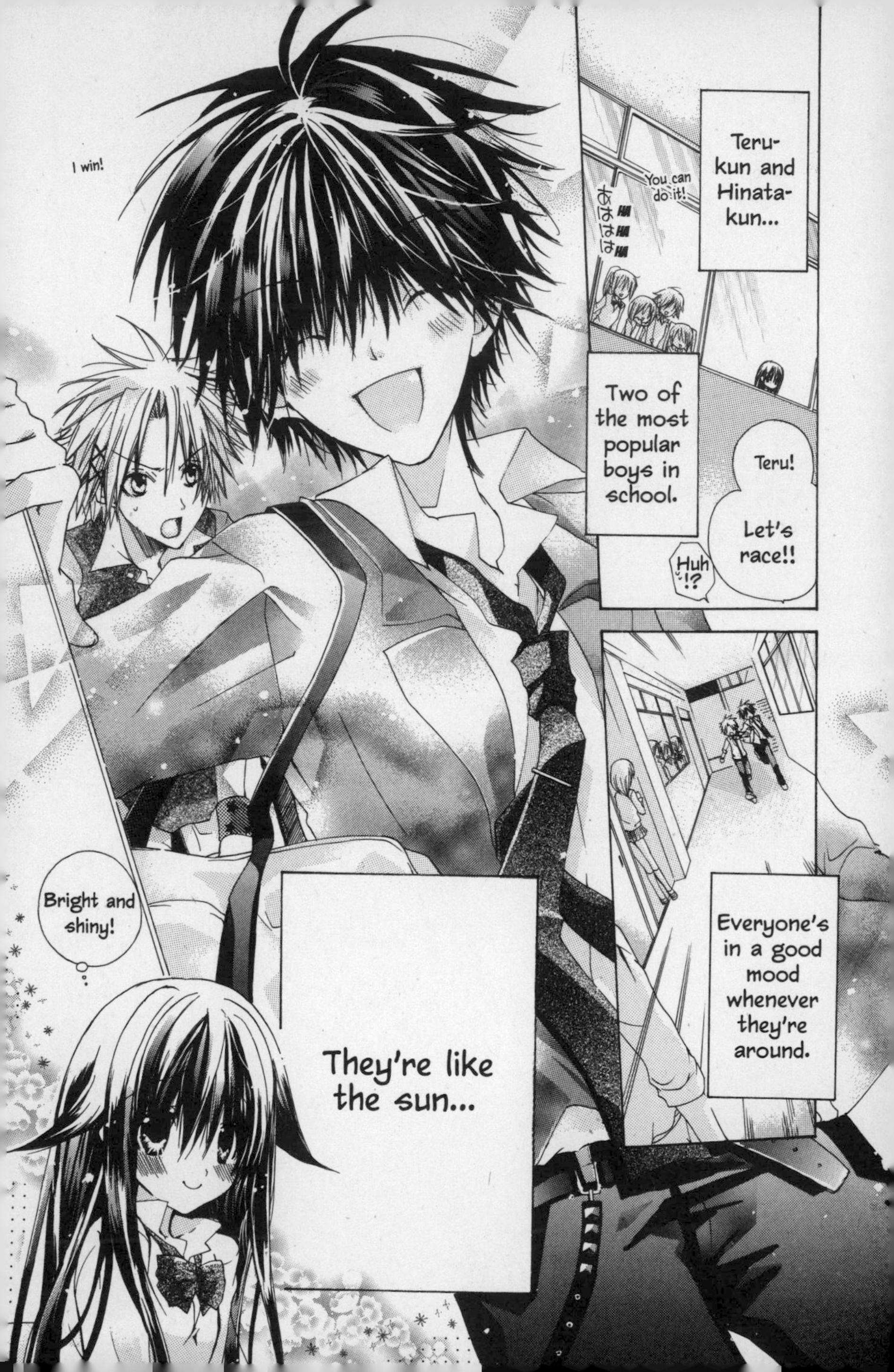
Teru-kun and Hinata-kun...
You can do it!
あははは HA HA HA
Two of the most popular boys in school.
Teru!
Let's race!!
Huh!?
Everyone's in a good mood whenever they're around.
I win!
They're like the sun...
Bright and shiny!

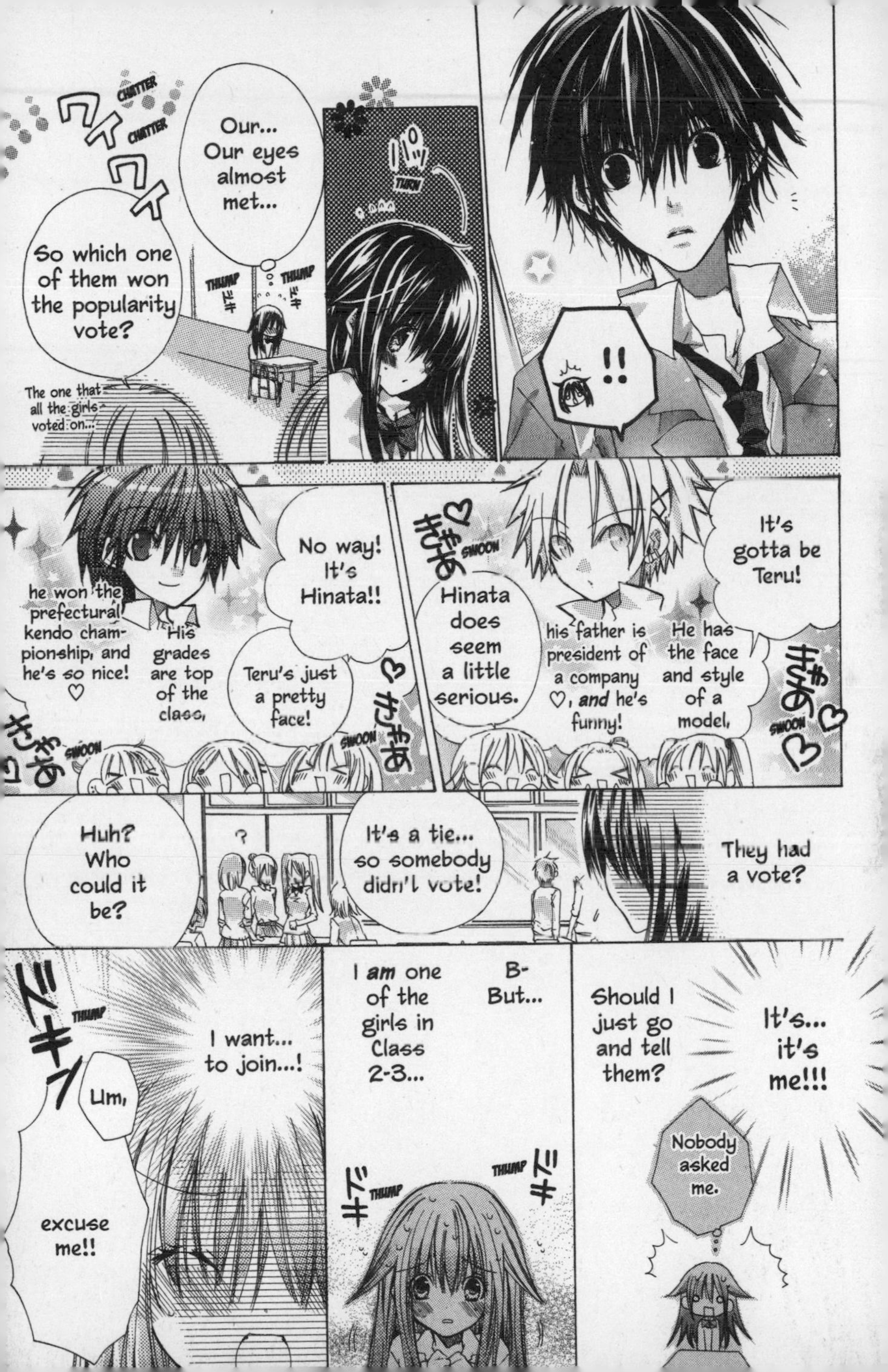
!!
パッ TURN
ワイワイ CHATTER CHATTER
Our... Our eyes almost met...
So which one of them won the popularity vote?
ドキ THUMP ドキ THUMP
The one that all the girls voted on...
It's gotta be Teru!
He has the face and style of a model,
his father is president of a company ♡, and he's funny!
きゃあ SWOON
Hinata does seem a little serious.
No way! It's Hinata!!
His grades are top of the class,
he won the prefectural kendo championship, and he's so nice! ♡
Teru's just a pretty face!
きゃあ SWOON
They had a vote?
It's a tie... so somebody didn't vote!
?
Huh? Who could it be?
It's... it's me!!!
Should I just go and tell them?
Nobody asked me.
B- But...
I am one of the girls in Class 2-3...
ドキ THUMP ドキ THUMP
I want... to join...!
ドキン THUMP
Um, excuse me!!

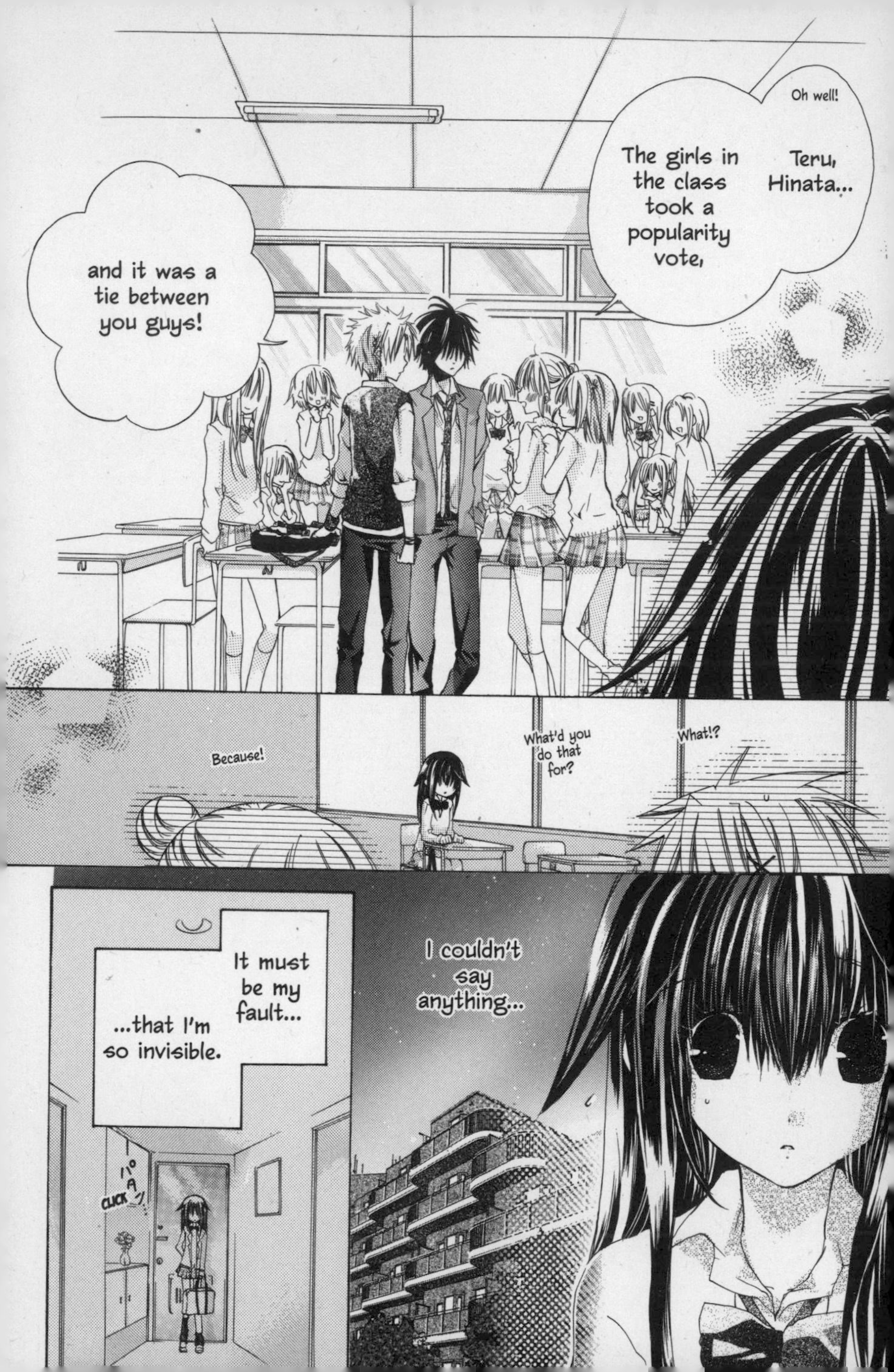
Oh well!
Teru, Hinata...
The girls in the class took a popularity vote,
and it was a tie between you guys!
What!?
What'd you do that for?
Because!
I couldn't say anything...
It must be my fault...
...that I'm so invisible.
CLICK

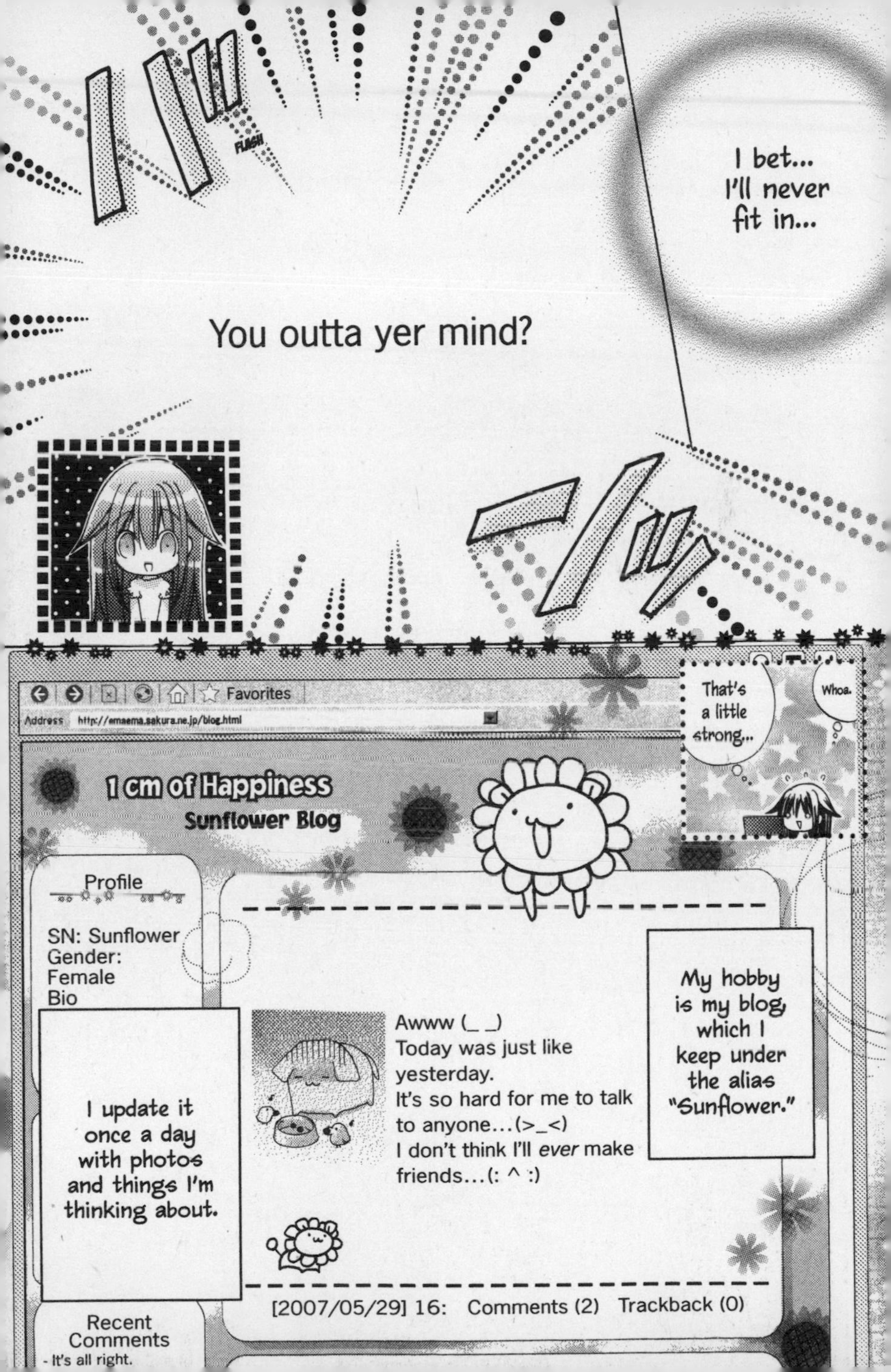
I bet... I'll never fit in...
FLASH
You outta yer mind?
Whoa.
That's a little strong...
My hobby is my blog, which I keep under the alias "Sunflower."
Favorites
Address http://emaema.sakura.ne.jp/blog.html
1 cm of Happiness
Sunflower Blog
Profile
SN: Sunflower
Gender: Female
Bio
Awww (_ _)
Today was just like yesterday.
It's so hard for me to talk to anyone…(>_<)
I don't think I'll *ever* make friends…(: ^ :)
[2007/05/29] 16: Comments (2) Trackback (0)
Recent Comments
- It's all right.
I update it once a day with photos and things I'm thinking about.

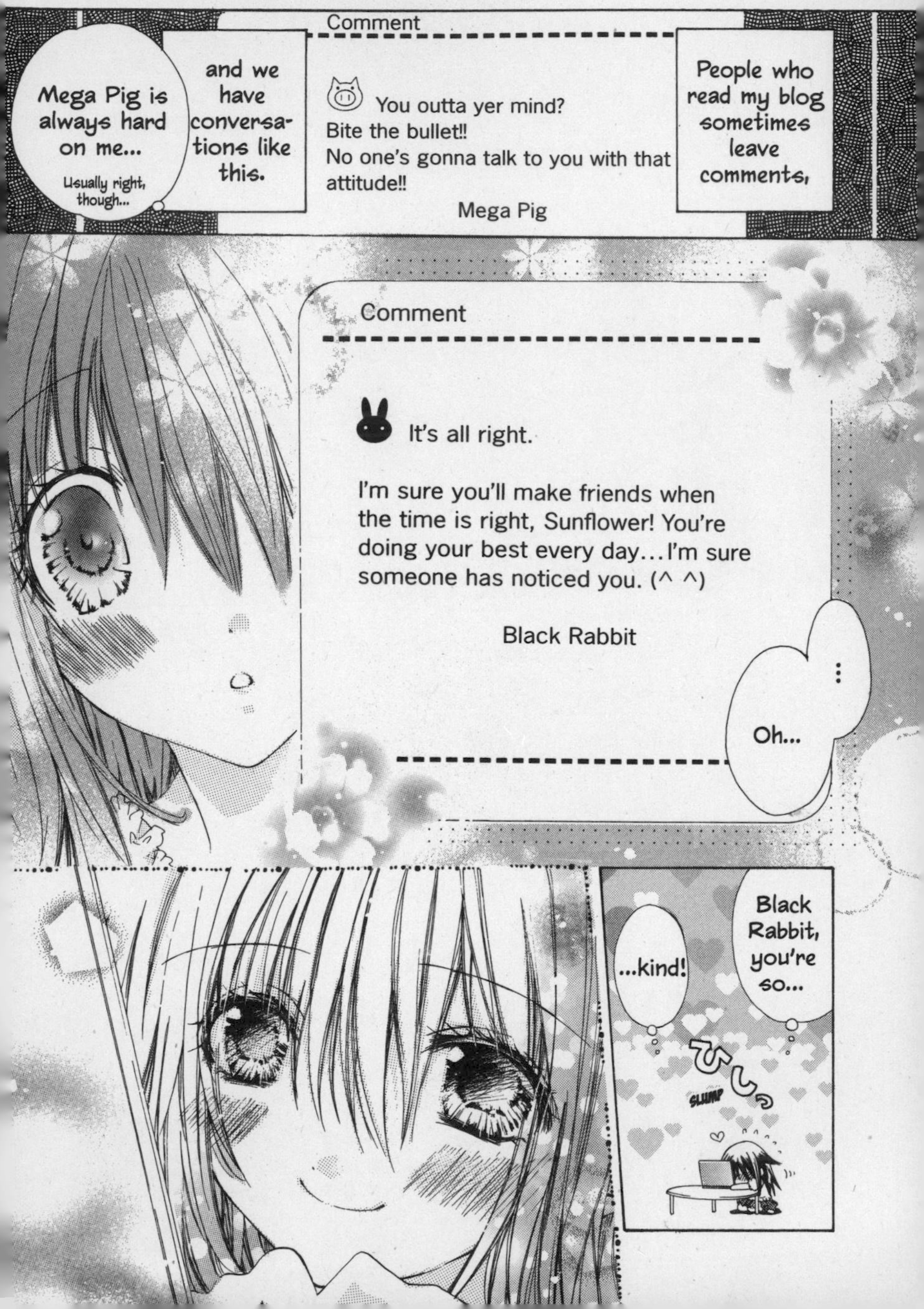
People who read my blog sometimes leave comments,
Comment
You outta yer mind?
Bite the bullet!!
No one's gonna talk to you with that attitude!!
Mega Pig
and we have conversa-tions like this.
Mega Pig is always hard on me...
Usually right, though...
Comment
It's all right.
I'm sure you'll make friends when the time is right, Sunflower! You're doing your best every day... I'm sure someone has noticed you. (^ ^)
Black Rabbit
...
Oh...
Black Rabbit, you're so...
...kind!
SLUMP

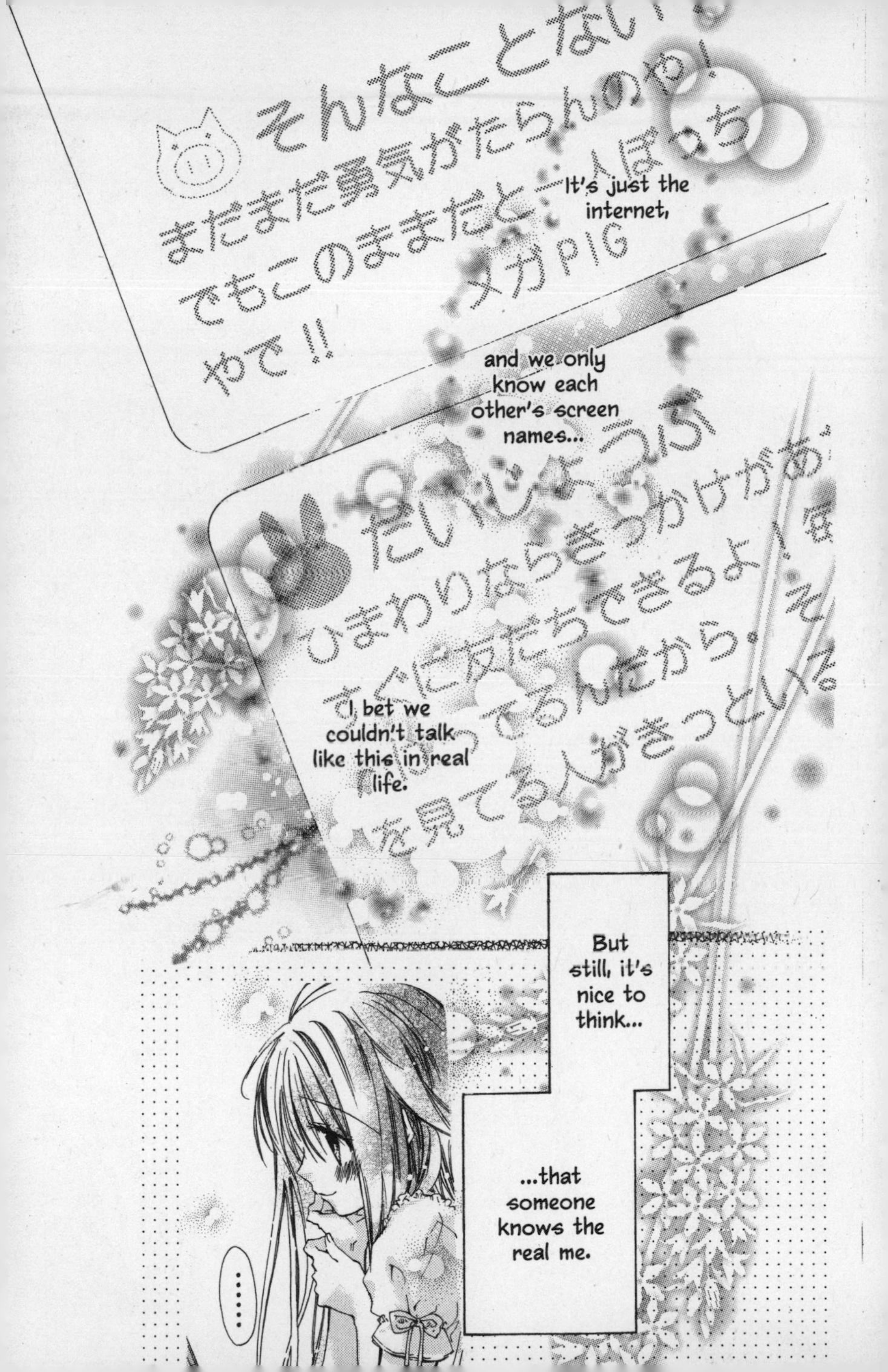
そんなことない！
まだまだ勇気がたらんのや！
でもこのままだと一人ぼっち
やで!!
メガPIG
It's just the internet,
and we only know each other's screen names...
だいじょうぶ
ひまわりならきっかけがあ
すぐに友だちできるよ！
I bet we couldn't talk like this in real life.
But still, it's nice to think...
...that someone knows the real me.
......

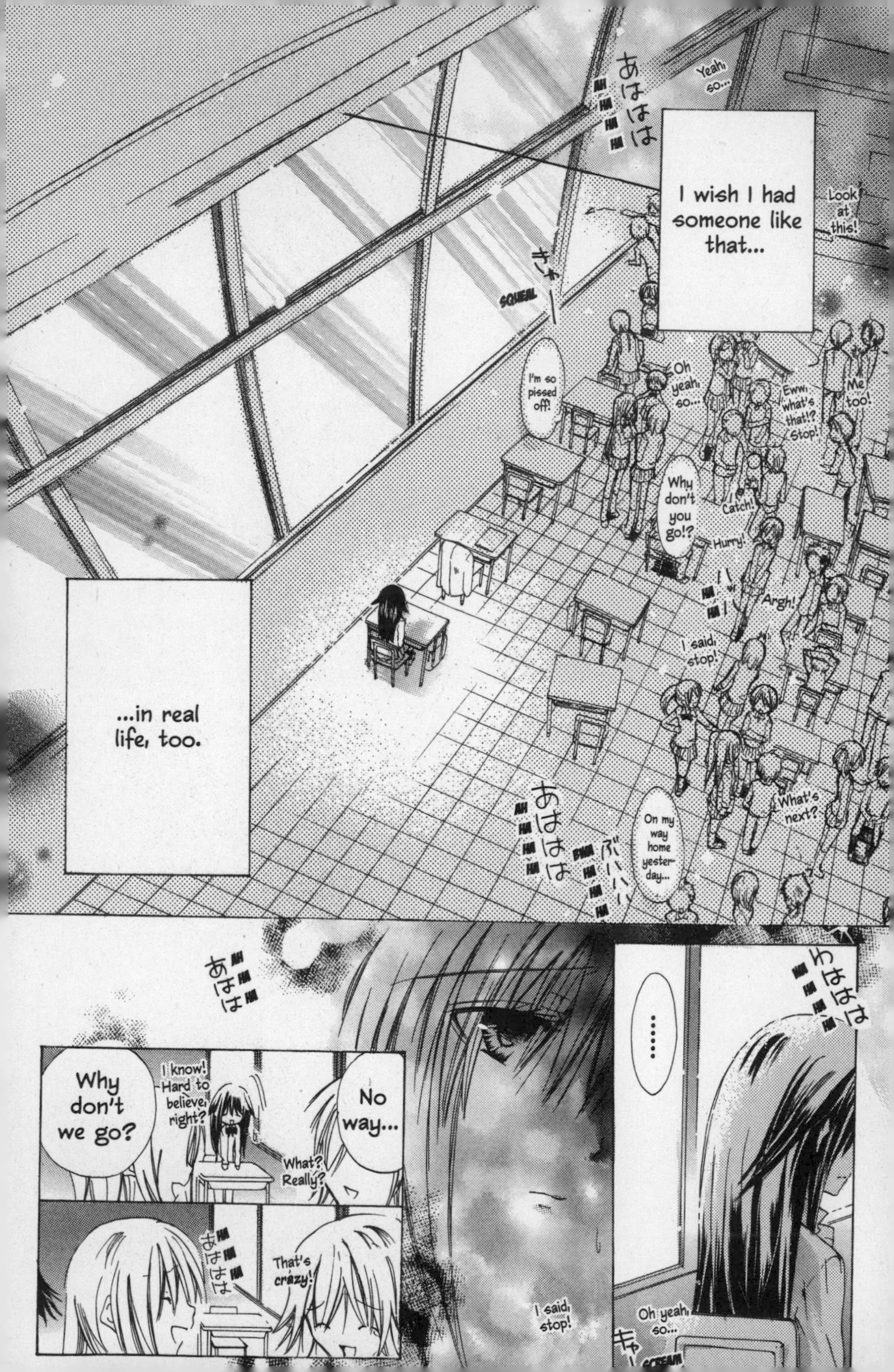
Yeah, so...
I wish I had someone like that...
Look at this!
あははは
AH HA HA HA
きゃー
SQUEAL
Me too!
Eww, what's that!? Stop!
Oh yeah, so...
I'm so pissed off!
Why don't you go!?
Catch!
Hurry!
HA HA
Argh!
I said, stop!
What's next?
On my way home yesterday...
ぶははは
BWA HA HA HA
あははは
AH HA HA HA
...in real life, too.
わははは
HA HA HA HA
......
Oh yeah, so...
きゃ
SCREAM
あはは
AH HA HA
I said, stop!
No way...
I know! Hard to believe, right?
Why don't we go?
What? Really?
That's crazy!
あはは
HA HA HA

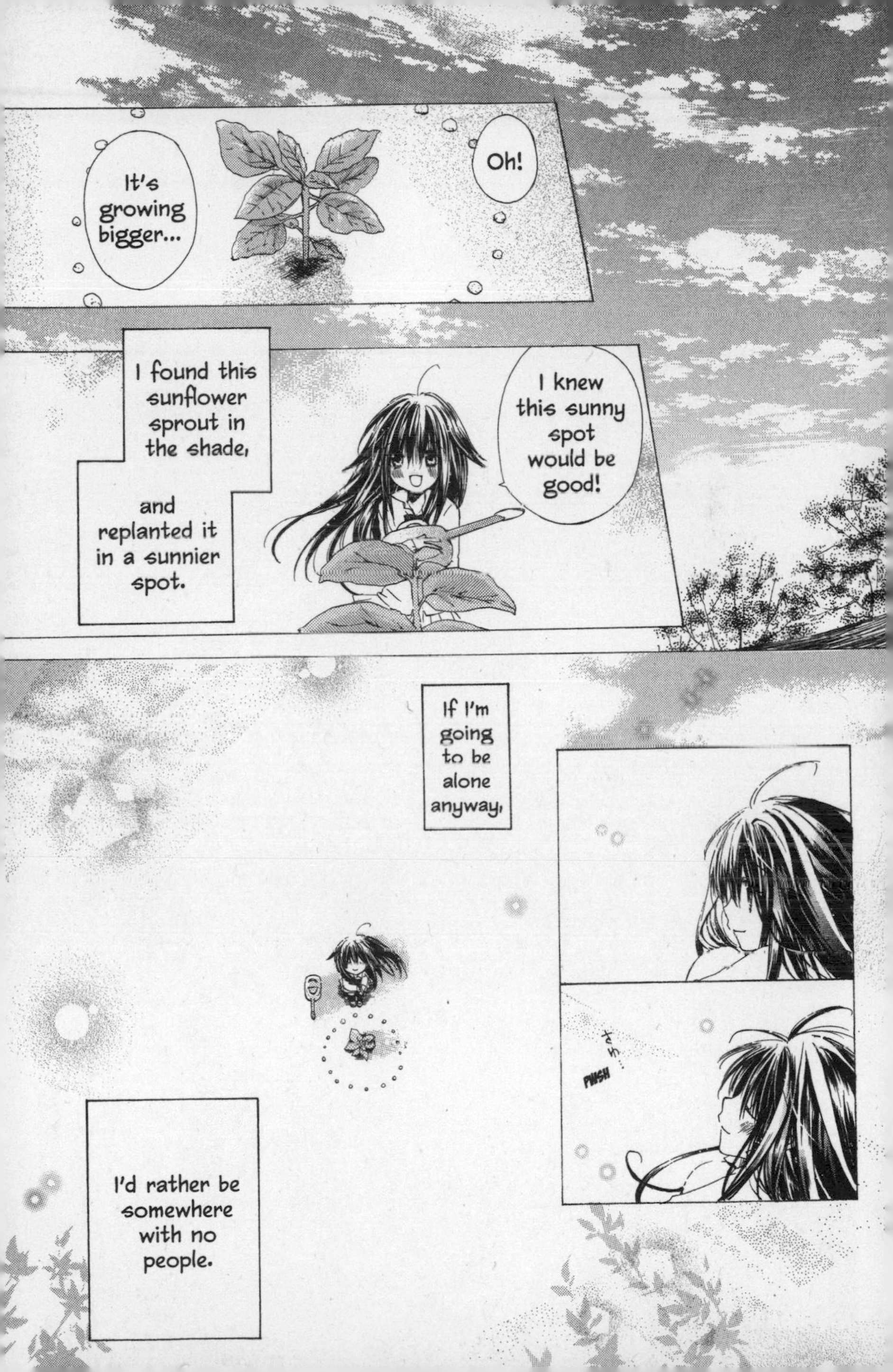
Oh!
It's growing bigger...
I knew this sunny spot would be good!
I found this sunflower sprout in the shade,
and replanted it in a sunnier spot.
PUSH
If I'm going to be alone anyway,
I'd rather be somewhere with no people.

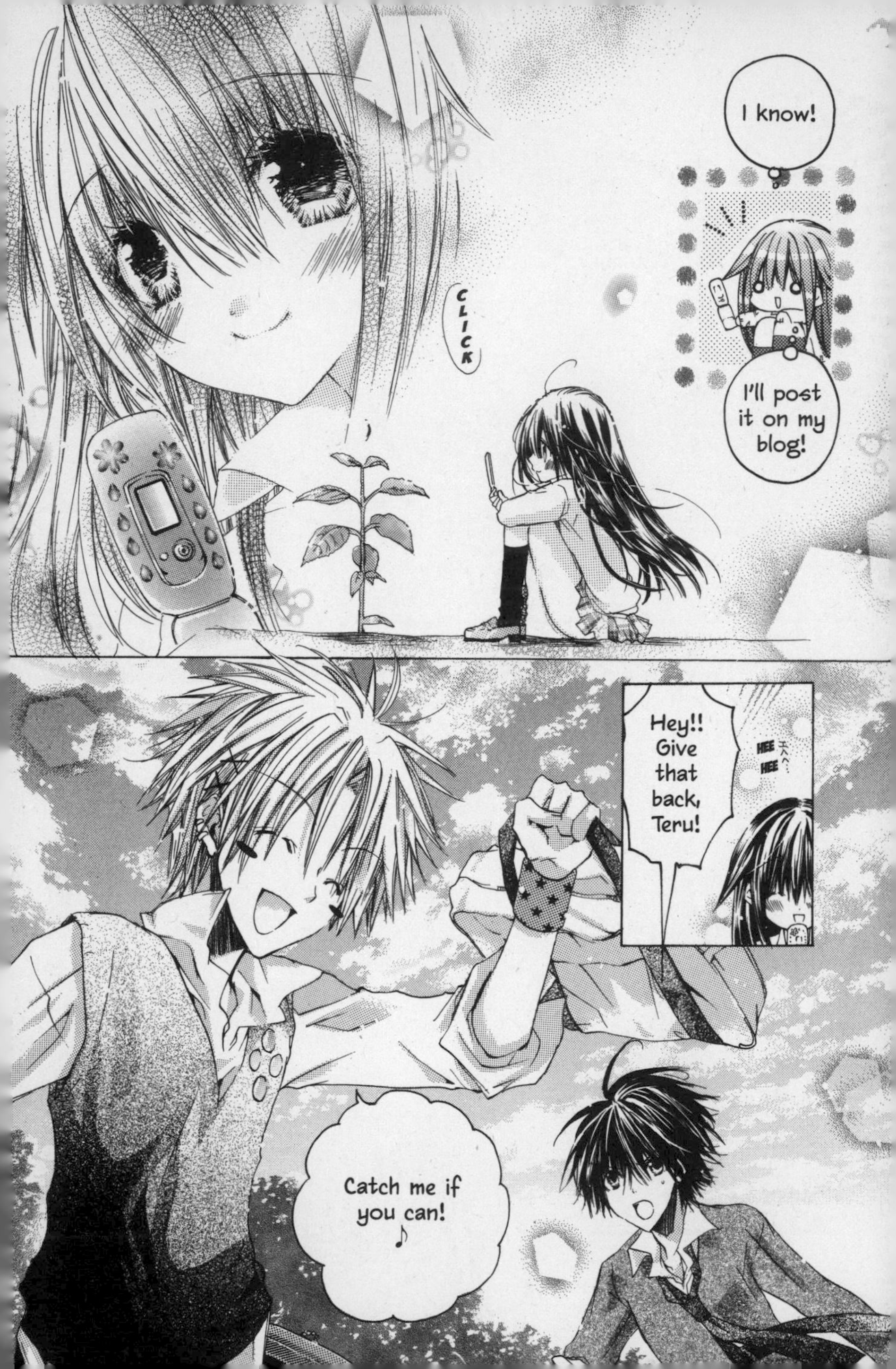
I know!
I'll post it on my blog!
CLICK
HEE HEE
Hey!! Give that back, Teru!
Catch me if you can! ♪

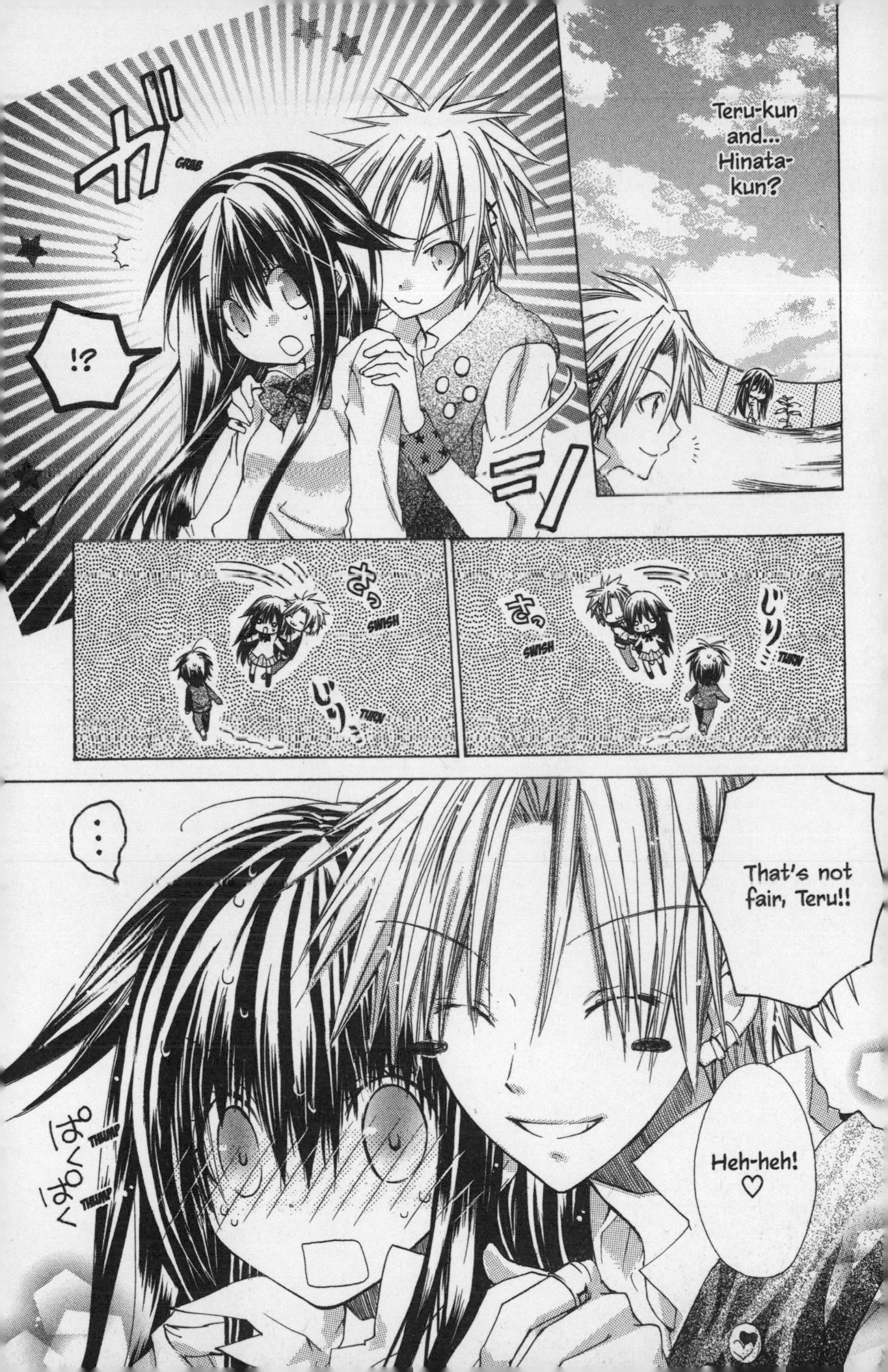

Teru-kun and... Hinata-kun?
GRIP
!?
TURN
SWISH
SWISH
TURN
That's not fair, Teru!!
...
Heh-heh! ♡
THUMP
THUMP

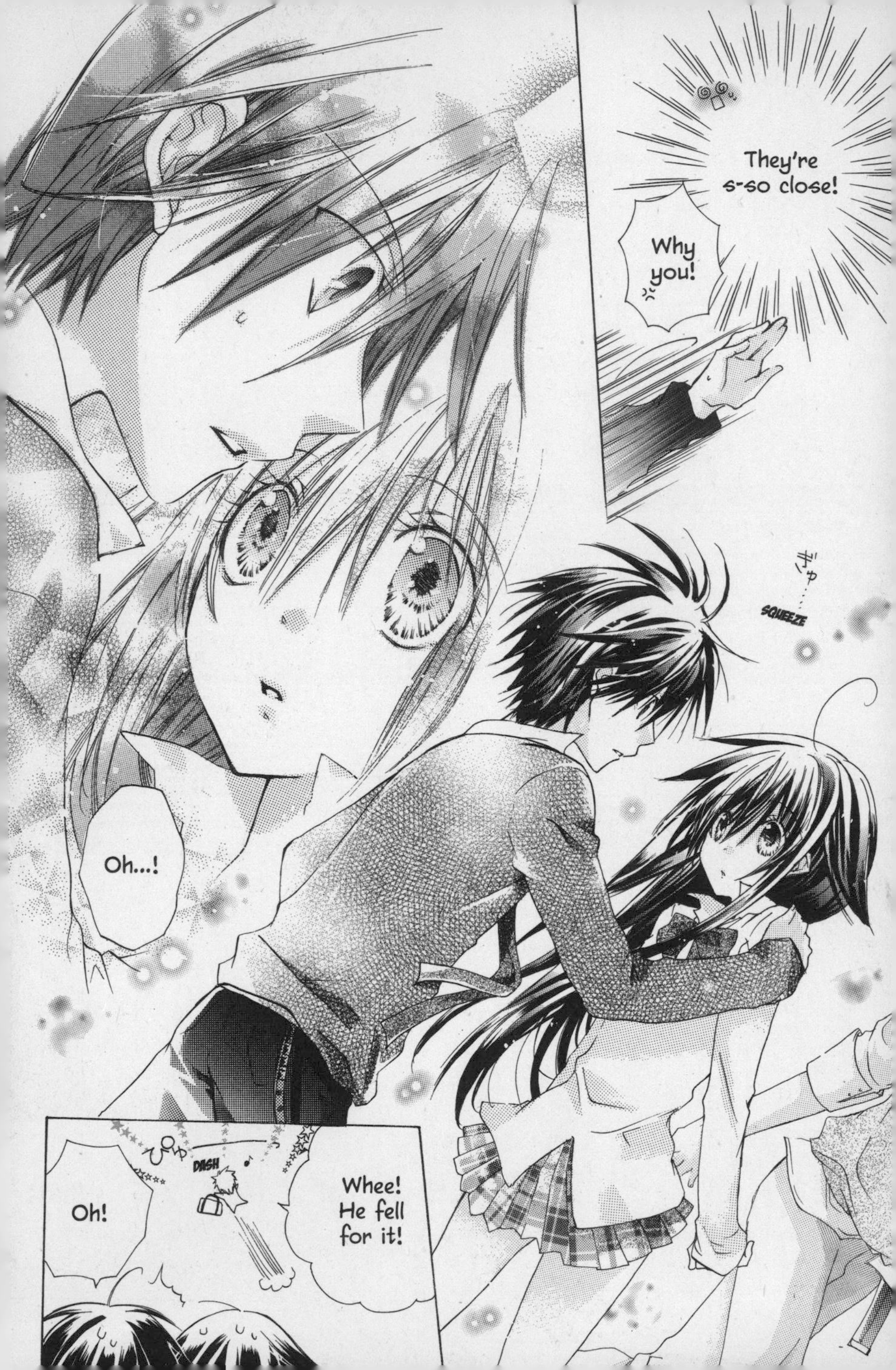

They're s-so close!
Why you!
ぎゅ…
SQUEEZE
Oh...!
Whee! He fell for it!
DASH
Oh!

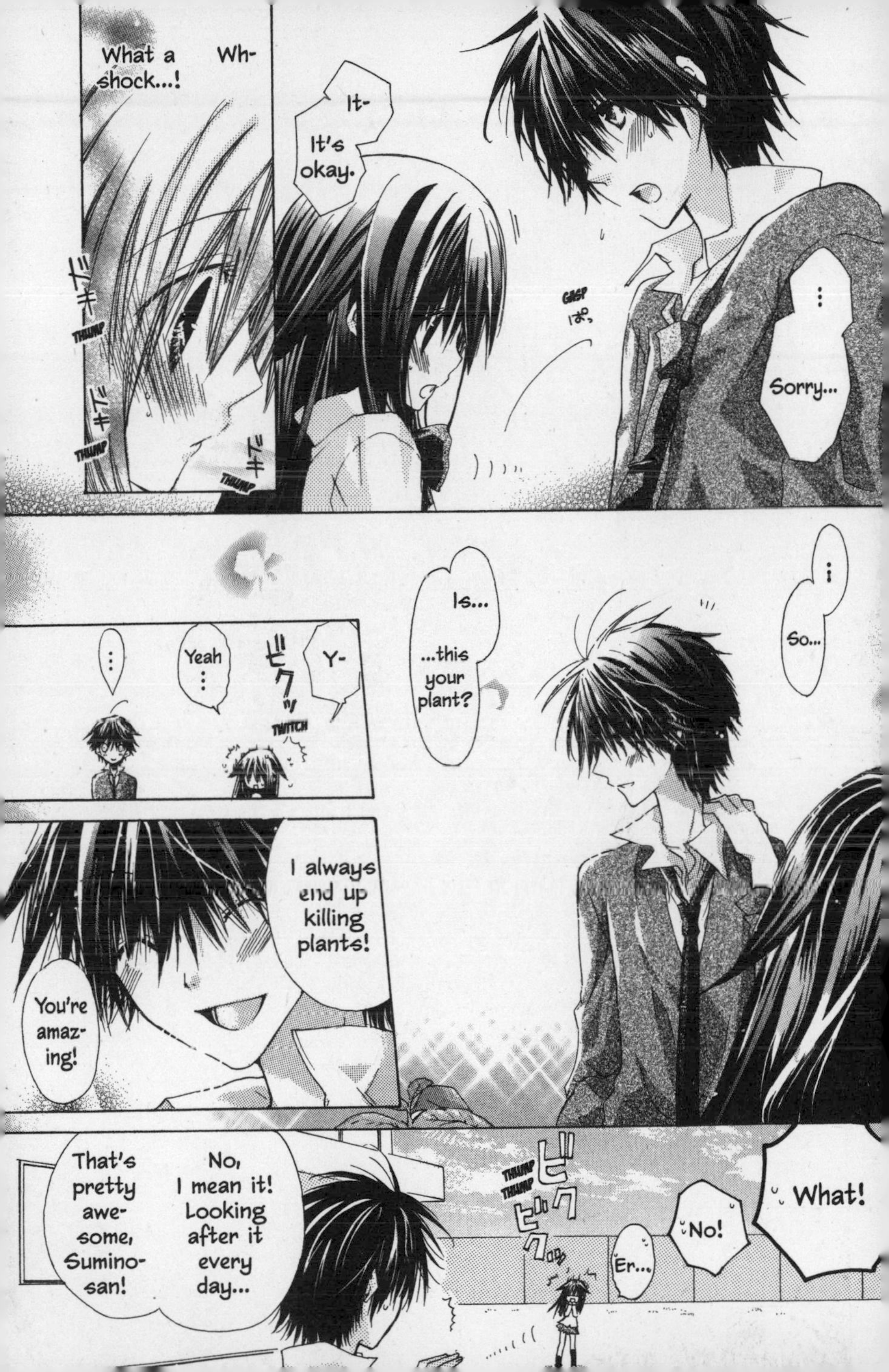

...
Sorry...
GASP
ぱっ
It-
It's okay.
Wh-
What a shock...!
ドキ
THUMP
ドキ
THUMP
ドキ
THUMP
...
So...
Is...
...this your plant?
Y-
ビクッ
TWITCH
Yeah...
...
I always end up killing plants!
You're amazing!
What!
No!
Er...
ビクビク
THUMP THUMP
No, I mean it! Looking after it every day...
That's pretty awesome, Sumino-san!

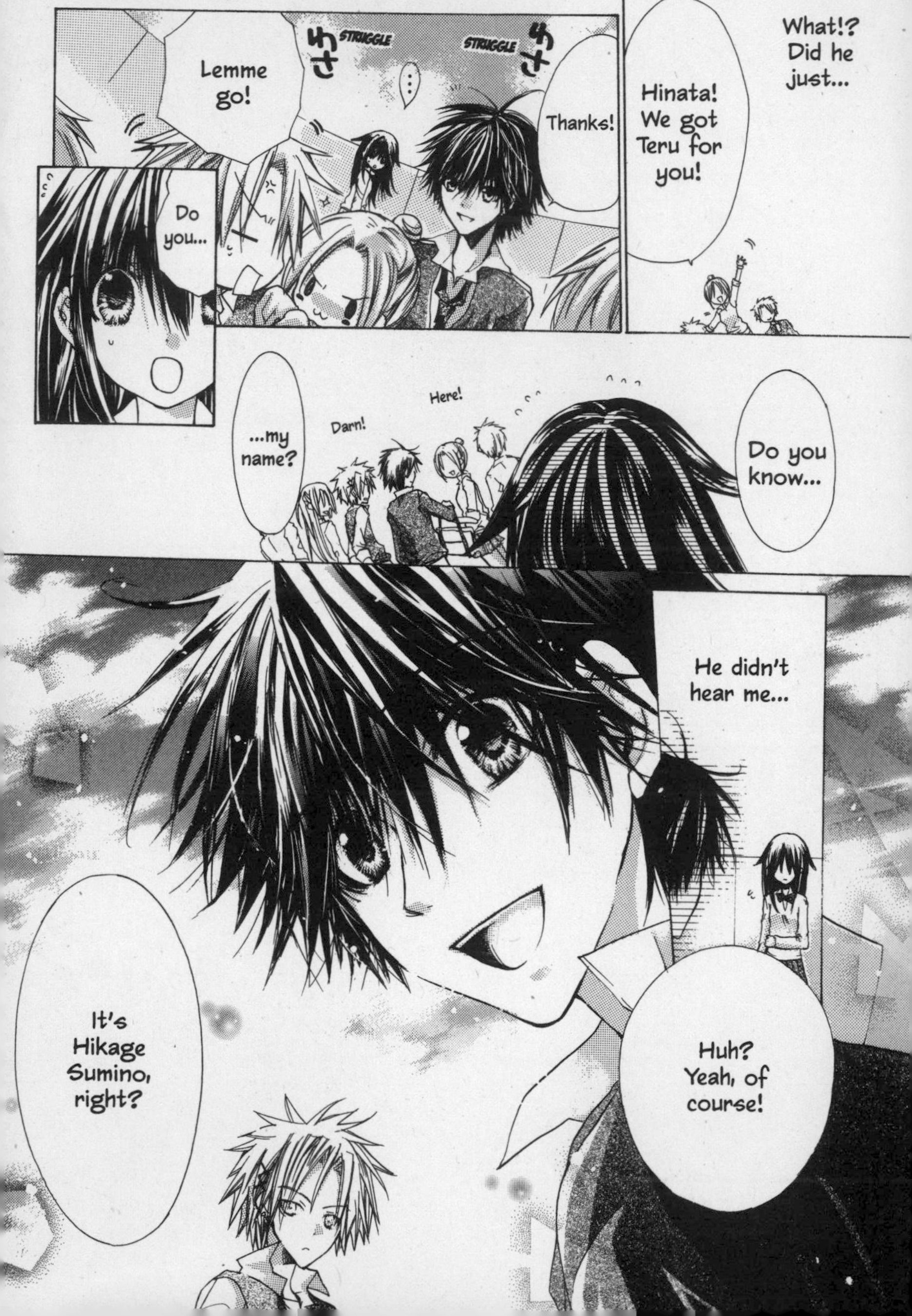
What!? Did he just...
Hinata! We got Teru for you!
STRUGGLE
Thanks!
STRUGGLE
...
Lemme go!
Do you...
Do you know...
Here!
Darn!
...my name?
He didn't hear me...
Huh? Yeah, of course!
It's Hikage Sumino, right?

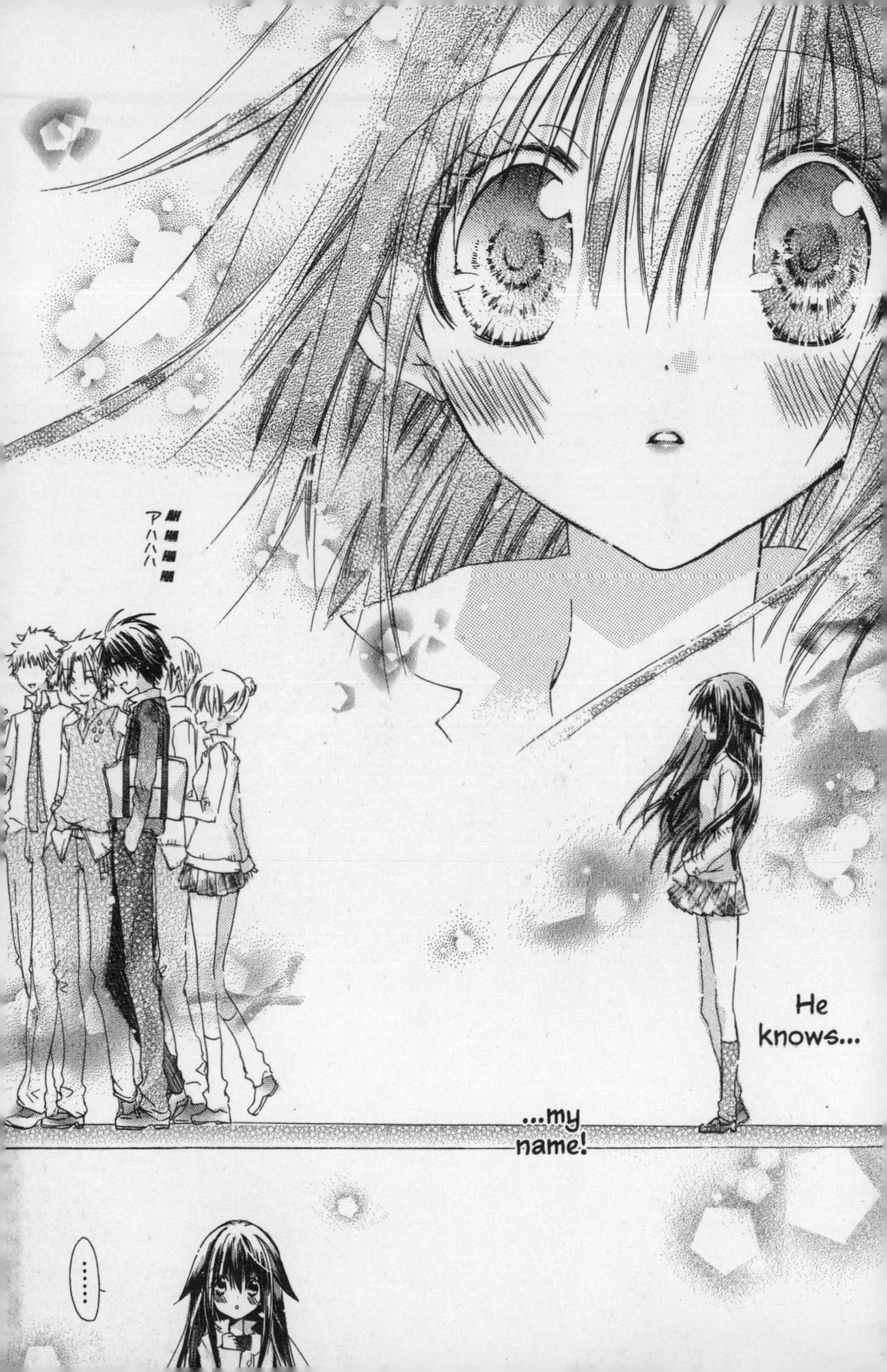
アハハハ
He knows...
...my name!
......

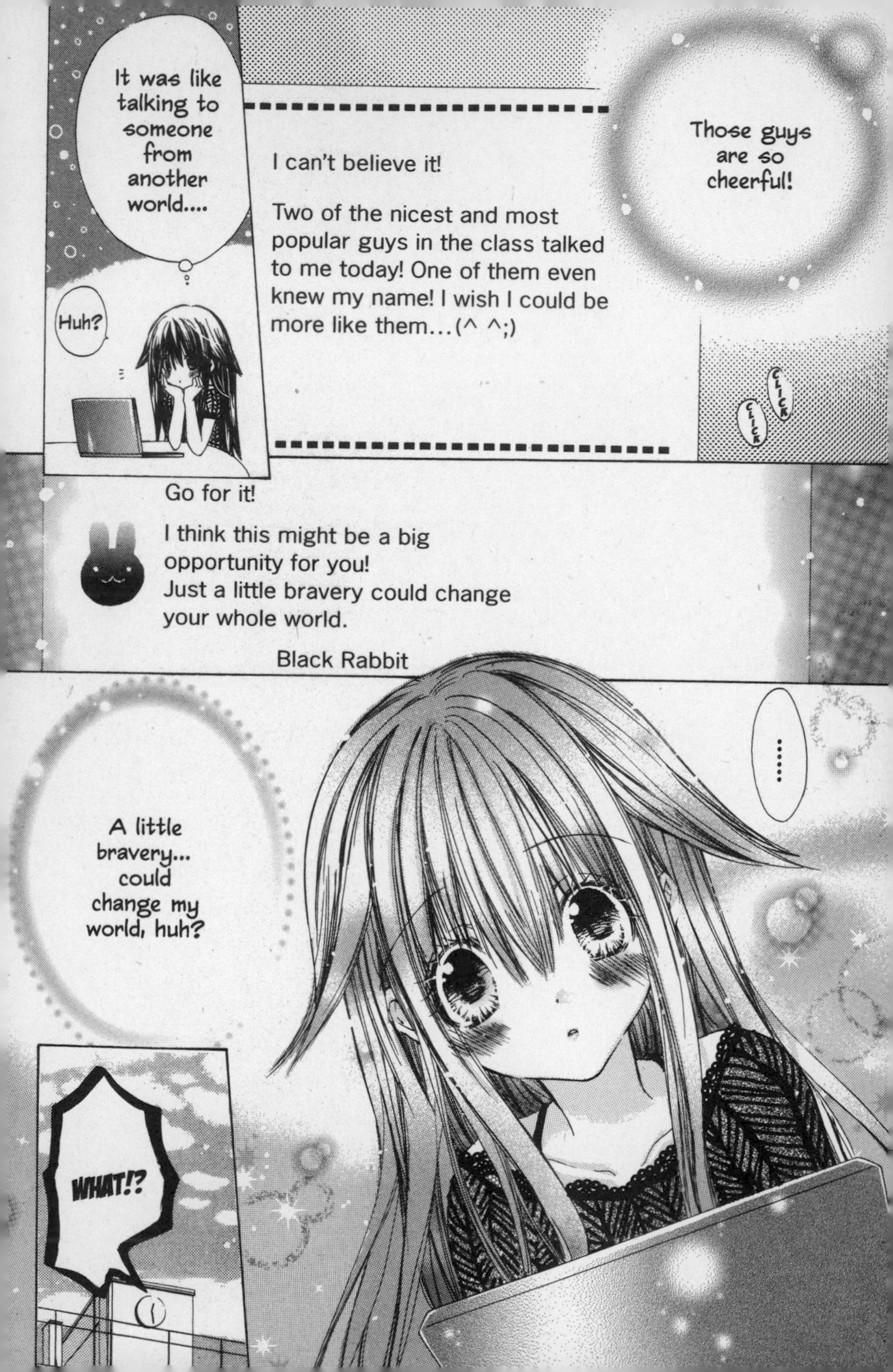

Those guys are so cheerful!
CLICK CLICK
I can't believe it!
Two of the nicest and most popular guys in the class talked to me today! One of them even knew my name! I wish I could be more like them...(^ ^;)
It was like talking to someone from another world....
Huh?
Go for it!
I think this might be a big opportunity for you!
Just a little bravery could change your whole world.
Black Rabbit
......
A little bravery... could change my world, huh?
WHAT!?

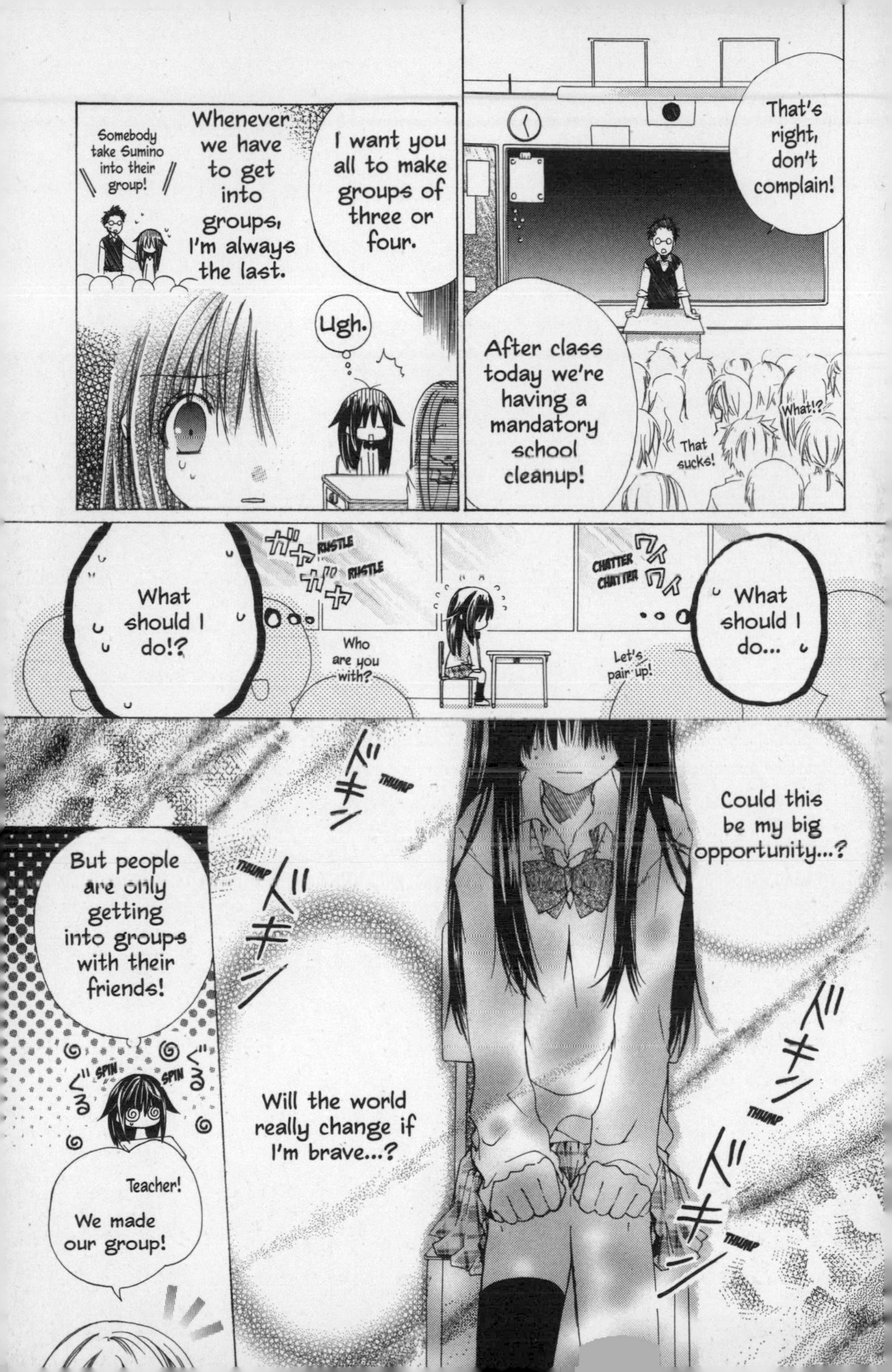

That's right, don't complain!
What!?
That sucks!
After class today we're having a mandatory school cleanup!
I want you all to make groups of three or four.
Whenever we have to get into groups, I'm always the last.
Somebody take Sumino into their group!
Ugh.
What should I do...
CHATTER CHATTER
Let's pair up!
Who are you with?
RUSTLE RUSTLE
What should I do!?
Could this be my big opportunity...?
THUMP
THUMP
THUMP
THUMP
Will the world really change if I'm brave...?
But people are only getting into groups with their friends!
SPIN SPIN
Teacher!
We made our group!

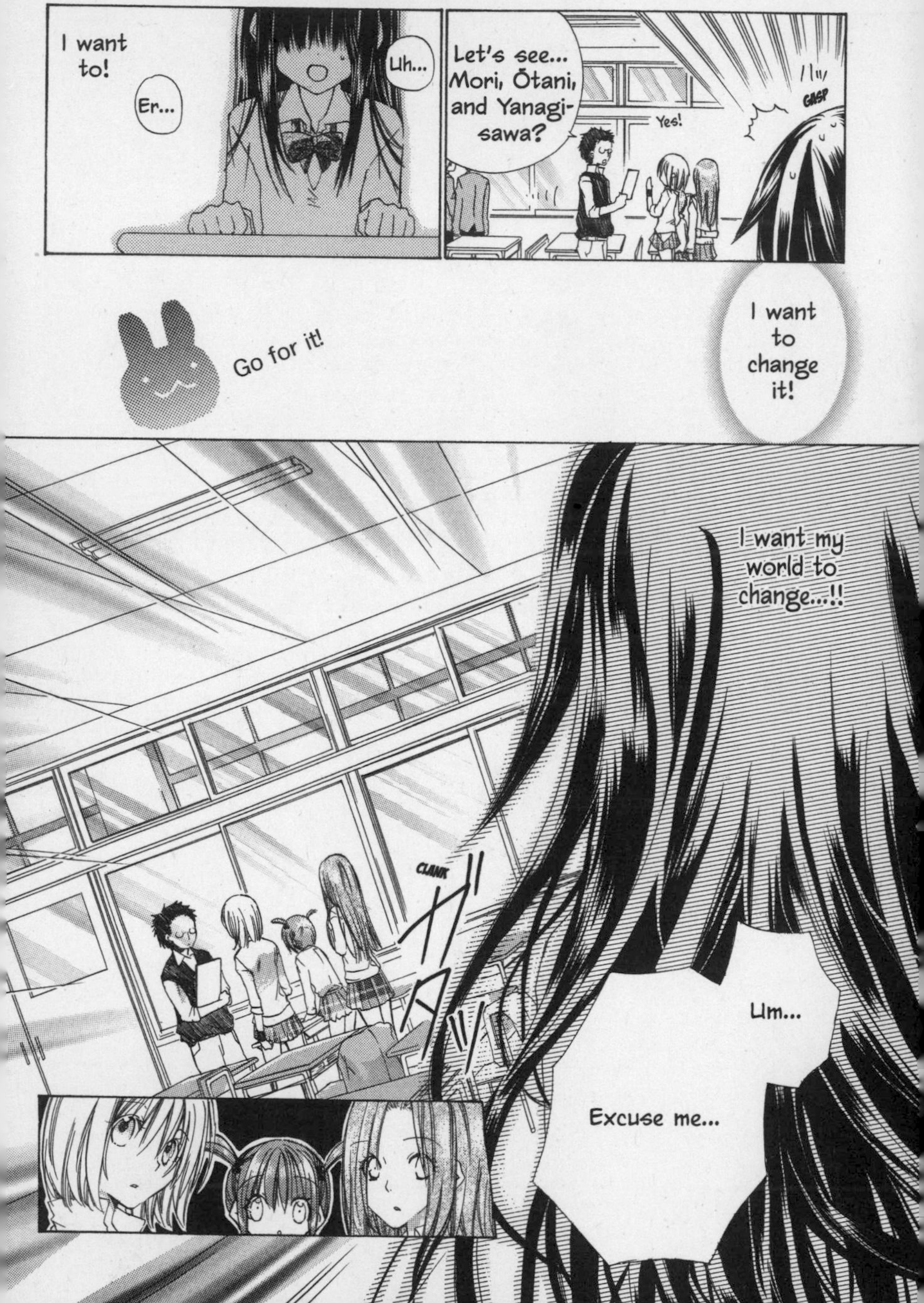
Let's see... Mori, Ōtani, and Yanagi-sawa?
Yes!
GASP
Uh...
I want to!
Er...
I want to change it!
Go for it!
I want my world to change...!!
CLANK
Um...
Excuse me...

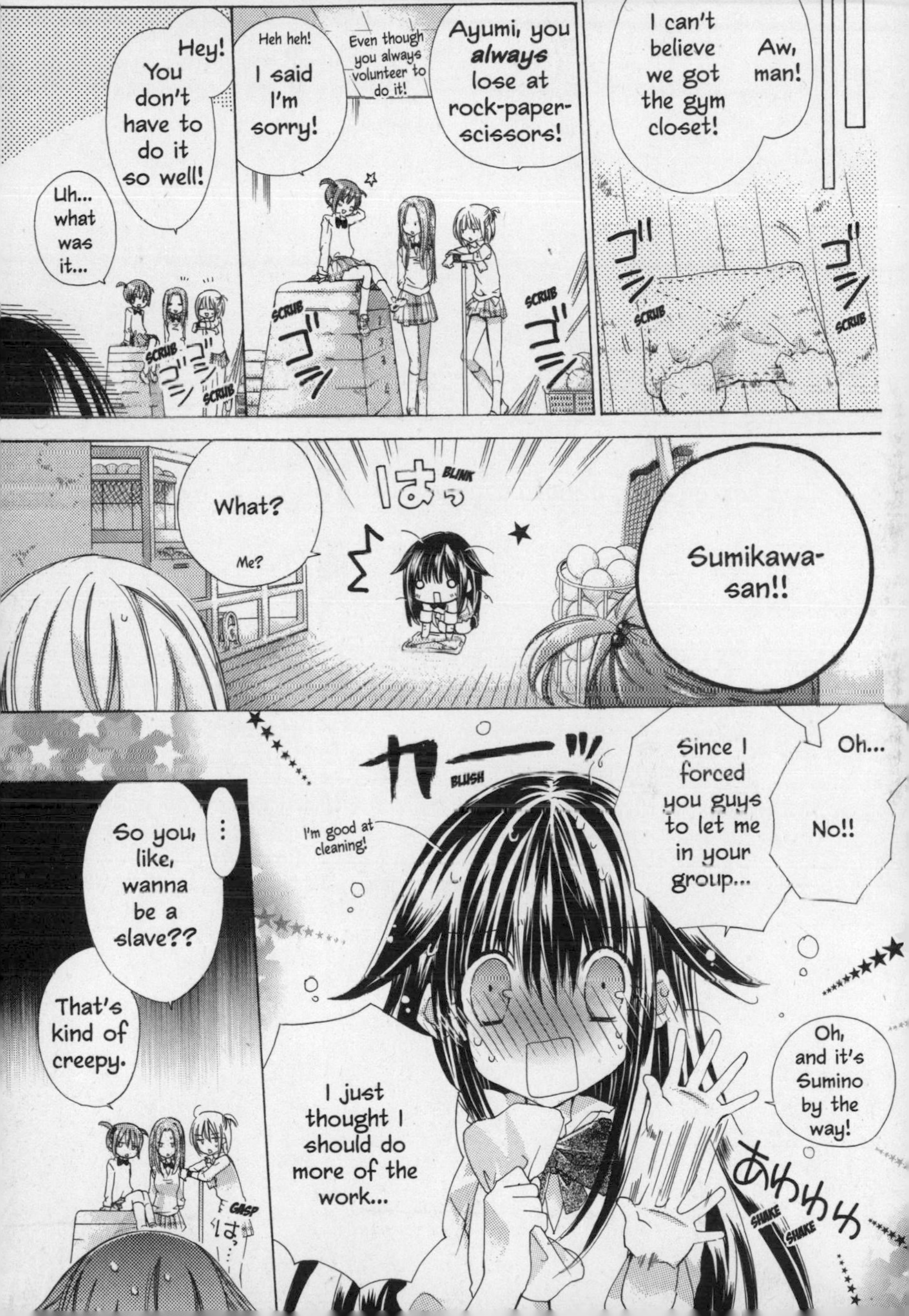
Aw, man!
I can't believe we got the gym closet!
ゴシ SCRUB
ゴシ SCRUB
Ayumi, you **always** lose at rock-paper-scissors!
Even though you always volunteer to do it!
Heh heh! I said I'm sorry!
ゴシ SCRUB
ゴシ SCRUB
Hey! You don't have to do it so well!
Uh... what was it...
ゴシ SCRUB
ゴシ SCRUB
Sumikawa-san!!
はっ BLINK
What?
Me?
Oh...
No!!
Since I forced you guys to let me in your group...
カーッ BLUSH
I'm good at cleaning!
Oh, and it's Sumino by the way!
I just thought I should do more of the work...
あわわわ SHAKE SHAKE
…
So you, like, wanna be a slave??
That's kind of creepy.
はっ GASP

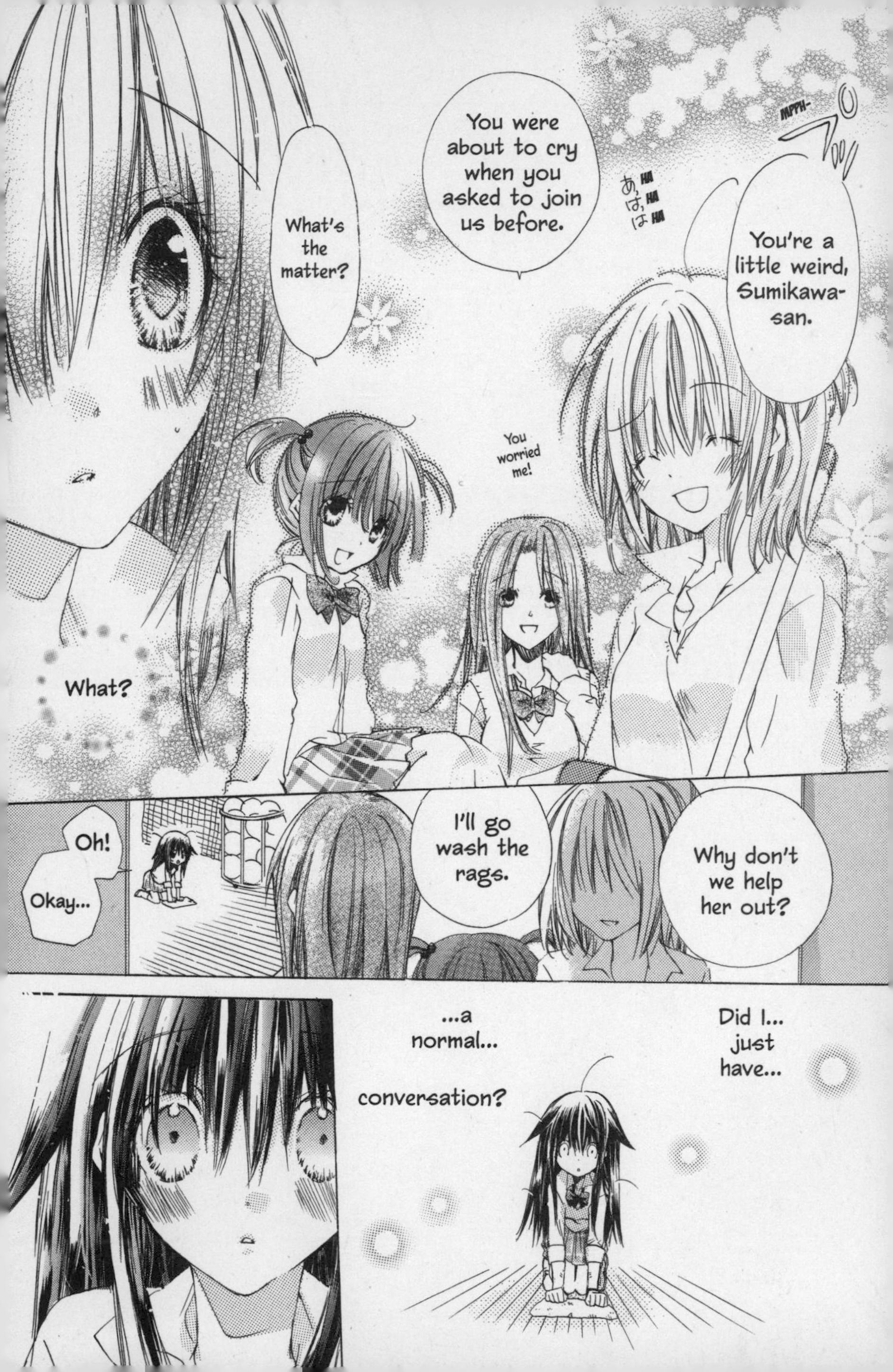
MPPH-
You're a little weird, Sumikawa-san.
あはは HA HA HA
You were about to cry when you asked to join us before.
You worried me!
What's the matter?
What?
Why don't we help her out?
I'll go wash the rags.
Oh!
Okay...
Did I... just have...
...a normal...
conversation?

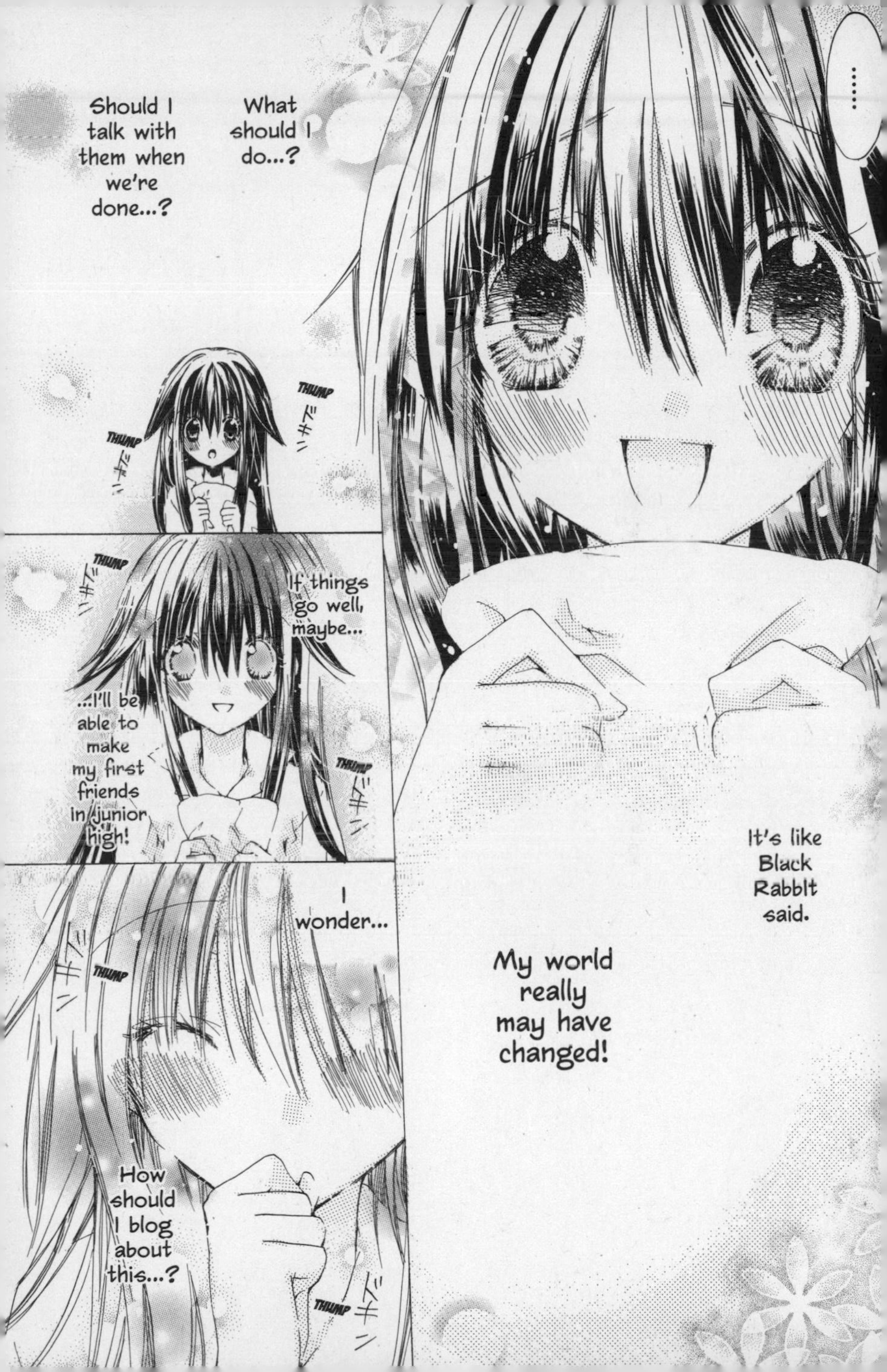
......
It's like Black Rabbit said.
My world really may have changed!
What should I do...?
Should I talk with them when we're done...?
THUMP
THUMP
If things go well, maybe...
...I'll be able to make my first friends in junior high!
THUMP
THUMP
I wonder...
How should I blog about this...?
THUMP
THUMP

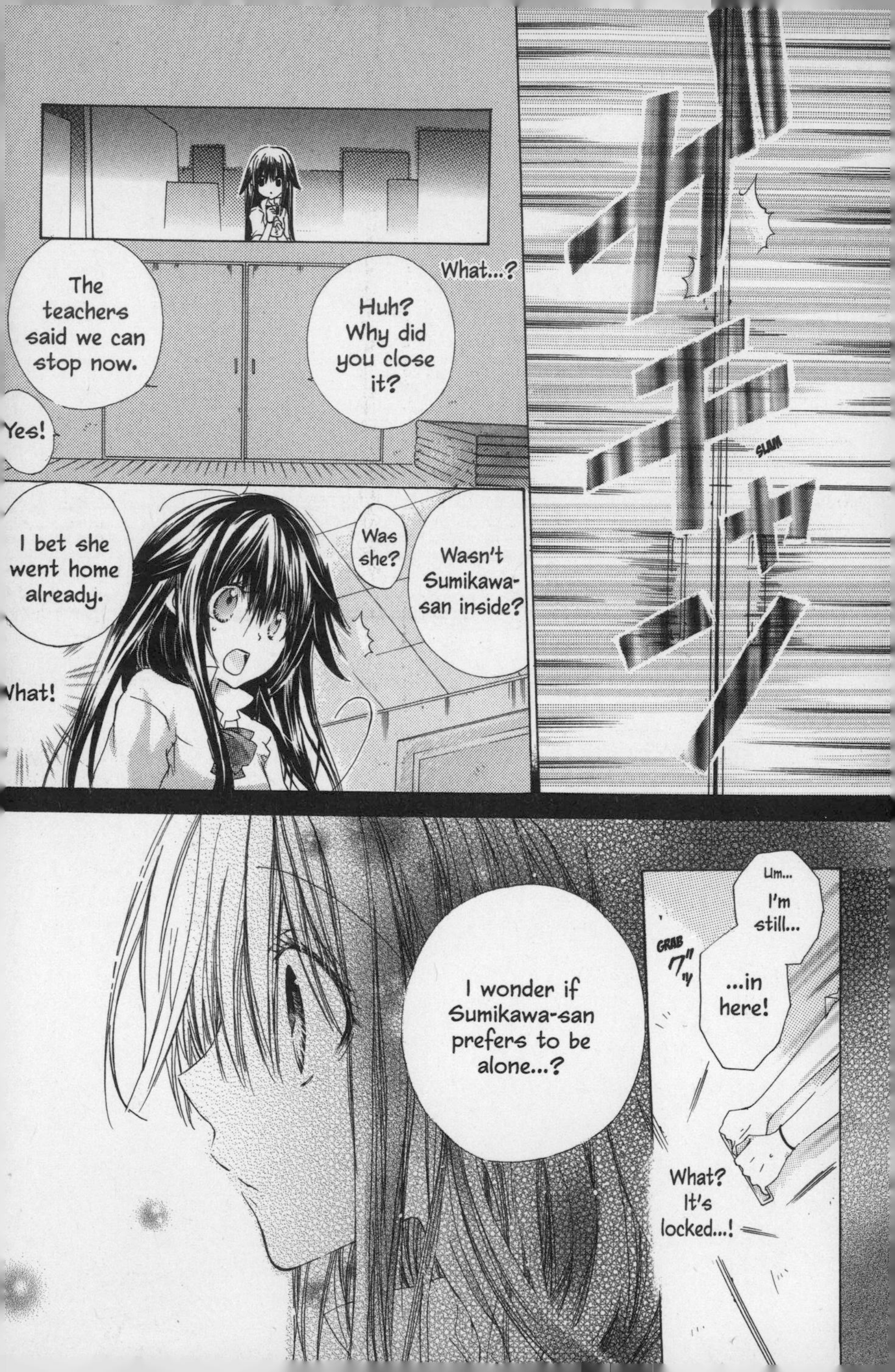
SLAM
What...?
Huh? Why did you close it?
The teachers said we can stop now.
Yes!
Wasn't Sumikawa-san inside?
Was she?
I bet she went home already.
What!
Um... I'm still...
GRAB
...in here!
What? It's locked...!
I wonder if Sumikawa-san prefers to be alone...?

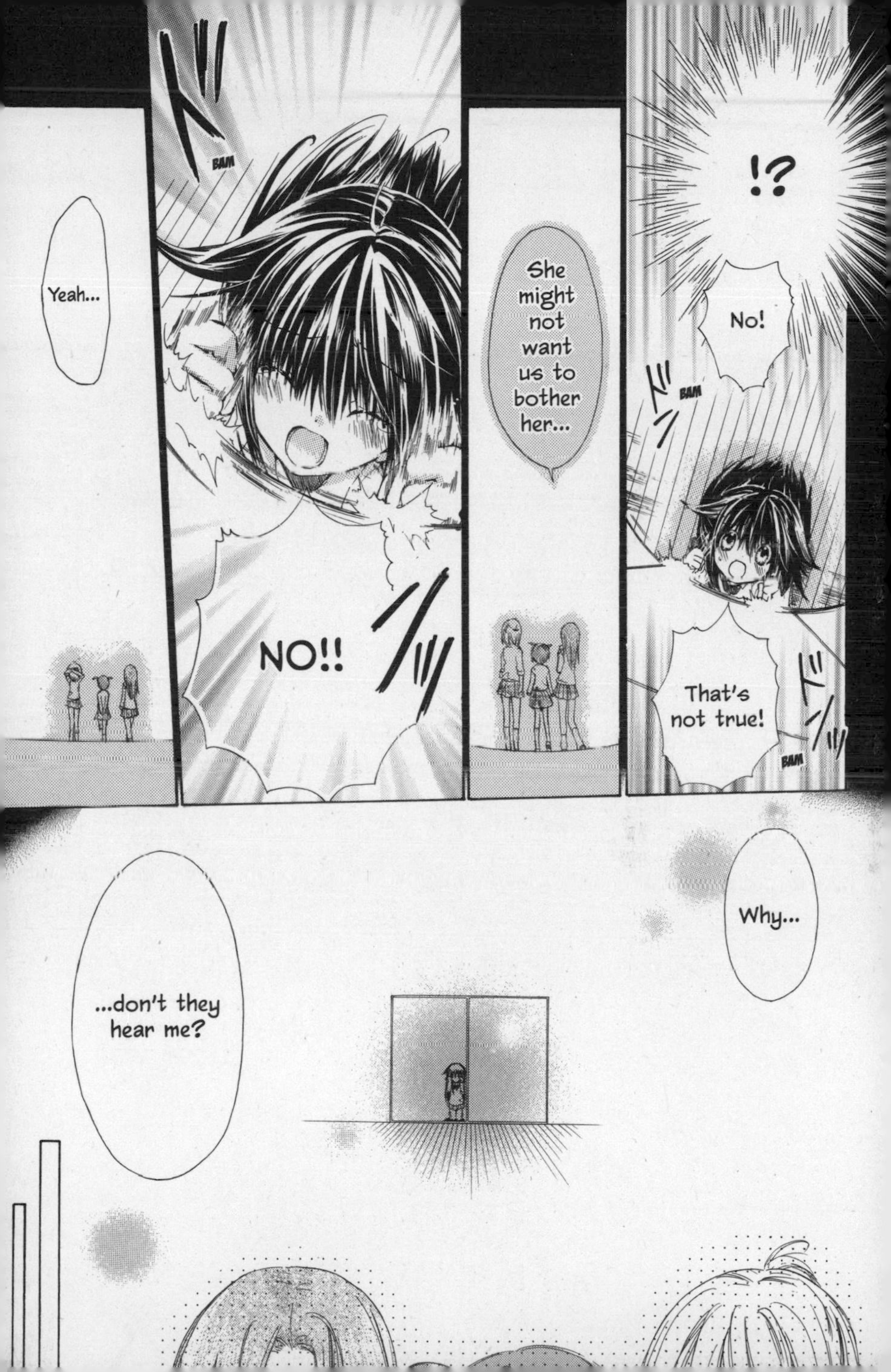
!?
No!
BAM
That's not true!
BAM
She might not want us to bother her...
BAM
NO!!
Yeah...
Why...
...don't they hear me?

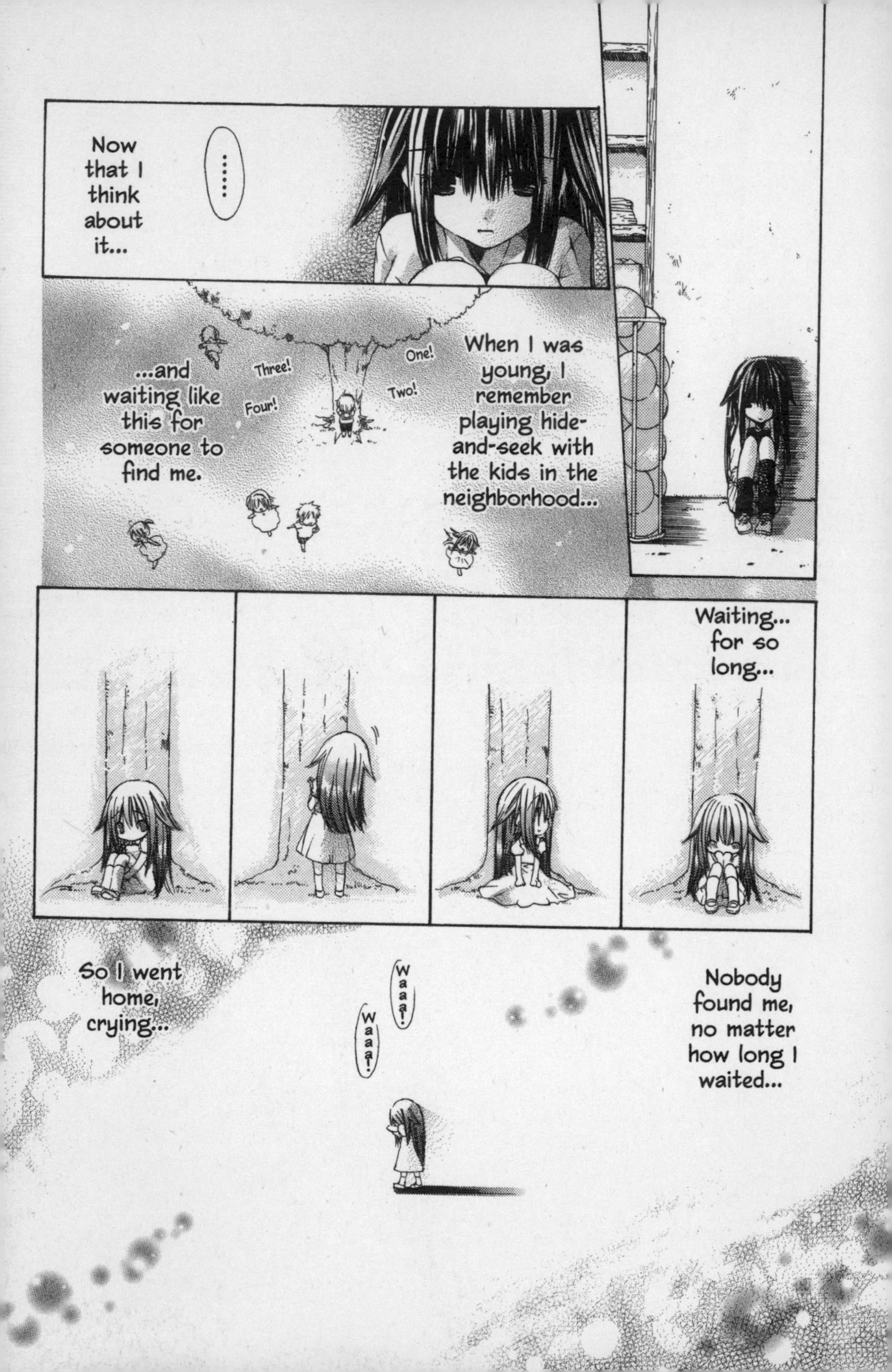

Now that I think about it...
......
When I was young, I remember playing hide-and-seek with the kids in the neighborhood...
One!
Two!
Three!
Four!
...and waiting like this for someone to find me.
Waiting... for so long...
Nobody found me, no matter how long I waited...
Waaa!
Waaa!
So I went home, crying...

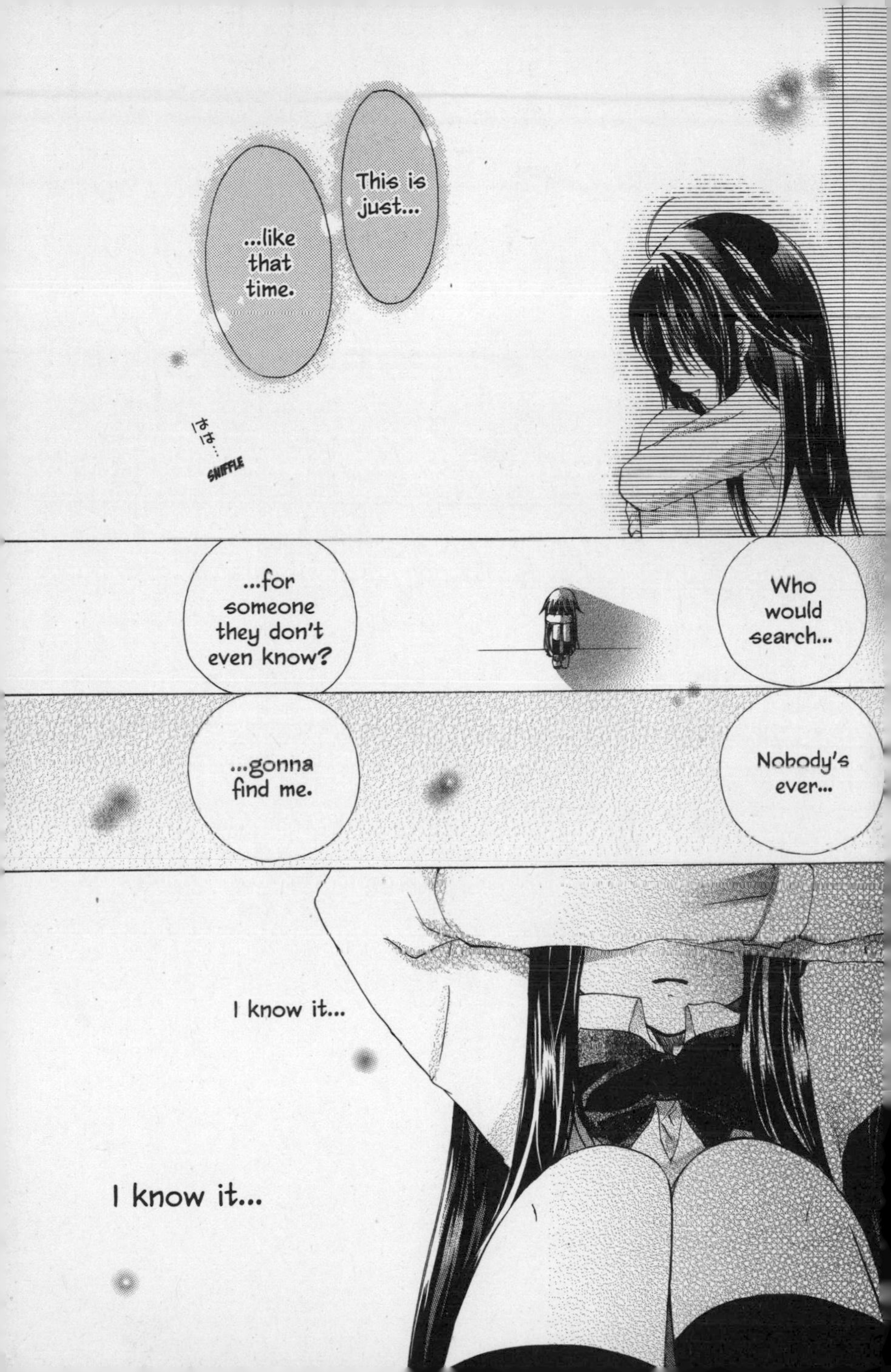
This is just...
...like that time.
はは…
SNIFFLE
Who would search...
...for someone they don't even know?
Nobody's ever...
...gonna find me.
I know it...
I know it...

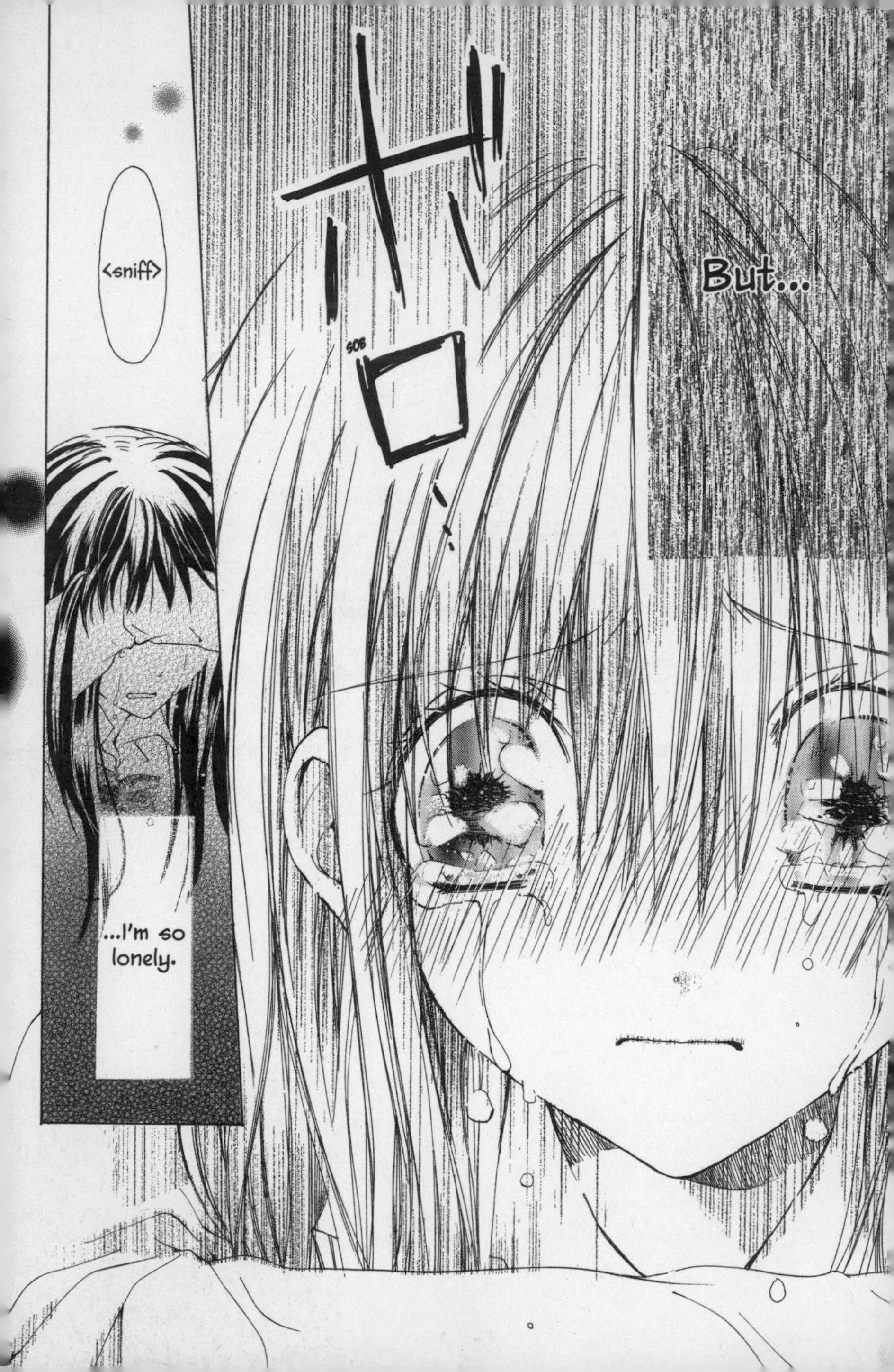
But...
SOB
<sniff>
...I'm so lonely.

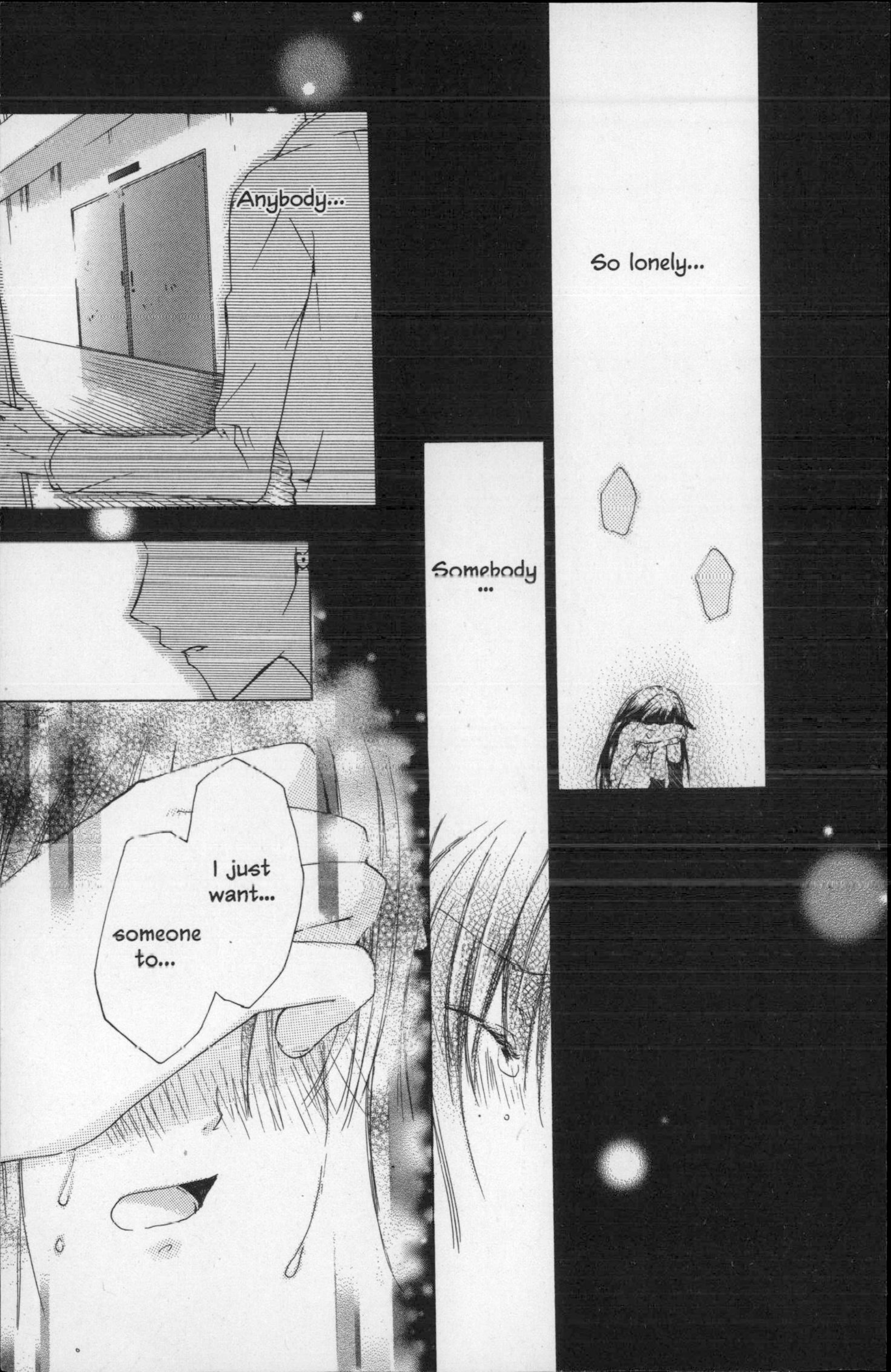

So lonely...
Somebody...
Anybody...
I just want... someone to...

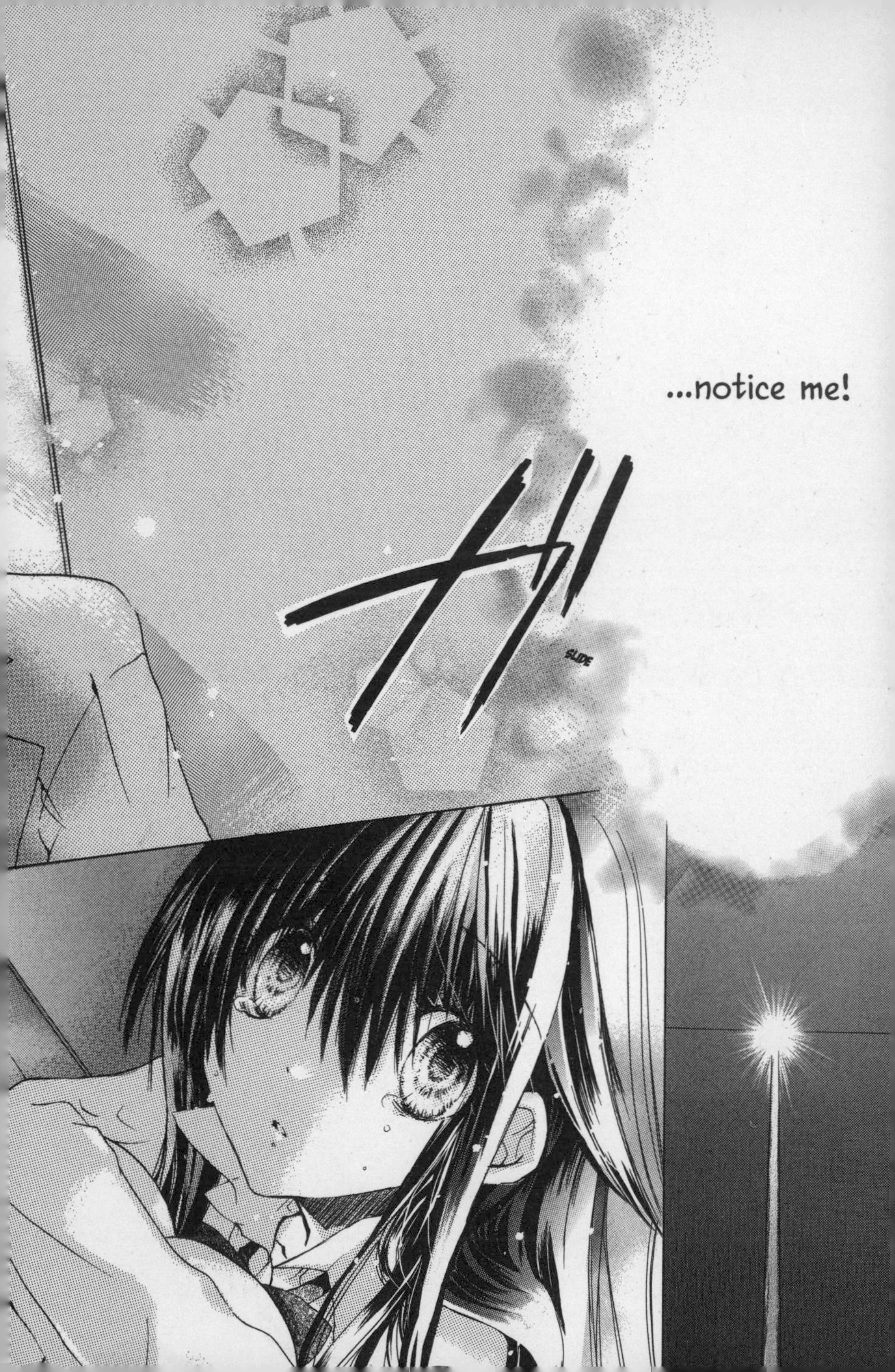
...notice me!
SLIDE

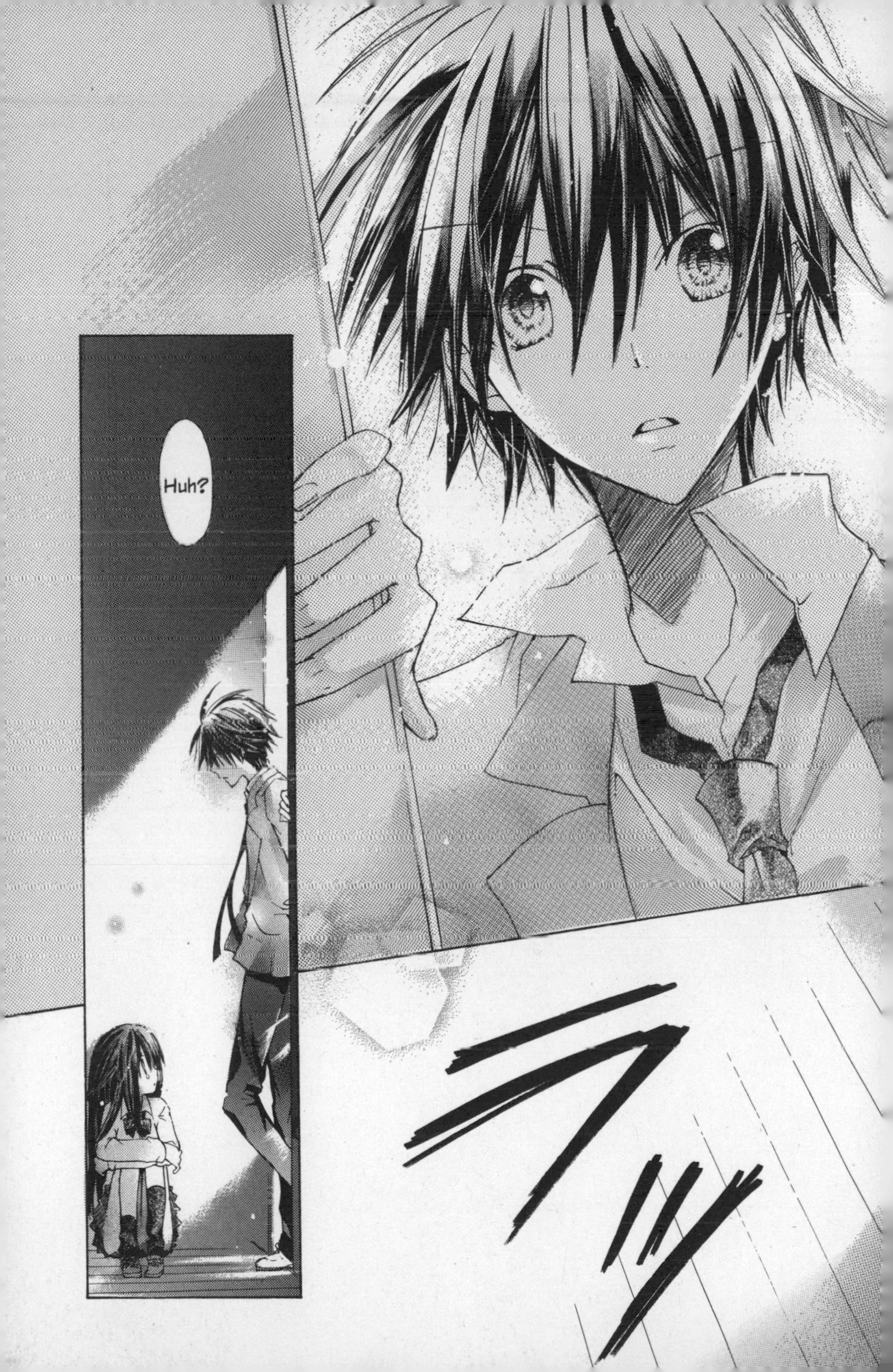
ラッ
Huh?

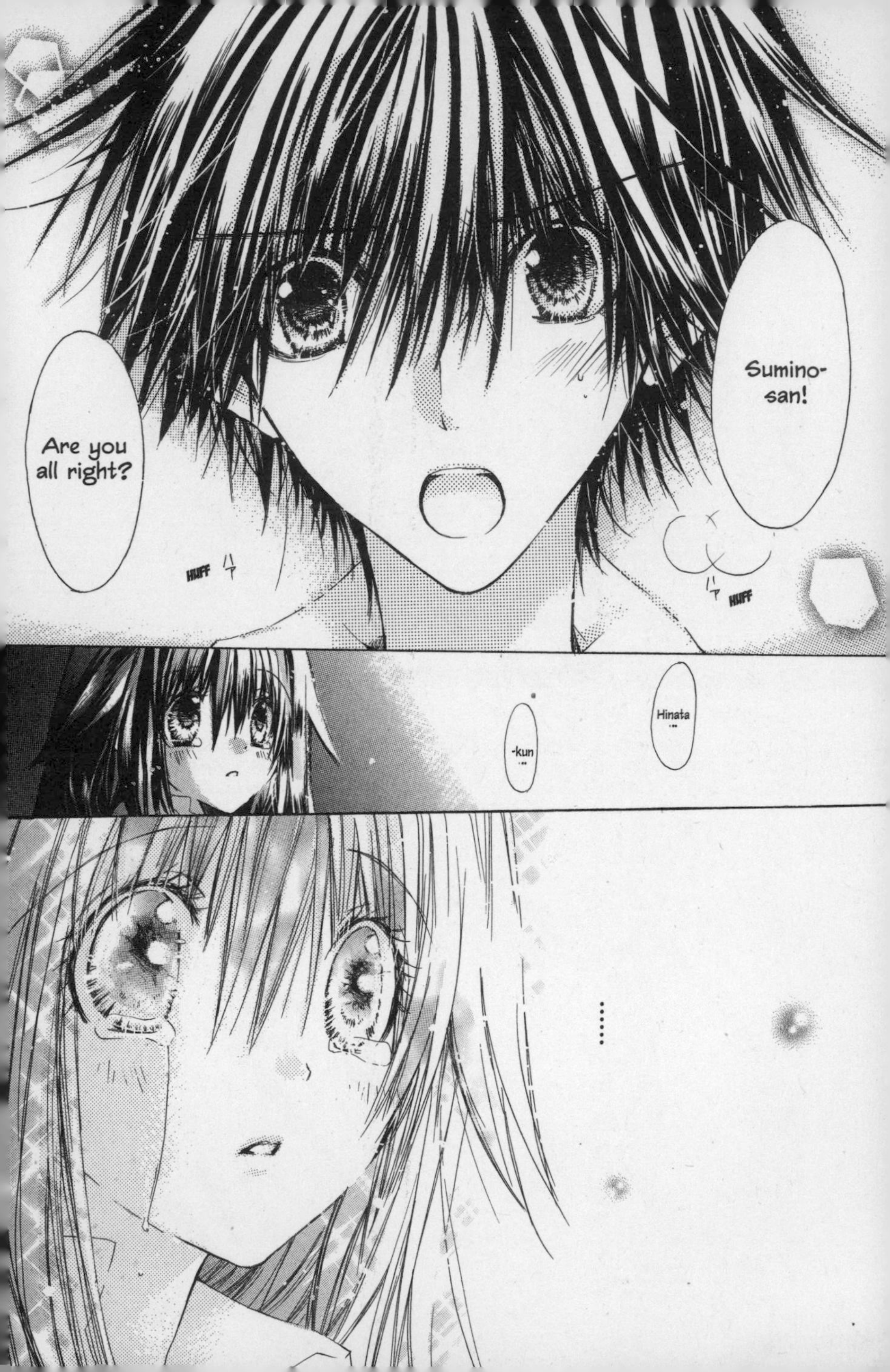

Sumino-san!
HUFF
Are you all right?
HUFF
Hinata...
-kun...
......

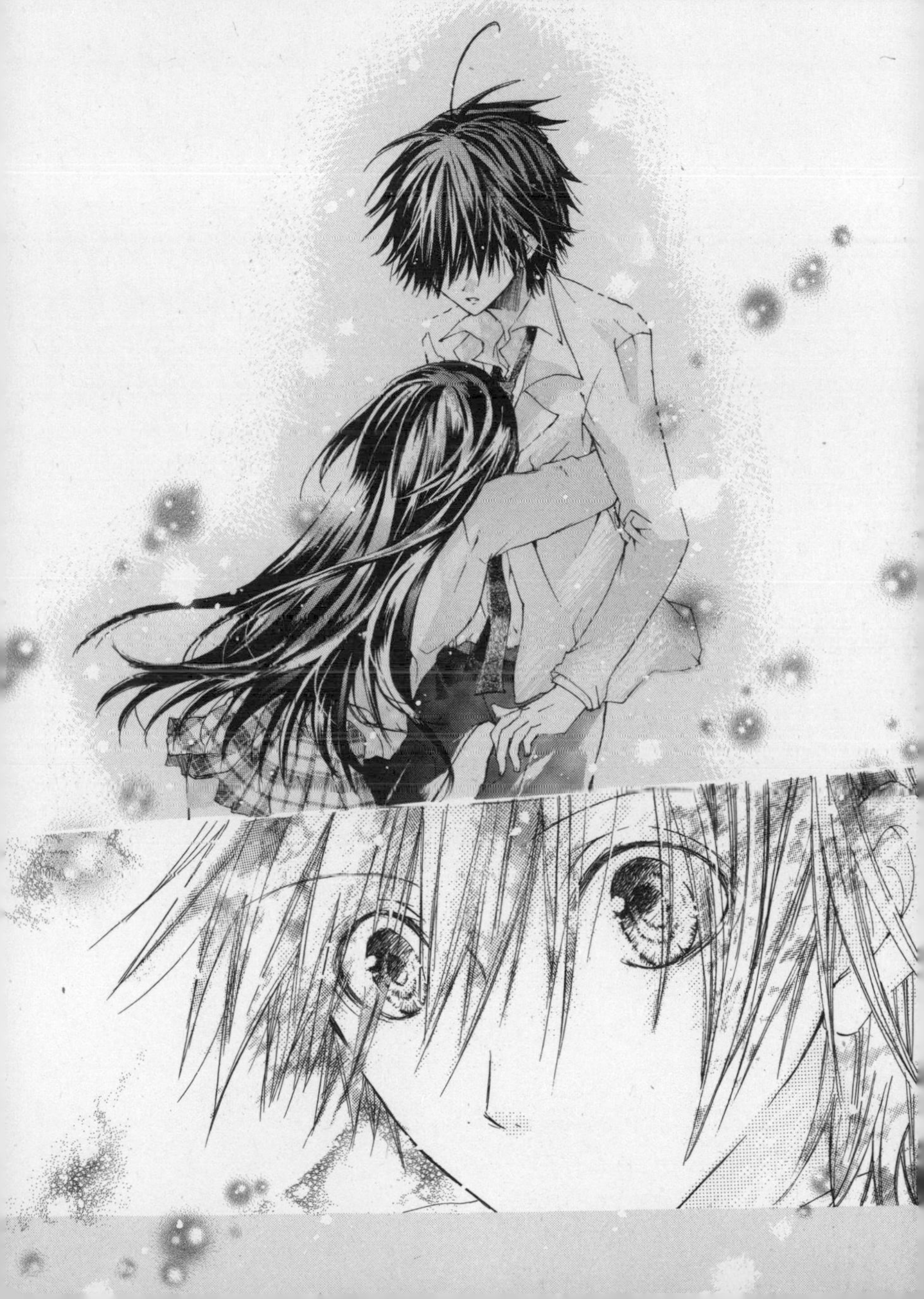

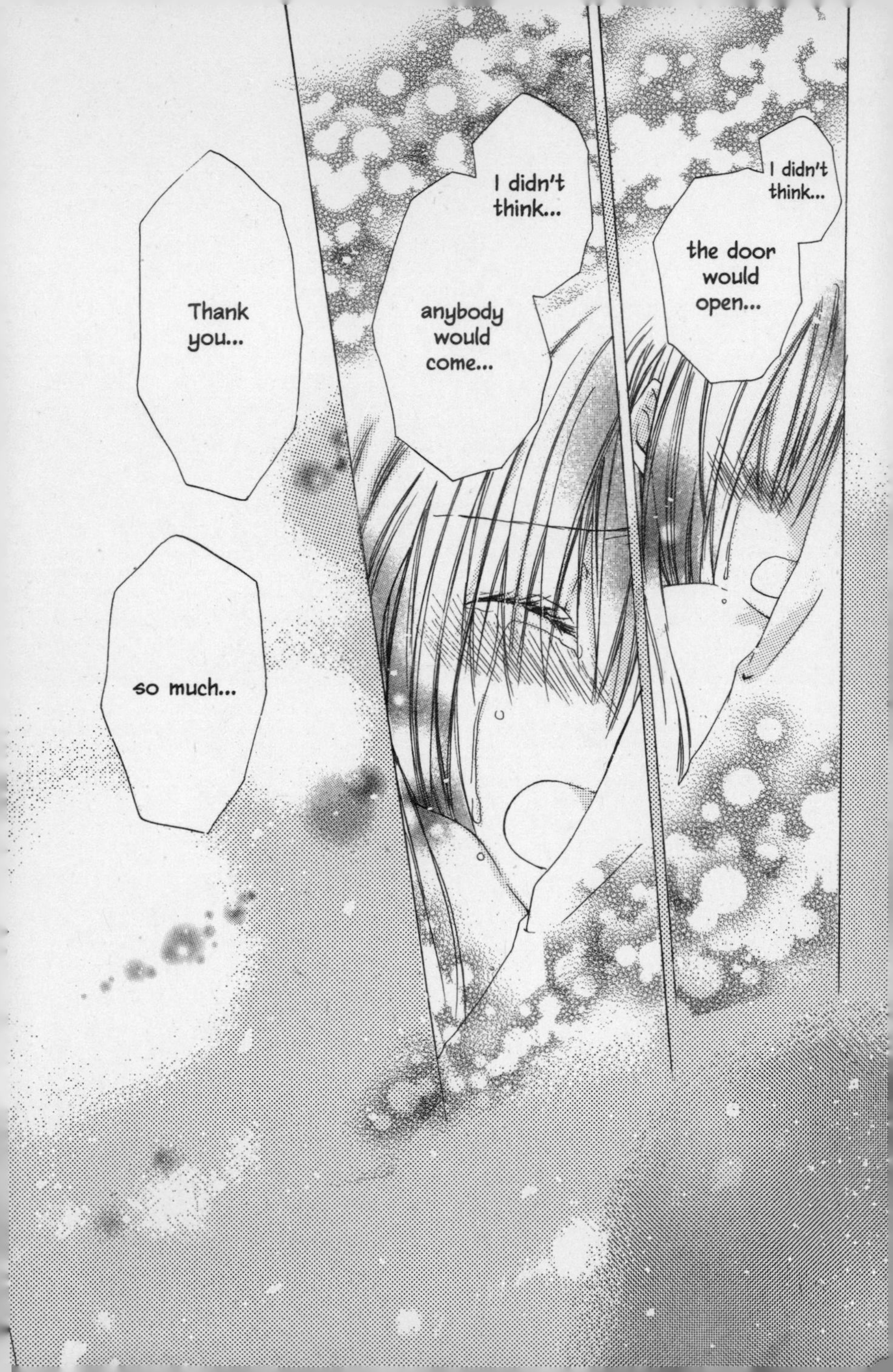
I didn't think...
the door would open...
I didn't think...
anybody would come...
Thank you...
so much...

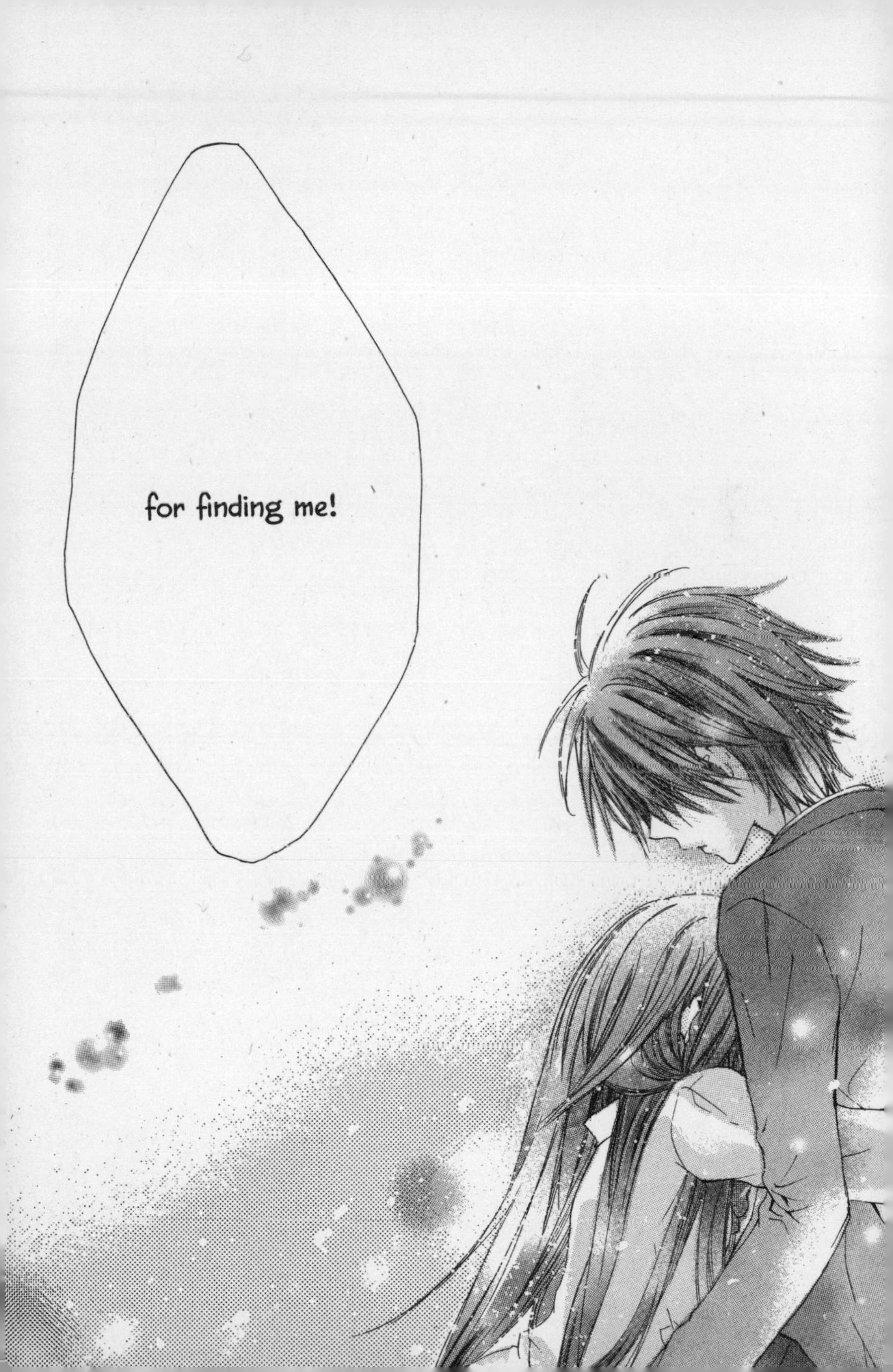
for finding me!

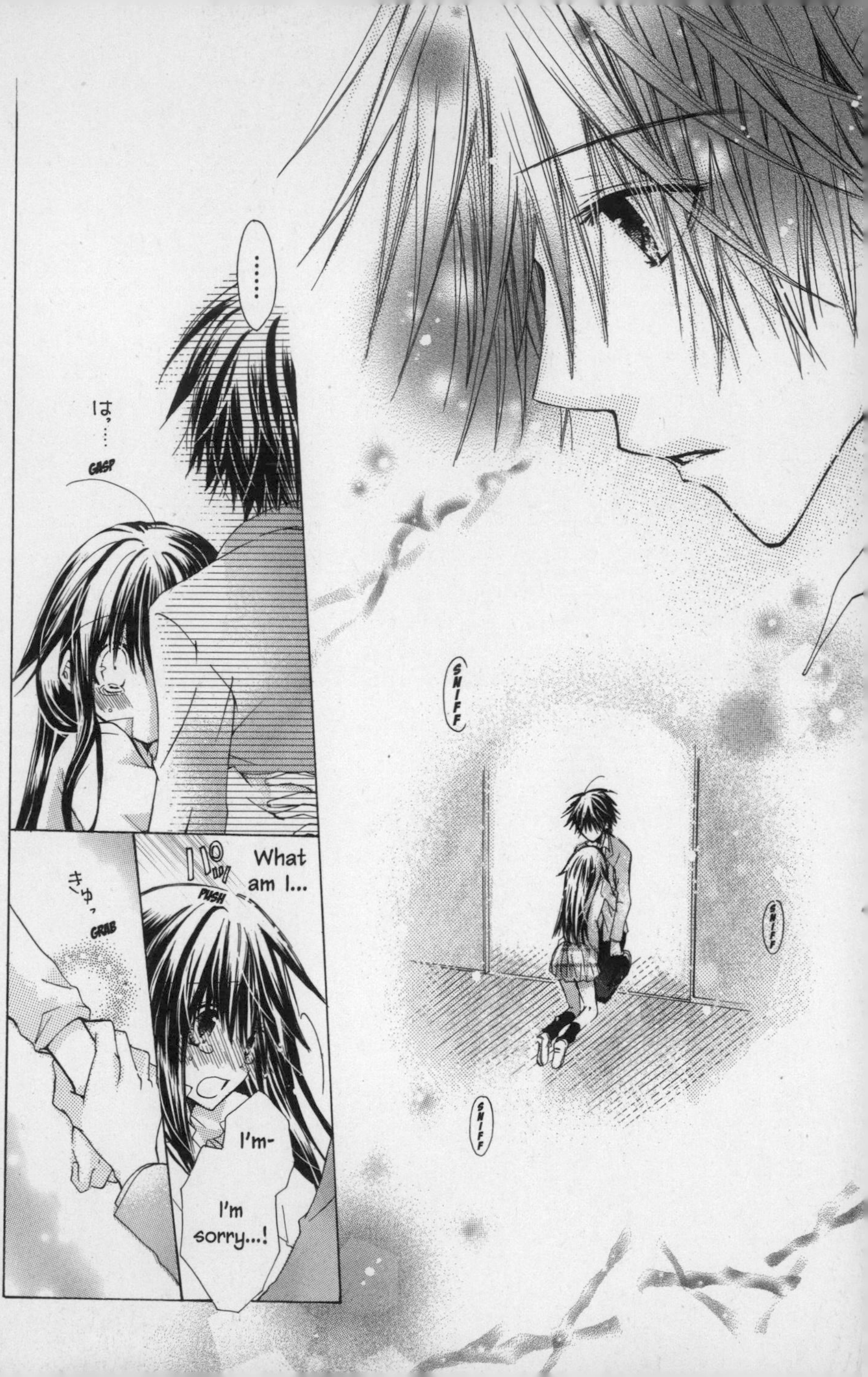
SNIFF
SNIFF
SNIFF
......
はっ……
GASP
What am I...
PUSH
I'm-
I'm sorry...!
きゅっ
GRAB

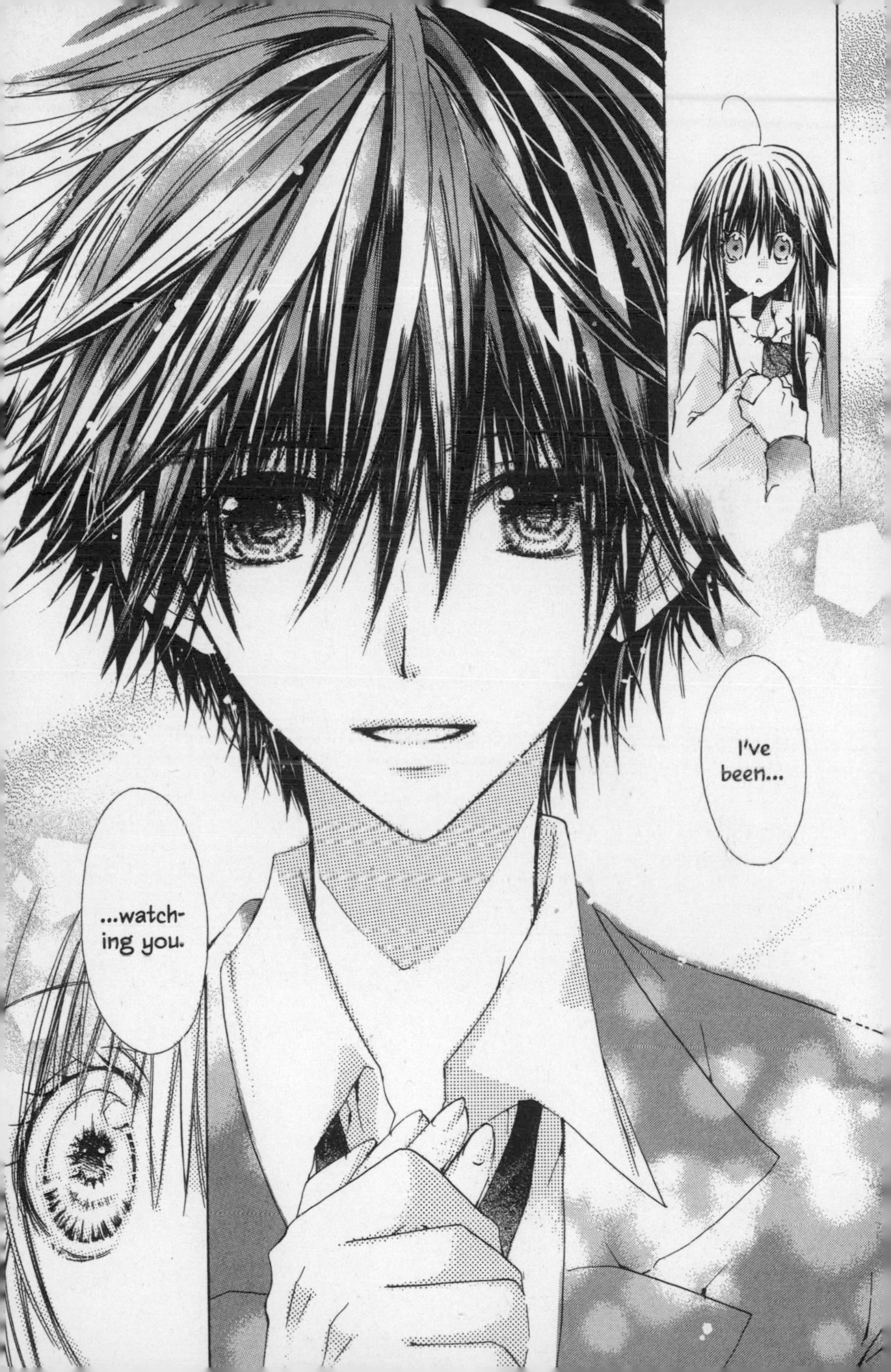
I've been...
...watch-ing you.

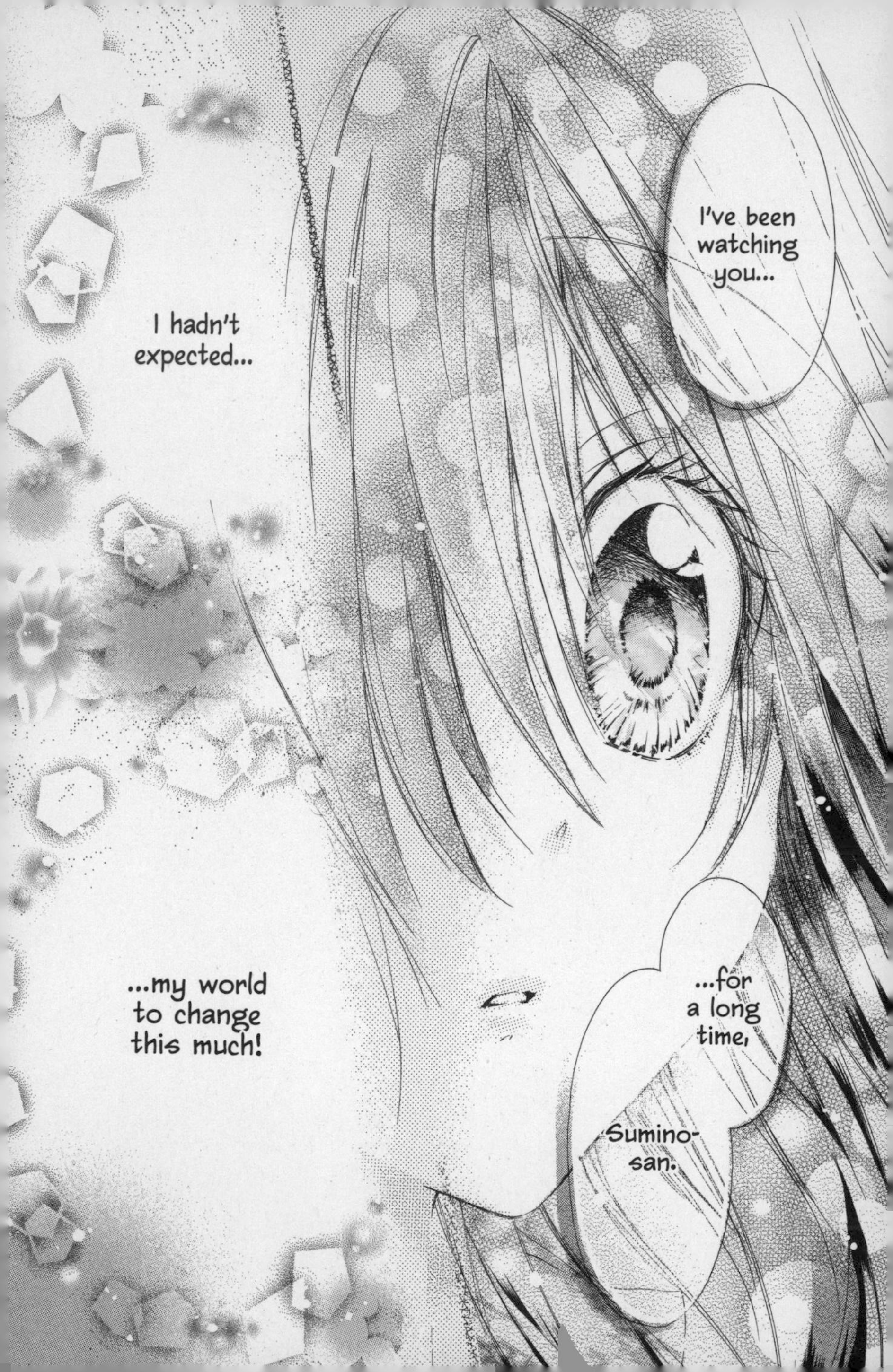
I've been watching you...
...for a long time,
Sumino-san.
I hadn't expected...
...my world to change this much!

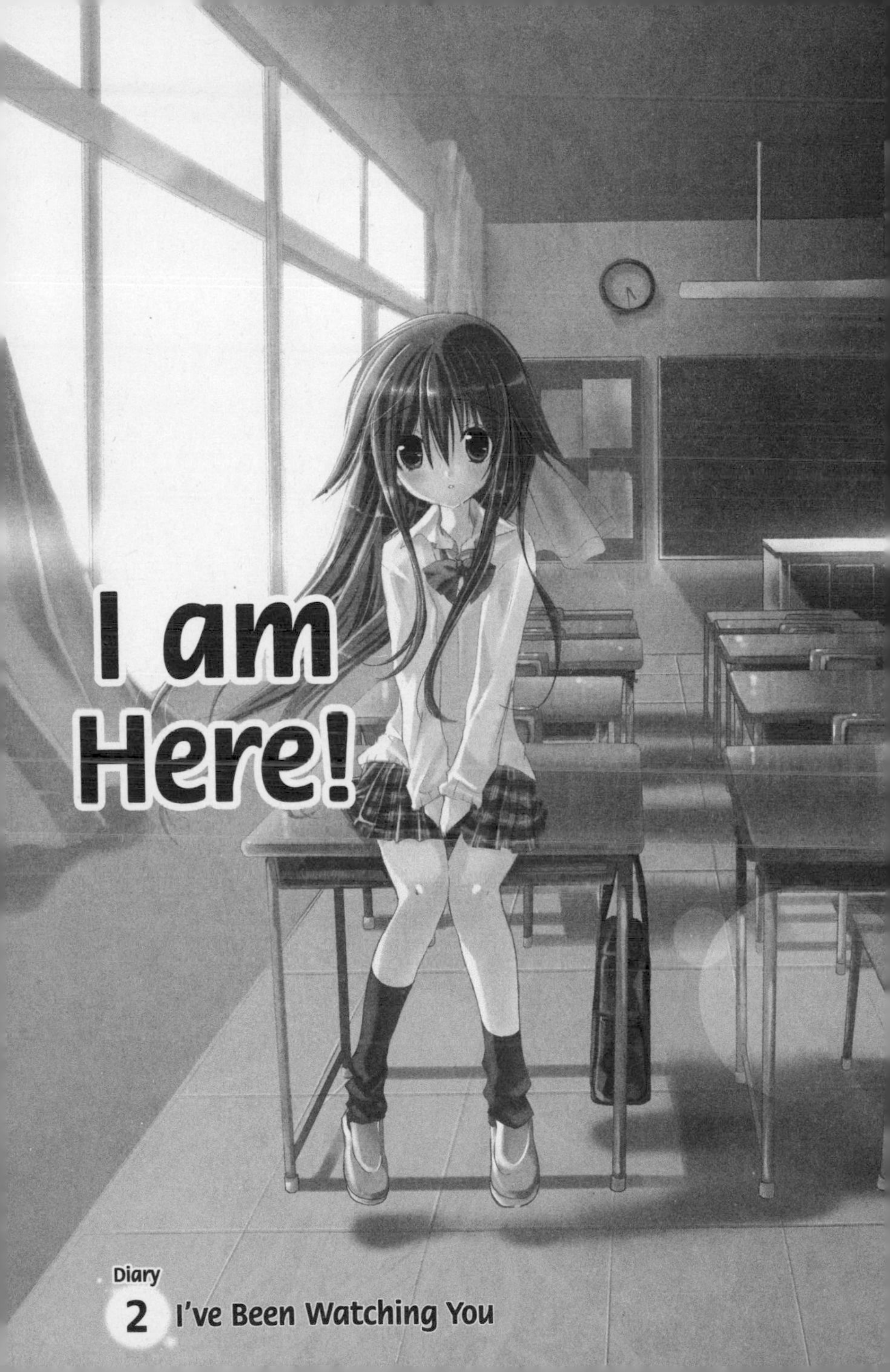
I am Here!
Diary
2 I've Been Watching You

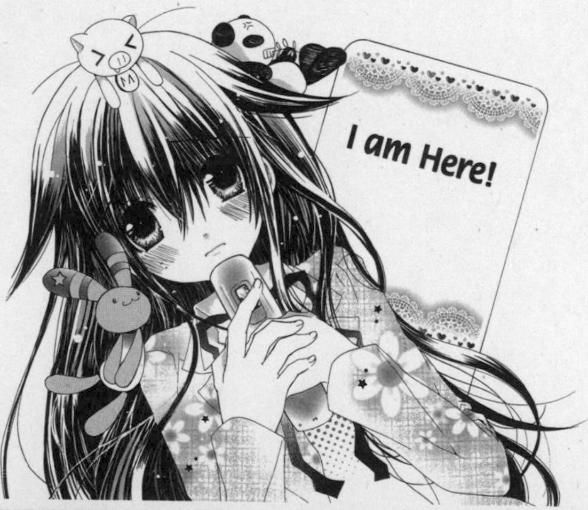
I am Here!

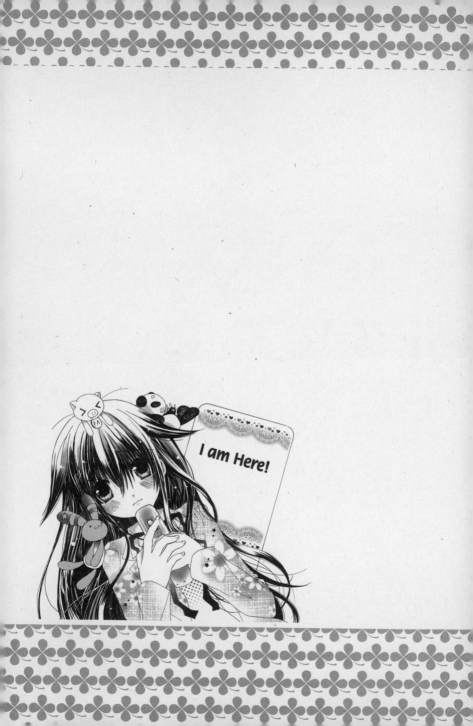

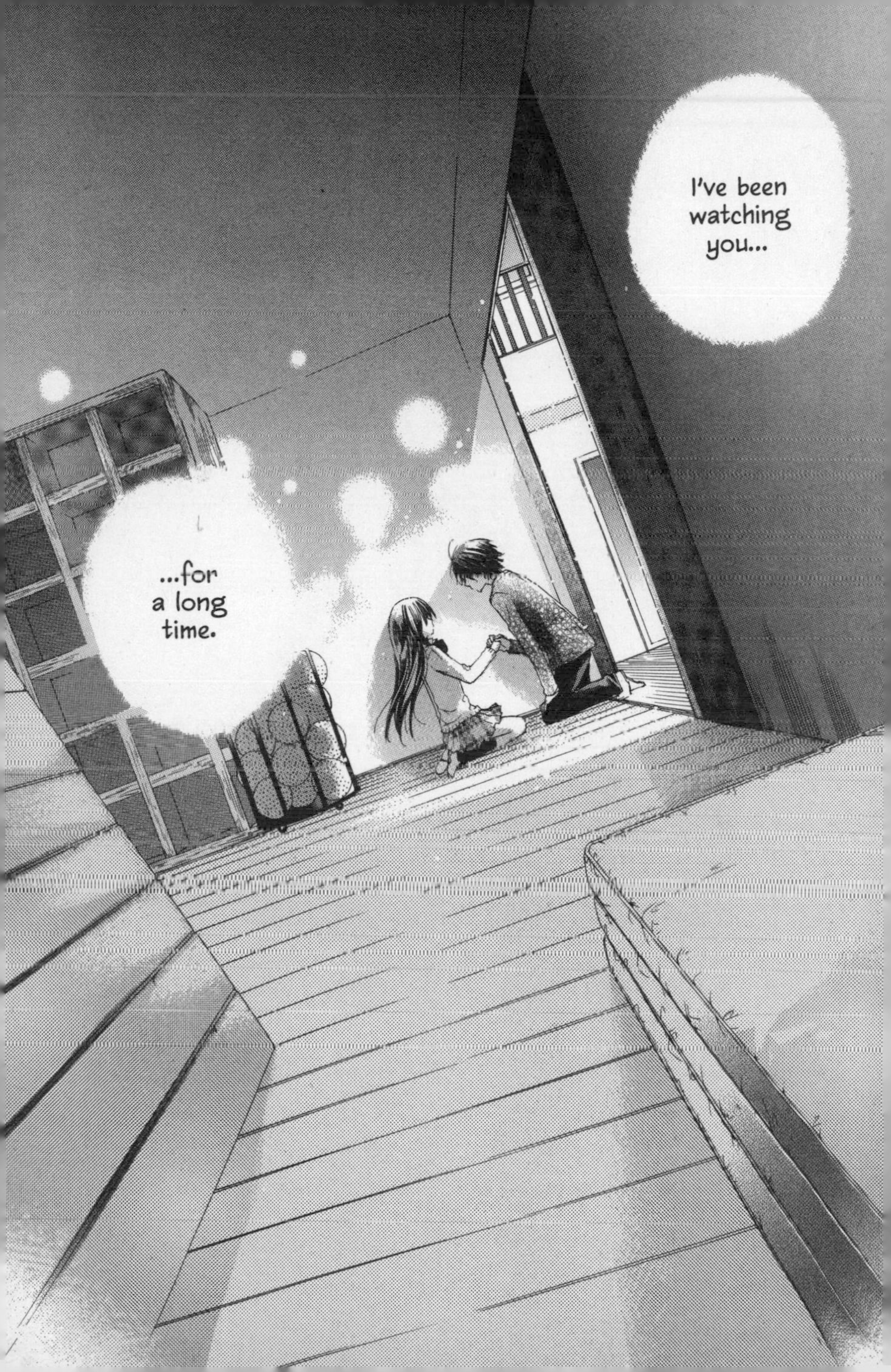
I've been watching you...
...for a long time.

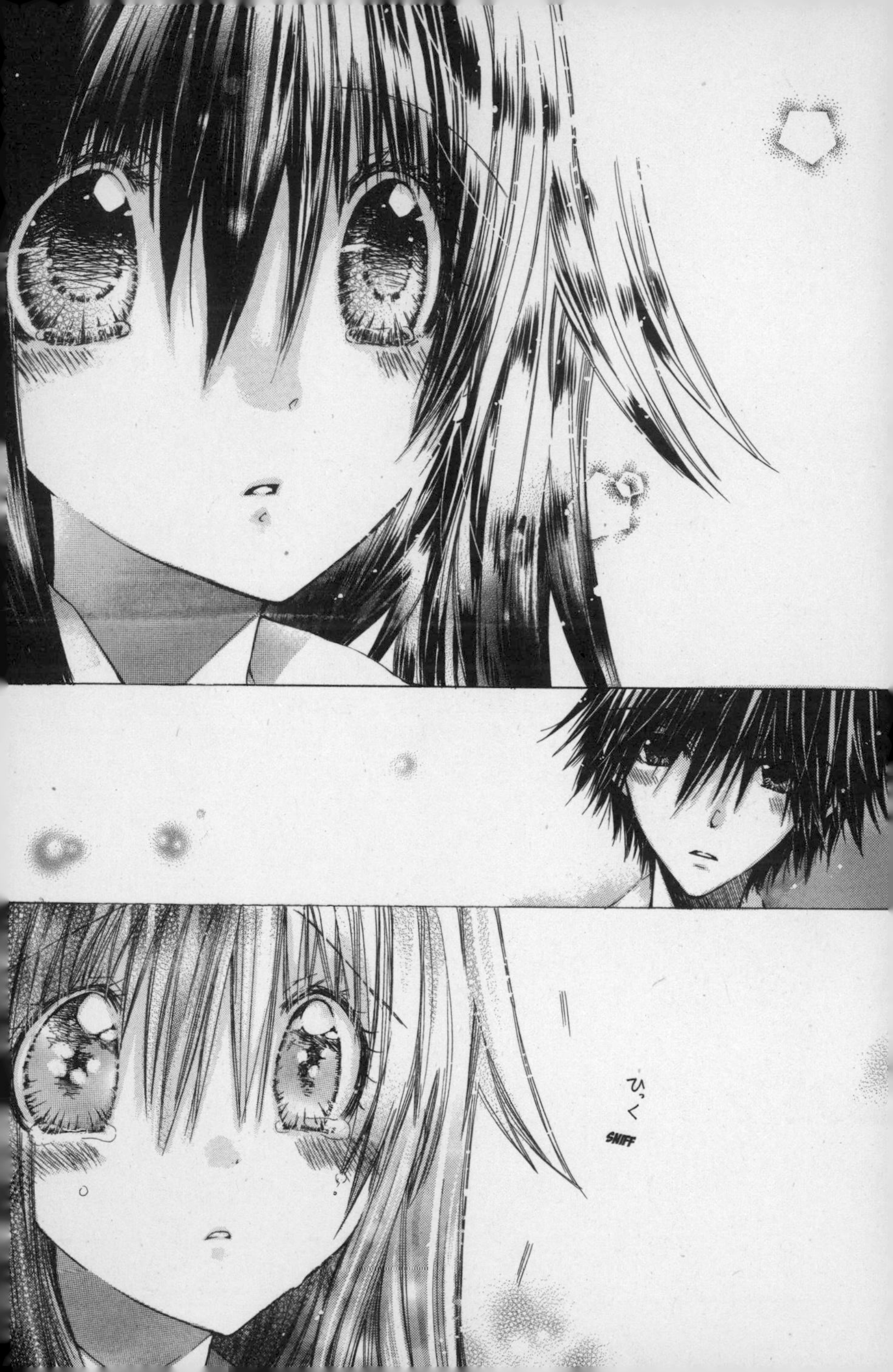
ぴっく
SNIFF

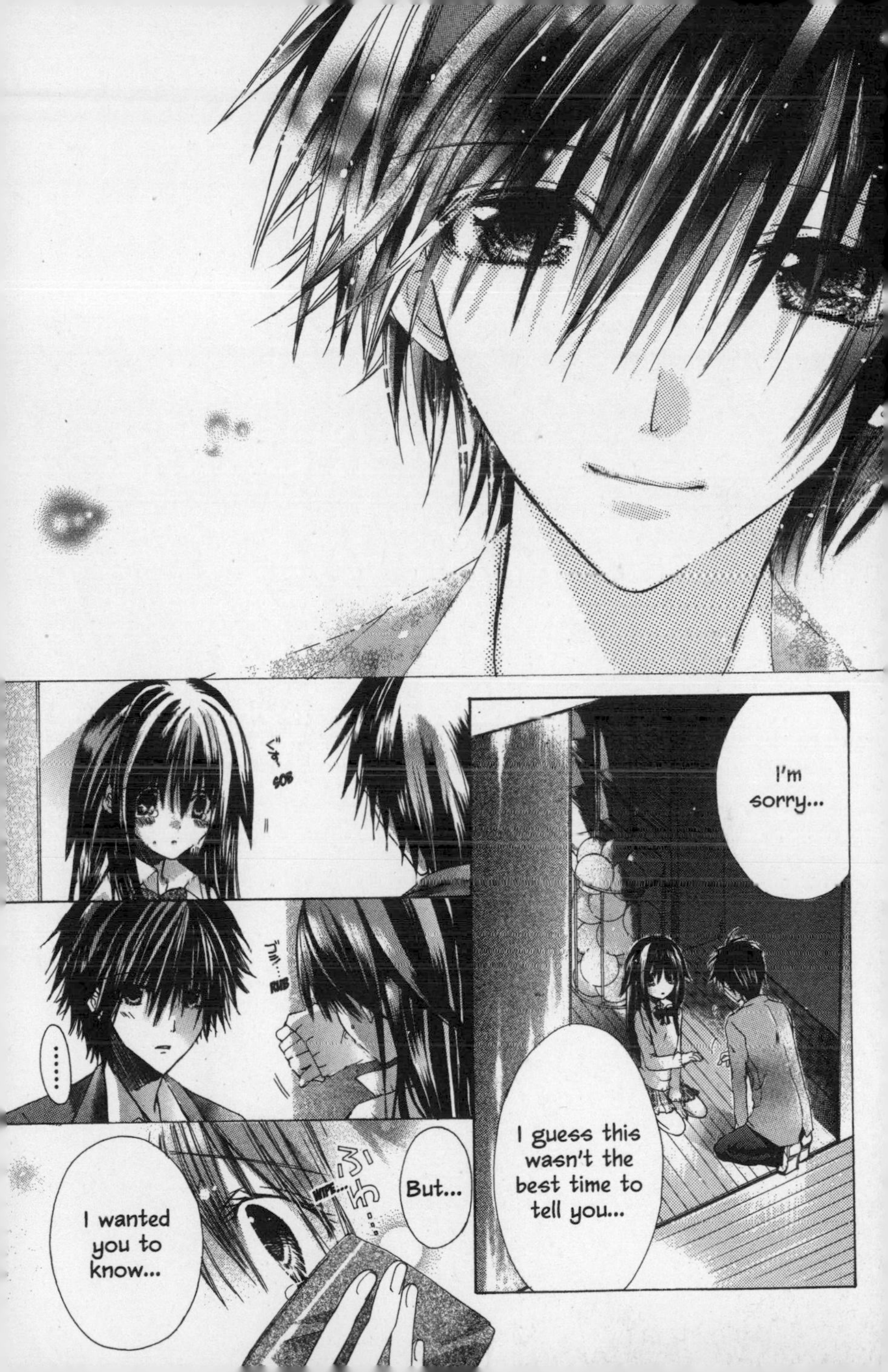
I'm sorry...
I guess this wasn't the best time to tell you...
SOB
RUB
......
WIPE...
But...
I wanted you to know...

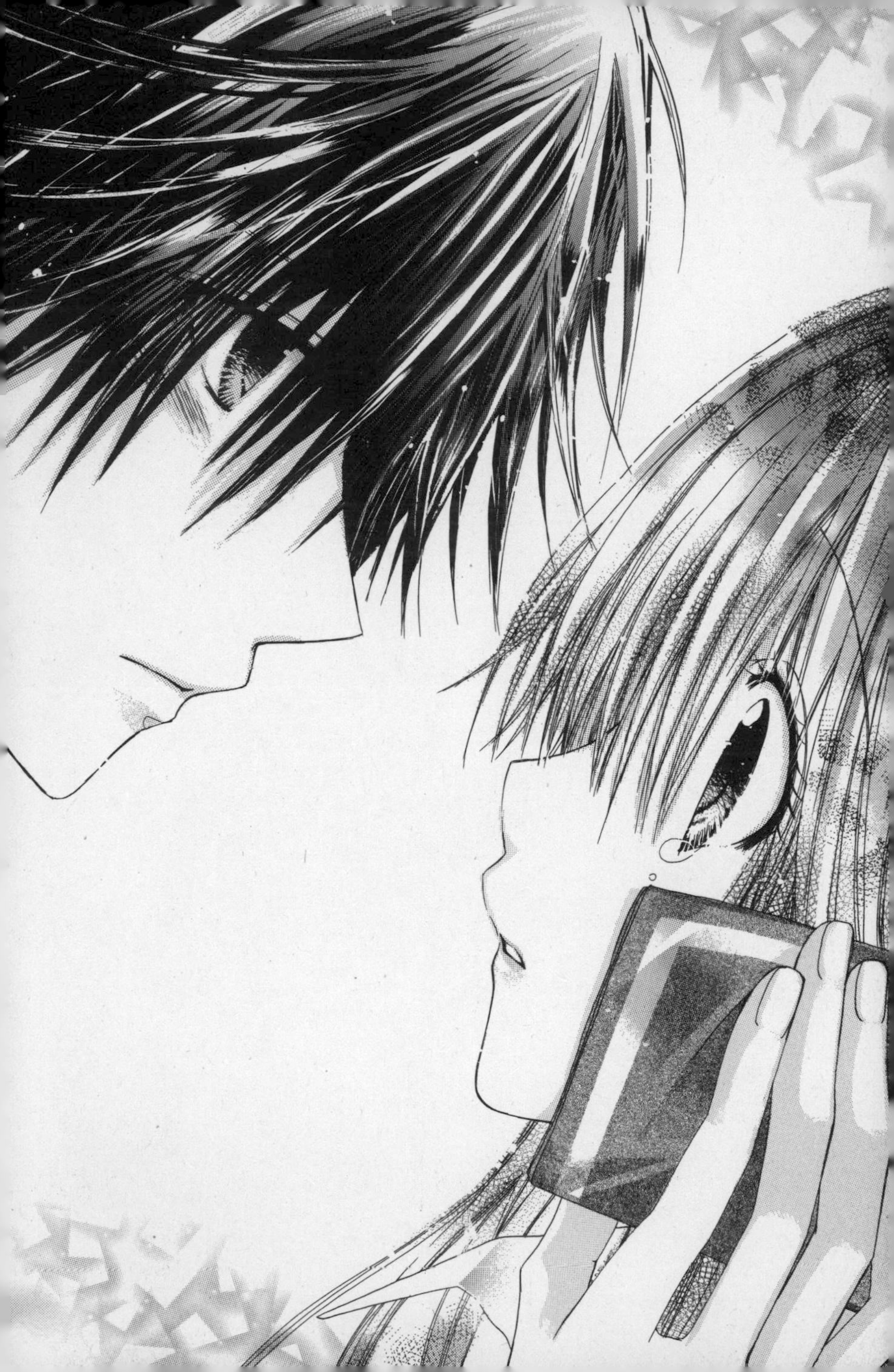

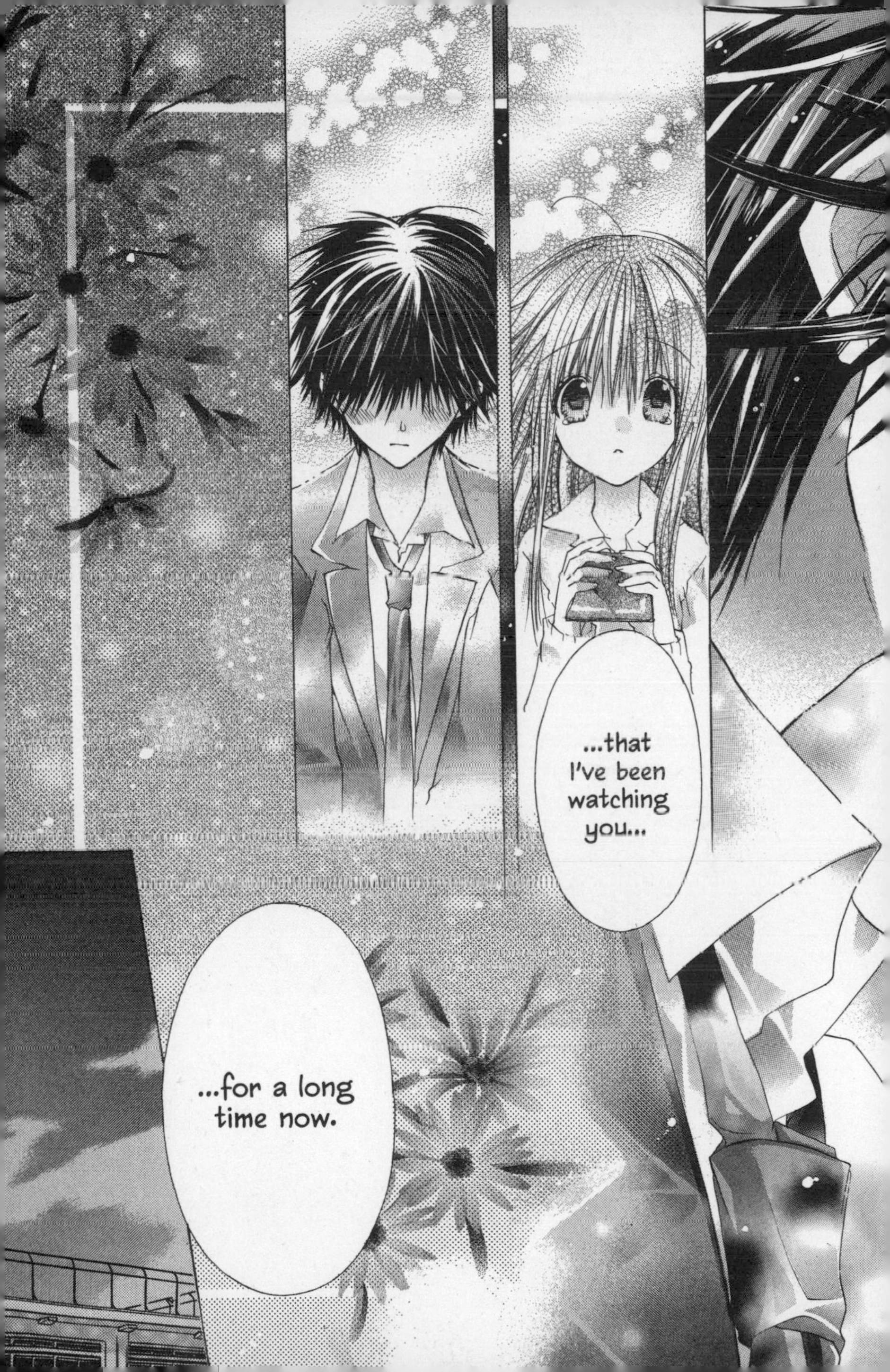
...that I've been watching you...
...for a long time now.

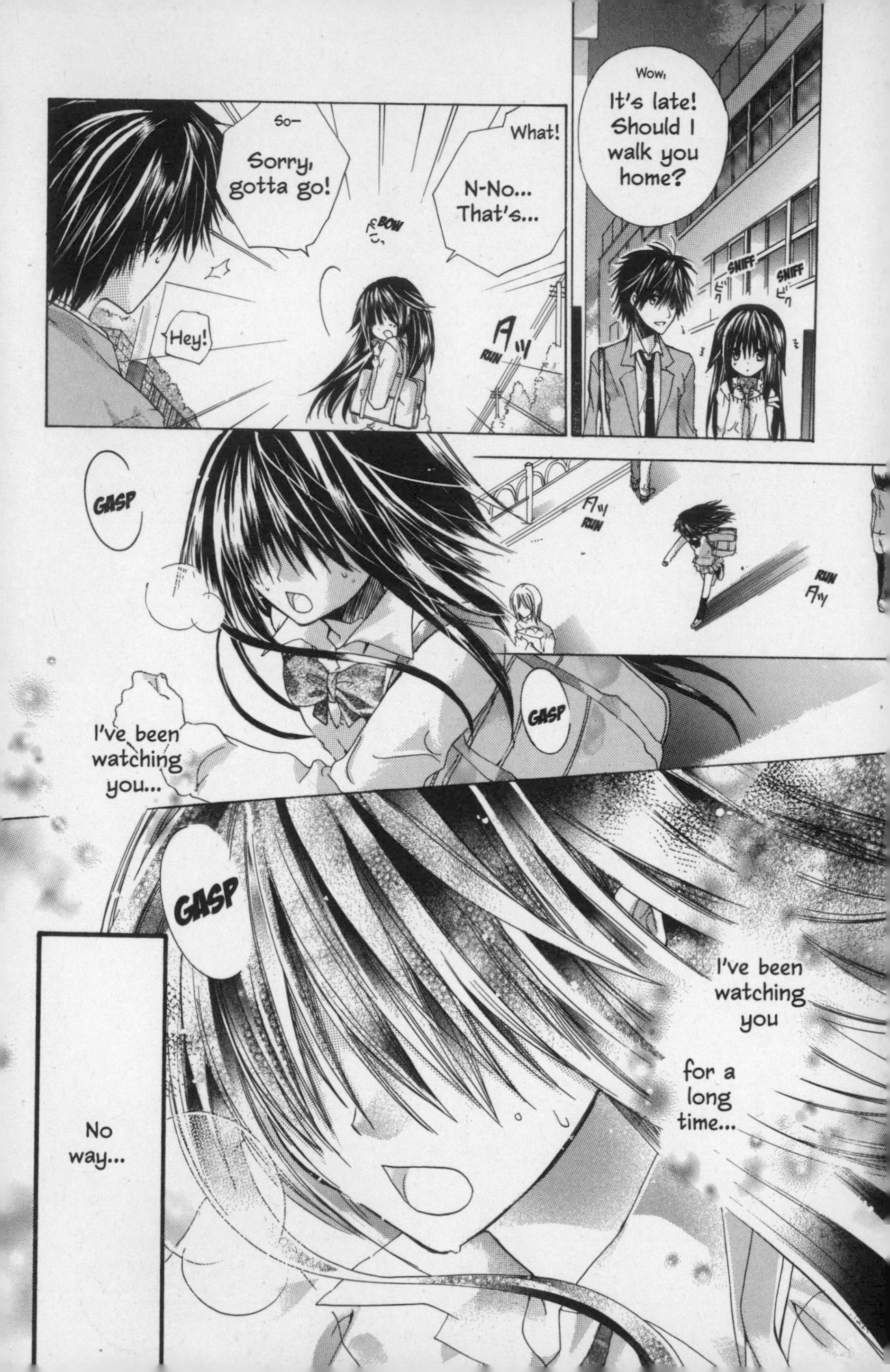
Wow,
It's late! Should I walk you home?
SNIFF
SNIFF
What!
N-No... That's...
So–
Sorry, gotta go!
BOW
RUN
Hey!
RUN
RUN
GASP
GASP
I've been watching you...
I've been watching you
for a long time...
GASP
No way...

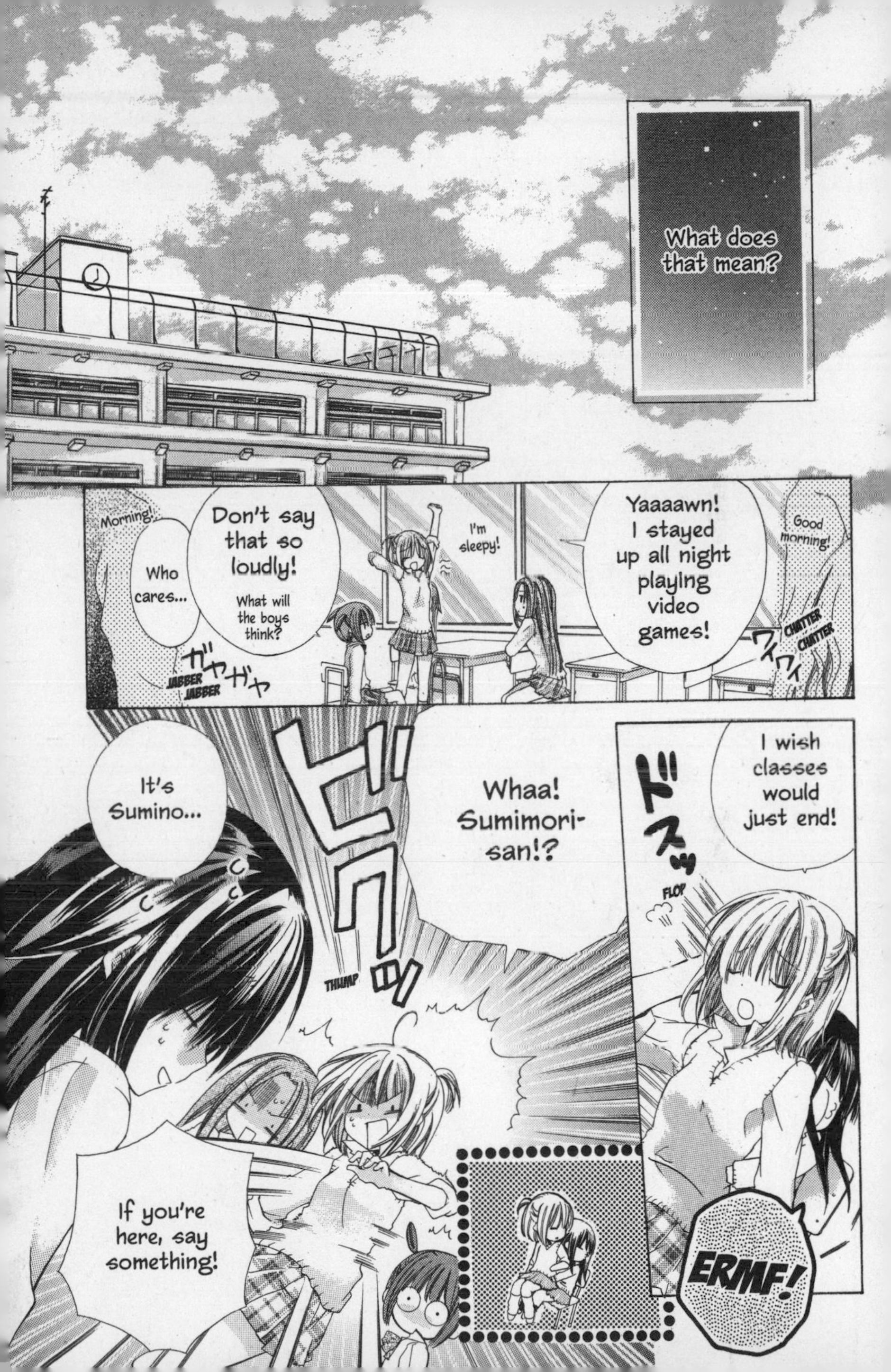

What does that mean?
Good morning!
ワイワイ CHATTER CHATTER
Yaaaawn! I stayed up all night playing video games!
I'm sleepy!
Don't say that so loudly!
What will the boys think?
Who cares...
Morning!
ガヤガヤ JABBER JABBER
I wish classes would just end!
ドスッ FLOP
ERMF!
Whaa! Sumimori-san!?
ドクッ THUMP
It's Sumino...
If you're here, say something!

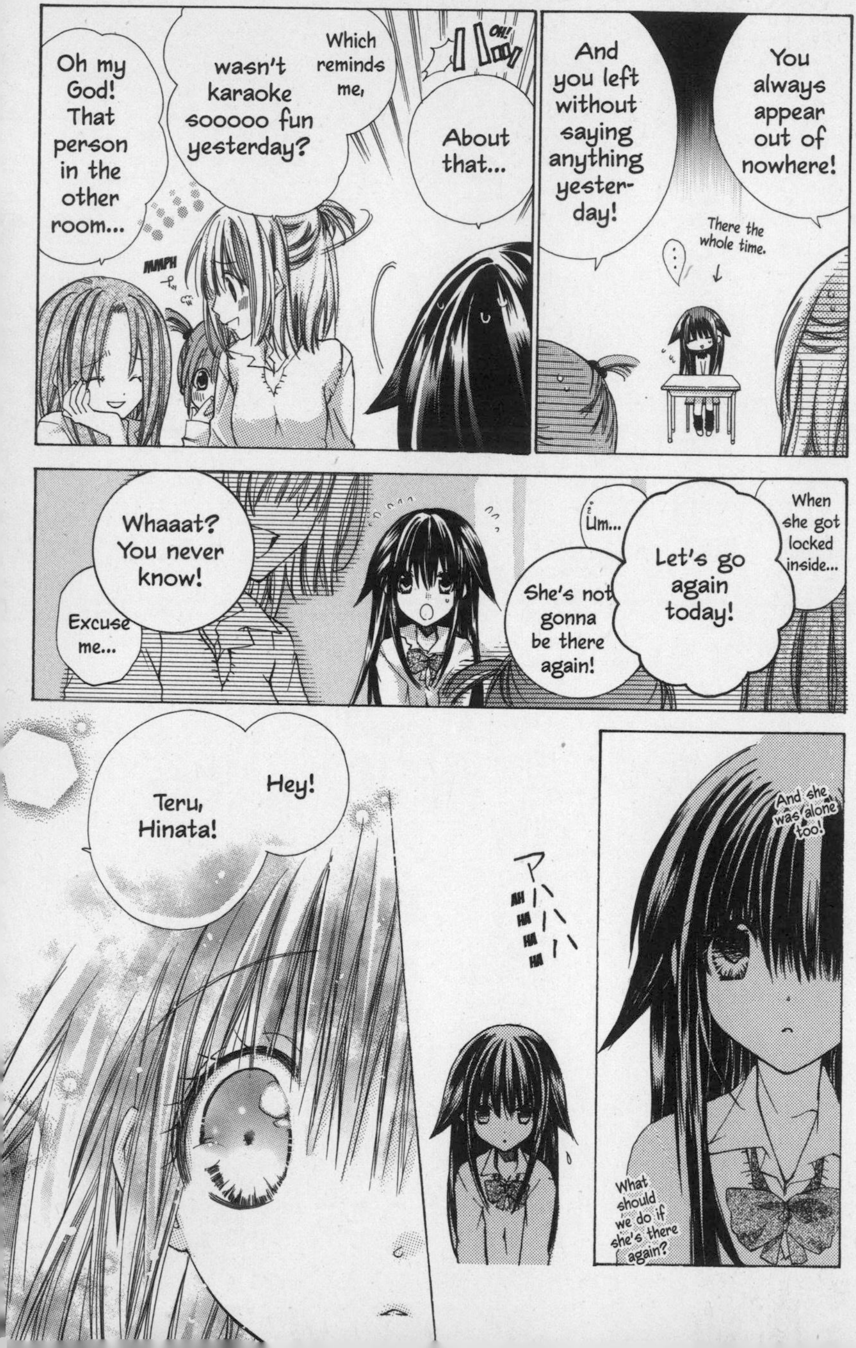

You always appear out of nowhere!
And you left without saying anything yester-day!
There the whole time.
OH!
About that...
Which reminds me,
wasn't karaoke sooooo fun yesterday?
Oh my God! That person in the other room...
MMPH
When she got locked inside...
Let's go again today!
Um...
She's not gonna be there again!
Whaaat? You never know!
Excuse me...
And she was alone too!
What should we do if she's there again?
アハハハ
AH HA HA HA
Hey!
Teru, Hinata!

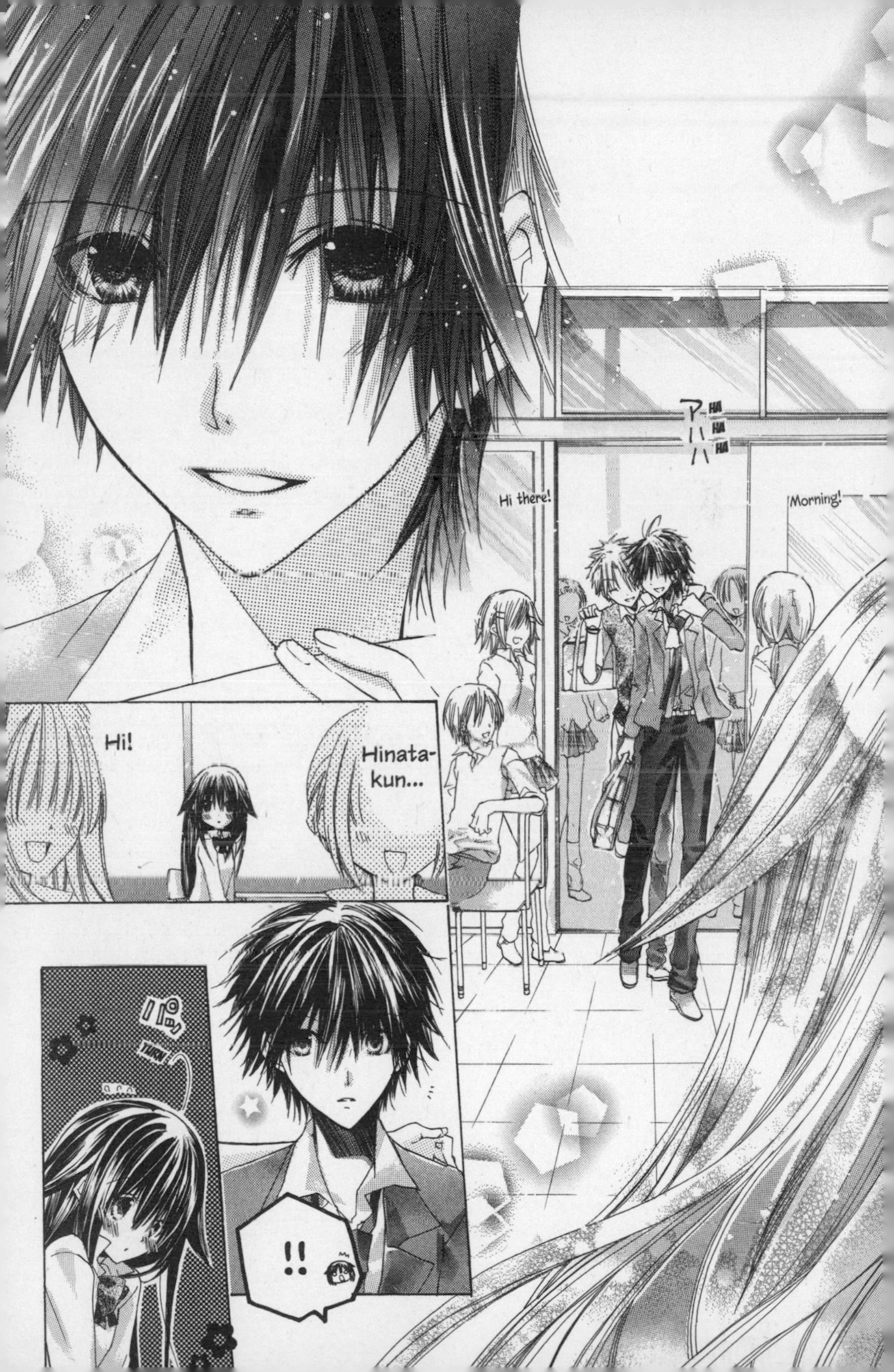

HA HA HA
Morning!
Hi there!
Hinata-kun...
Hi!
!!

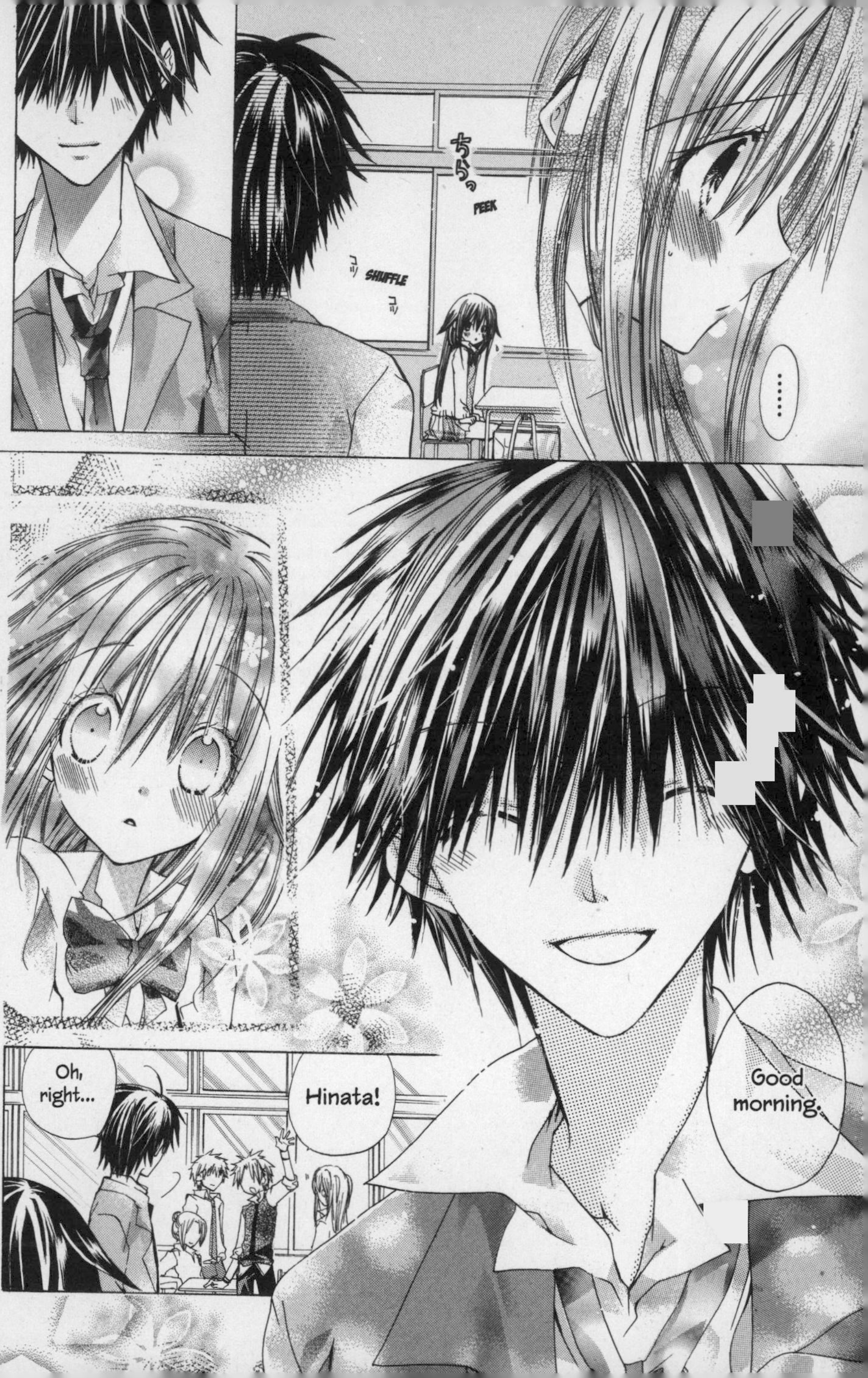
......
ちらっ
PEEK
SHUFFLE
Good morning.
Hinata!
Oh, right...

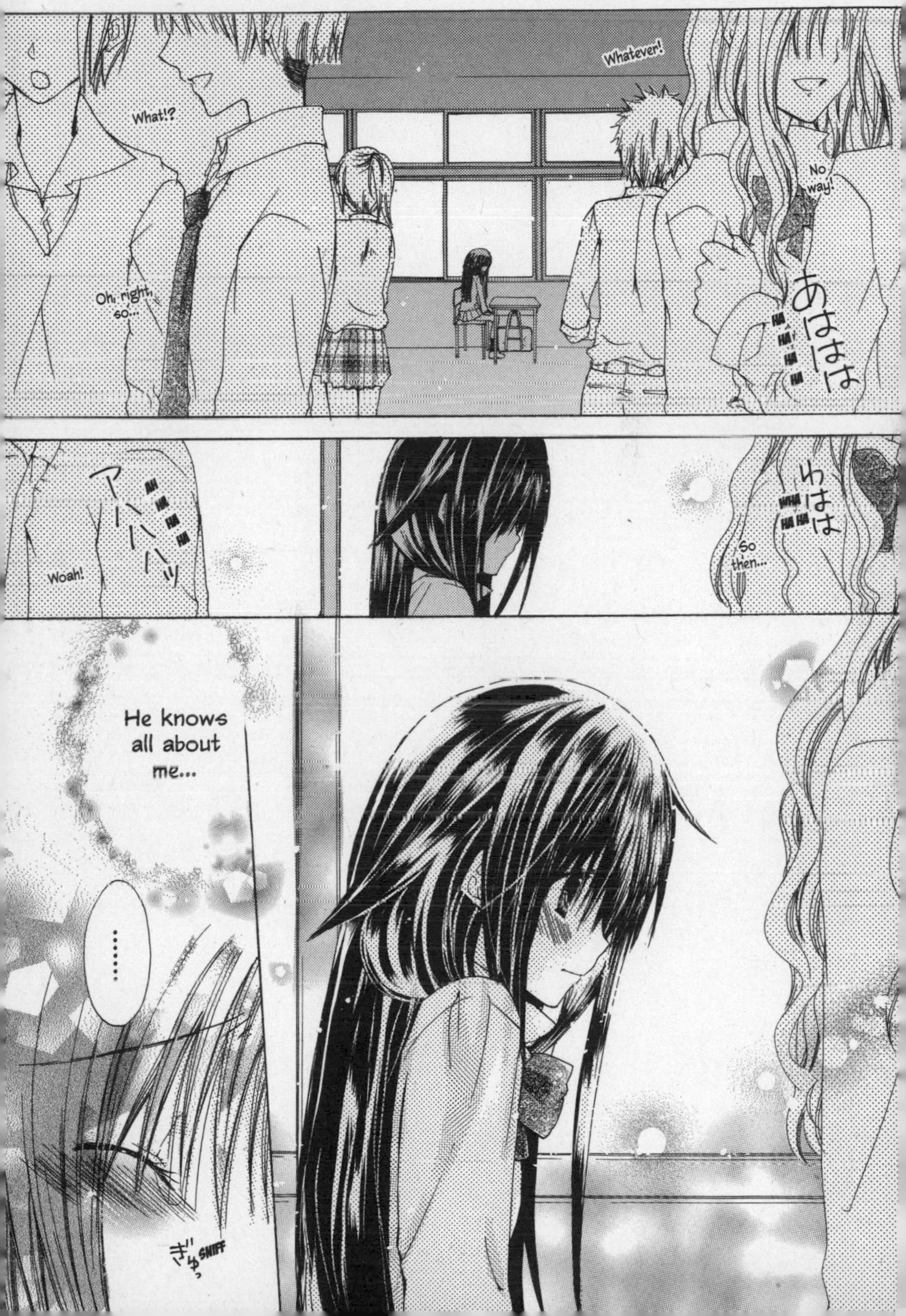

No way!
あははは
HA HA HA HA
Whatever!
What!?
Oh, right, so...
わはは
WHA HA HA
So then...
アハハハッ
AH HA HA HA
Woah!
He knows all about me...
......
ぎゅっ
SNIFF

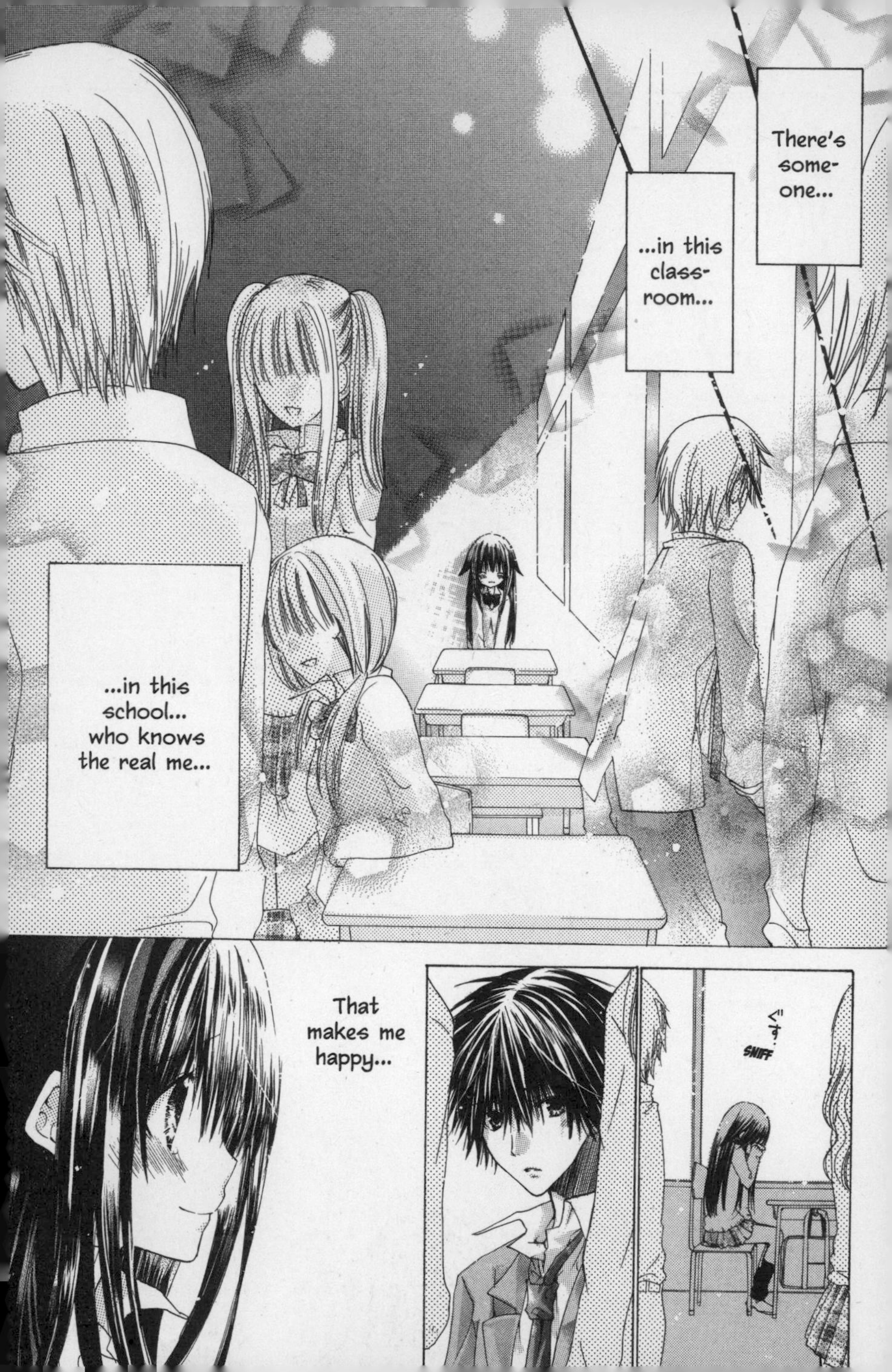

There's some-one...
...in this class-room...
...in this school... who knows the real me...
ぐす…
SNIFF
That makes me happy...

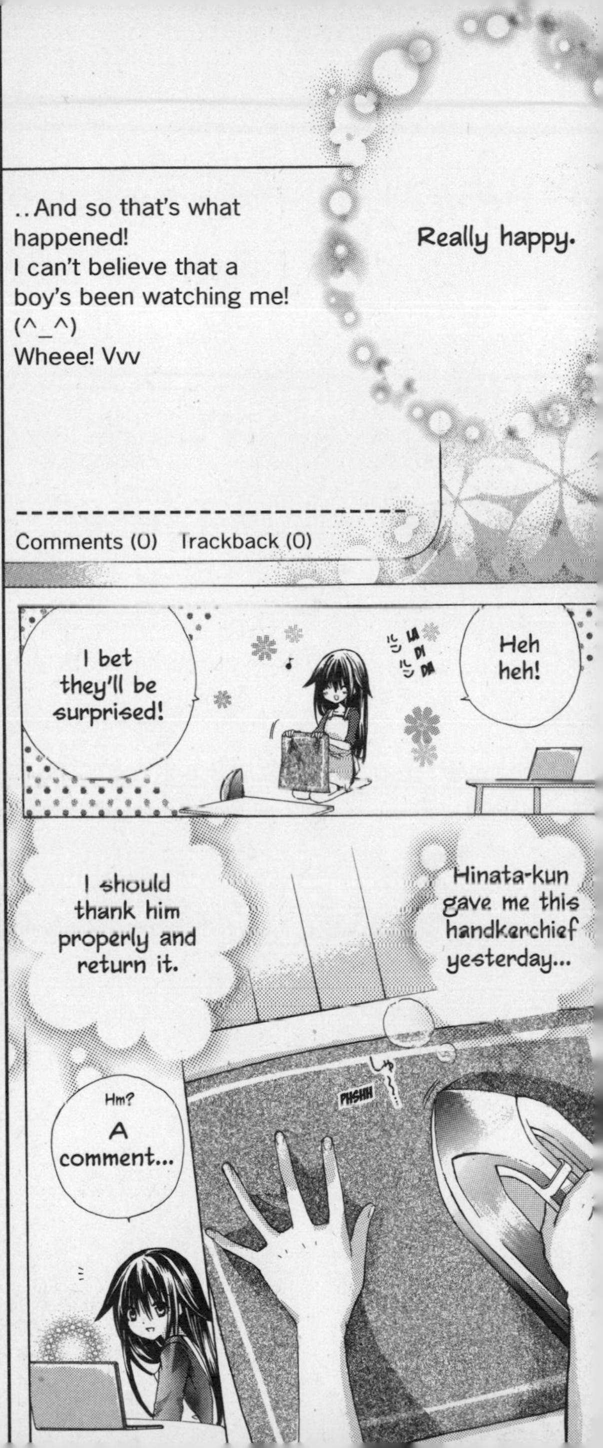
Really happy.
..And so that's what happened!
I can't believe that a boy's been watching me!
(^_^)
Wheee! Vvv
Comments (0) Trackback (0)
Heh heh!
LA DI DA
I bet they'll be surprised!
Hinata-kun gave me this handkerchief yesterday...
I should thank him properly and return it.
PHSHH
Hm? A comment...

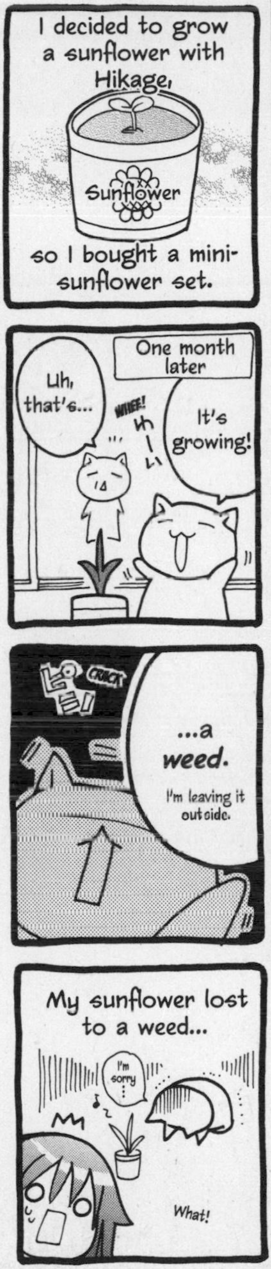
I decided to grow a sunflower with Hikage,
Sunflower
so I bought a mini-sunflower set.
One month later
It's growing!
WHEE!
Uh, that's...
CRACK
...a weed.
I'm leaving it outside.
My sunflower lost to a weed...
I'm sorry
What!

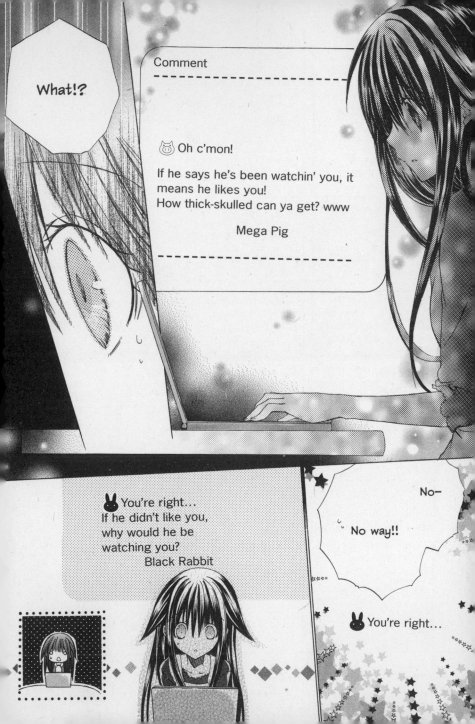

What!?

Comment

- -

Oh c'mon!

If he says he's been watchin' you, it
means he likes you!
How thick-skulled can ya get? www

Mega Pig

- -

You're right...
If he didn't like you,
why would he be
watching you?
Black Rabbit

No—

No way!!

You're right...

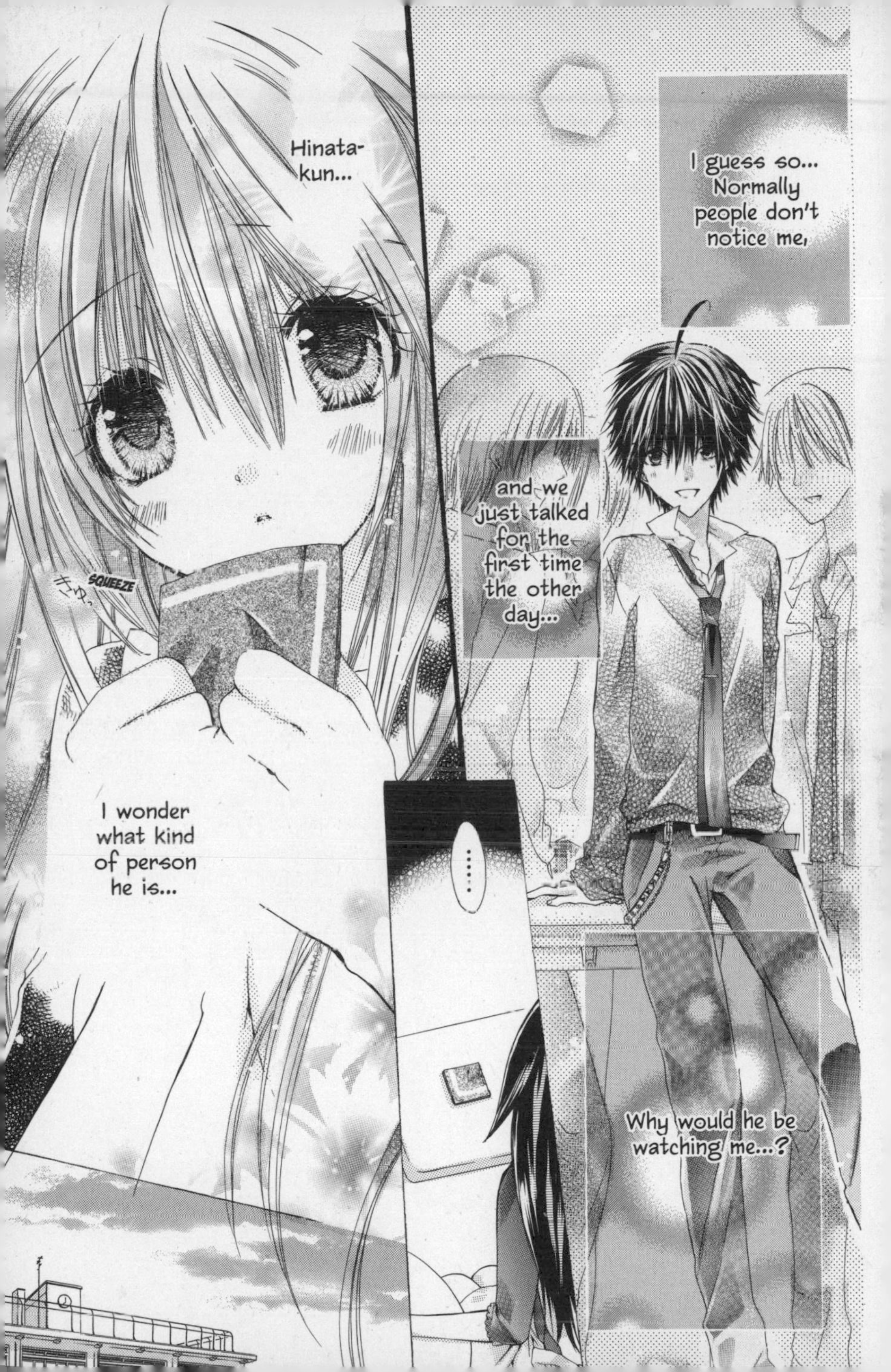
I guess so... Normally people don't notice me,
and we just talked for the first time the other day...
Why would he be watching me...?
......
Hinata-kun...
SQUEEZE
I wonder what kind of person he is...

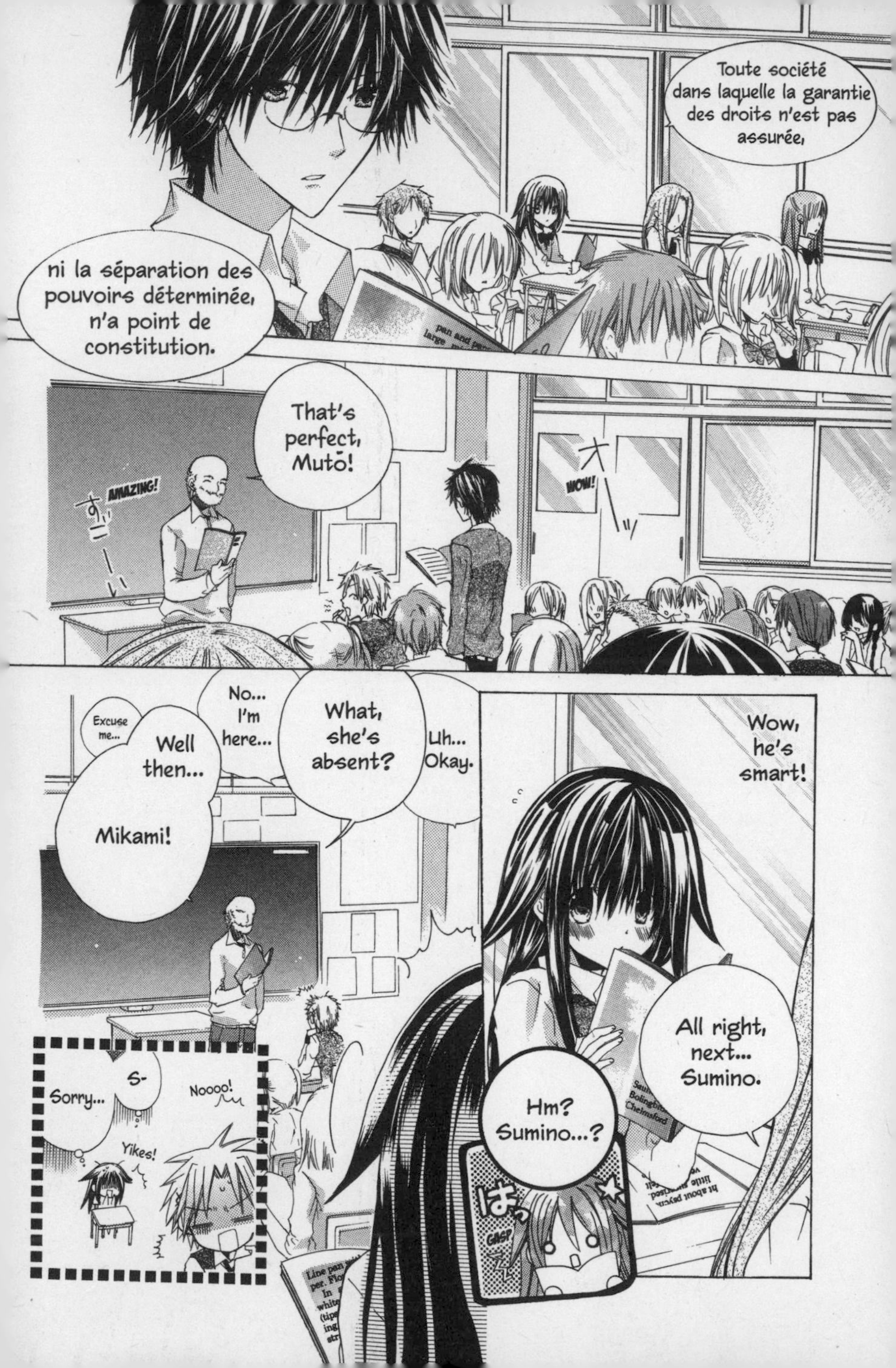

Toute société dans laquelle la garantie des droits n'est pas assurée,
ni la séparation des pouvoirs déterminée, n'a point de constitution.
That's perfect, Mutō!
WOW!
AMAZING!
Wow, he's smart!
All right, next... Sumino.
Hm? Sumino...?
GASP
Uh... Okay.
What, she's absent?
No... I'm here...
Excuse me...
Well then...
Mikami!
Noooo!
S-
Sorry...
Yikes!

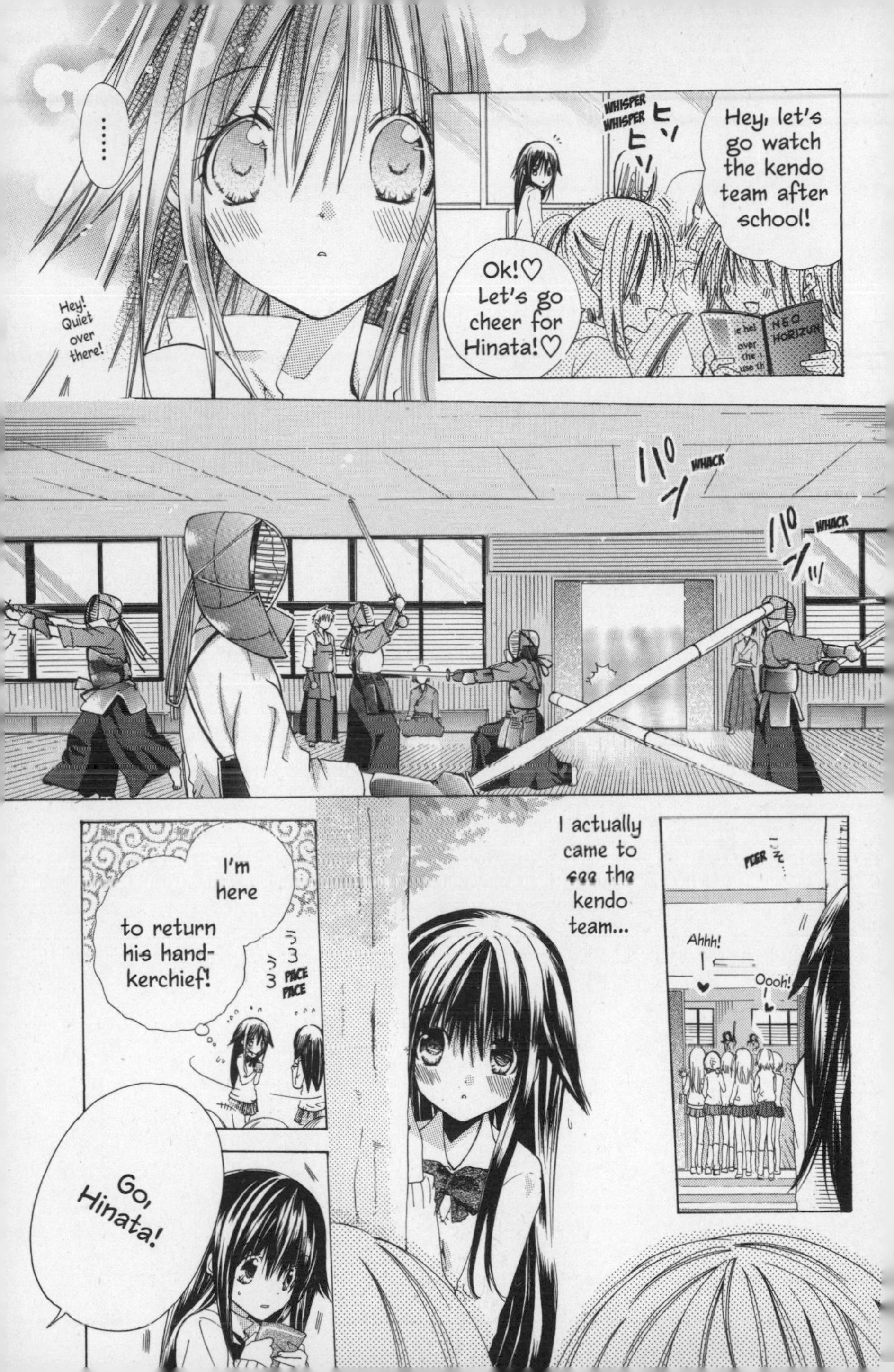

WHISPER WHISPER
Hey, let's go watch the kendo team after school!
Ok!♡ Let's go cheer for Hinata!♡
NEO HORIZON
......
Hey! Quiet over there!
WHACK
WHACK
PEER
Ahhh!
Oooh!
I actually came to see the kendo team...
I'm here to return his handkerchief!
PACE PACE
Go, Hinata!

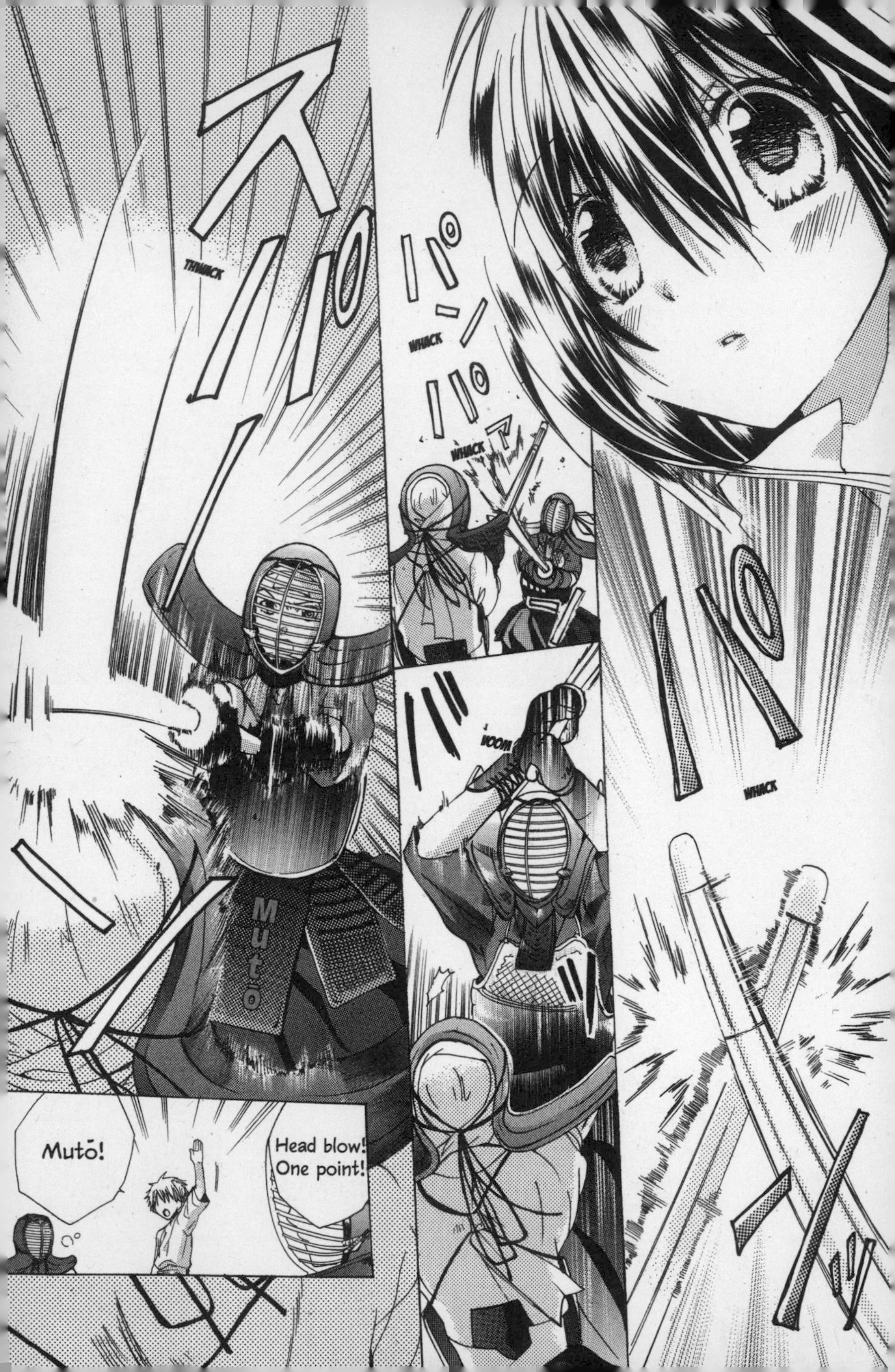
WHACK
WHACK
WHACK
VOOM
THWACK
Mutō
Head blow! One point!
Mutō!

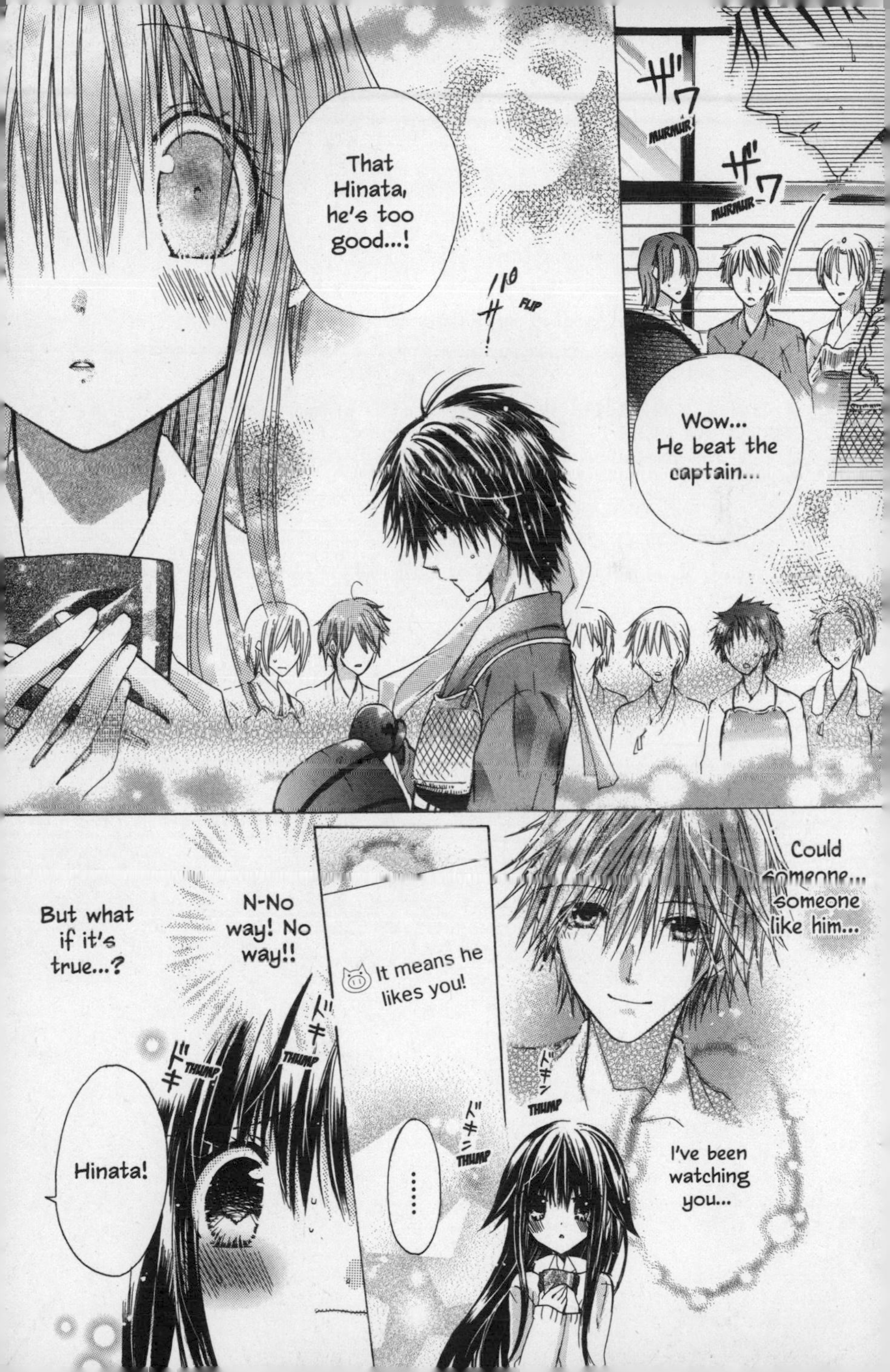

ザワ
MURMUR
ザワ
MURMUR
Wow... He beat the captain...
That Hinata, he's too good...!
パサ
FLIP
Could someone... someone like him...
I've been watching you...
THUMP
It means he likes you!
THUMP
......
N-No way! No way!!
But what if it's true...?
THUMP
THUMP
Hinata!

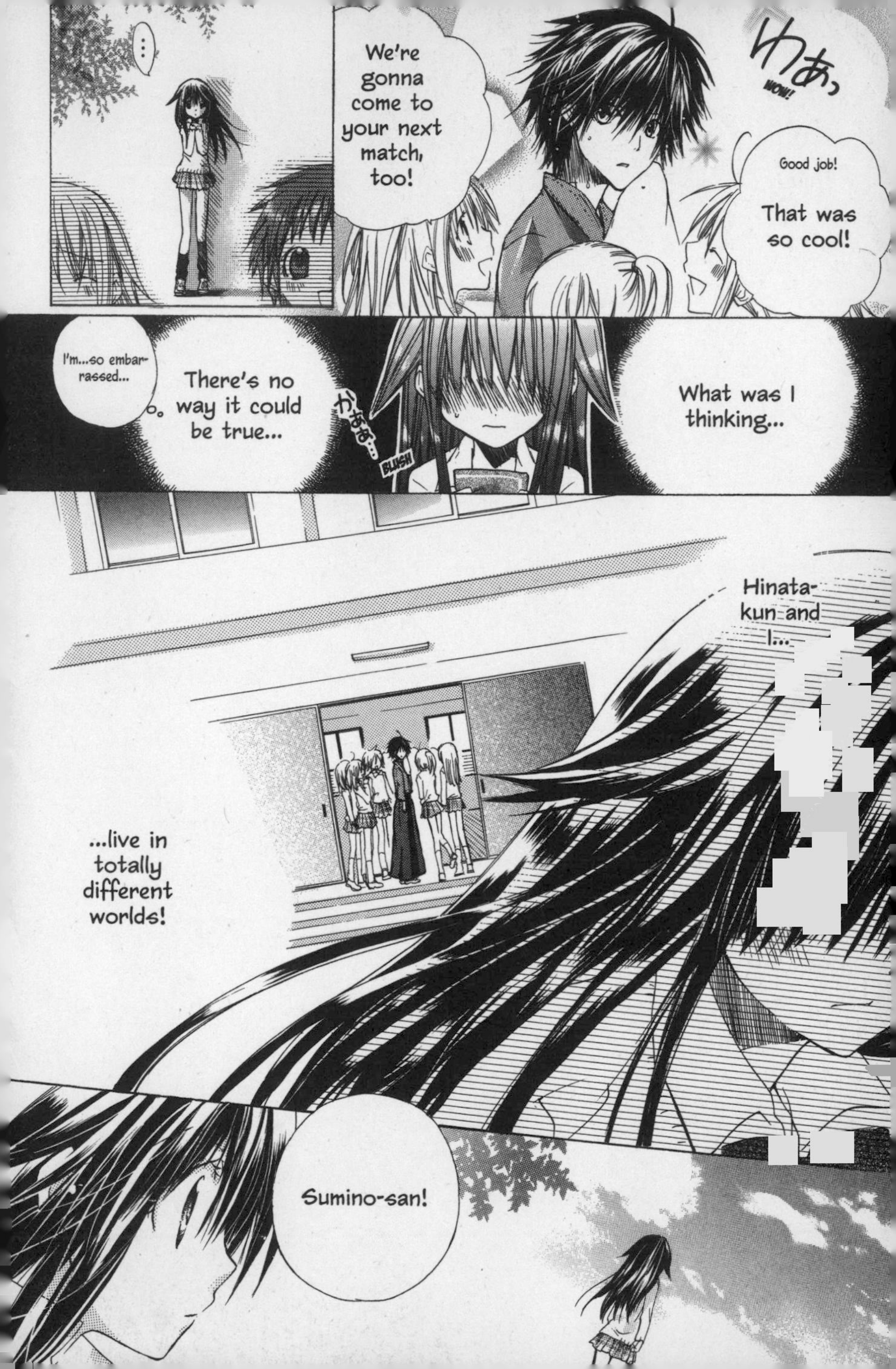
わあっ
WOW!
Good job!
That was so cool!
We're gonna come to your next match, too!
...
What was I thinking...
There's no way it could be true...
かあぁ...
BLUSH
I'm...so embarrassed...
Hinata-kun and I...
...live in totally different worlds!
Sumino-san!

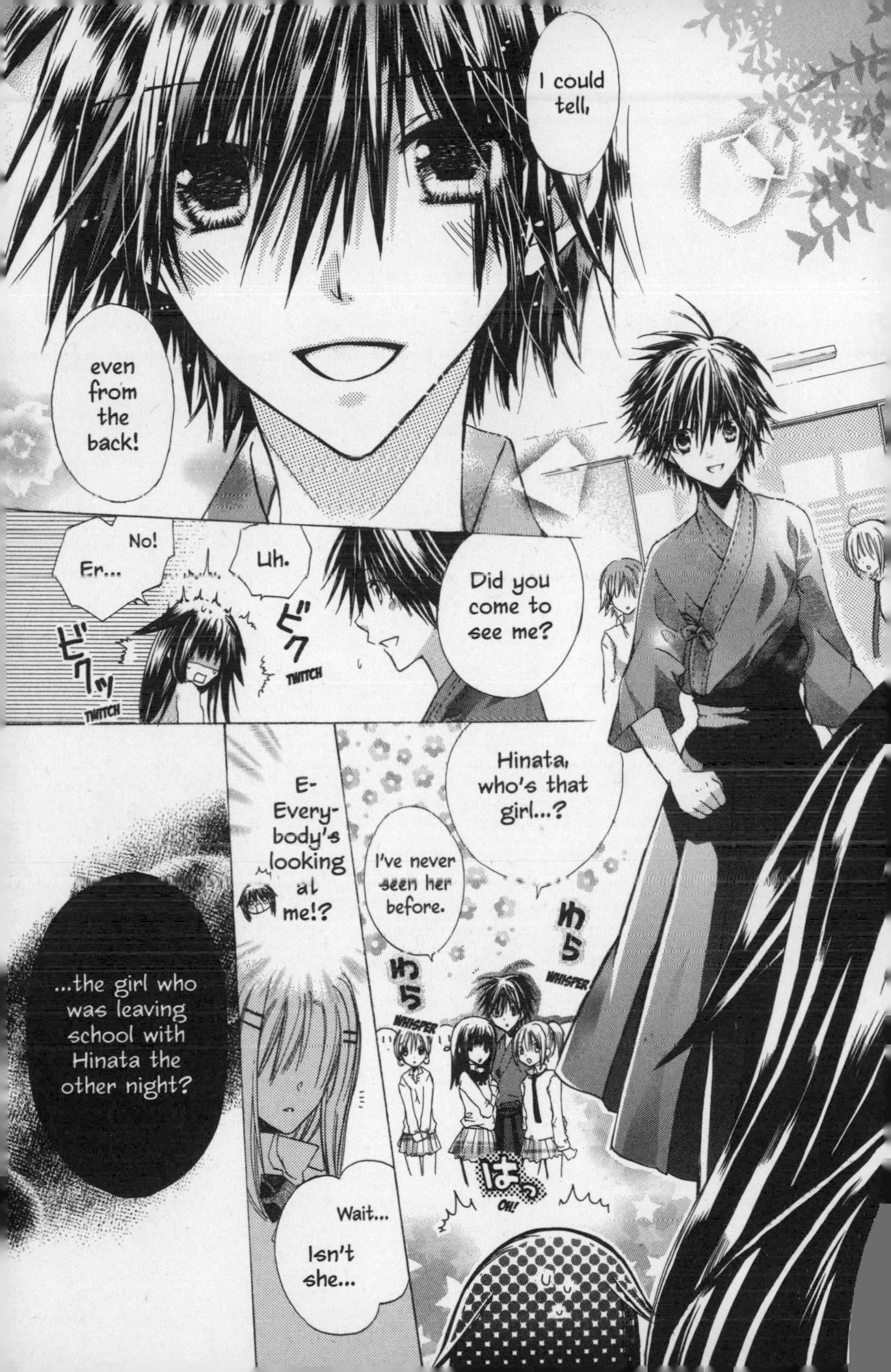
I could tell,
even from the back!
Did you come to see me?
Uh.
ビク
TWITCH
No! Er...
ビクッ
TWITCH
Hinata, who's that girl...?
I've never seen her before.
WHISPER
WHISPER
はっ
OH!
E- Every-body's looking at me!?
Wait... Isn't she...
...the girl who was leaving school with Hinata the other night?

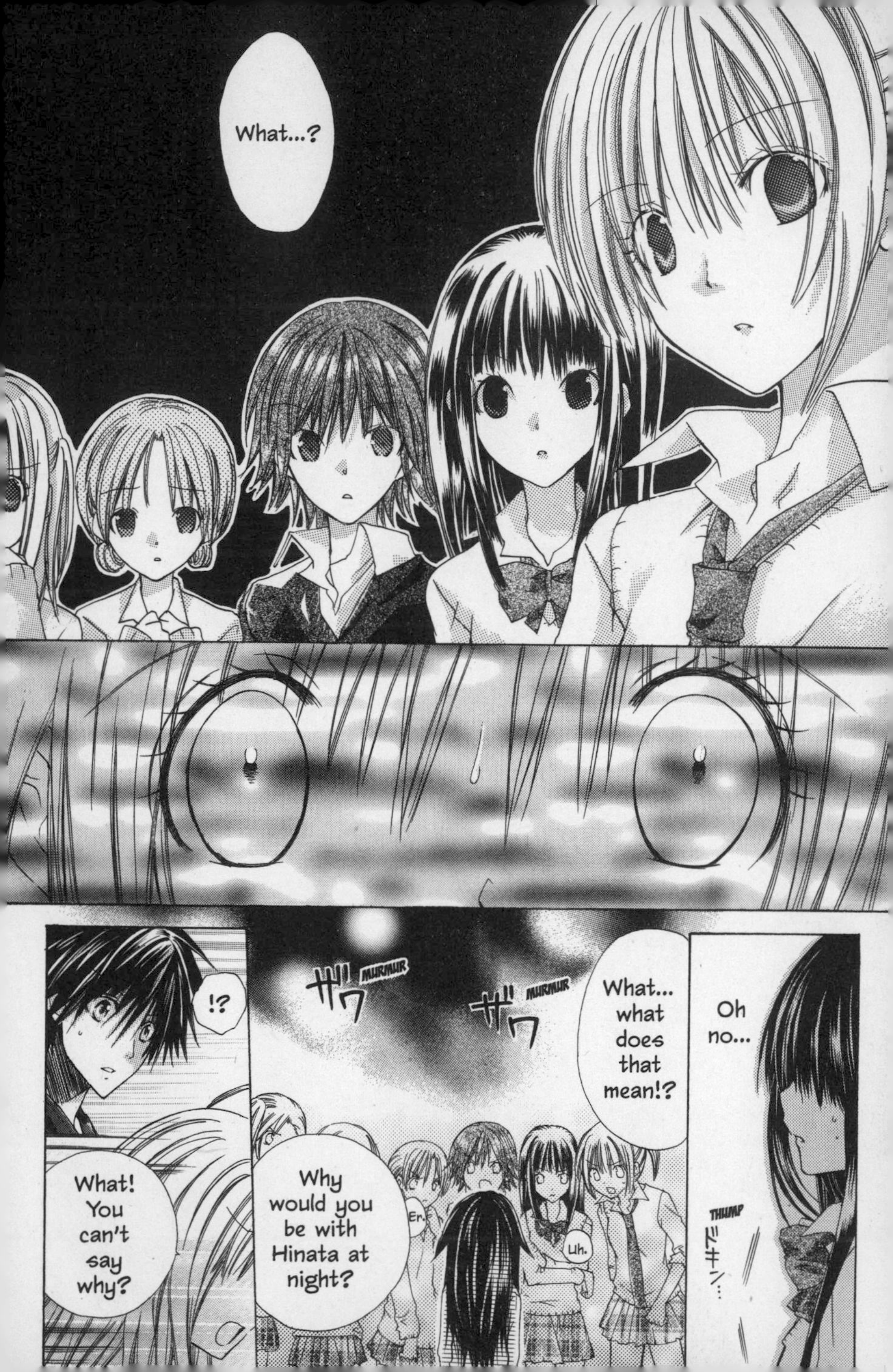
What...?
Oh no...
ドキン…
THUMP
What... what does that mean!?
ザワ
MURMUR
ザワ
MURMUR
Uh.
Er.
Why would you be with Hinata at night?
!?
What! You can't say why?

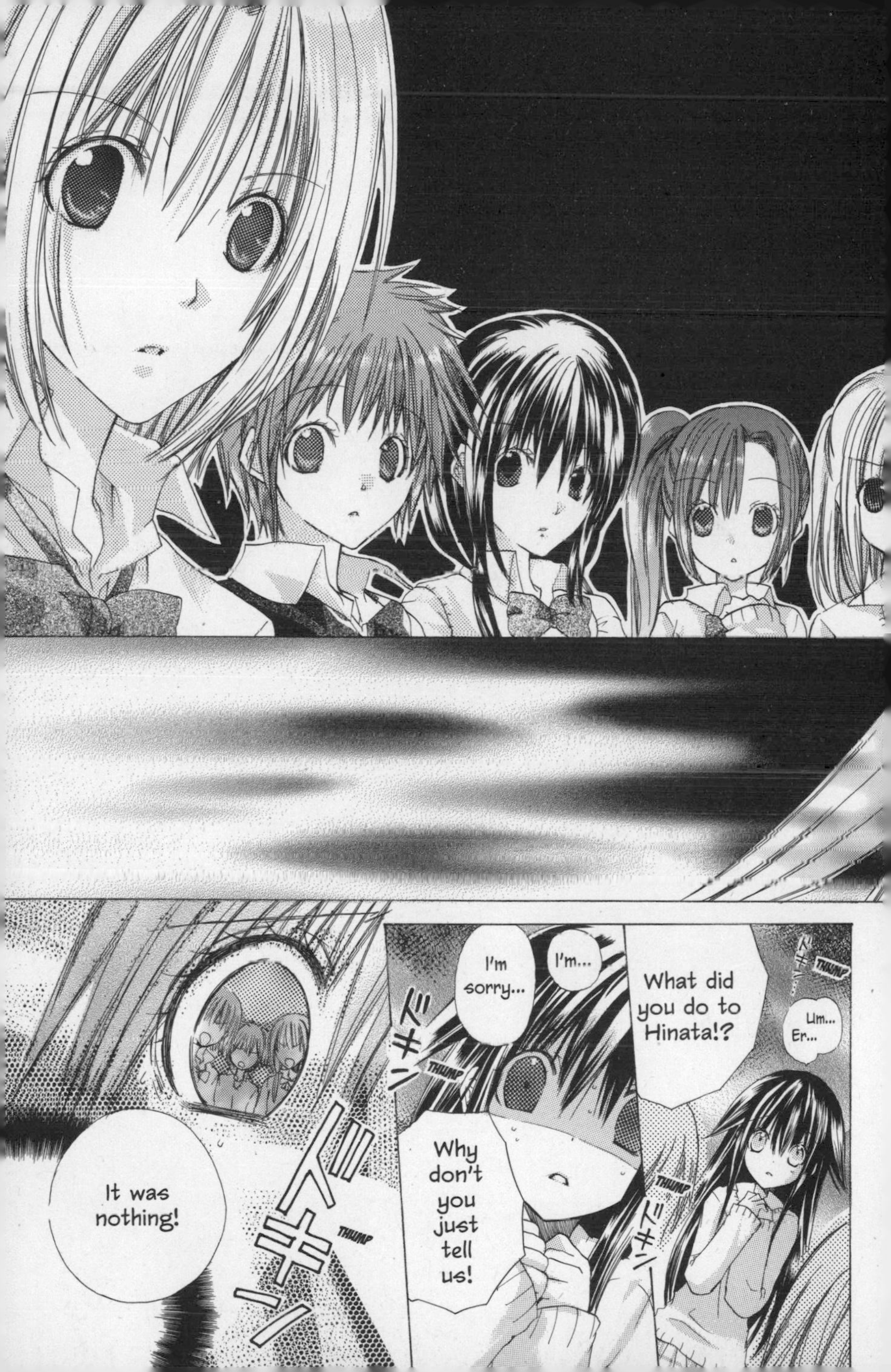
THUMP
Um... Er...
What did you do to Hinata!?
I'm...
I'm sorry...
ドキン
THUMP
Why don't you just tell us!
ドキン
THUMP
ドキン
THUMP
It was nothing!

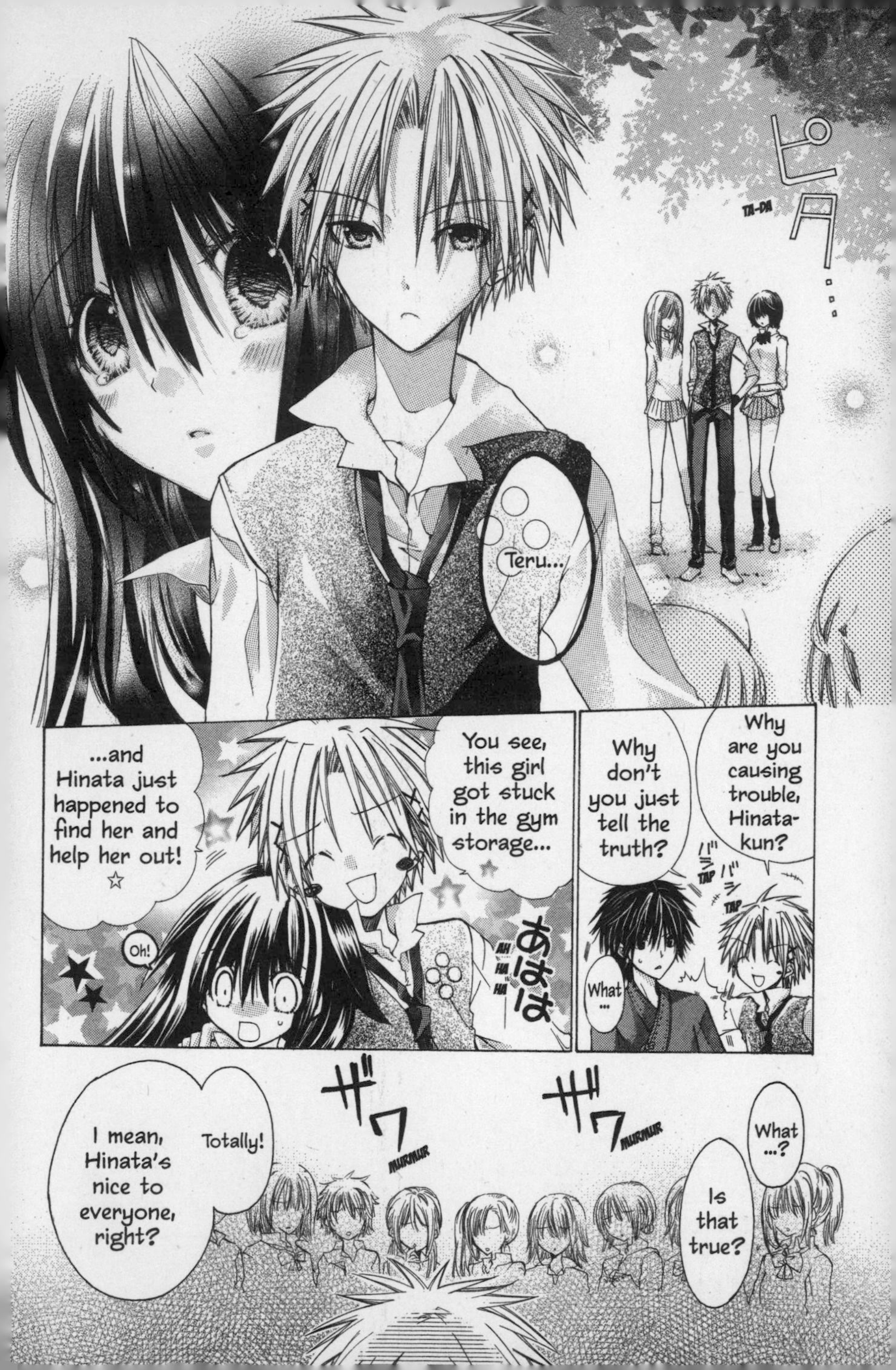
ピタ...
TA-DA
Teru...
Why are you causing trouble, Hinata-kun?
Why don't you just tell the truth?
バシ TAP バシ TAP
What...
You see, this girl got stuck in the gym storage...
...and Hinata just happened to find her and help her out! ☆
あはは AH HA HA
Oh!
What...?
Is that true?
ザワ MURMUR ザワ MURMUR
Totally!
I mean, Hinata's nice to everyone, right?

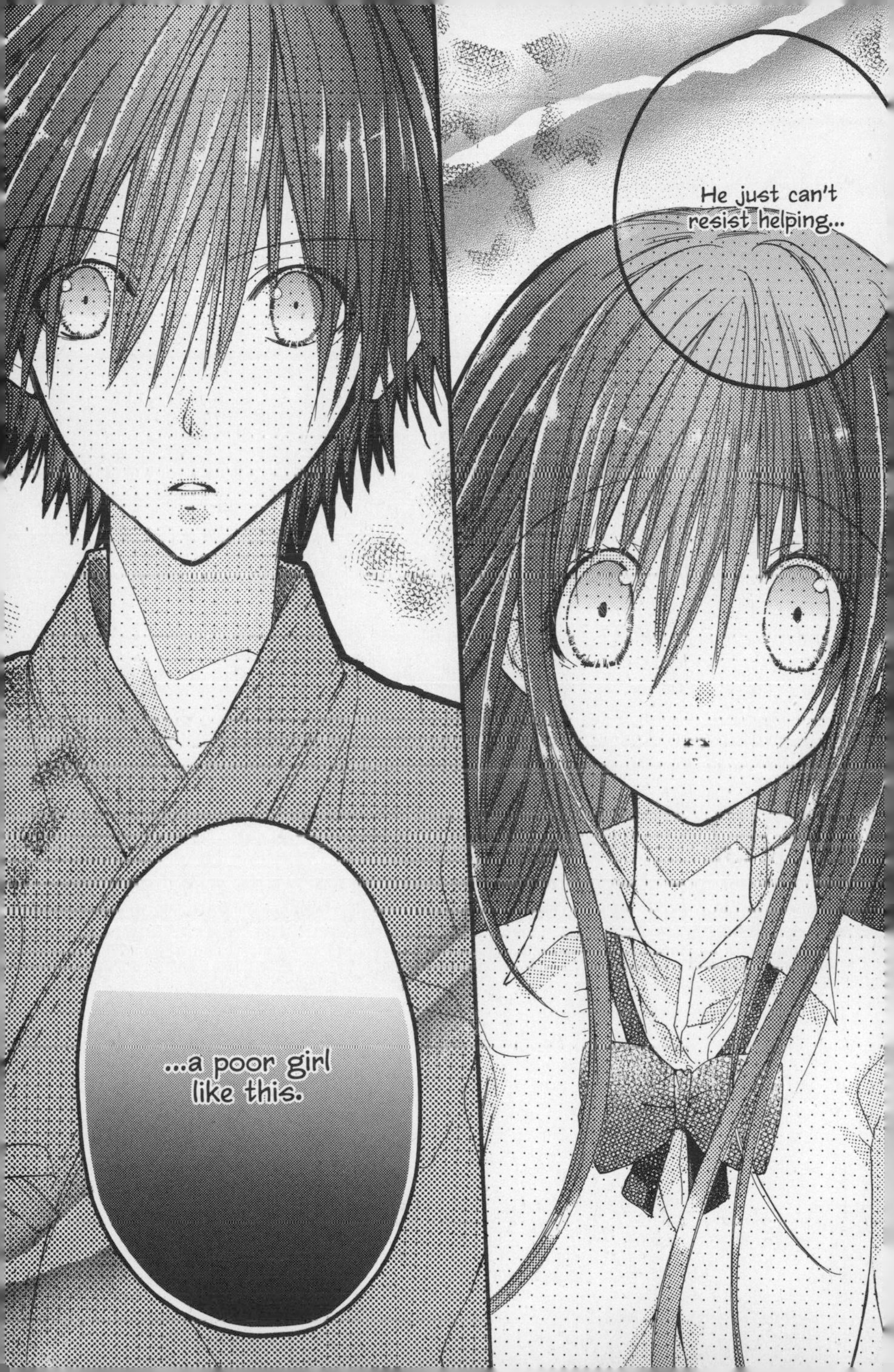
He just can't resist helping...
...a poor girl like this.

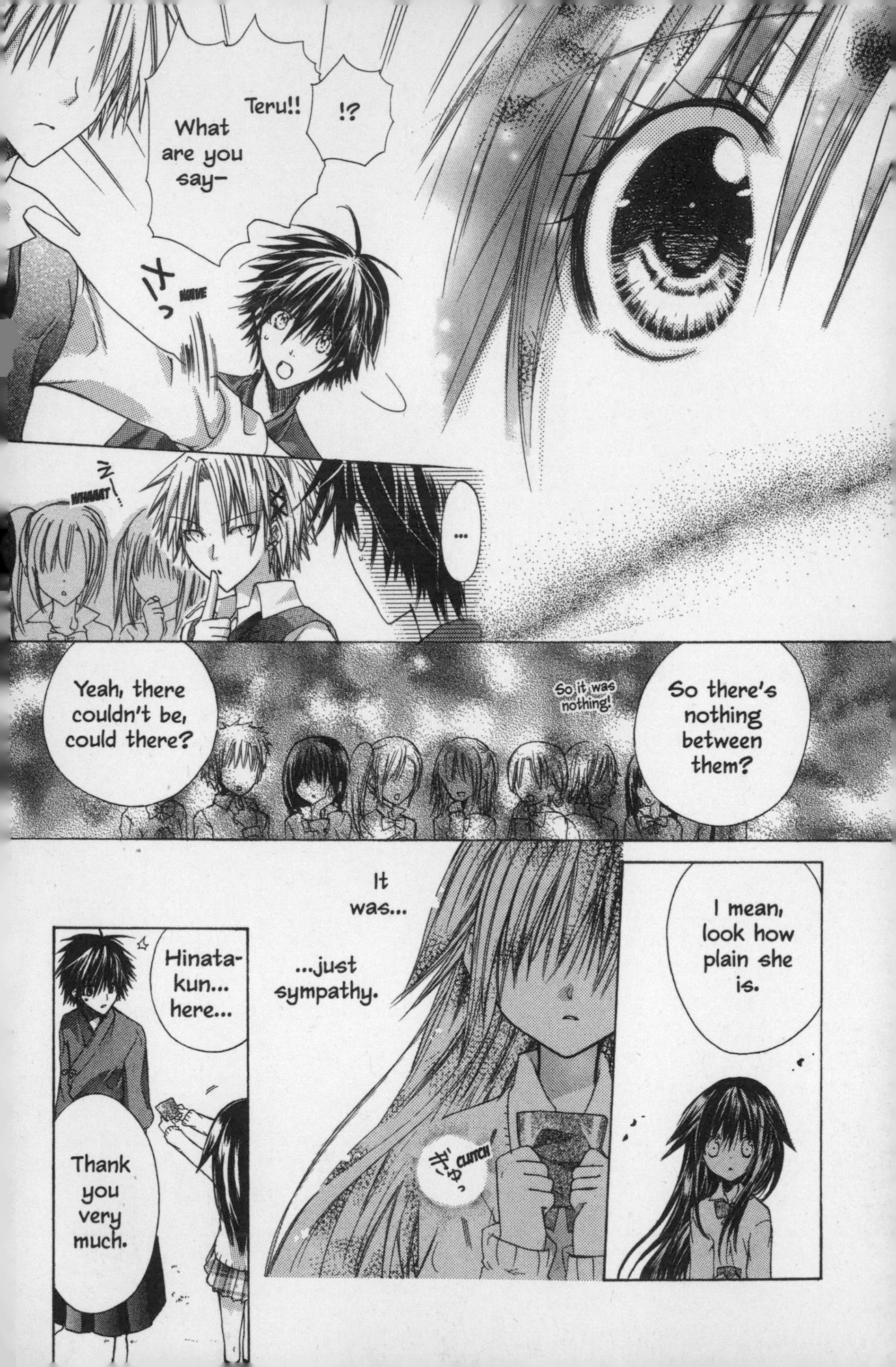
!?
Teru!! What are you say-
WAVE
...
WHAAAT
So there's nothing between them?
So it was nothing!
Yeah, there couldn't be, could there?
I mean, look how plain she is.
It was...
...just sympathy.
CLUTCH
Hinata-kun... here...
Thank you very much.

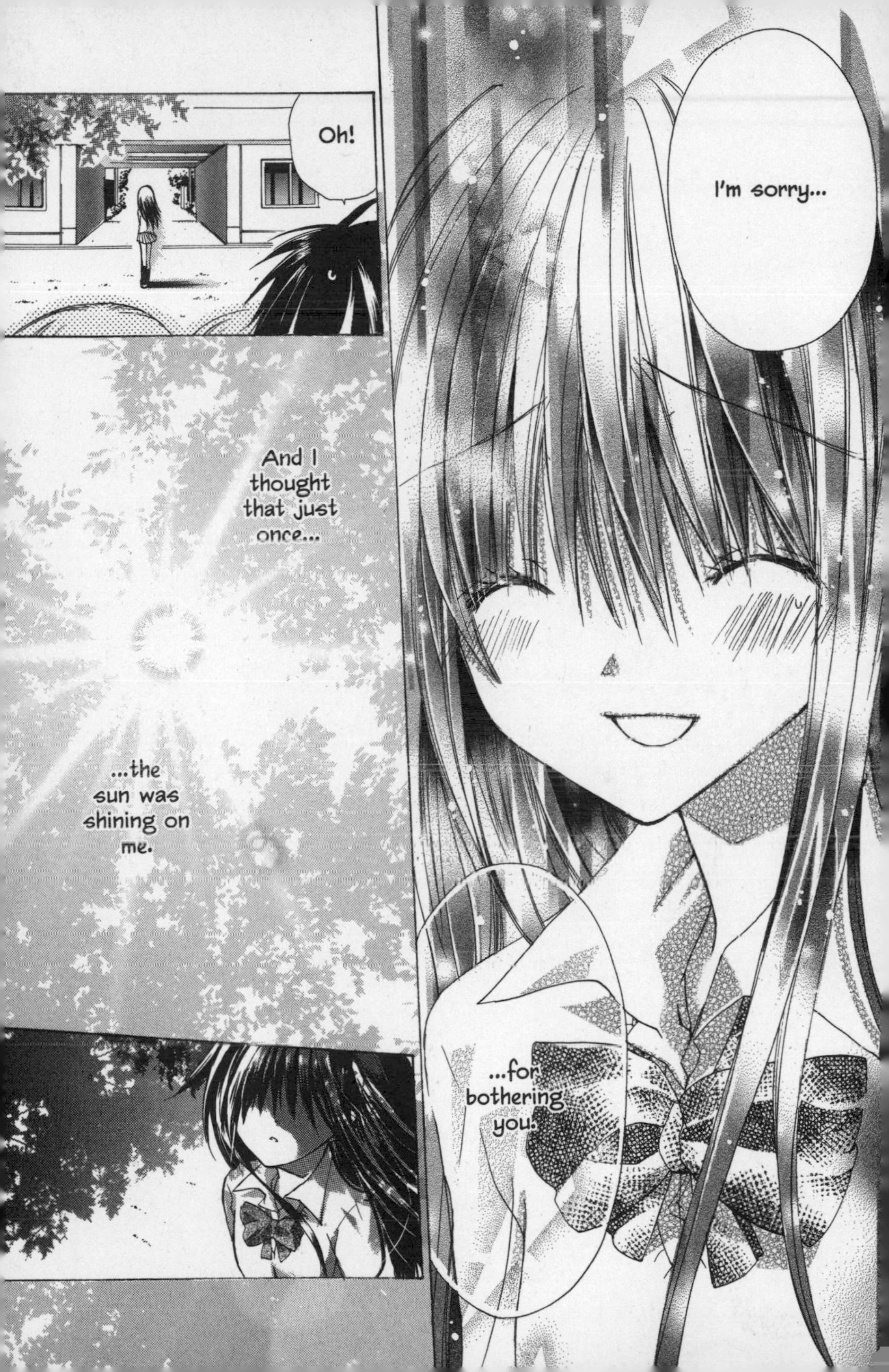
I'm sorry...
...for bothering you.
Oh!
And I thought that just once...
...the sun was shining on me.

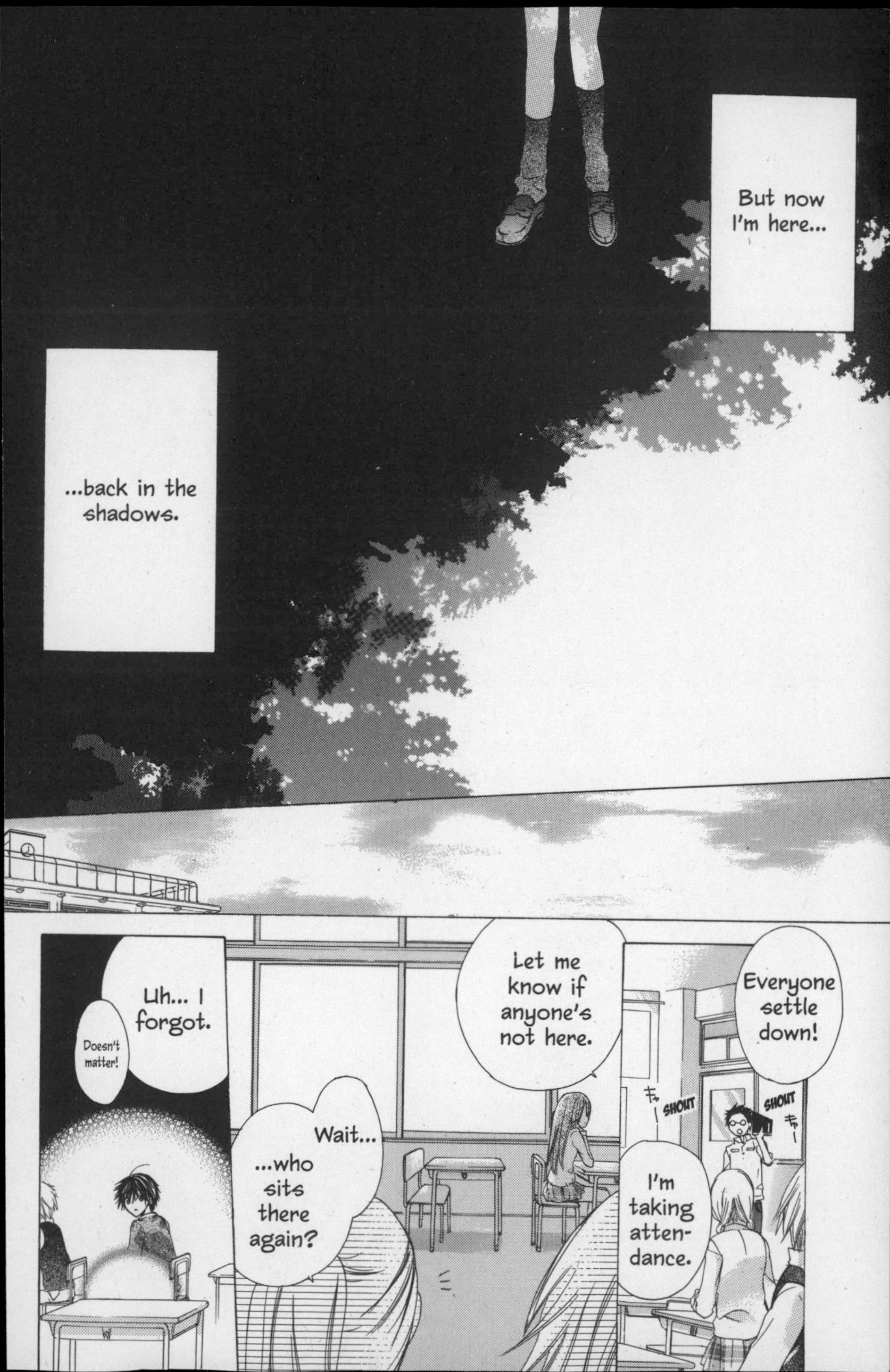
But now I'm here...
...back in the shadows.
Everyone settle down!
SHOUT
SHOUT
I'm taking attendance.
Let me know if anyone's not here.
Wait... ...who sits there again?
Uh... I forgot.
Doesn't matter!

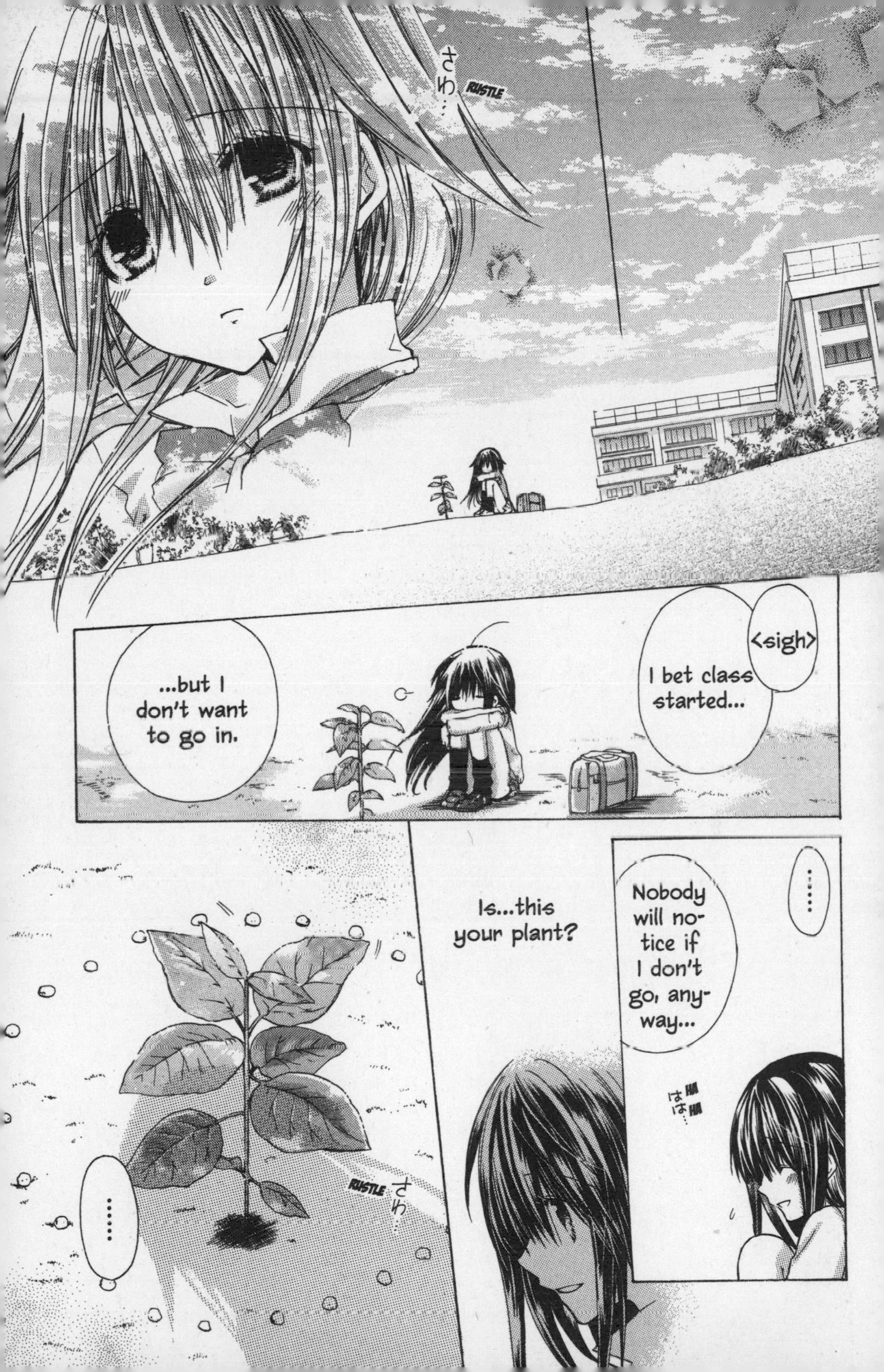
さわ… RUSTLE
<sigh>
I bet class started...
...but I don't want to go in.
......
Nobody will notice if I don't go, anyway...
ははっ… HA HA
Is...this your plant?
RUSTLE さわ…
......

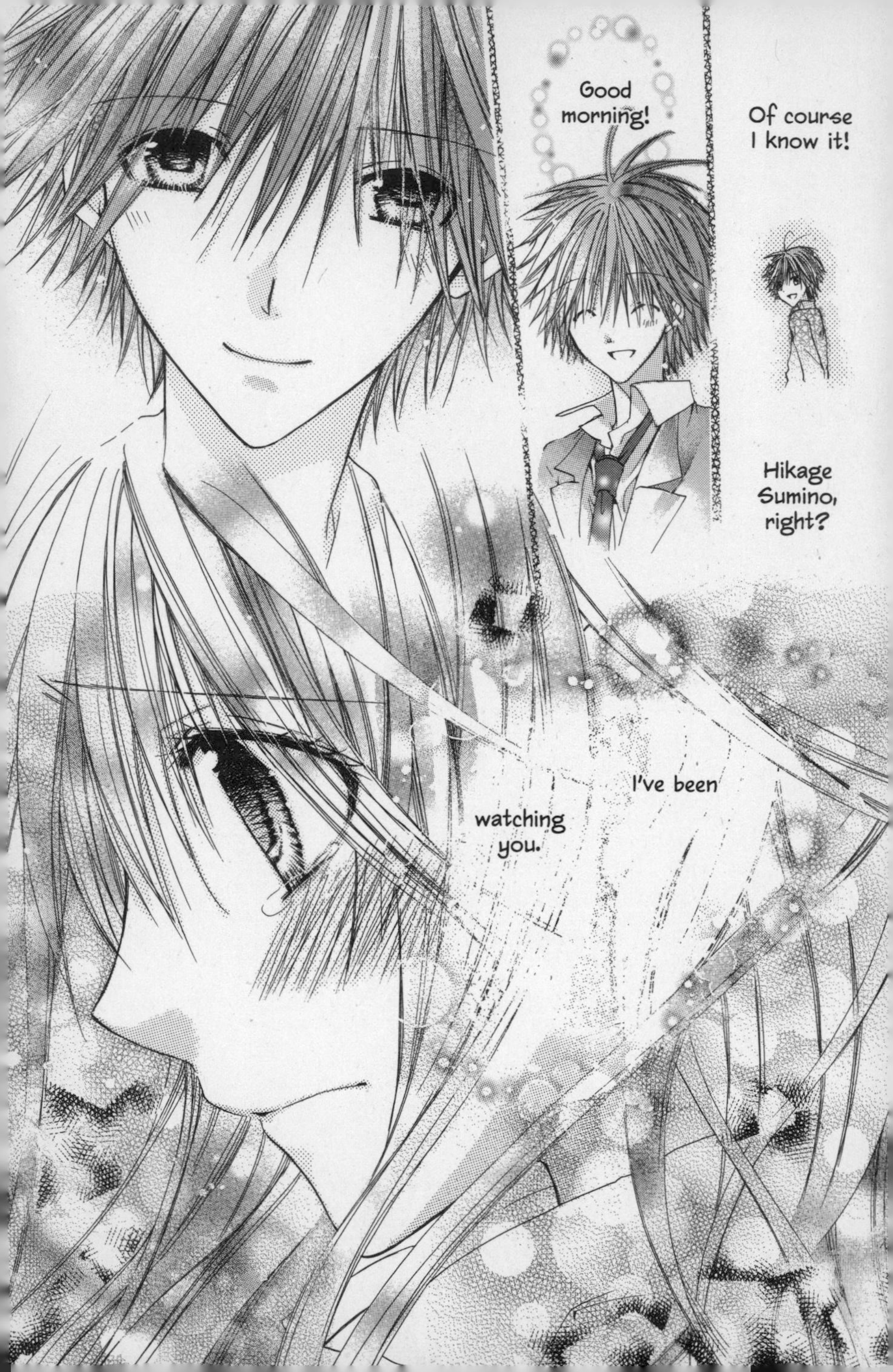
Of course I know it!
Hikage Sumino, right?
Good morning!
I've been
watching you.

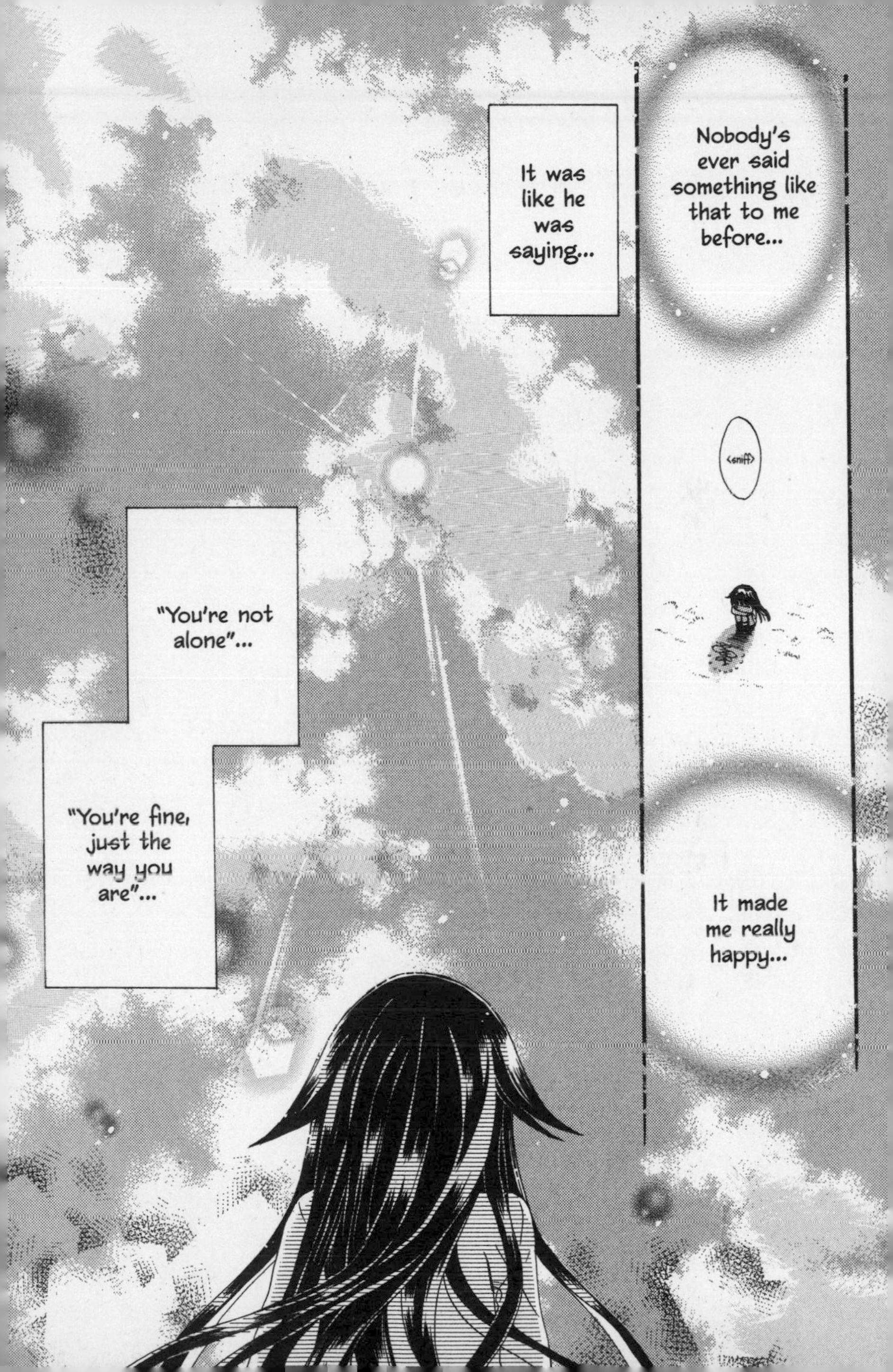
Nobody's ever said something like that to me before...
<sniff>
It made me really happy...
It was like he was saying...
"You're not alone"...
"You're fine, just the way you are"...

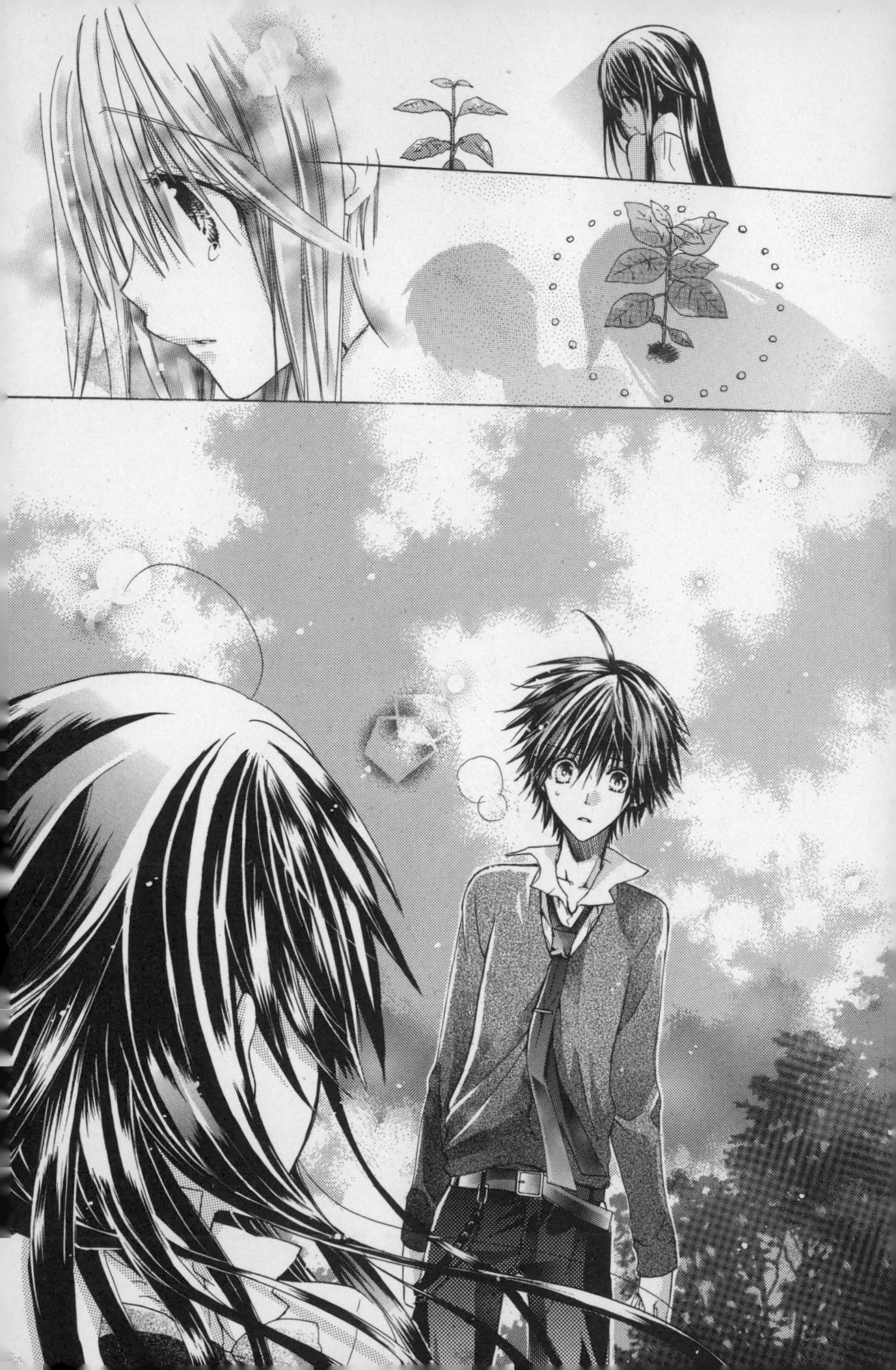

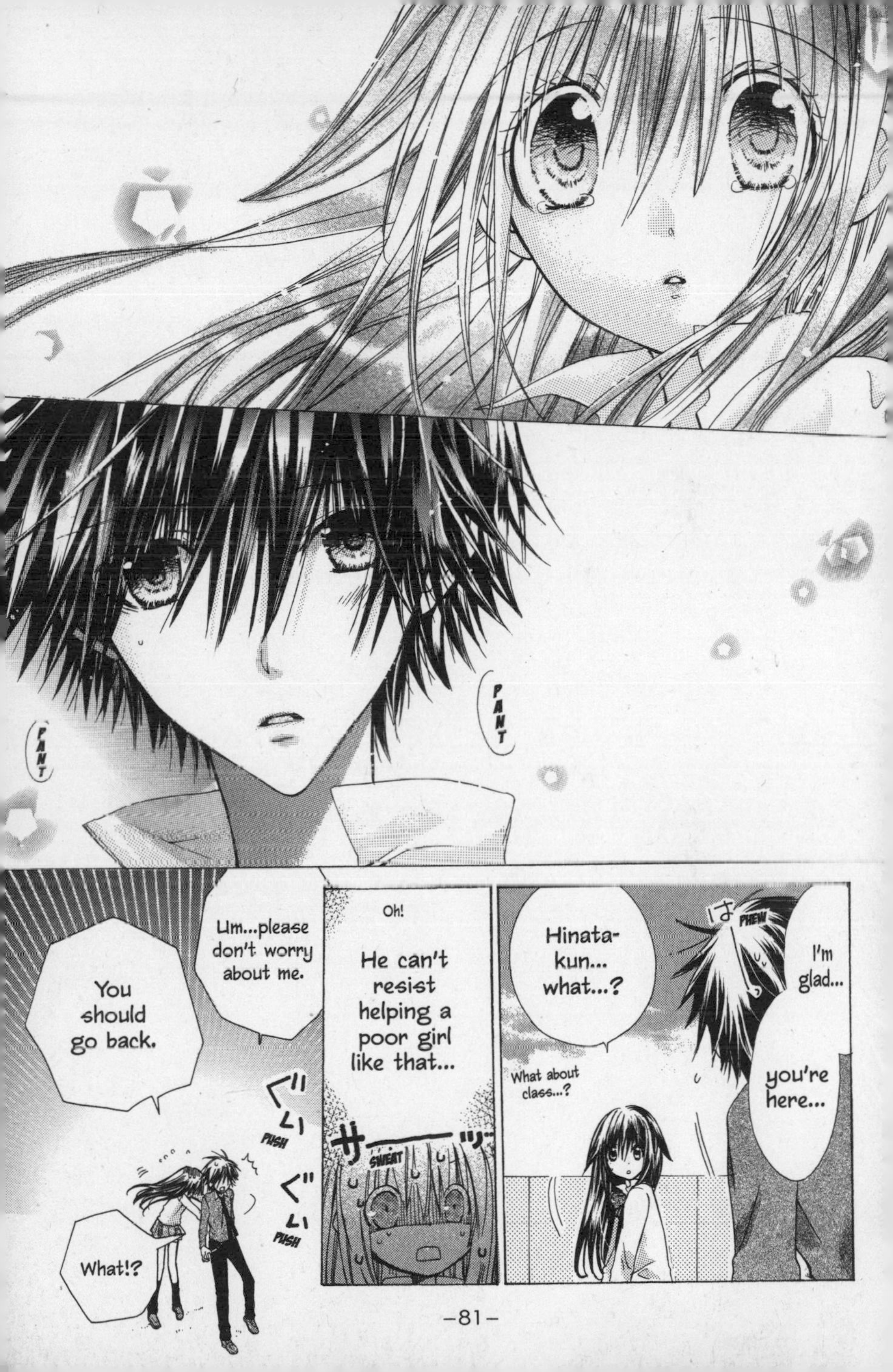
PANT
PANT
は
PHEW
I'm glad...
you're here...
Hinata-kun... what...?
What about class...?
Oh!
He can't resist helping a poor girl like that...
サーーッ
SWEAT
Um...please don't worry about me.
You should go back.
ぐい
PUSH
ぐい
PUSH
What!?

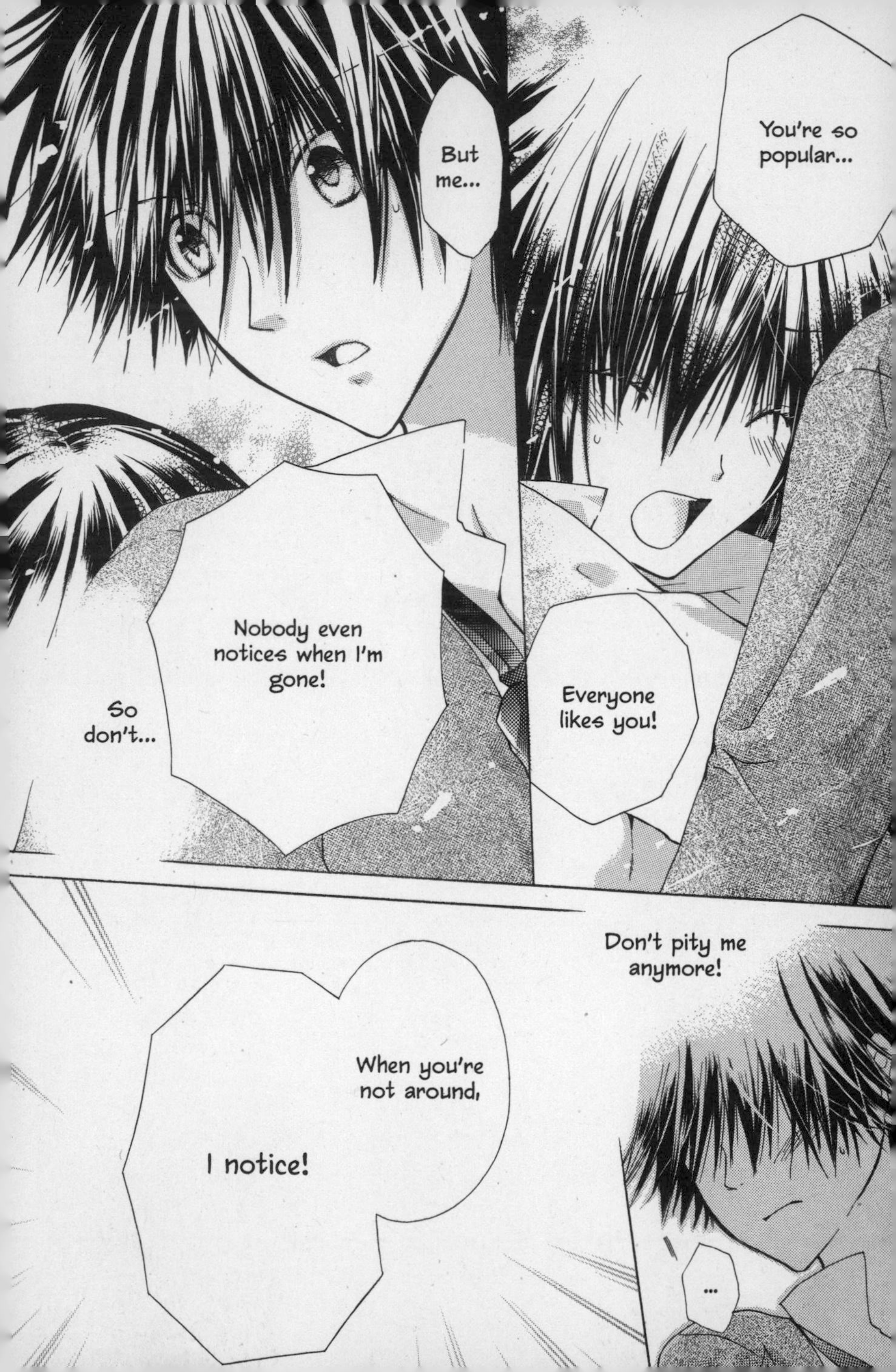

You're so popular...
Everyone likes you!
But me...
Nobody even notices when I'm gone!
So don't...
Don't pity me anymore!
When you're not around,
I notice!
...

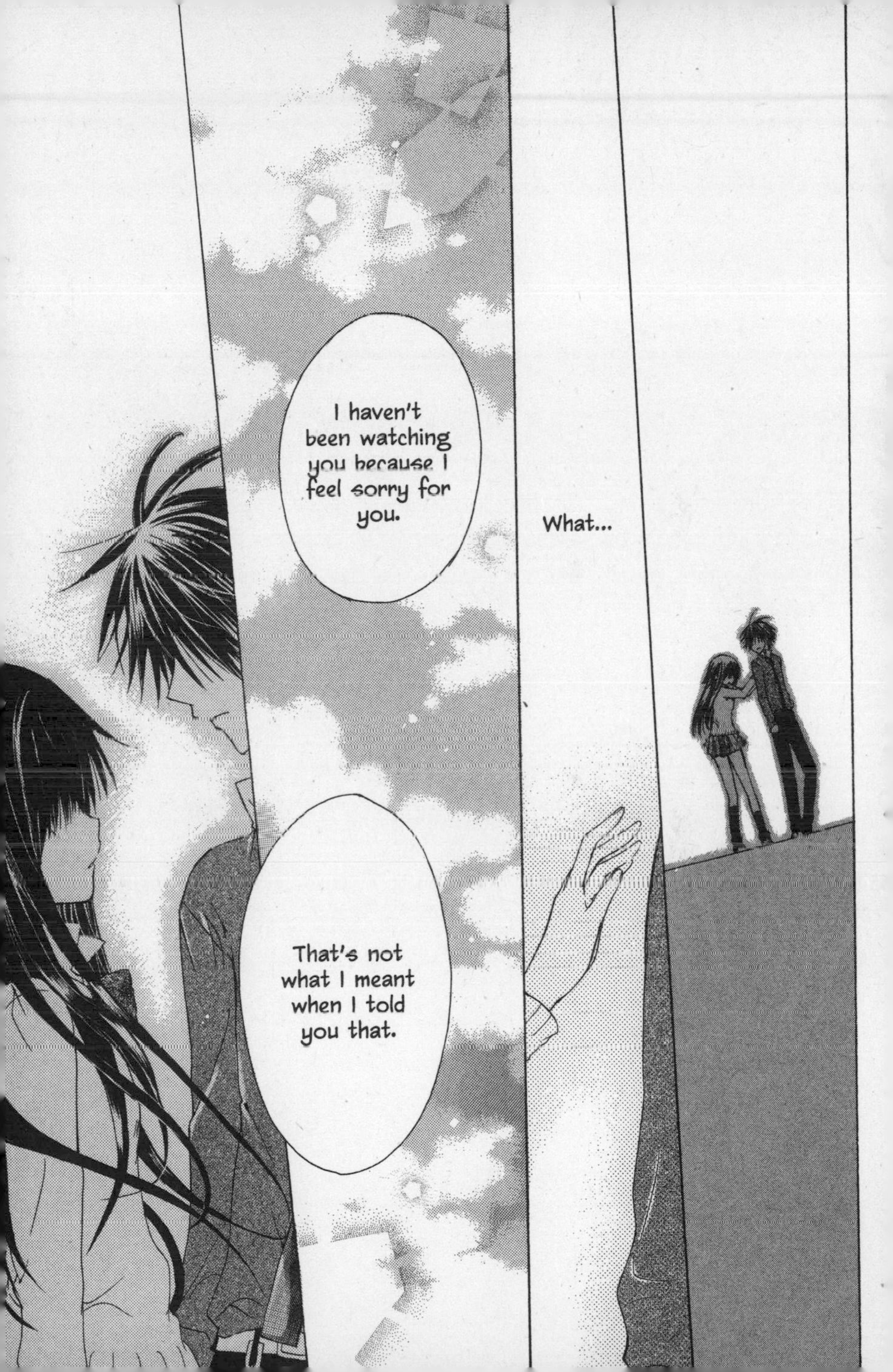
What...
I haven't been watching you because I feel sorry for you.
That's not what I meant when I told you that.

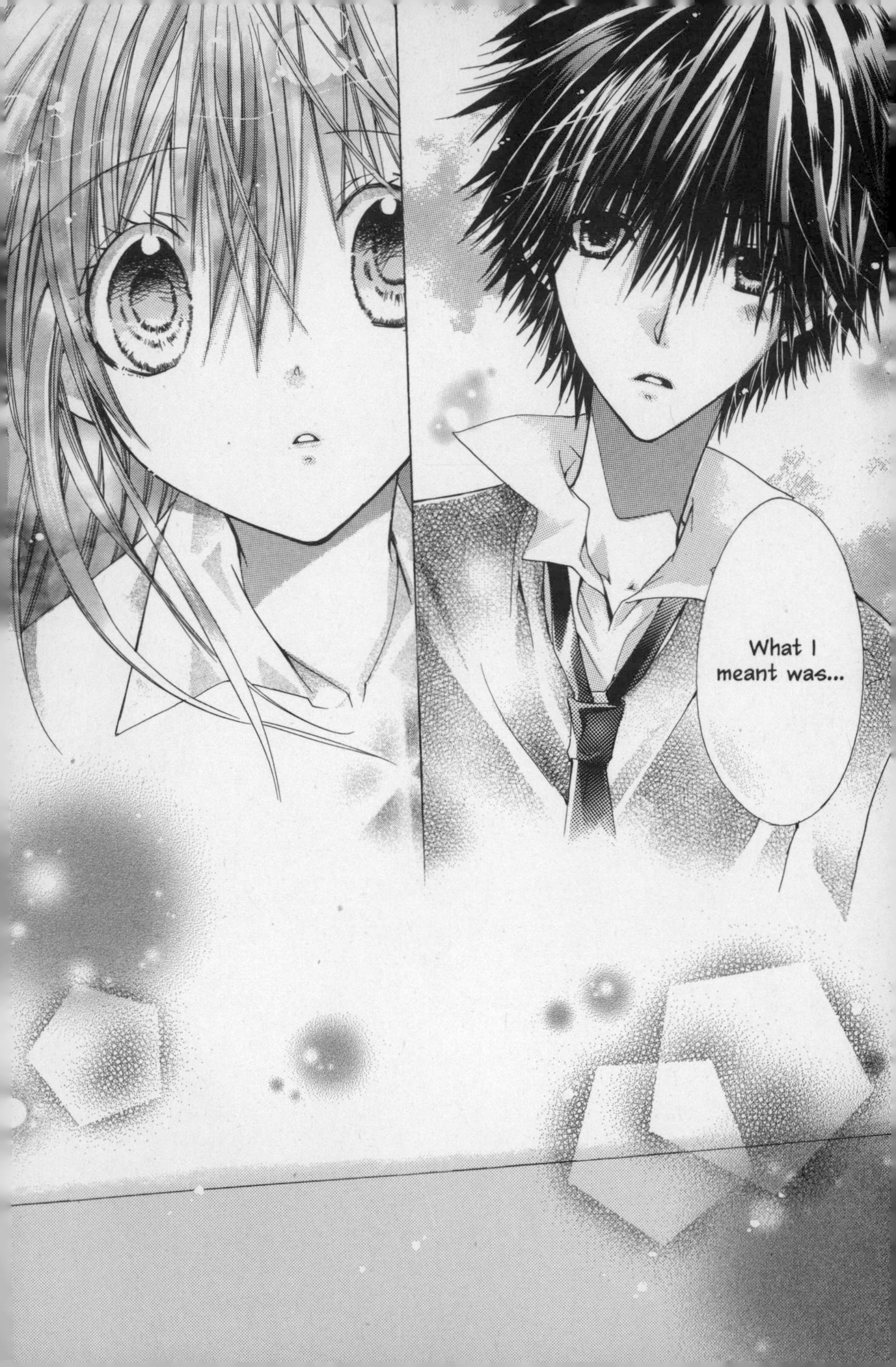
What I meant was...

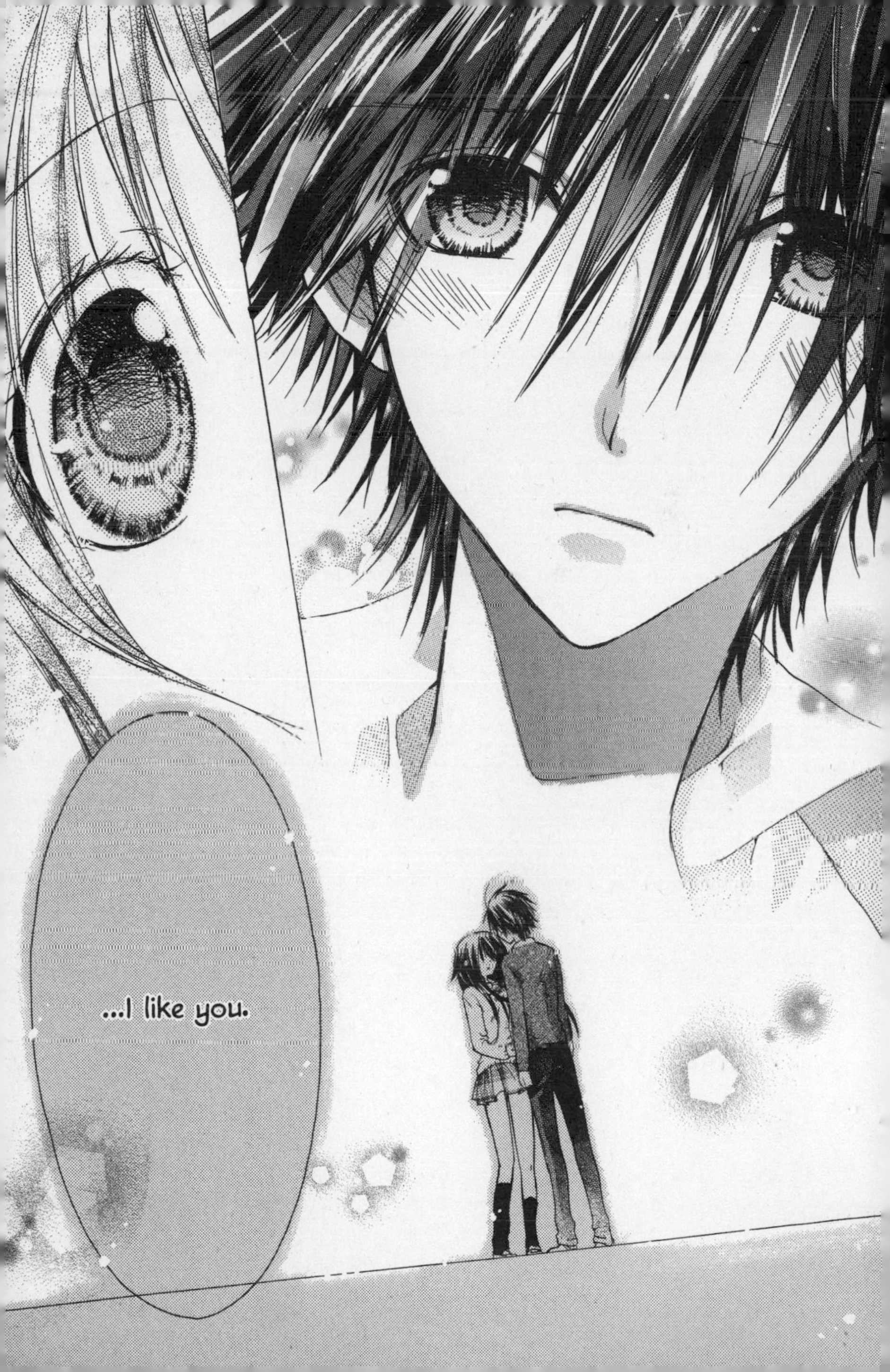
...I like you.

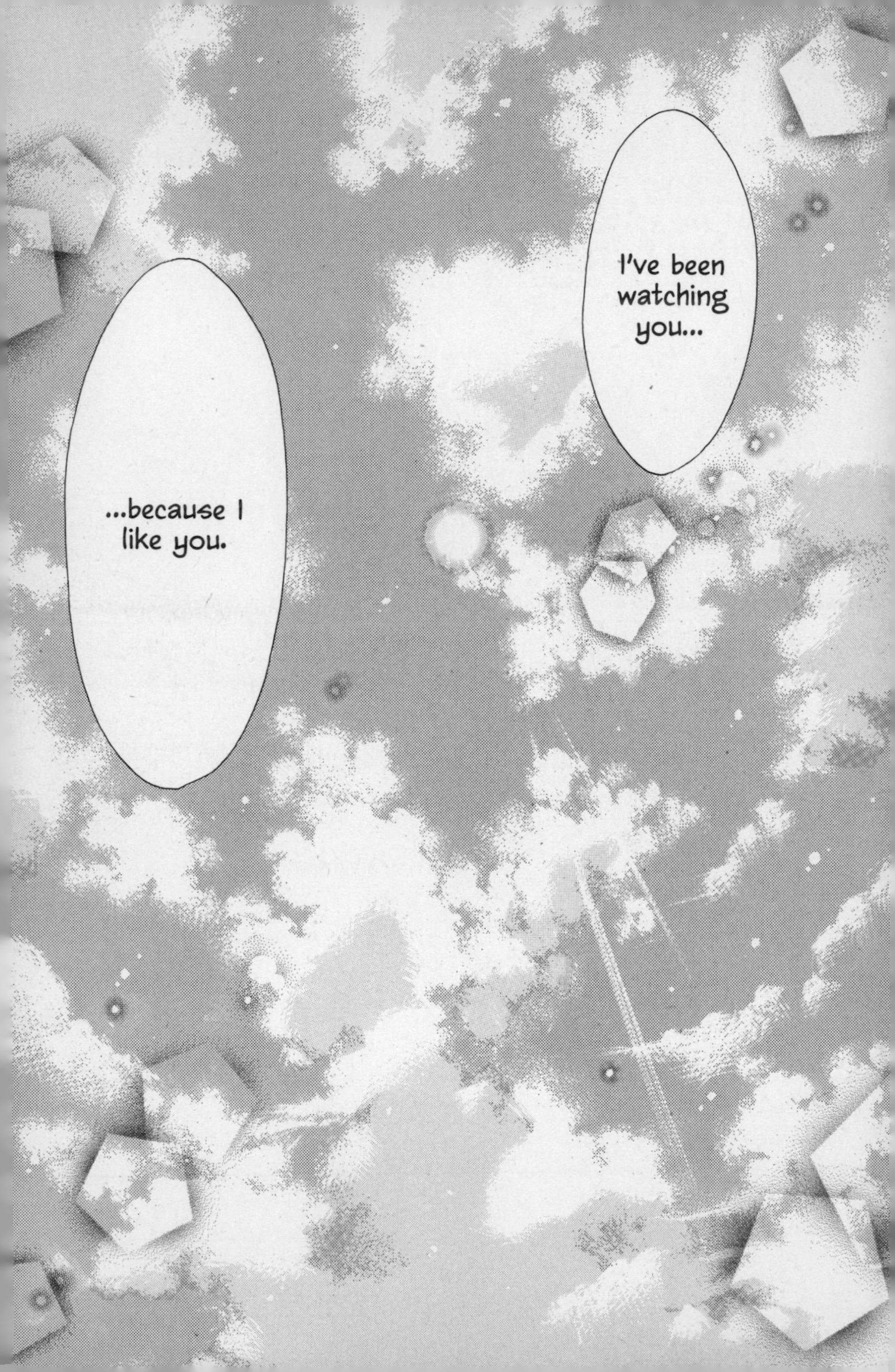
I've been watching you...
...because I like you.

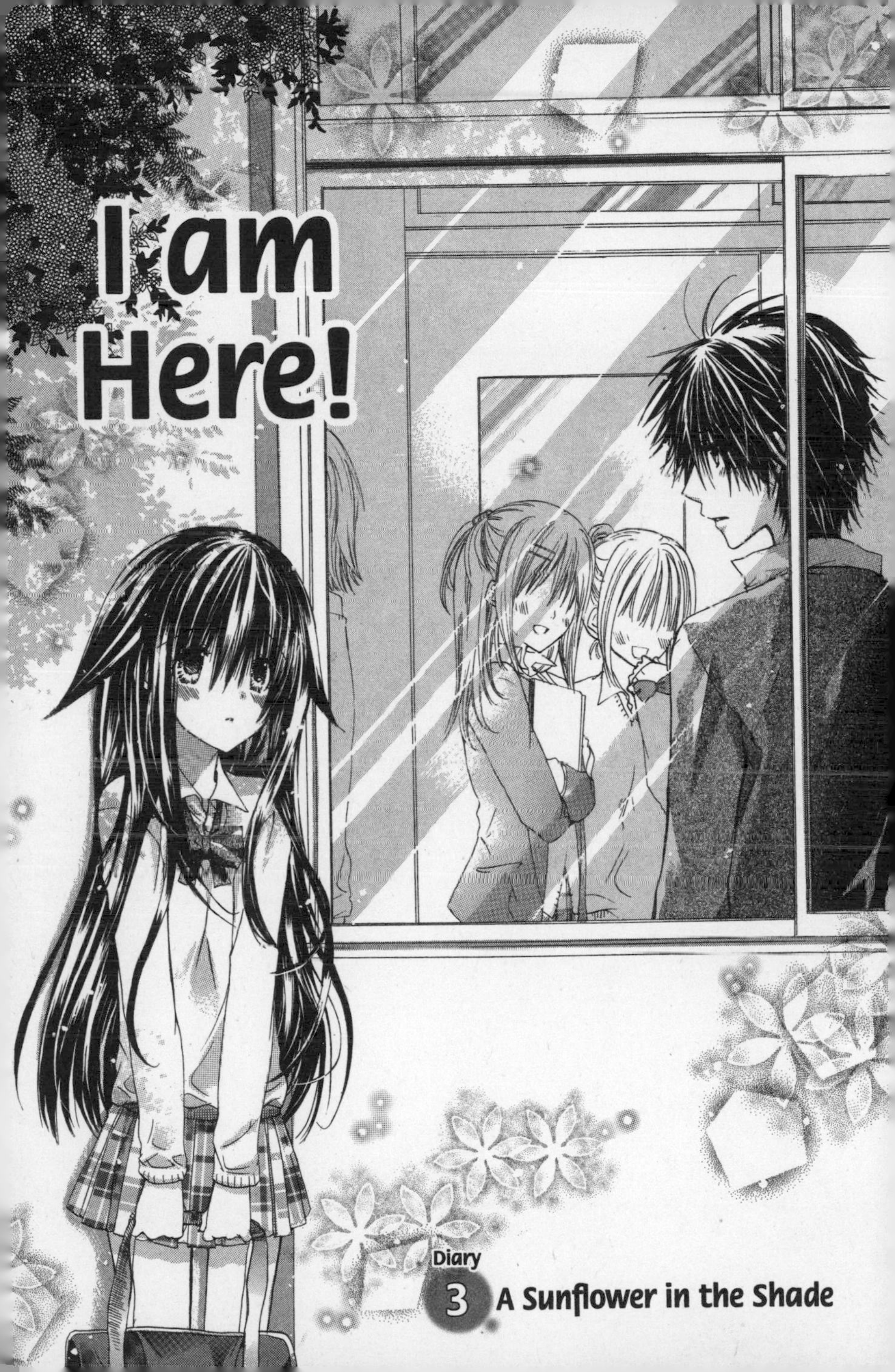
I am Here!
Diary 3 A Sunflower in the Shade

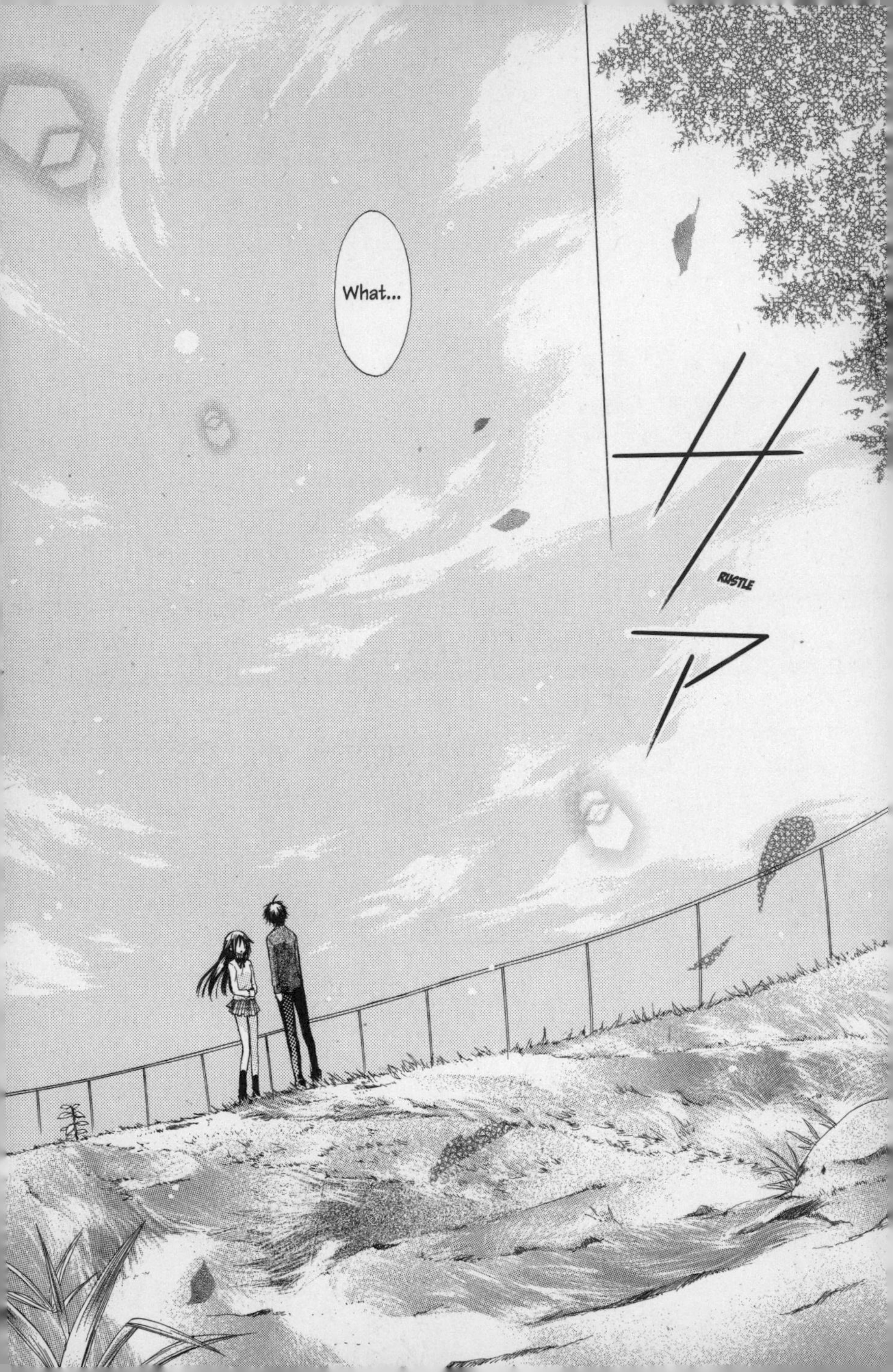
RUSTLE
What...

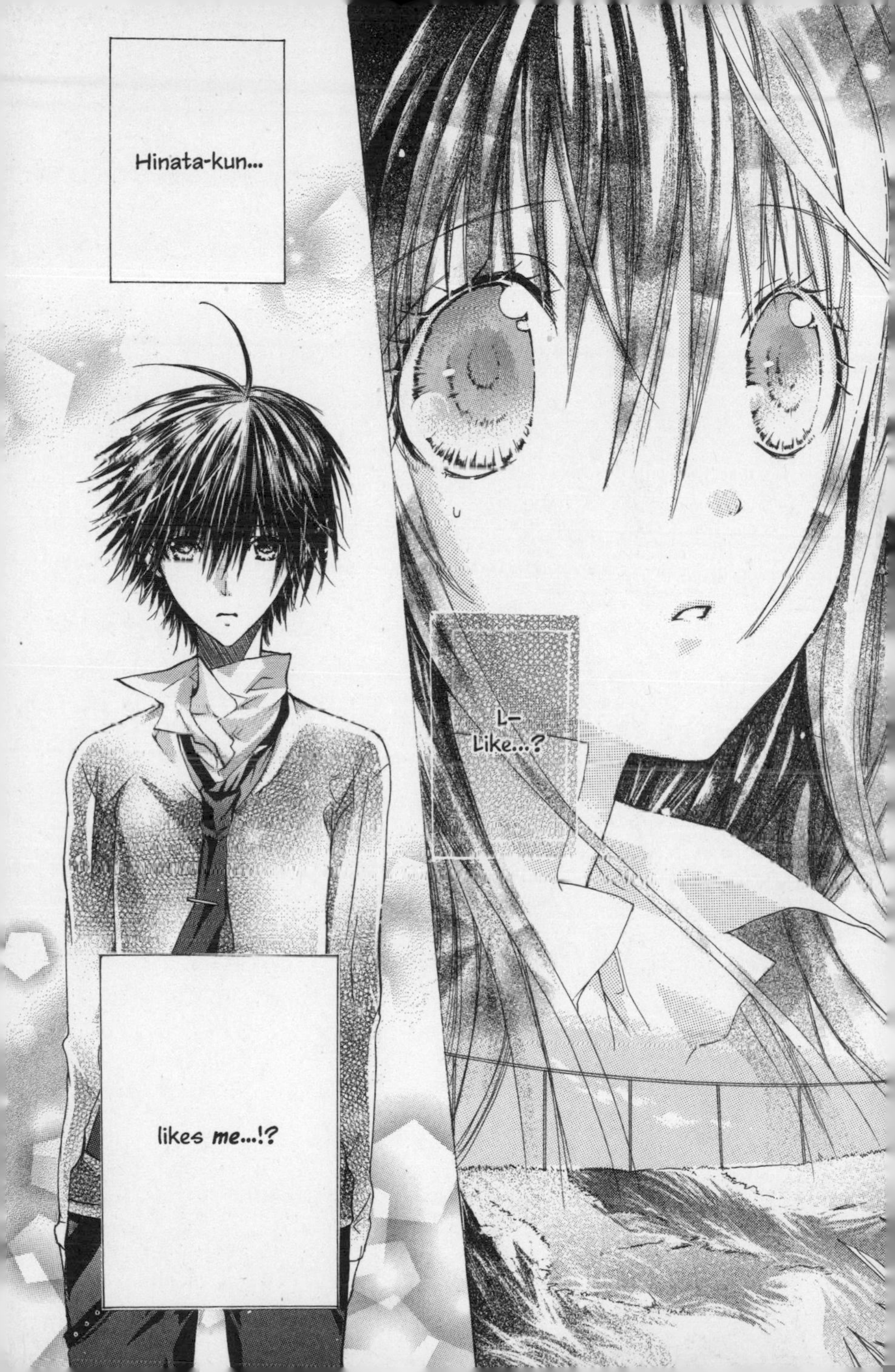
L–
Like...?
Hinata-kun...
likes me...!?

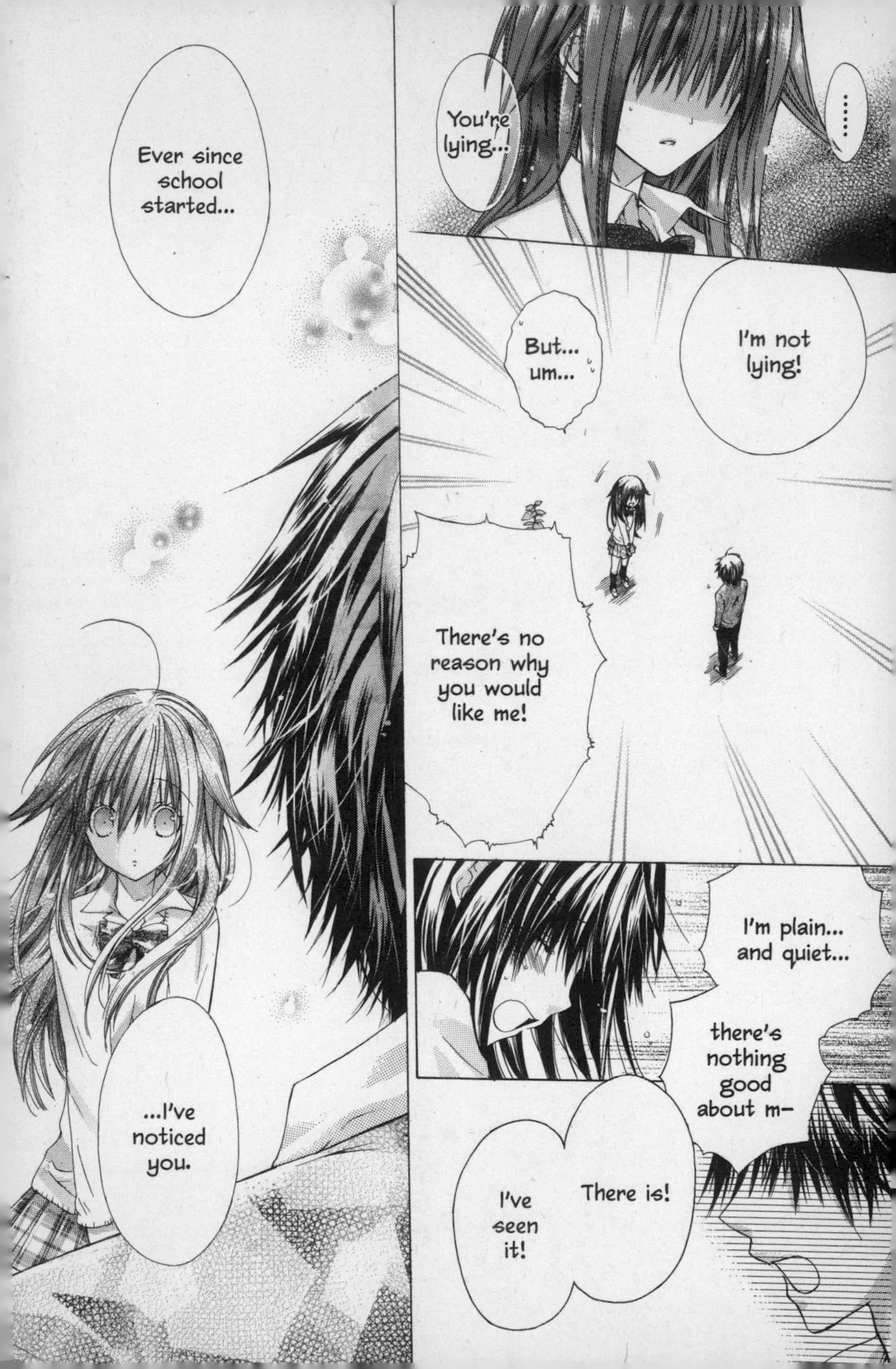
Ever since school started...
...I've noticed you.
......
You're lying...
I'm not lying!
But... um...
There's no reason why you would like me!
I'm plain... and quiet...
there's nothing good about m—
There is!
I've seen it!

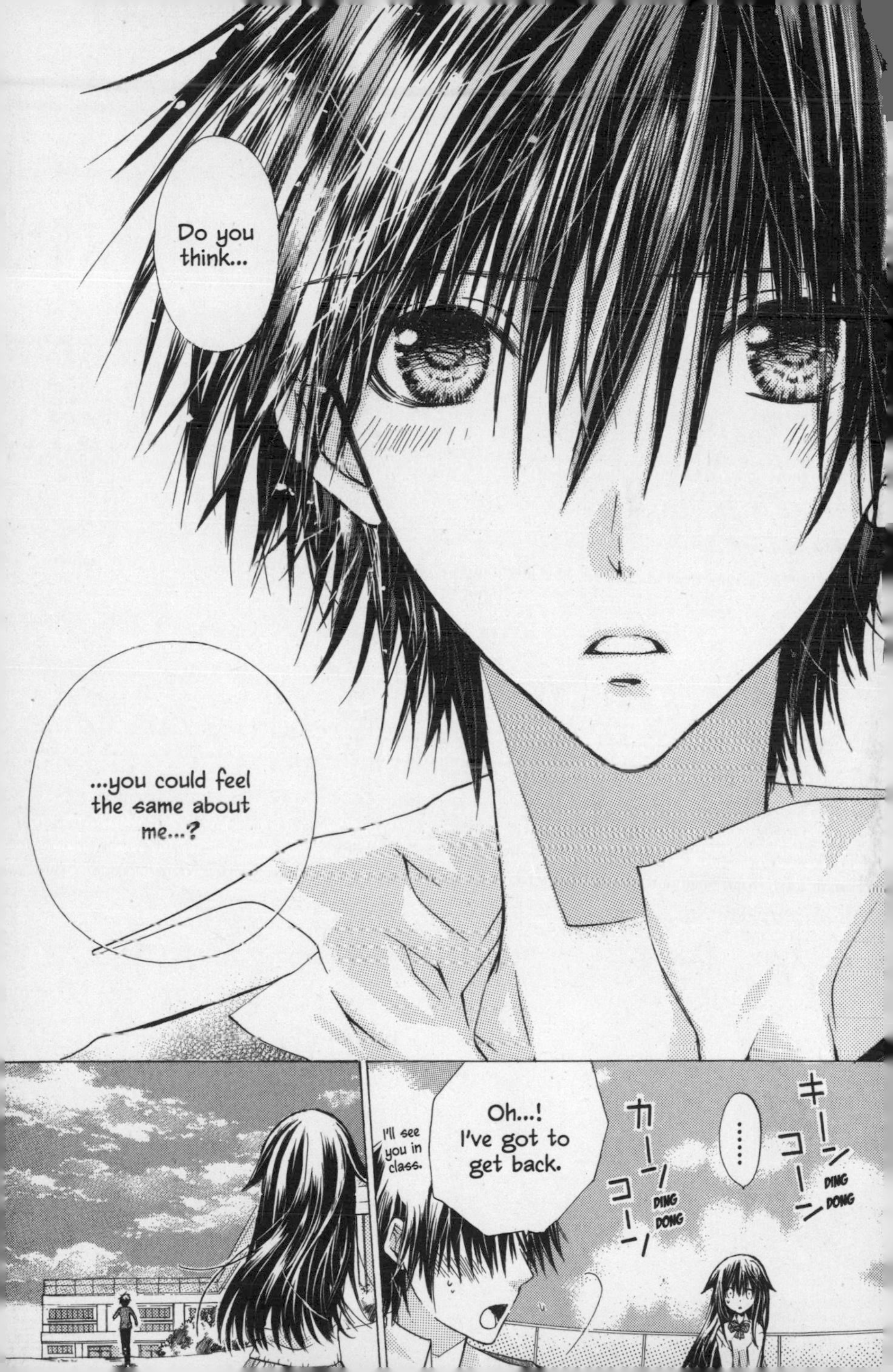
Do you think...
...you could feel the same about me...?
キーンコーン
DING DONG
カーンコーン
DING DONG
......
Oh...! I've got to get back.
I'll see you in class.

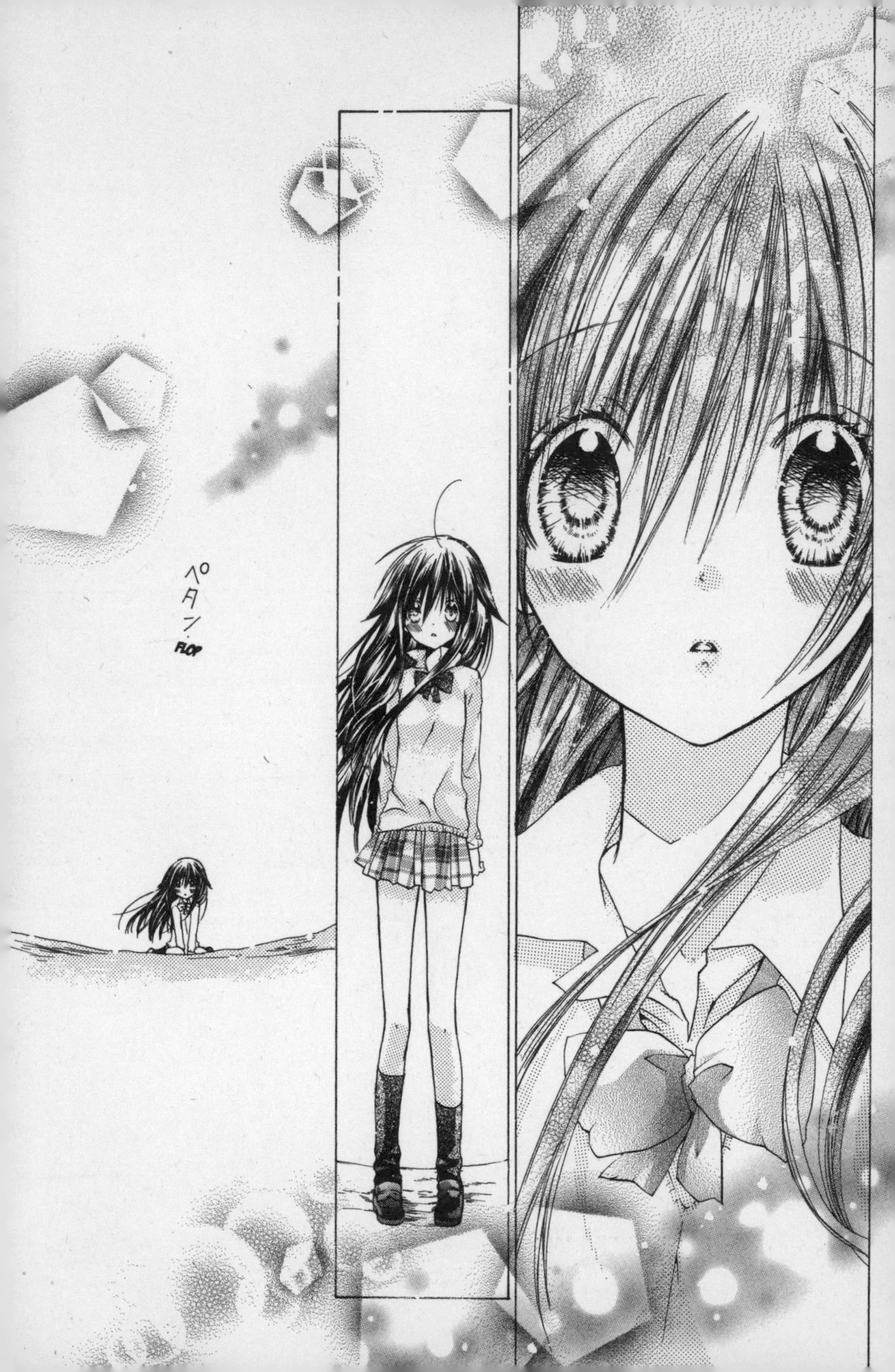
ペタン
FLOP

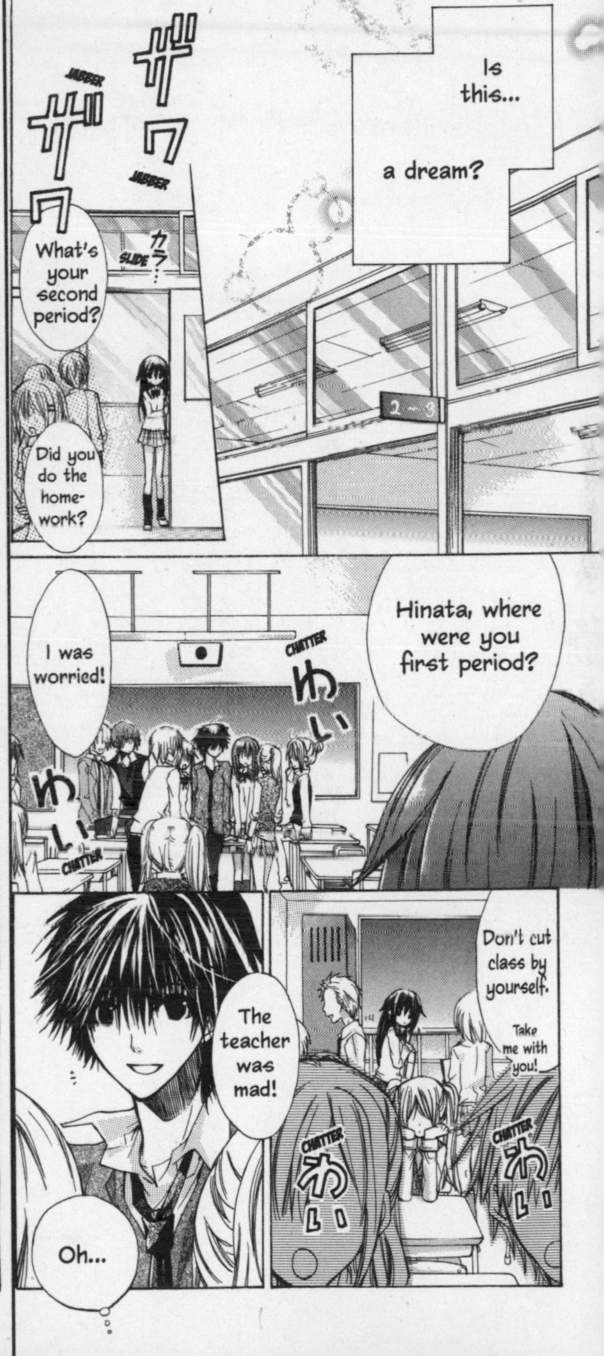
Is this...
a dream?
ザワ JABBER
ザワ JABBER
カラ... SLIDE
What's your second period?
Did you do the home-work?
Hinata, where were you first period?
わい CHATTER
I was worried!
わい CHATTER
Don't cut class by yourself.
Take me with you!
わい CHATTER
わい CHATTER
The teacher was mad!
Oh...

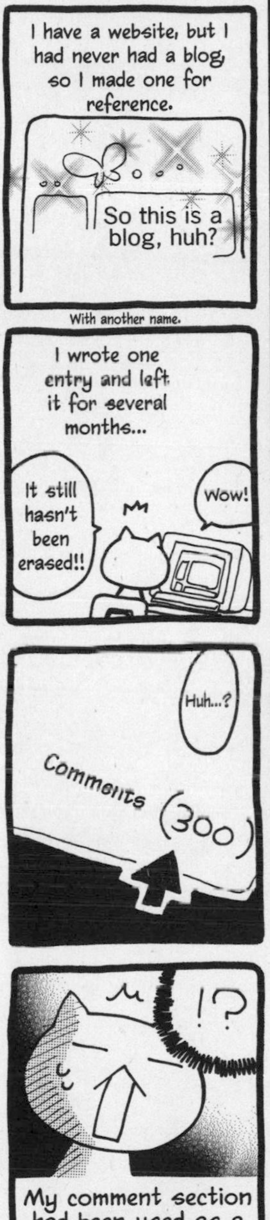
I have a website, but I had never had a blog, so I made one for reference.
So this is a blog, huh?
With another name.
I wrote one entry and left it for several months...
Wow!
It still hasn't been erased!!
Huh...?
Comments (300)
!?
My comment section had been used as a chat room.
The internet is really something!

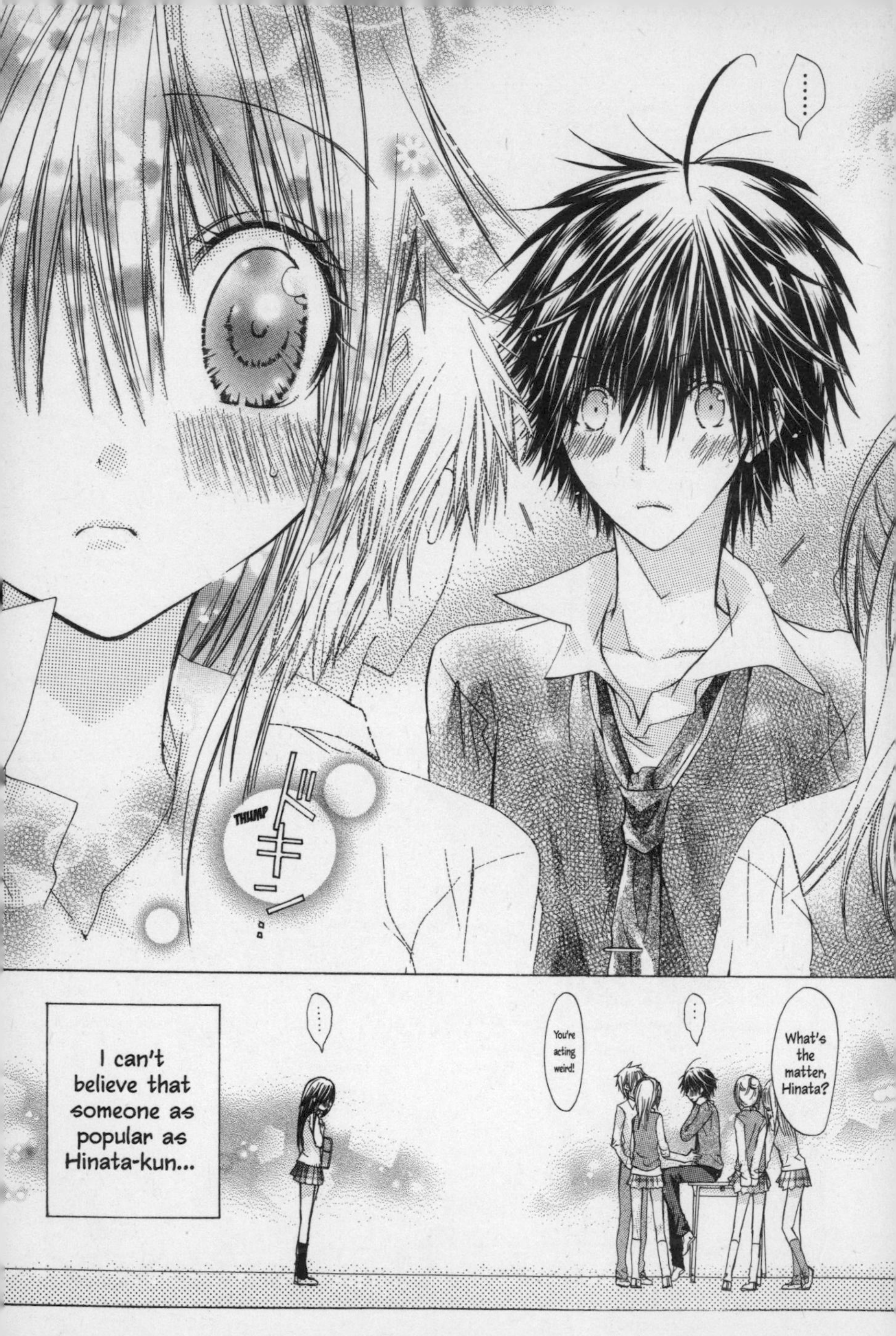

......
THUMP
What's the matter, Hinata?
...
You're acting weird!
...
I can't believe that someone as popular as Hinata-kun...

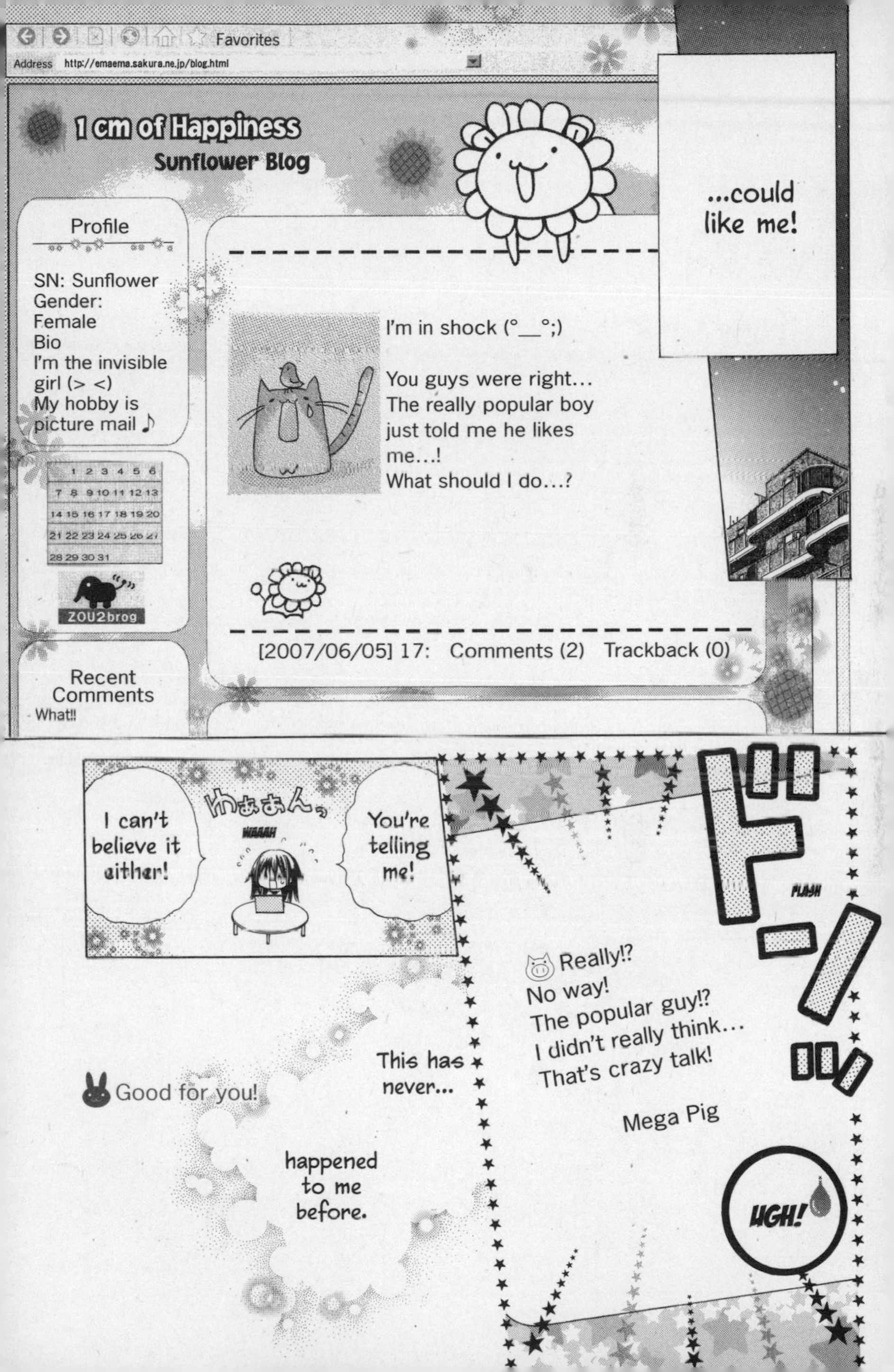
...could like me!
Favorites
Address http://emaema.sakura.ne.jp/blog.html
1 cm of Happiness
Sunflower Blog
Profile
SN: Sunflower
Gender: Female
Bio
I'm the invisible girl (> <)
My hobby is picture mail ♪
1 2 3 4 5 6
7 8 9 10 11 12 13
14 15 16 17 18 19 20
21 22 23 24 25 26 27
28 29 30 31
ZOU2brog
Recent Comments
What!!
I'm in shock (°__°;)
You guys were right...
The really popular boy just told me he likes me...!
What should I do...?
[2007/06/05] 17: Comments (2) Trackback (0)
ドーン!!
FLASH
Really!?
No way!
The popular guy!?
I didn't really think...
That's crazy talk!
Mega Pig
UGH!
You're telling me!
WAAAH
I can't believe it either!
This has never...
happened to me before.
Good for you!

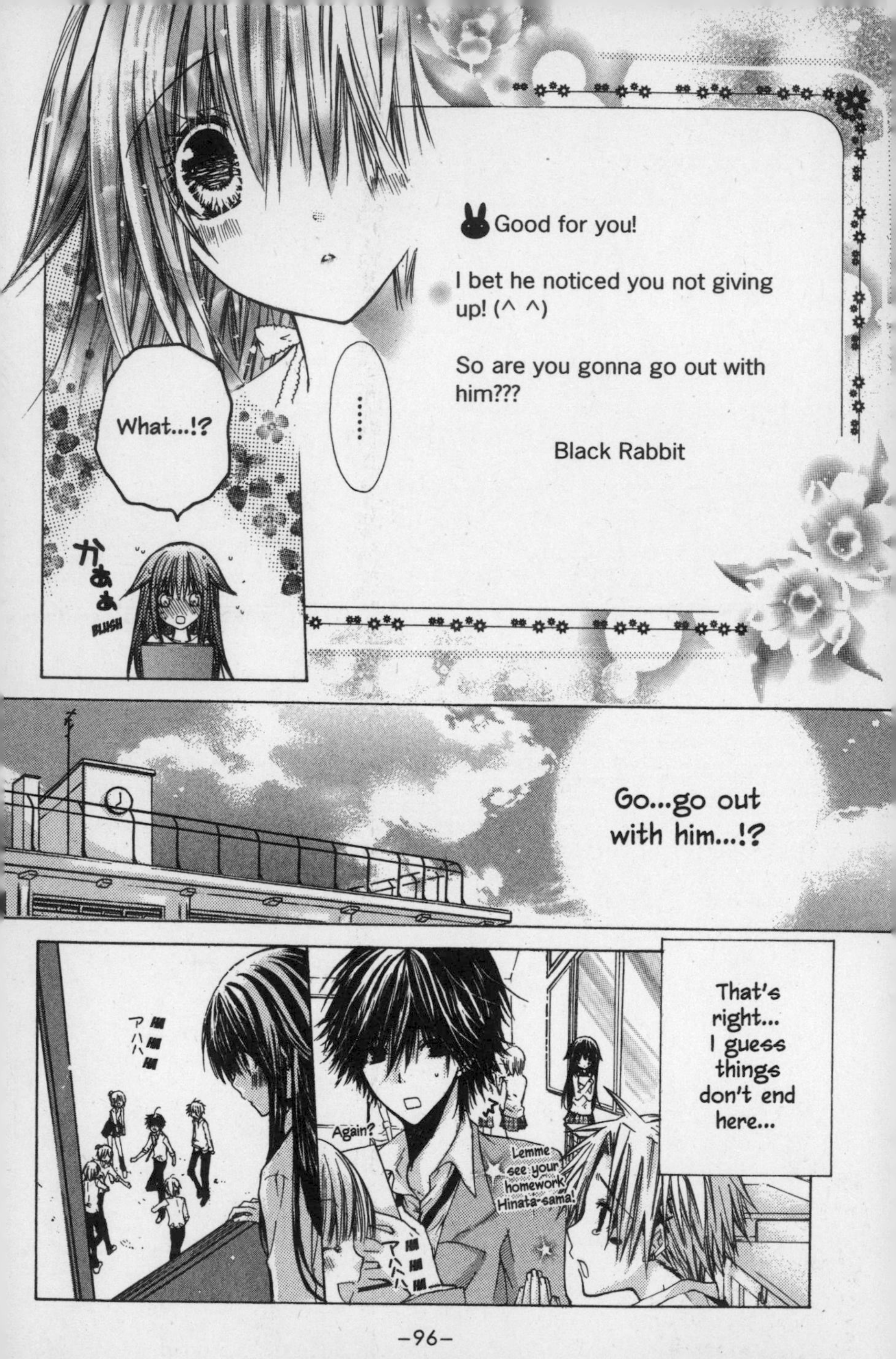
Good for you!
I bet he noticed you not giving up! (^ ^)
So are you gonna go out with him???
Black Rabbit
......
What...!?
かあぁ
BLUSH
Go...go out with him...!?
That's right... I guess things don't end here...
Lemme see your homework Hinata-sama!
Again?
アハハ
HA HA HA
アハハ
HA HA HA

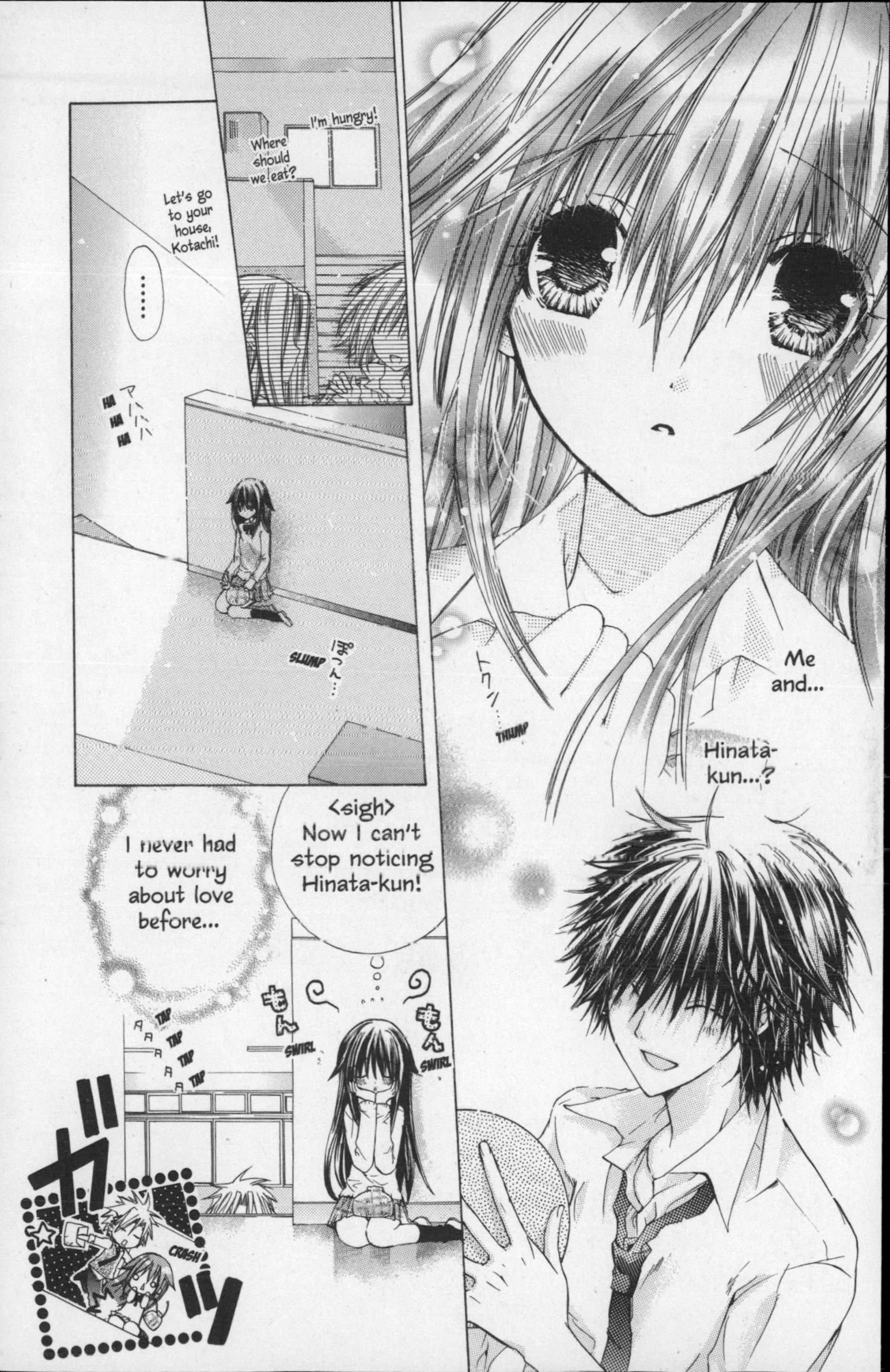
THUMP
Me and...
Hinata-kun...?
I'm hungry!
Where should we eat?
Let's go to your house, Kotachi!
......
HA HA HA
SLUMP
<sigh> Now I can't stop noticing Hinata-kun!
I never had to worry about love before...
SWIRL
SWIRL
TAP TAP TAP TAP
CRASH

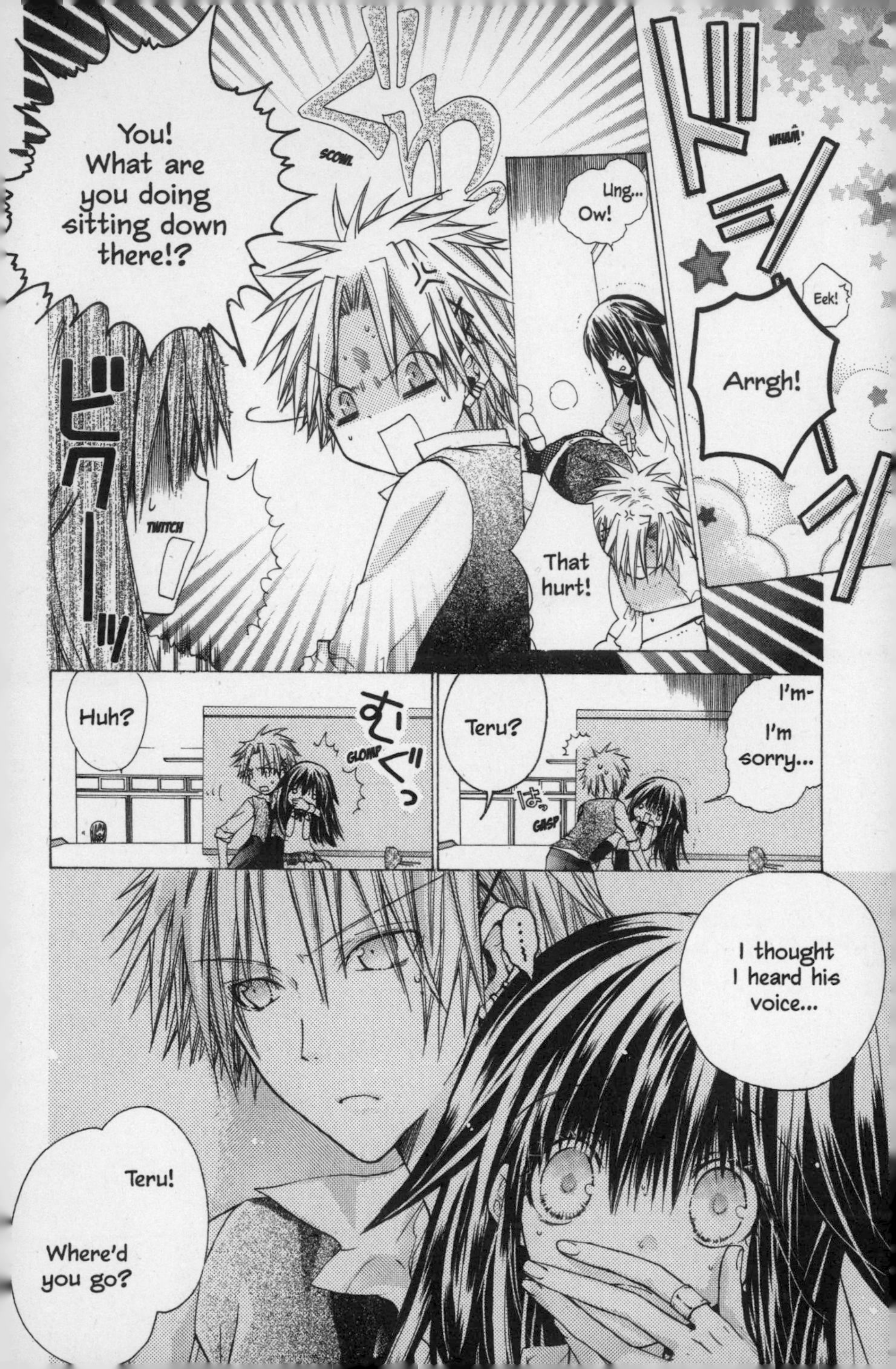
WHAM
Eek!
Arrgh!
Ung... Ow!
That hurt!
SCOWL
You! What are you doing sitting down there!?
TWITCH
I'm- I'm sorry...
Teru?
GASP
GLOMP
Huh?
I thought I heard his voice...
...
Teru!
Where'd you go?

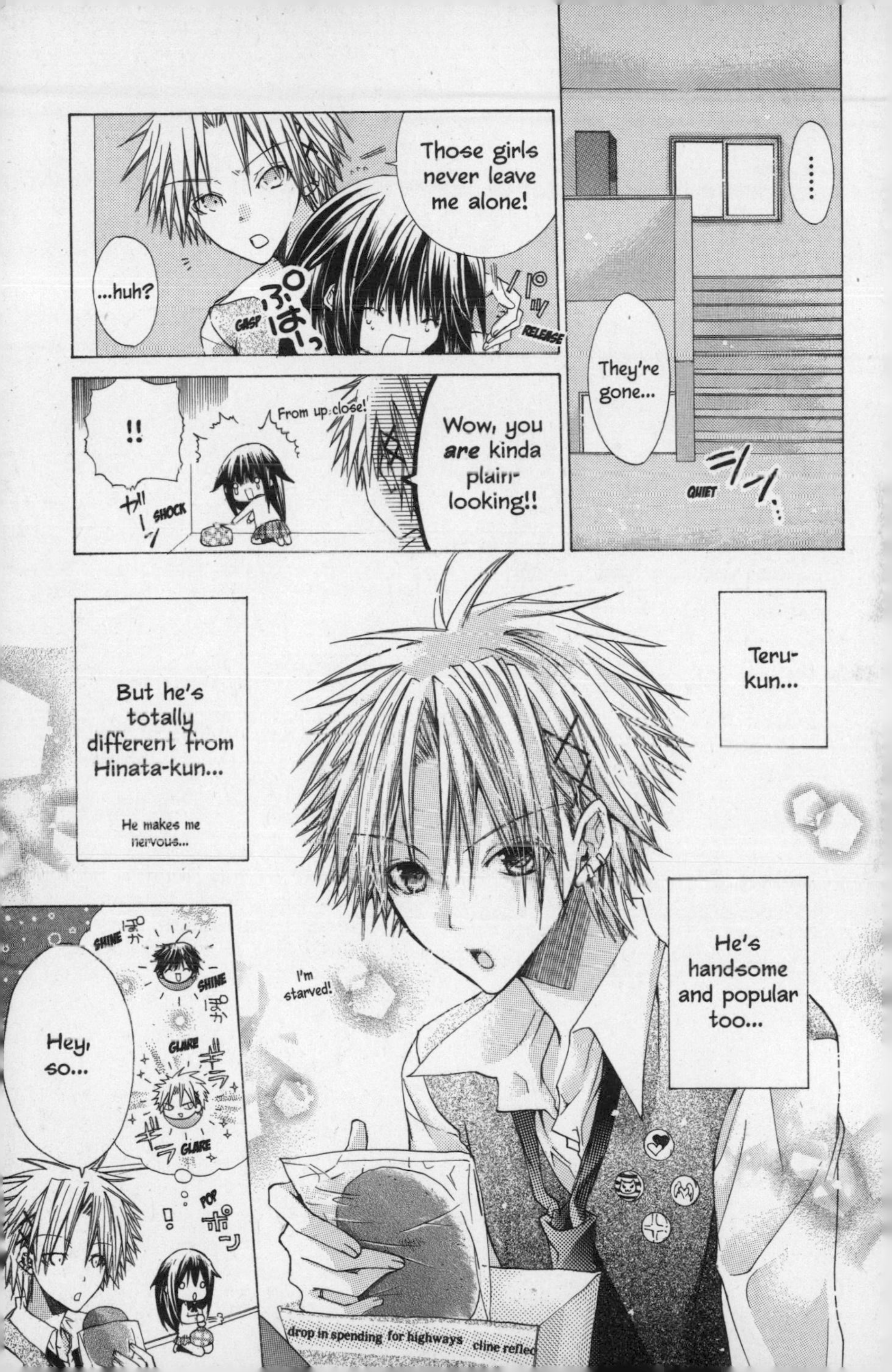

......
They're gone...
QUIET
Those girls never leave me alone!
...huh?
GASP
RELEASE
Wow, you are kinda plain-looking!!
From up close!
!!
SHOCK
Teru-kun...
But he's totally different from Hinata-kun...
He makes me nervous...
He's handsome and popular too...
I'm starved!
drop in spending for highways cline refle
Hey, so...
SHINE
SHINE
GLARE
GLARE
!
POP

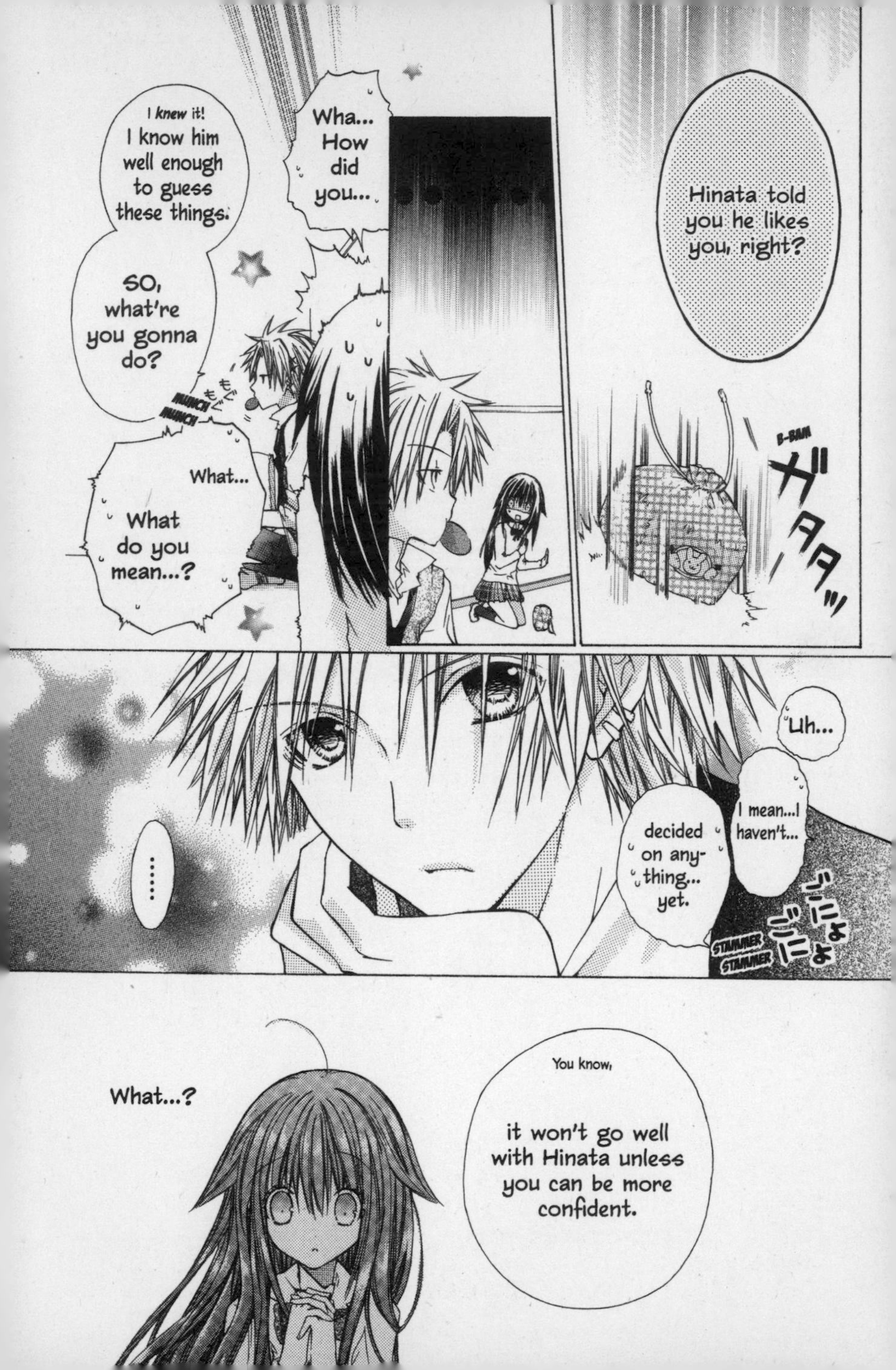

Hinata told you he likes you, right?
B-BAM
ガタタッ
Wha... How did you...
I *knew* it! I know him well enough to guess these things.
SO, what're you gonna do?
もぐもぐ
MUNCH MUNCH
What... What do you mean...?
Uh...
I mean...I haven't...
decided on any-thing... yet.
ごにょごにょ
STAMMER STAMMER
......
You know, it won't go well with Hinata unless you can be more confident.
What...?

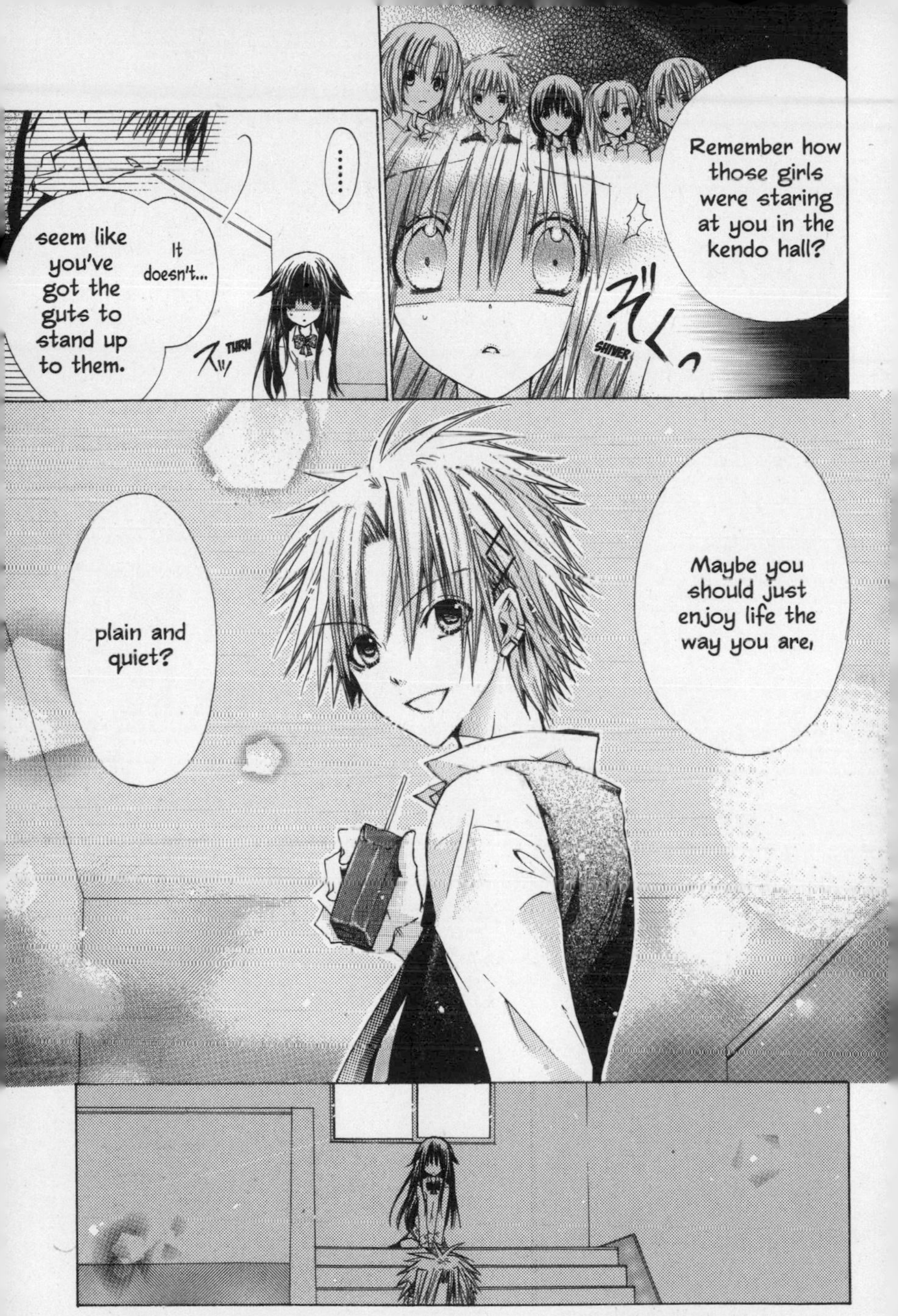
Remember how those girls were staring at you in the kendo hall?
SHIVER
......
It doesn't...
seem like you've got the guts to stand up to them.
TURN
Maybe you should just enjoy life the way you are,
plain and quiet?

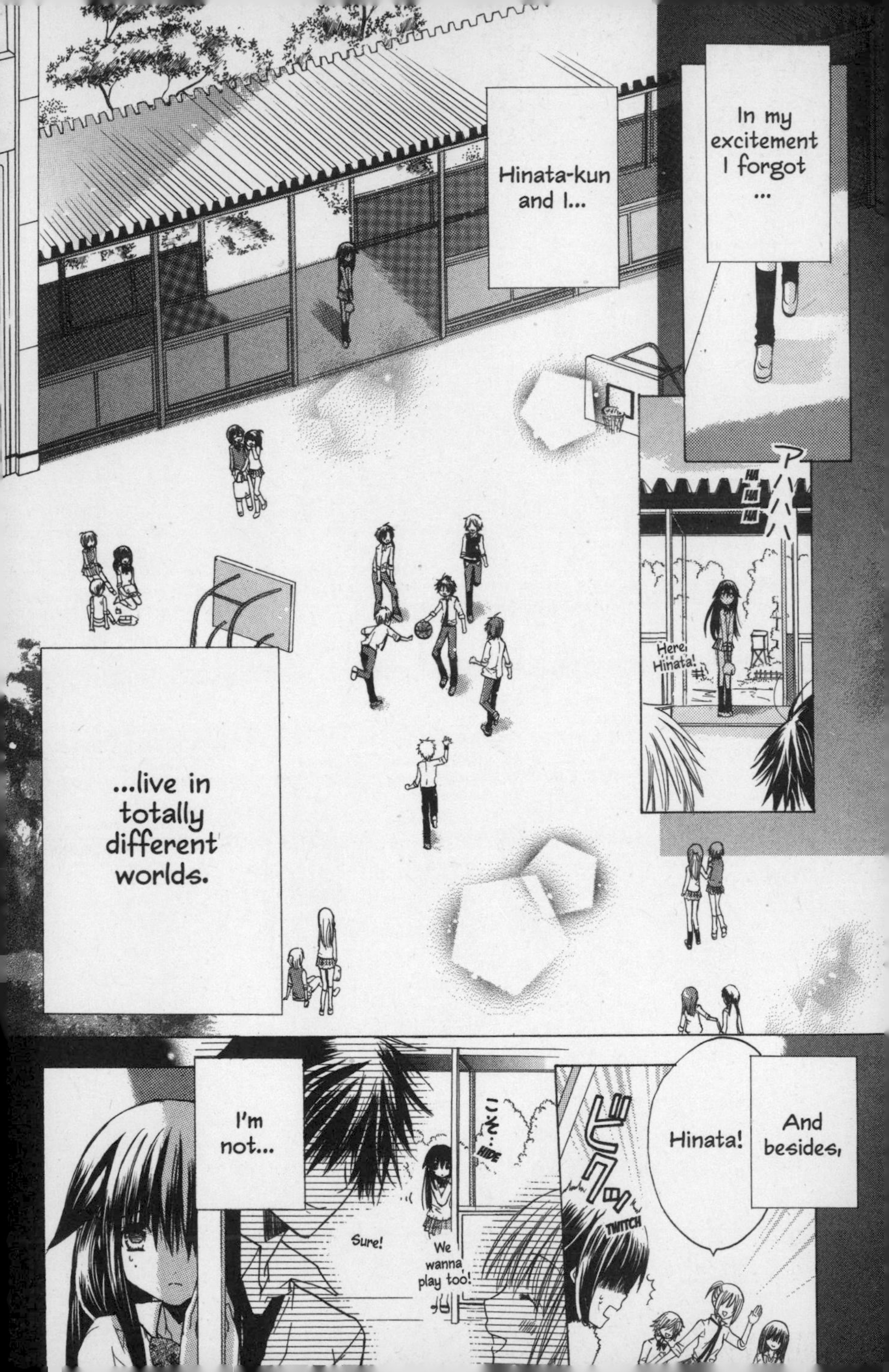
In my excitement I forgot...
Hinata-kun and I...
HA
HA
HA
Here, Hinata!
...live in totally different worlds.
And besides,
Hinata!
TWITCH
HIDE
Sure!
We wanna play too!
I'm not...

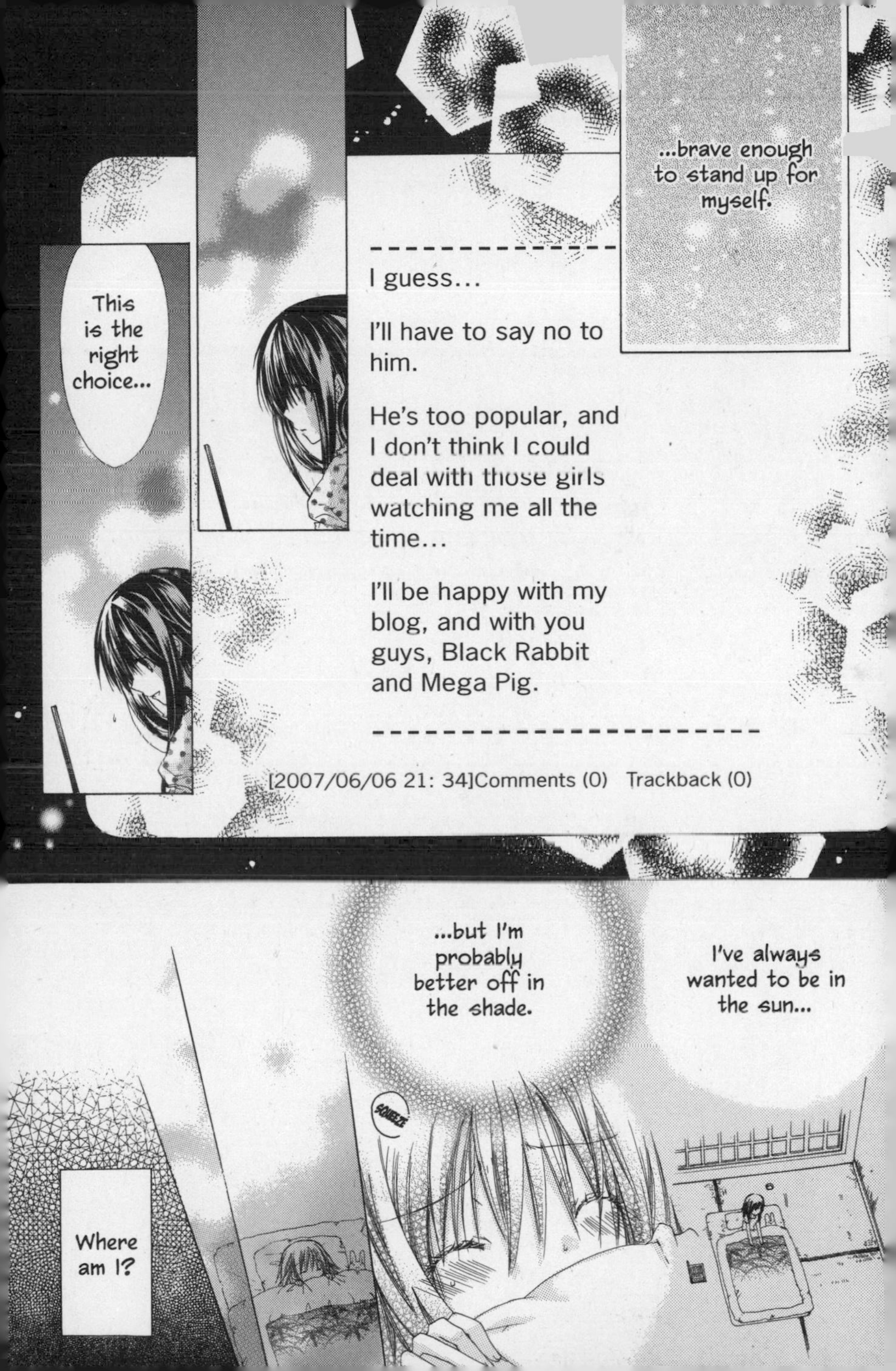
...brave enough to stand up for myself.
I guess...
I'll have to say no to him.
He's too popular, and I don't think I could deal with those girls watching me all the time...
I'll be happy with my blog, and with you guys, Black Rabbit and Mega Pig.
[2007/06/06 21: 34]Comments (0) Trackback (0)
This is the right choice...
I've always wanted to be in the sun...
...but I'm probably better off in the shade.
SQUEEZE
Where am I?

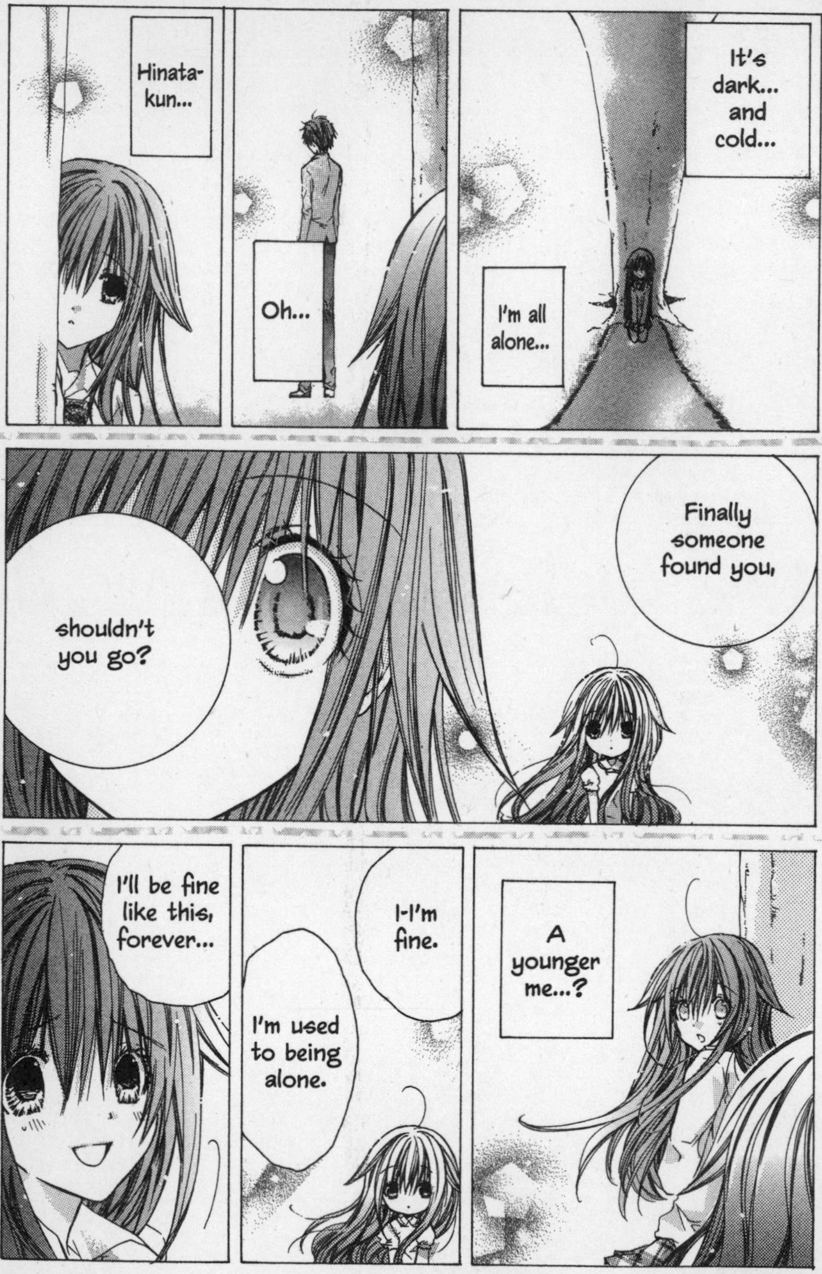
It's dark... and cold...
I'm all alone...
Oh...
Hinata-kun...
Finally someone found you,
shouldn't you go?
A younger me...?
I-I'm fine.
I'm used to being alone.
I'll be fine like this, forever...

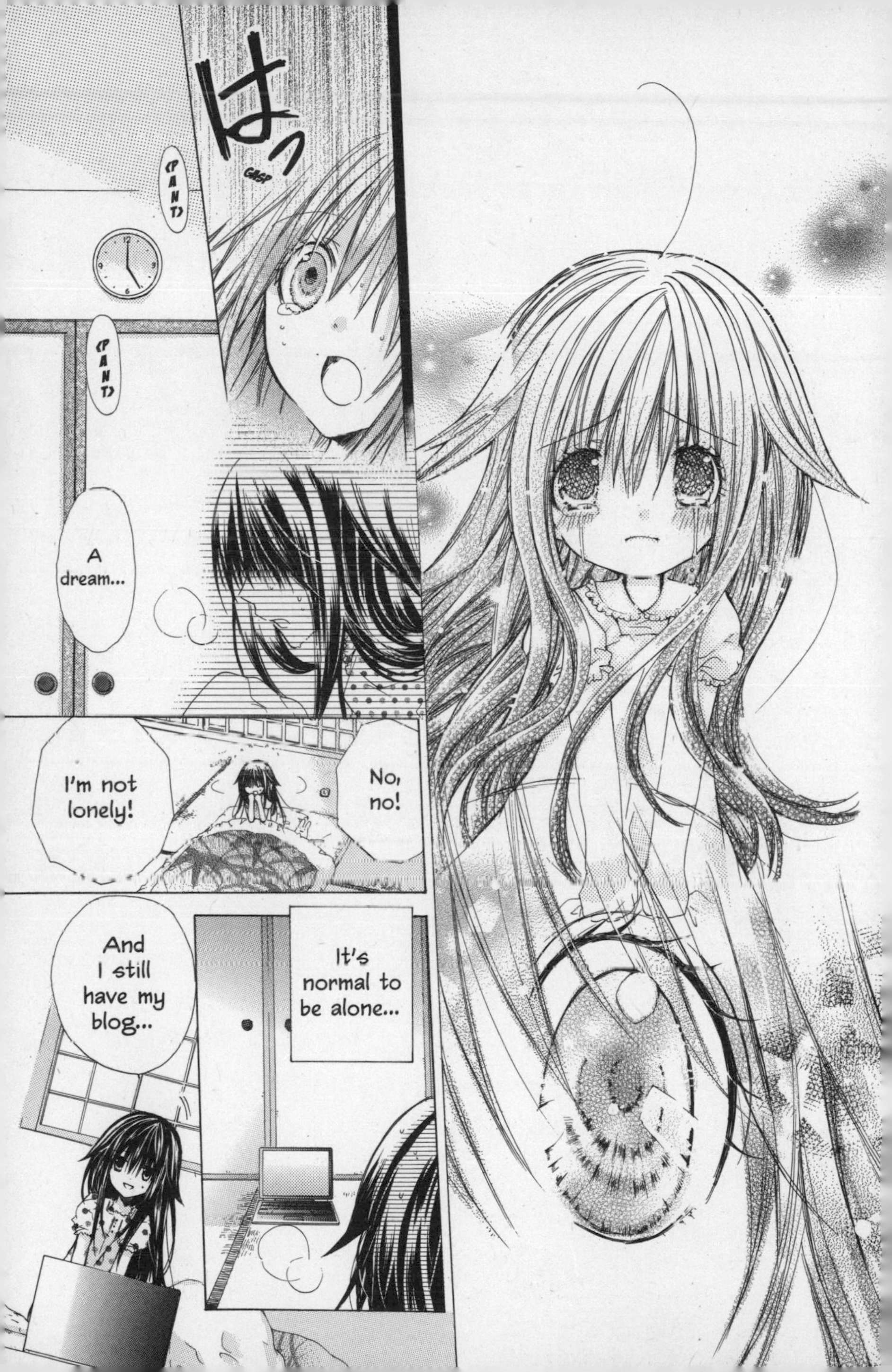

はっ
GASP
<PANT>
<PANT>
A dream...
No, no!
I'm not lonely!
It's normal to be alone...
And I still have my blog...

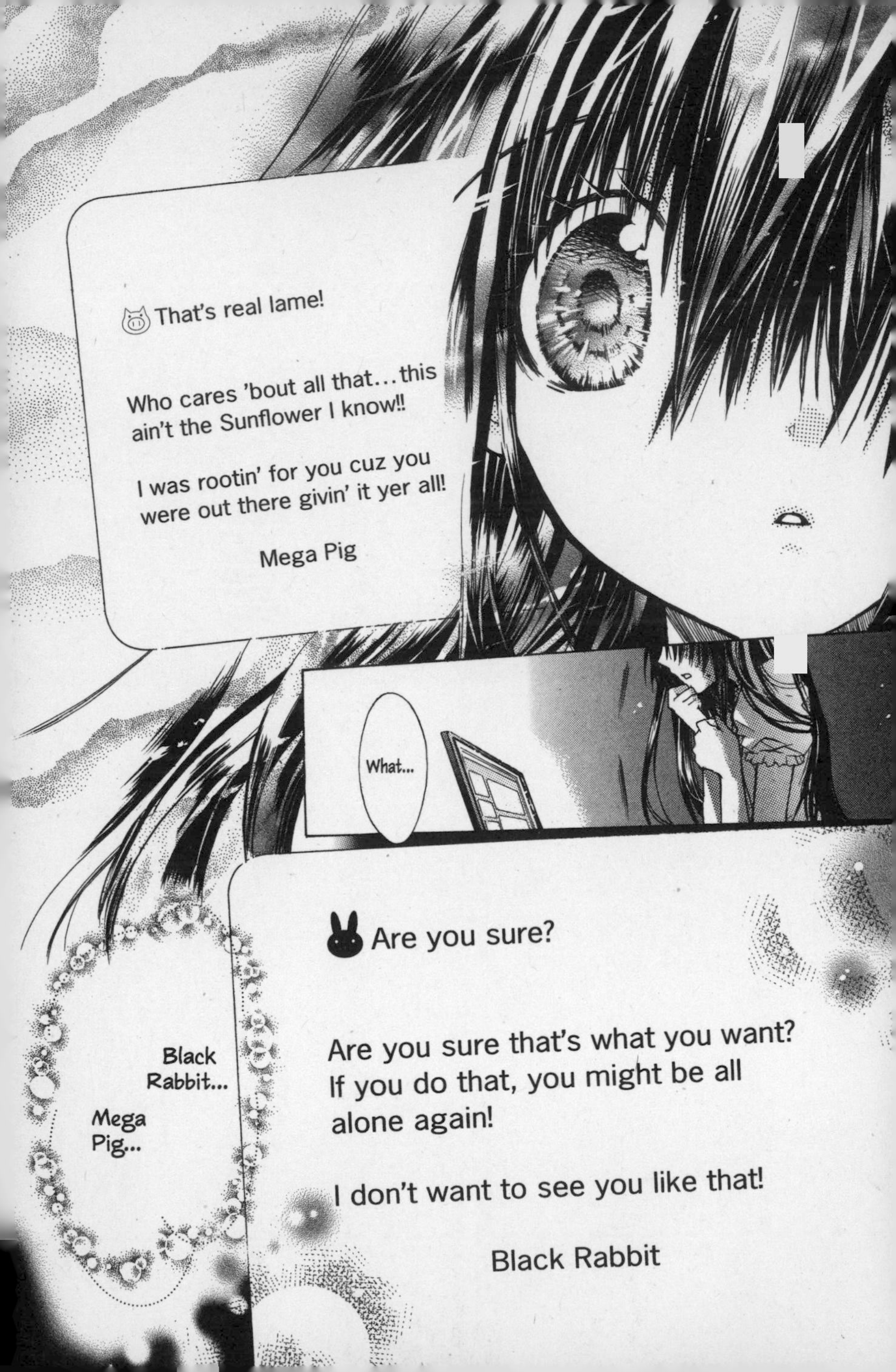
That's real lame!
Who cares 'bout all that... this ain't the Sunflower I know!!
I was rootin' for you cuz you were out there givin' it yer all!
Mega Pig
What...
Are you sure?
Are you sure that's what you want? If you do that, you might be all alone again!
I don't want to see you like that!
Black Rabbit
Black Rabbit...
Mega Pig...

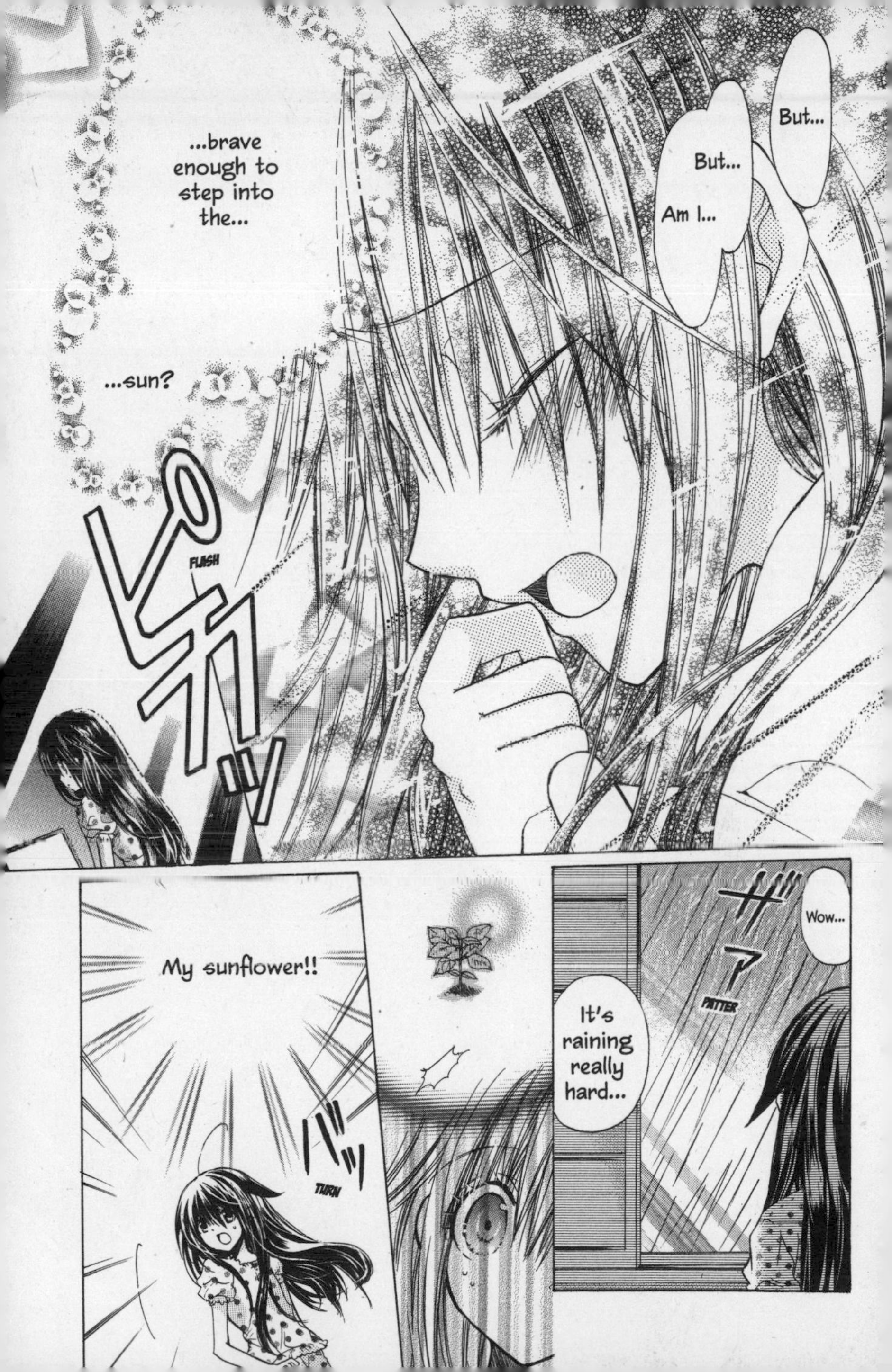

But...
But...
Am I...
...brave enough to step into the...
...sun?
FLASH
Wow...
PATTER
It's raining really hard...
My sunflower!!
TURN

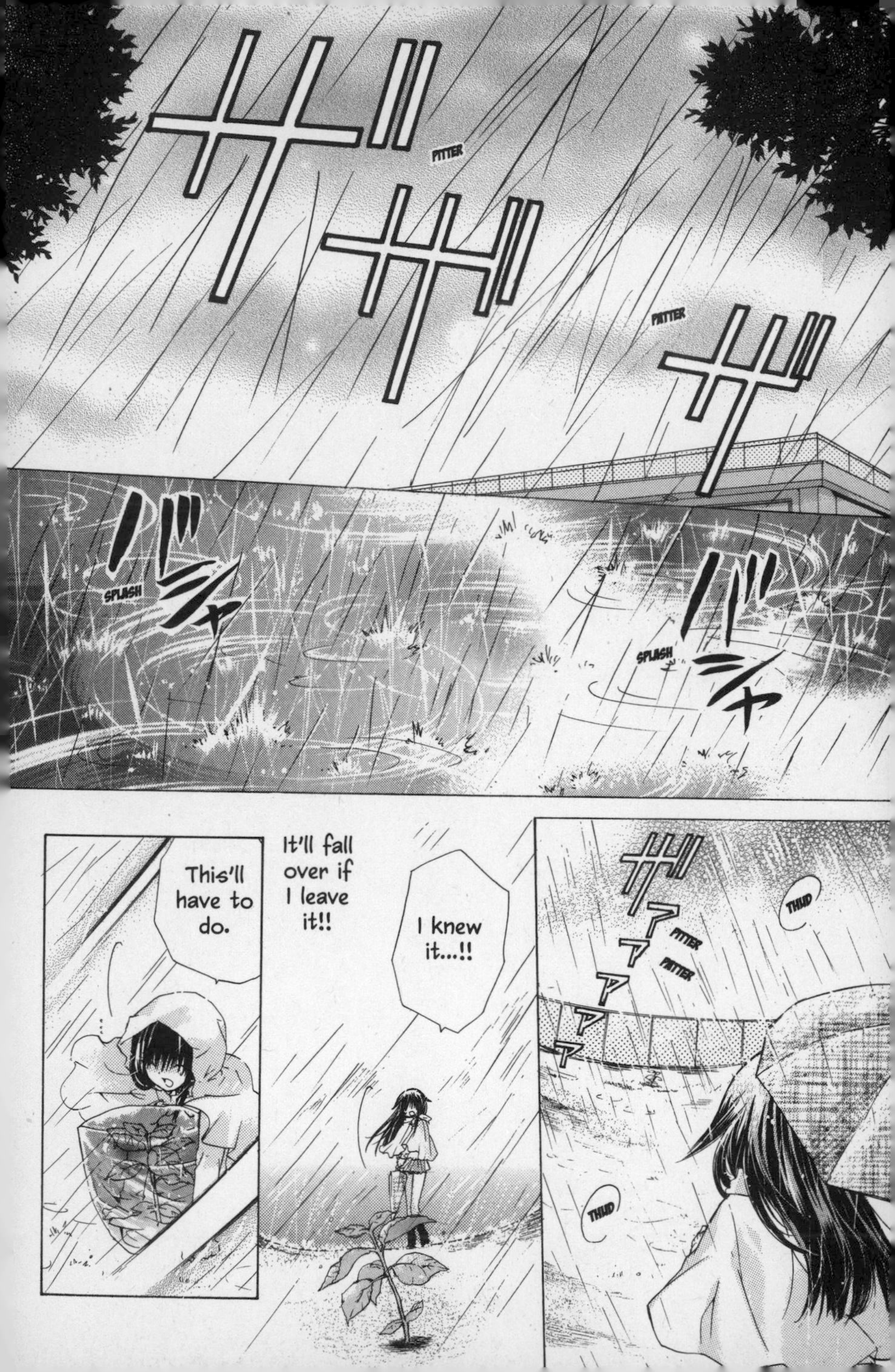
PITTER
PITTER
SPLASH
SPLASH
PITTER
PATTER
THUD
THUD
I knew it...!!
It'll fall over if I leave it!!
This'll have to do.

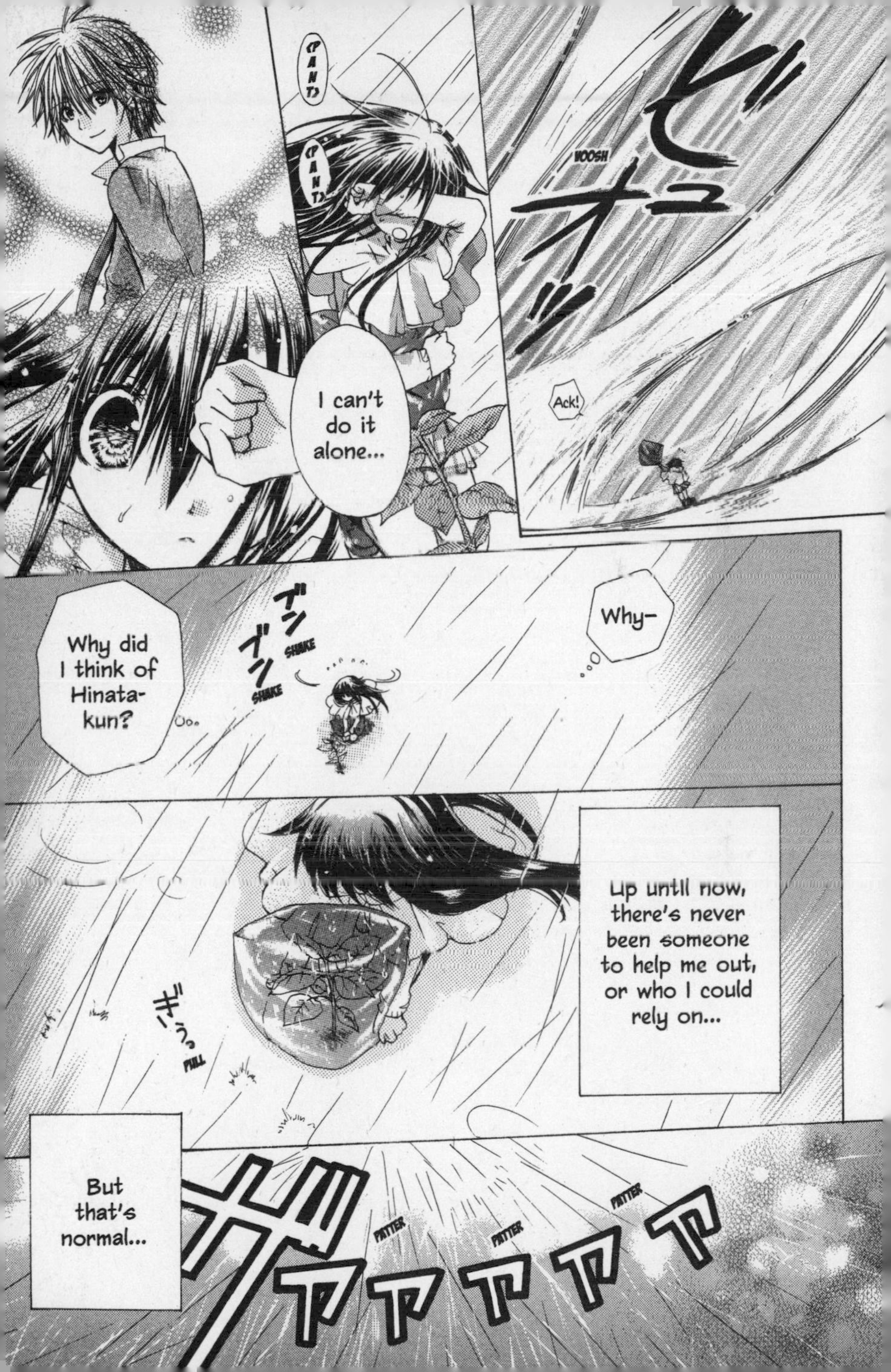

VOOSH
Ack!
<PANT>
<PANT>
I can't do it alone...
Why-
SHAKE
SHAKE
Why did I think of Hinata-kun?
Up until now, there's never been someone to help me out, or who I could rely on...
PULL
PATTER
PATTER
PATTER
But that's normal...

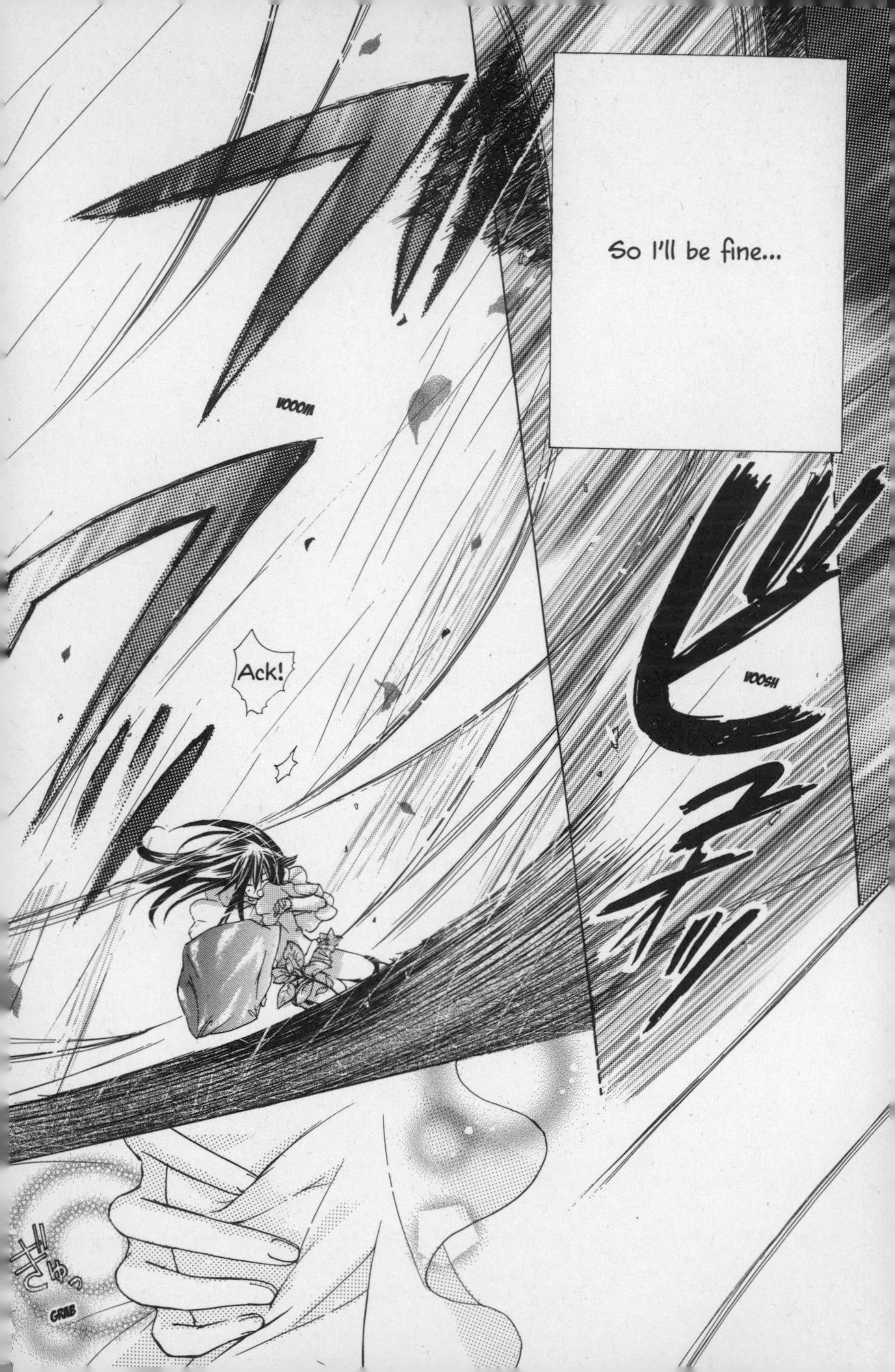
So I'll be fine...
VOOSH
VOOOM
Ack!
GRAB

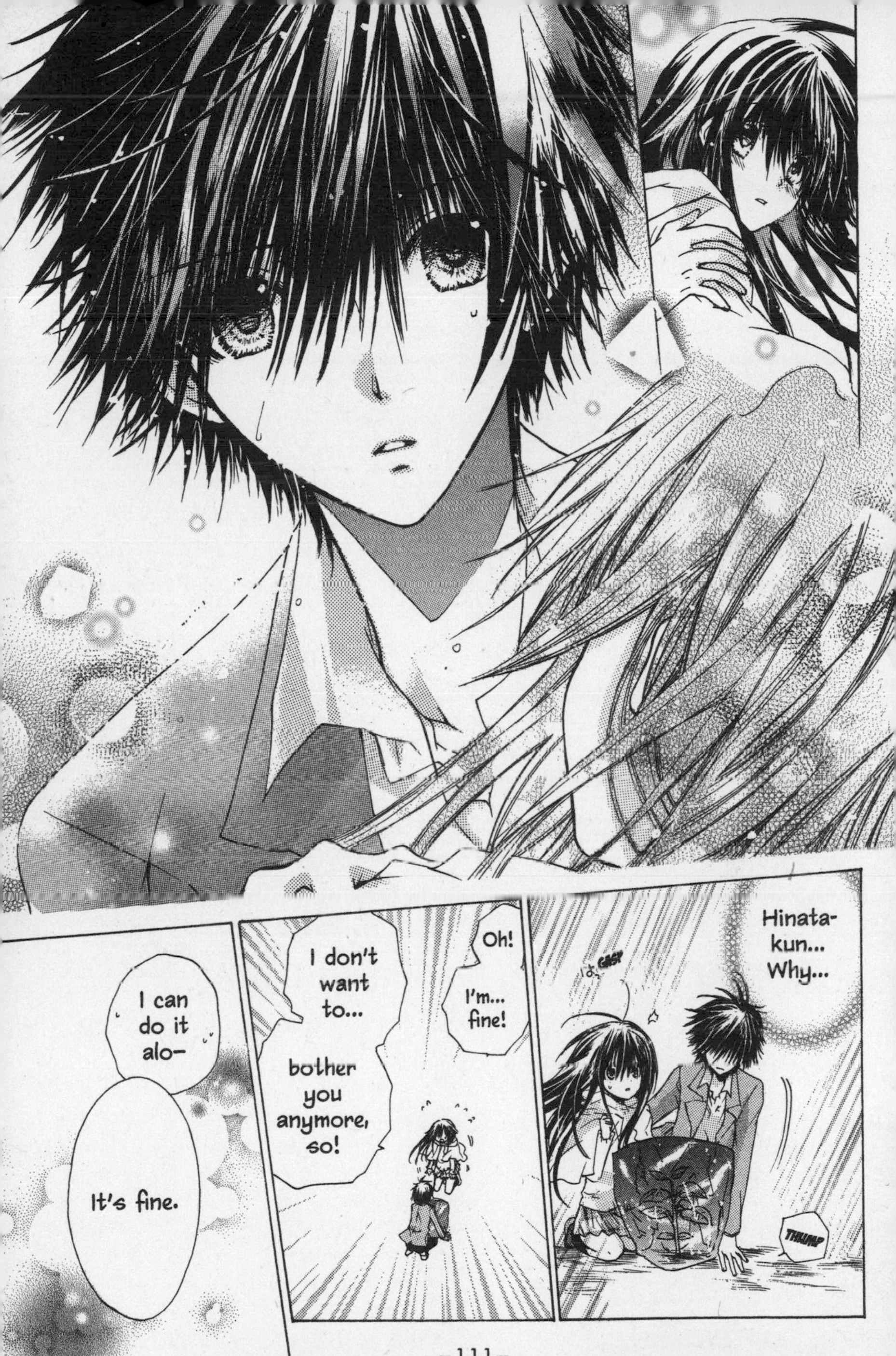
Hinata-kun... Why...
GASP
THUMP
Oh!
I'm... fine!
I don't want to...
bother you anymore, so!
I can do it alo-
It's fine.

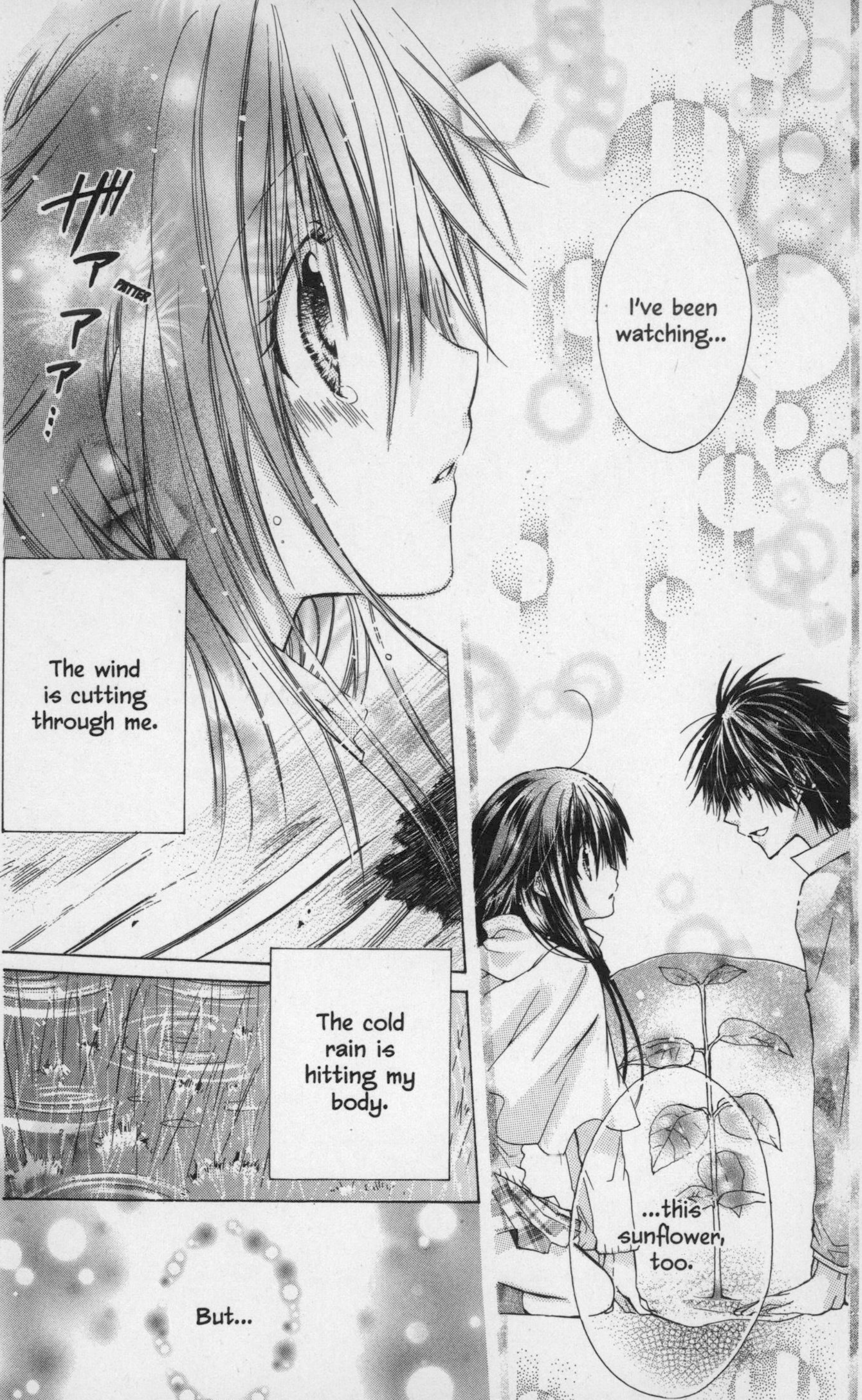
I've been watching...
...this sunflower, too.
ザァァァ…
PATTER
The wind is cutting through me.
The cold rain is hitting my body.
But...

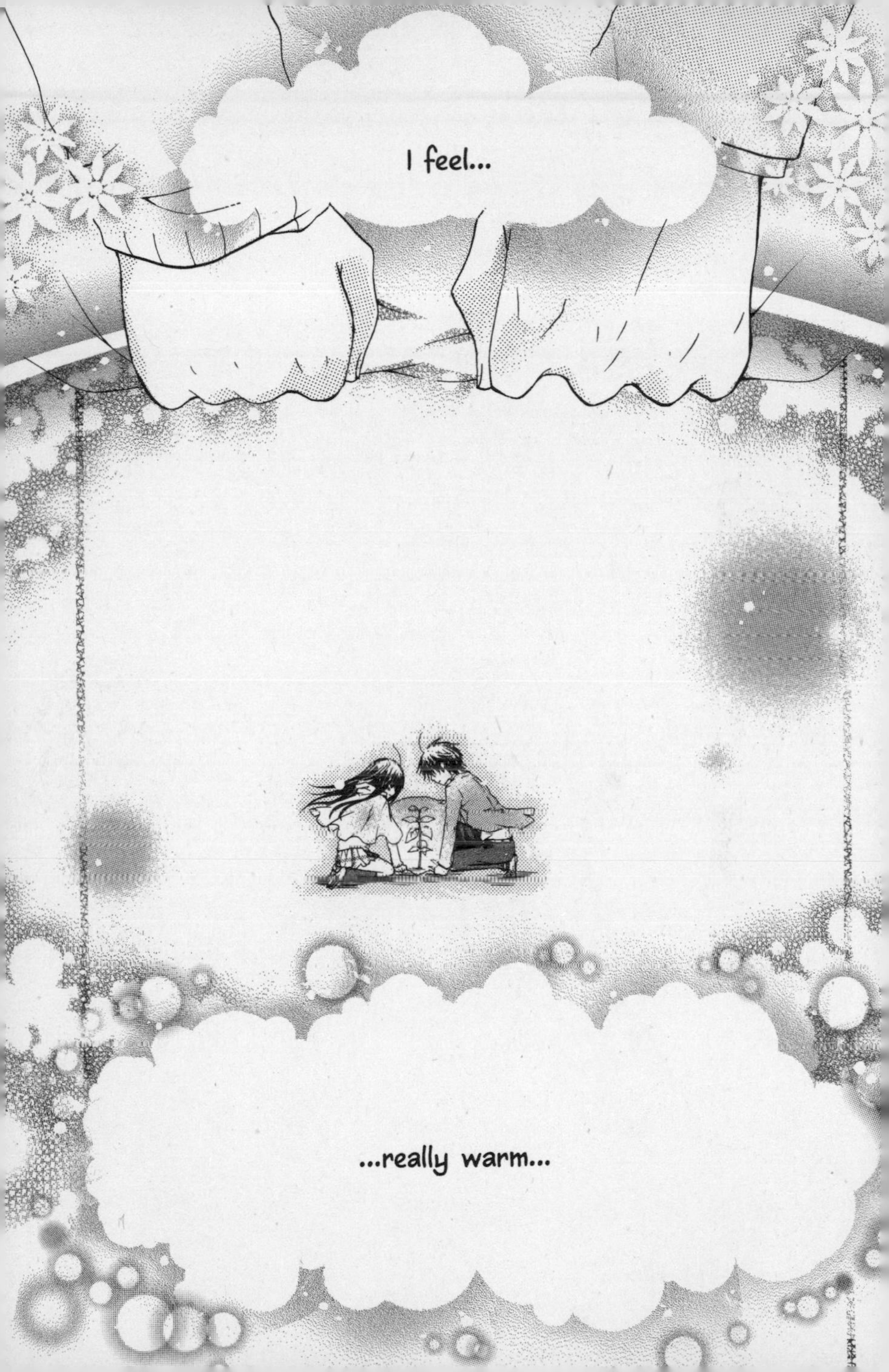
I feel...
...really warm...

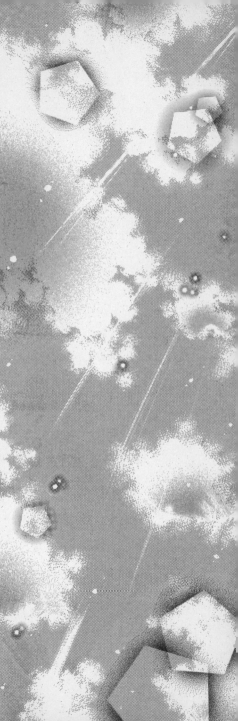

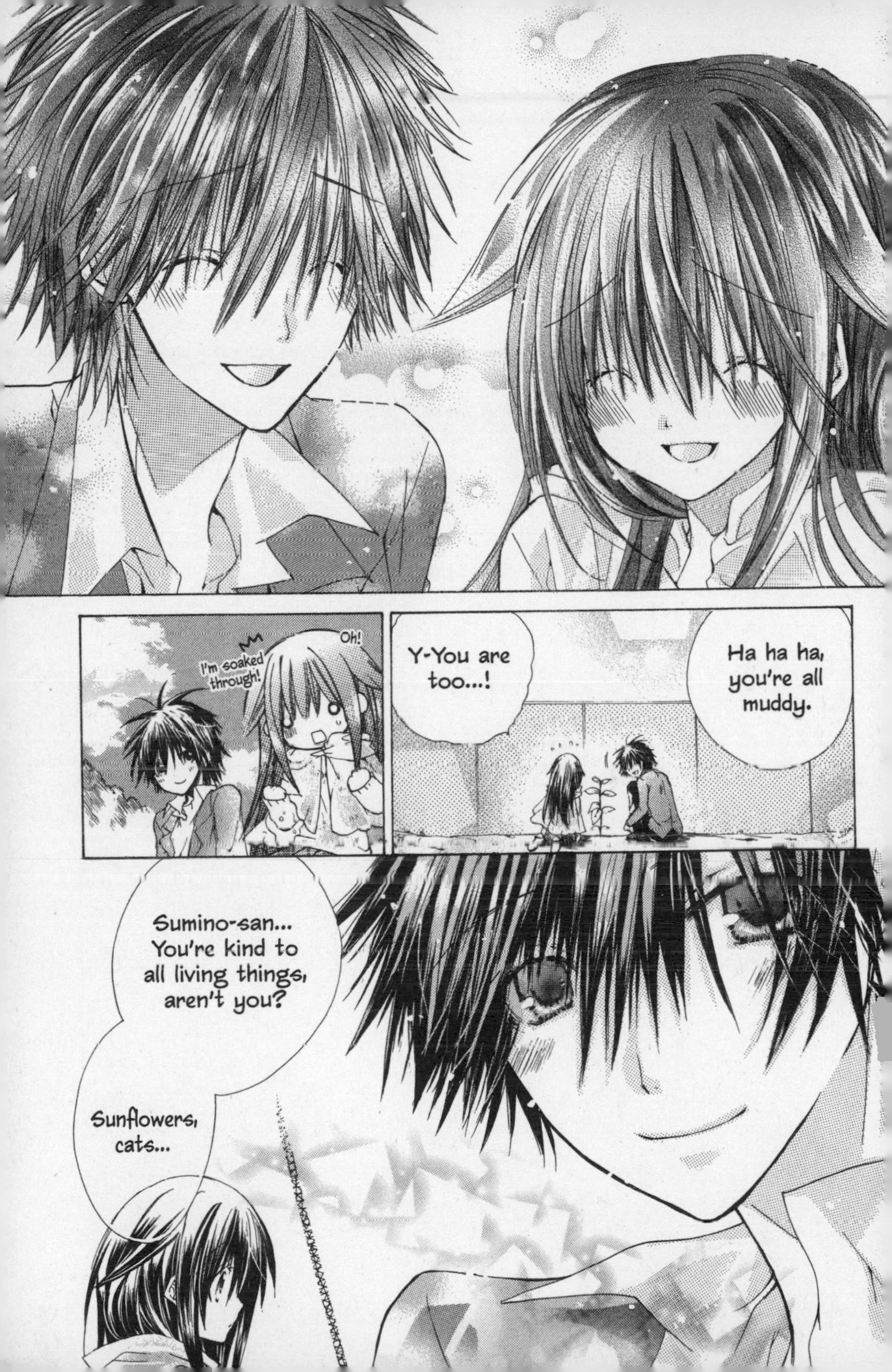
Ha ha ha, you're all muddy.
Y-You are too...!
Oh!
I'm soaked through!
Sumino-san... You're kind to all living things, aren't you?
Sunflowers, cats...

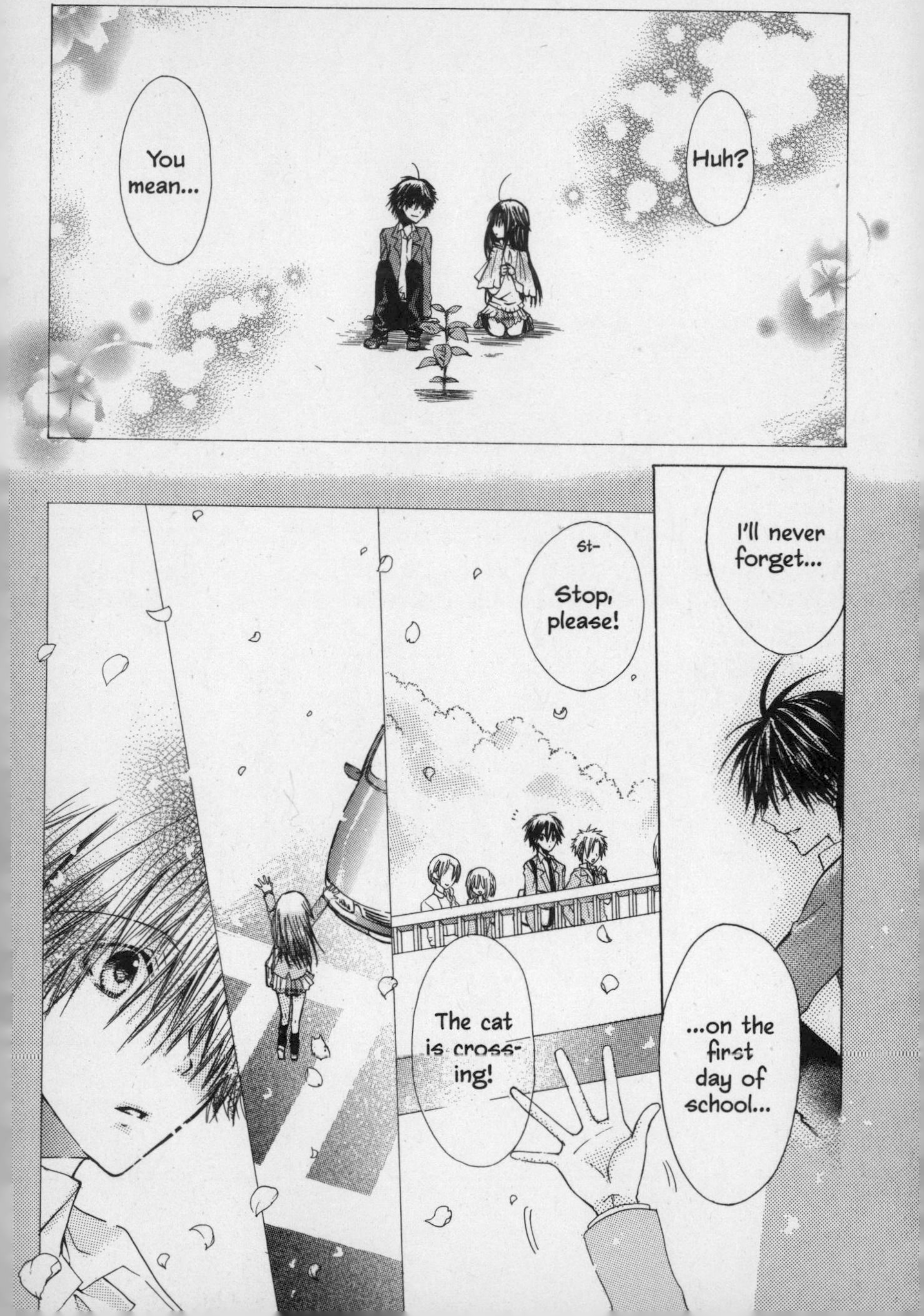
Huh?
You mean...
I'll never forget...
...on the first day of school...
St-
Stop, please!
The cat is crossing!

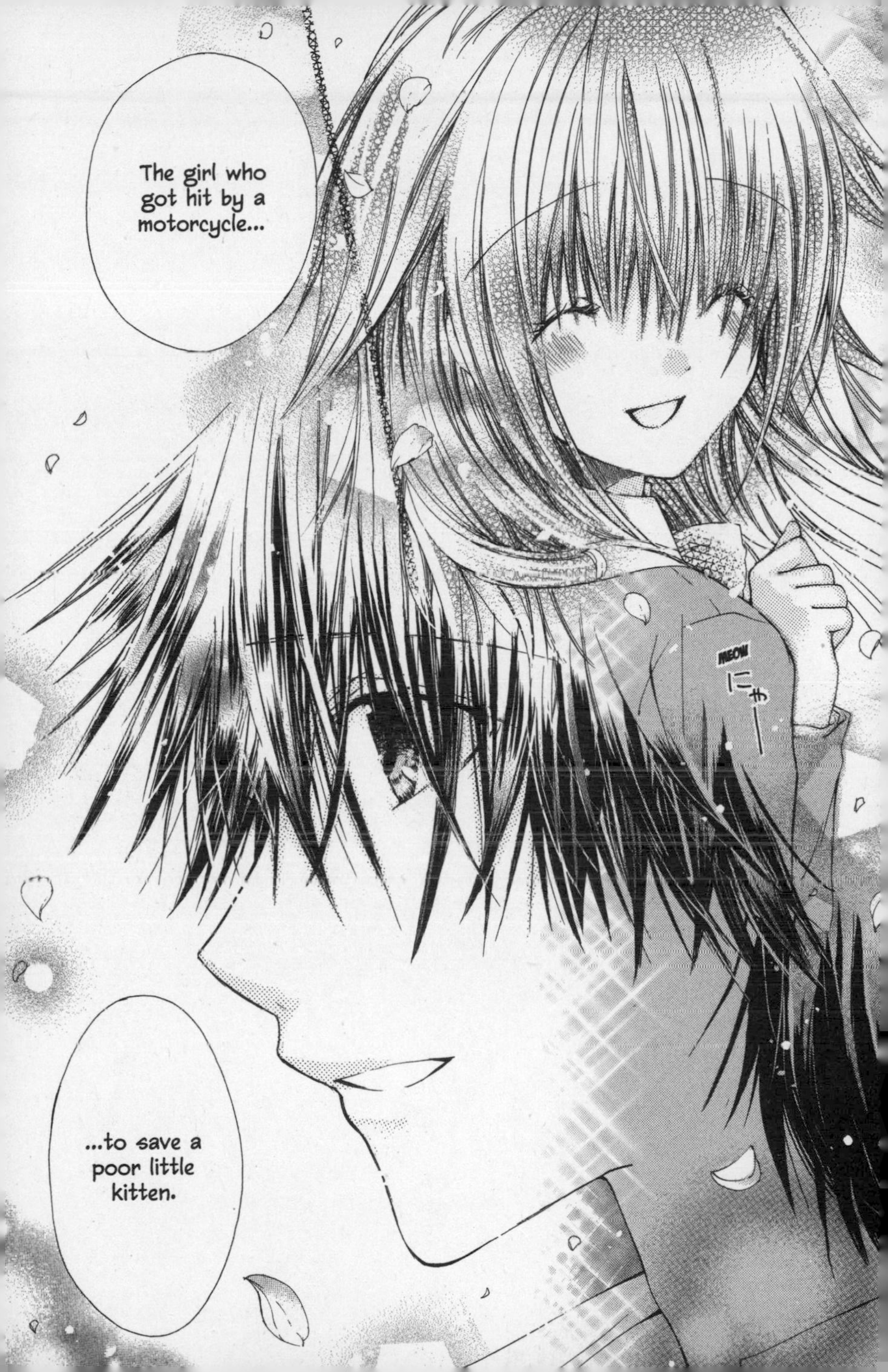
The girl who got hit by a motorcycle...
MEOW
にゃー
...to save a poor little kitten.

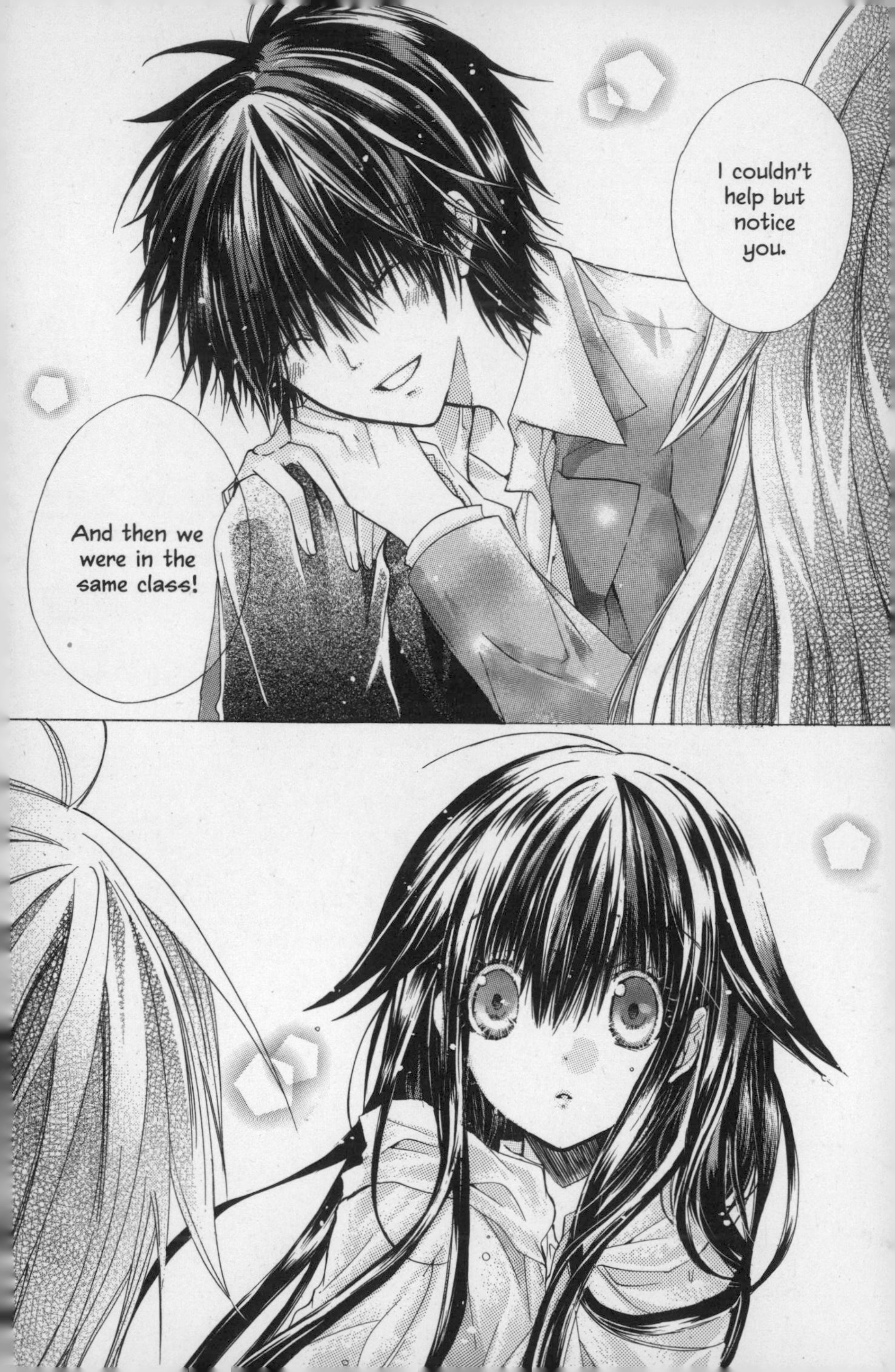
I couldn't help but notice you.
And then we were in the same class!

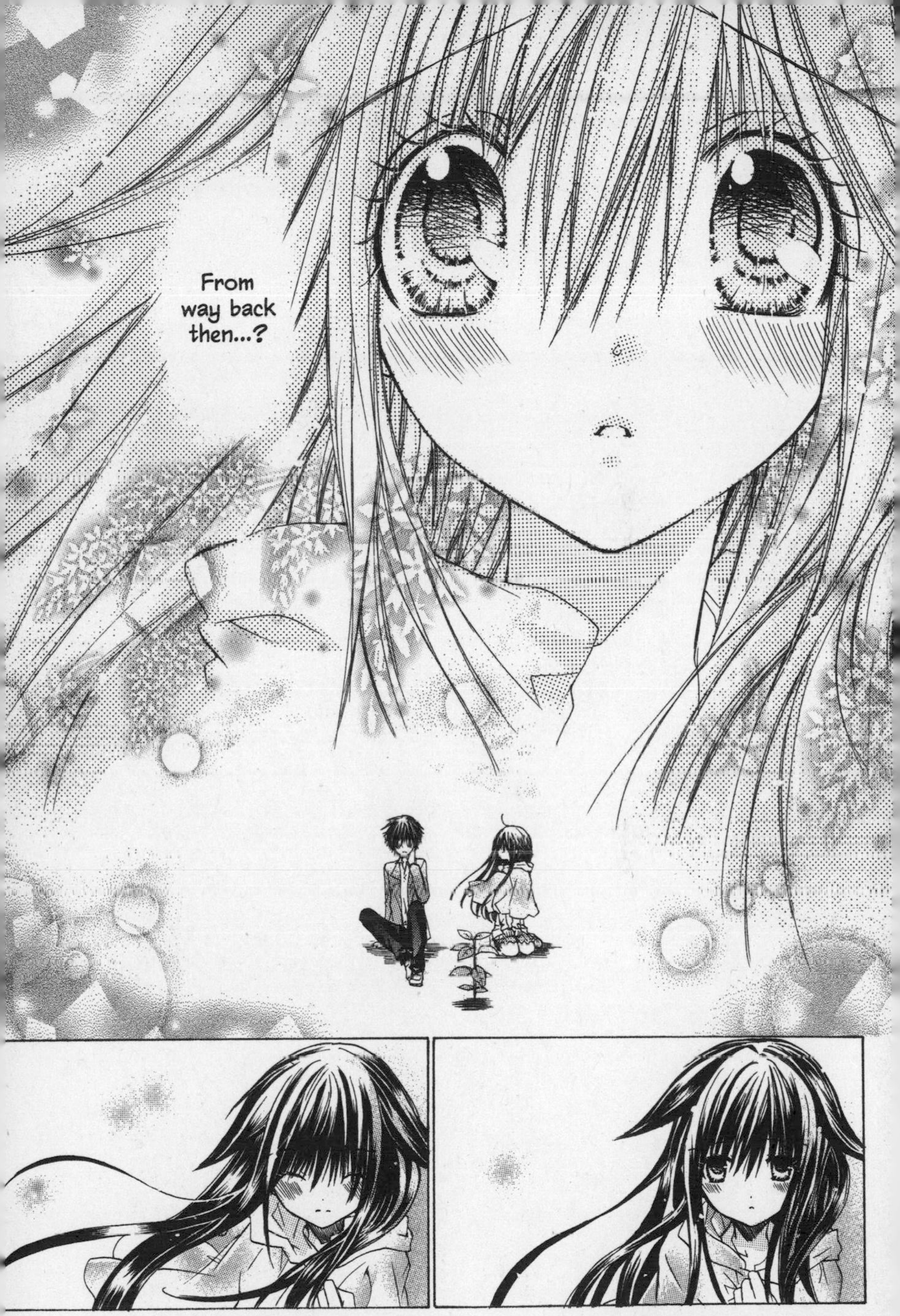
From way back then...?

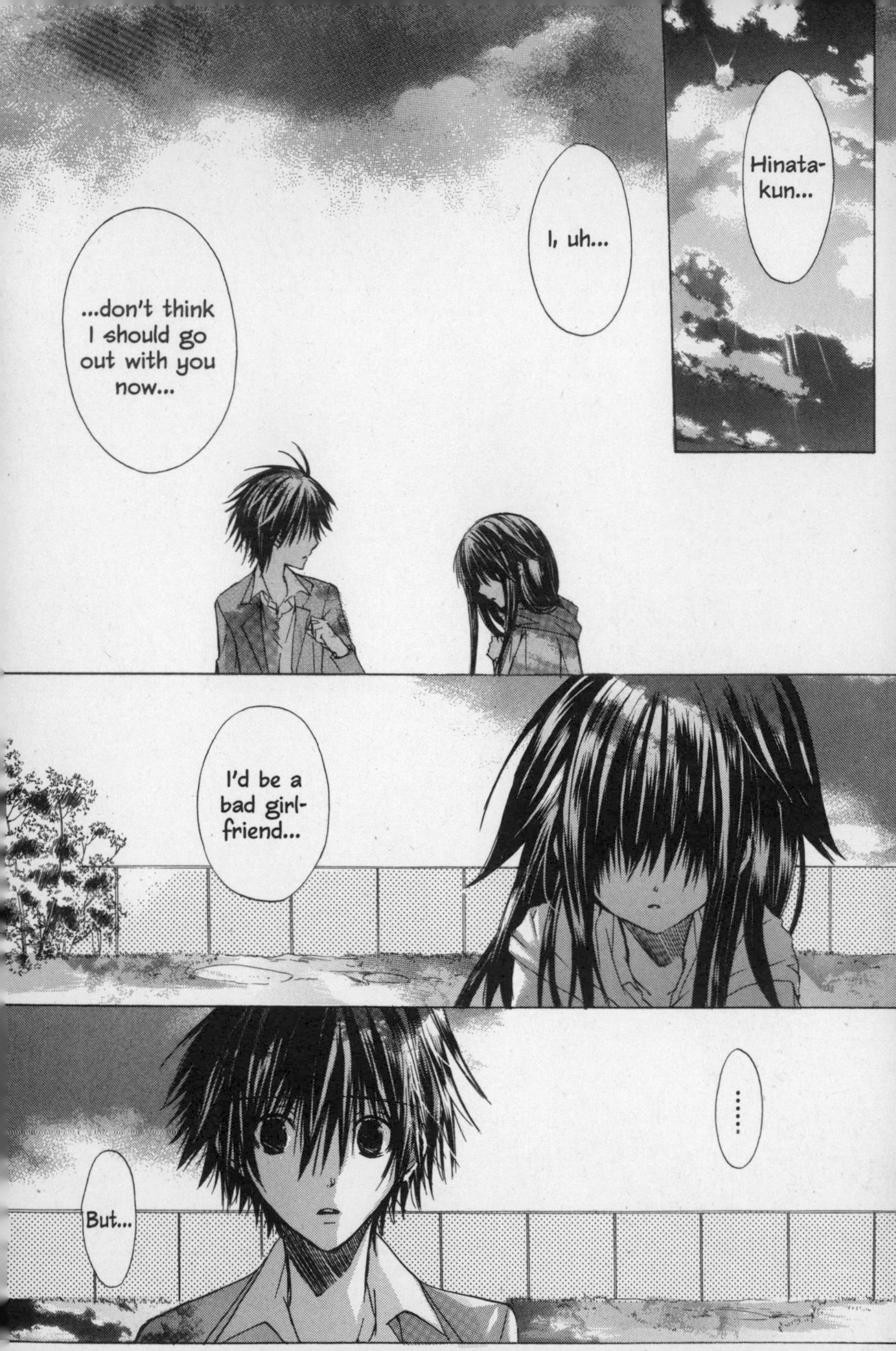
Hinata-kun...
I, uh...
...don't think I should go out with you now...
I'd be a bad girl-friend...
......
But...

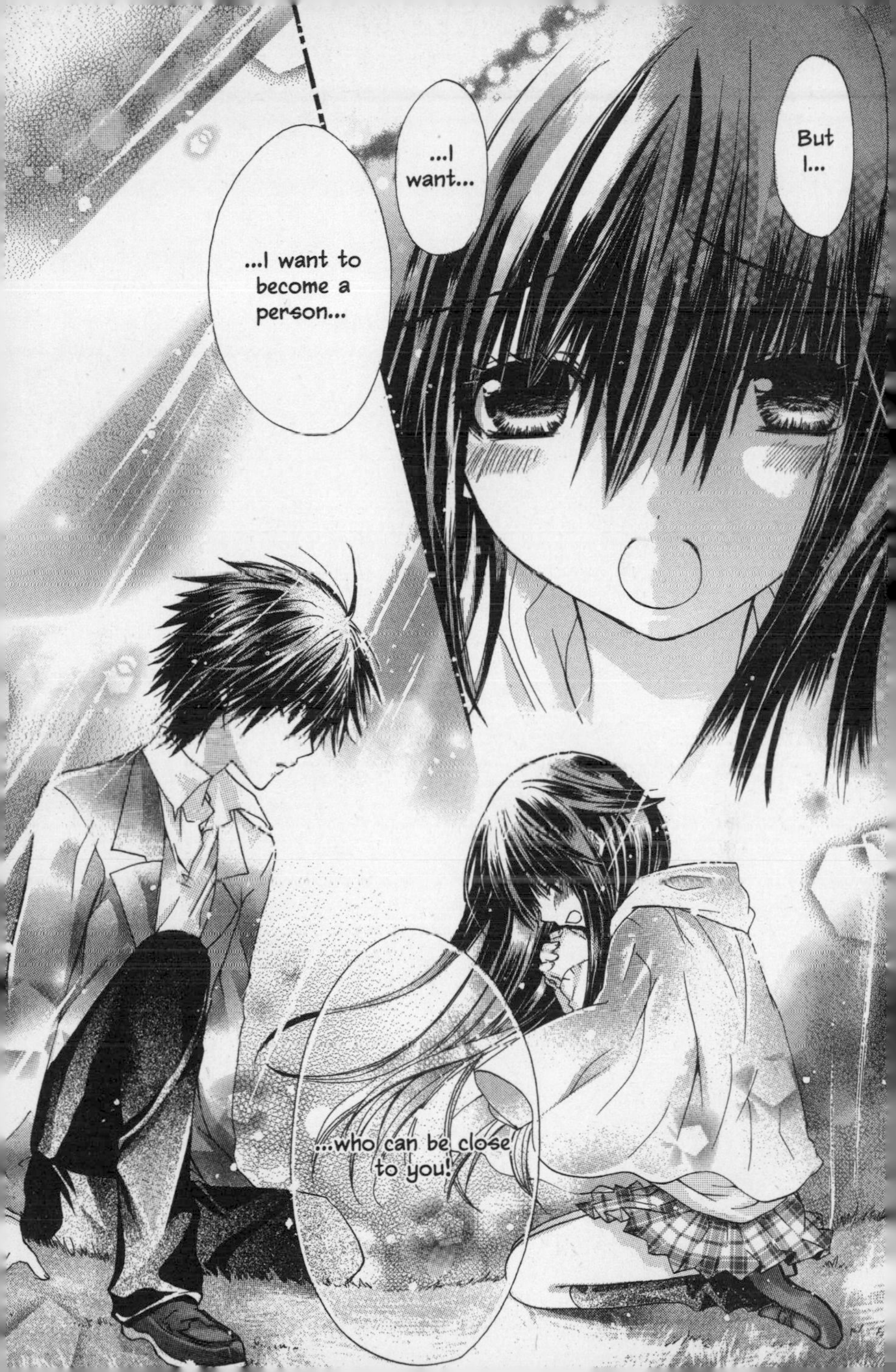
But I...
...I want...
...I want to become a person...
...who can be close to you!

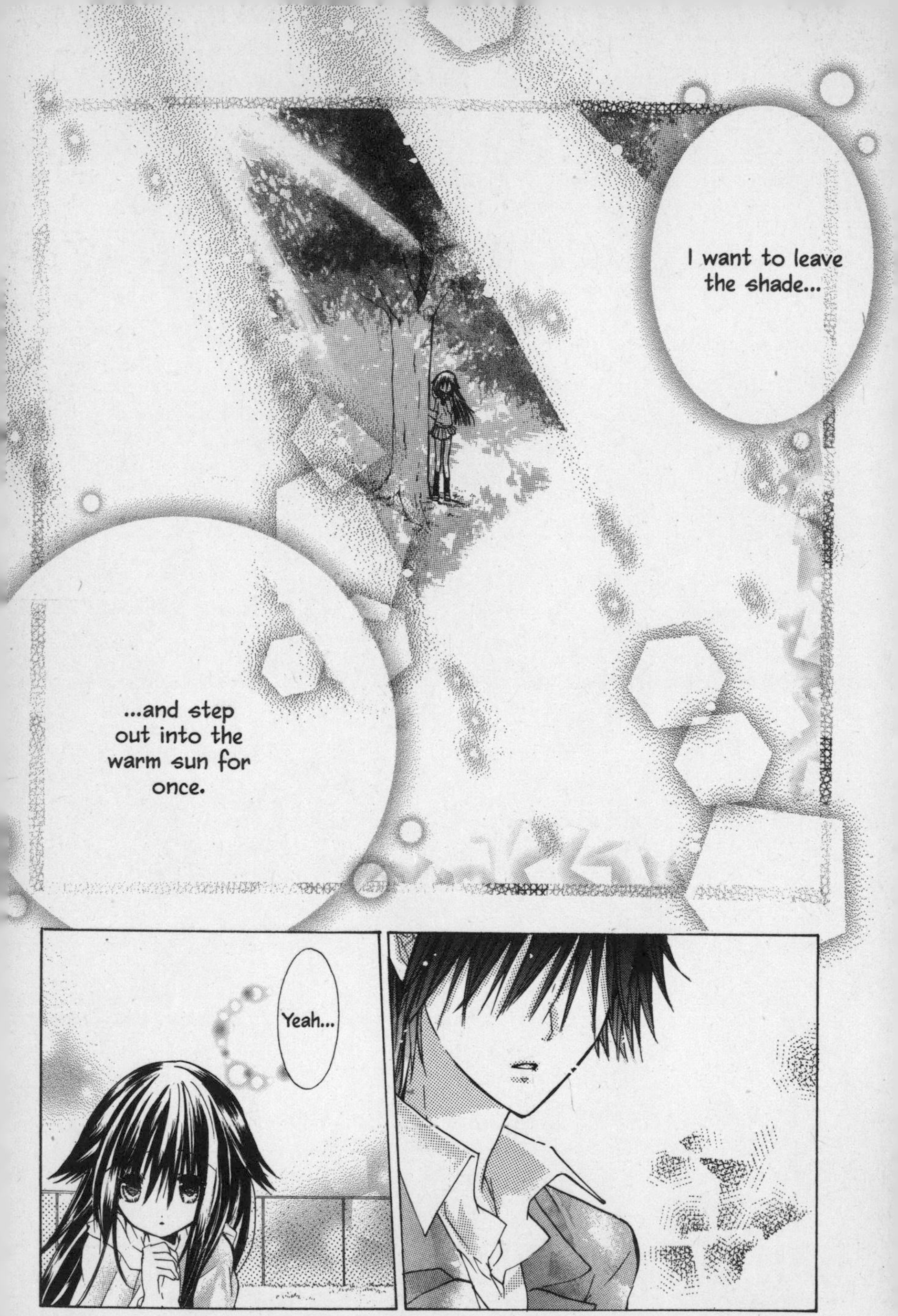
I want to leave the shade...
...and step out into the warm sun for once.
Yeah...

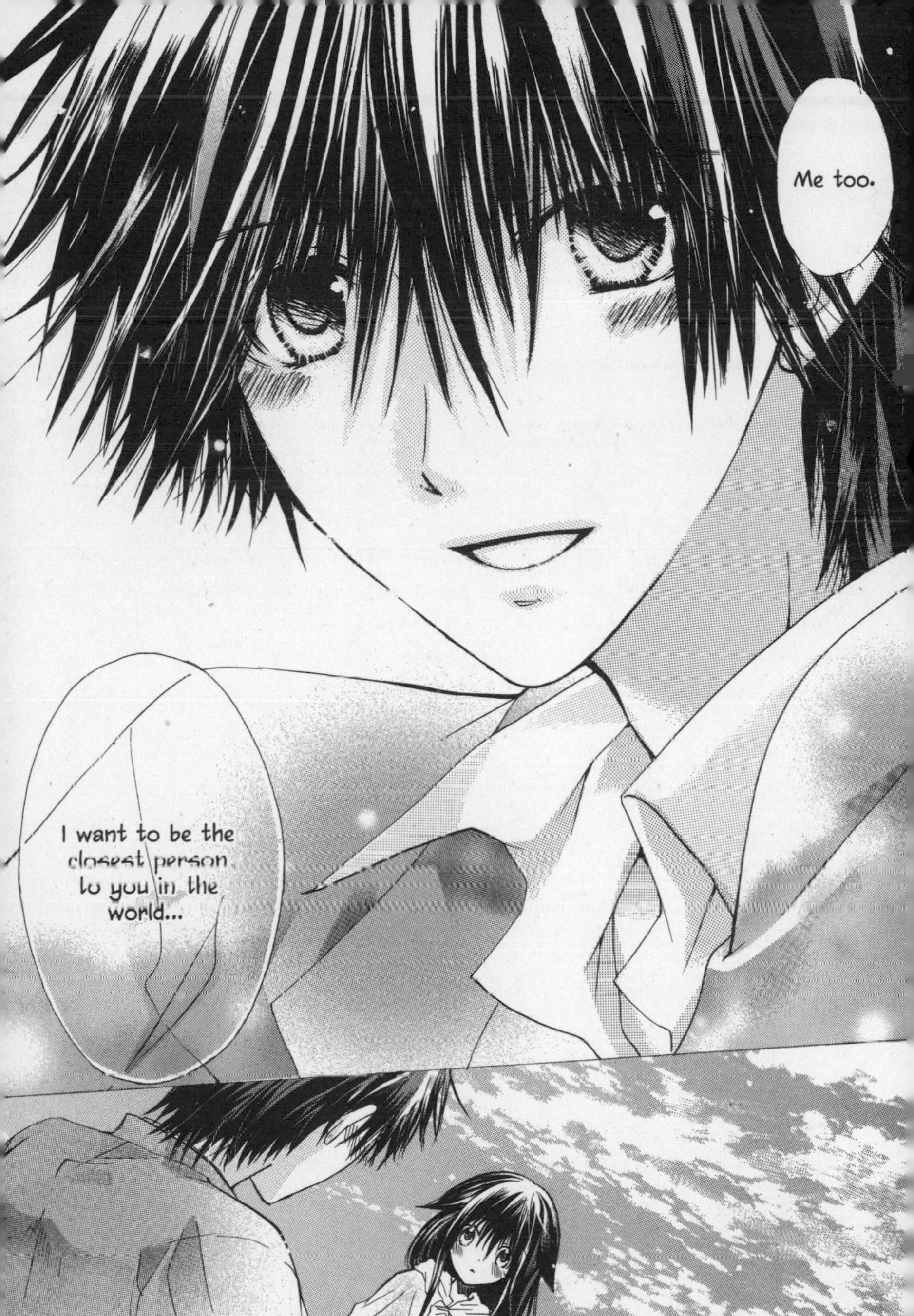
Me too.
I want to be the closest person to you in the world...

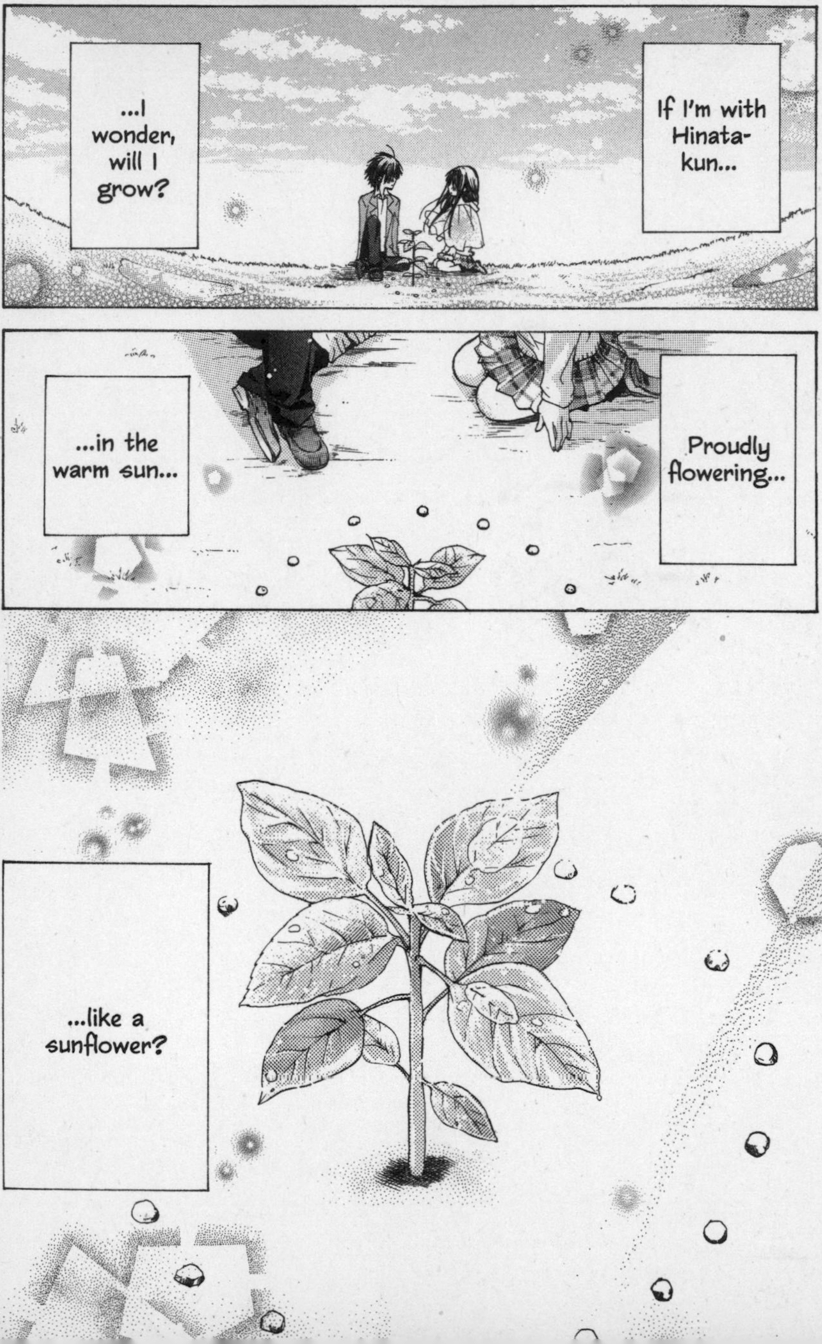
If I'm with Hinata-kun...
...I wonder, will I grow?
Proudly flowering...
...in the warm sun...
...like a sunflower?

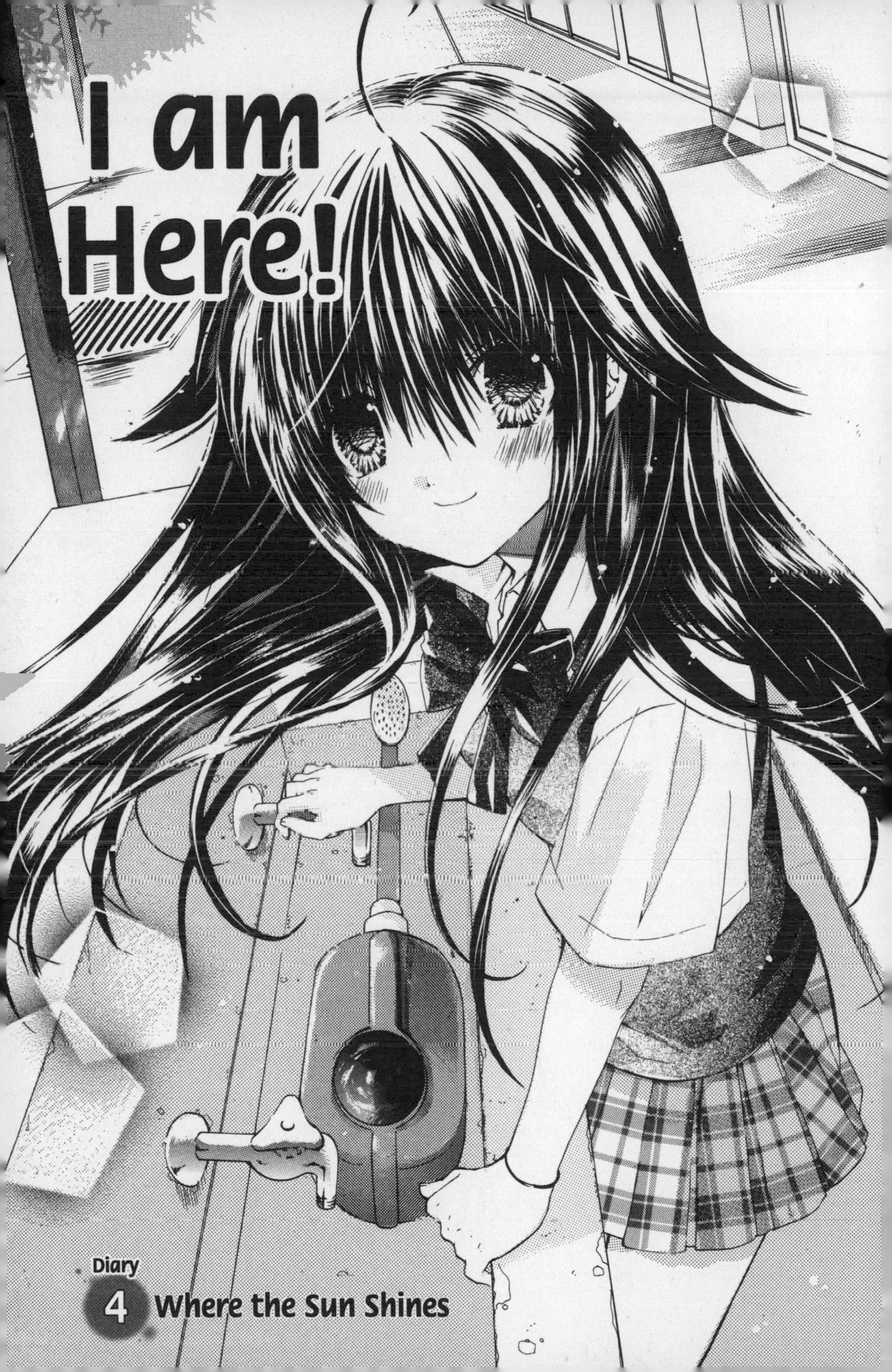
I am Here!
Diary
4 Where the Sun Shines

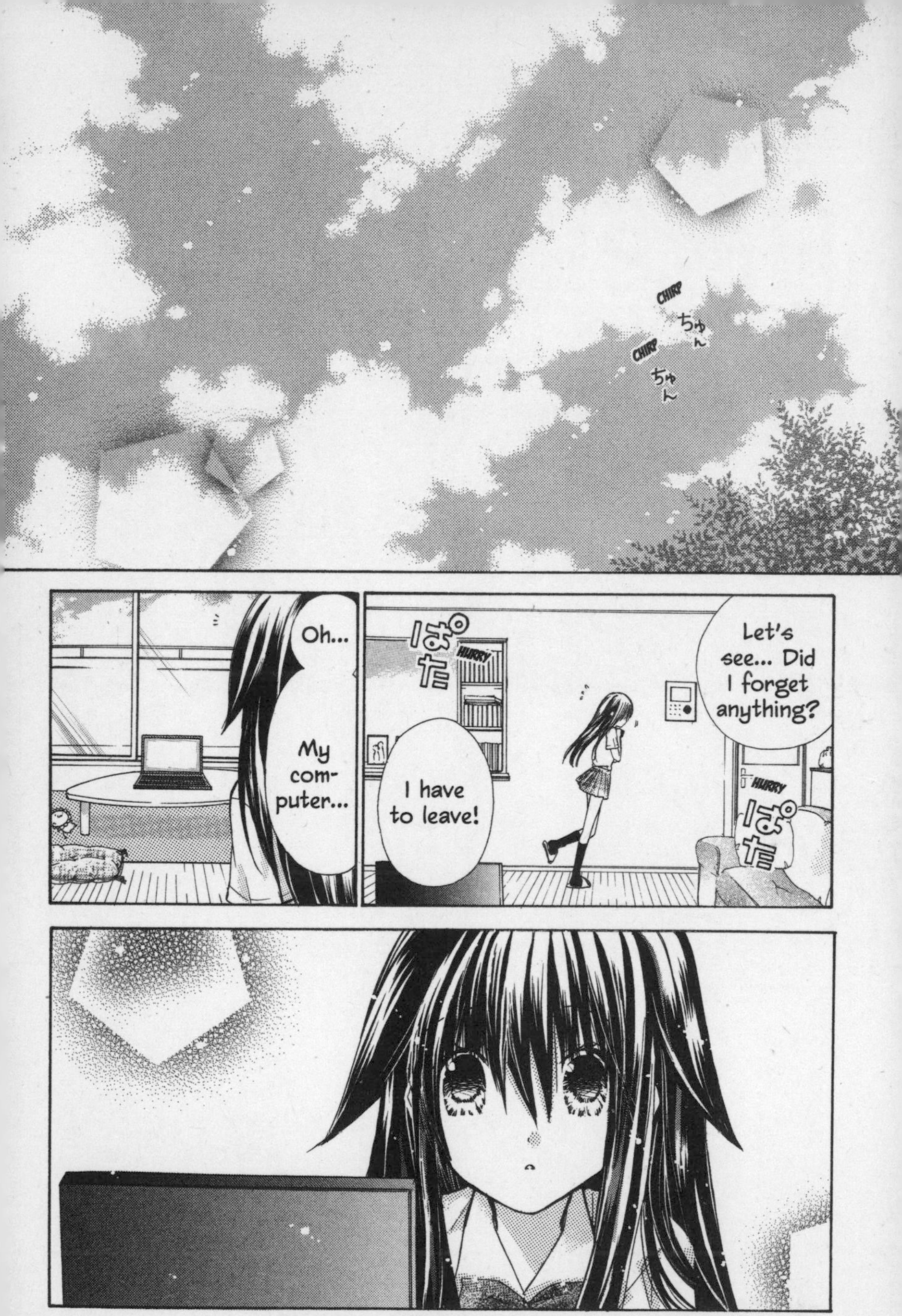
CHIRP
ちゅん
CHIRP
ちゅん
Let's see... Did I forget anything?
HURRY
ぱた
HURRY
ぱた
I have to leave!
Oh...
My computer...

1 cm of Happiness
Sunflower Blog

Profile

SN: Sunflower
Gender: Female
Bio
I'm the invisible
girl (> <)
My hobby is
picture mail ♪

1	2	3	4	5	6
7	8	9	10	11	12	13
14	15	16	17	18	19	20
21	22	23	24	25	26	27
28	29	30	31			

ZOU2brog

Recent Comments
About flowering
So high
maintenance!
Talk about it

It seems like the popular boy
has been watching me for over
a year now!

I can't imagine going out with
him now, but I'd like to change
into the kind of person who can
be close with him.

Black Rabbit, Mega Pig, I'm
sorry for making you guys
worry! My goal is now to
proudly flower like a sunflower.

[2007/06/08 20:15] Comments (2) Trackback (0)

Making a
decision like
this...

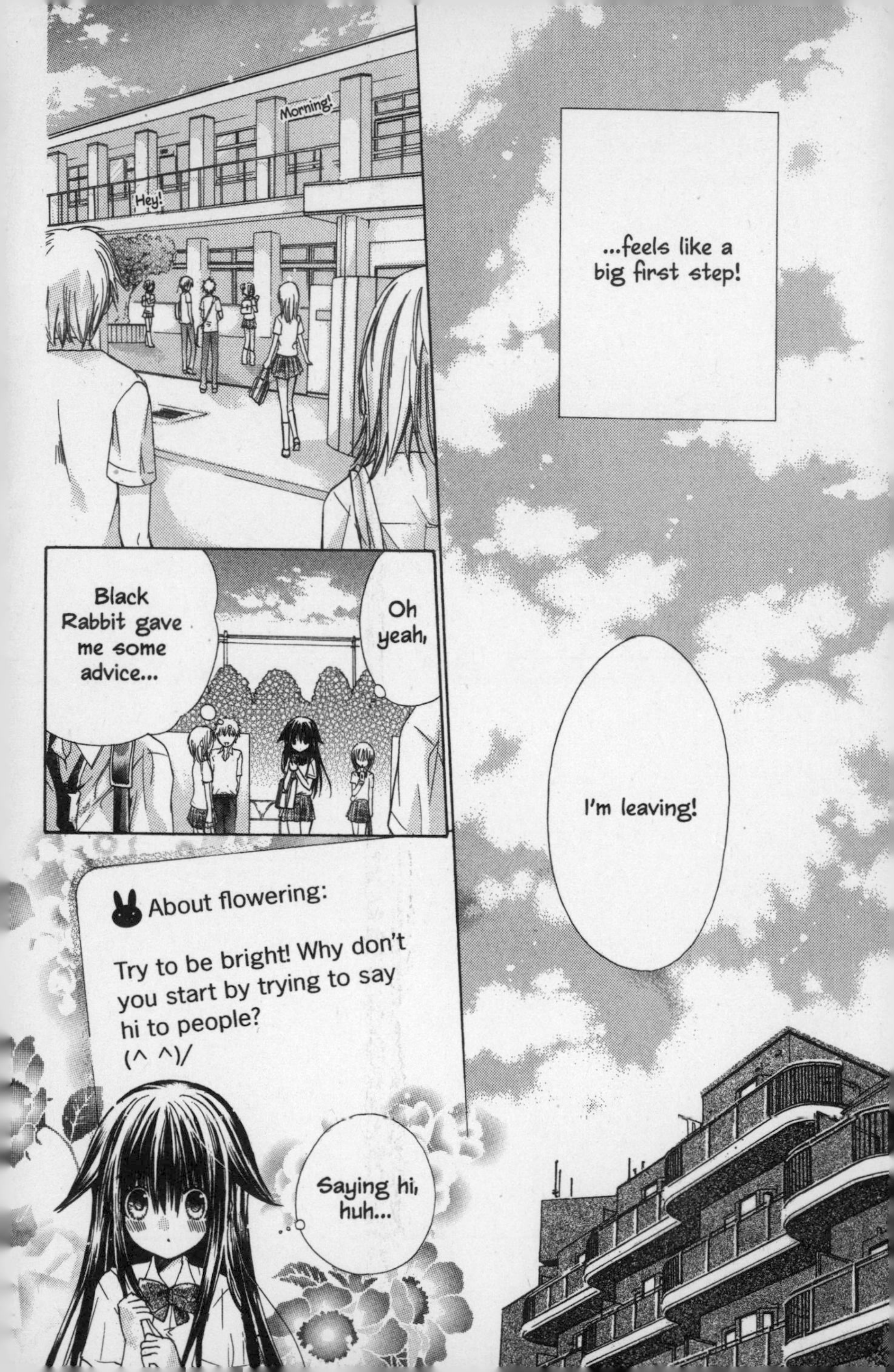

...feels like a big first step!
I'm leaving!
Morning!
Hey!
Oh yeah,
Black Rabbit gave me some advice...
About flowering:
Try to be bright! Why don't you start by trying to say hi to people?
(^ ^)/
Saying hi, huh...

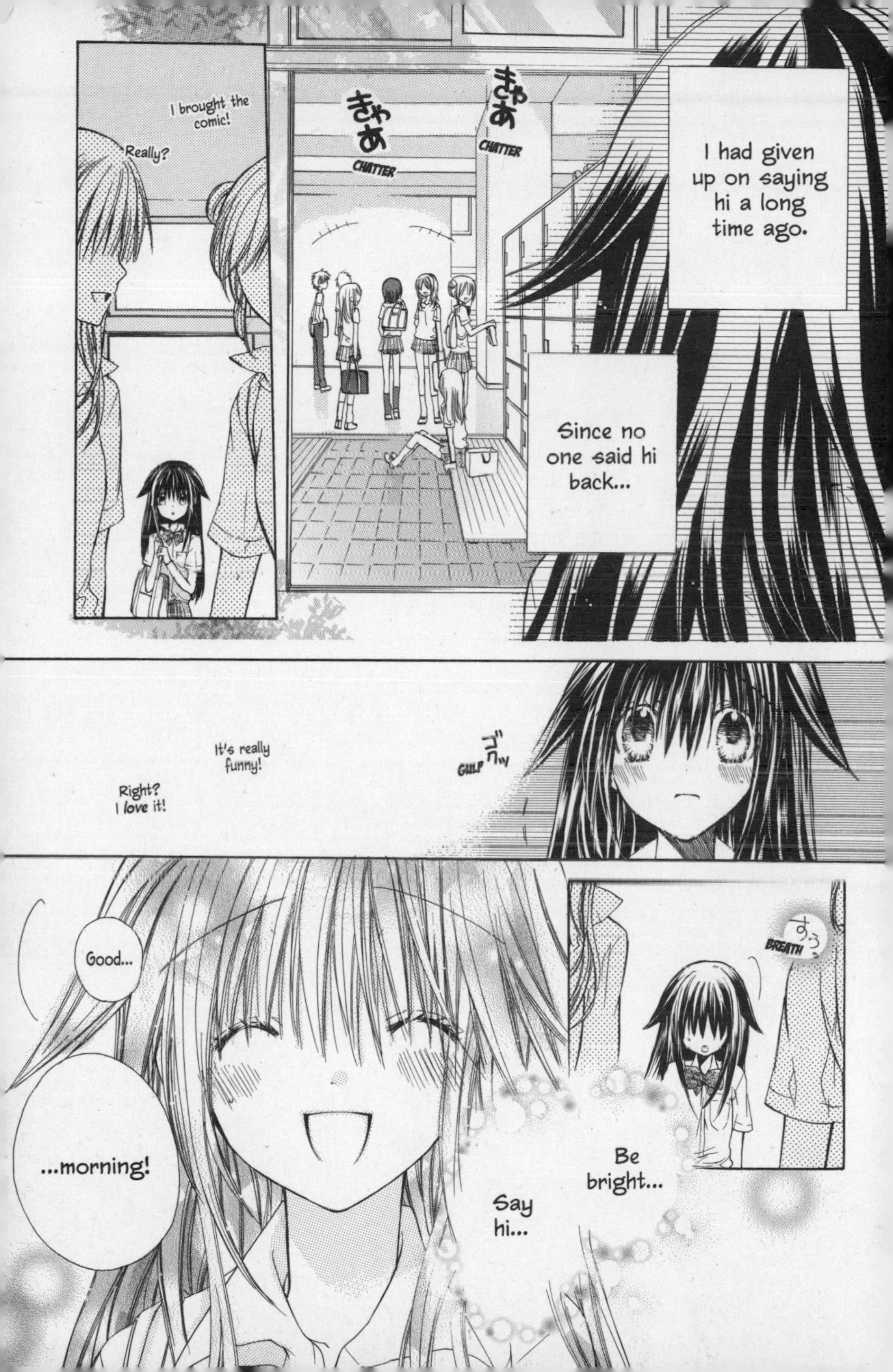
I had given up on saying hi a long time ago.
Since no one said hi back...
きゃあ
CHATTER
きゃあ
CHATTER
I brought the comic!
Really?
ゴクッ
GULP
It's really funny!
Right? I love it!
すぅ
BREATH
Be bright...
Say hi...
Good...
...morning!

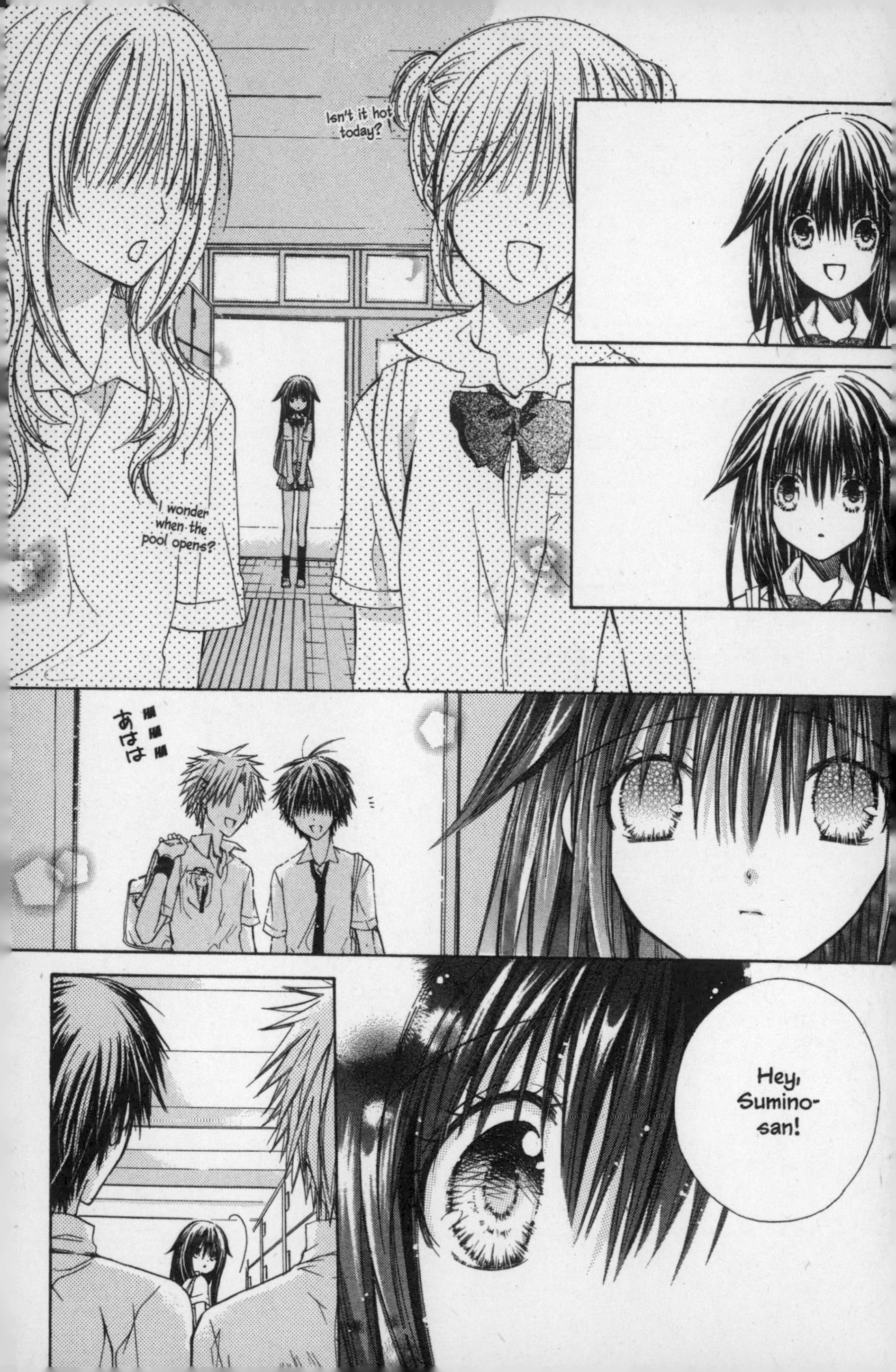
Isn't it hot today?
I wonder when the pool opens?
あはは HA HA HA
Hey, Sumino-san!

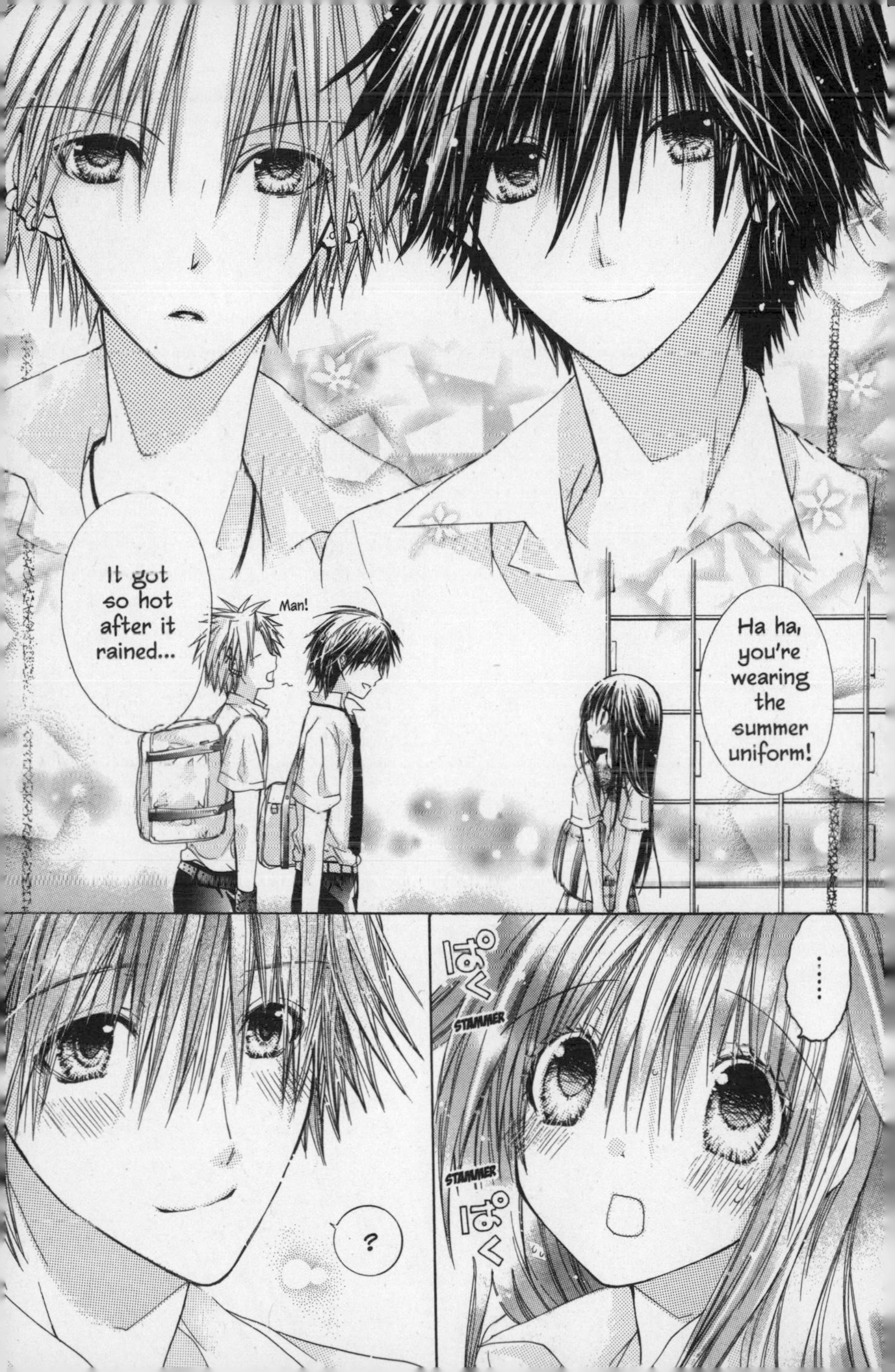

It got so hot after it rained...
Man!
Ha ha, you're wearing the summer uniform!
......
ぱく
STAMMER
STAMMER
ぱく
?

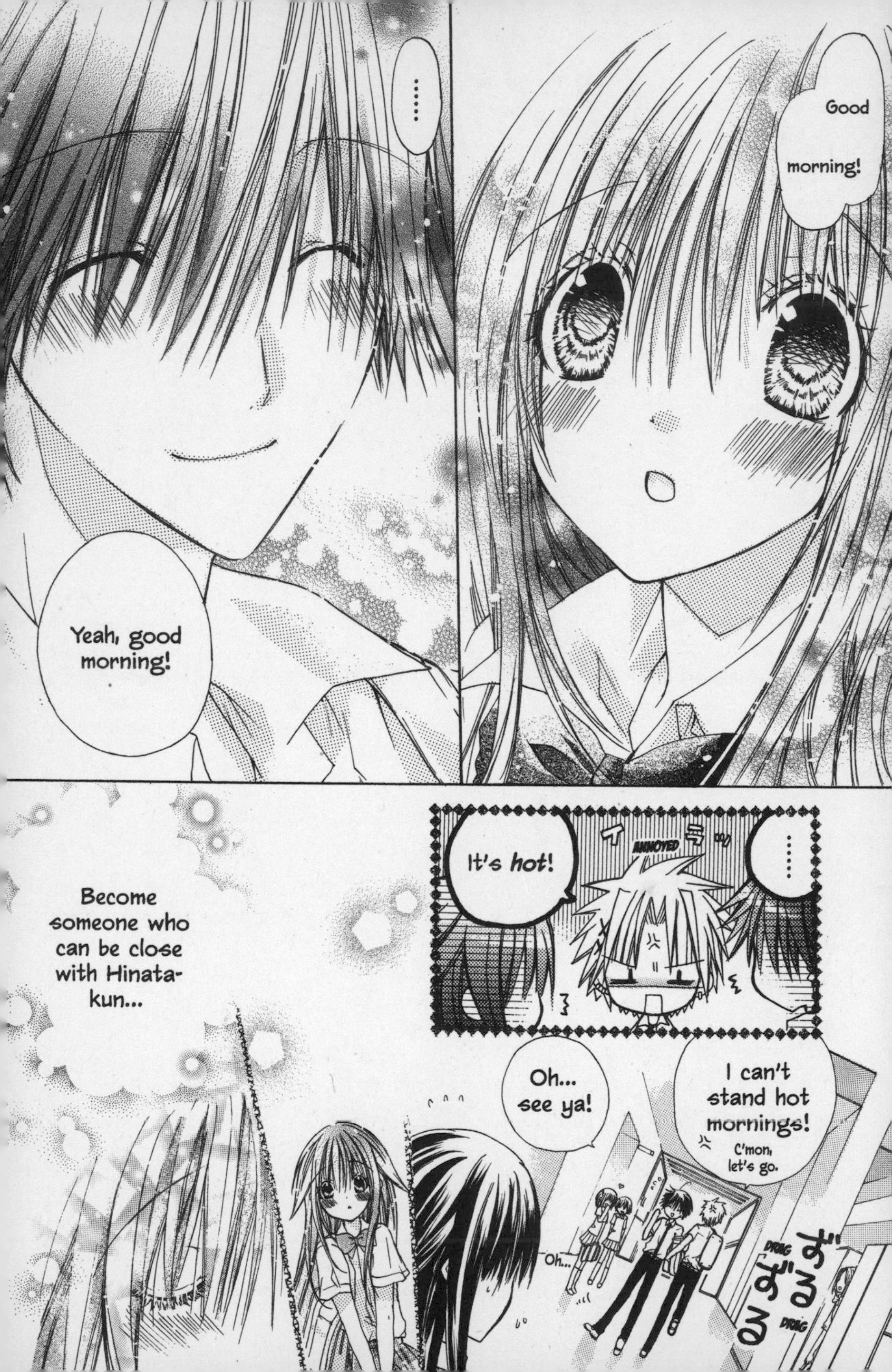

Good morning!
......
Yeah, good morning!
......
ANNOYED
It's hot!
I can't stand hot mornings!
C'mon, let's go.
Oh... see ya!
Oh...
DRAG
DRAG
Become someone who can be close with Hinata-kun...

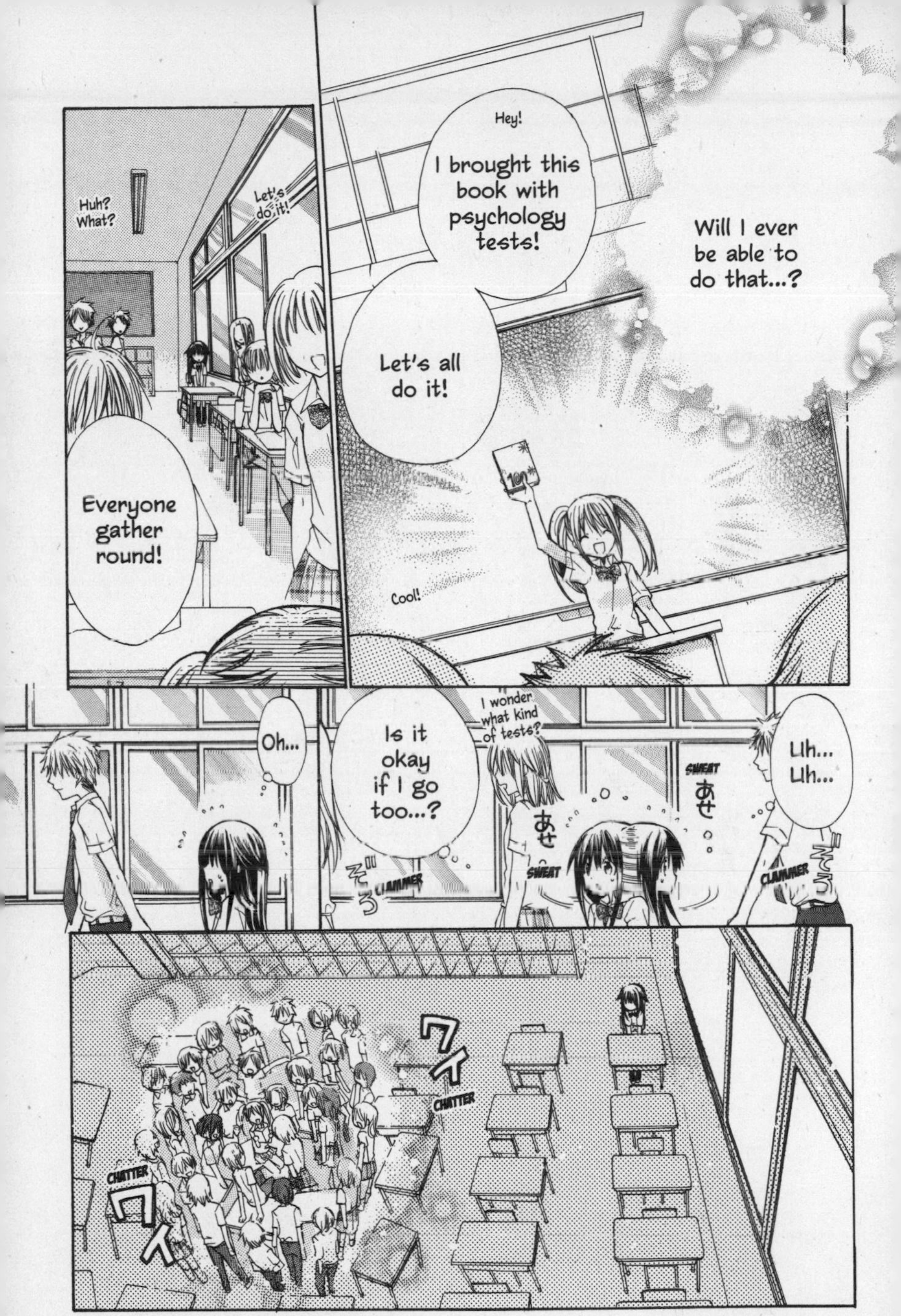
Will I ever be able to do that...?
Hey!
I brought this book with psychology tests!
Let's all do it!
Cool!
Let's do it!
Huh? What?
Everyone gather round!
Uh... Uh...
SWEAT
あせ
CLAMMER
ぞろ
I wonder what kind of tests?
あせ
SWEAT
Is it okay if I go too...?
ぞろ
CLAMMER
Oh...
ワイ
CHATTER
CHATTER
ワイ

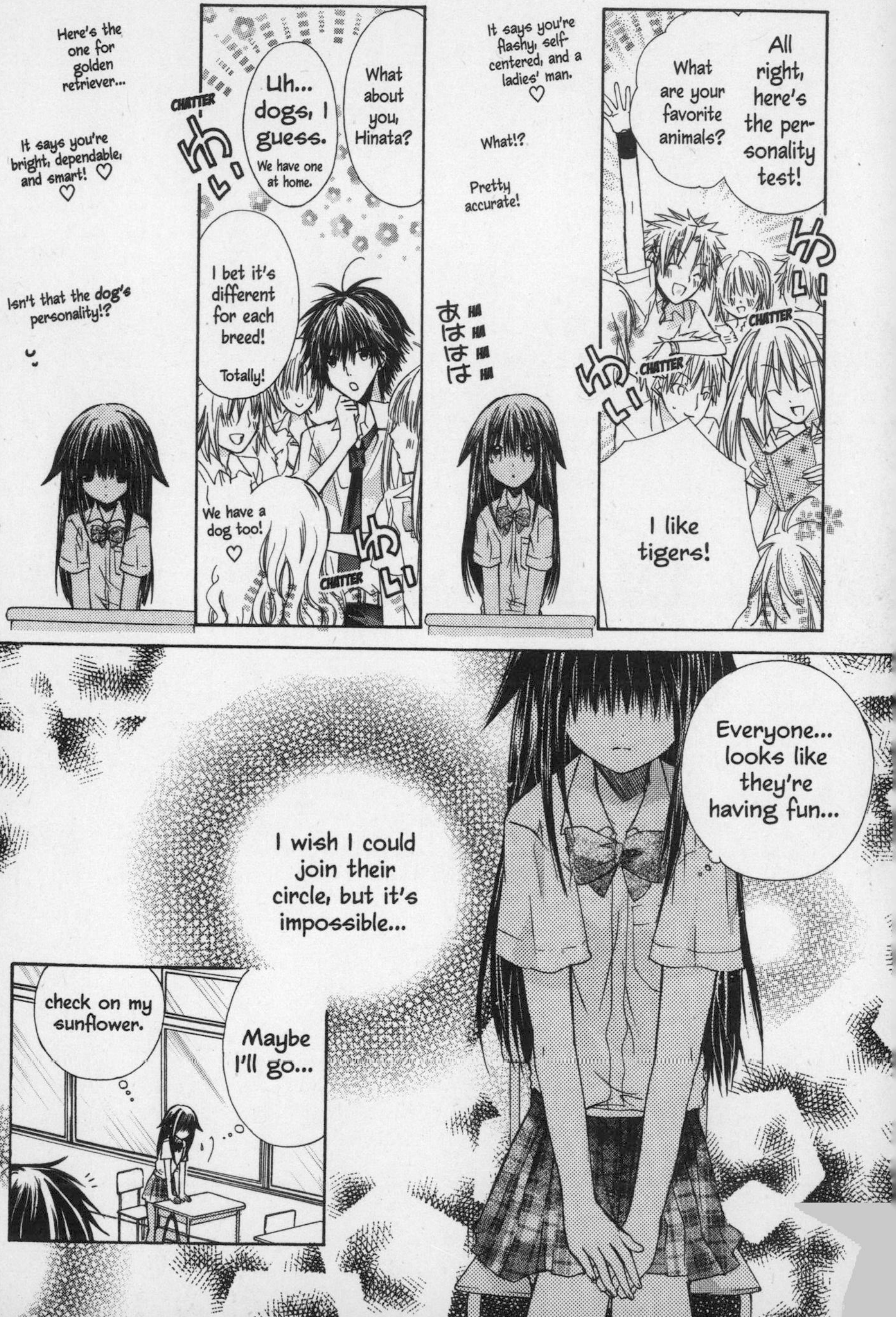
All right, here's the personality test!
What are your favorite animals?
CHATTER
CHATTER
I like tigers!
It says you're flashy, self-centered, and a ladies' man. ♡
What!?
Pretty accurate!
あははは HA HA HA HA
What about you, Hinata?
Uh... dogs, I guess.
We have one at home.
CHATTER
I bet it's different for each breed!
Totally!
We have a dog too! ♡
CHATTER
Here's the one for golden retriever...
It says you're bright, dependable, and smart! ♡ ♡
Isn't that the dog's personality!?
Everyone... looks like they're having fun...
I wish I could join their circle, but it's impossible...
Maybe I'll go...
check on my sunflower.

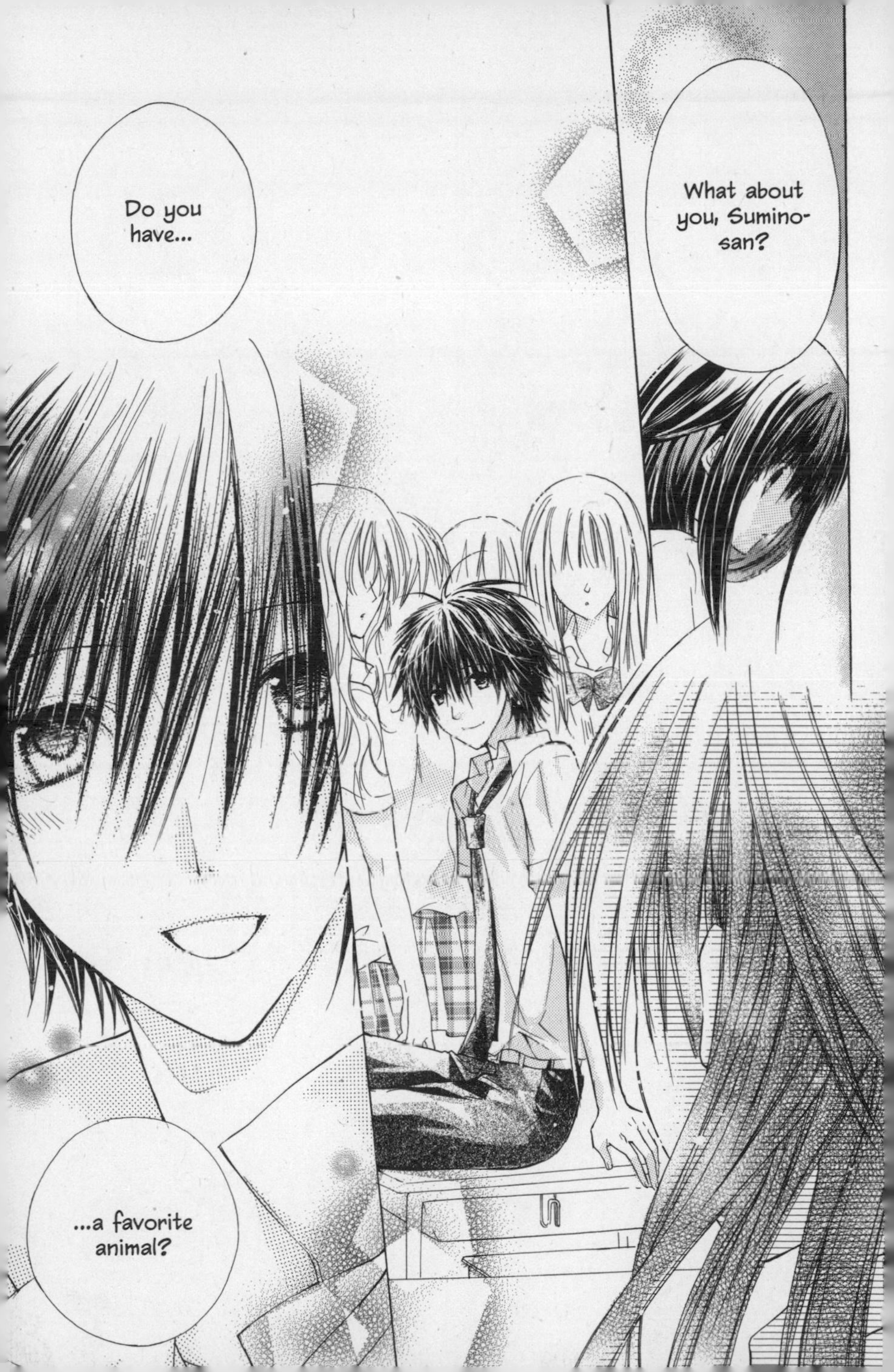
What about you, Sumino-san?
Do you have...
...a favorite animal?

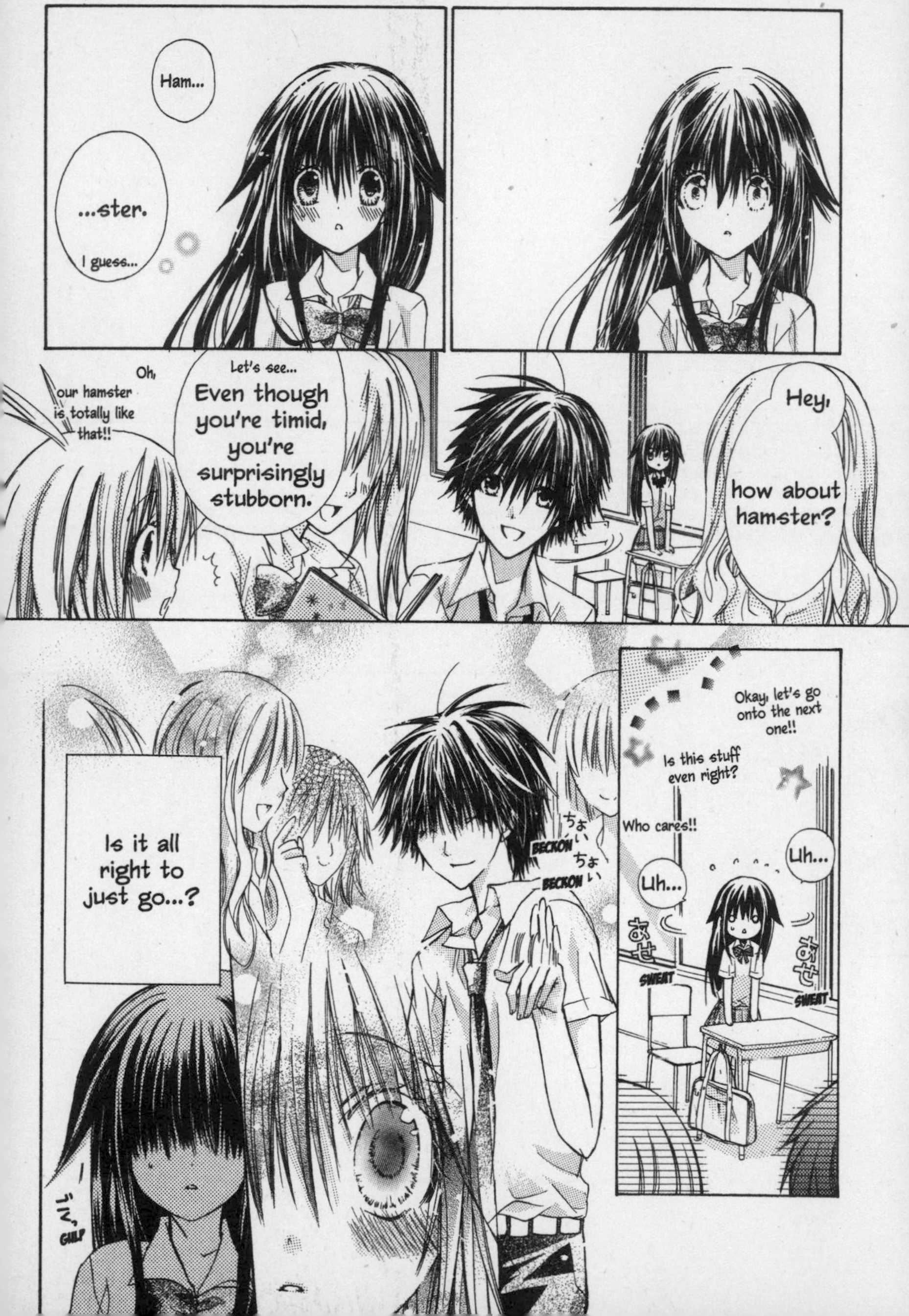

Ham...
...ster.
I guess...
Hey,
how about hamster?
Let's see...
Even though you're timid, you're surprisingly stubborn.
Oh, our hamster is totally like that!!
Okay, let's go onto the next one!!
Is this stuff even right?
Who cares!!
Uh...
Uh...
あせ SWEAT
あせ SWEAT
ちょい BECKON
ちょい BECKON
Is it all right to just go...?
GULP

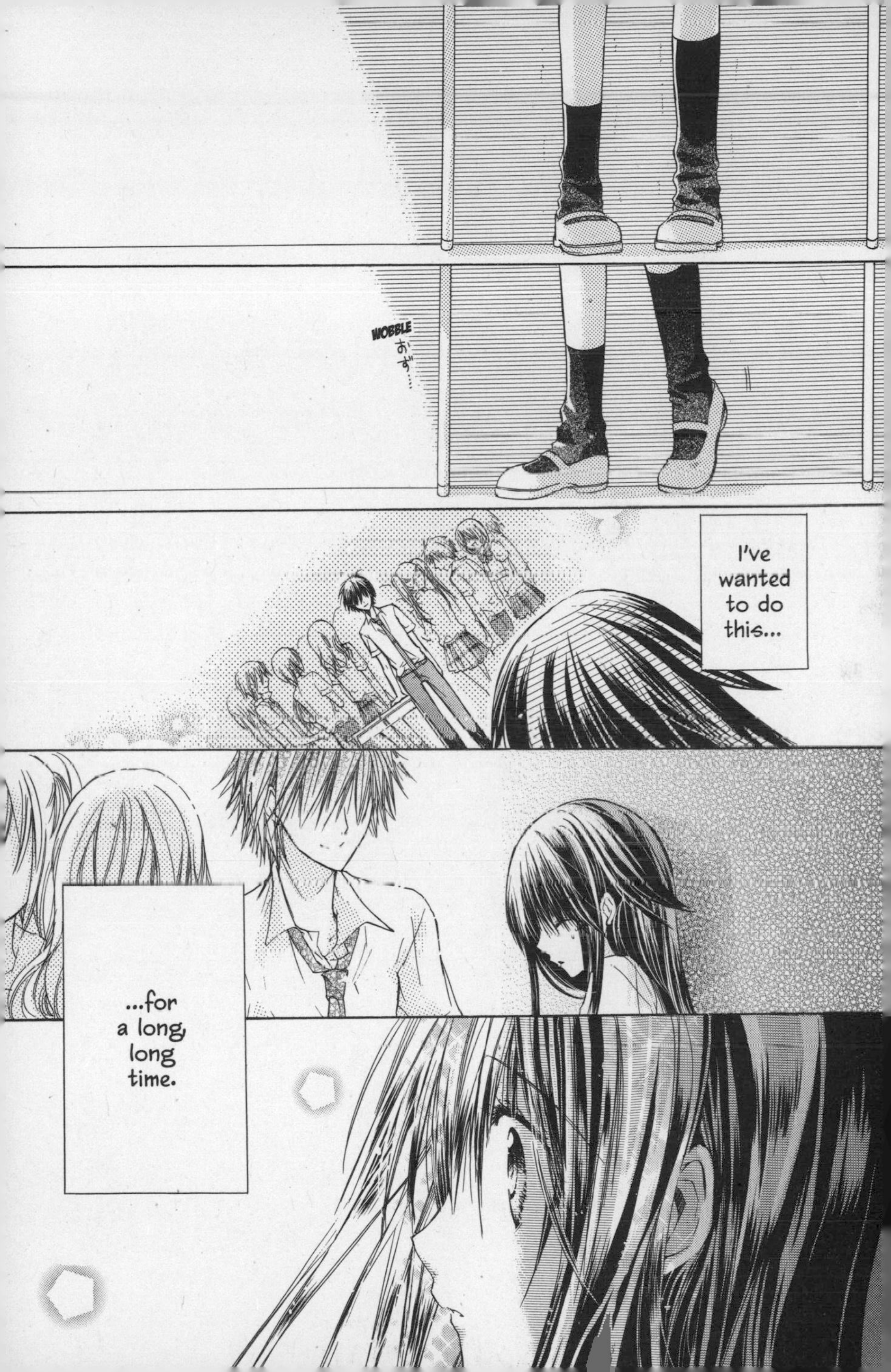
WOBBLE
おず…
I've wanted to do this...
...for a long, long time.

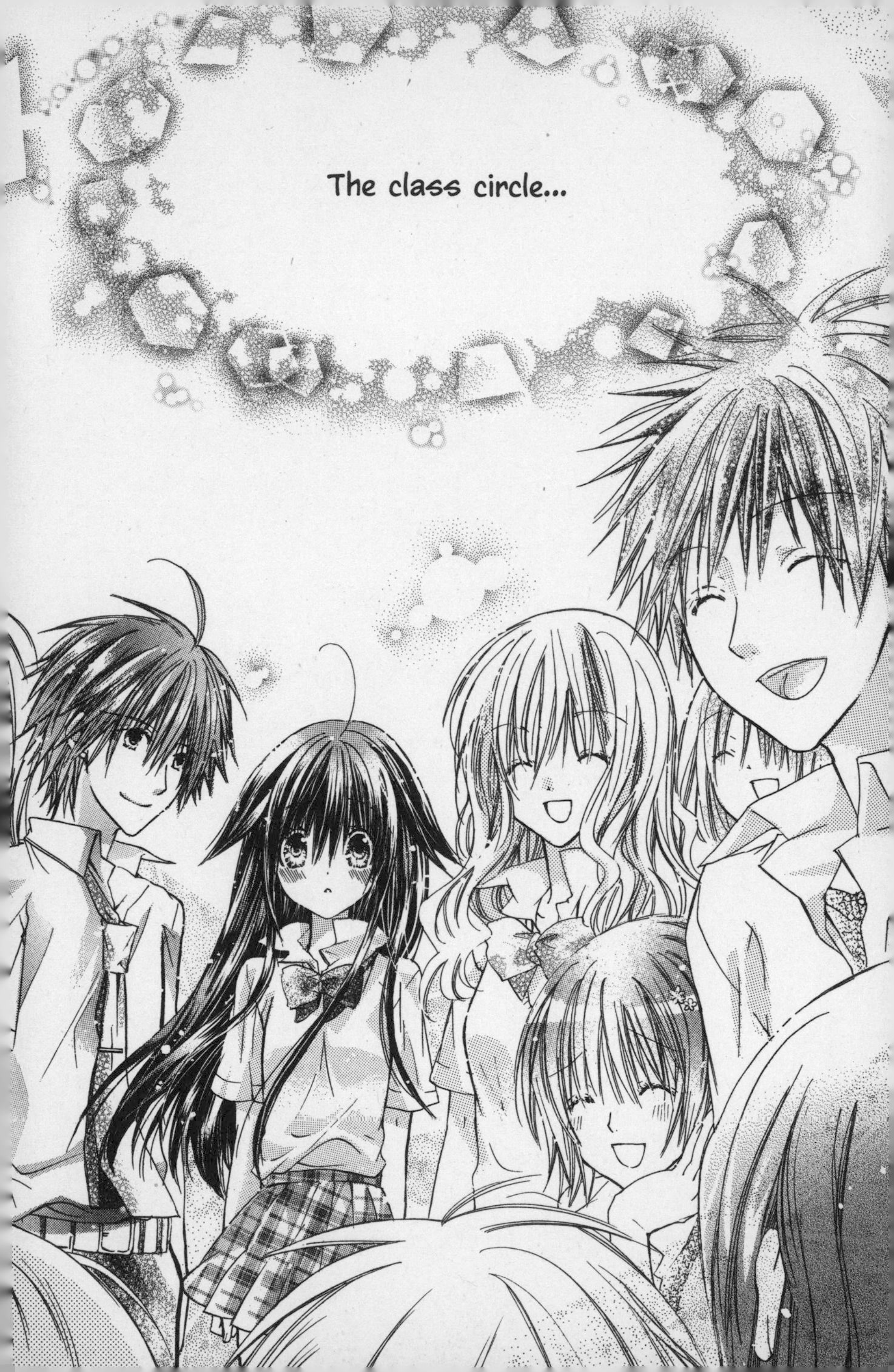
The class circle...

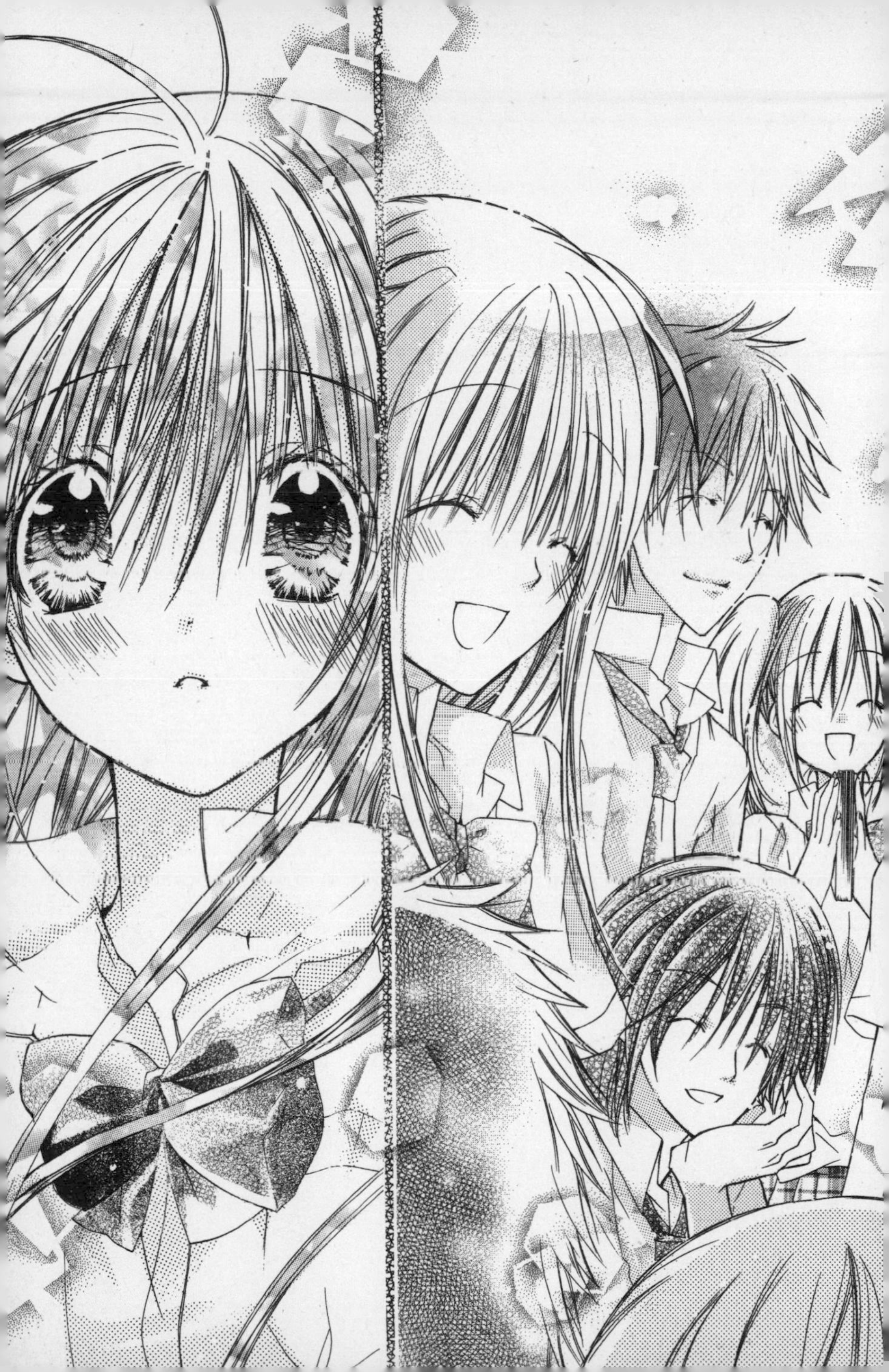

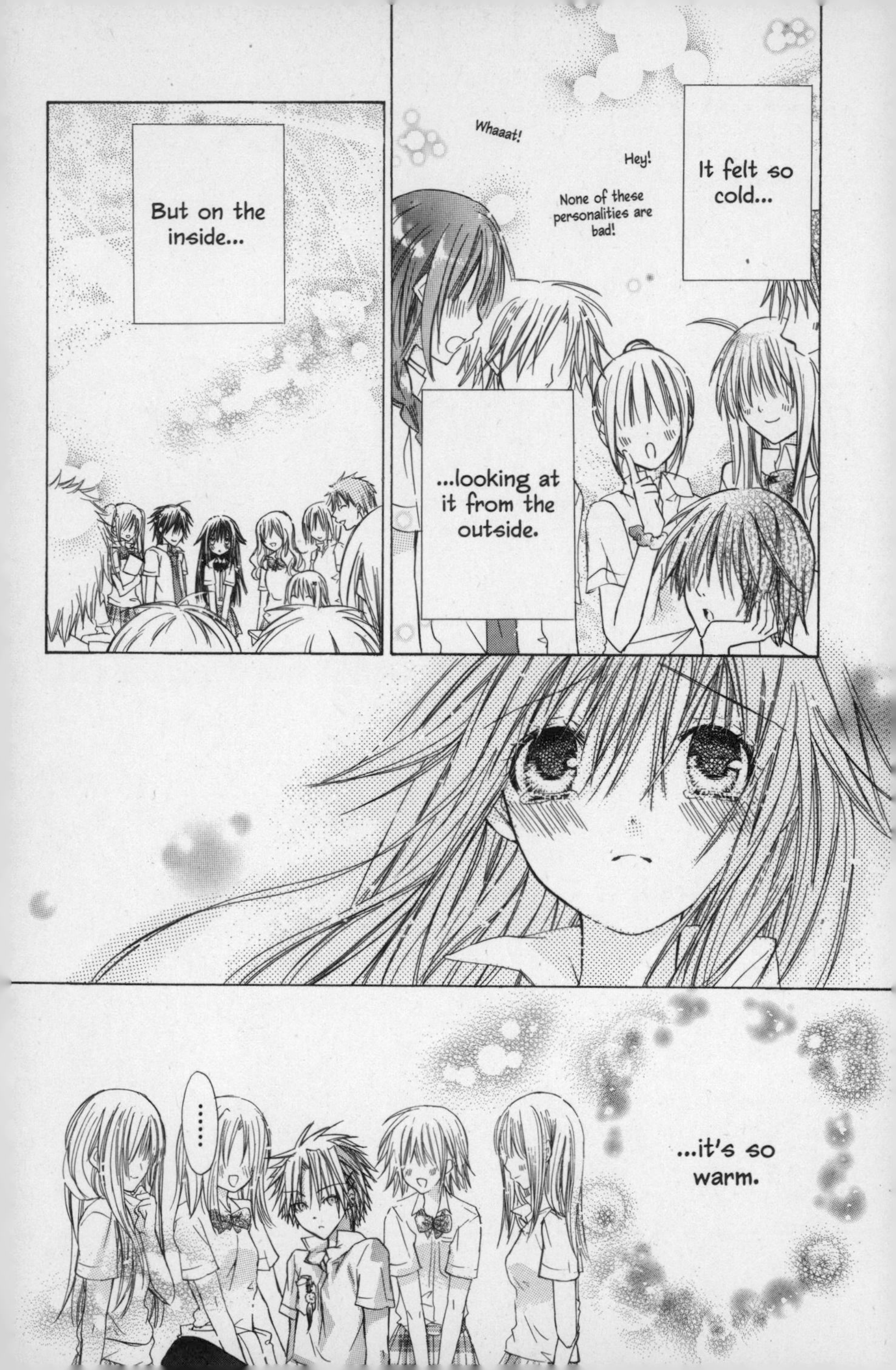
It felt so cold...
Hey!
Whaaat!
None of these personalities are bad!
...looking at it from the outside.
But on the inside...
......
...it's so warm.

‹sigh›

TAP

TAP

Guess what?

Because of the popular boy, I entered the class circle for the first time in junior high school!

I was just in the corner, but I still feel so happy!

I'm glad I met Hinata-kun...

Maybe I'll be able...

See?

Everything's goin' great! Hope there ain't no snags...
Mega Pig

...to live in the sun, after all.

す…SLIDE

We might make it!

I have to hurry too...

TAP TAP
てくてく

Do we have gym first period?

CHATTER

So annoying!

CHATTER

Hurry, let's go!

Wait!

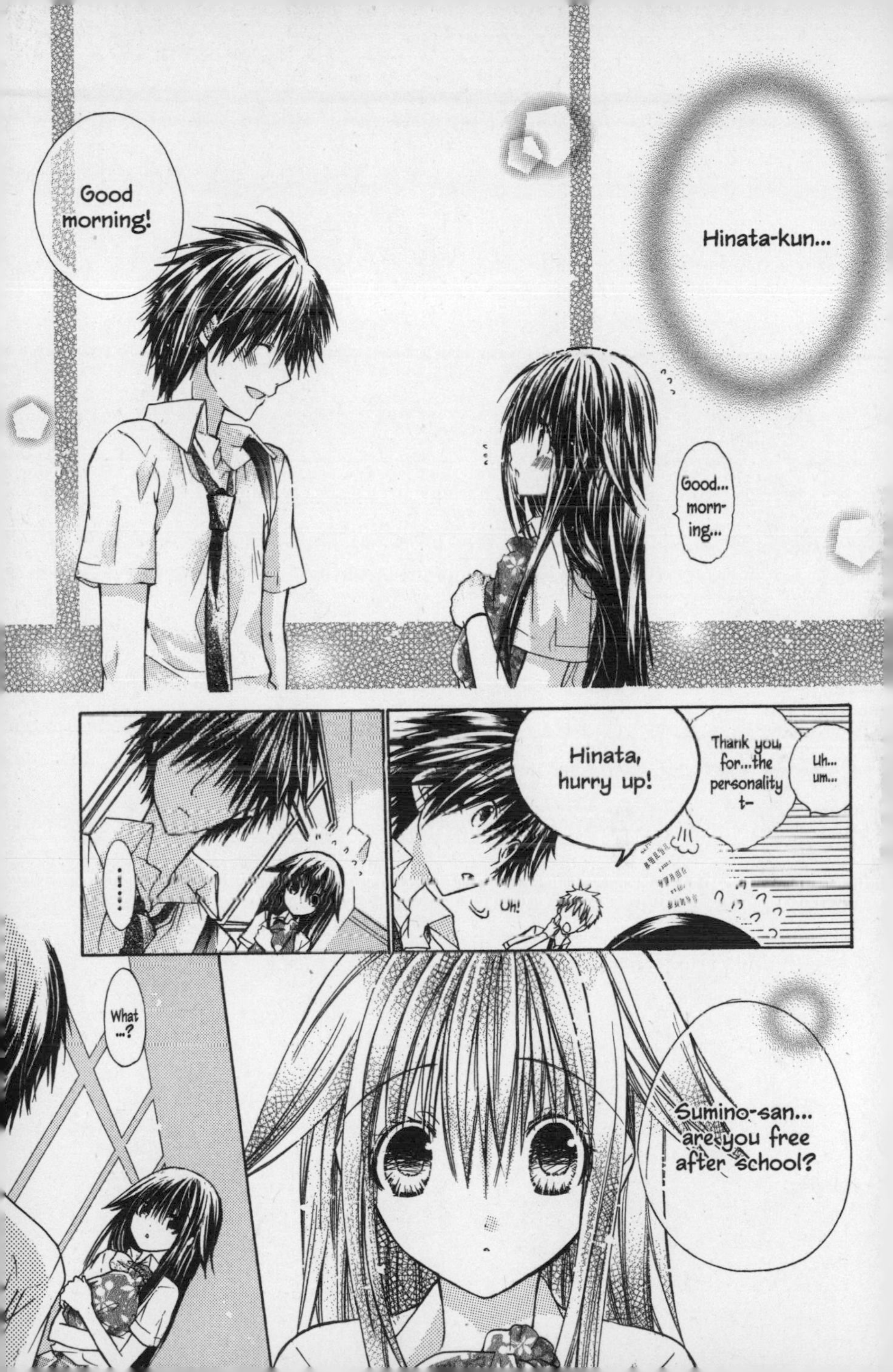
Hinata-kun...
Good morning!
Good... morn-ing...
Uh... um...
Thank you, for...the personality t-
Hinata, hurry up!
Uh!
......
Sumino-san... are you free after school?
What ...?

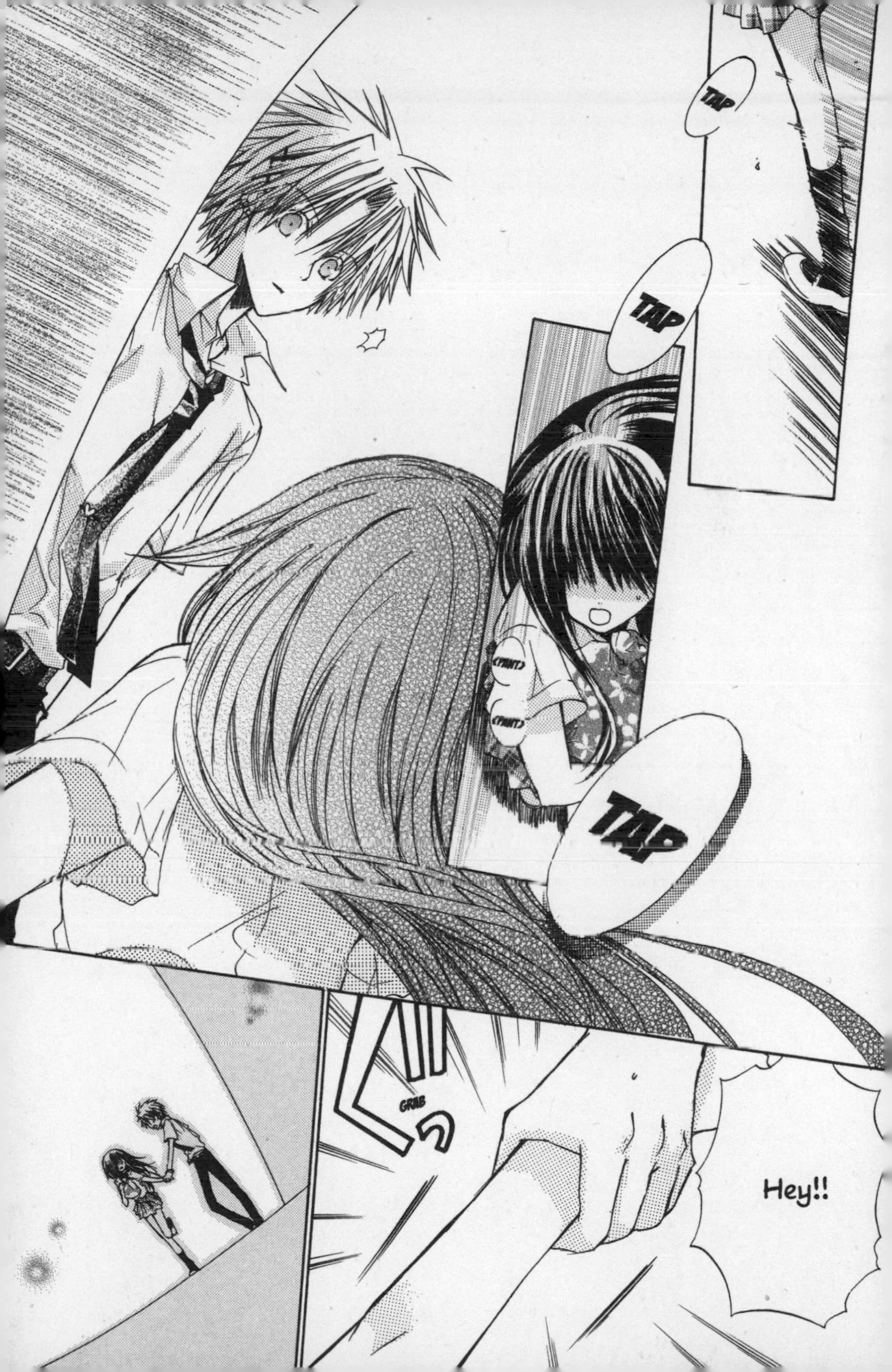
TAP
TAP
(PANT)
(PANT)
TAP
Hey!!
GRAB

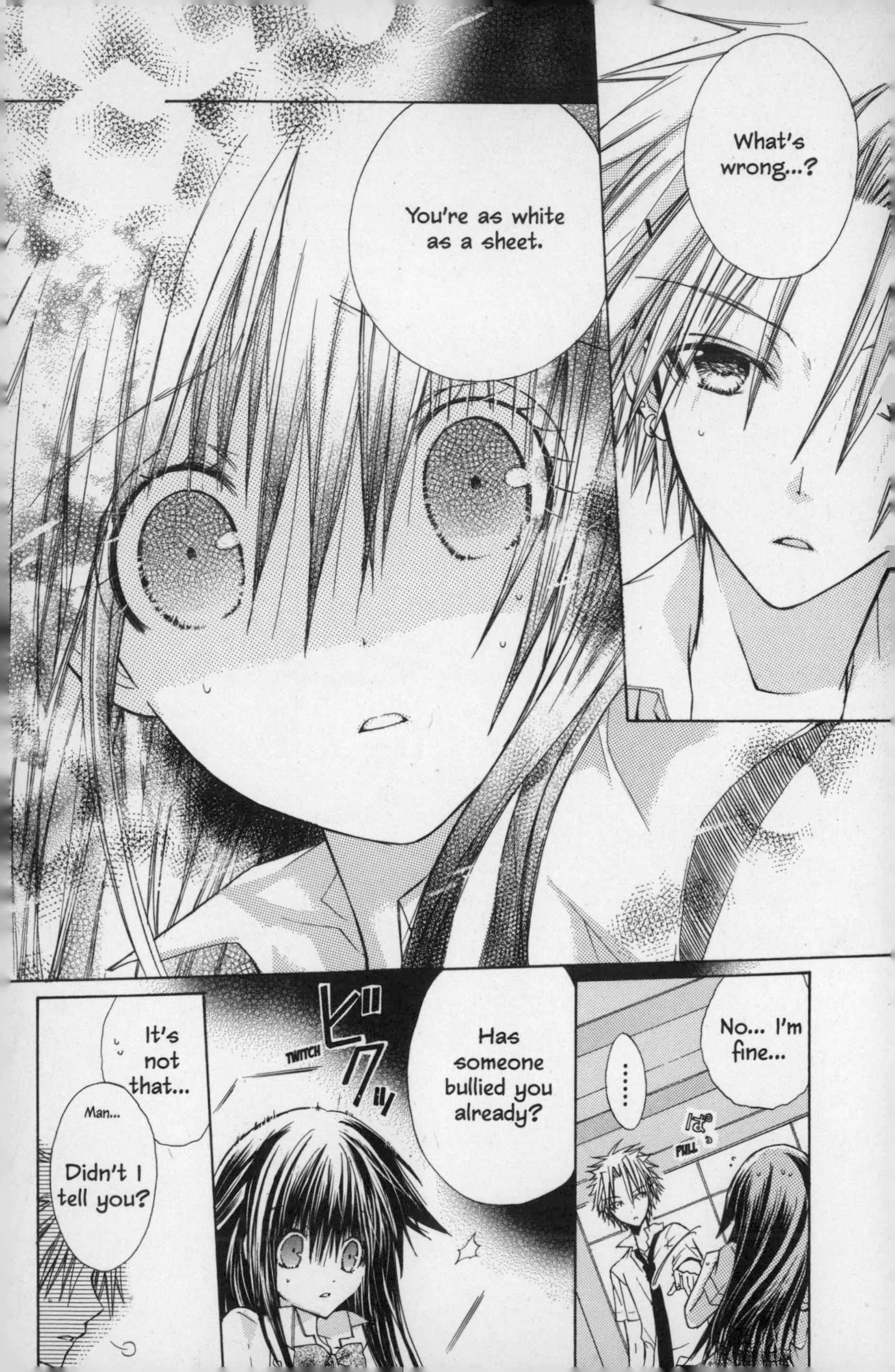
What's wrong...?
You're as white as a sheet.
No... I'm fine...
......
PULL
Has someone bullied you already?
ビクッ
TWITCH
It's not that...
Man...
Didn't I tell you?

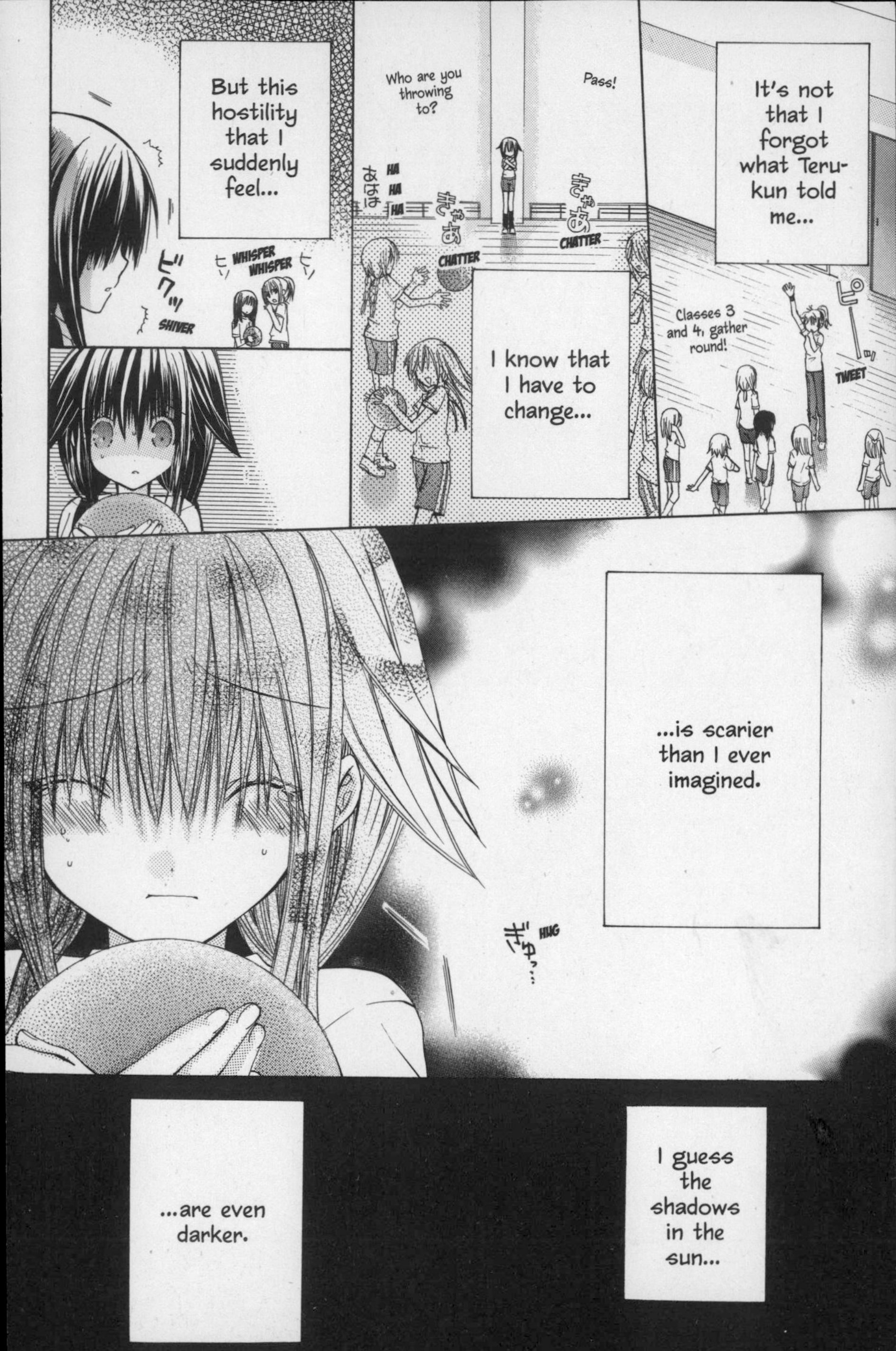

It's not that I forgot what Teru-kun told me...
Classes 3 and 4, gather round!
ピー
TWEET
Pass!
Who are you throwing to?
きゃあ
CHATTER
きゃあ
CHATTER
あはは
HA HA HA
I know that I have to change...
But this hostility that I suddenly feel...
ヒソ
ヒソ
WHISPER WHISPER
ビクッ
SHIVER
...is scarier than I ever imagined.
ぎゅ
HUG
I guess the shadows in the sun...
...are even darker.

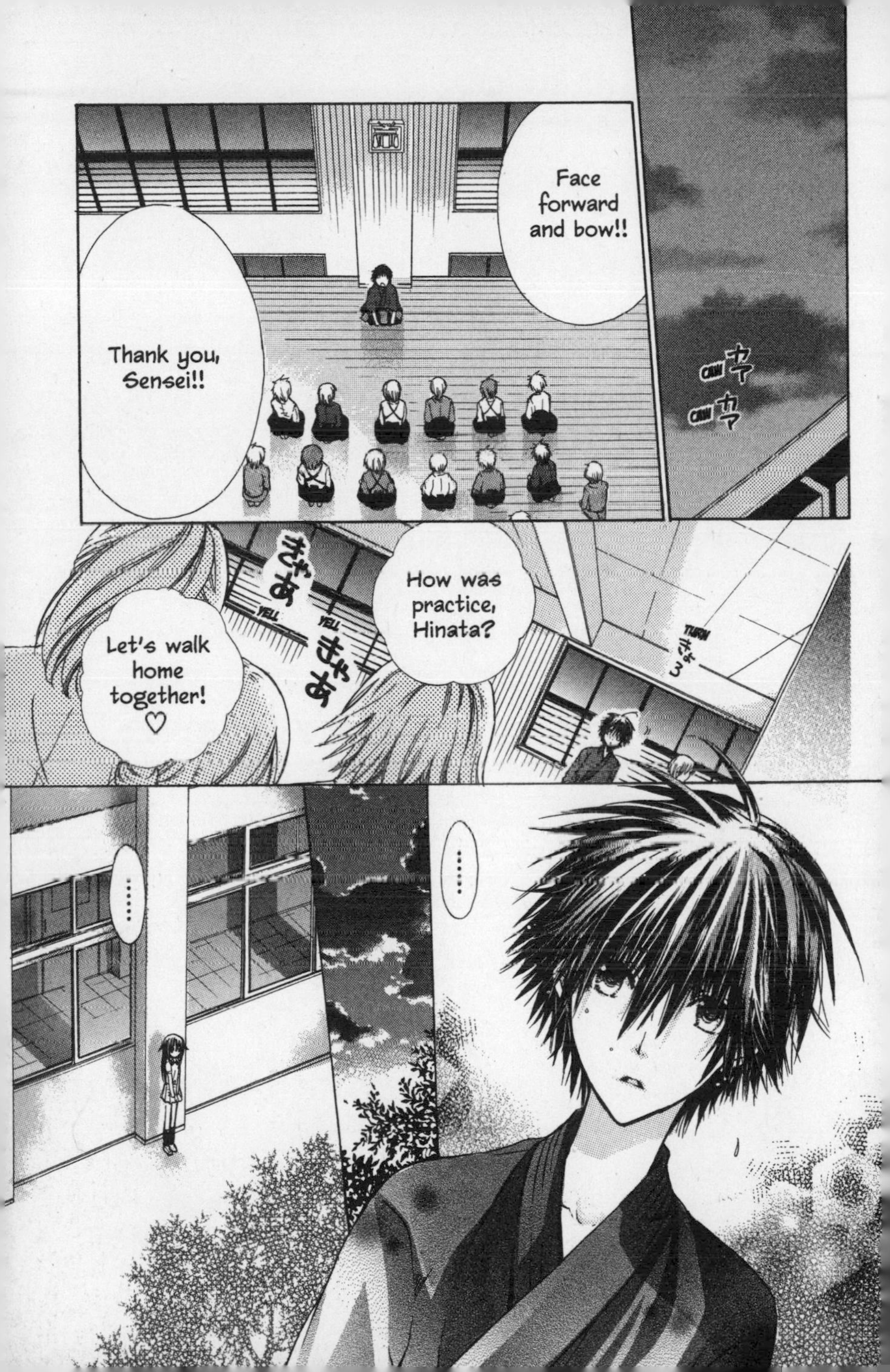
CAW カア
CAW カア
Face forward and bow!!
Thank you, Sensei!!
TURN
How was practice, Hinata?
YELL きゃあ
YELL きゃあ
Let's walk home together! ♡
……
……

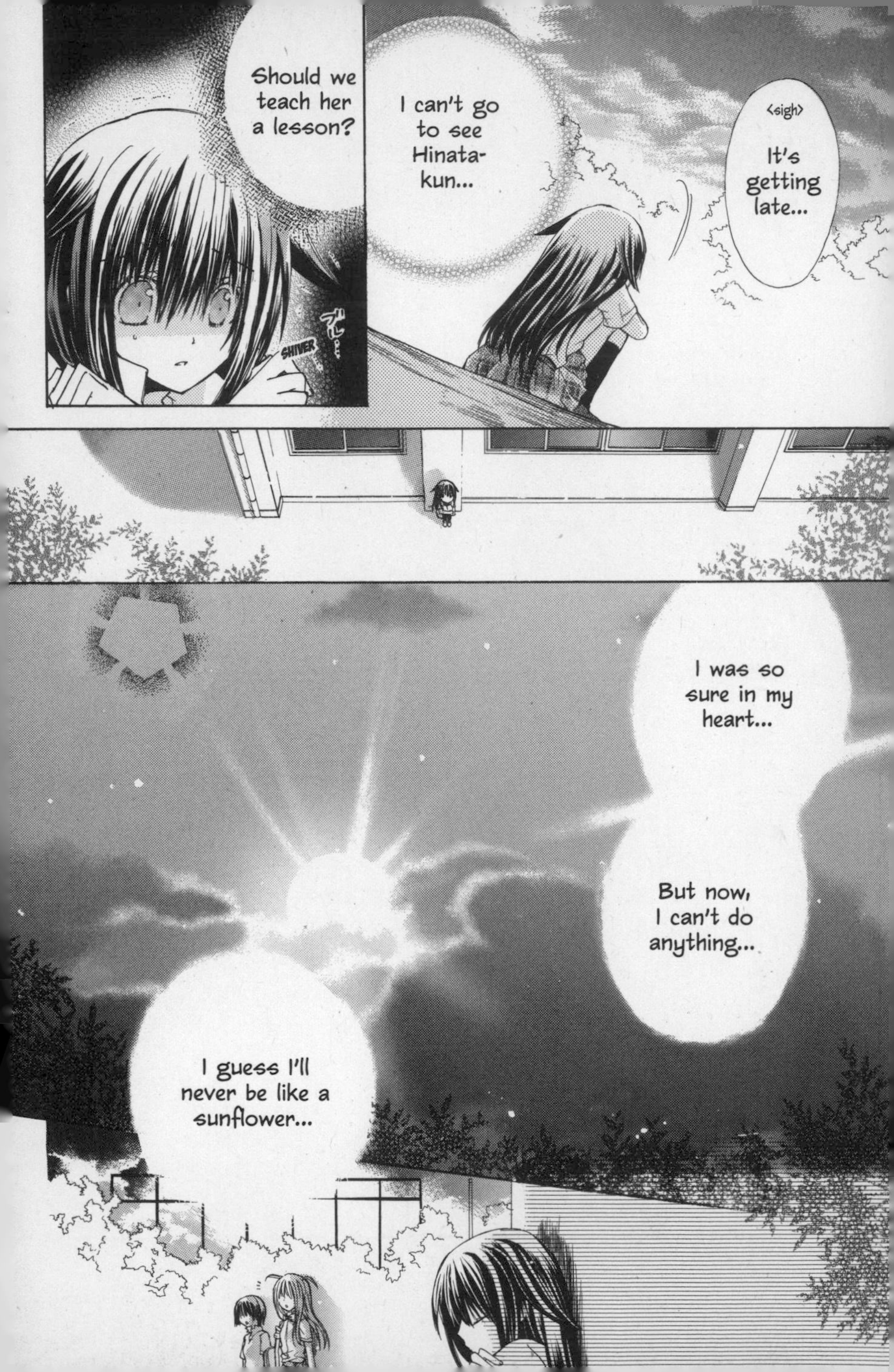
<sigh>
It's getting late...
I can't go to see Hinata-kun...
Should we teach her a lesson?
SHIVER
I was so sure in my heart...
But now, I can't do anything...
I guess I'll never be like a sunflower...

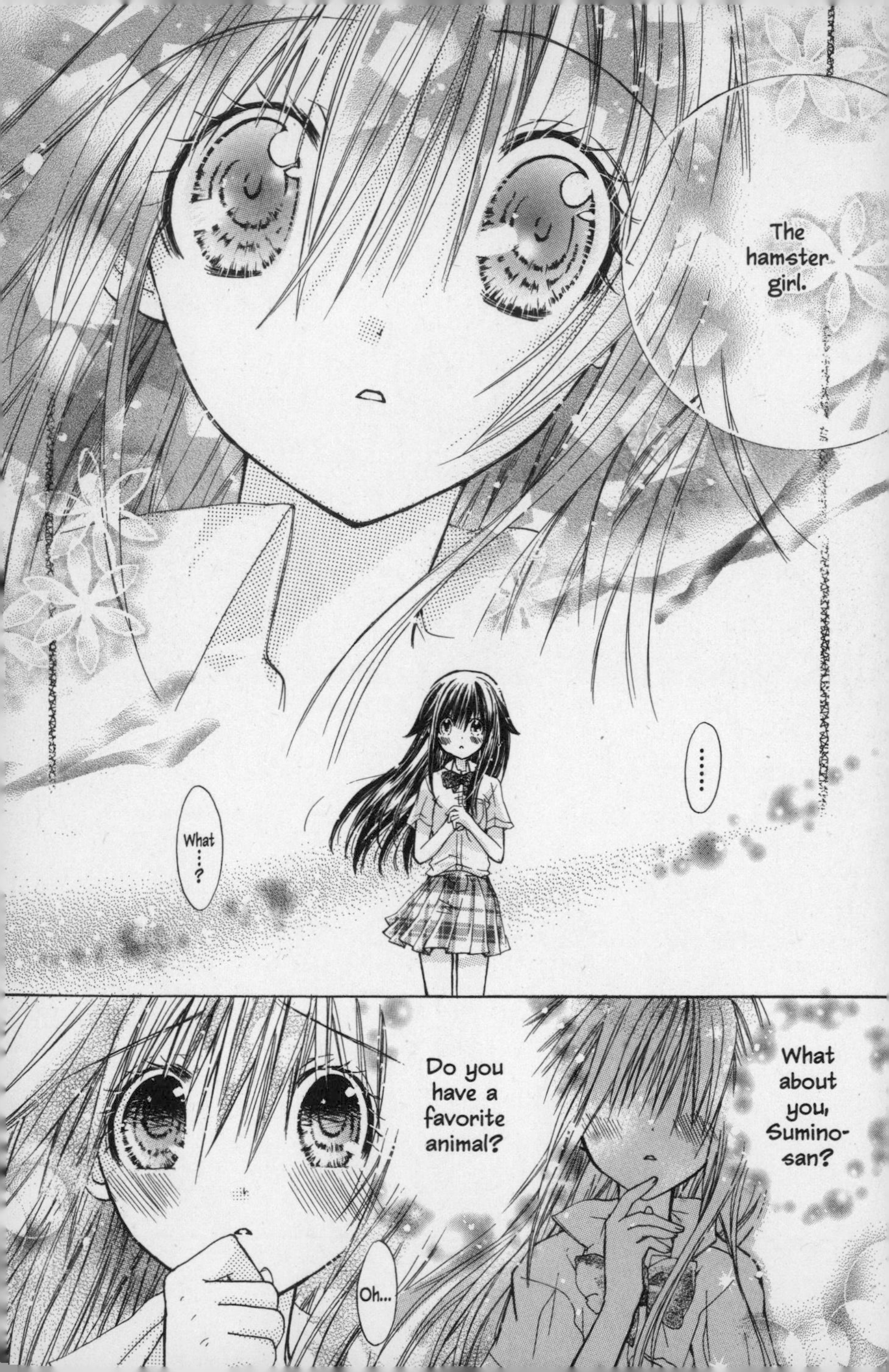
The hamster girl.
......
What...?
What about you, Sumino-san?
Do you have a favorite animal?
Oh...

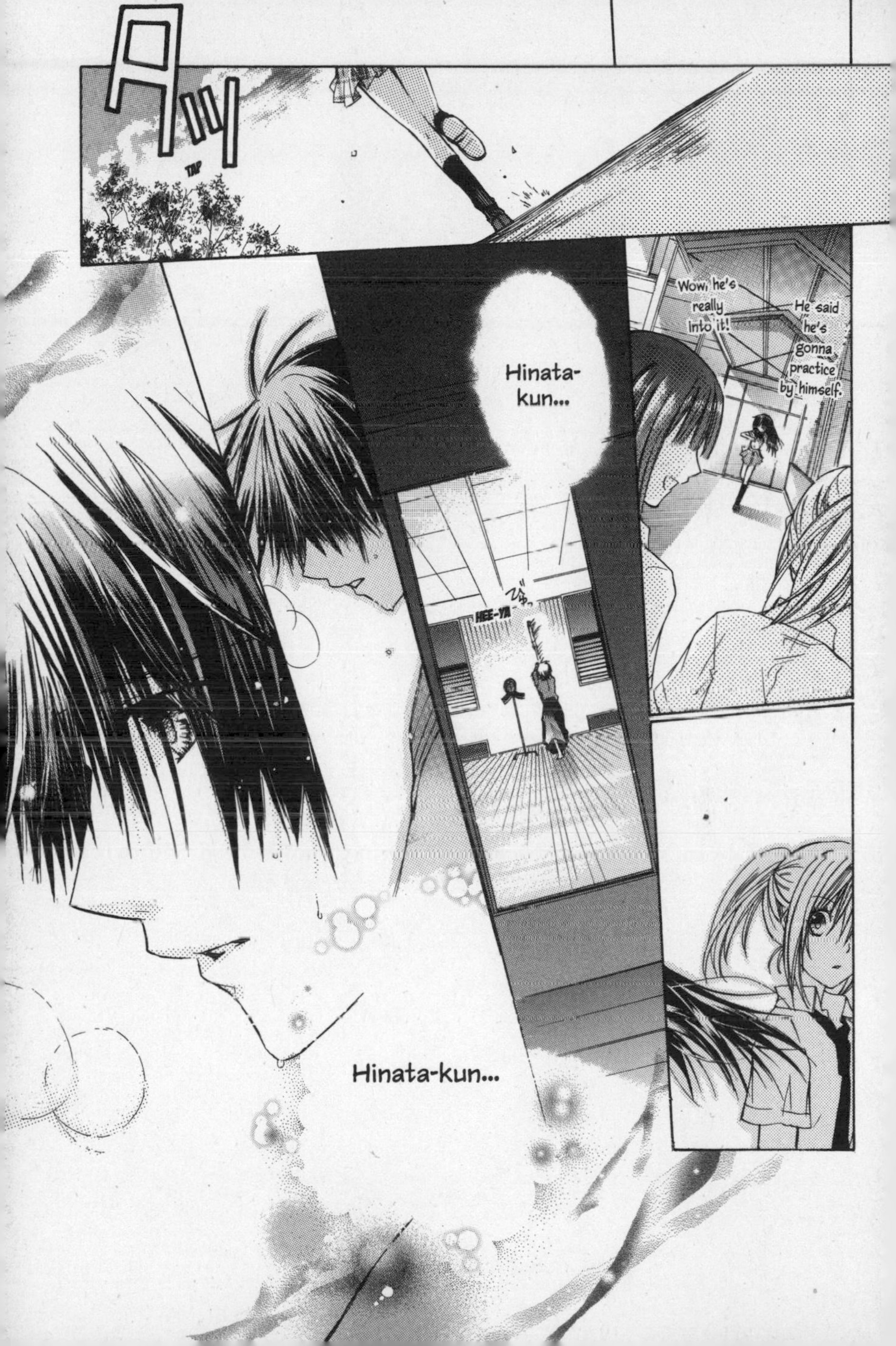
TAP
He said he's gonna practice by himself.
Wow, he's really into it!
Hinata-kun...
HEE-YA
Hinata-kun...

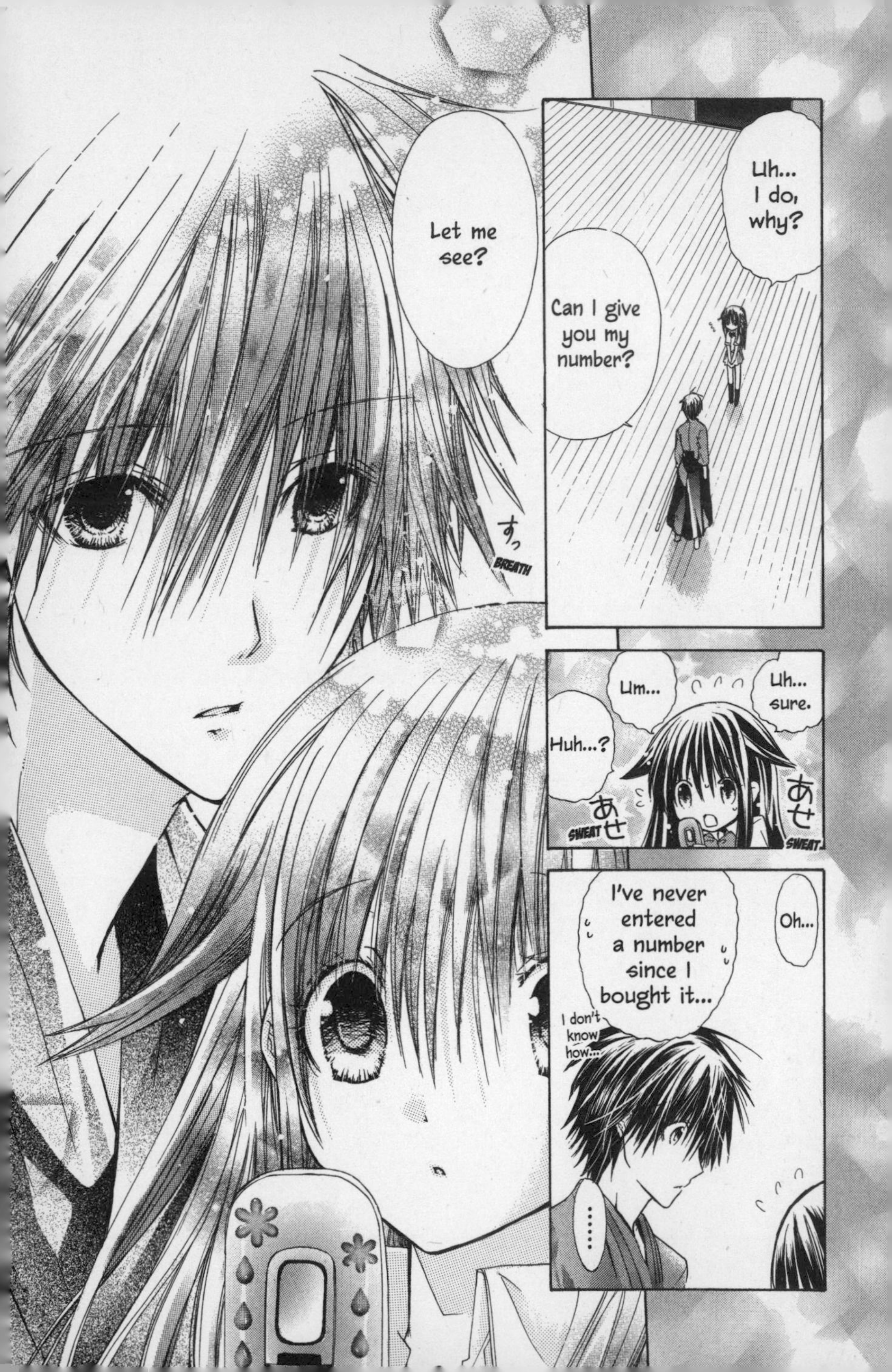
Uh... I do, why?
Can I give you my number?
Uh... sure.
Um...
Huh...?
あせ
SWEAT
あせ
SWEAT
Oh...
I've never entered a number since I bought it...
I don't know how...
......
Let me see?
すっ
BREATH

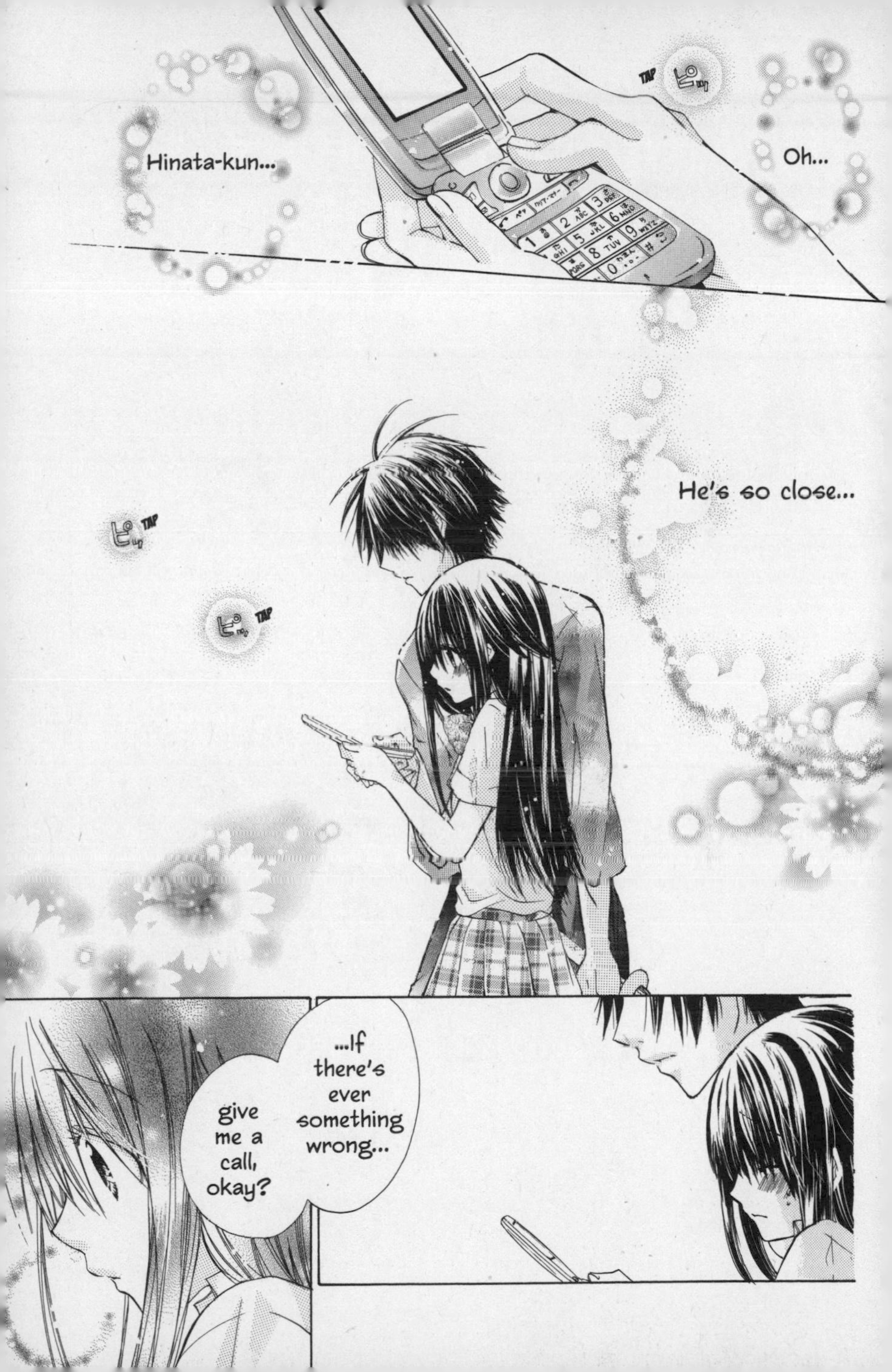

TAP ピッ
Oh...
Hinata-kun...
He's so close...
TAP ピッ
TAP ピッ
...If there's ever something wrong... give me a call, okay?

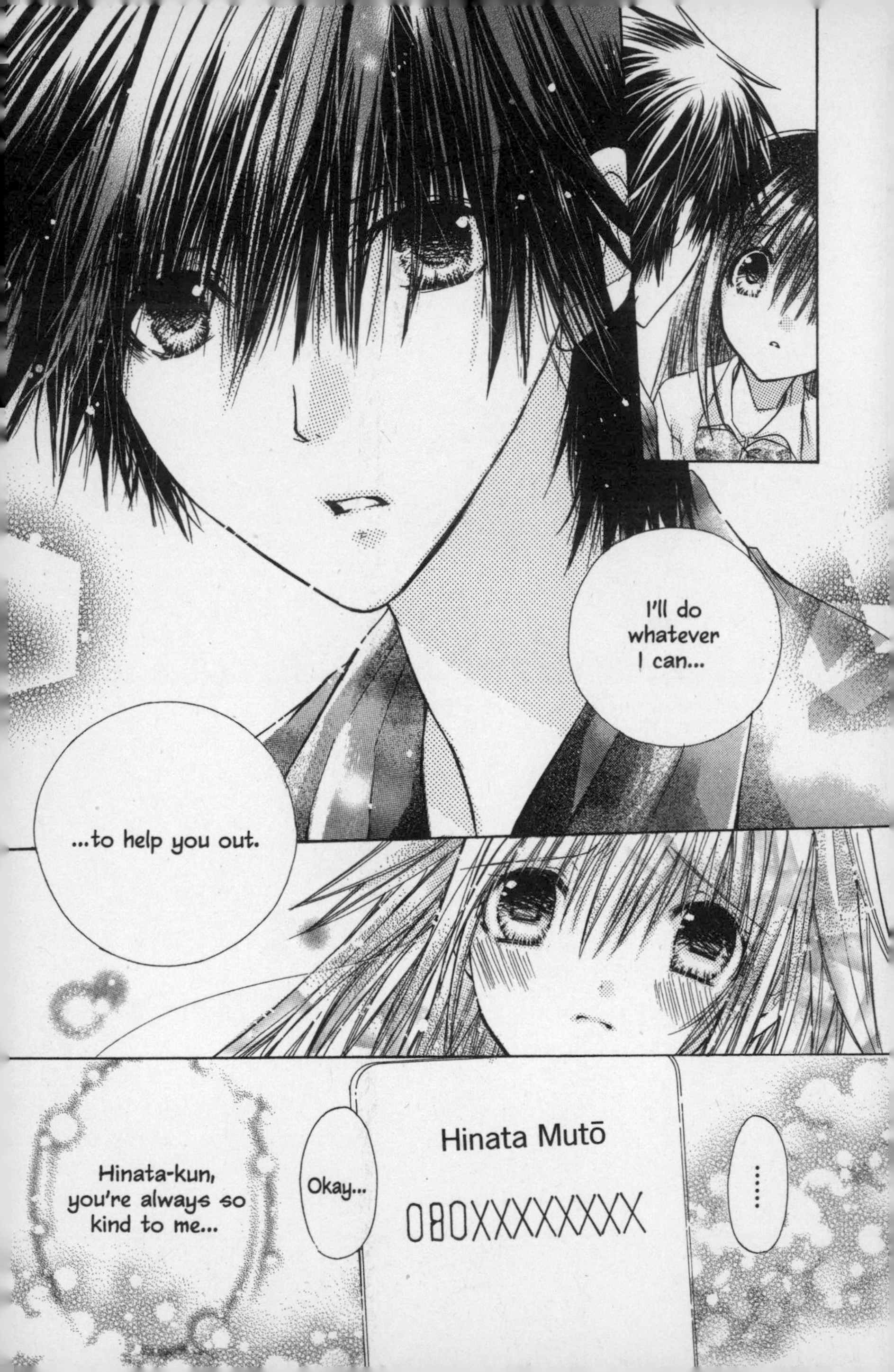
I'll do whatever I can...
...to help you out.
......
Hinata Mutō
080XXXXXXXX
Okay...
Hinata-kun, you're always so kind to me...

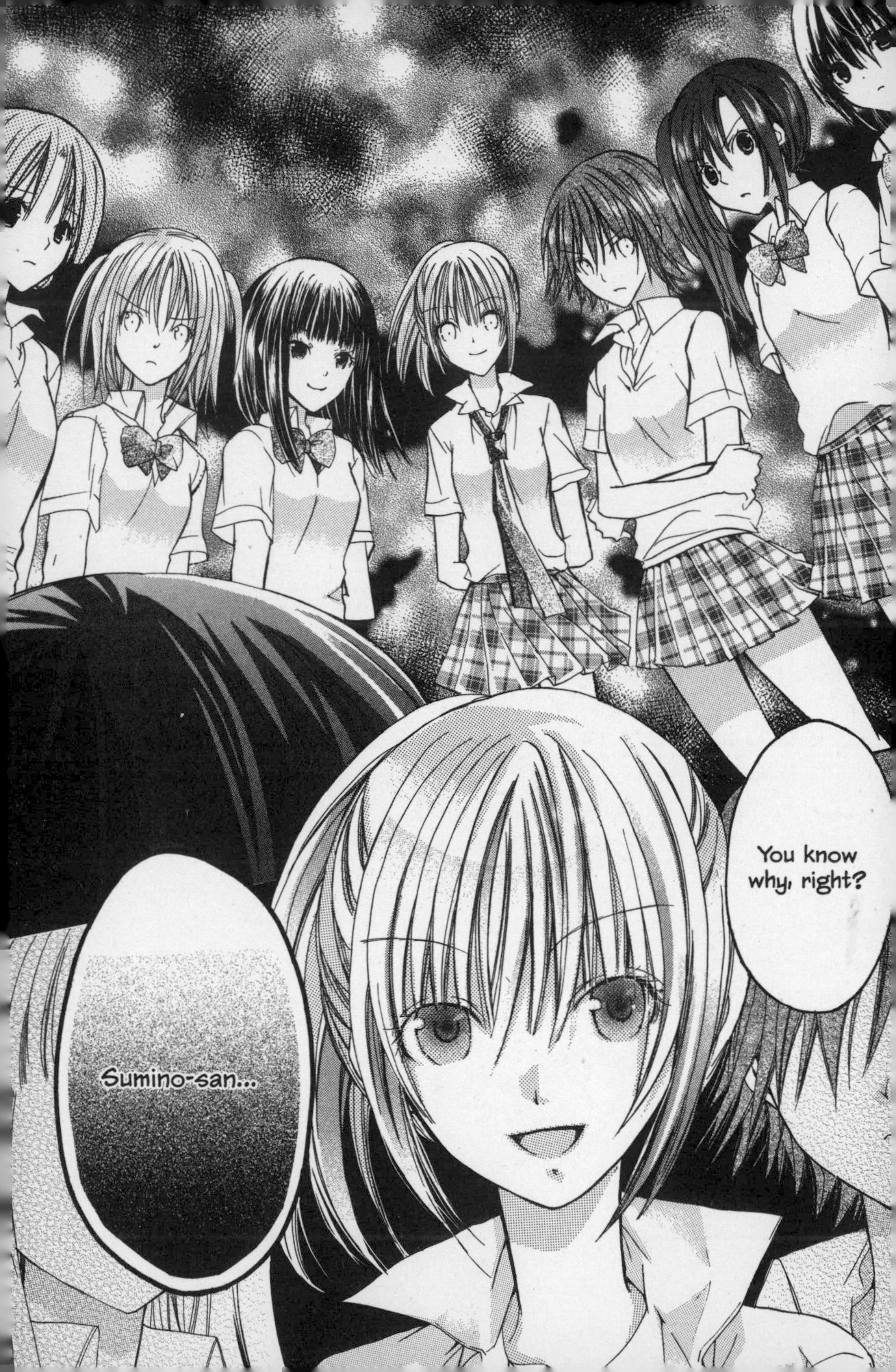
You know why, right?
Sumino-san...

Ema Tōyama

I think my Hikage-quotient is pretty high. A boy who was in my class for two years asked me "What's your name again?" on our graduation day.

That sucks. It's hard to know how to respond.

I dedicate this comic to all the people who've had experiences like that, and all the people who sometimes feel lonely.

PROFILE
Born May 23
Gemini
Blood Type B

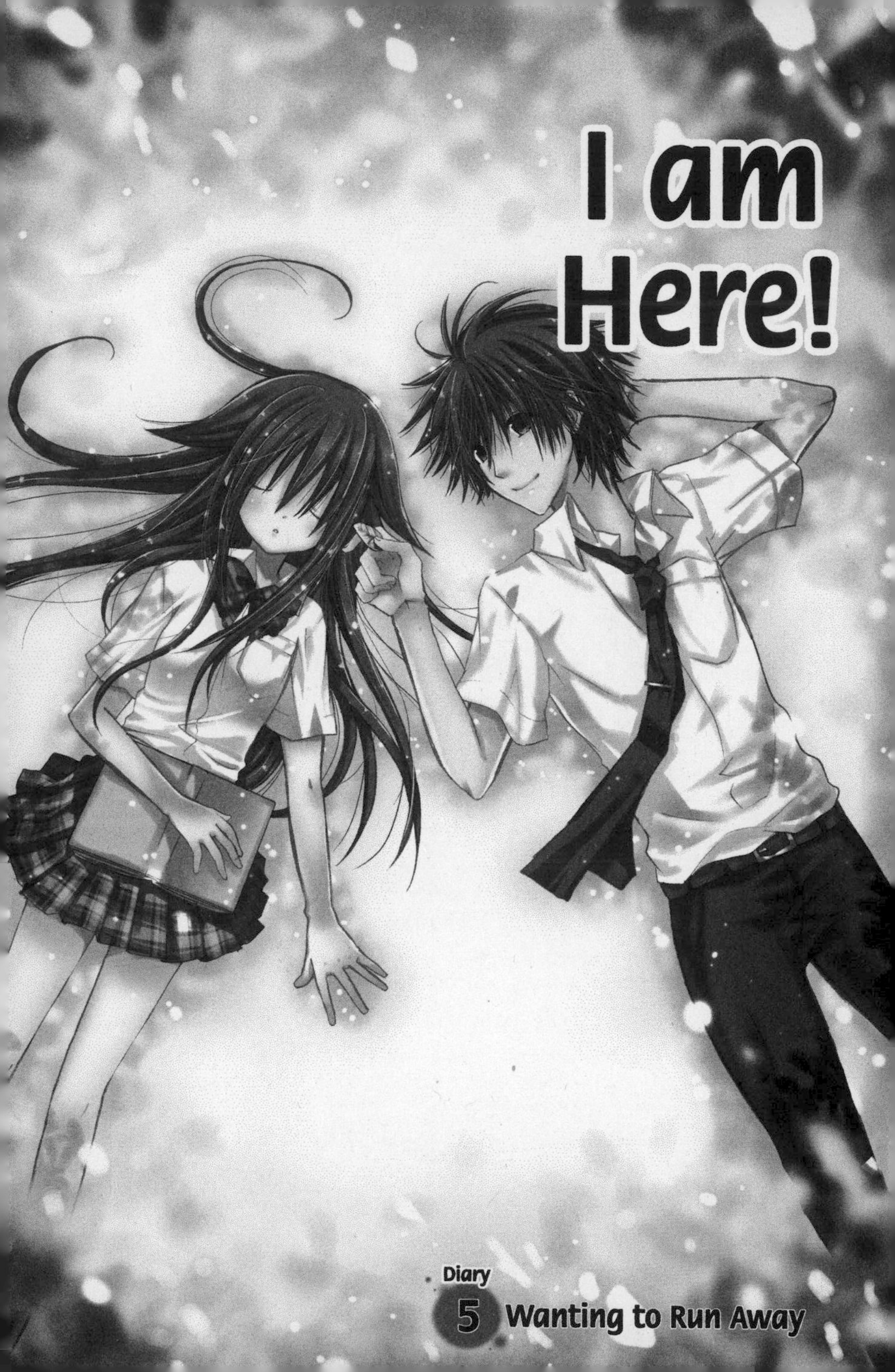
I am Here!
Diary
5 Wanting to Run Away

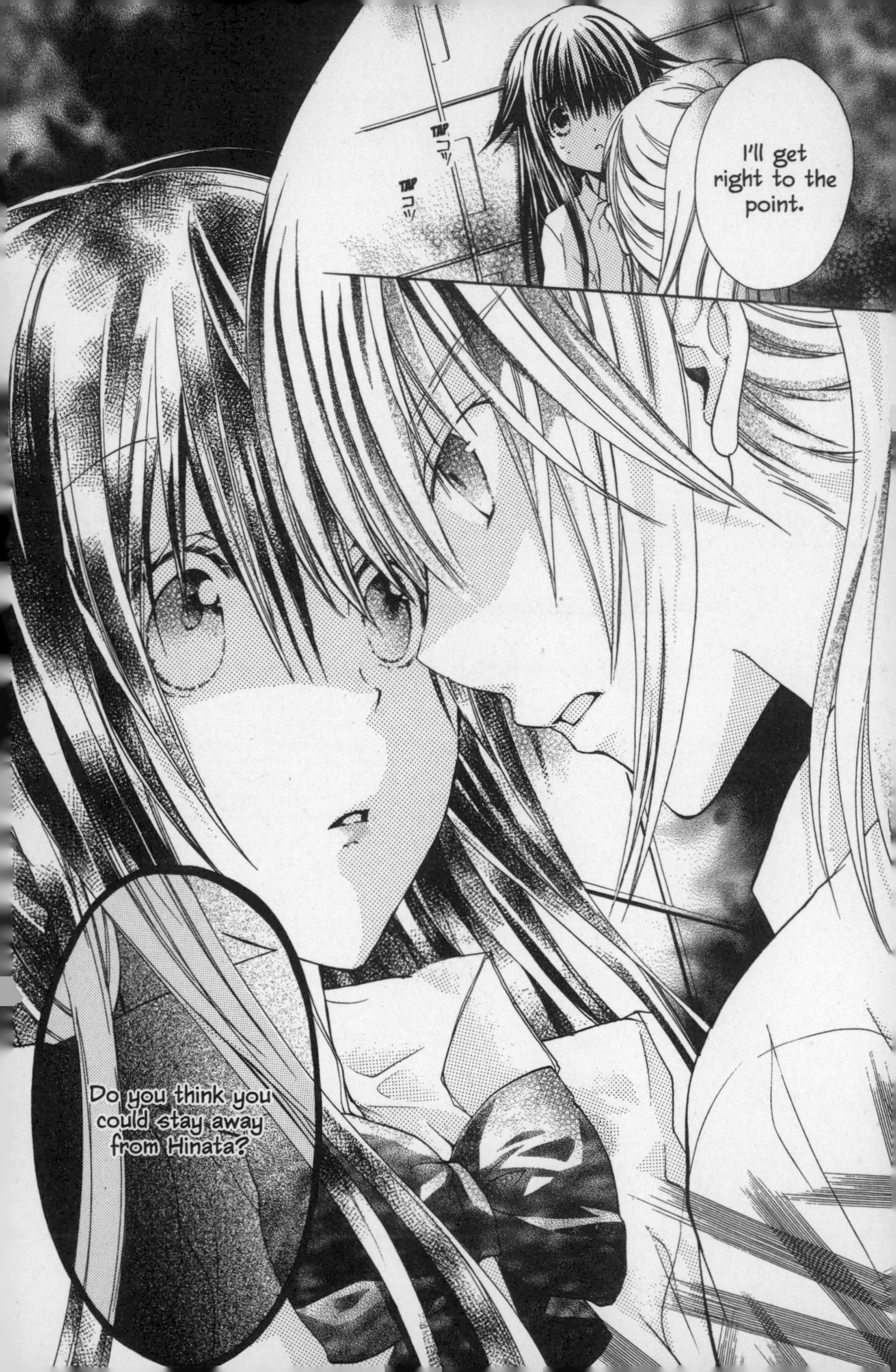
I'll get right to the point.
TAP
TAP
Do you think you could stay away from Hinata?

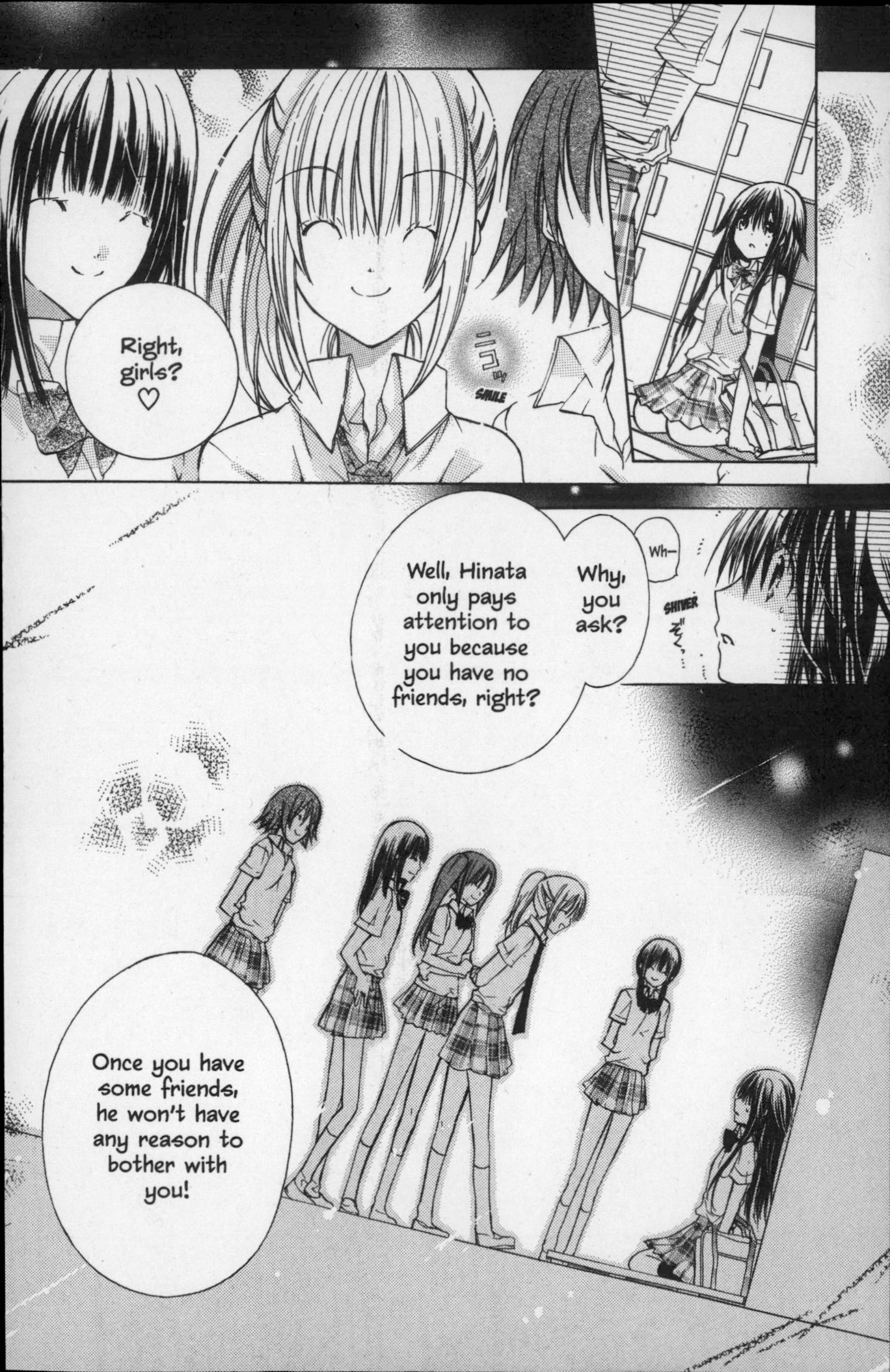
Right, girls? ♡
ニコッ
SMILE
Wh-
SHIVER
Why, you ask?
Well, Hinata only pays attention to you because you have no friends, right?
Once you have some friends, he won't have any reason to bother with you!

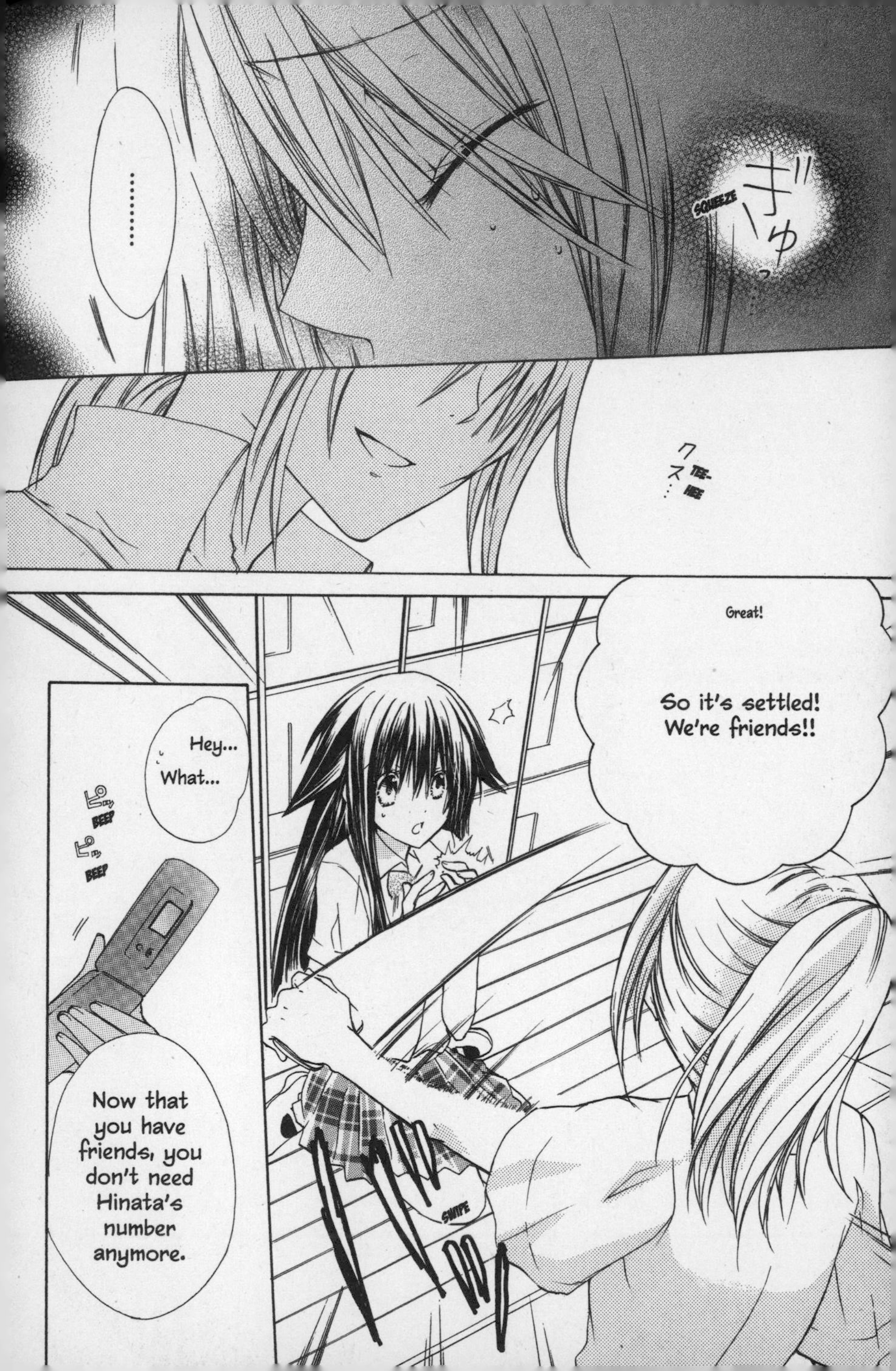

ぎゅっ
SQUEEZE
......
クス…
TEE-HEE
Great!
So it's settled! We're friends!!
Hey... What...
ピッ
BEEP
ピッ
BEEP
Now that you have friends, you don't need Hinata's number anymore.
SWIPE

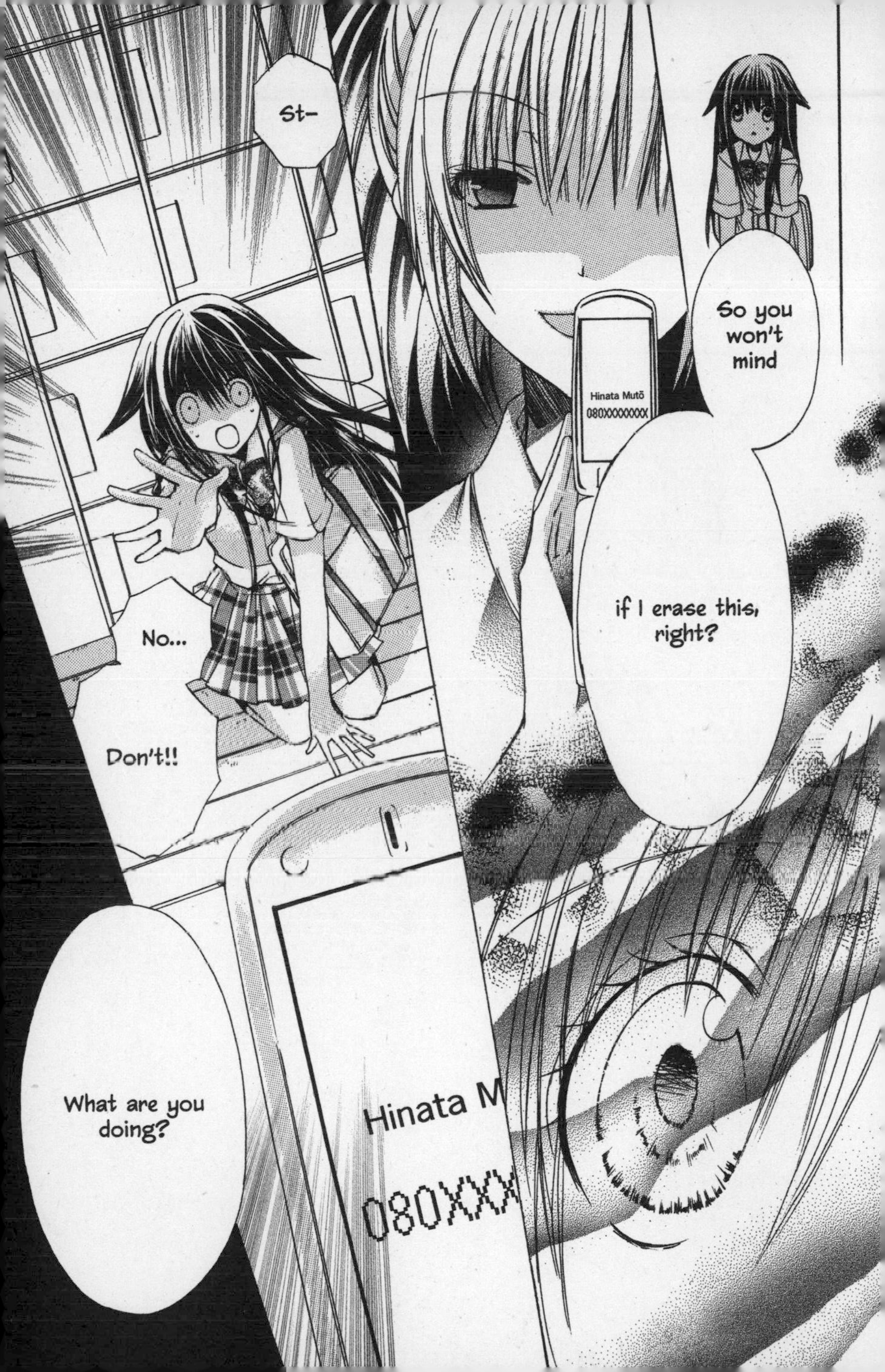
So you won't mind
Hinata Mutō
080XXXXXXXX
if I erase this, right?
St-
No...
Don't!!
Hinata M
080XXX
What are you doing?

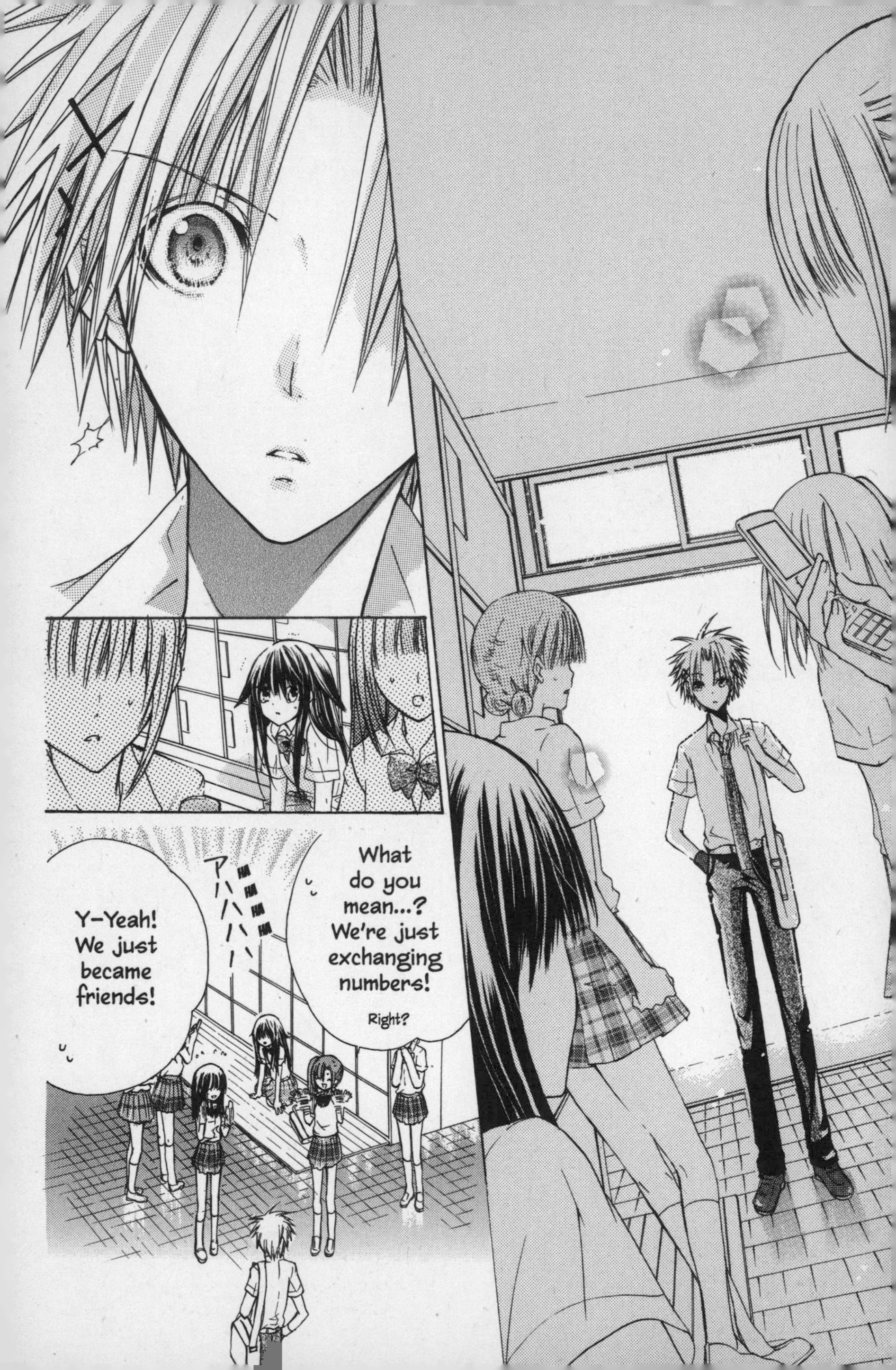
What do you mean...? We're just exchanging numbers!
Right?
HA HA HA HA HA
Y-Yeah! We just became friends!

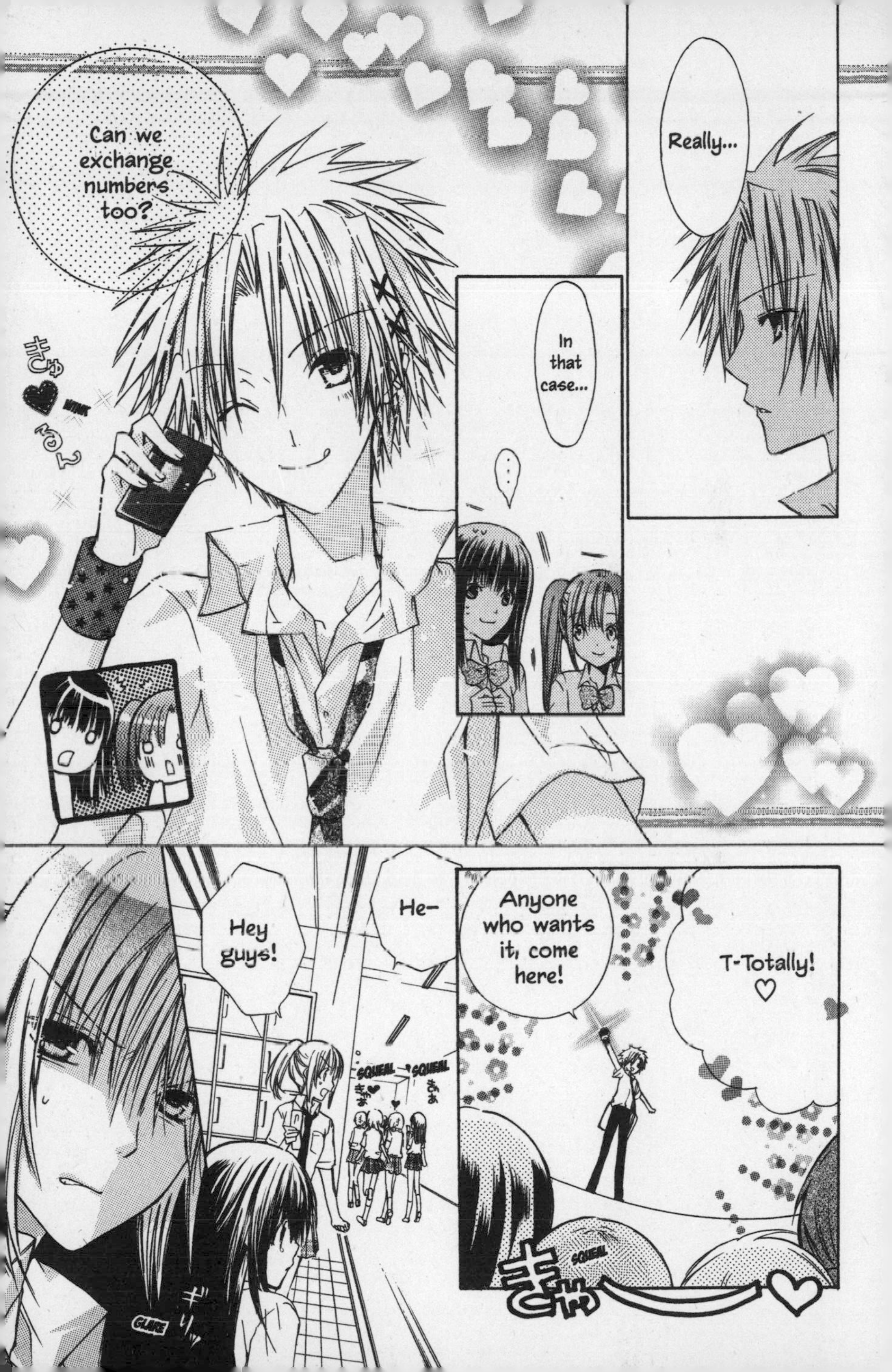
Really...
In that case...
...
Can we exchange numbers too?
きゅるん
WINK
Anyone who wants it, come here!
T-Totally! ♡
きゃ~
SQUEAL
He-
Hey guys!
SQUEAL
SQUEAL
きゃ
きゃあ
ギリッ
GLARE

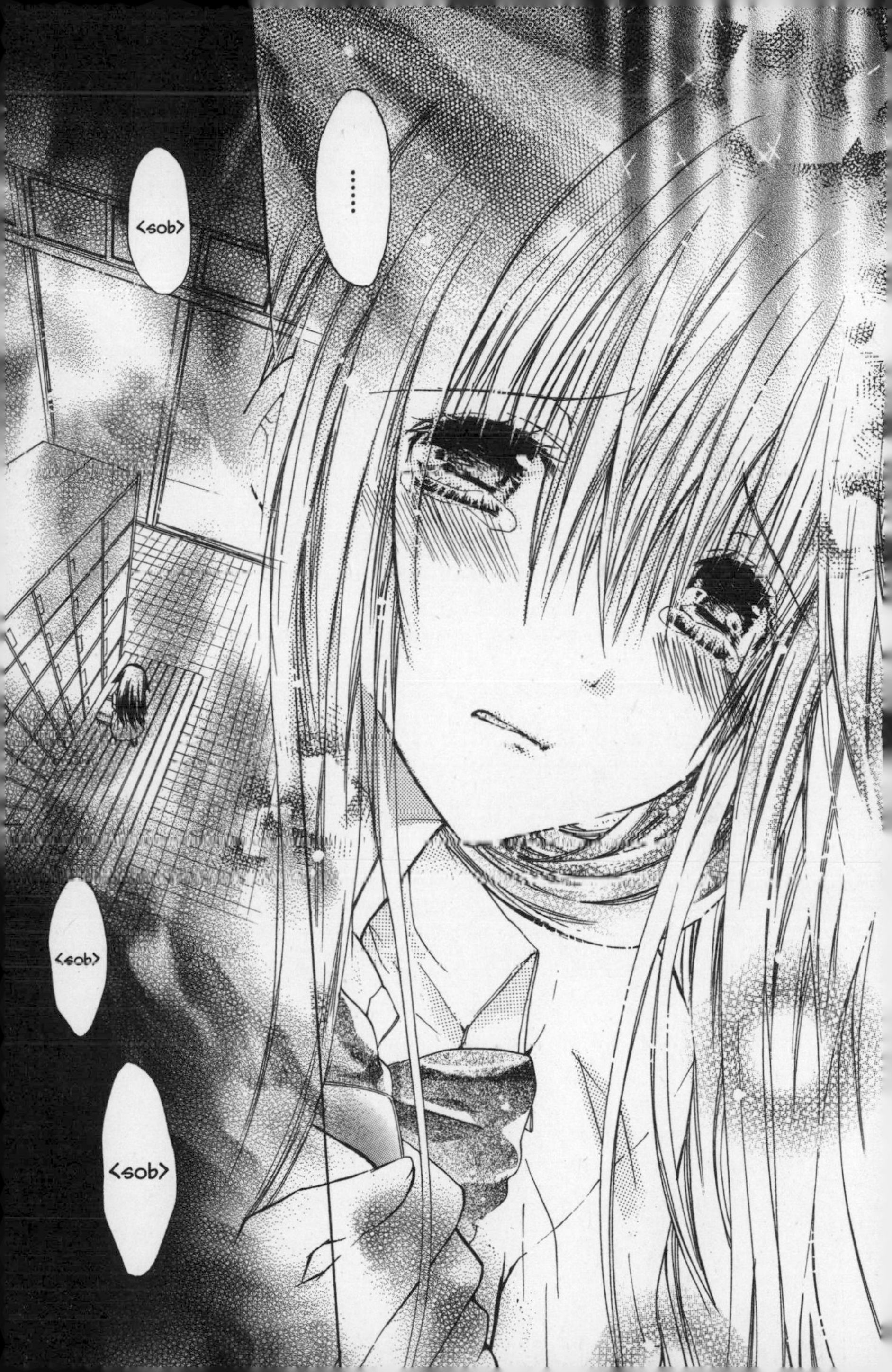
......
<sob>
<sob>
<sob>

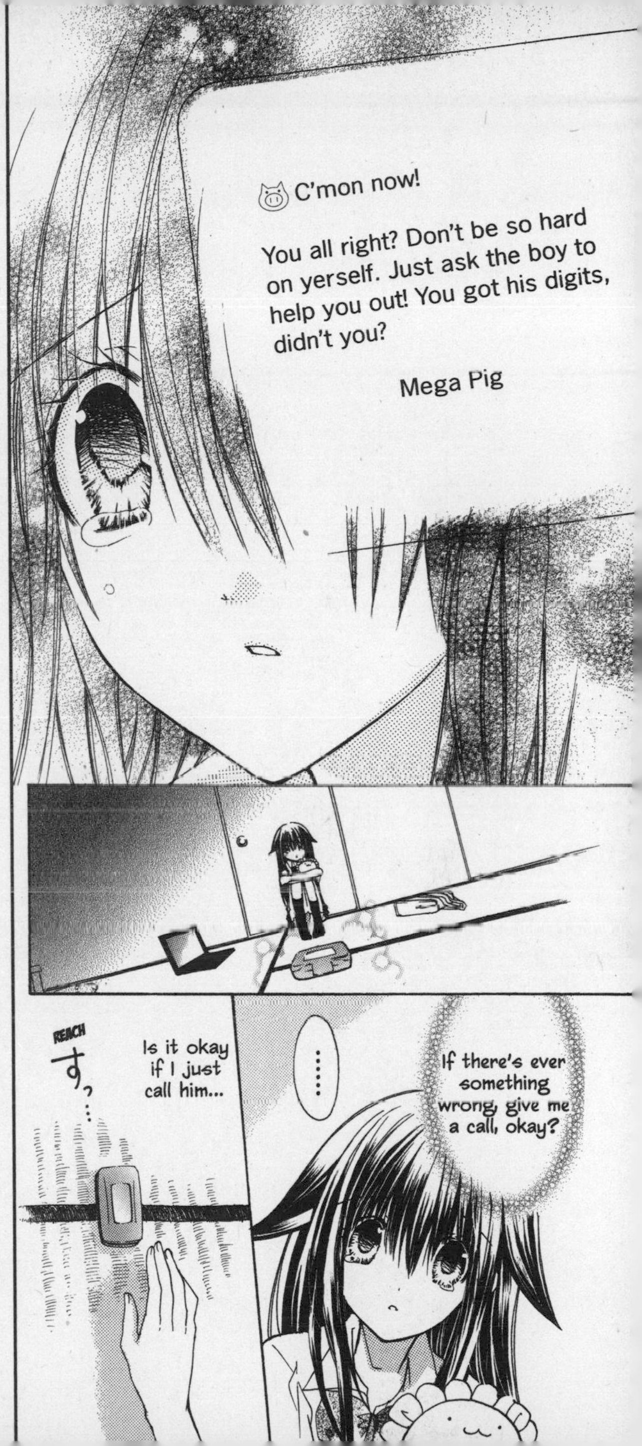
C'mon now!
You all right? Don't be so hard on yerself. Just ask the boy to help you out! You got his digits, didn't you?
Mega Pig
If there's ever something wrong, give me a call, okay?
......
REACH
すっ
Is it okay if I just call him...

Mahimahi

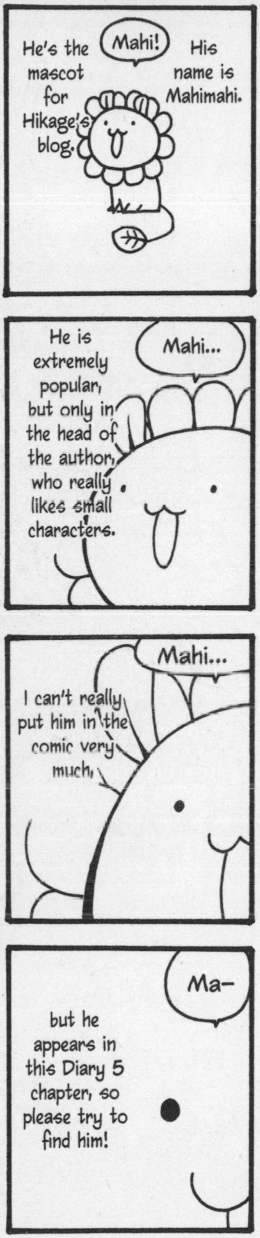
His name is Mahimahi.
Mahi!
He's the mascot for Hikage's blog.
Mahi...
He is extremely popular, but only in the head of the author, who really likes small characters.
Mahi...
I can't really put him in the comic very much,
Ma-
but he appears in this Diary 5 chapter, so please try to find him!

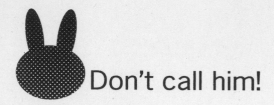# Don't call him!

What...

Black Rabbit...

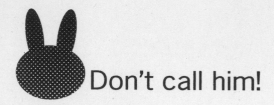Don't call him!

Since you decided that you were going to change, maybe you shouldn't rely on him...?

I don't think you're gonna make it through this unless you focus on changing yourself.

Black Rabbit

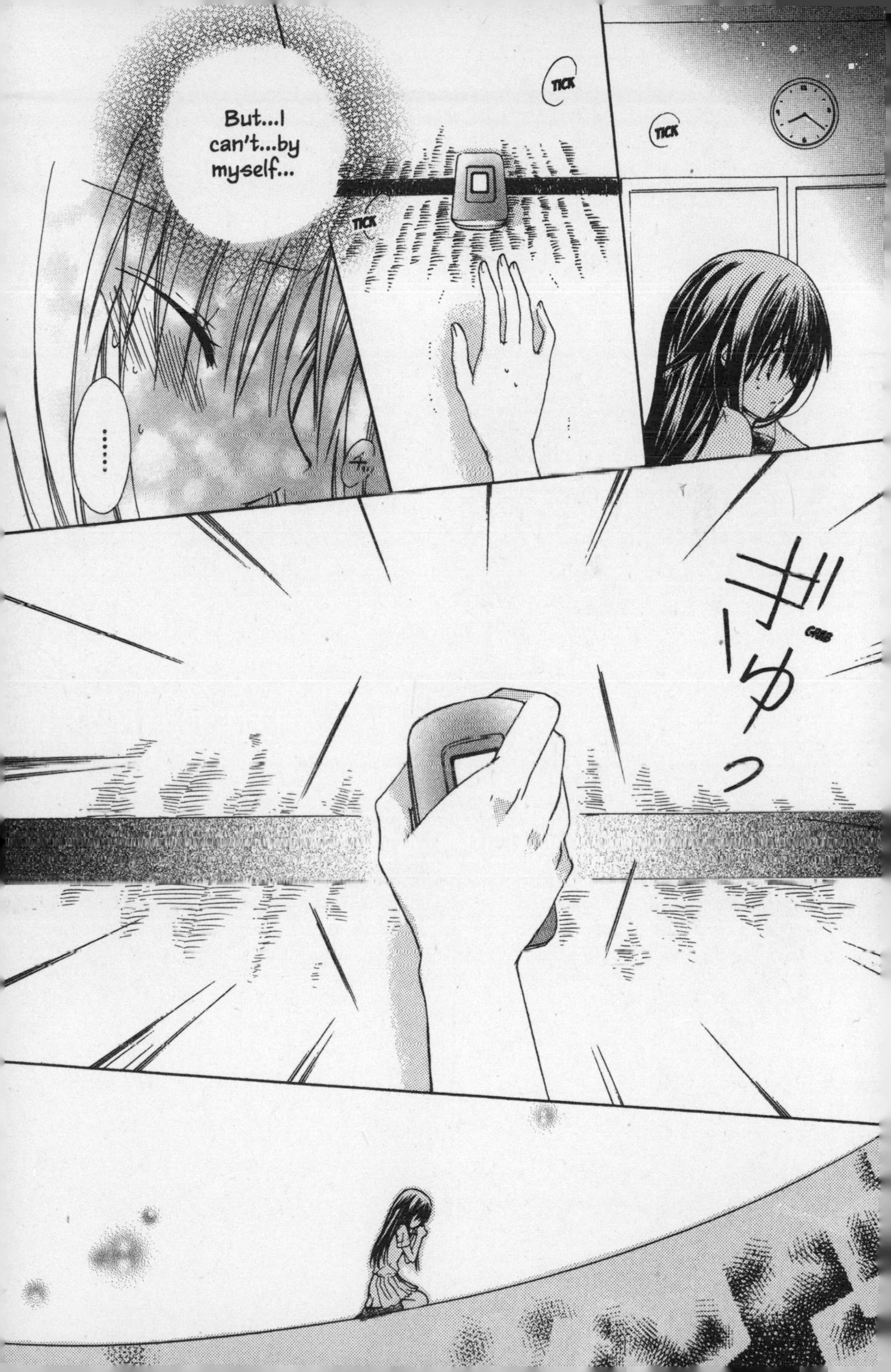
TICK
TICK
TICK
But...I can't...by myself...
......
ぎゅっ

RINNING

RINNING

I'll just...

THUMP

RINNING

THUMP

(SIGH)

Hinata Mutō
080XXXXXXX

I'll just let it ring
three times, and if
he doesn't answer,
I'll hang up...

CLICK

Hello?

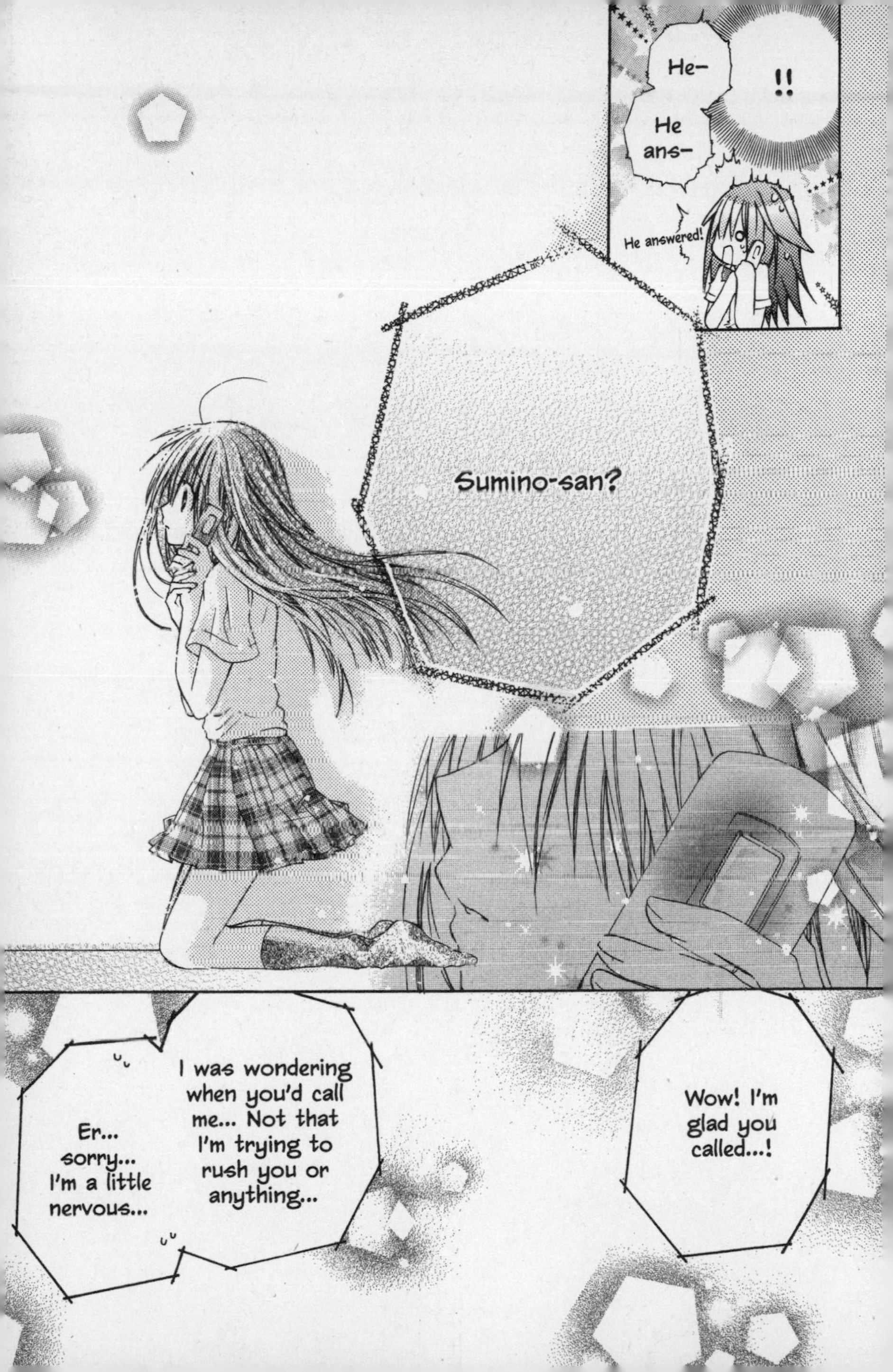
!!
He-
He ans-
He answered!
Sumino-san?
Wow! I'm glad you called...!
I was wondering when you'd call me... Not that I'm trying to rush you or anything...
Er... sorry... I'm a little nervous...

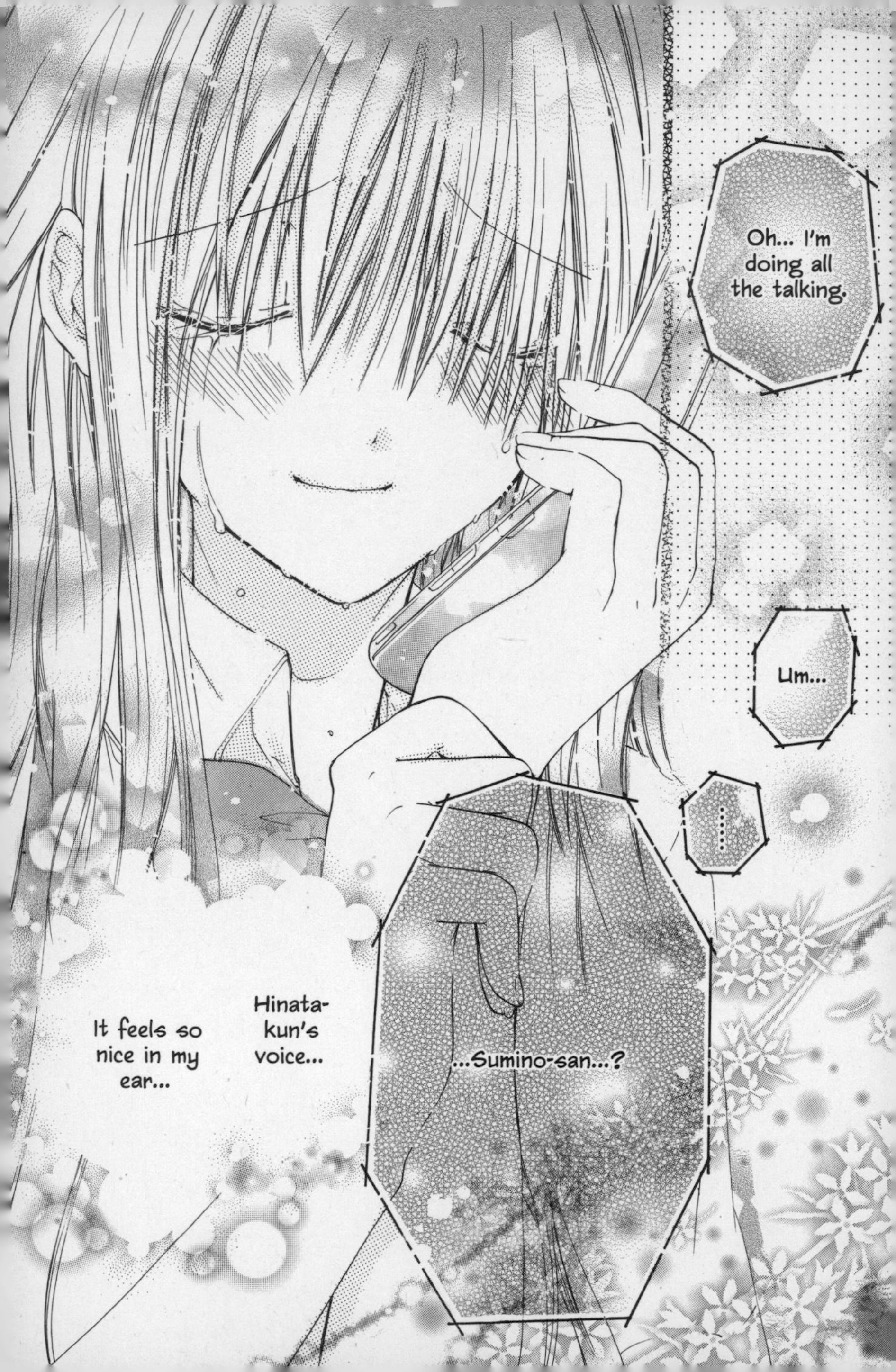
Oh... I'm doing all the talking.
Um...
......
...Sumino-san...?
Hinata-kun's voice...
It feels so nice in my ear...

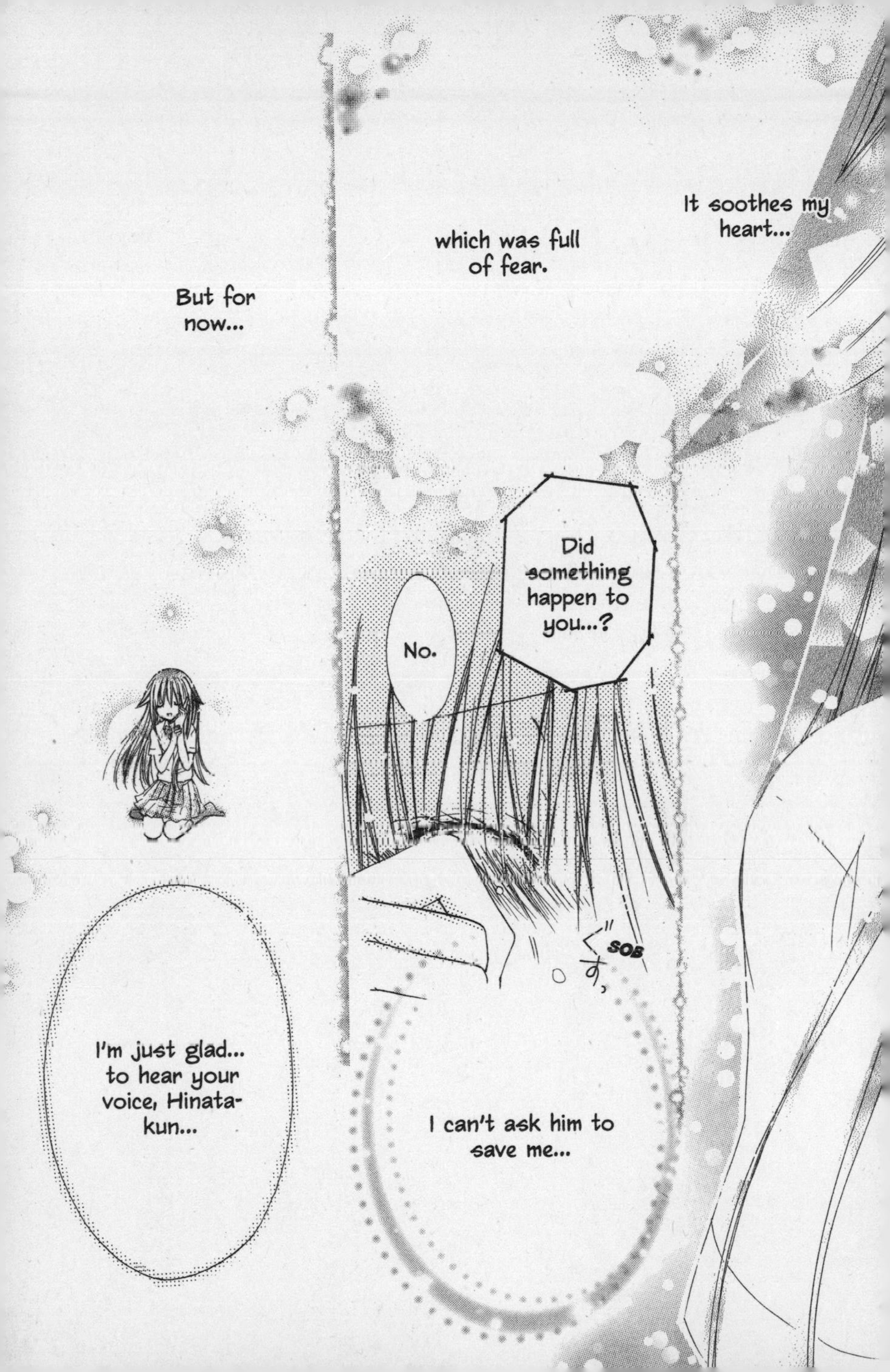
It soothes my heart...
which was full of fear.
Did something happen to you...?
No.
SOB
I can't ask him to save me...
But for now...
I'm just glad... to hear your voice, Hinata-kun...

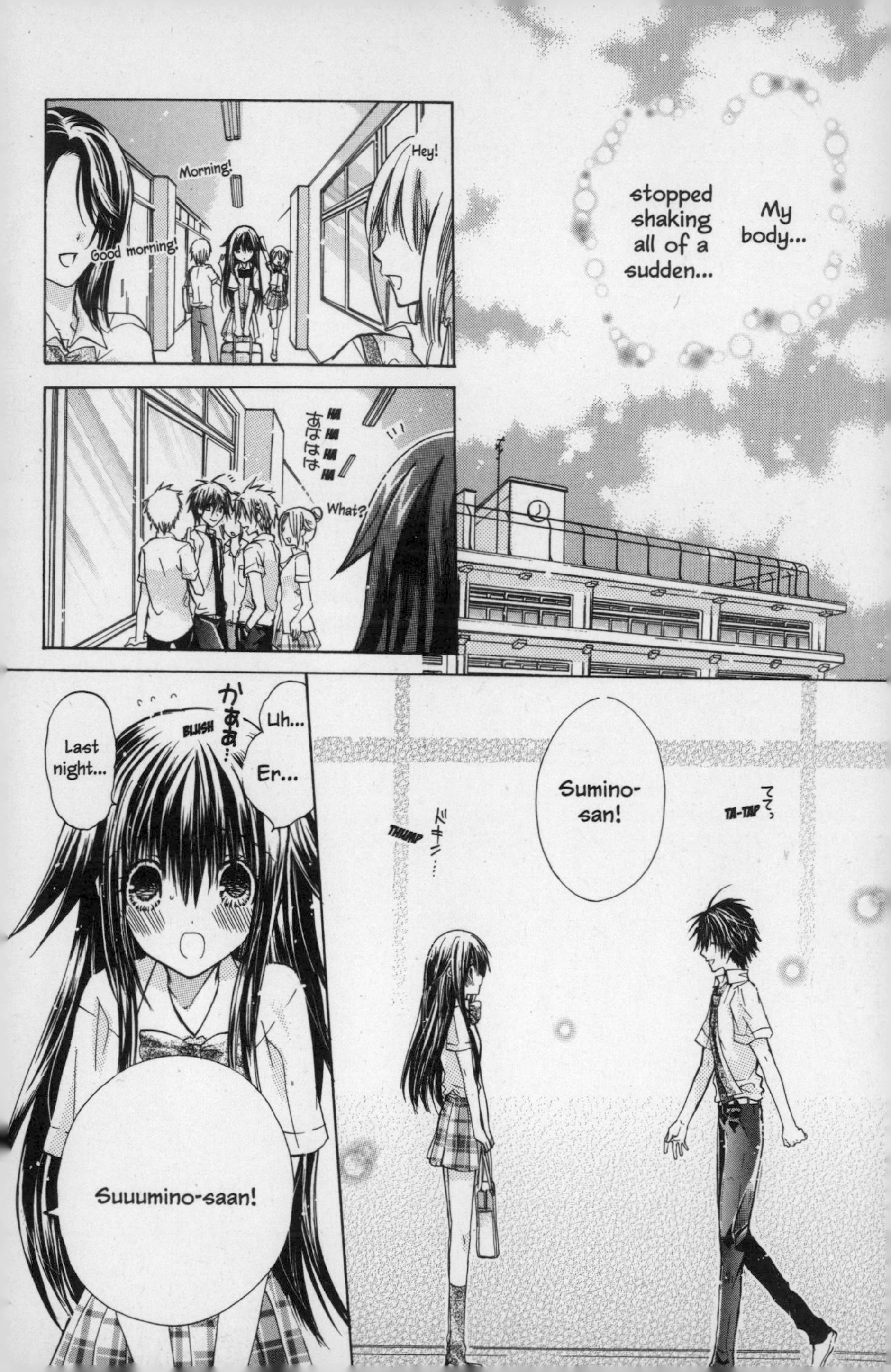
My body...
stopped shaking all of a sudden...
Hey!
Morning!
Good morning!
HA HA HA HA
あははは
What?
TA-TAP
てて
Sumino-san!
THUMP
ドキーン…
Uh...
Er...
BLUSH
かあぁ…
Last night...
Suuumino-saan!

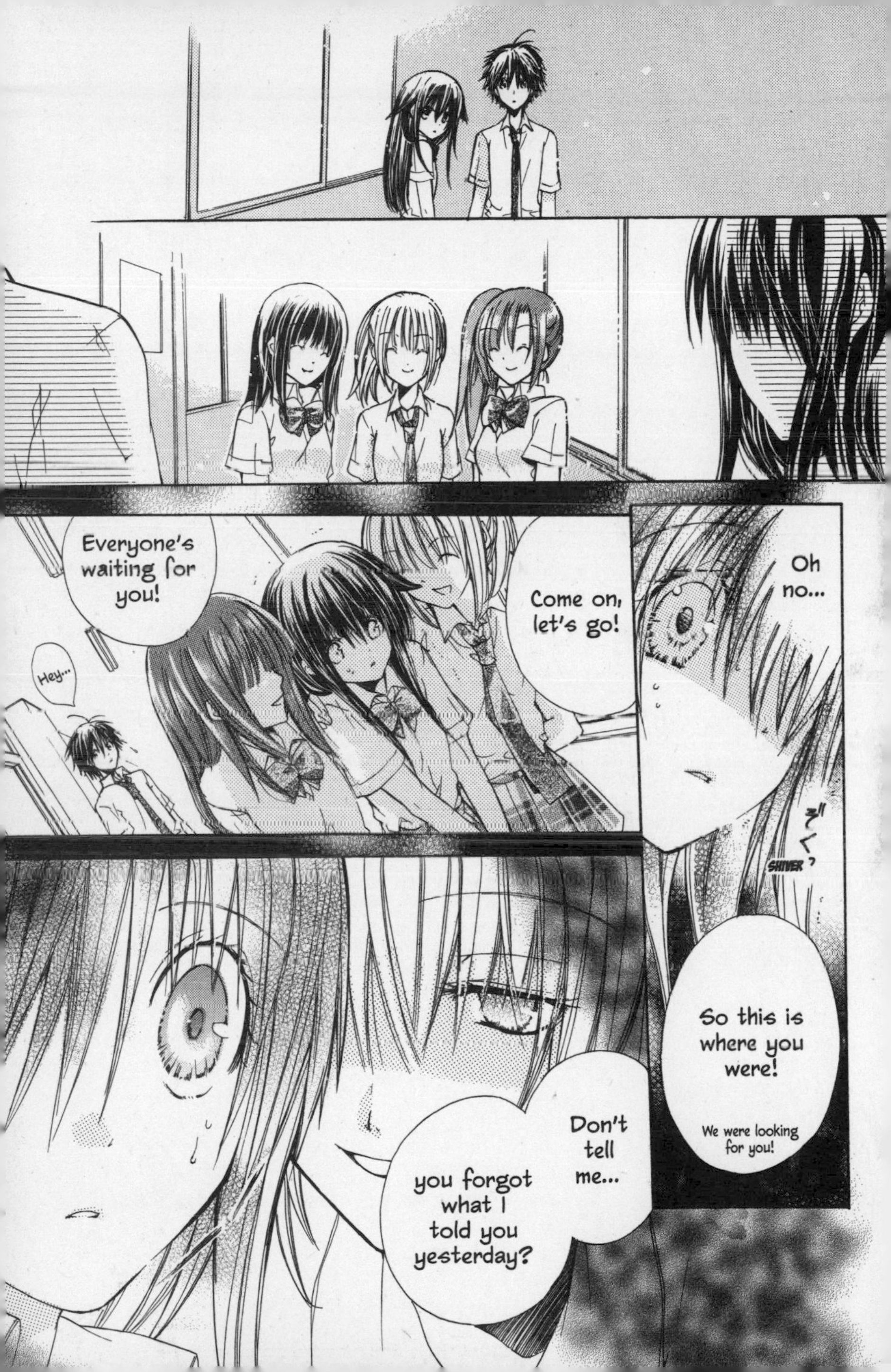
Oh no...
Come on, let's go!
Everyone's waiting for you!
Hey...
SHIVER
So this is where you were!
We were looking for you!
Don't tell me...
you forgot what I told you yesterday?

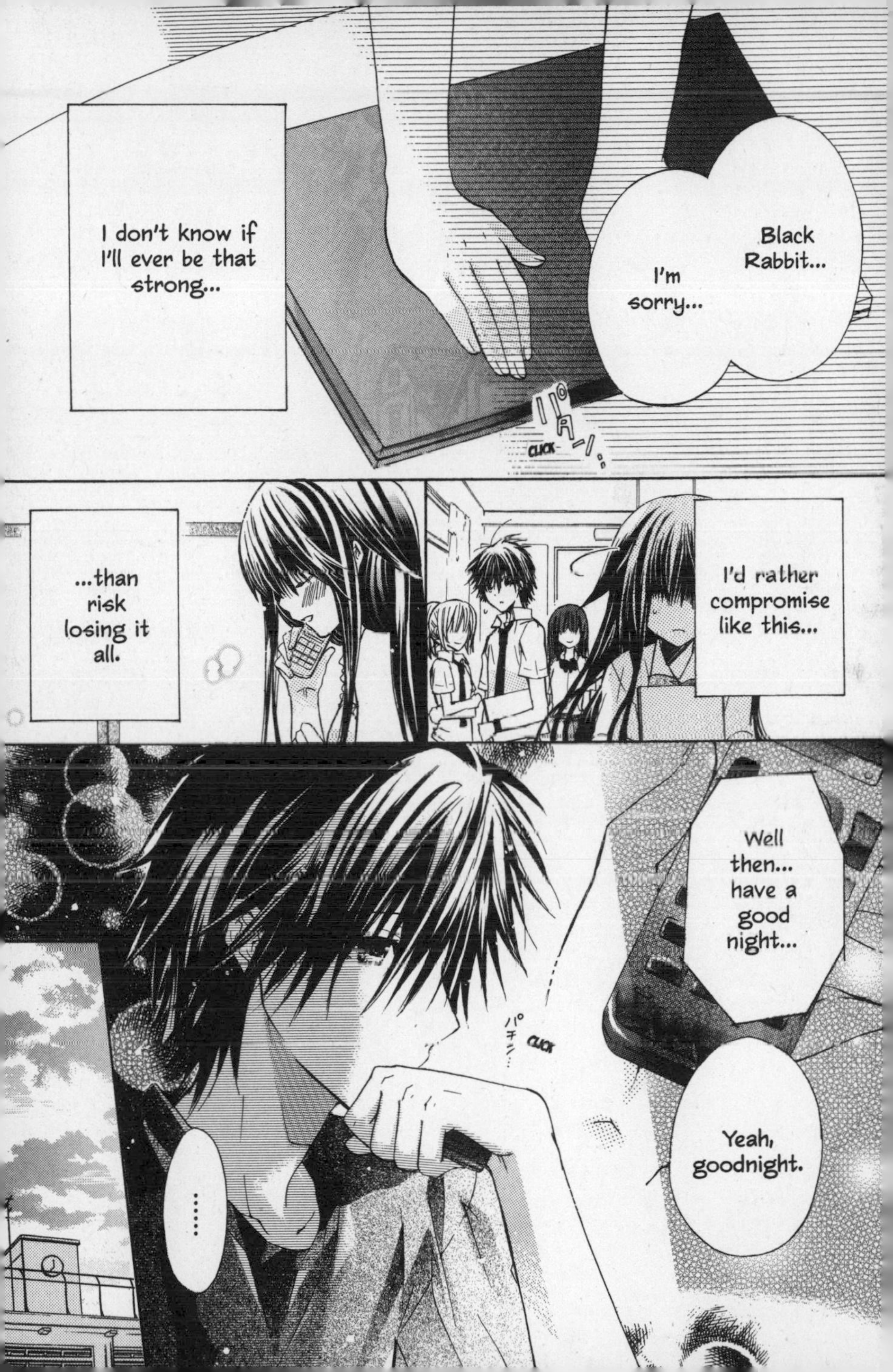
Black Rabbit... I'm sorry...
I don't know if I'll ever be that strong...
CLICK
I'd rather compromise like this...
...than risk losing it all.
Well then... have a good night...
CLICK
Yeah, goodnight.
......

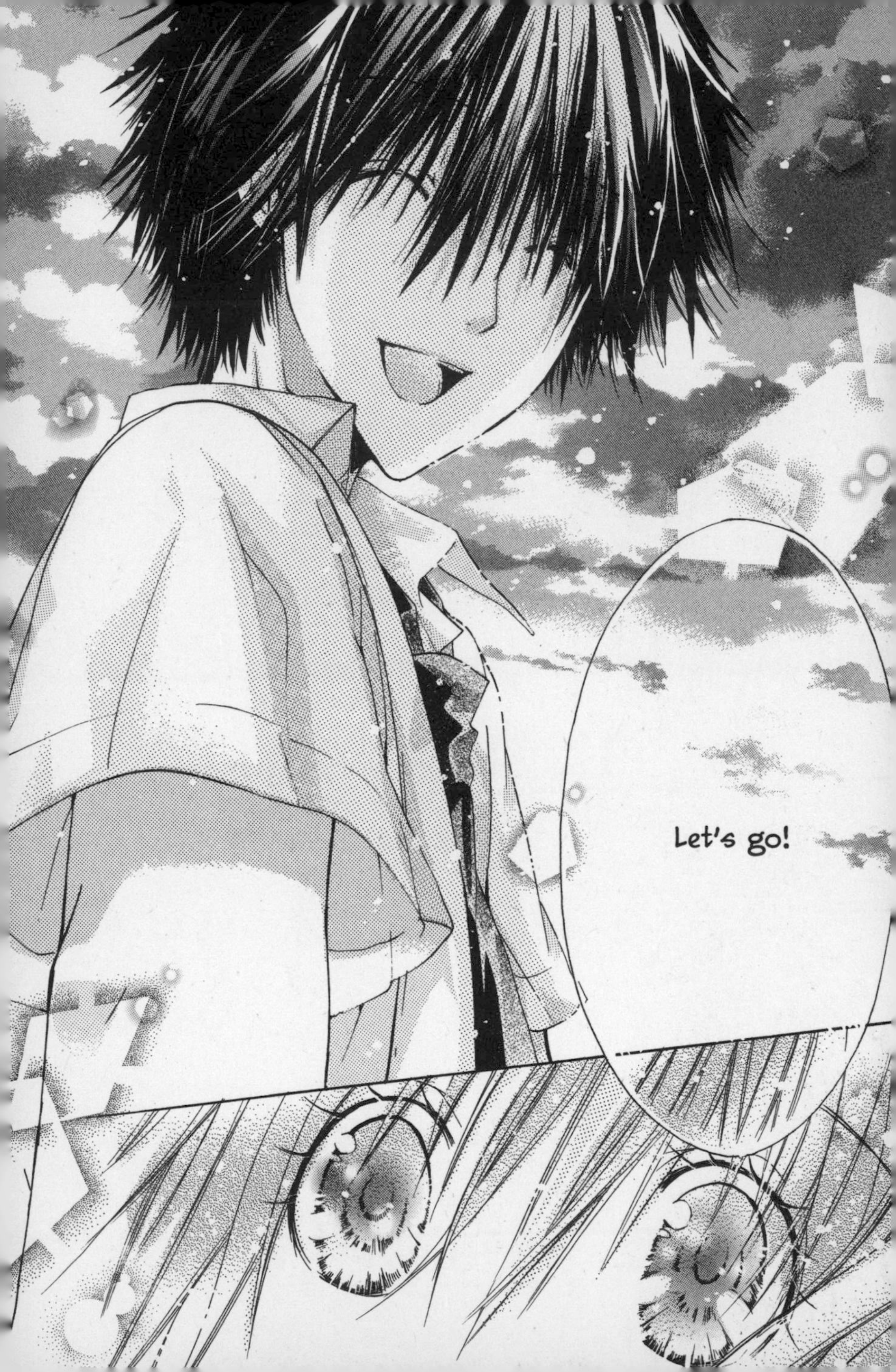
Let's go!

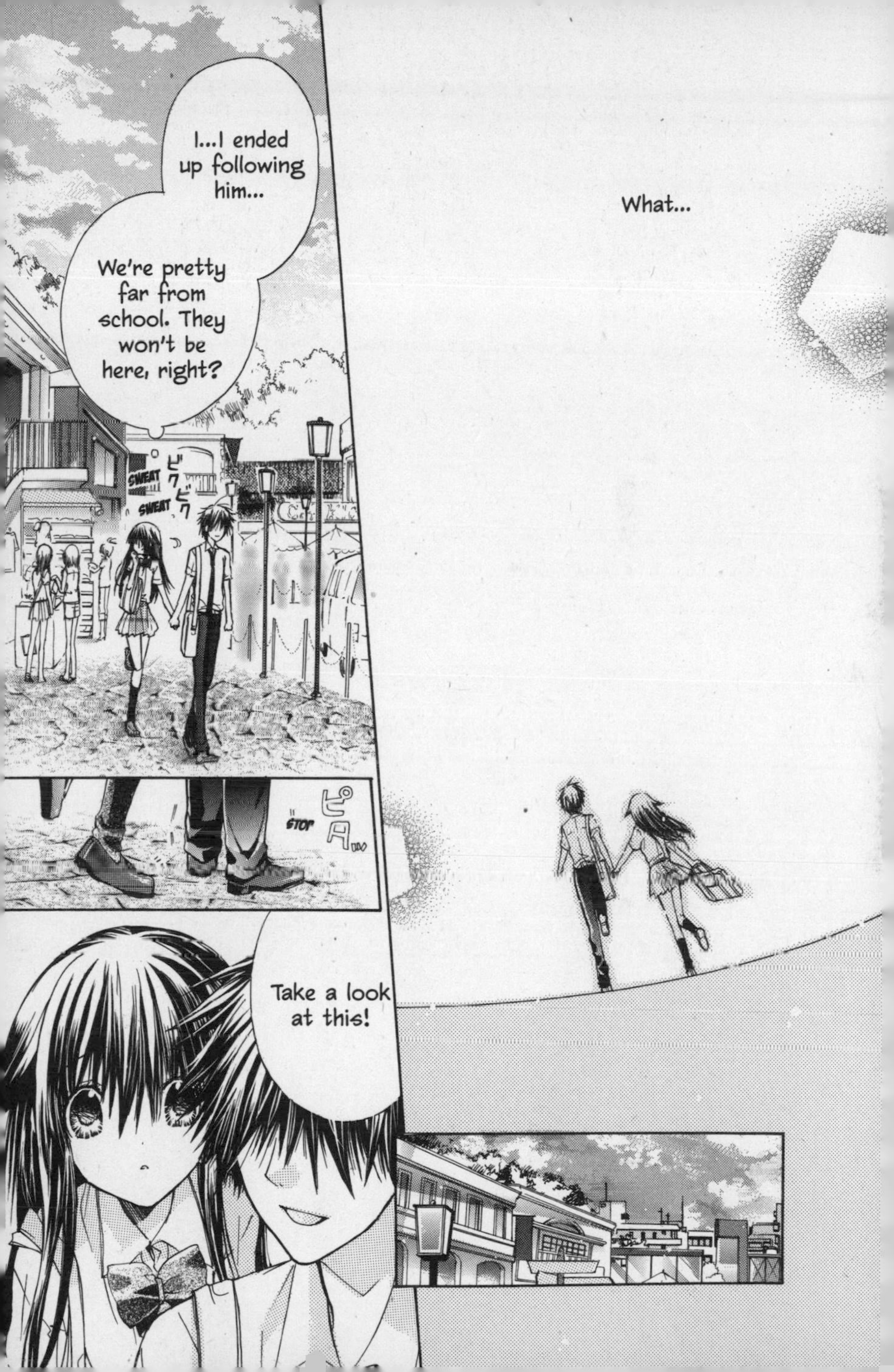
What...
I...I ended up following him...
We're pretty far from school. They won't be here, right?
SWEAT
SWEAT
STOP
Take a look at this!

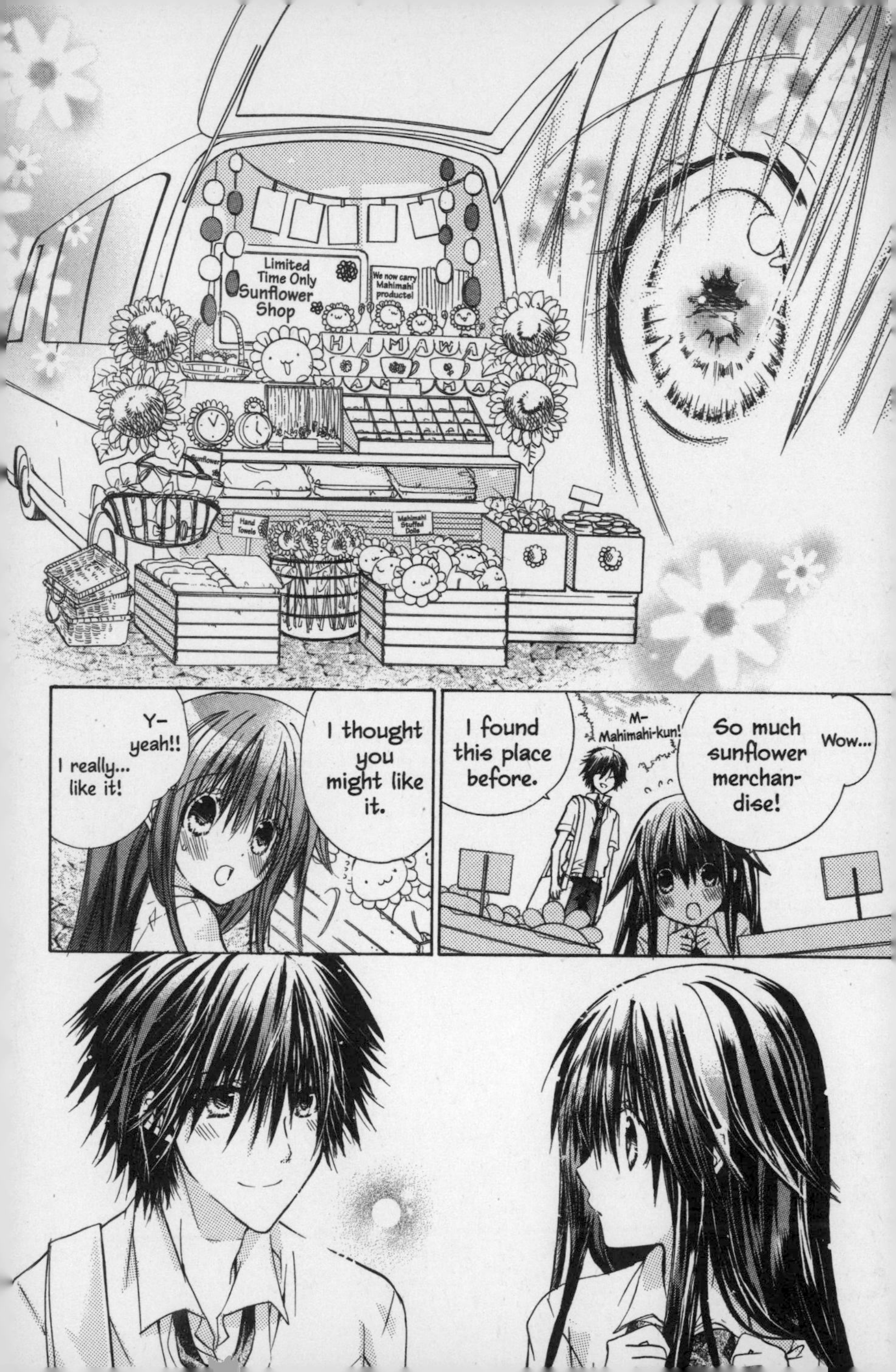
Limited Time Only Sunflower Shop
We now carry Mahimahi products!
Sunflower
Hand Towels
Mahimahi Stuffed Dolls
Wow...
So much sunflower merchan-dise!
M-Mahimahi-kun!
I found this place before.
I thought you might like it.
Y-yeah!!
I really... like it!

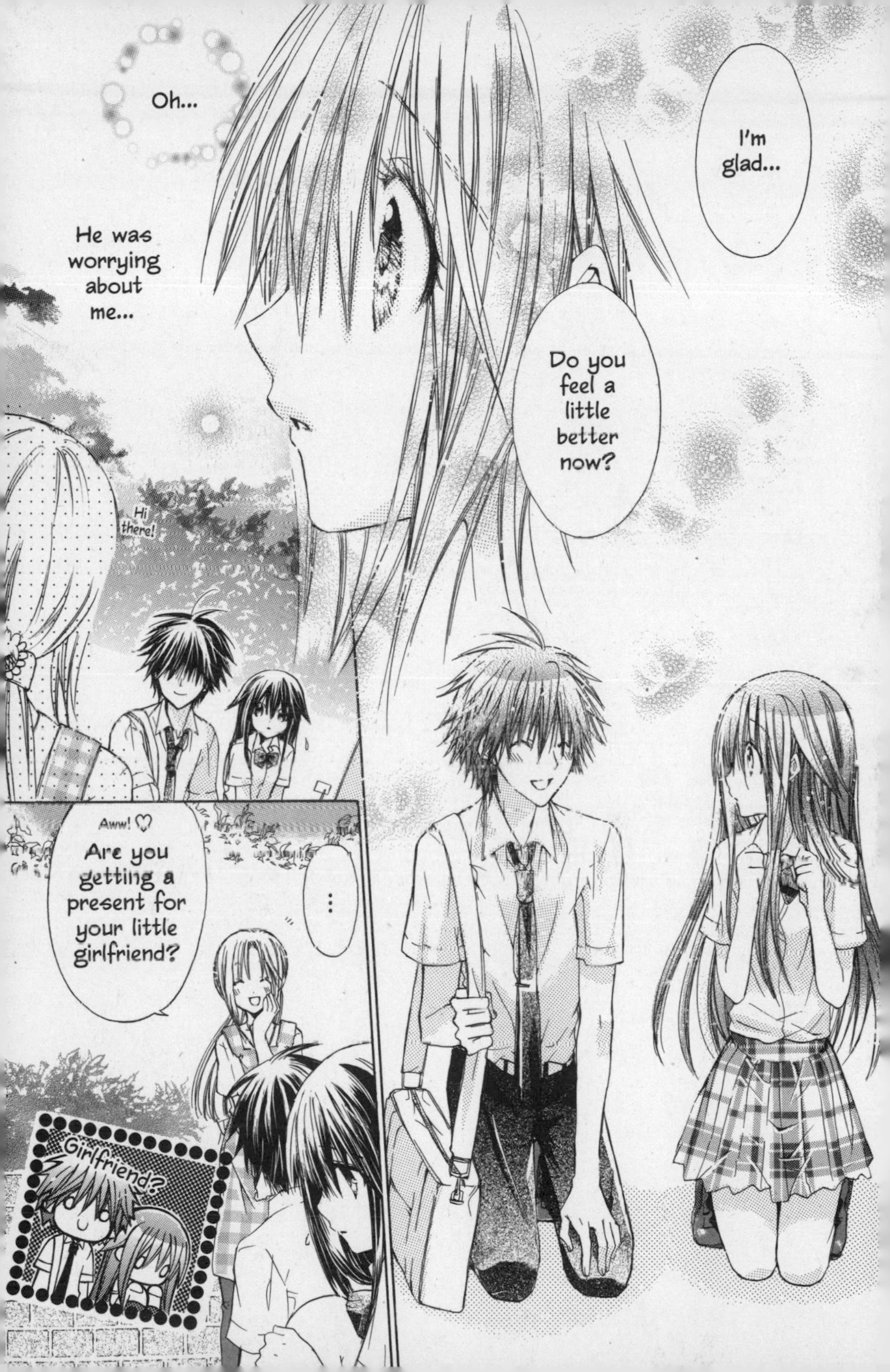
I'm glad...
Do you feel a little better now?
Oh...
He was worrying about me...
Hi there!
...
Aww! ♡
Are you getting a present for your little girlfriend?
Girlfriend?

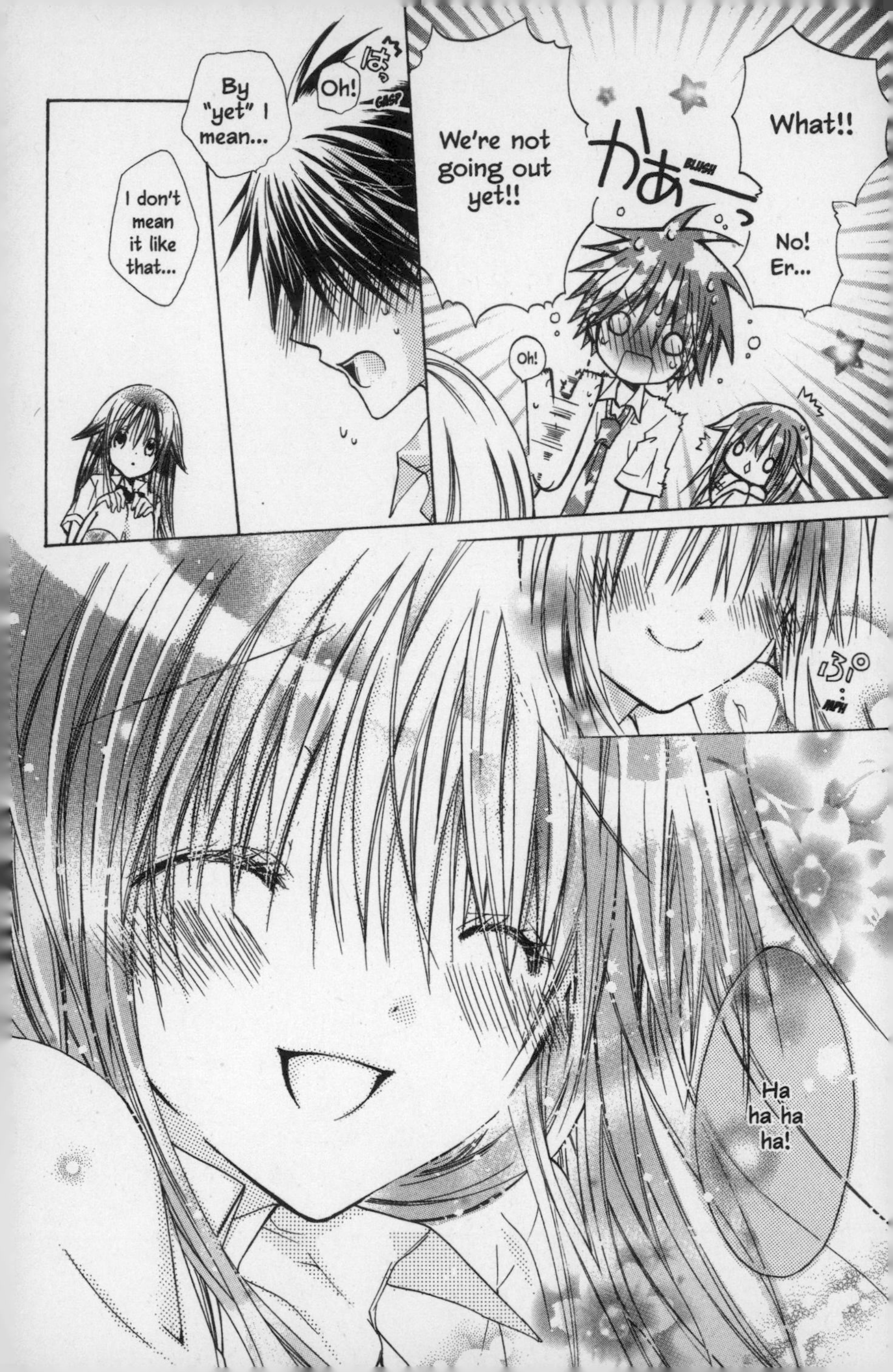

What!!
かあー
BLUSH
No! Er...
We're not going out yet!!
Oh!
ぱっ
GASP
Oh!
By "yet" I mean...
I don't mean it like that...
ぷ
MPH
Ha ha ha ha!

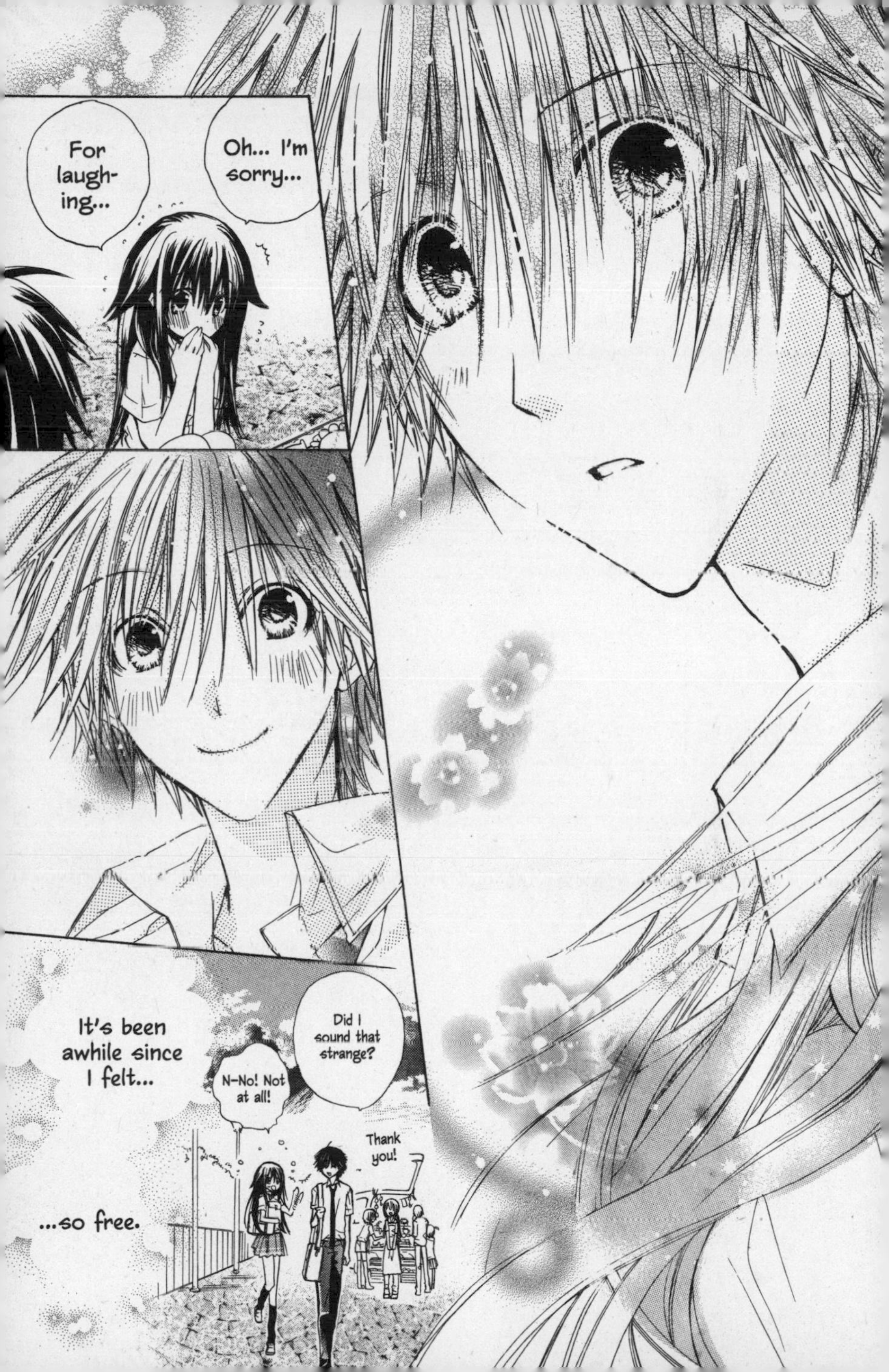
Oh... I'm sorry...
For laughing...
Did I sound that strange?
N-No! Not at all!
Thank you!
It's been awhile since I felt...
...so free.

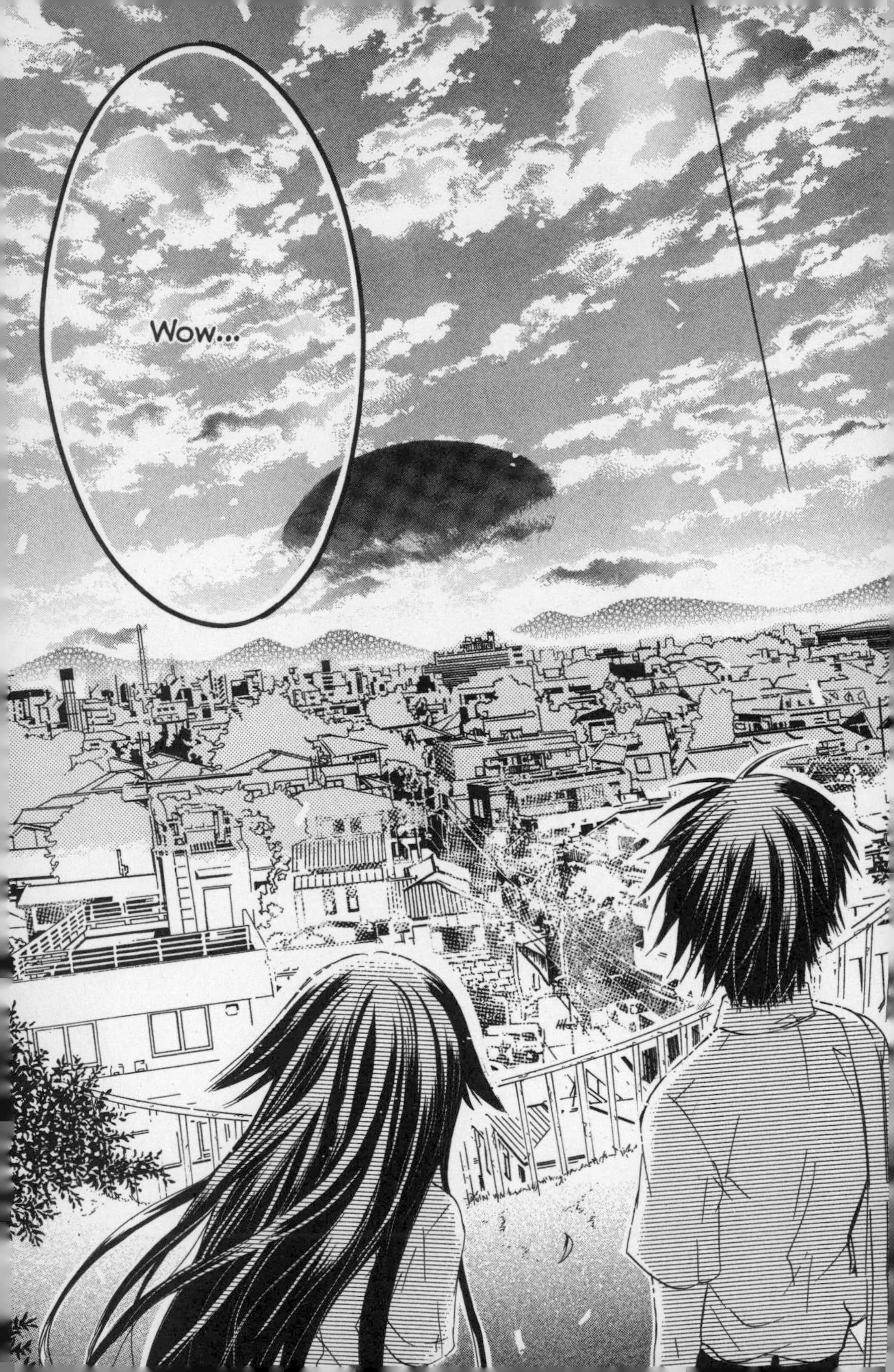
Wow...

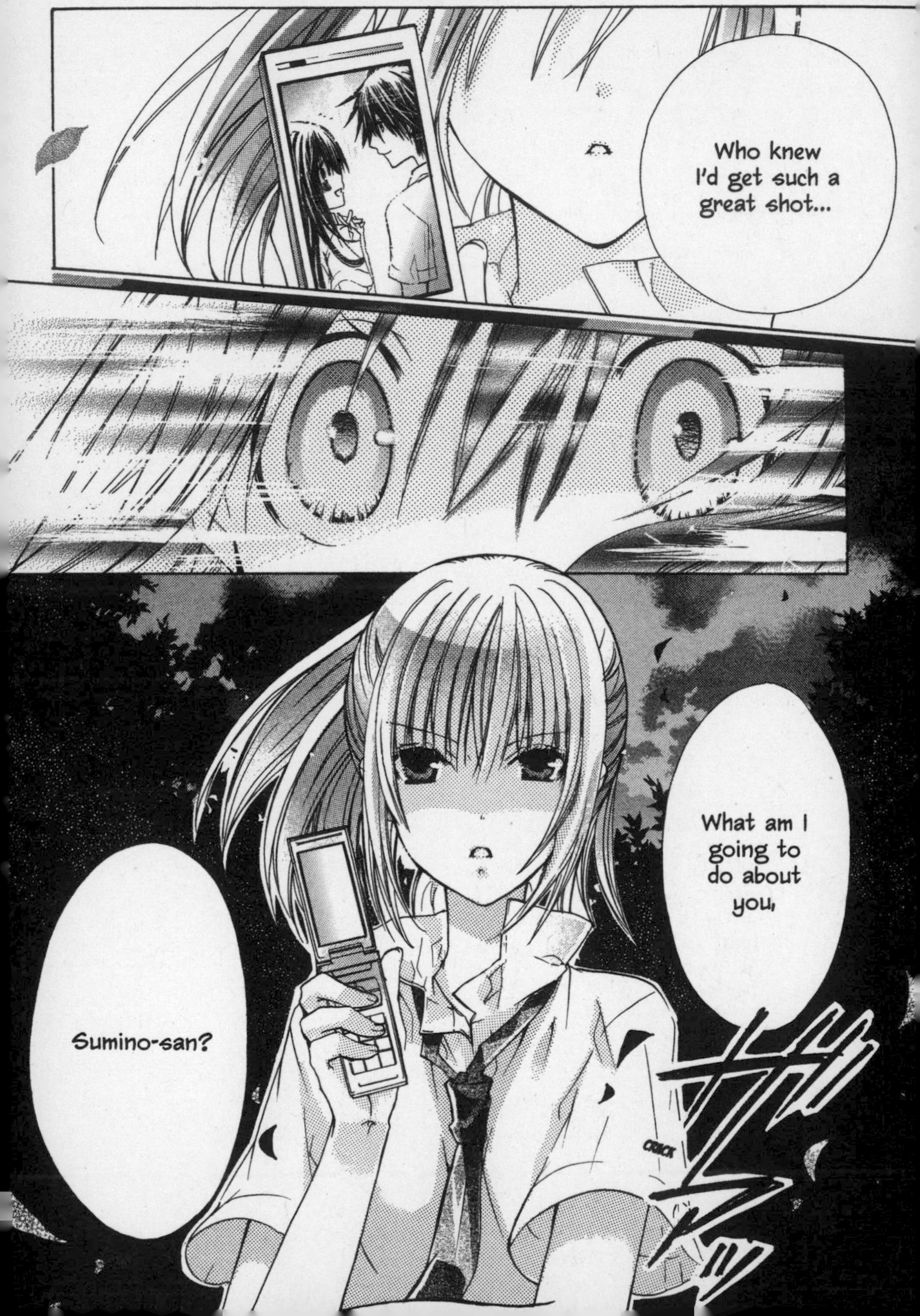
Who knew I'd get such a great shot...
What am I going to do about you,
Sumino-san?
CRACK

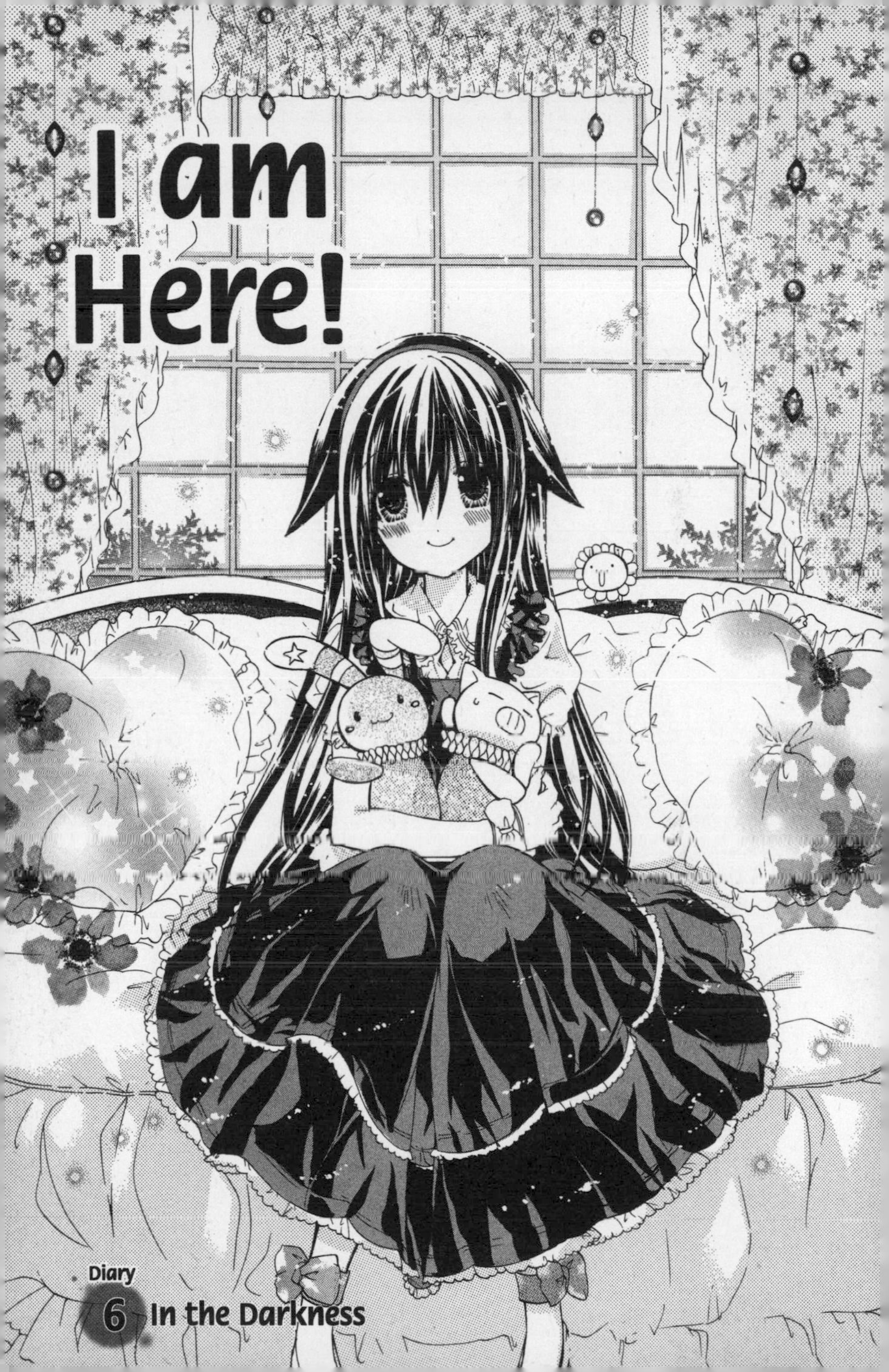
I am Here!
Diary
6 In the Darkness

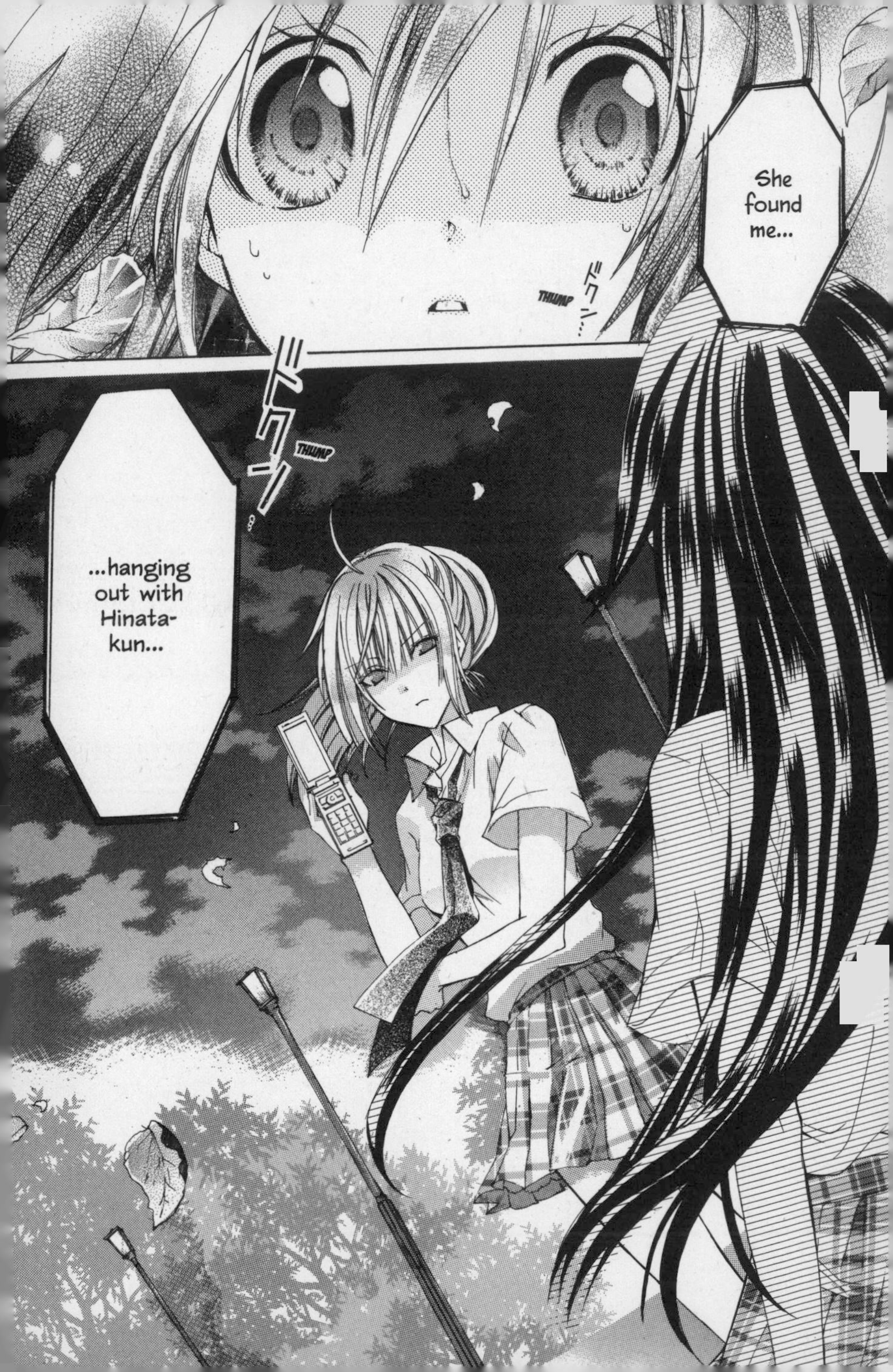
She found me...
THUMP
ドクン…
ドクン…
THUMP
...hanging out with Hinata-kun...

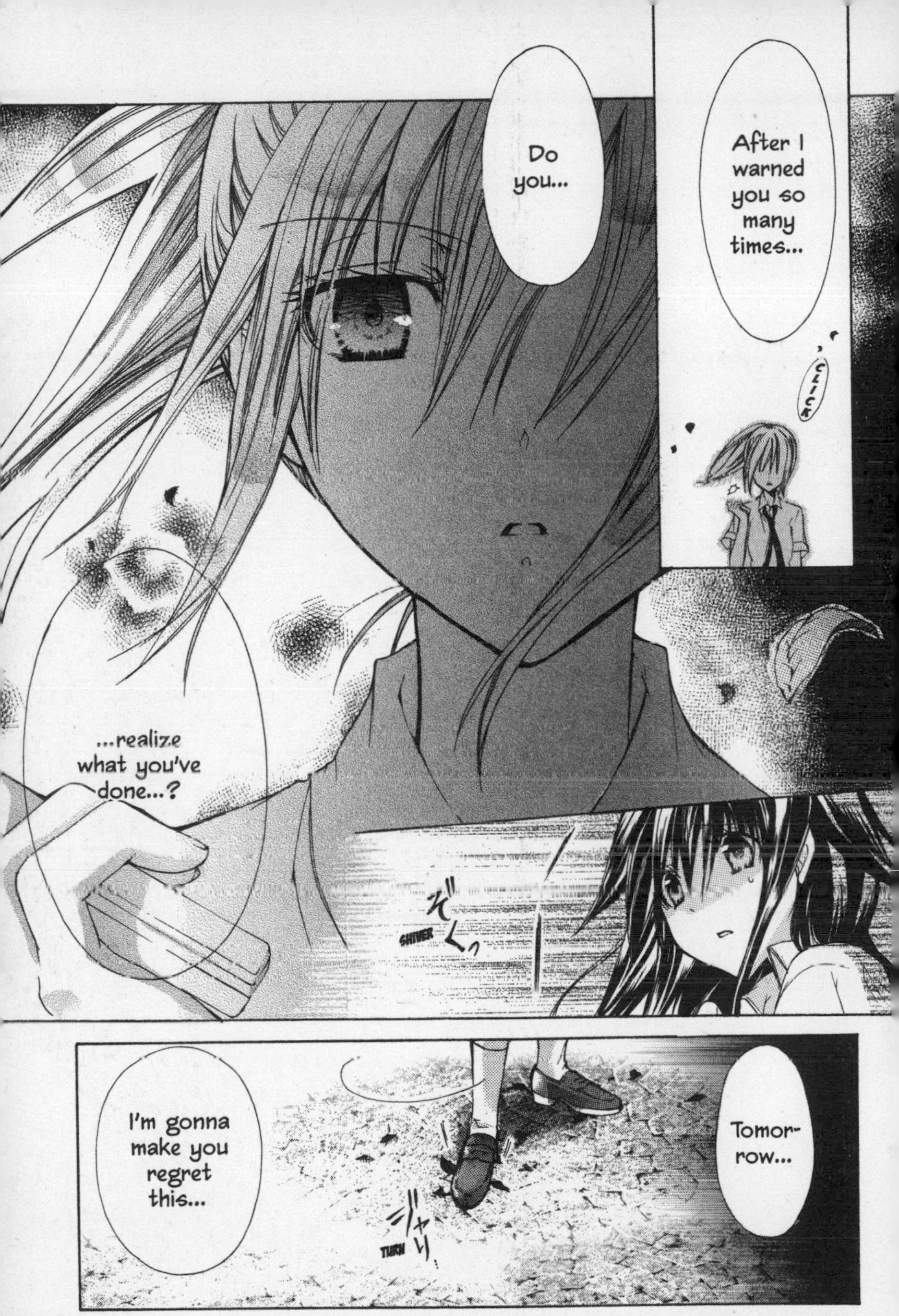
After I warned you so many times...
CLICK
Do you...
...realize what you've done...?
SHIVER
ぞくっ
Tomor-row...
I'm gonna make you regret this...
TURN
ジャリ

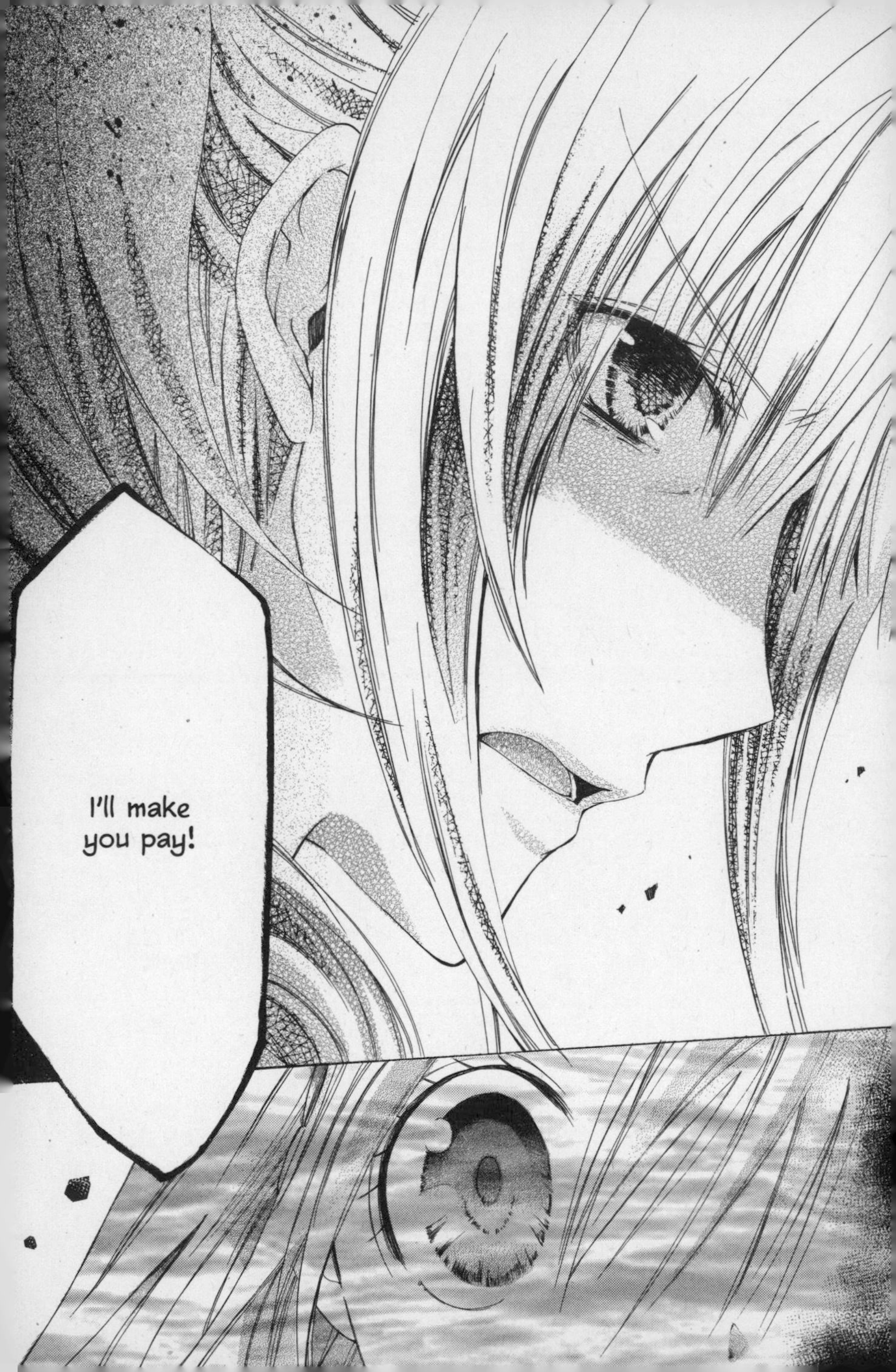
I'll make you pay!

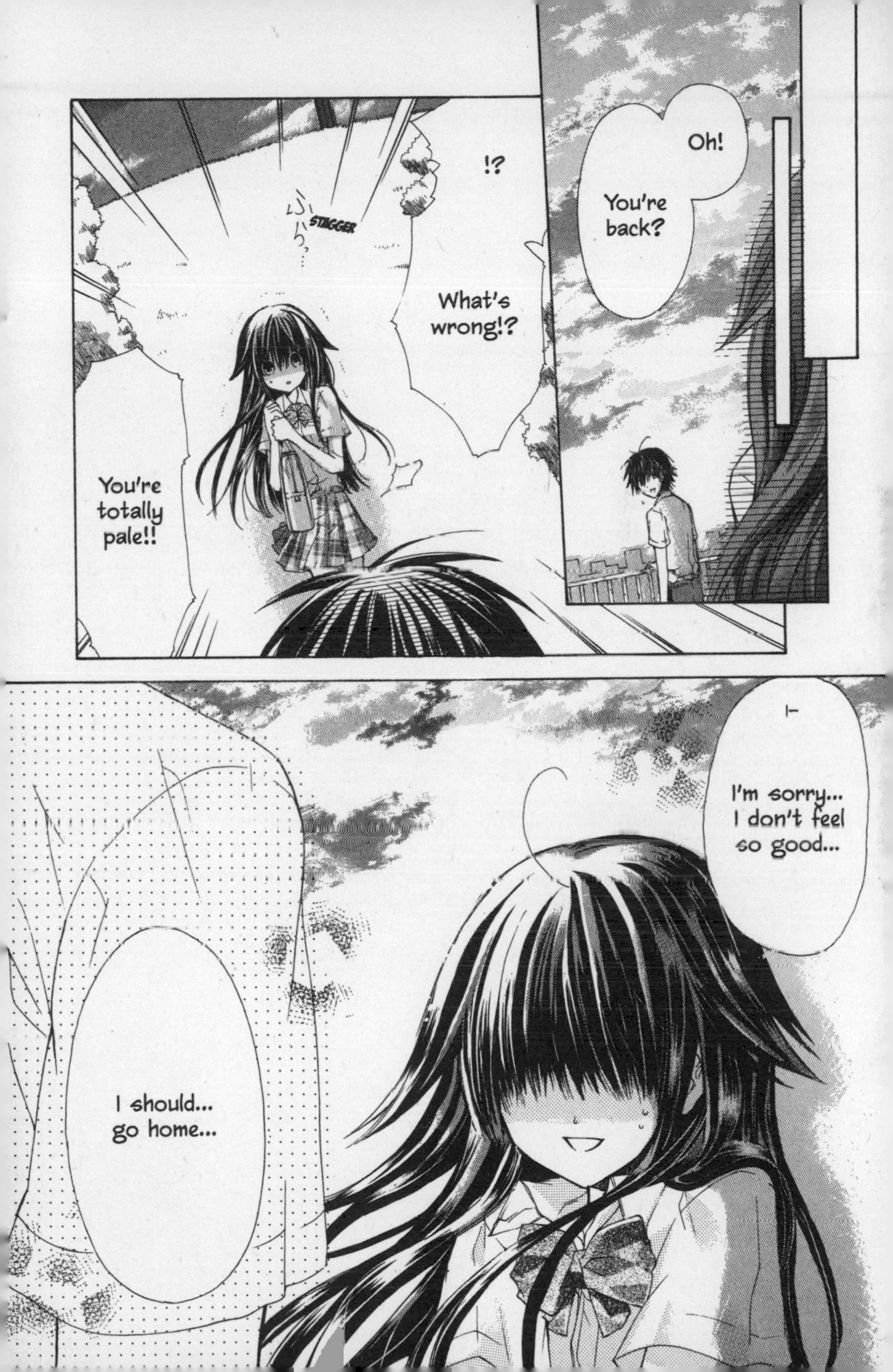
Oh!
You're back?
!?
STAGGER
What's wrong!?
You're totally pale!!
I–
I'm sorry... I don't feel so good...
I should... go home...

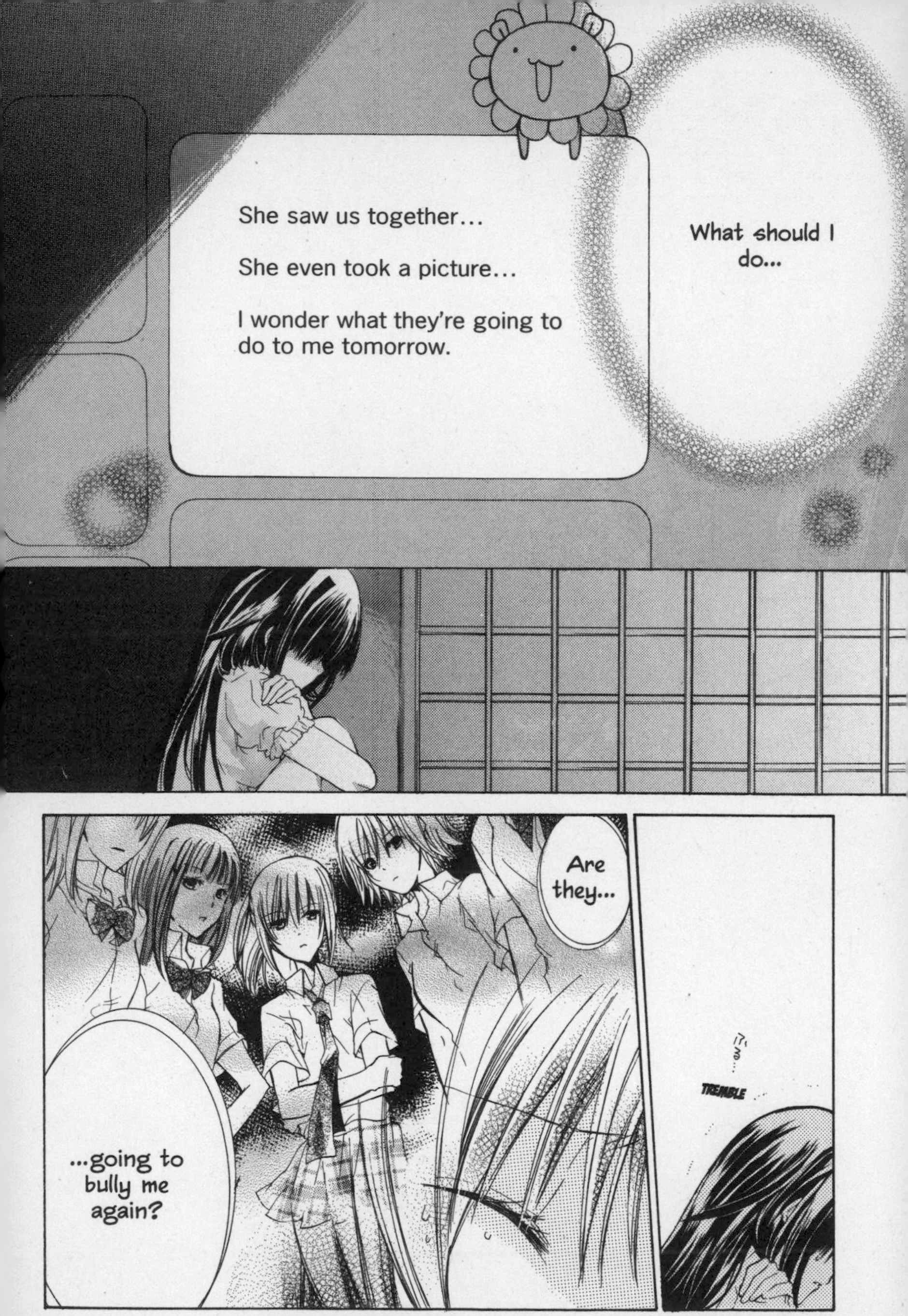
She saw us together...
She even took a picture...
I wonder what they're going to do to me tomorrow.
What should I do...
ぶる...
TREMBLE
Are they...
...going to bully me again?

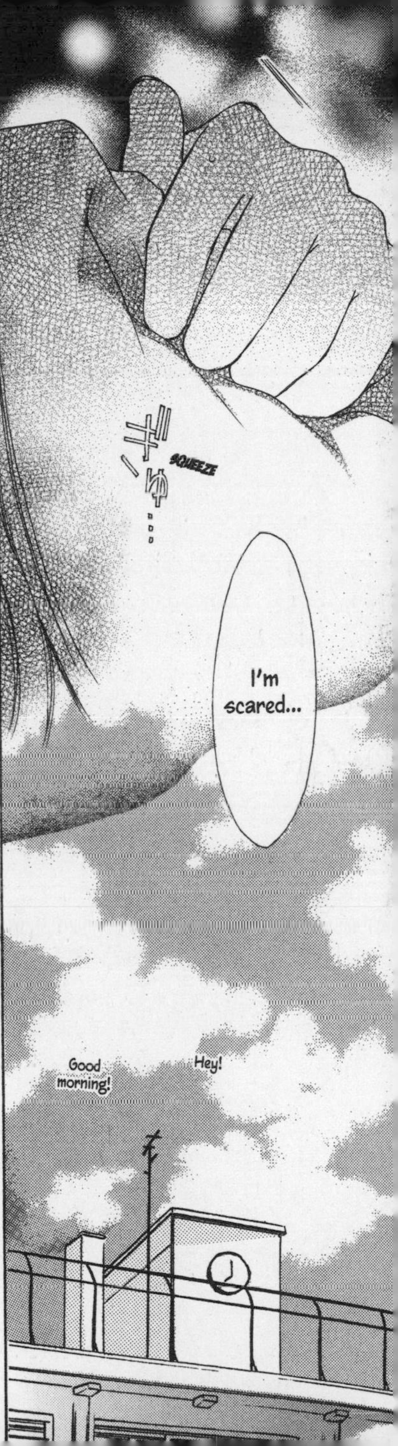
ぎゅ…
SQUEEZE
I'm scared...
Hey!
Good morning!

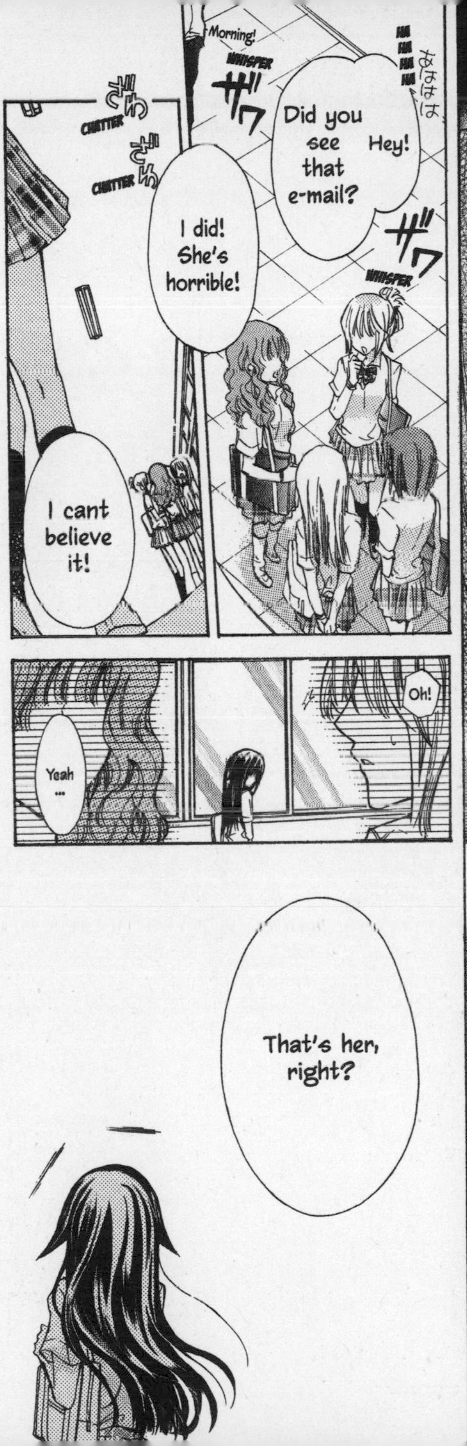
Morning!
HA HA HA HA
あははは
ザワ
WHISPER
Hey!
Did you see that e-mail?
ザワ
WHISPER
I did! She's horrible!
ざわ
CHATTER
ざわ
CHATTER
I cant believe it!
Oh!
Yeah ...
That's her, right?

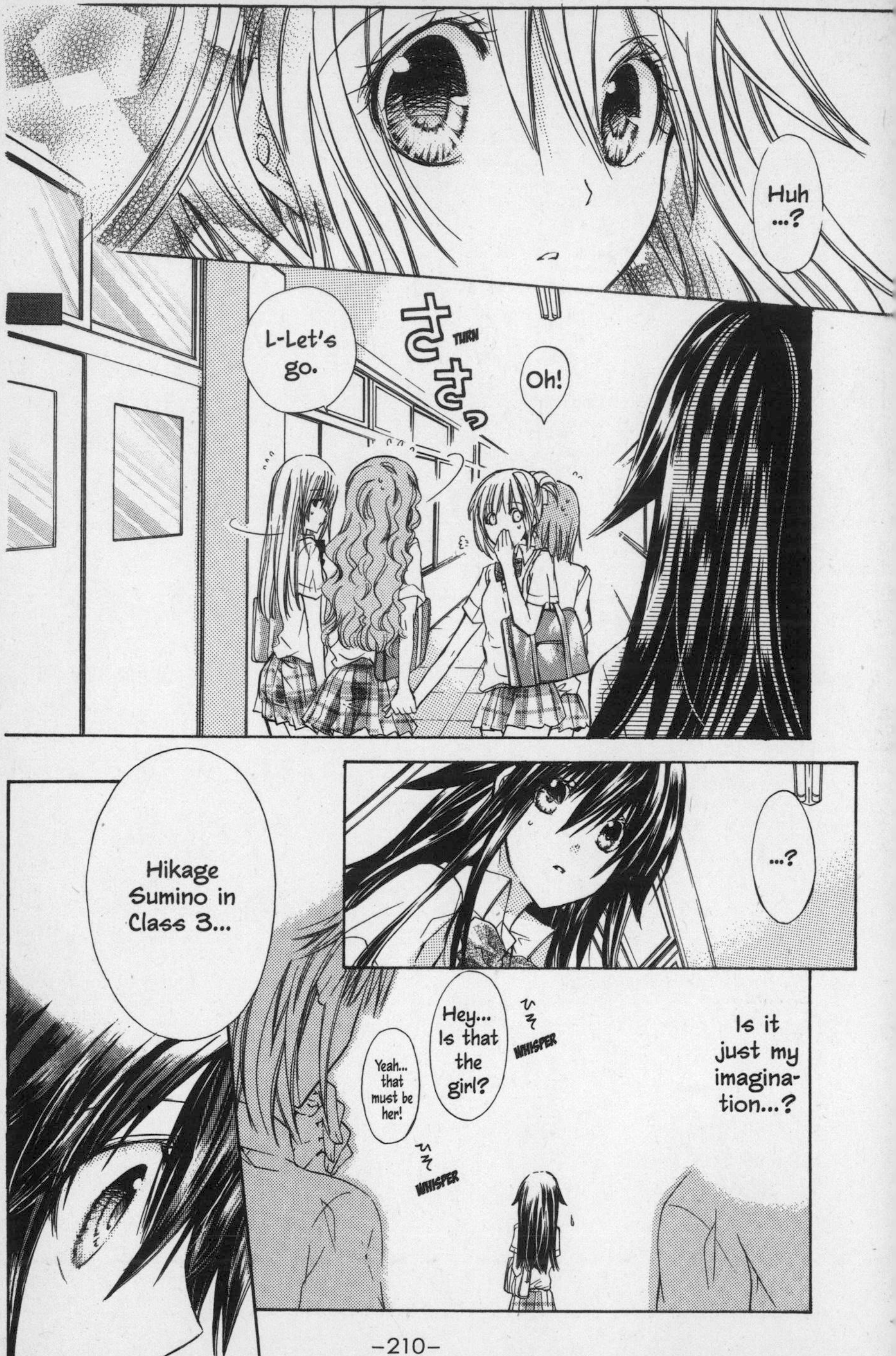

Huh ...?
Oh!
ささっ
TURN
L-Let's go.
...?
Is it just my imagination...?
Hey... Is that the girl?
ひそ
WHISPER
Yeah... that must be her!
ひそ
WHISPER
Hikage Sumino in Class 3...

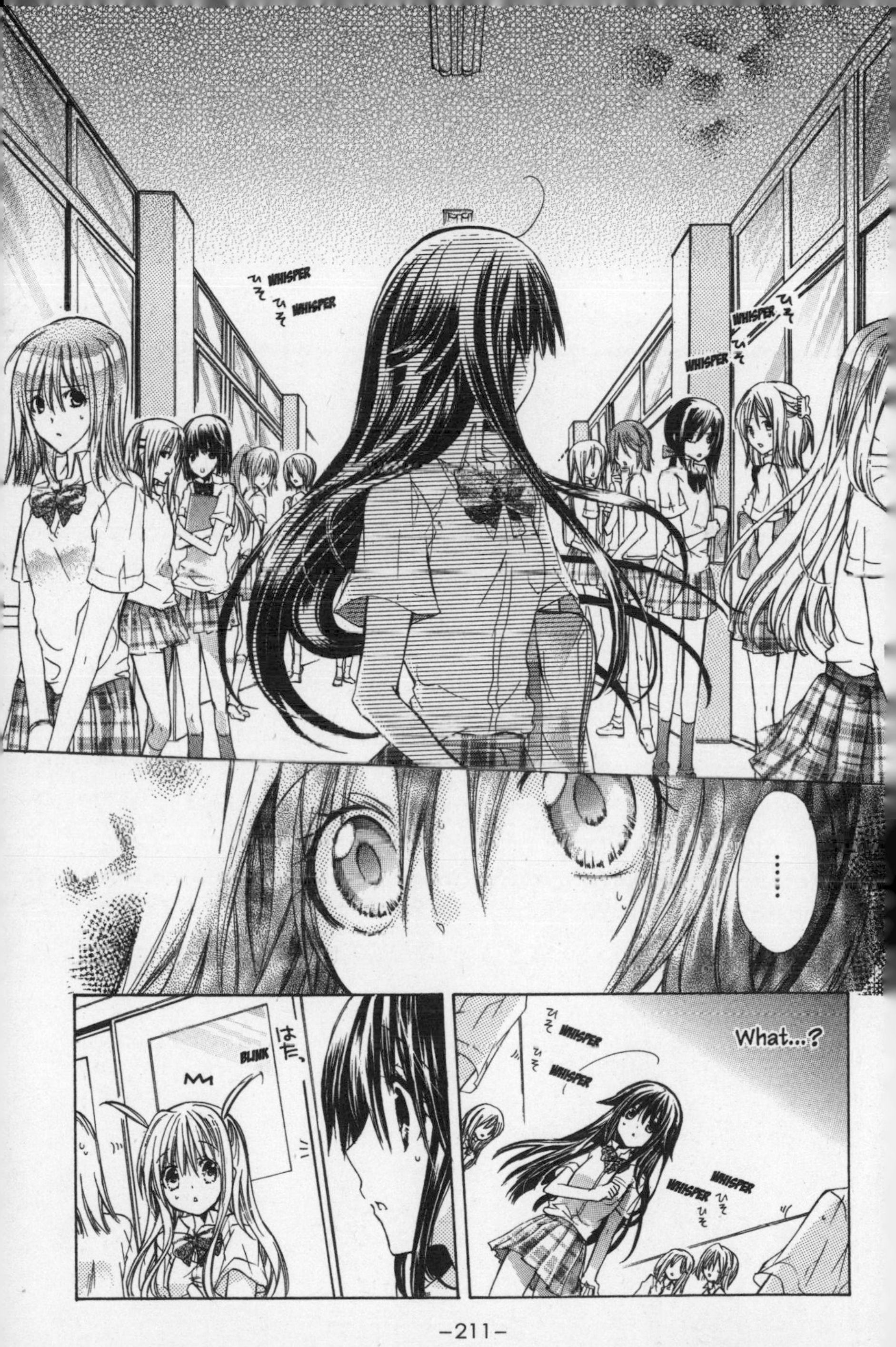

WHISPER ひそ
WHISPER ひそ
ひそ WHISPER
ひそ WHISPER
......
What...?
ひそ WHISPER
ひそ WHISPER
WHISPER ひそ
WHISPER ひそ
はた、
BLINK

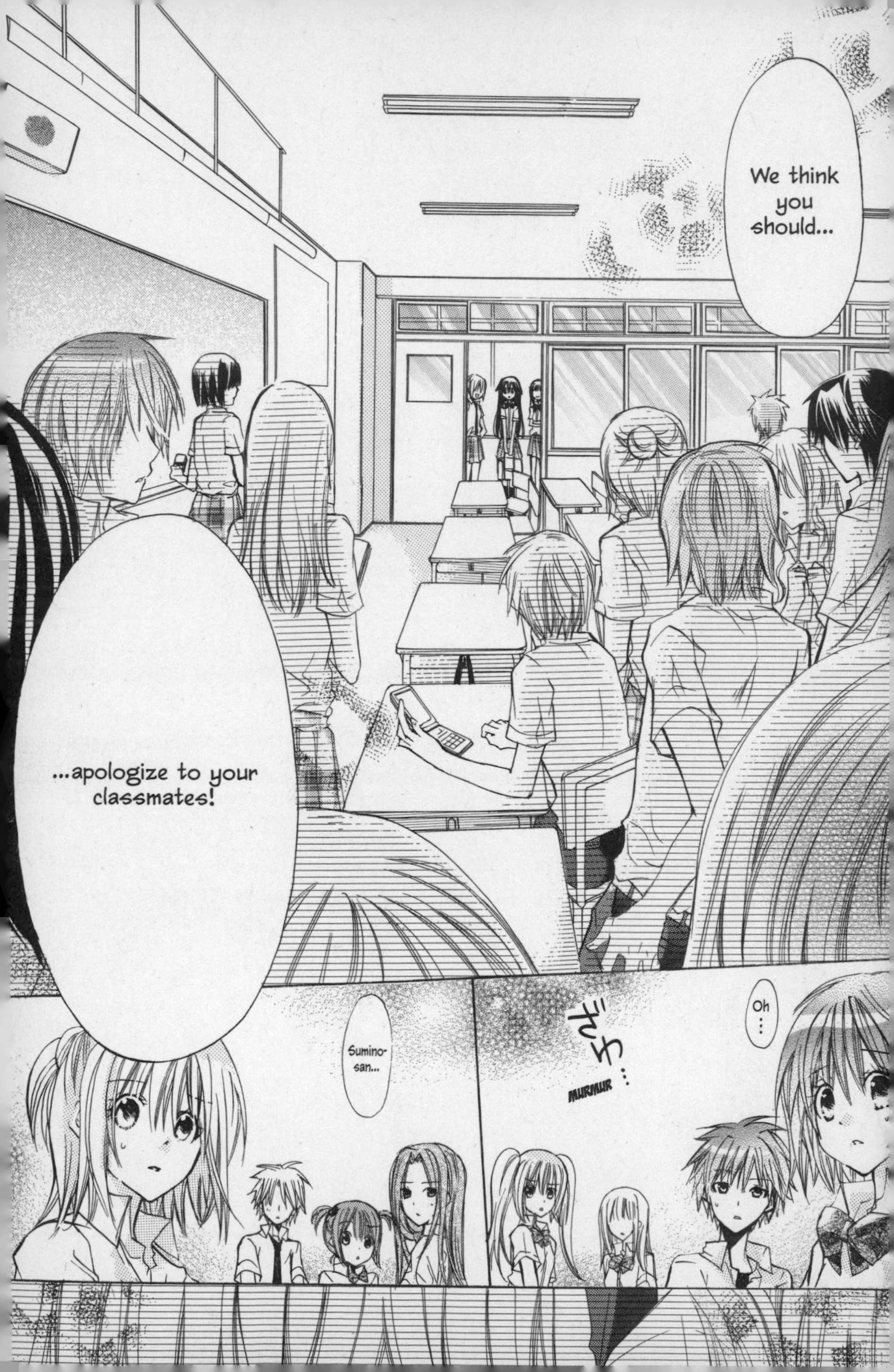
We think you should...
...apologize to your classmates!
Oh...
ざわ...
MURMUR
Sumino-san...

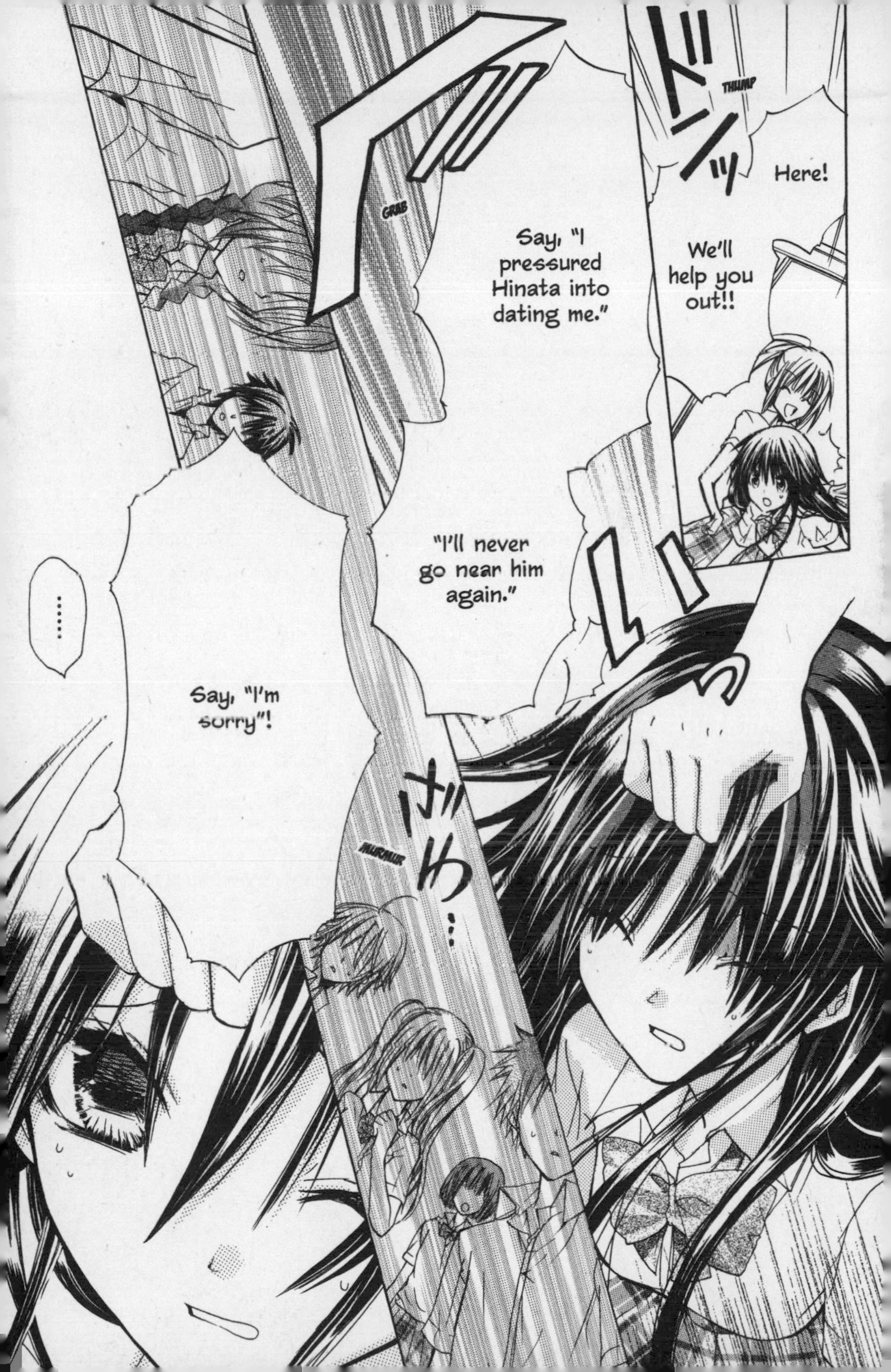
THUMP
Here!
We'll help you out!!
GRAB
Say, "I pressured Hinata into dating me."
"I'll never go near him again."
Say, "I'm sorry"!
......
MURMUR

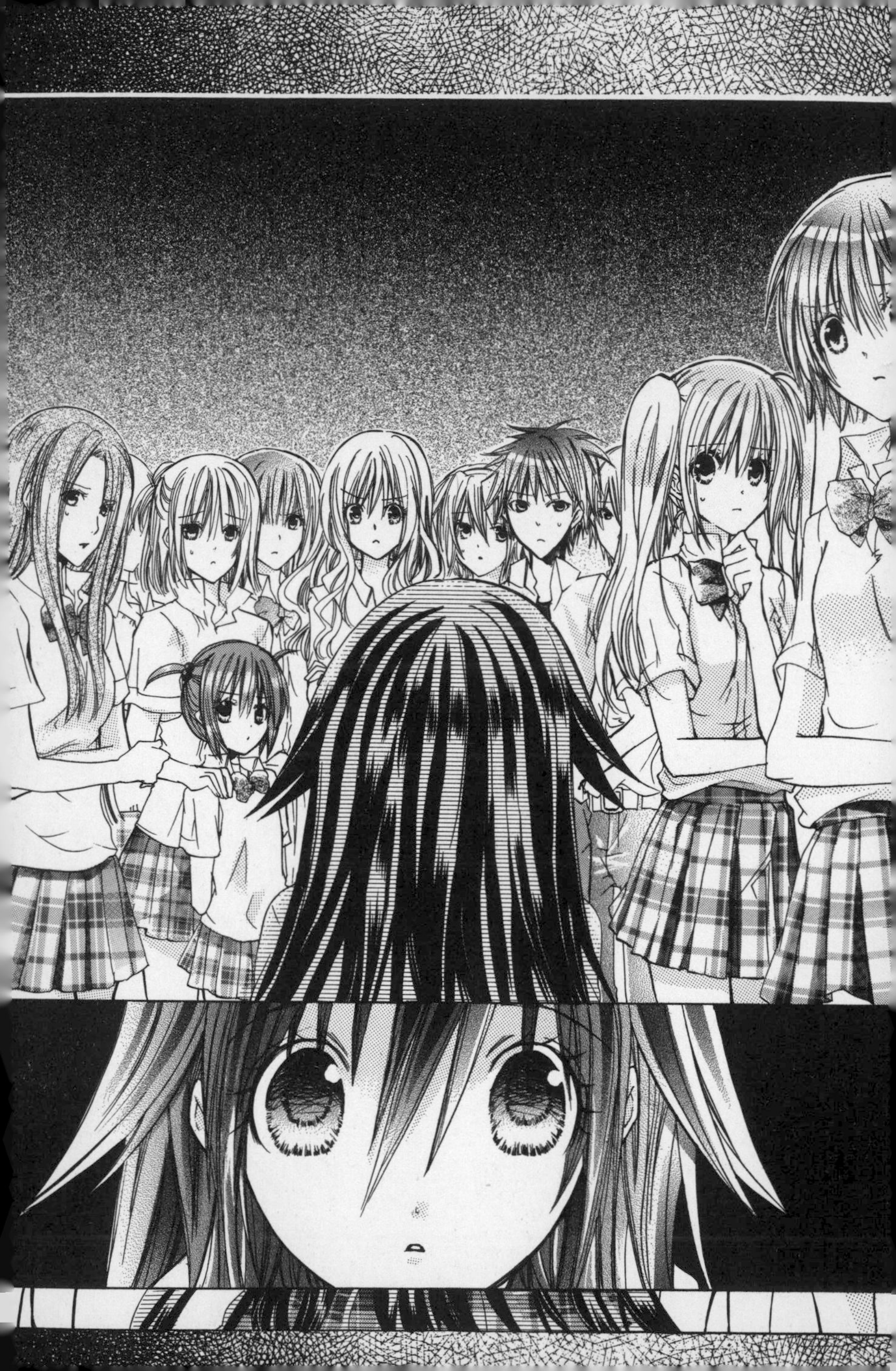

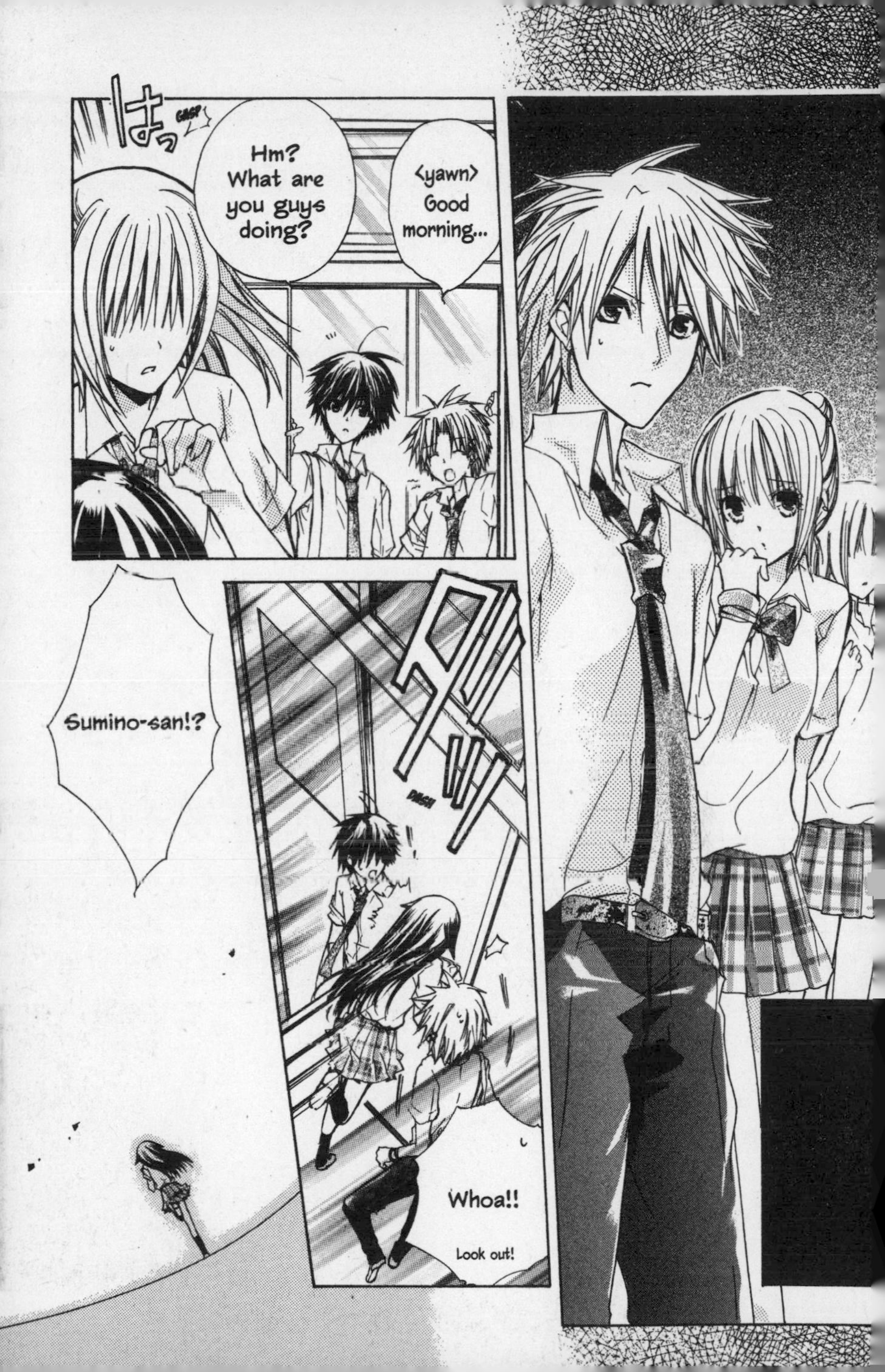
<yawn> Good morning...
Hm? What are you guys doing?
はっ GASP
DASH
Whoa!!
Look out!
Sumino-san!?

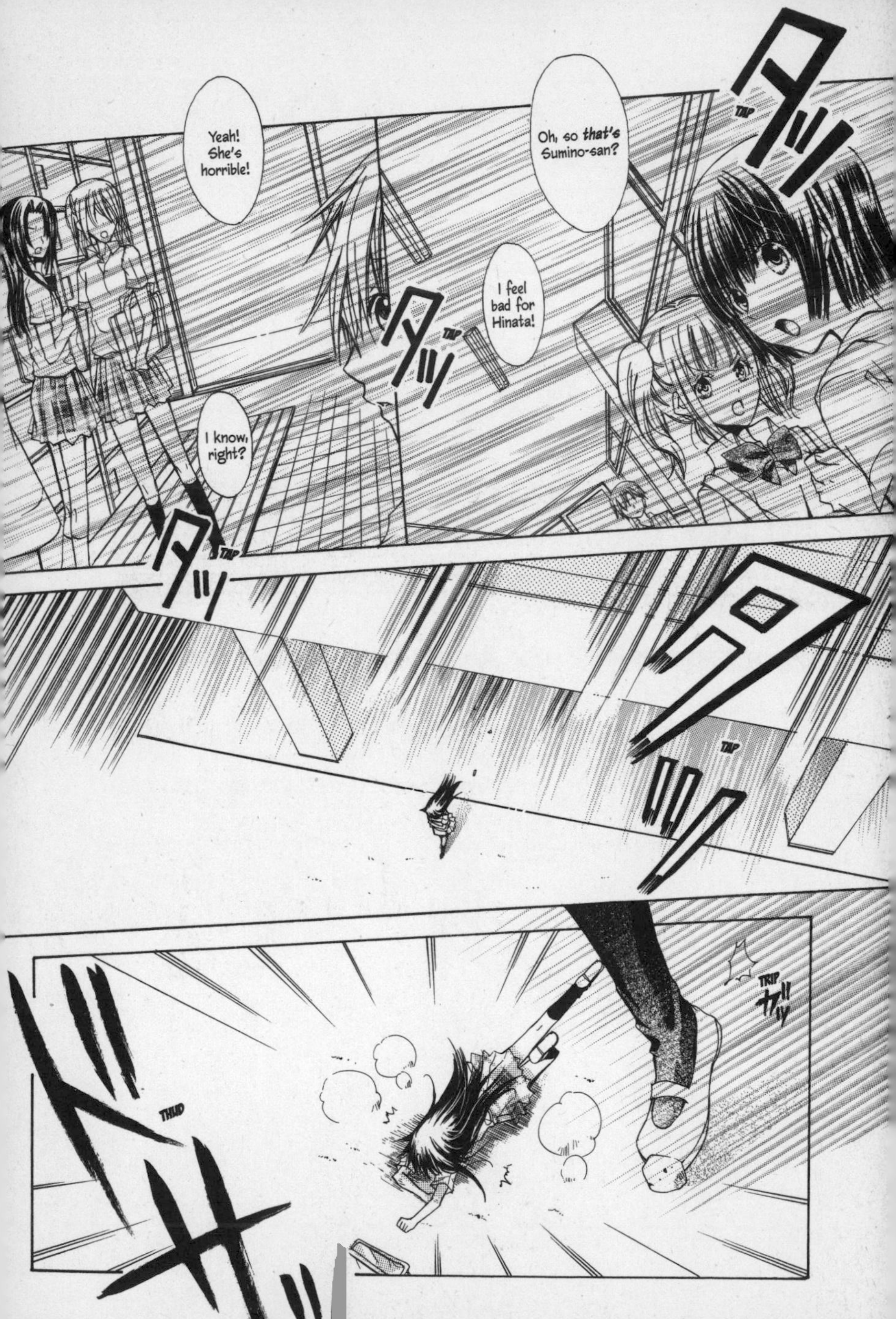
TAP
Oh, so *that's* Sumino-san?
I feel bad for Hinata!
TAP
Yeah! She's horrible!
I know, right?
TAP
TAP
TRIP
THUD

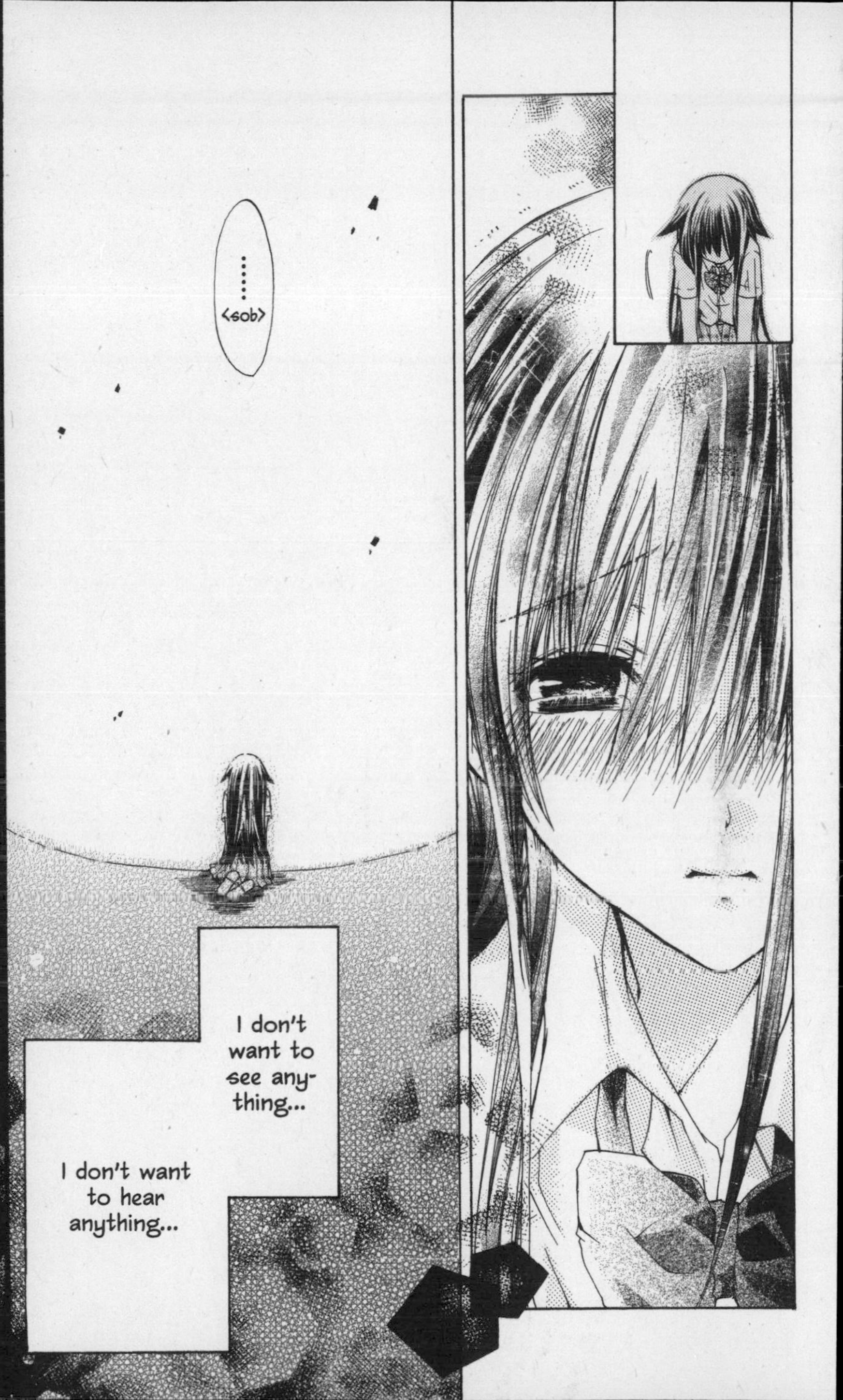
......
<sob>
I don't want to see any-thing...
I don't want to hear anything...

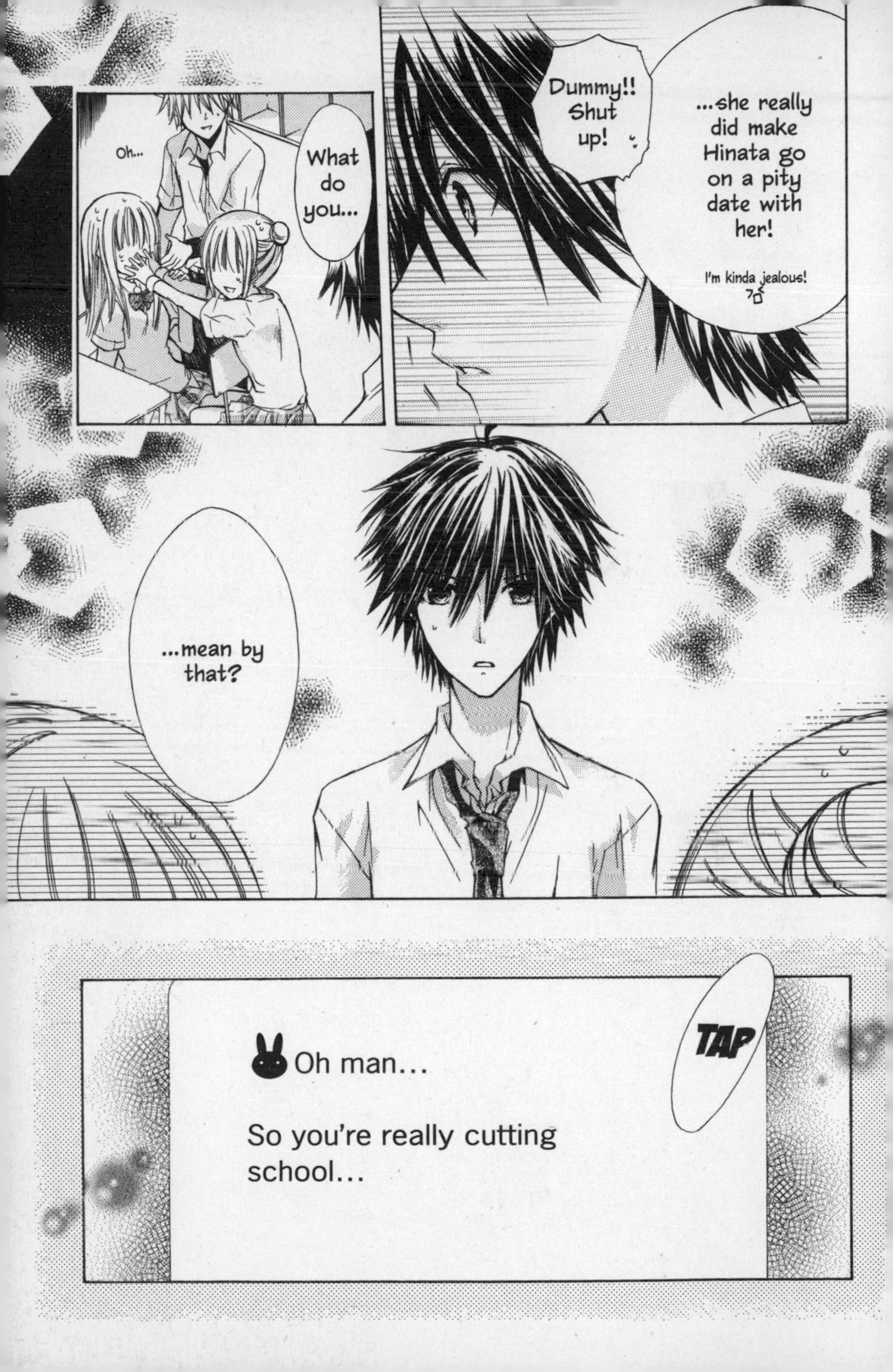
...she really did make Hinata go on a pity date with her!
I'm kinda jealous!
Dummy!! Shut up!
What do you...
Oh...
...mean by that?
TAP
Oh man...
So you're really cutting school...

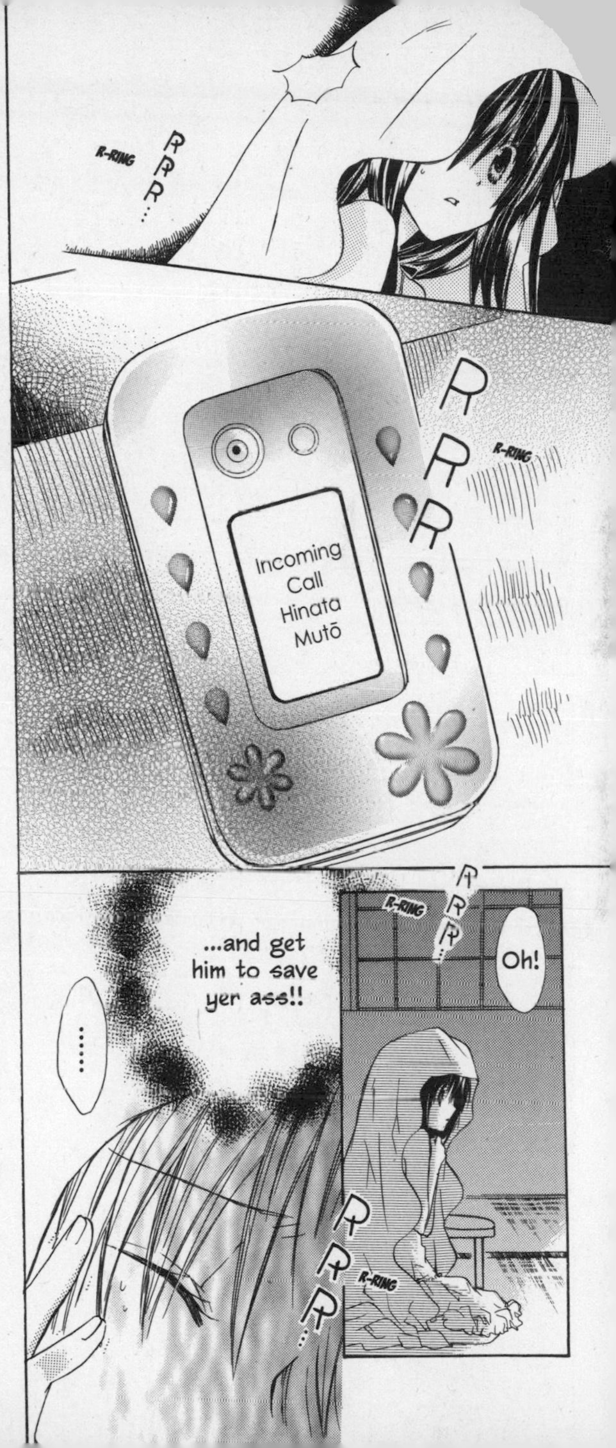
R-RING
RRR...
RRR
R-RING
Incoming Call Hinata Mutō
R-RING
RRR...
Oh!
RRR...
R-RING
...and get him to save yer ass!!
......

A No-Good Conversation

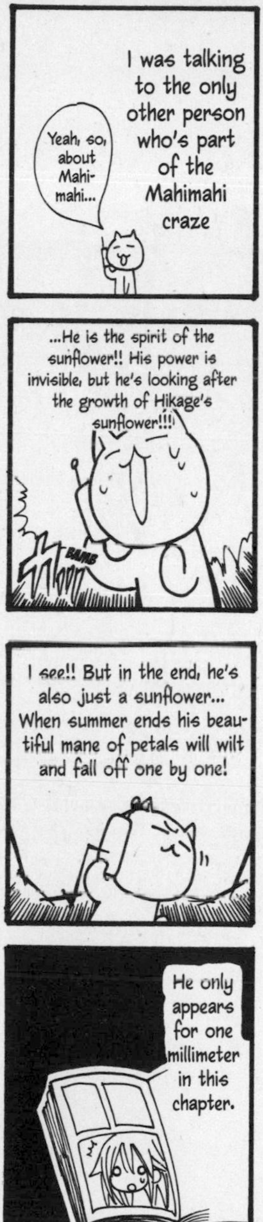
I was talking to the only other person who's part of the Mahimahi craze
Yeah, so, about Mahi-mahi...
...He is the spirit of the sunflower!! His power is invisible, but he's looking after the growth of Hikage's sunflower!!!
BAMB
I see!! But in the end, he's also just a sunflower... When summer ends his beau-tiful mane of petals will wilt and fall off one by one!
He only appears for one millimeter in this chapter.

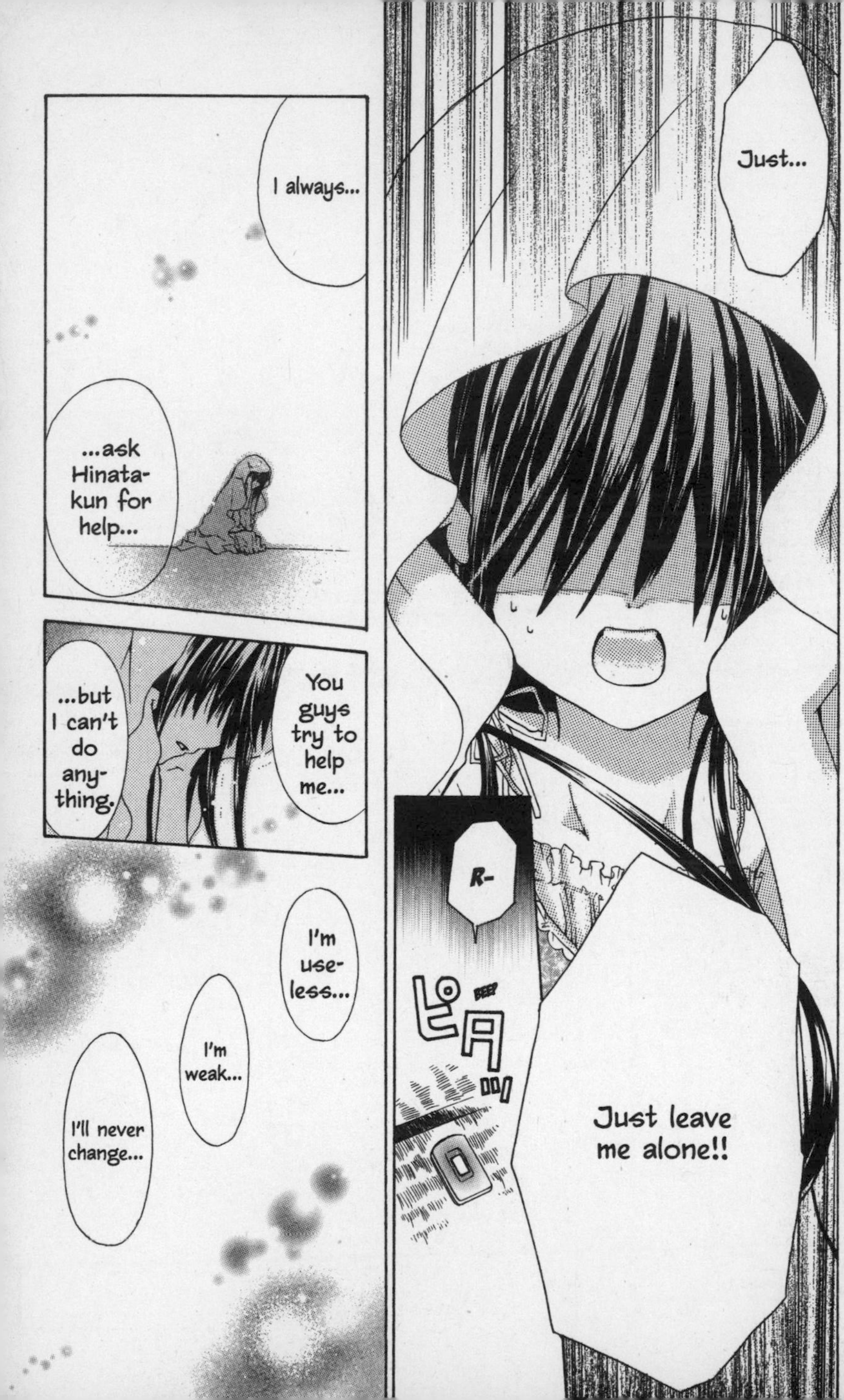
Just...
R-
BEEP
Just leave me alone!!
I always...
...ask Hinata-kun for help...
You guys try to help me...
...but I can't do anything.
I'm useless...
I'm weak...
I'll never change...

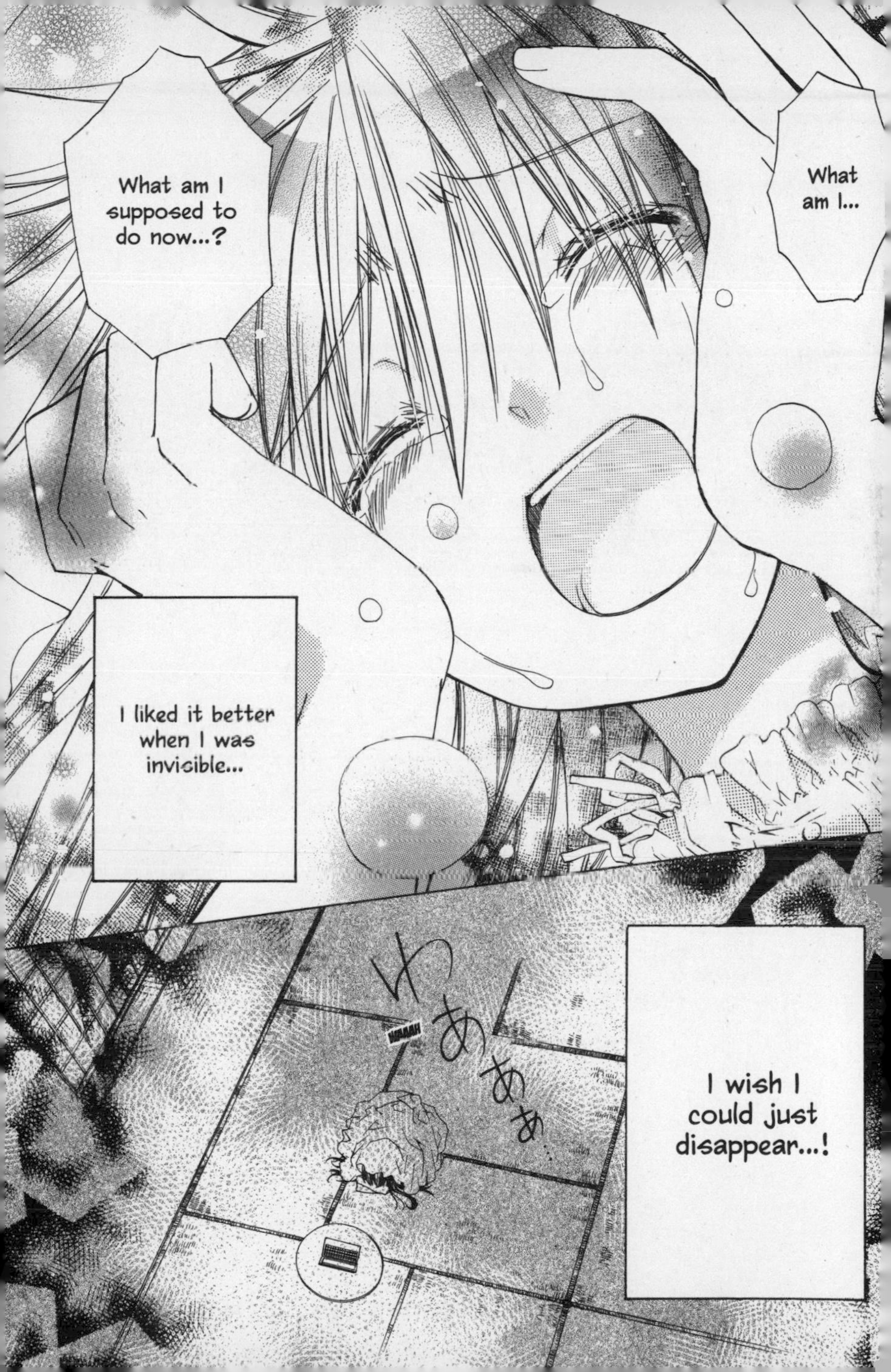

What am I...
What am I supposed to do now...?
I liked it better when I was invisible...
I wish I could just disappear...!
WAAAH
わああぁ…

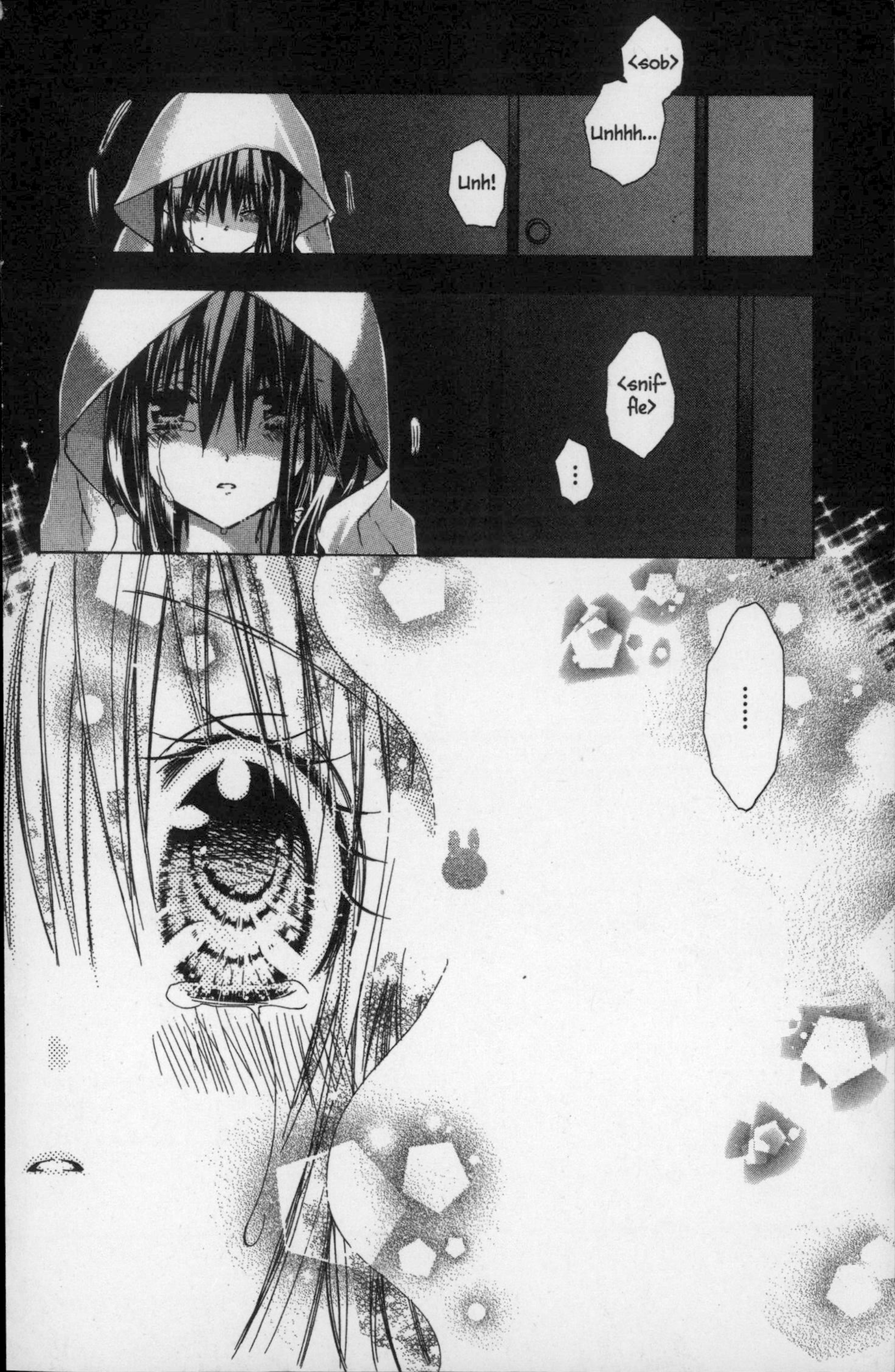
<sob>
Unhhh...
Unh!
<snif-fle>
...
......

🐰 It's fine!

I'm sorry for telling you to try harder when it was so painful that you couldn't even go to school... Don't blame yourself...

Black Rabbit

...What...

Huh ...

🐷 That's right...

We may have piled a little too much on yer plate...

I think we shoulda understood yer position better...

Why...?

You don't even know my real name or what I look like...!

Why are you guys still being nice to me!?

All I do is bother you guys... So **why**...!?

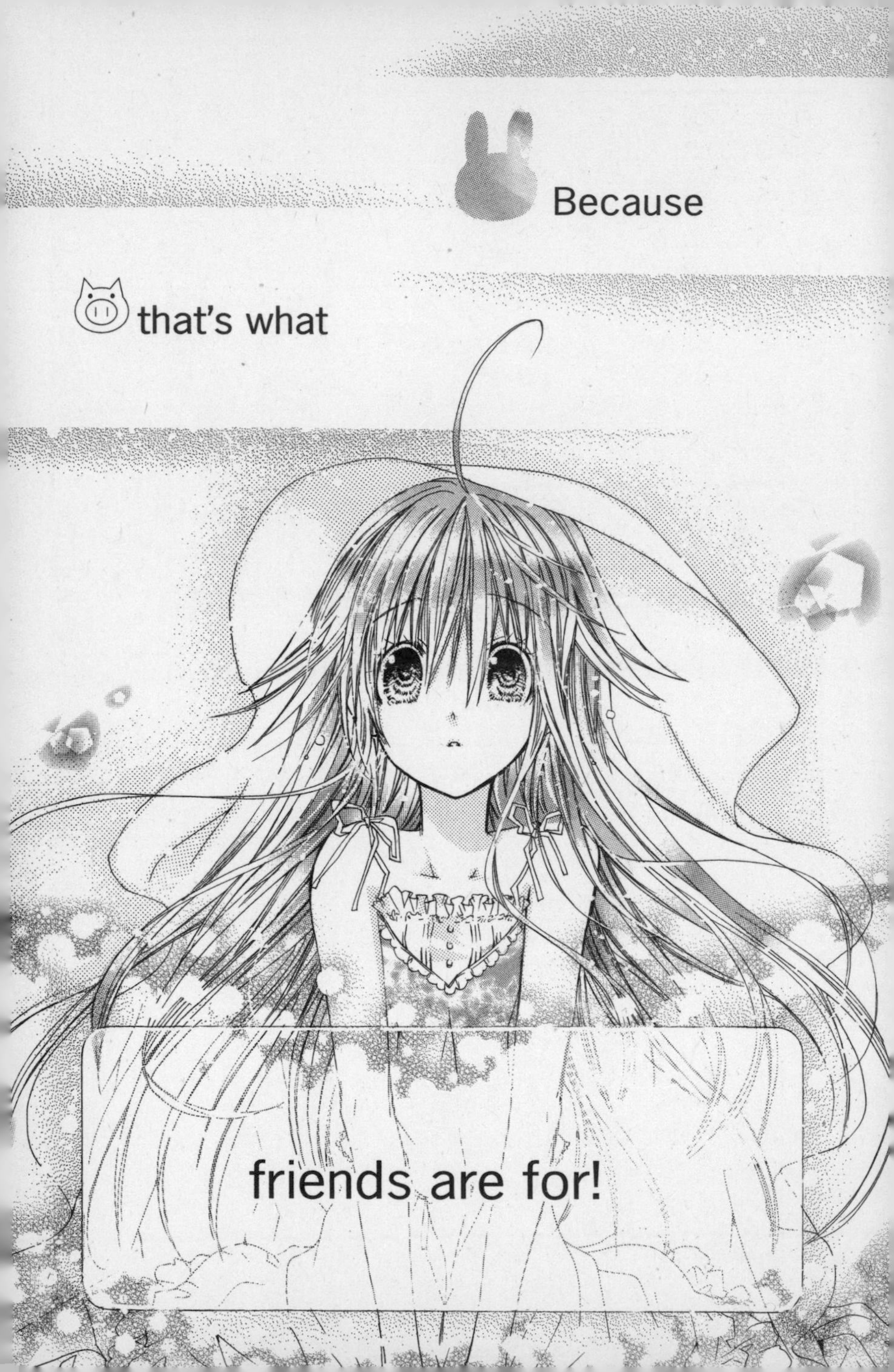
Because
that's what
friends are for!

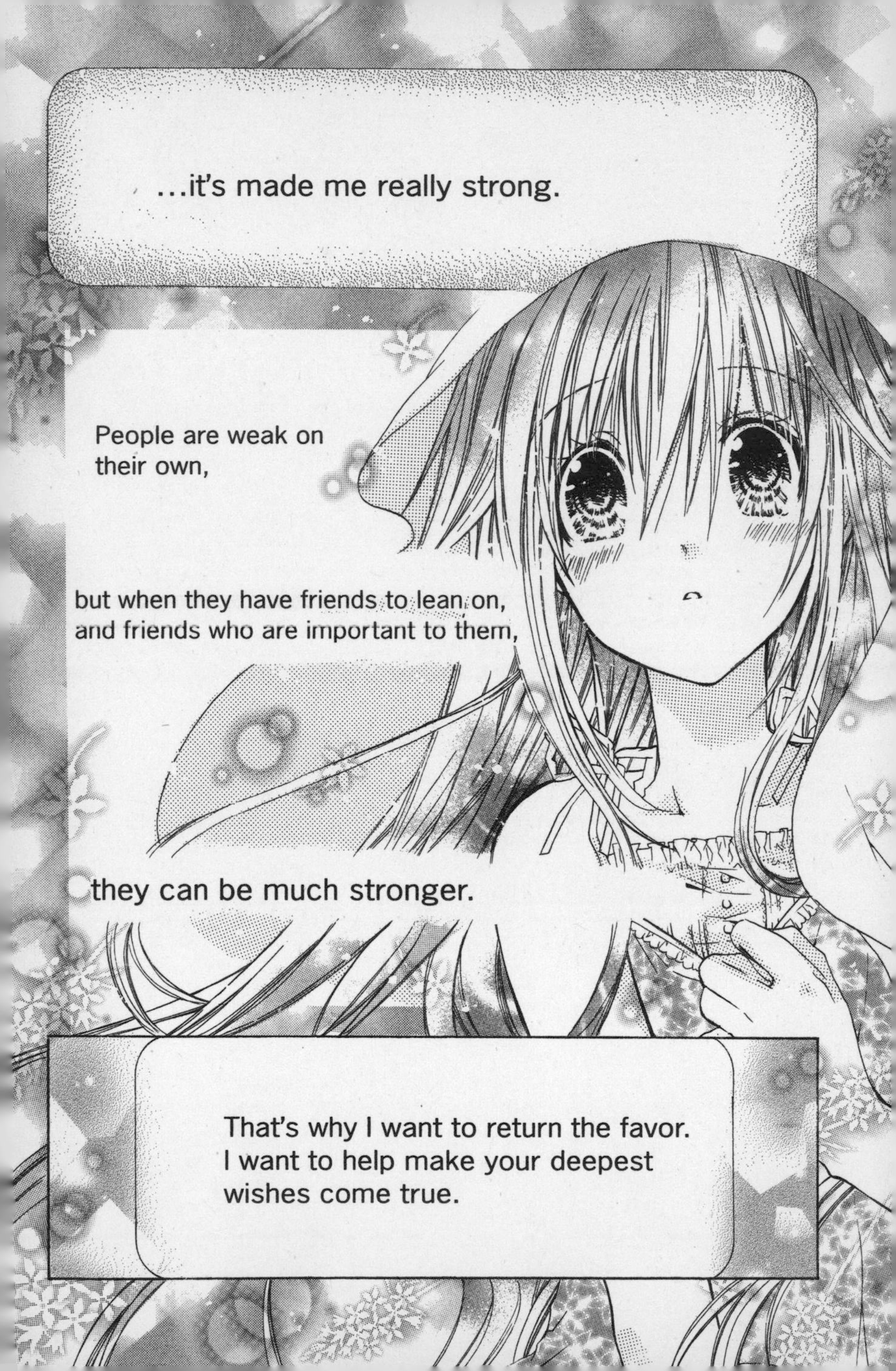
...it's made me really strong.
People are weak on their own,
but when they have friends to lean on, and friends who are important to them,
they can be much stronger.
That's why I want to return the favor. I want to help make your deepest wishes come true.

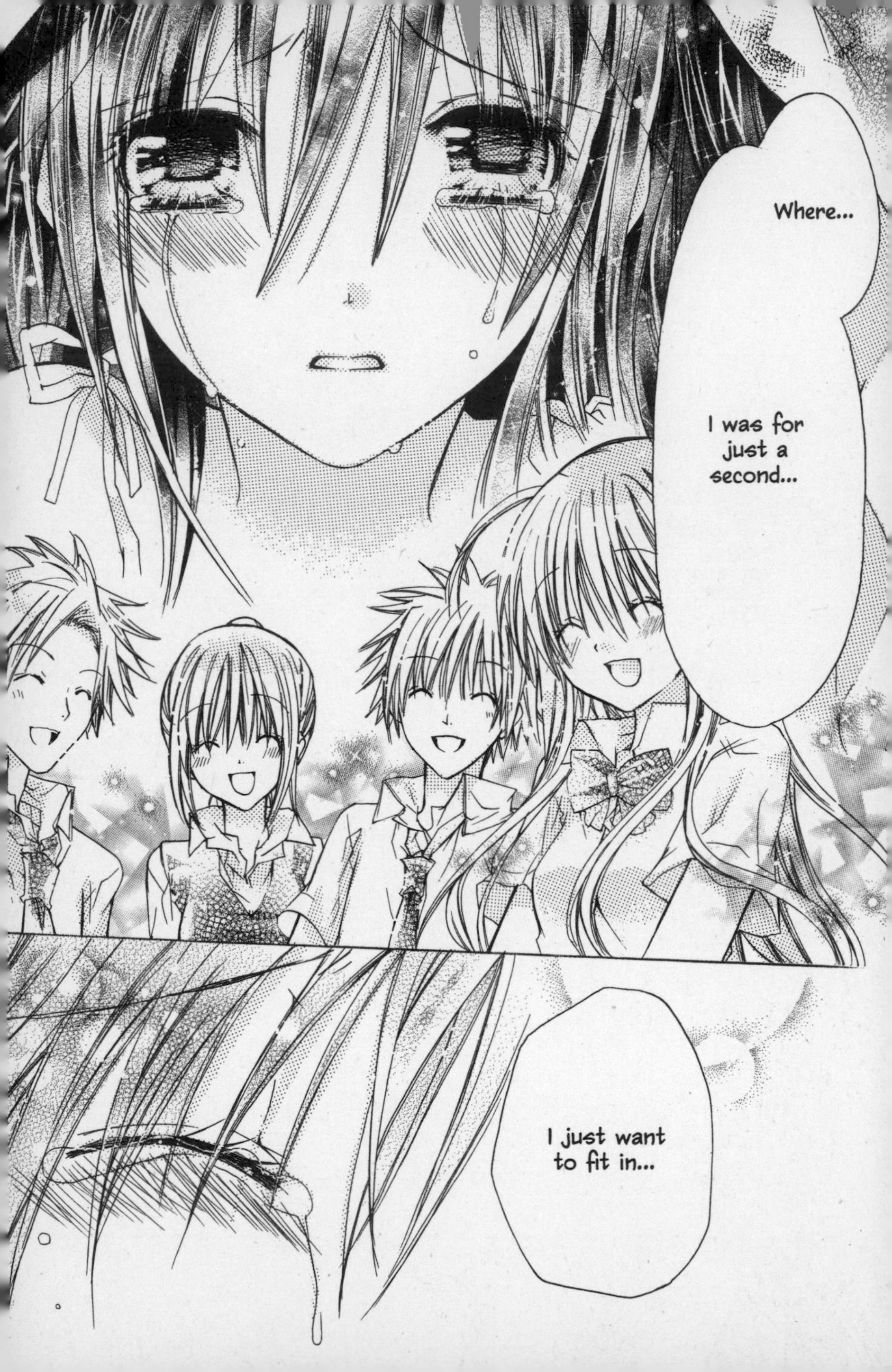
Where...
I was for just a second...
I just want to fit in...

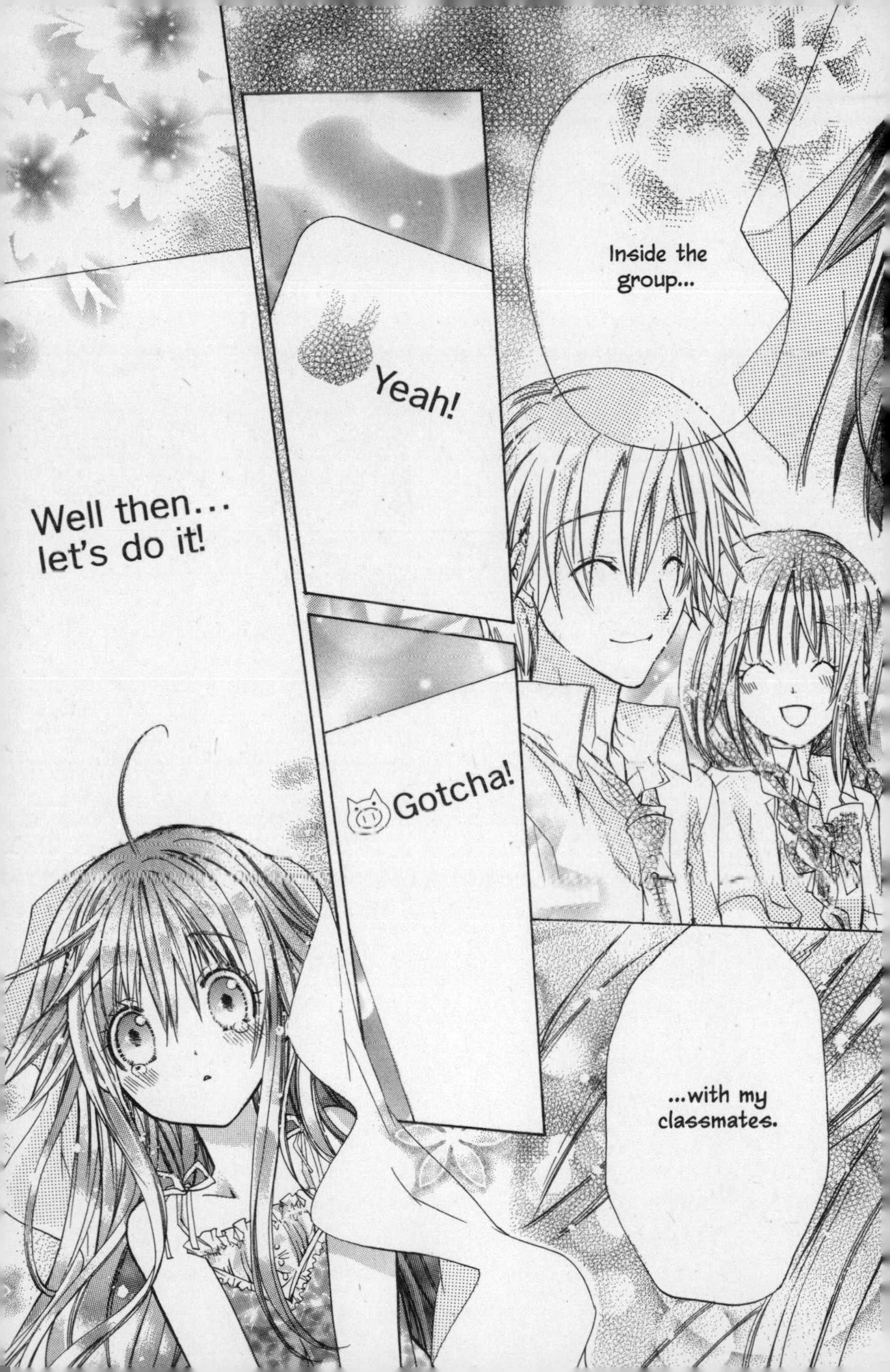
Inside the group...
...with my classmates.
Yeah!
Gotcha!
Well then... let's do it!

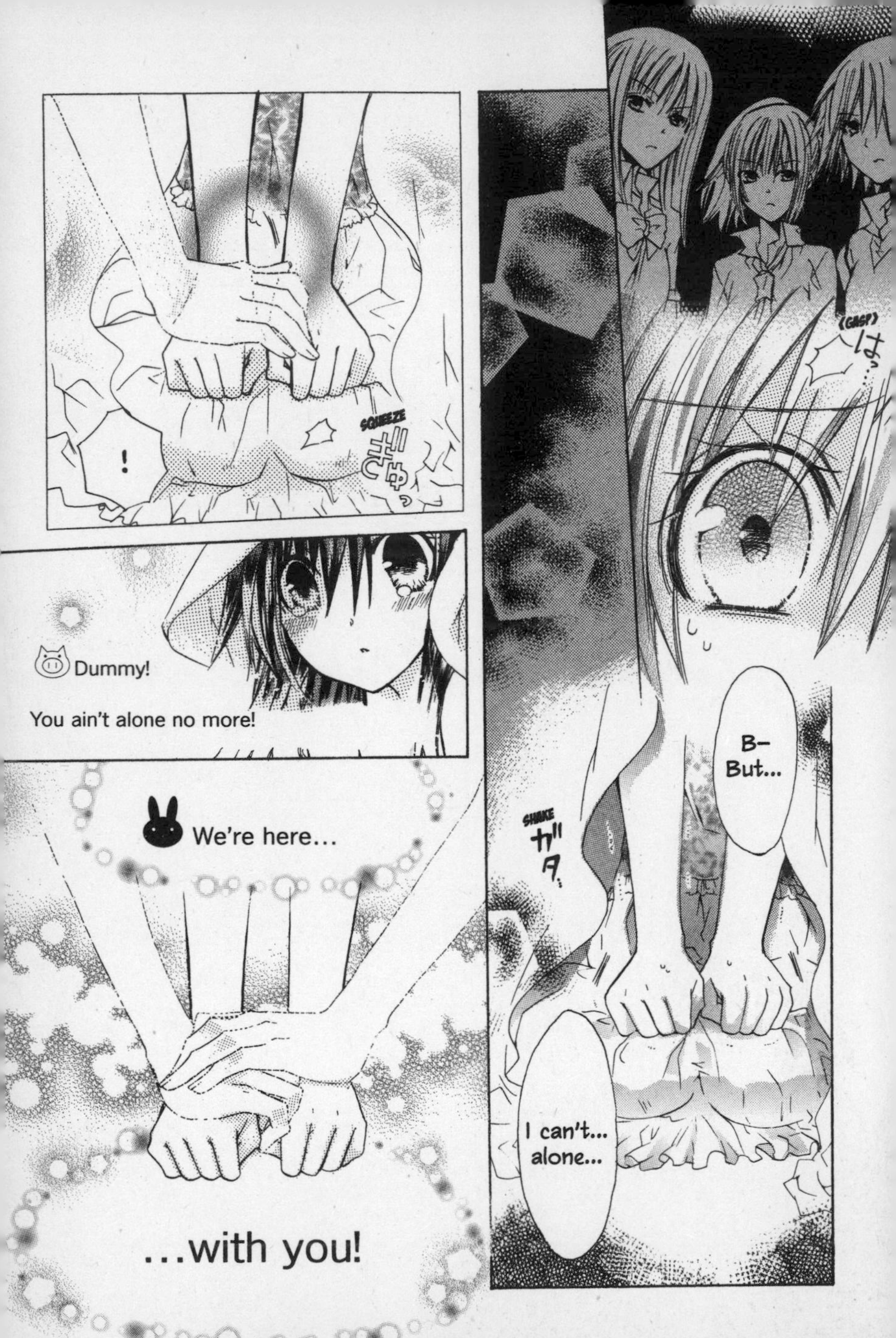
(GASP)
は…
SHAKE
ガタ
B–But...
I can't... alone...
SQUEEZE
ぎゅっ
!
Dummy!
You ain't alone no more!
We're here…
…with you!

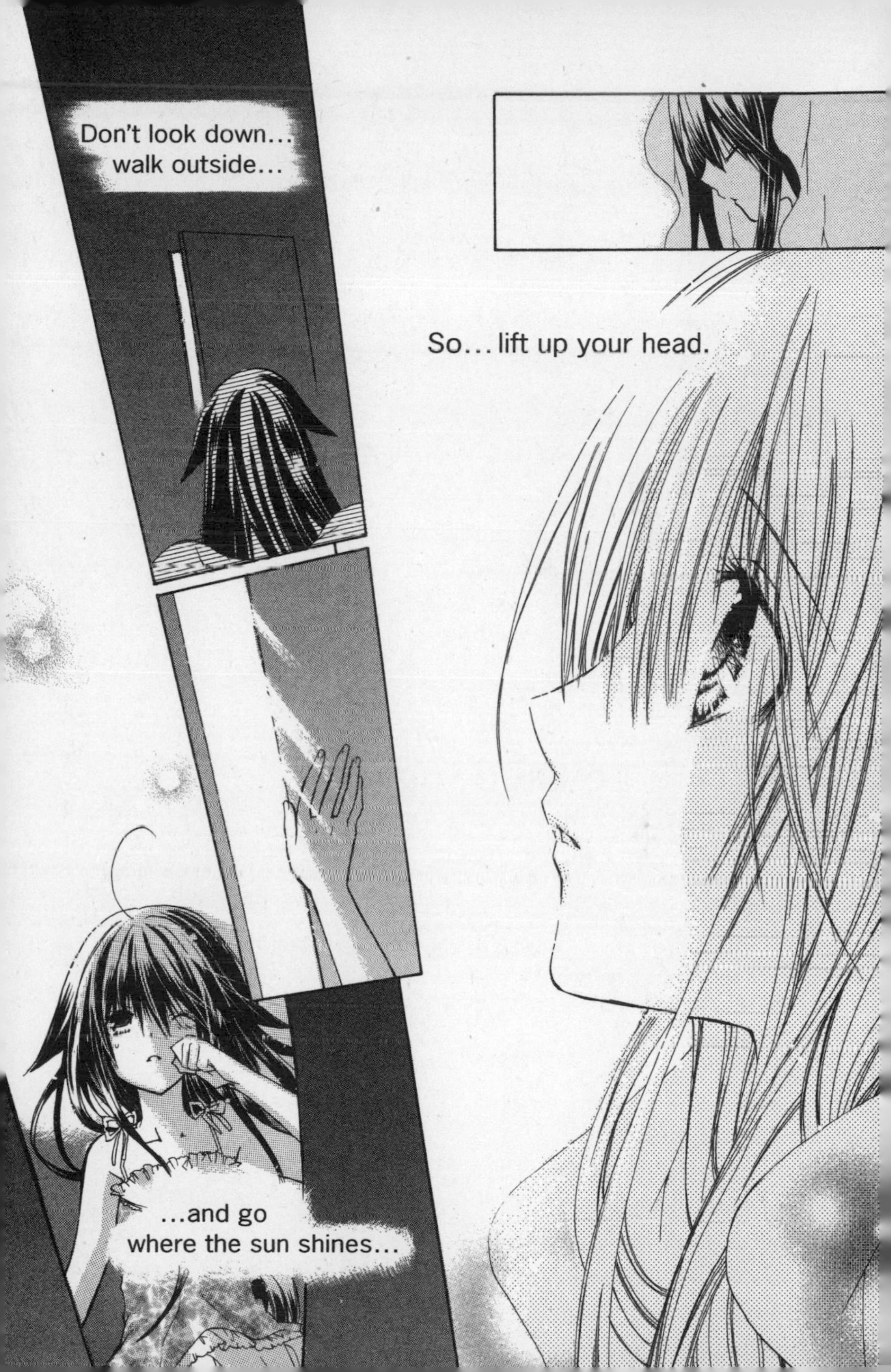
So… lift up your head.
Don't look down… walk outside…
…and go where the sun shines…

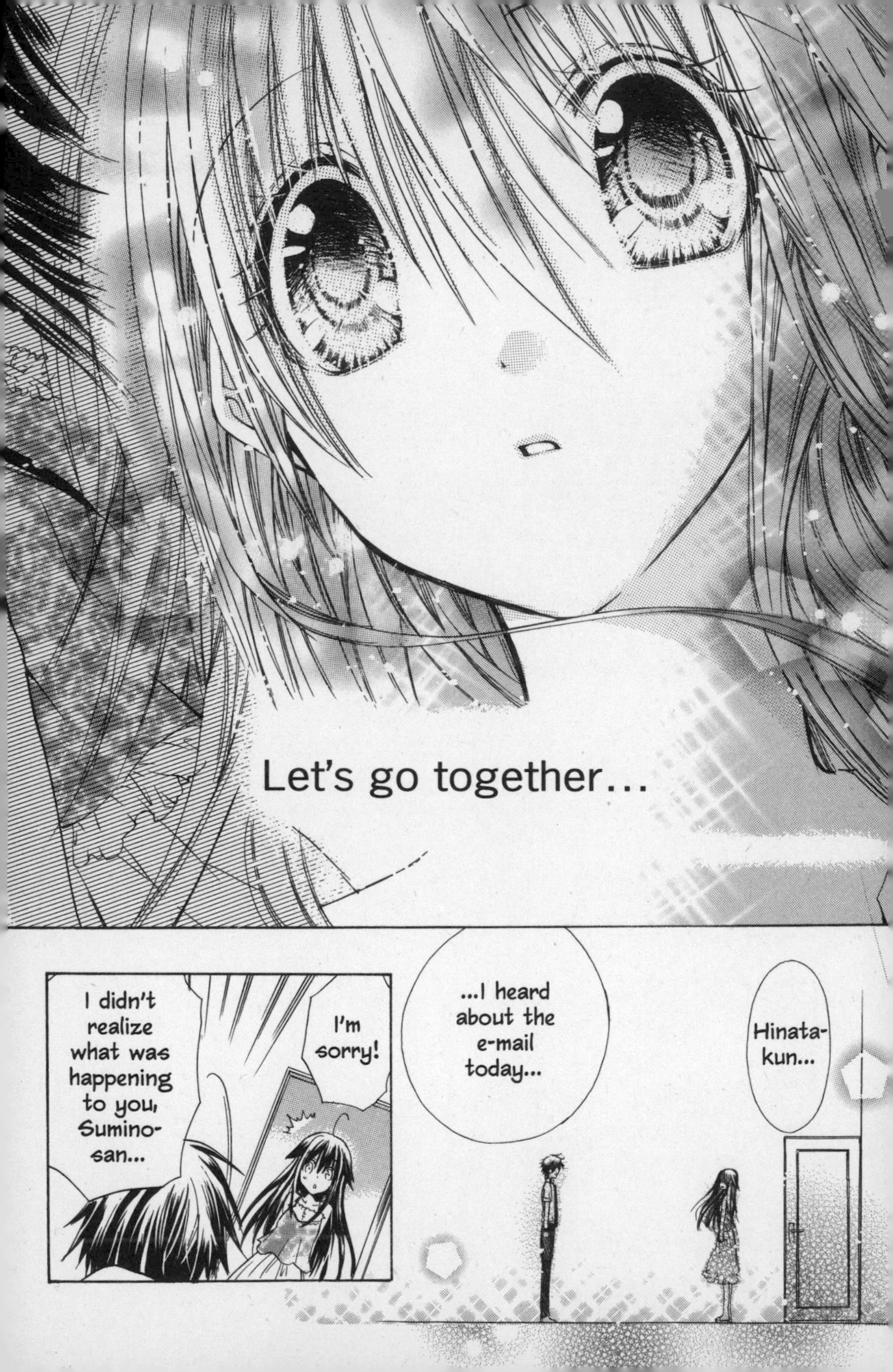
Let's go together…
Hinata-kun...
...I heard about the e-mail today...
I'm sorry!
I didn't realize what was happening to you, Sumino-san...

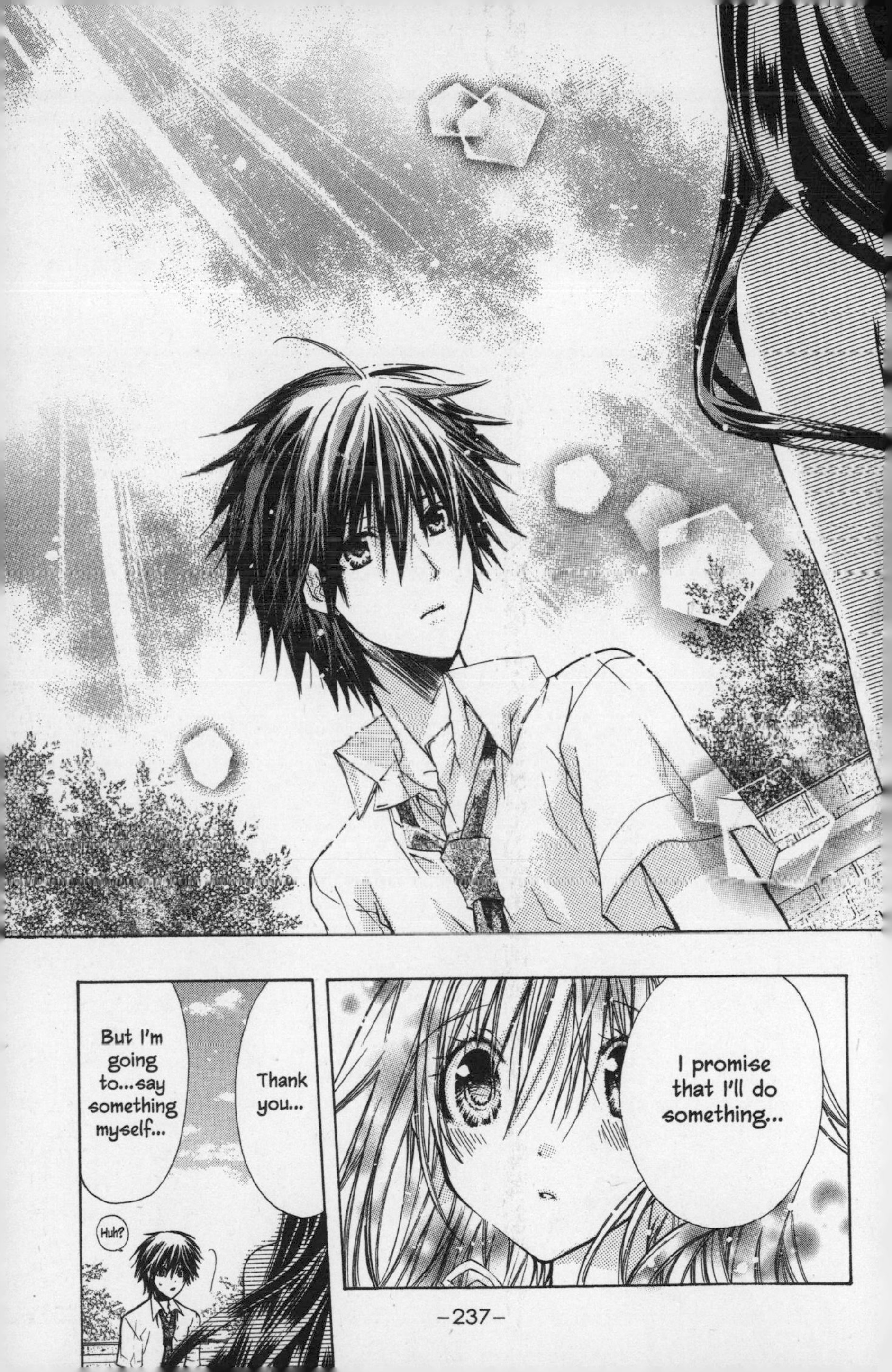
I promise that I'll do something...
Thank you...
But I'm going to...say something myself...
Huh?

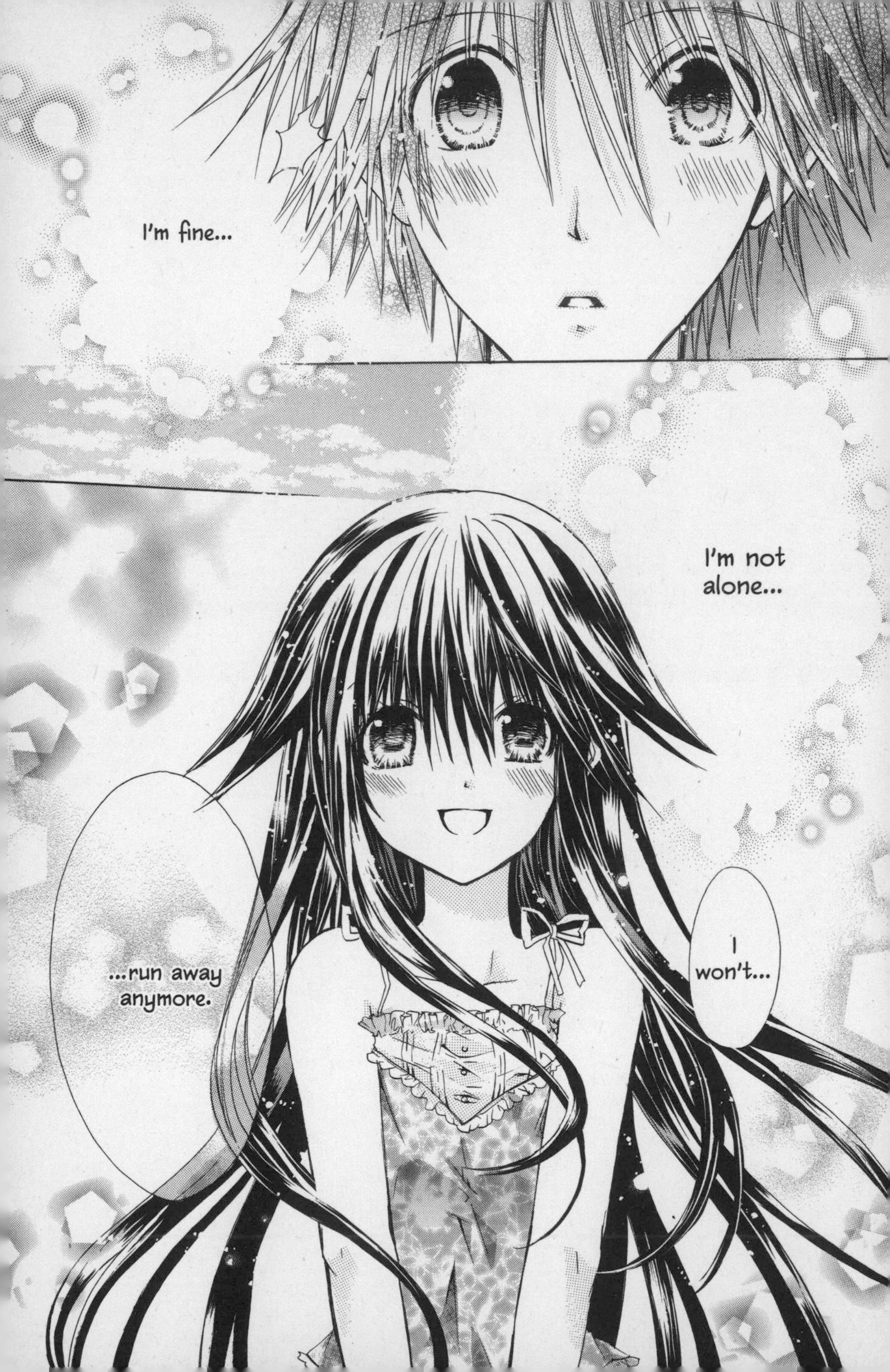
I'm fine...
I'm not alone...
I won't...
...run away anymore.

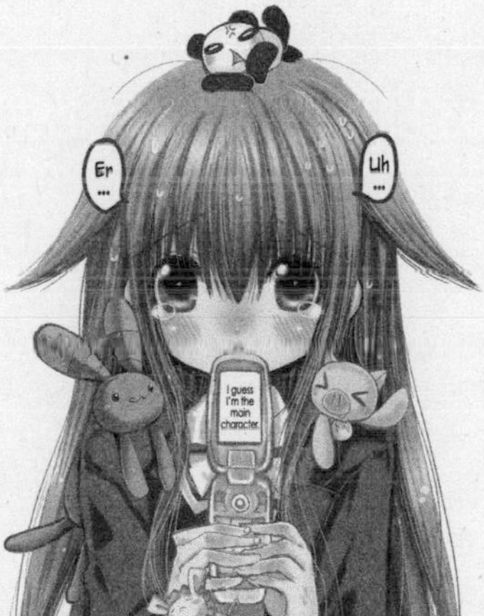
Uh...
Er...
I guess I'm the main character.

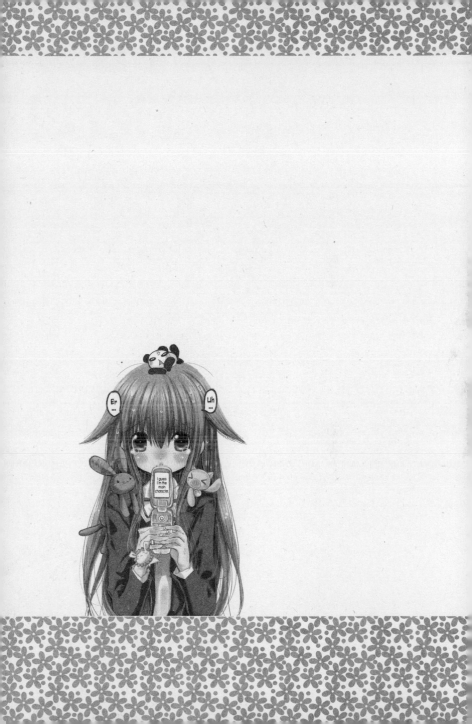

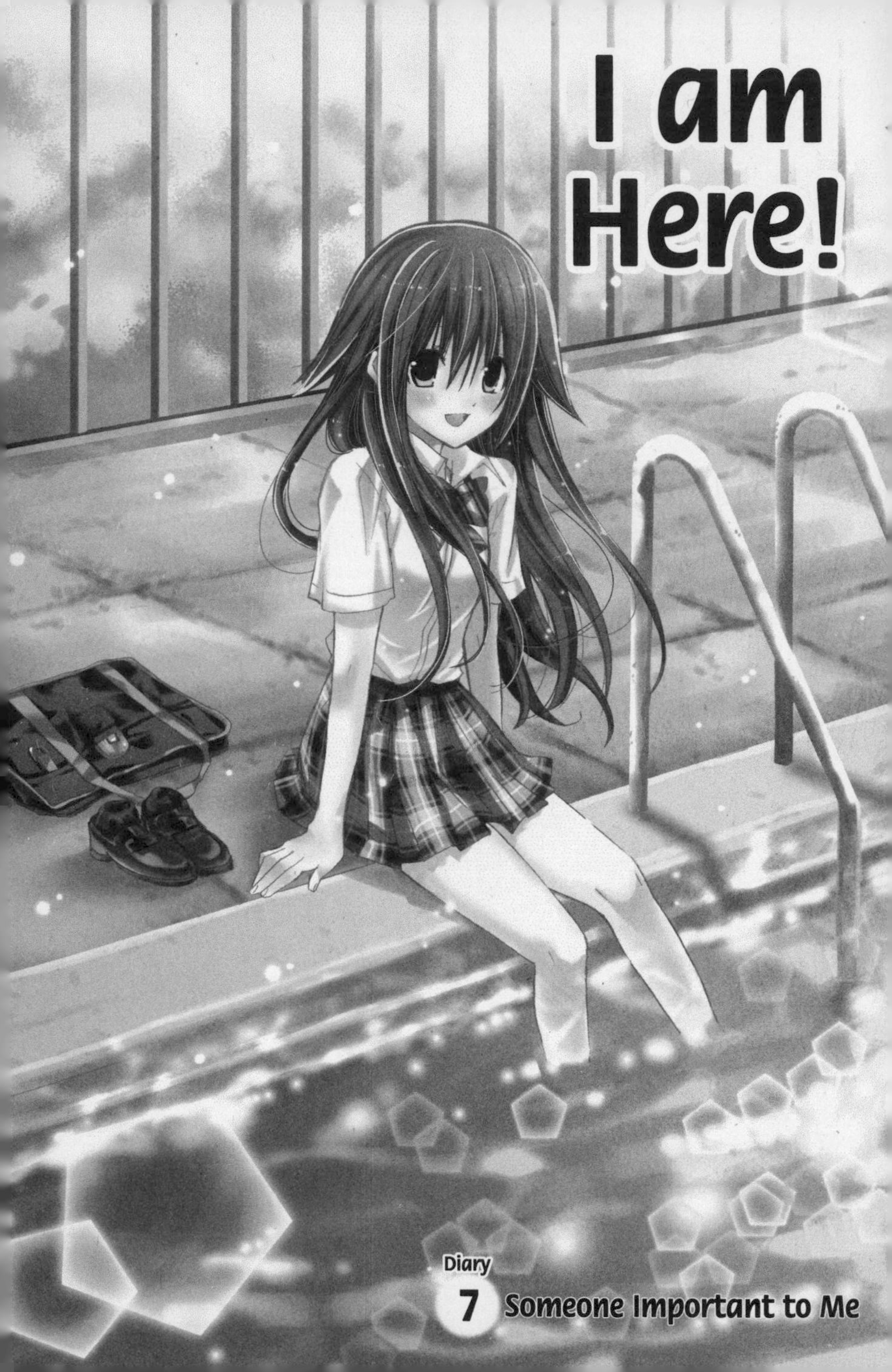
I am Here!
Diary
7 Someone Important to Me

2 - 3

Wow!

So Sumino-san didn't come today either...

Awesome! I bet she'll never go near Hinata again!

It's so annoying that we're not in his class!

Jeez!

Huh? But Hinata's not here either.

Neither is Teru!

Huh?

Oh... Aya...

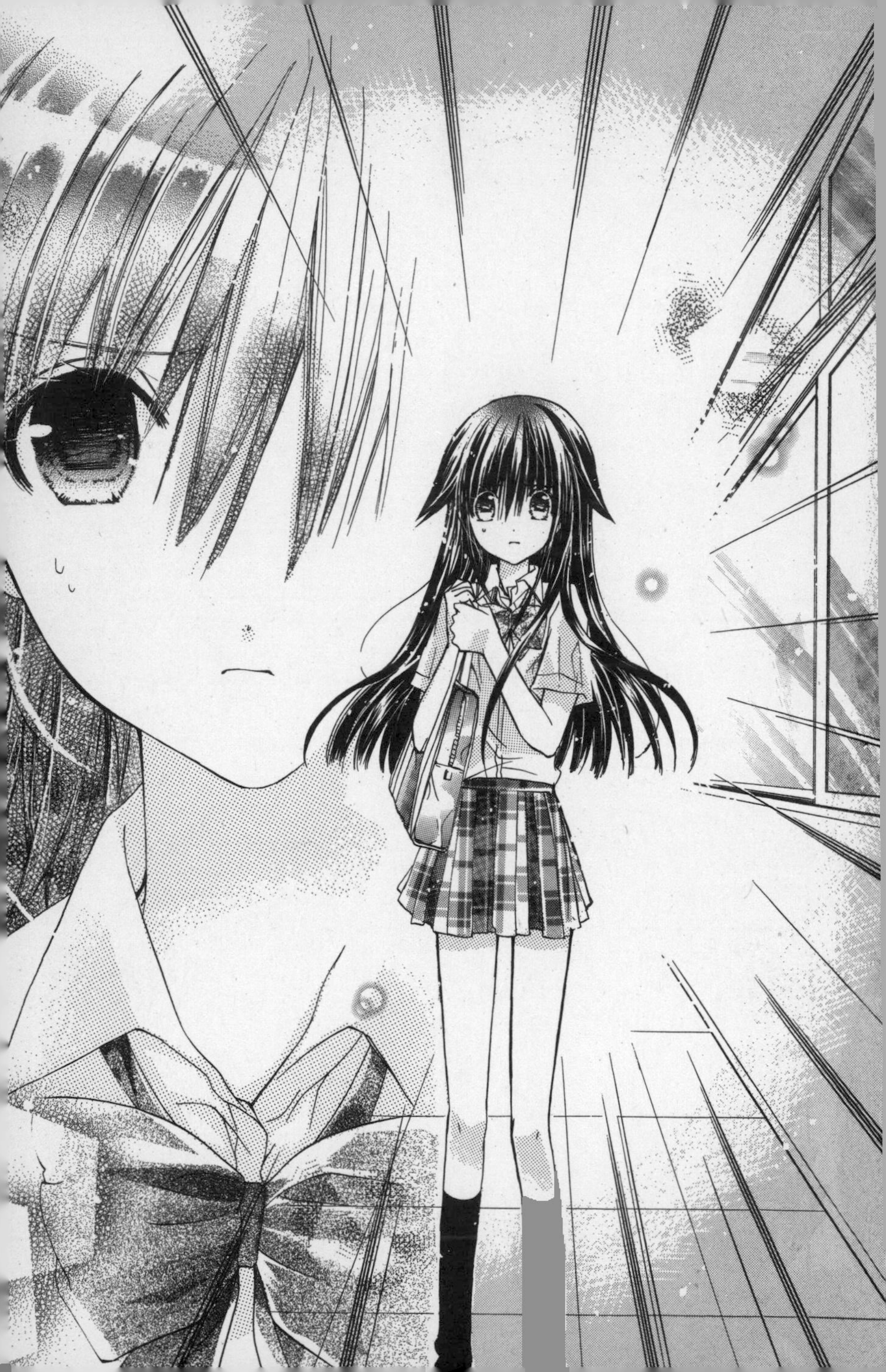

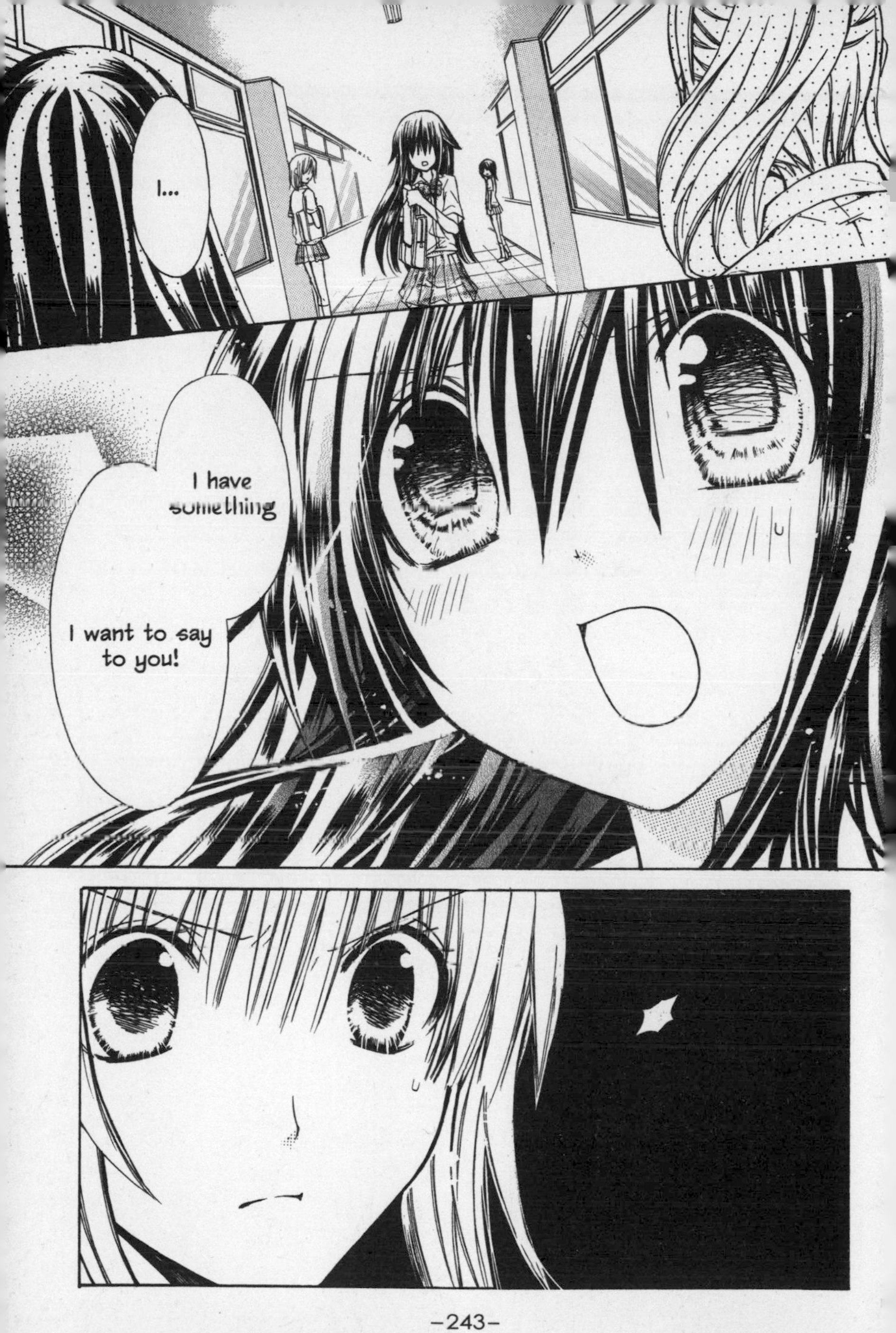
I...
I have something I want to say to you!

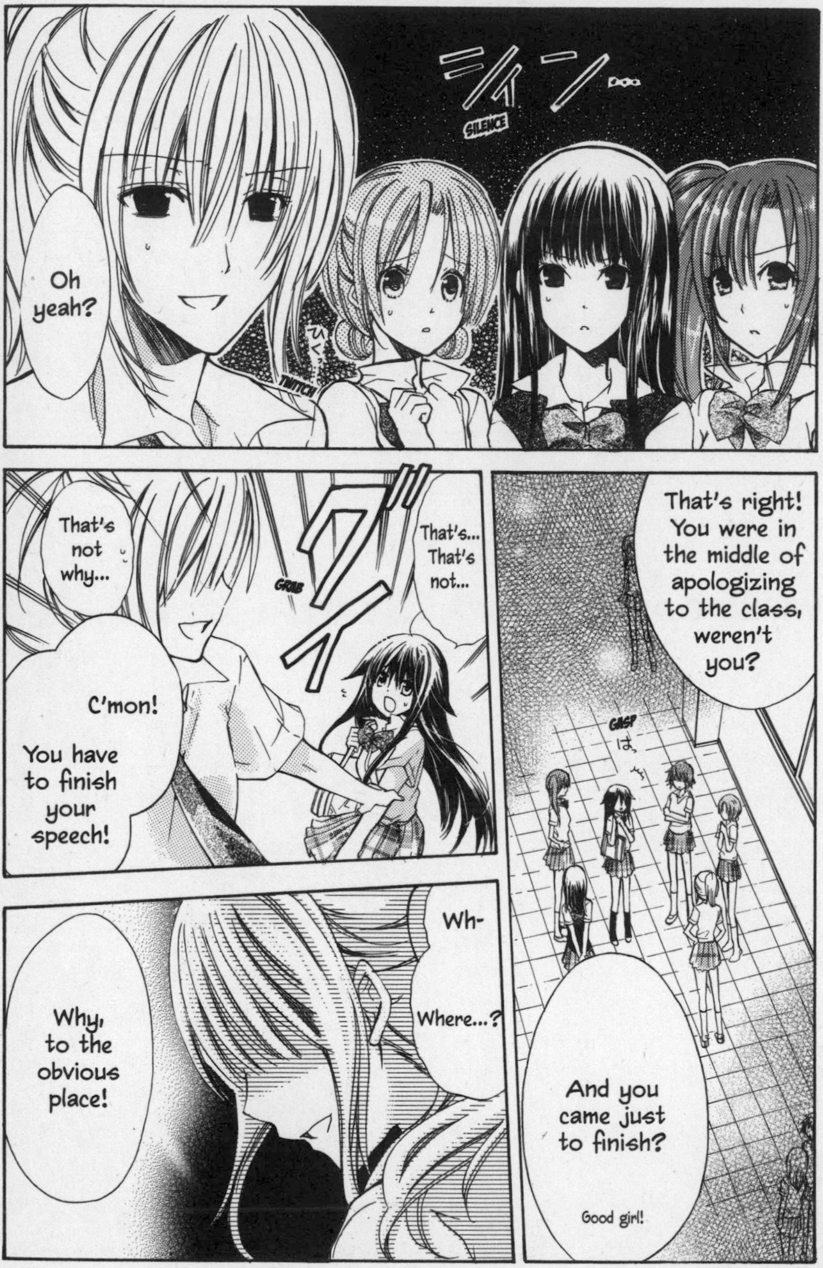
シィーン…
SILENCE
ひくっ
TWITCH
Oh yeah?
That's right! You were in the middle of apologizing to the class, weren't you?
GASP
は
And you came just to finish?
Good girl!
That's... That's not...
グイ
GRAB
That's not why...
C'mon!
You have to finish your speech!
Wh-
Where...?
Why, to the obvious place!

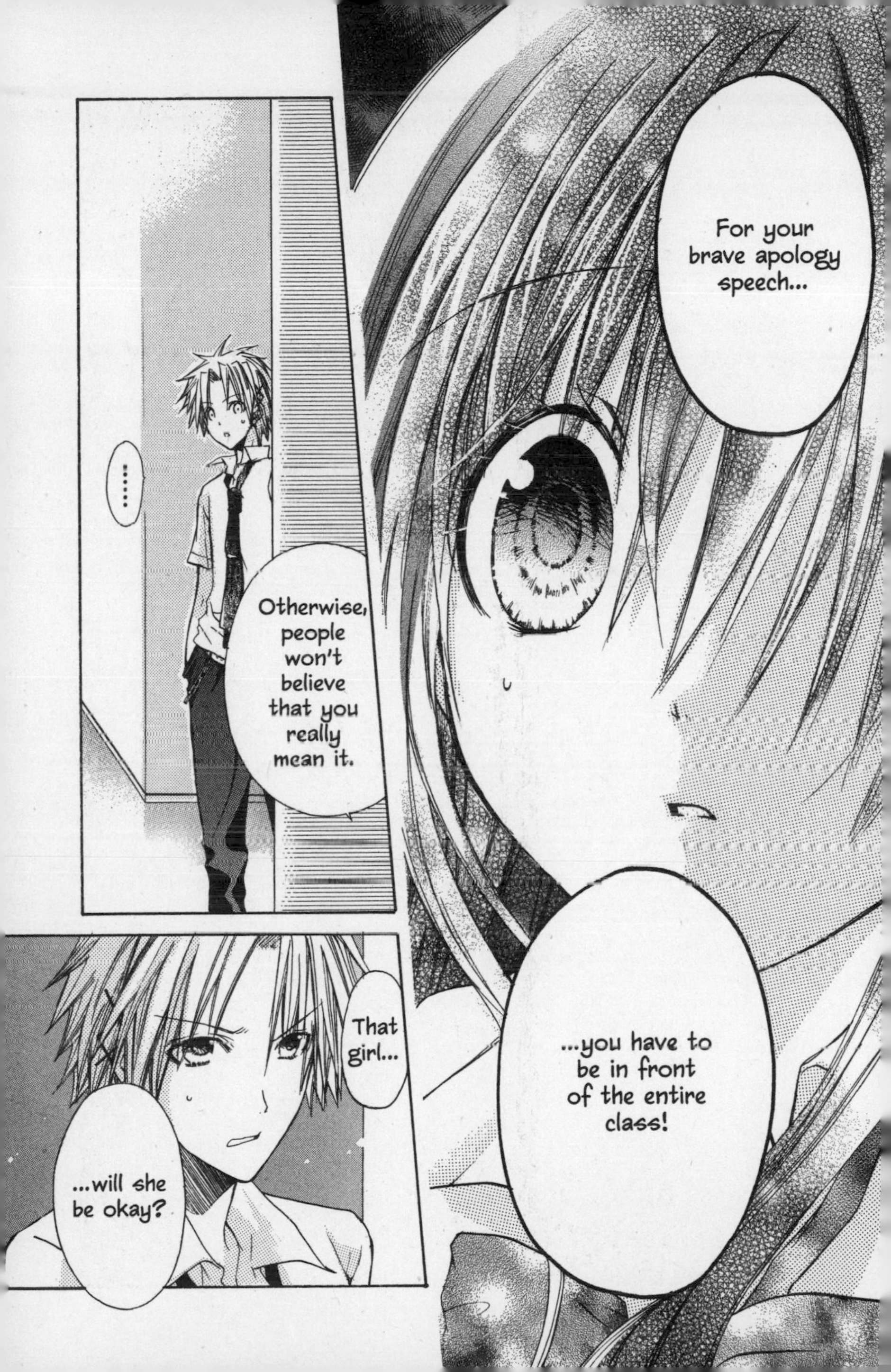
For your brave apology speech...
...you have to be in front of the entire class!
Otherwise, people won't believe that you really mean it.
......
That girl...
...will she be okay?

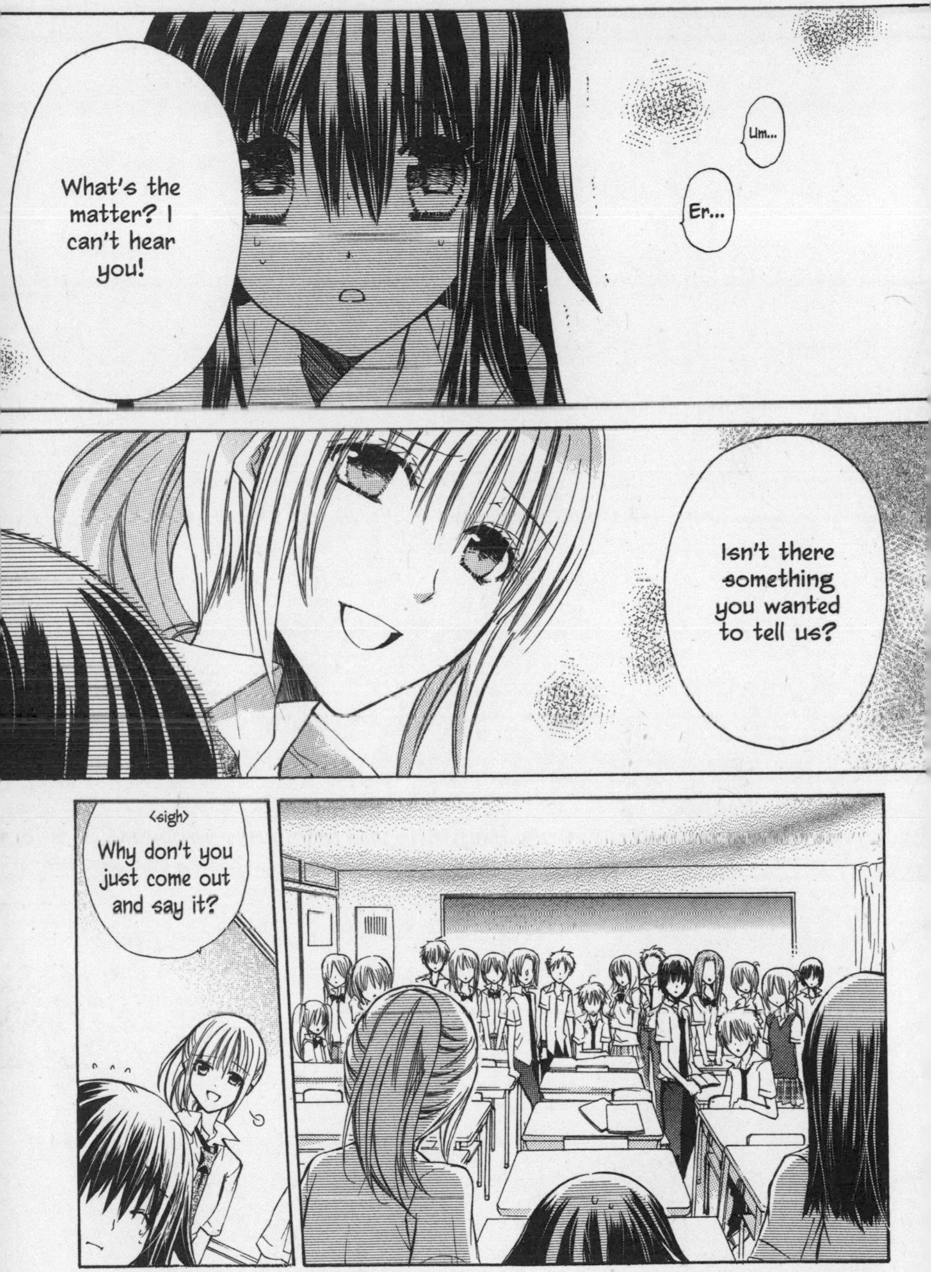
Um...
Er...
What's the matter? I can't hear you!
Isn't there something you wanted to tell us?
<sigh>
Why don't you just come out and say it?

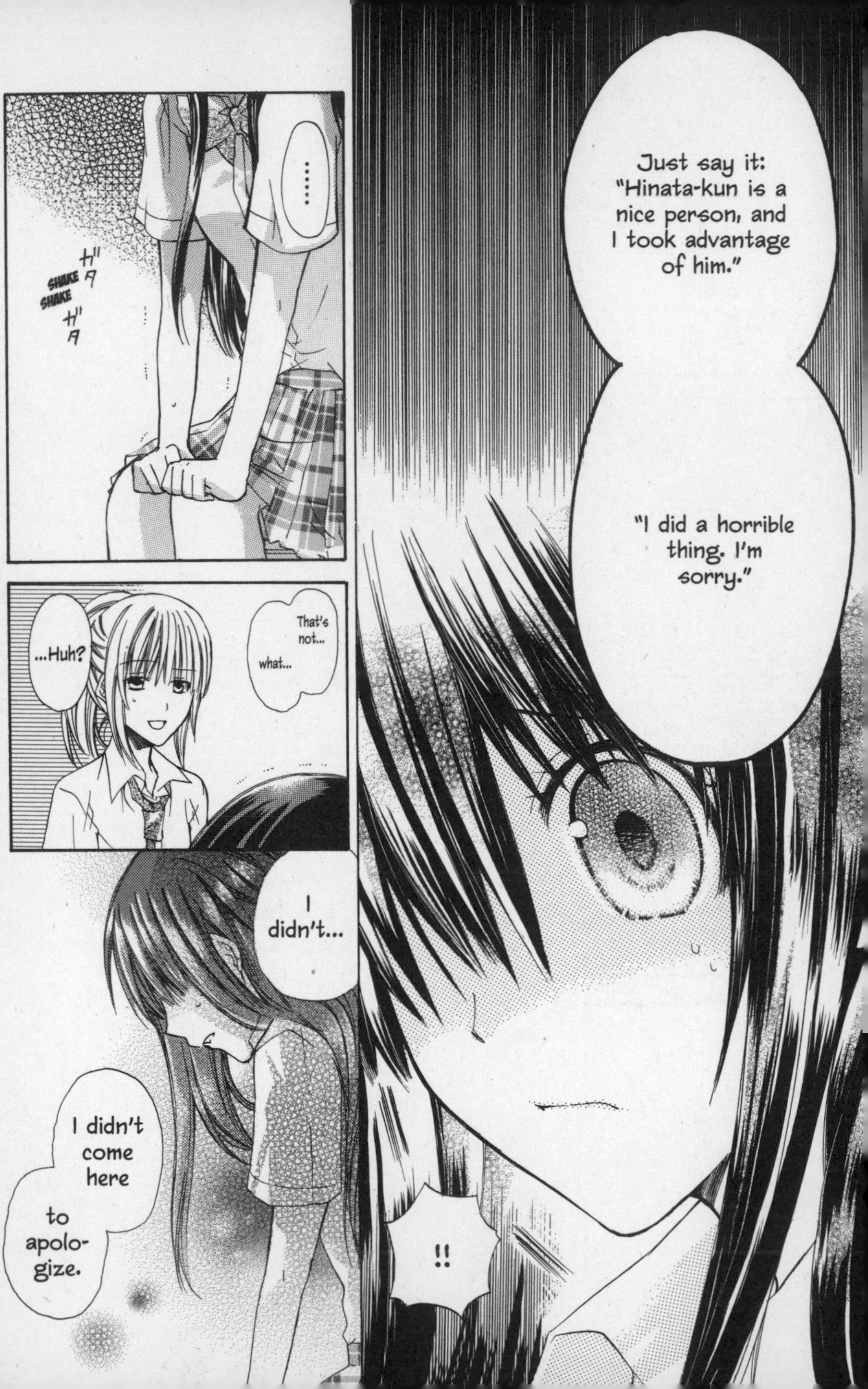
Just say it: "Hinata-kun is a nice person, and I took advantage of him."
"I did a horrible thing. I'm sorry."
!!
......
ガタ ガタ
SHAKE SHAKE
That's not... what...
...Huh?
I didn't...
I didn't come here to apologize.

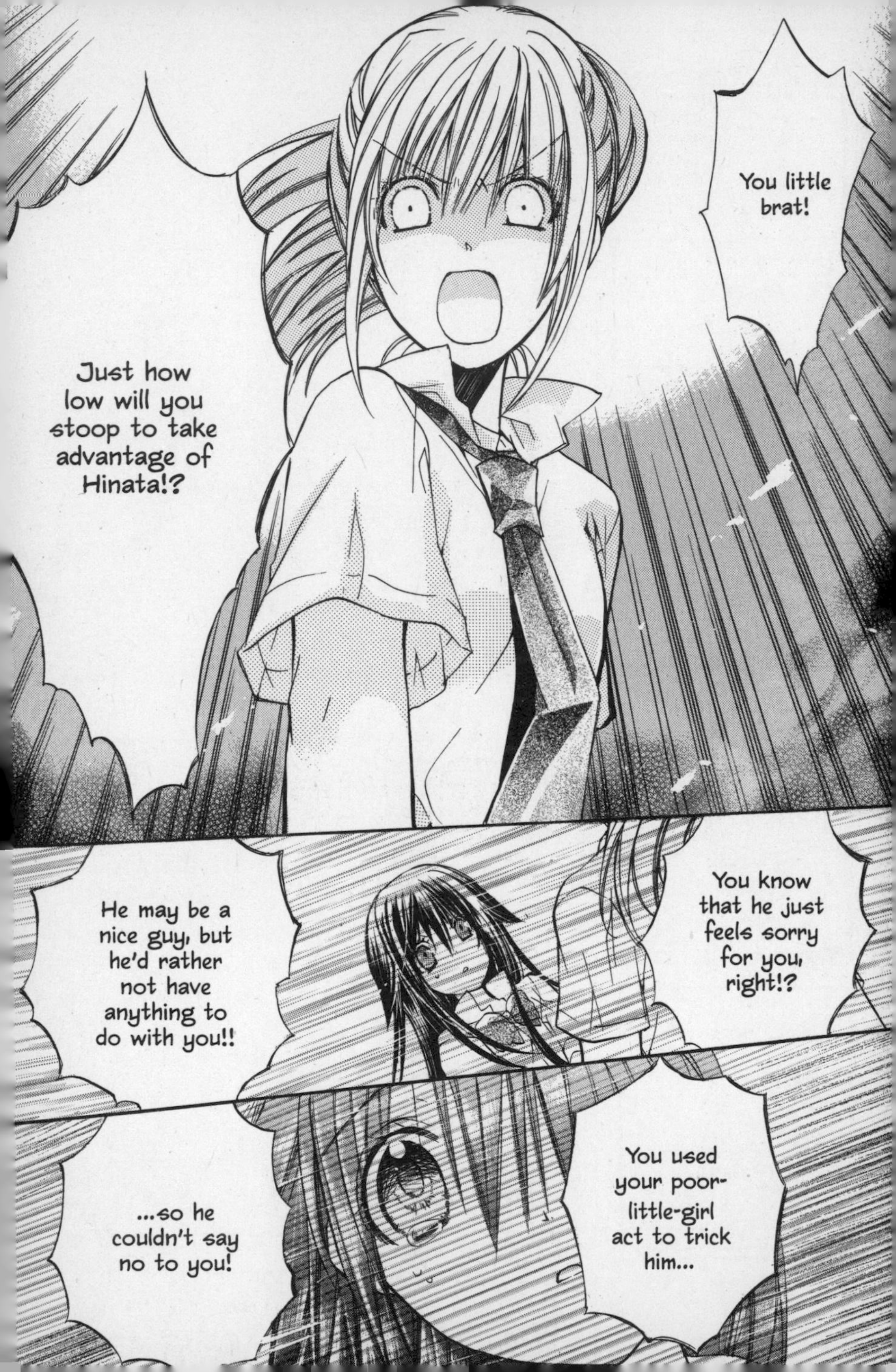
You little brat!
Just how low will you stoop to take advantage of Hinata!?
You know that he just feels sorry for you, right!?
He may be a nice guy, but he'd rather not have anything to do with you!!
You used your poor-little-girl act to trick him...
...so he couldn't say no to you!

A Shock

Postal delivery!

Well... I'll just accept this and move on...

Let's see...

So this issue's appendix is going to be file format?

Sunflower HIMAWARI

Oh! The name...

Even my editor's office didn't know about him.

It's supposed to be "Mahimahi"...

Get it into your head that he's only hanging out with you out of pity!!

WHISPER

You're right...

She should just give up and apologize already...

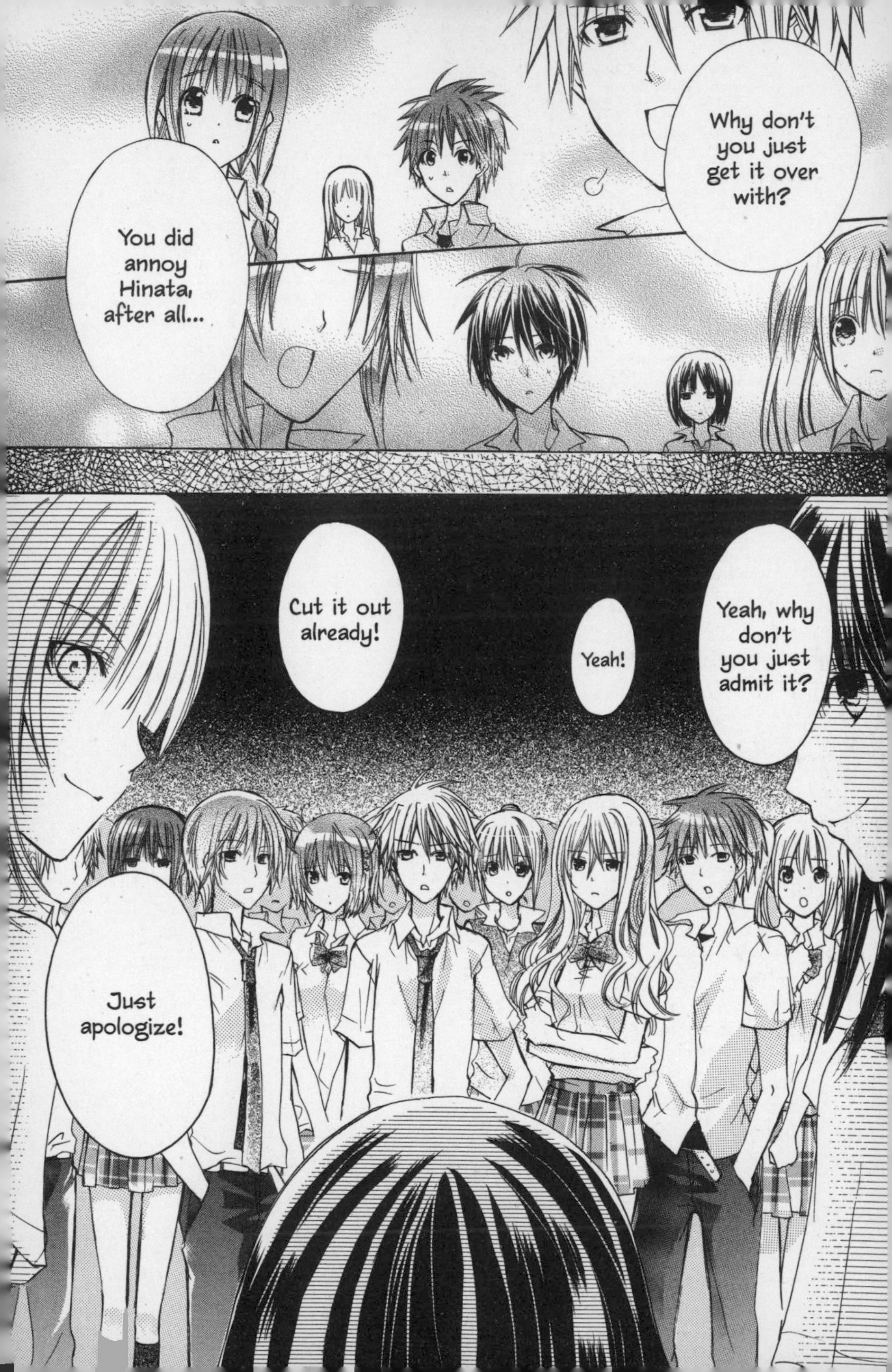
Why don't you just get it over with?
You did annoy Hinata, after all...
Yeah, why don't you just admit it?
Yeah!
Cut it out already!
Just apologize!

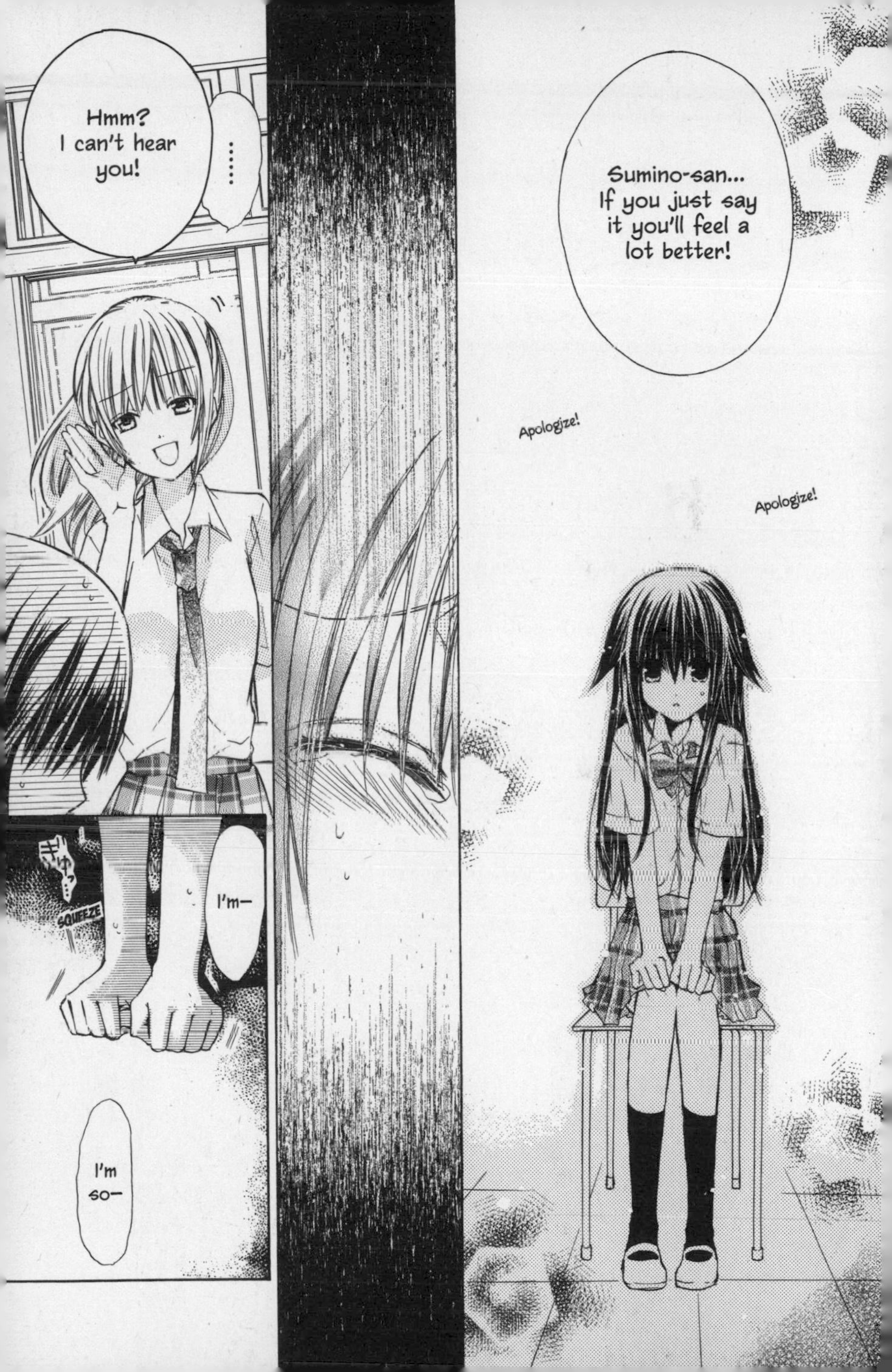

Sumino-san... If you just say it you'll feel a lot better!
Apologize!
Apologize!
……
Hmm? I can't hear you!
SQUEEZE
I'm—
I'm so—

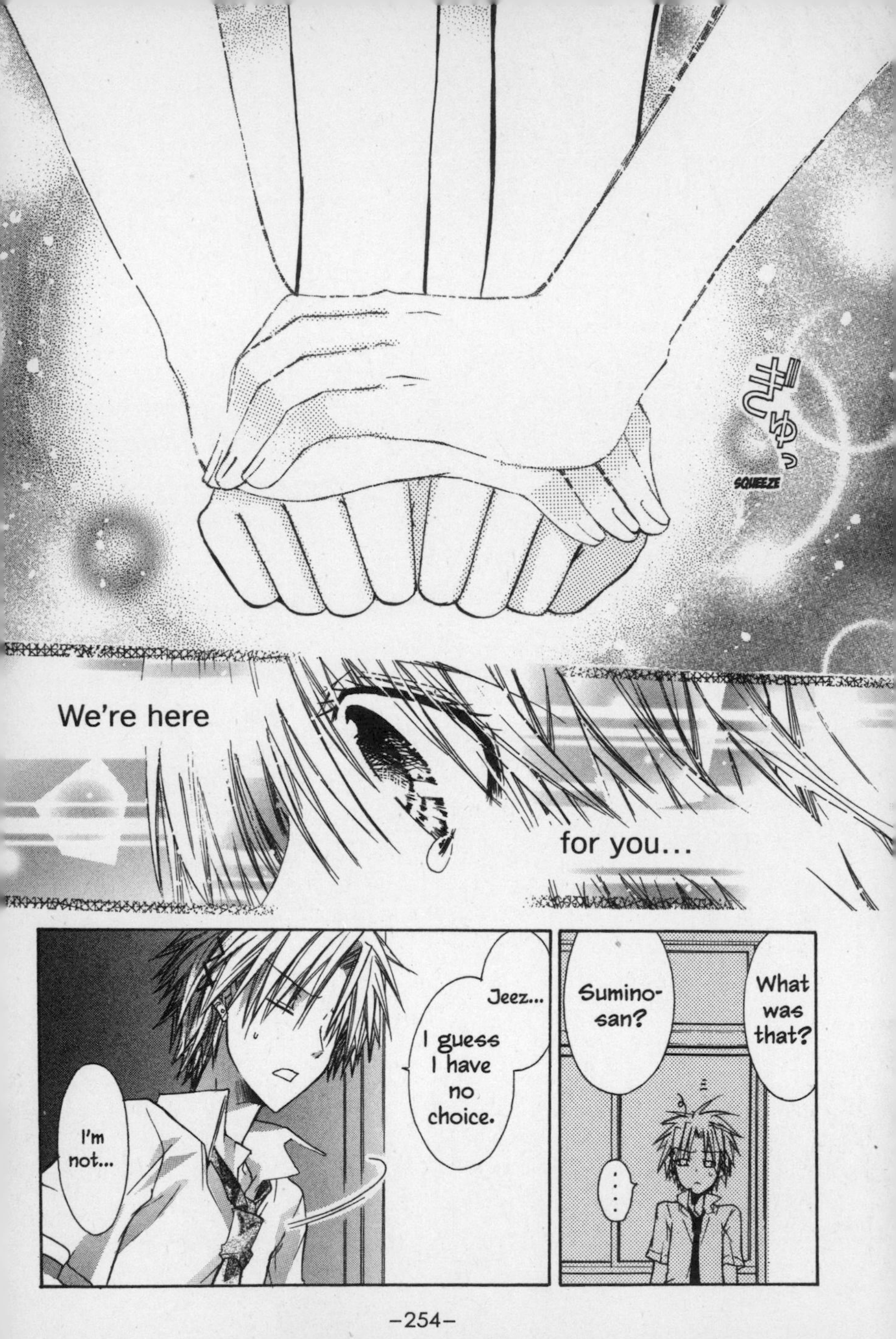
ぎゅっ
SQUEEZE
We're here
for you…
What was that?
Sumino-san?
…
Jeez...
I guess I have no choice.
I'm not...

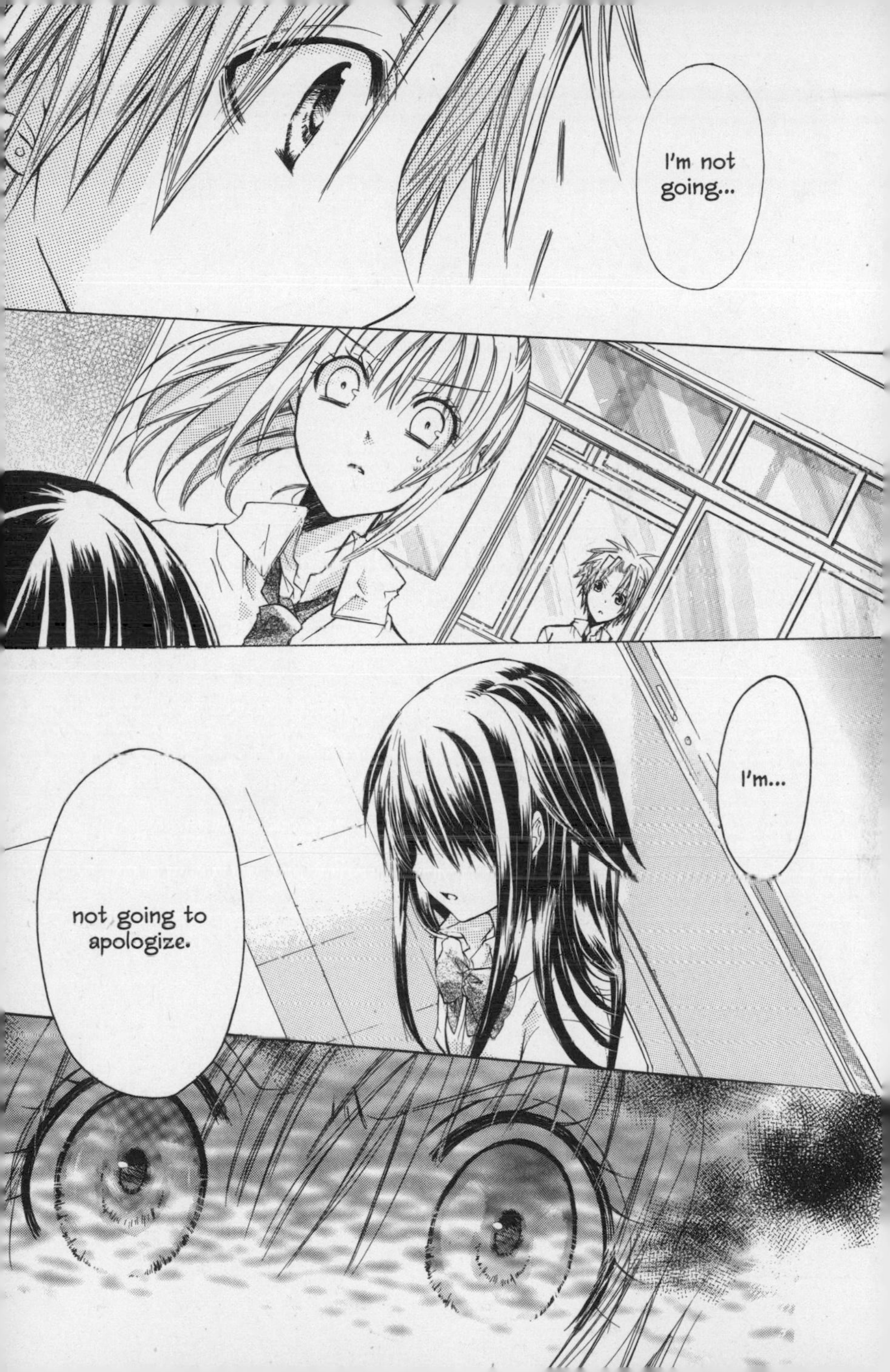
I'm not going...
I'm...
not going to apologize.

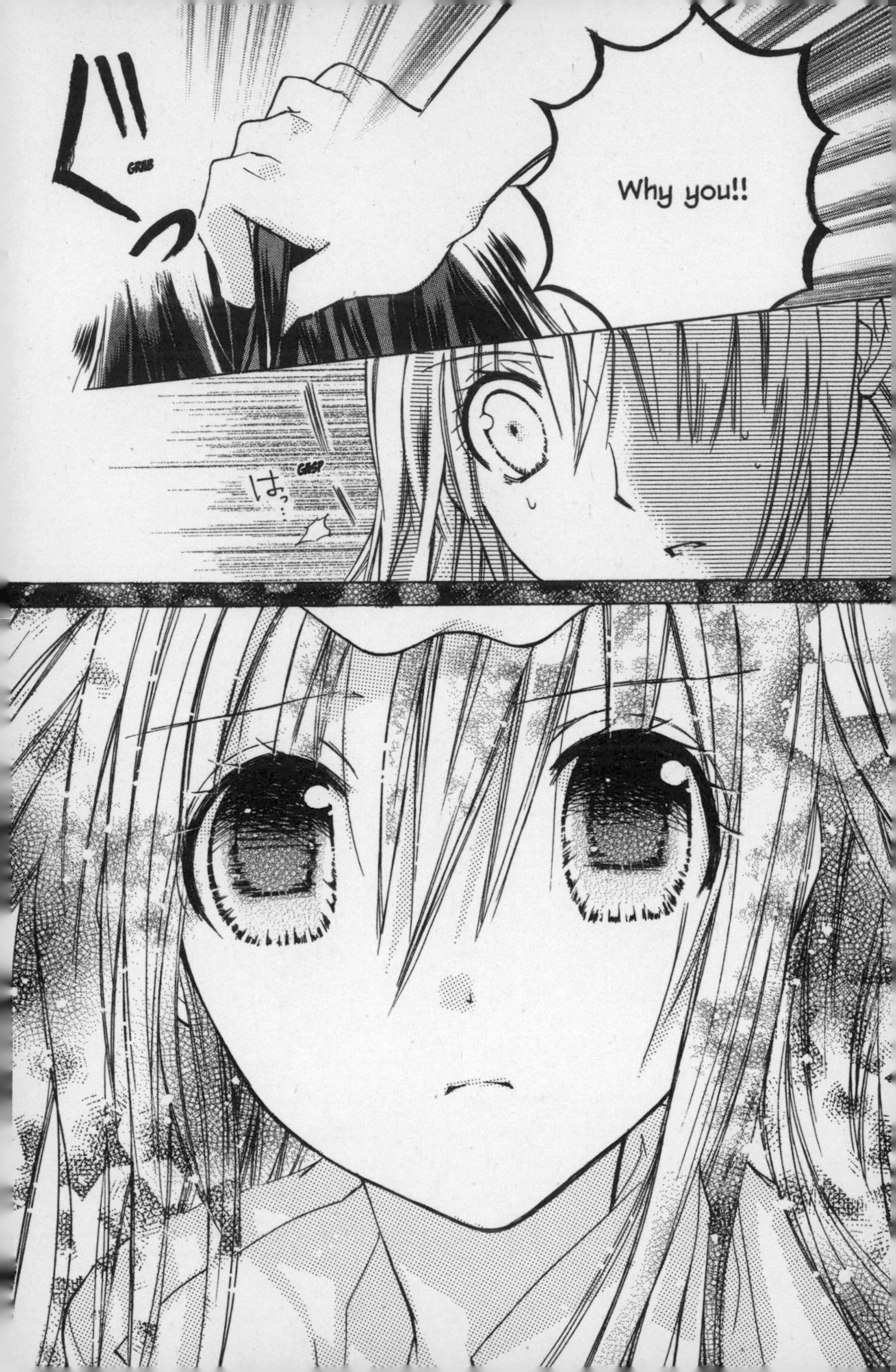
Why you!!
ぐっ
GRIB
はっ…
GASP

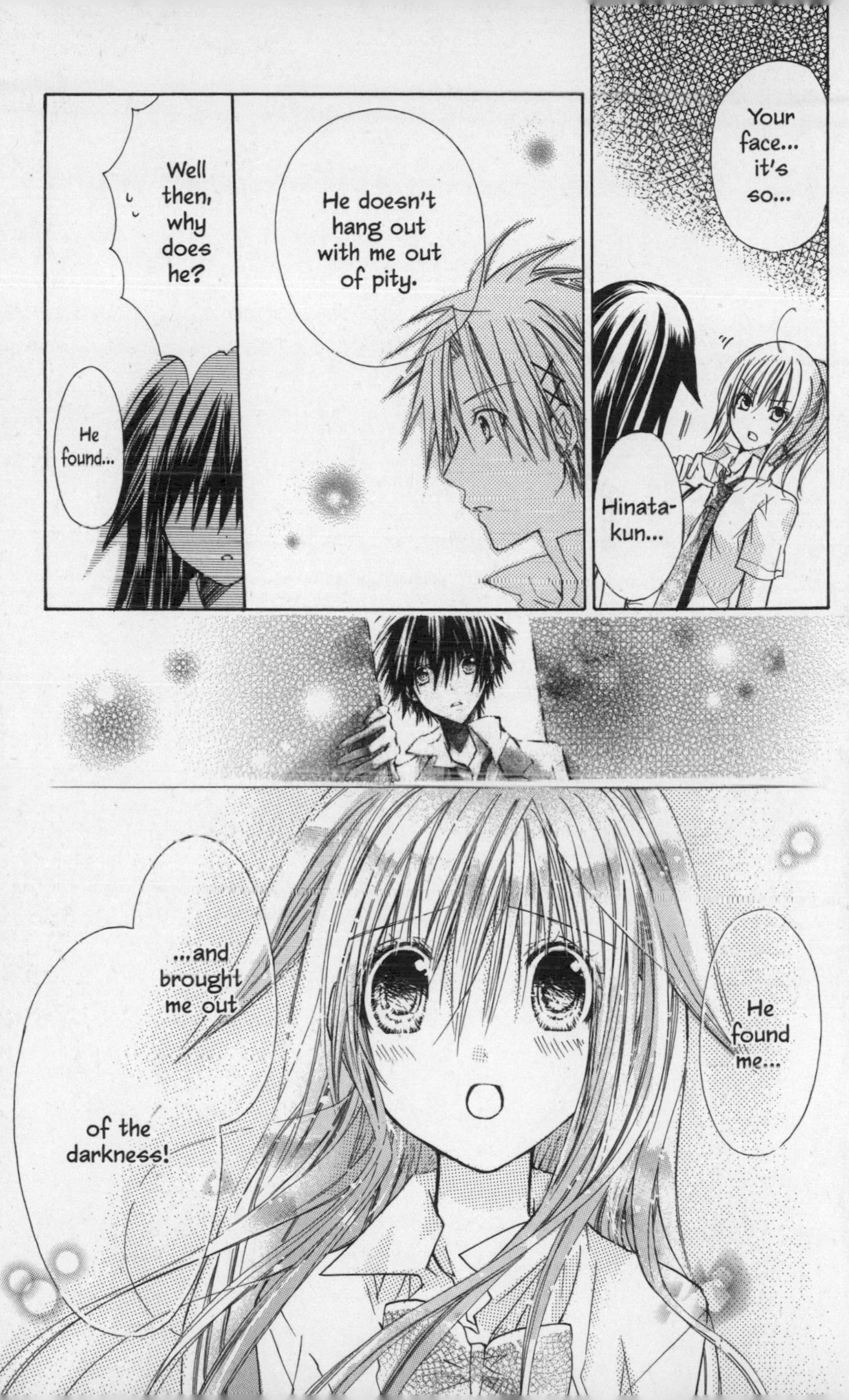
Your face... it's so...
Hinata-kun...
He doesn't hang out with me out of pity.
Well then, why does he?
He found...
He found me...
...and brought me out
of the darkness!

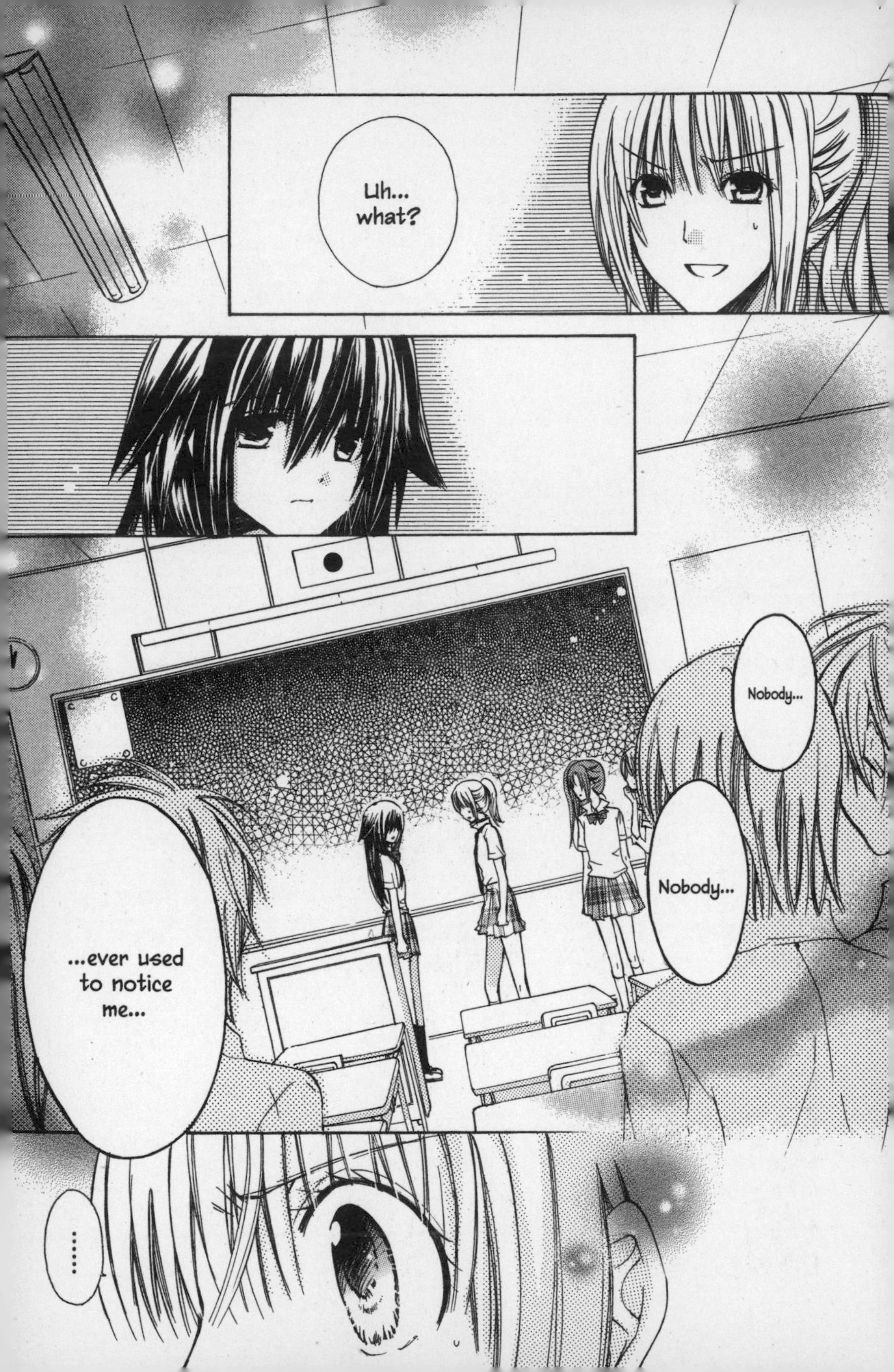
Uh... what?
Nobody...
Nobody...
...ever used to notice me...
......

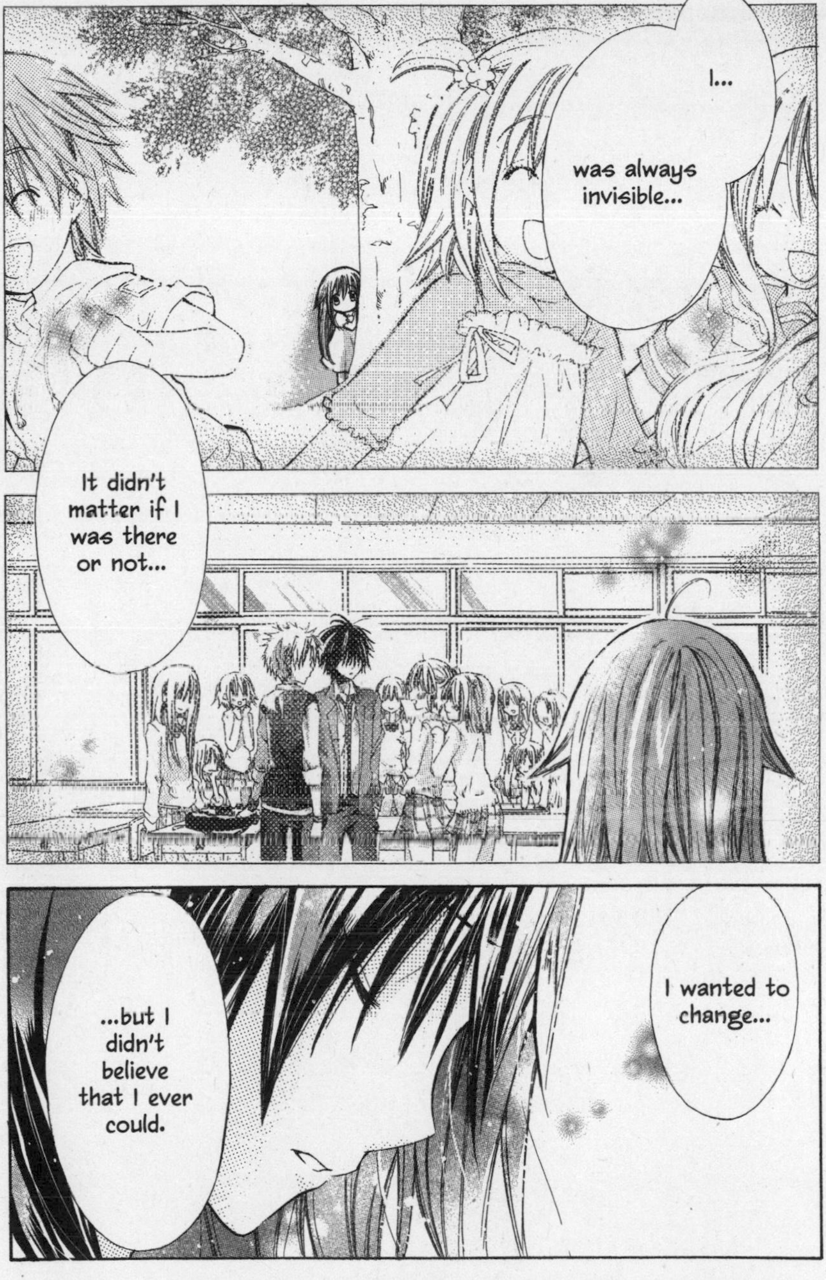
I...
was always invisible...
It didn't matter if I was there or not...
I wanted to change...
...but I didn't believe that I ever could.

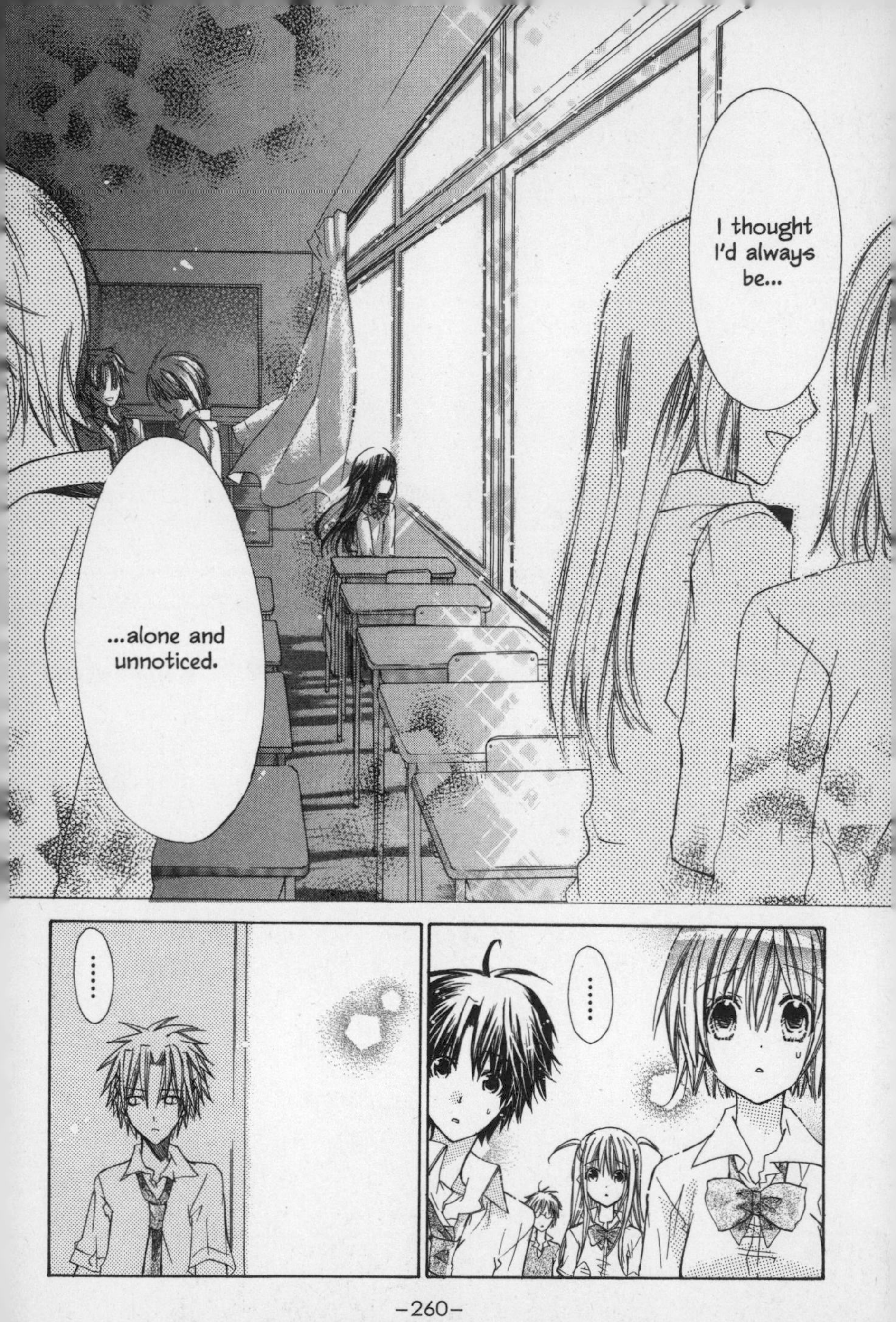
I thought I'd always be...
...alone and unnoticed.
......
......

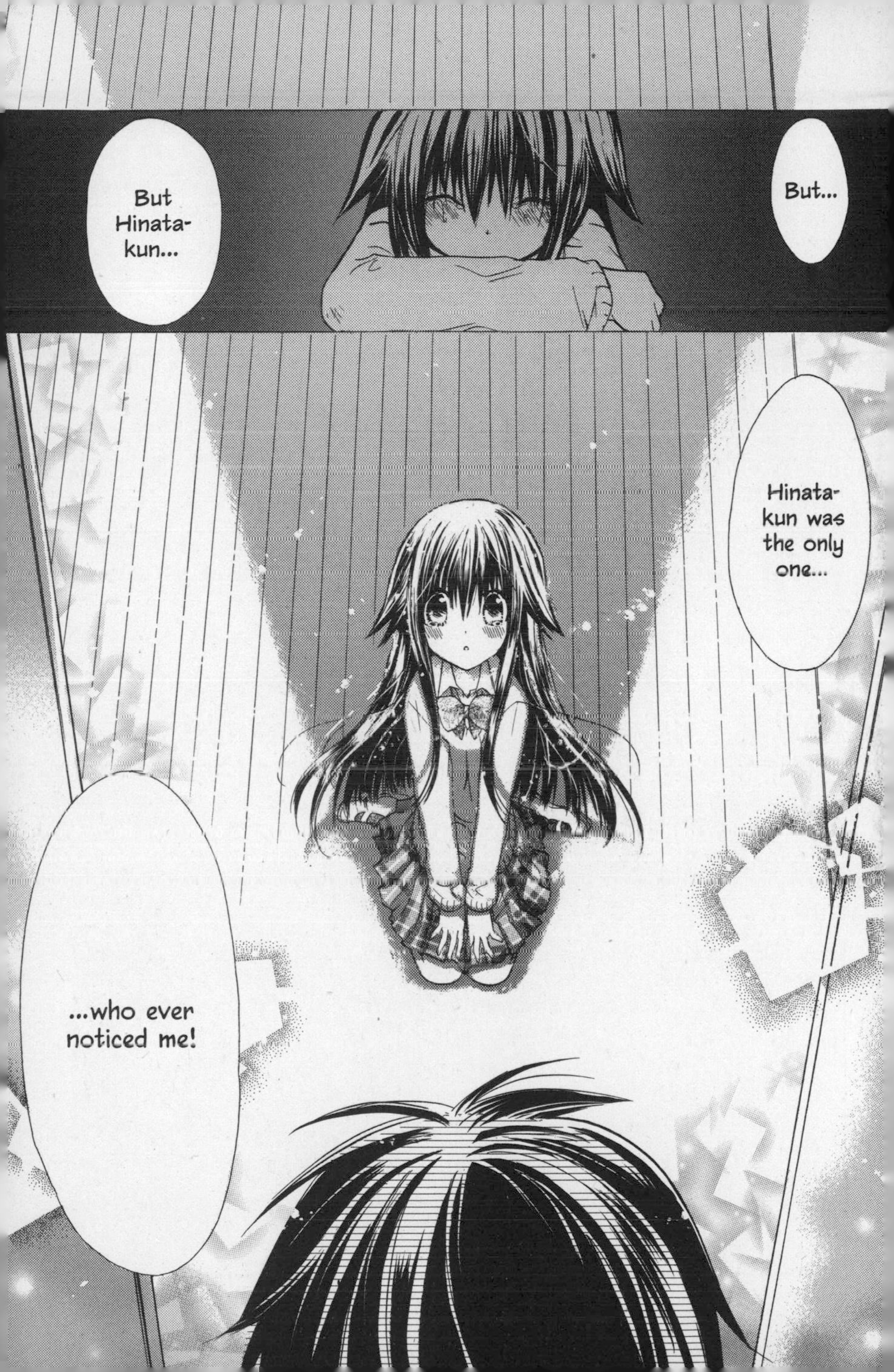
But...
But Hinata-kun...
Hinata-kun was the only one...
...who ever noticed me!

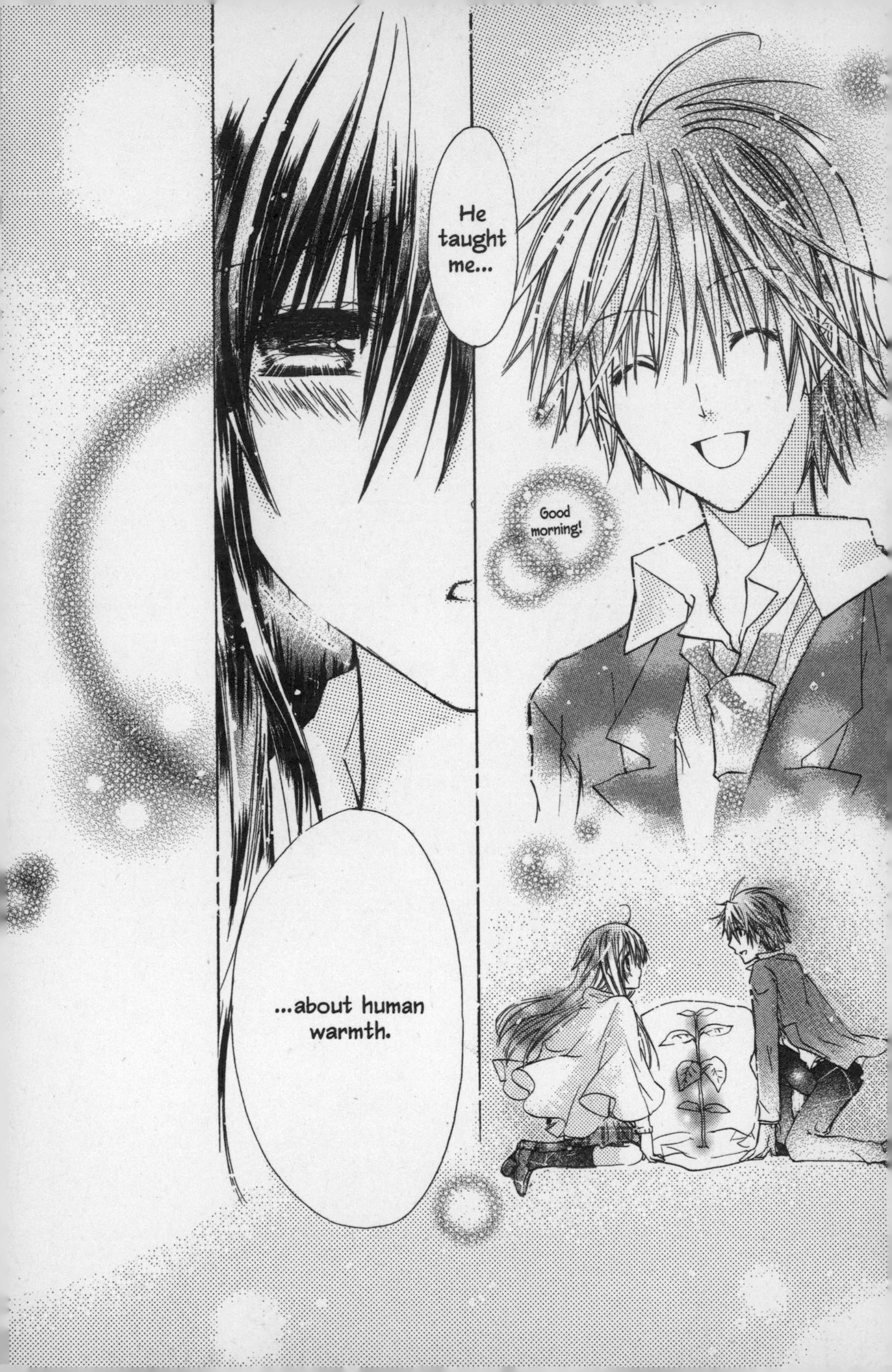
Good morning!
He taught me...
...about human warmth.

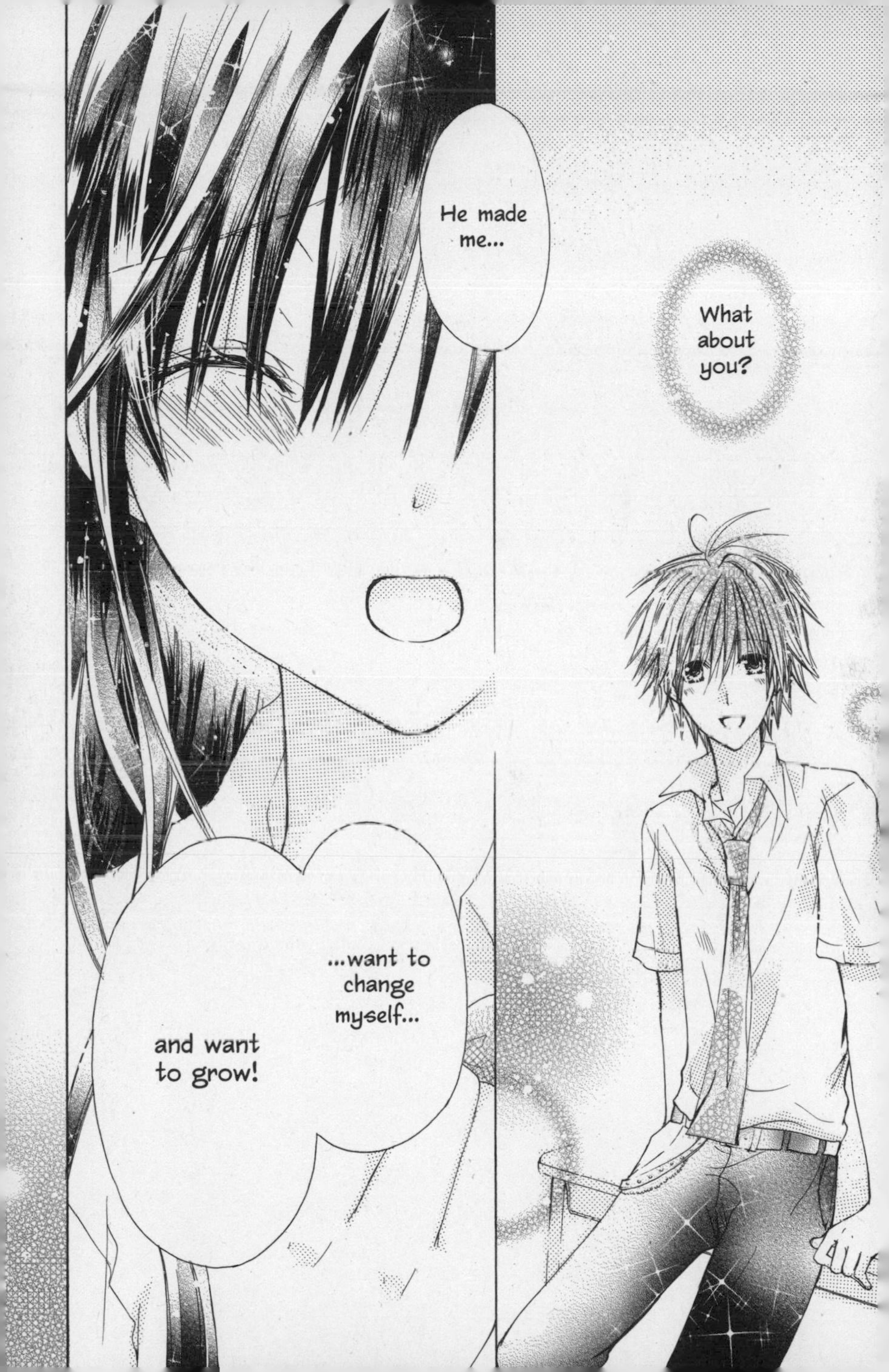
What about you?
He made me...
...want to change myself...
and want to grow!

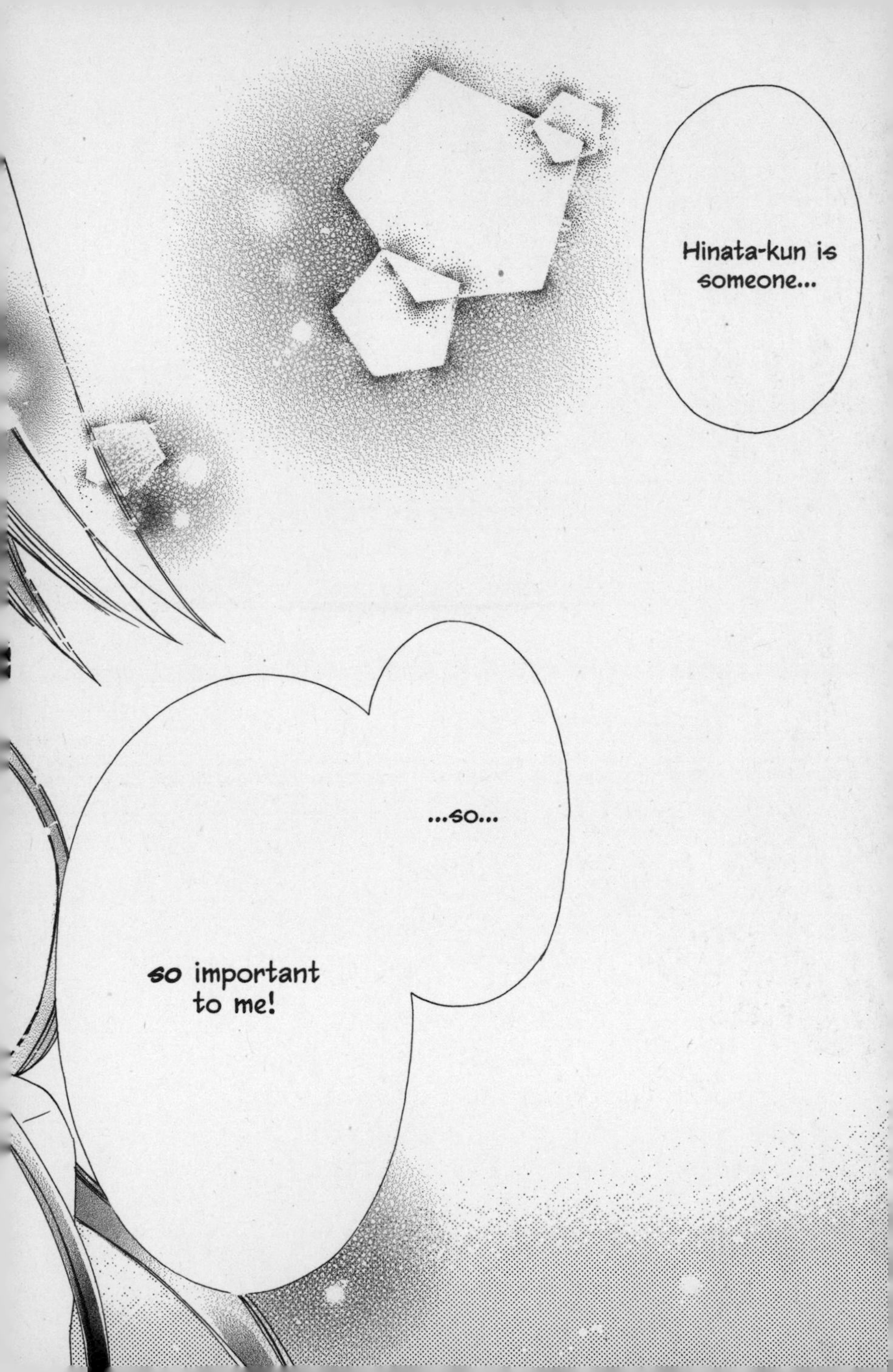
Hinata-kun is someone...
...so...
so important to me!

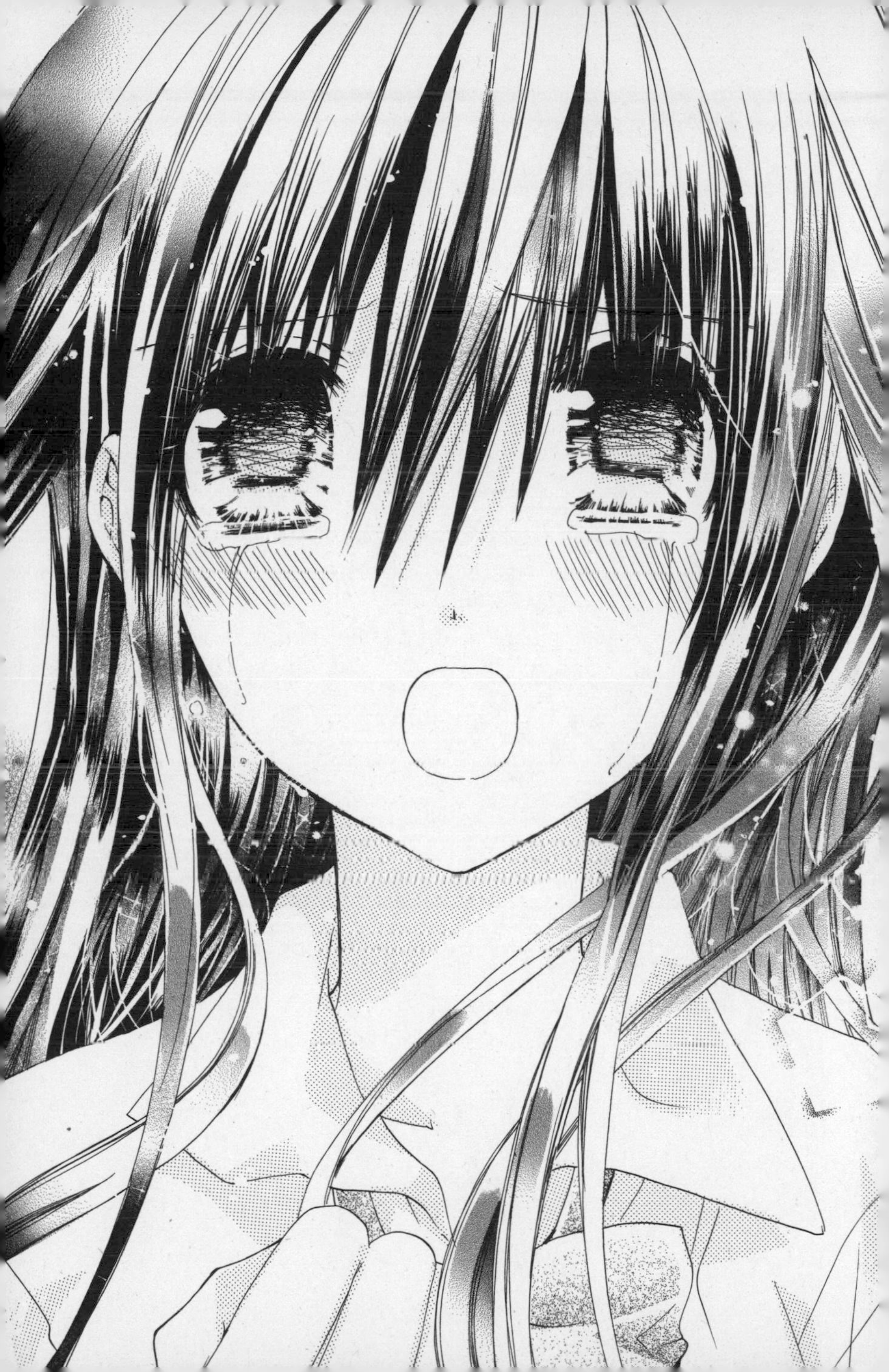

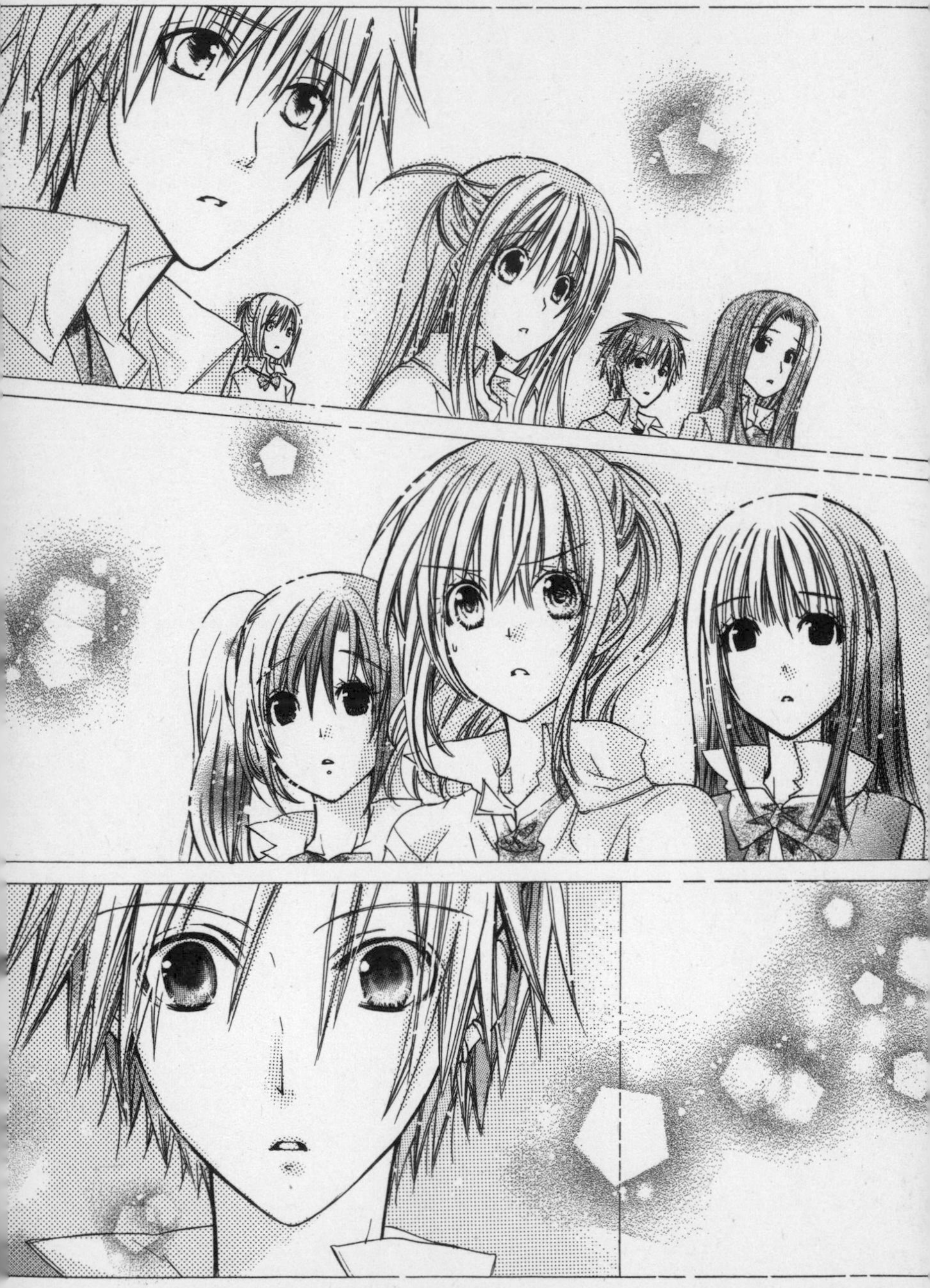

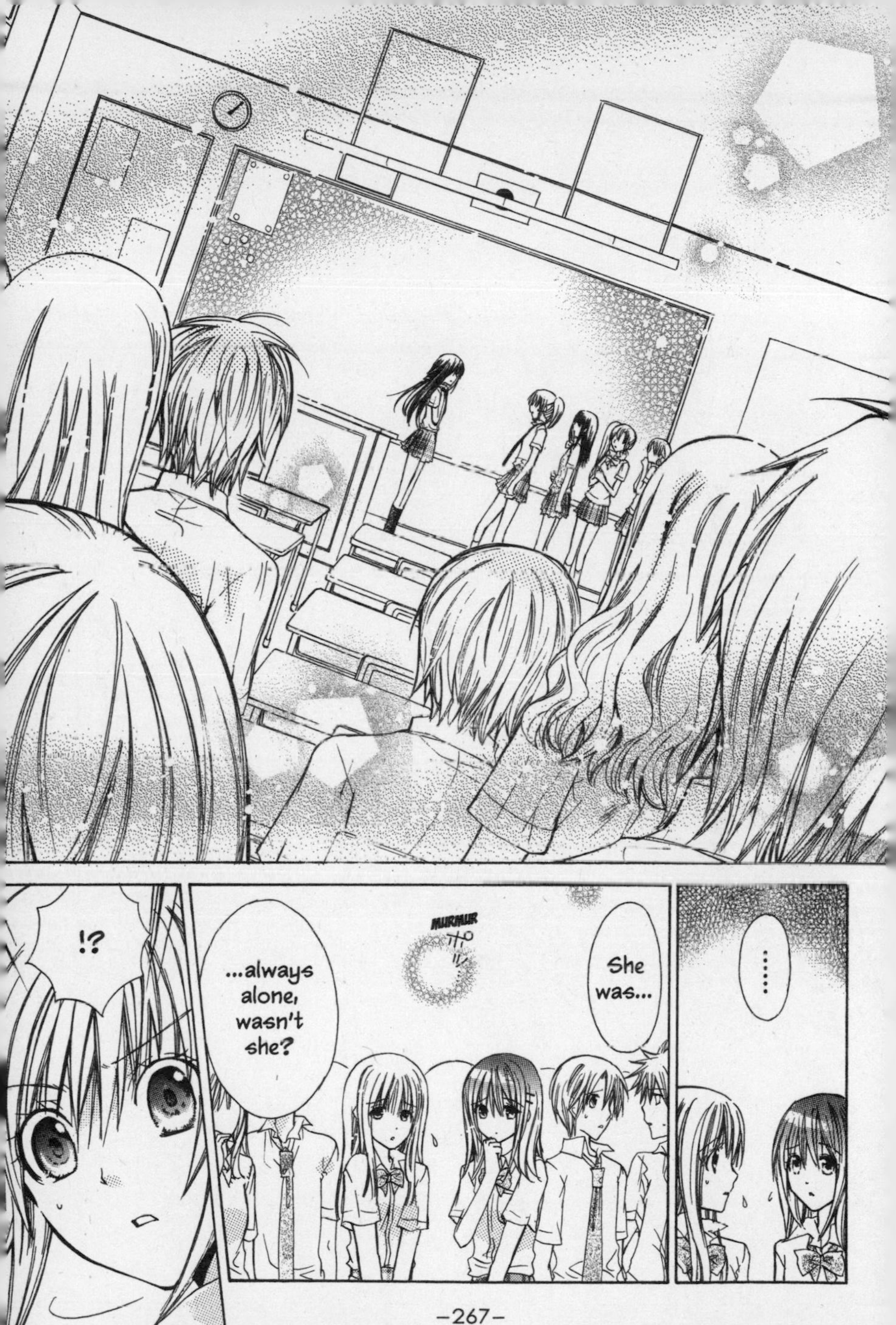
......
She was...
MURMUR
...always alone, wasn't she?
!?

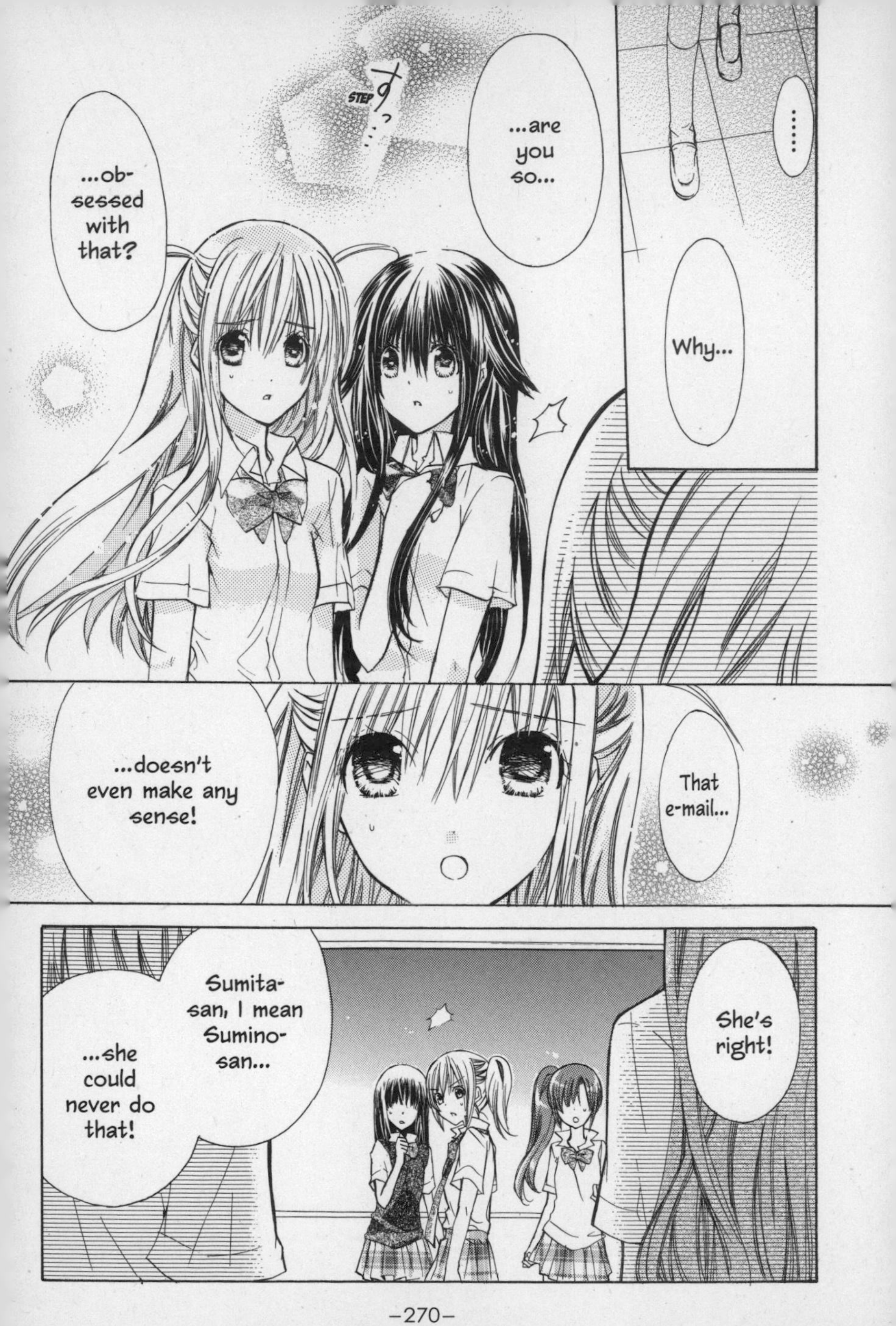

......
Why...
...are you so...
STEP
...ob-sessed with that?
That e-mail...
...doesn't even make any sense!
She's right!
Sumita-san, I mean Sumino-san...
...she could never do that!

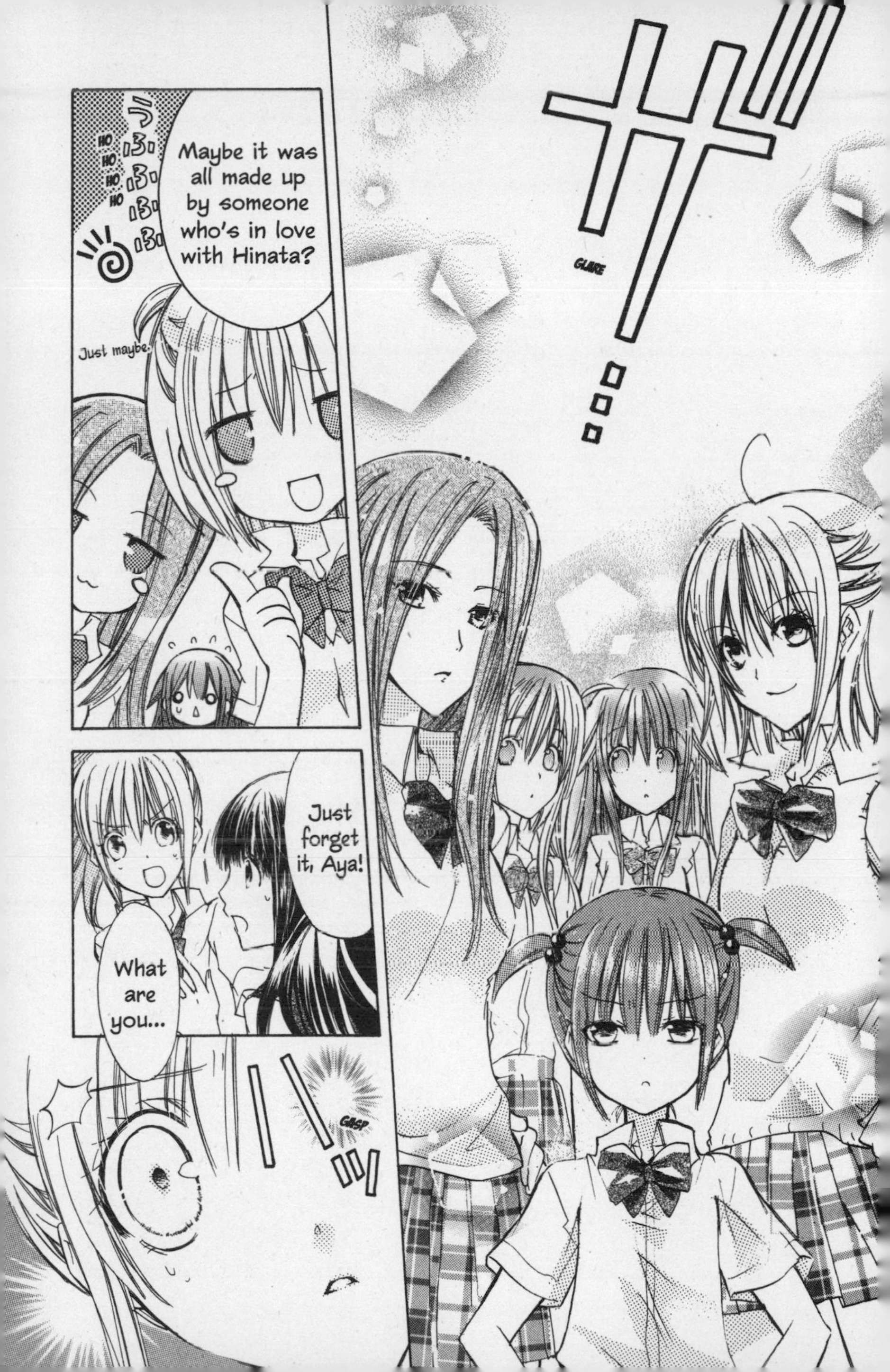

ザ
GLARE
Maybe it was all made up by someone who's in love with Hinata?
うふふふふ
HO HO HO HO
Just maybe.
Just forget it, Aya!
What are you...
GASP

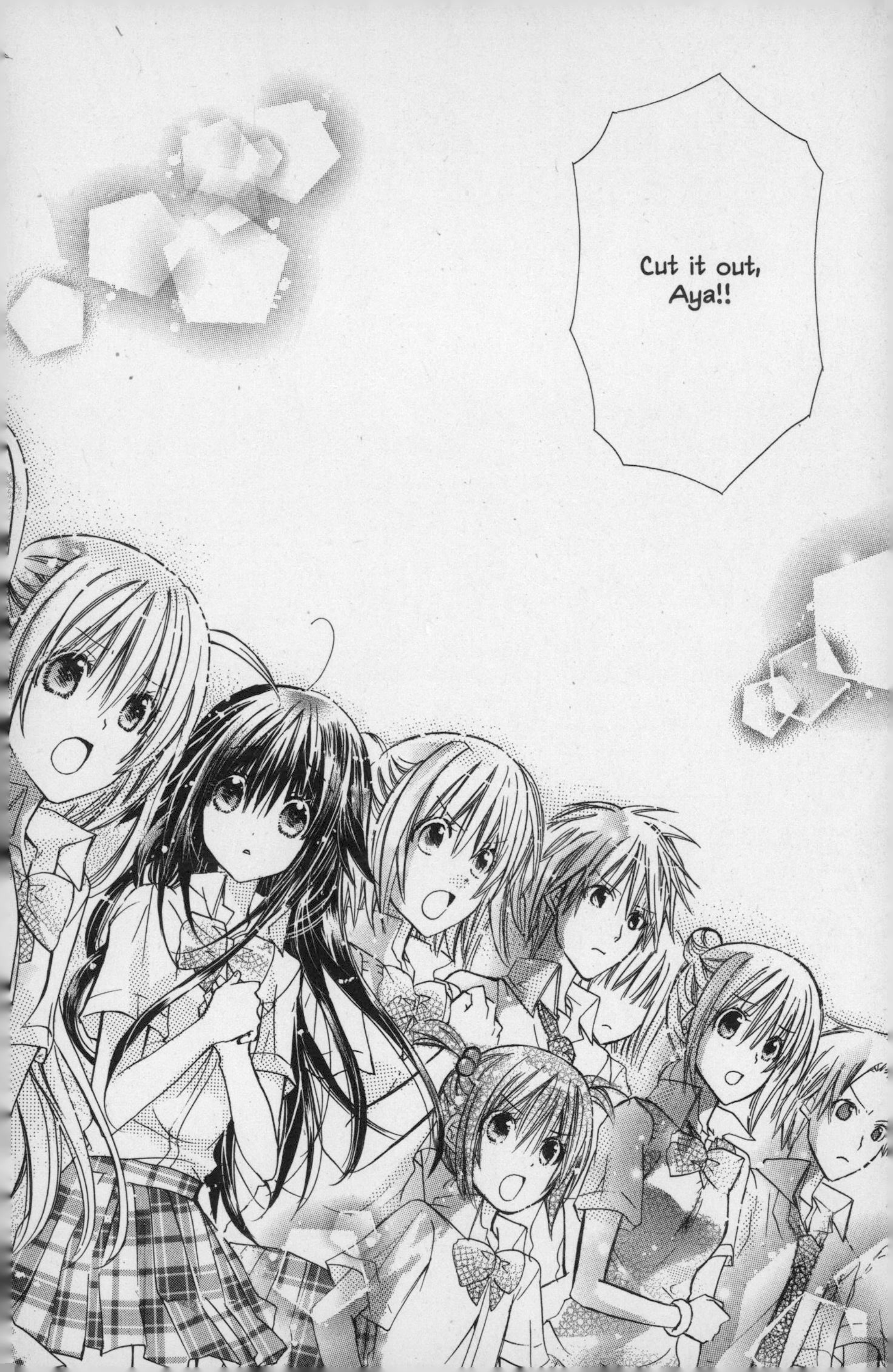
Cut it out, Aya!!

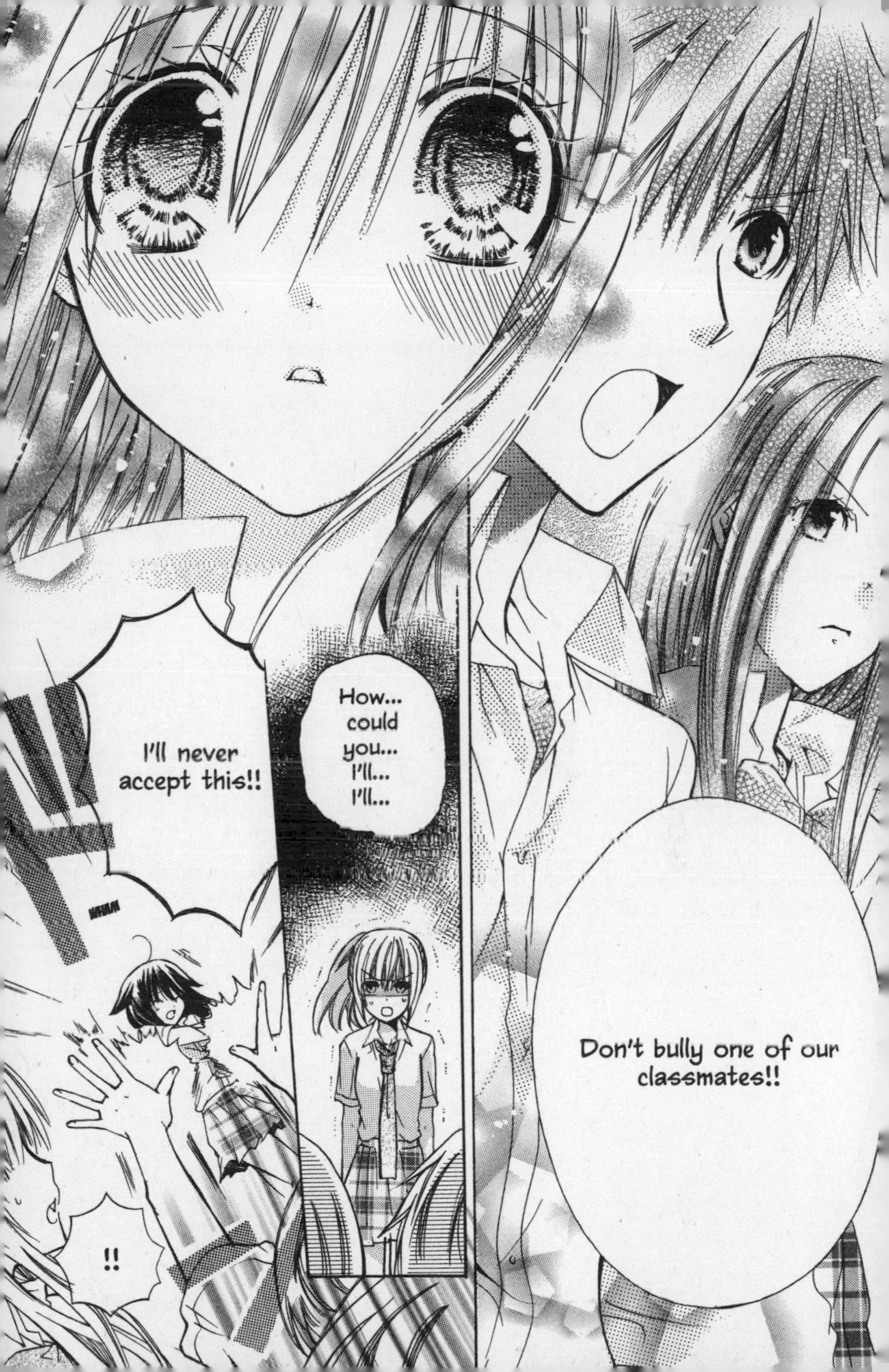
Don't bully one of our classmates!!
How... could you... I'll... I'll...
I'll never accept this!!
!!

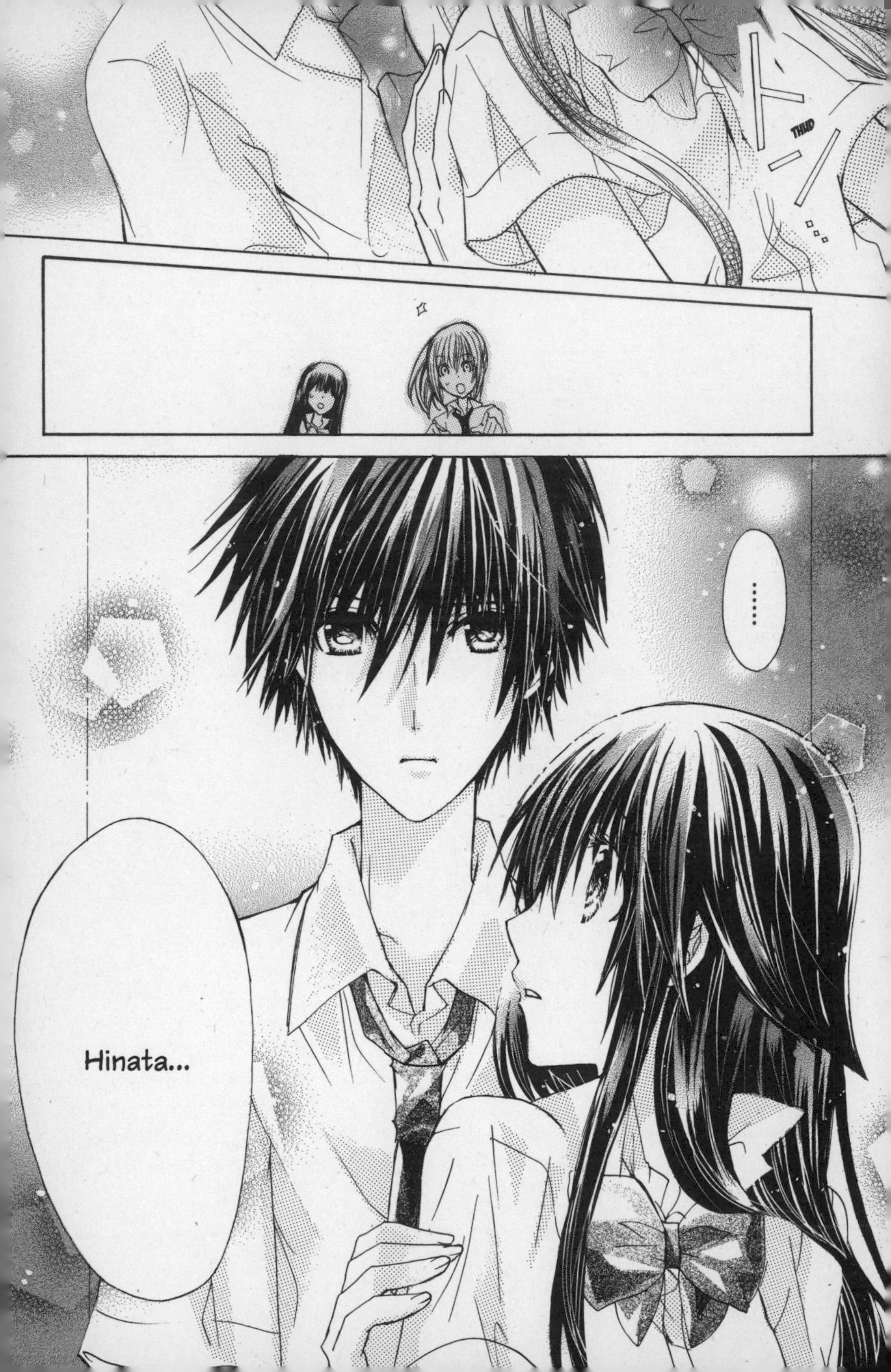
THUD
......
Hinata...

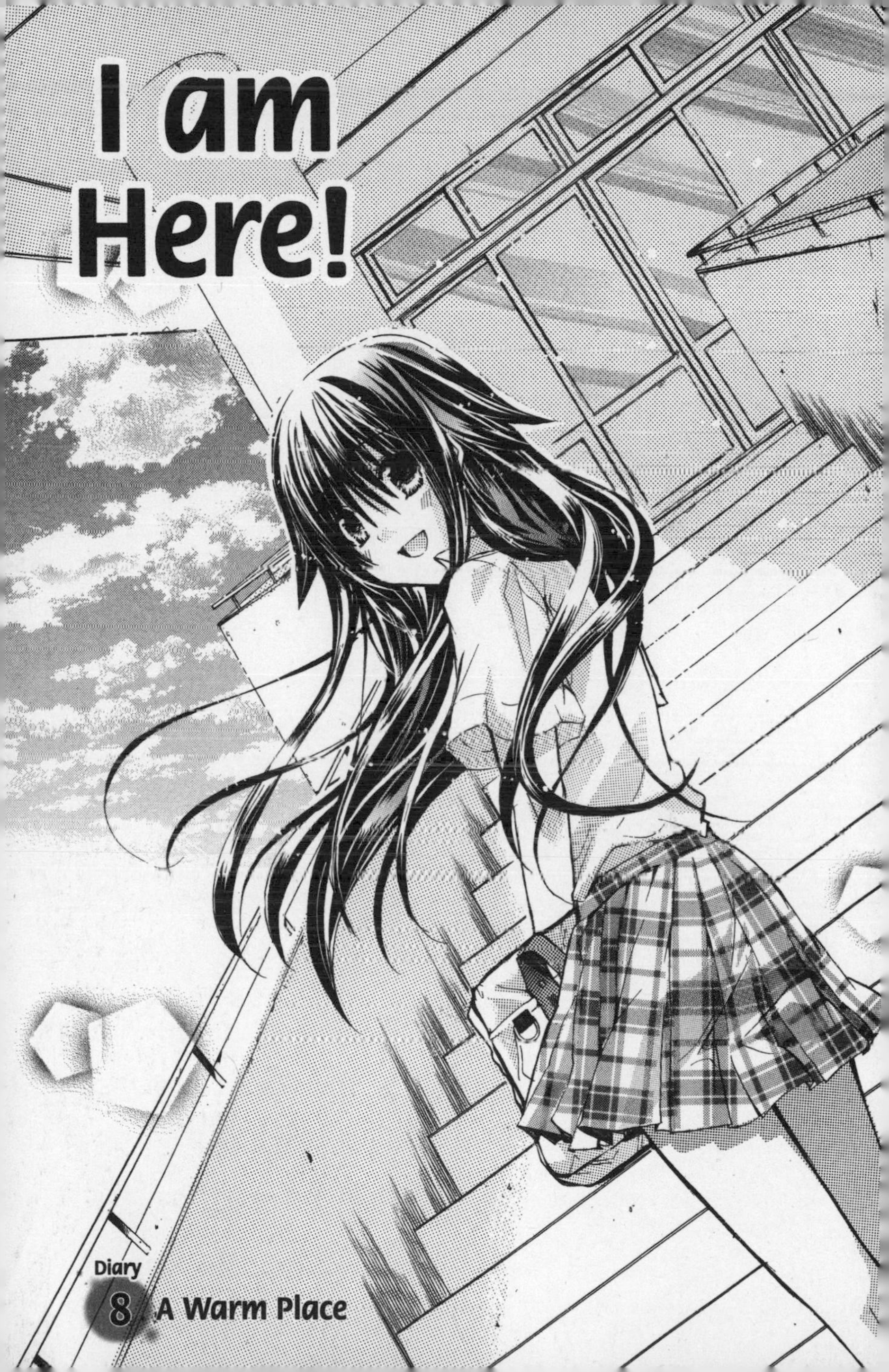
I am Here!
Diary 8 A Warm Place

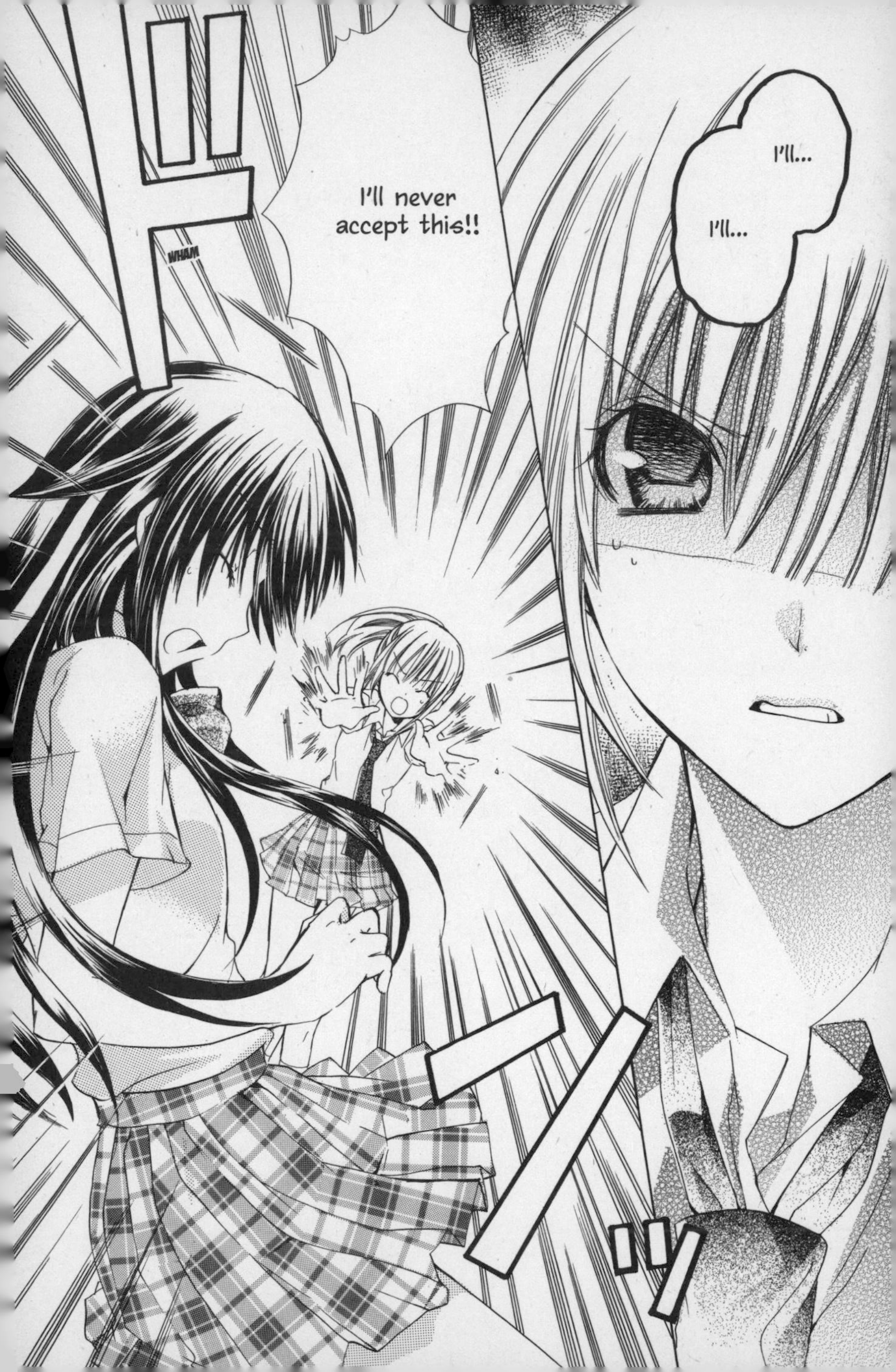
I'll...
I'll...
I'll never accept this!!
WHAM

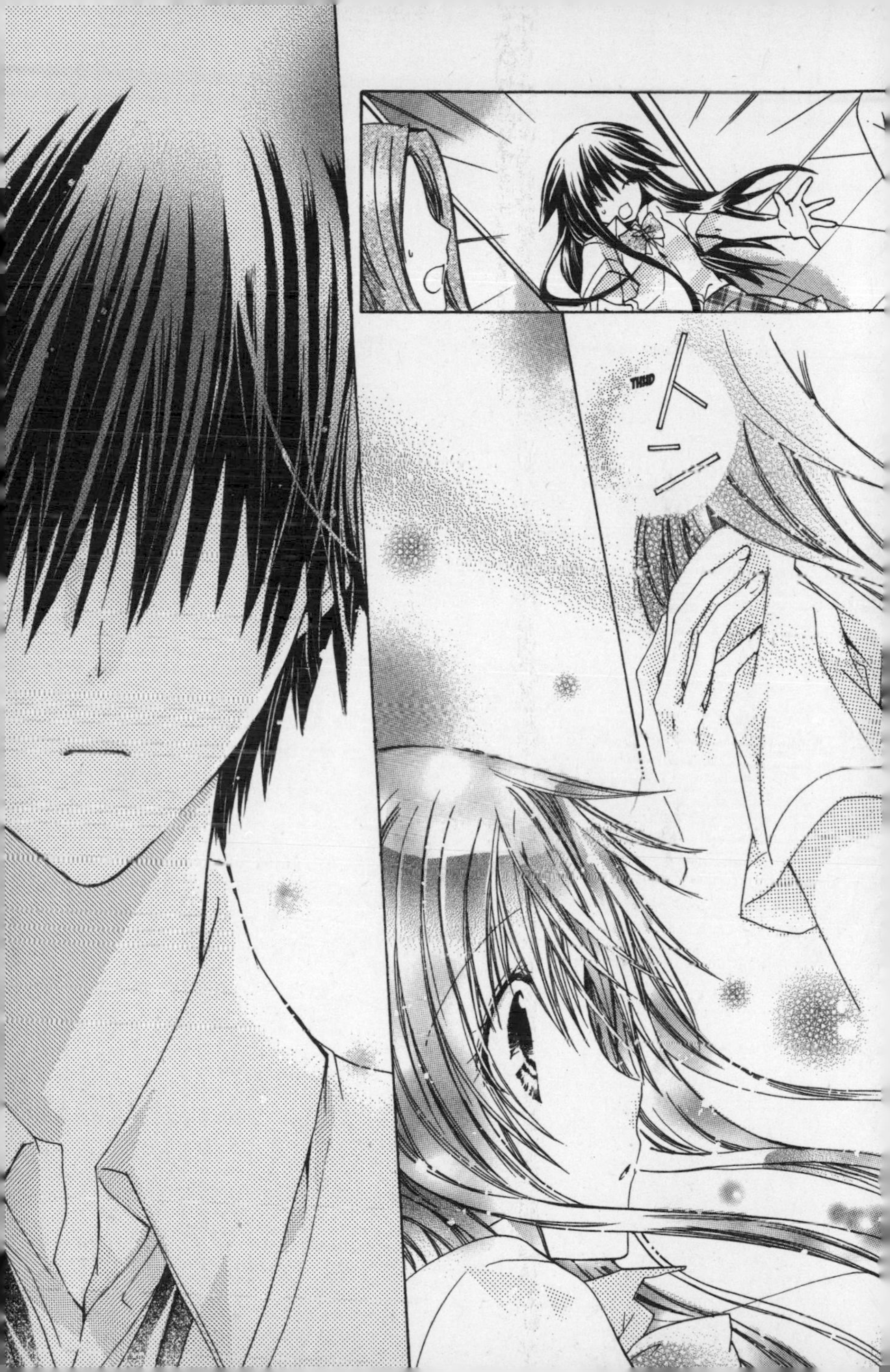
THUD

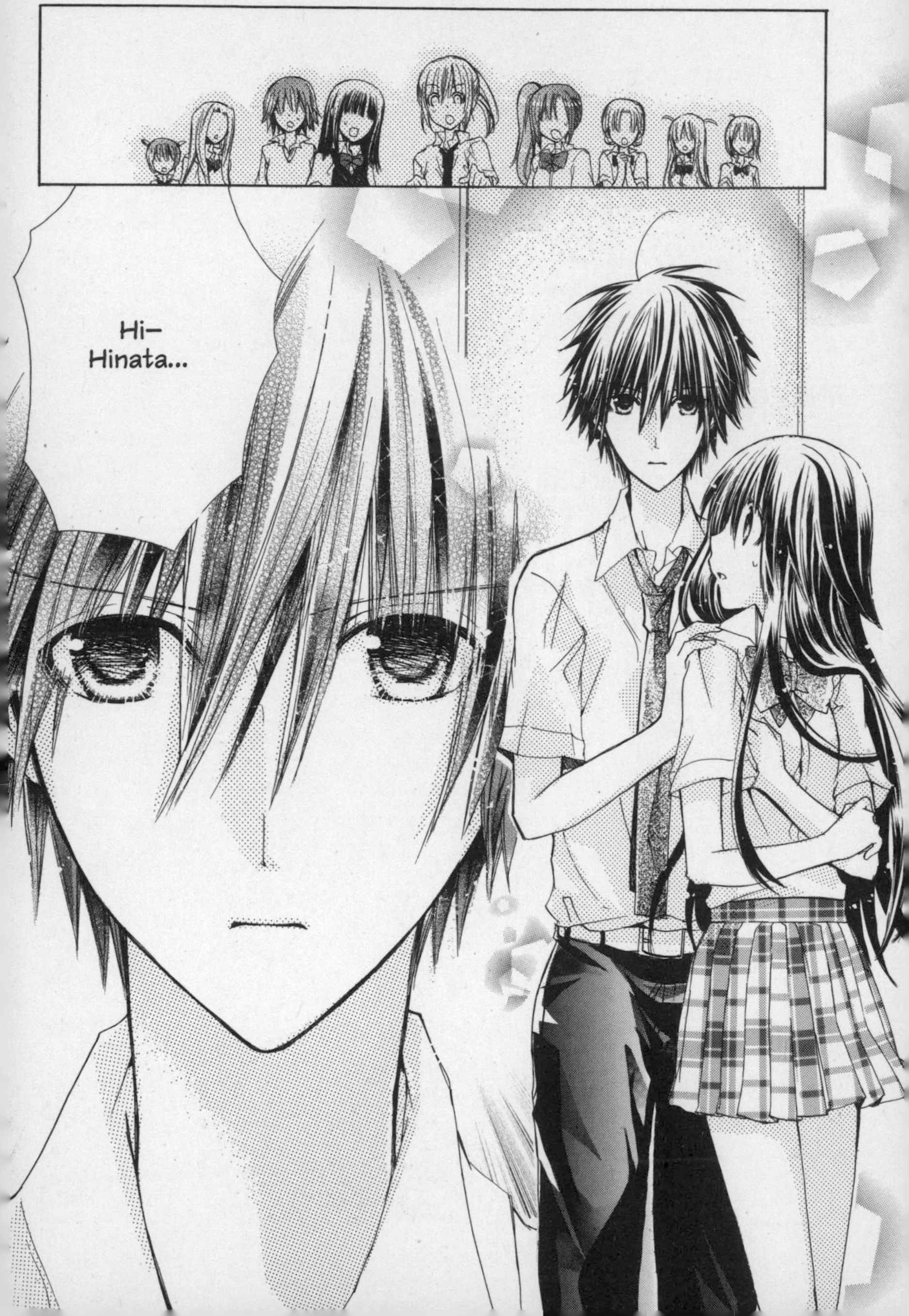
Hi–
Hinata...

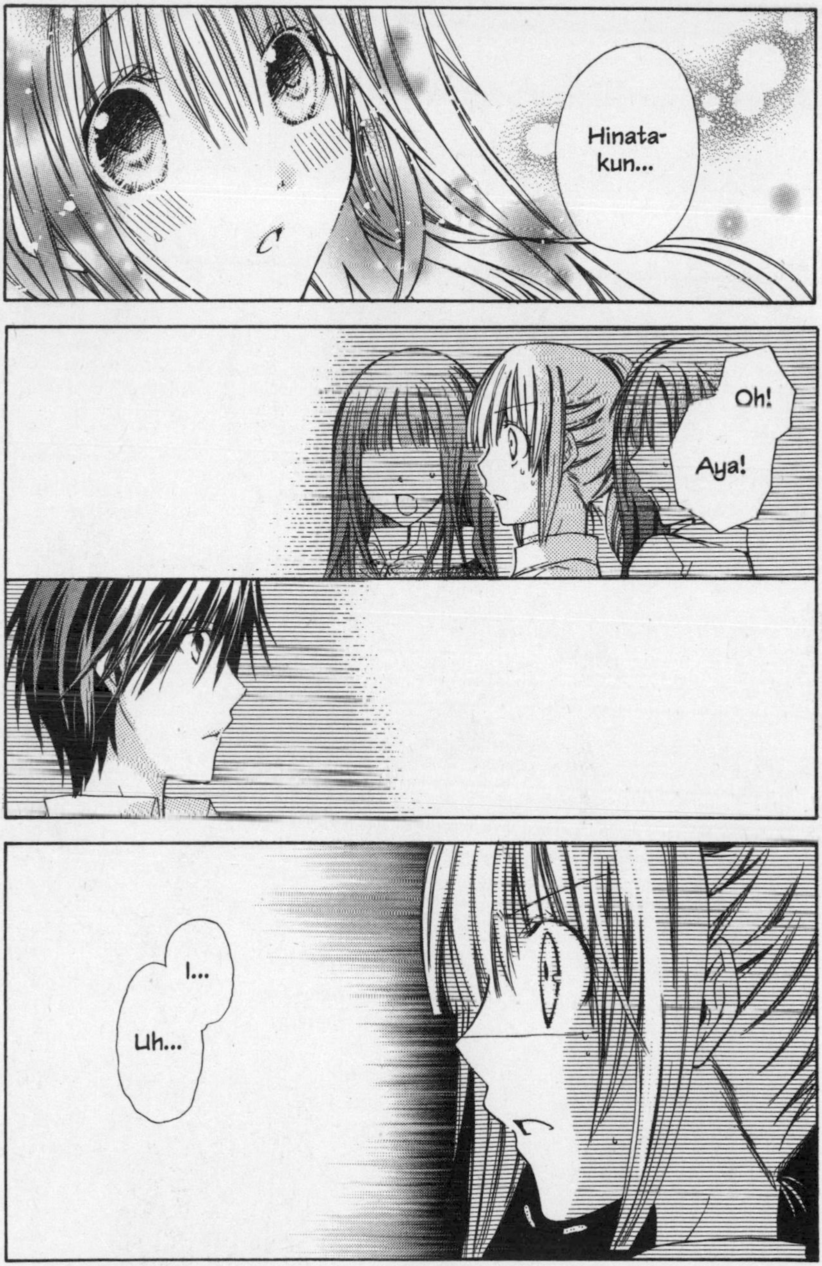
Hinata-kun...
Oh!
Aya!
I...
Uh...

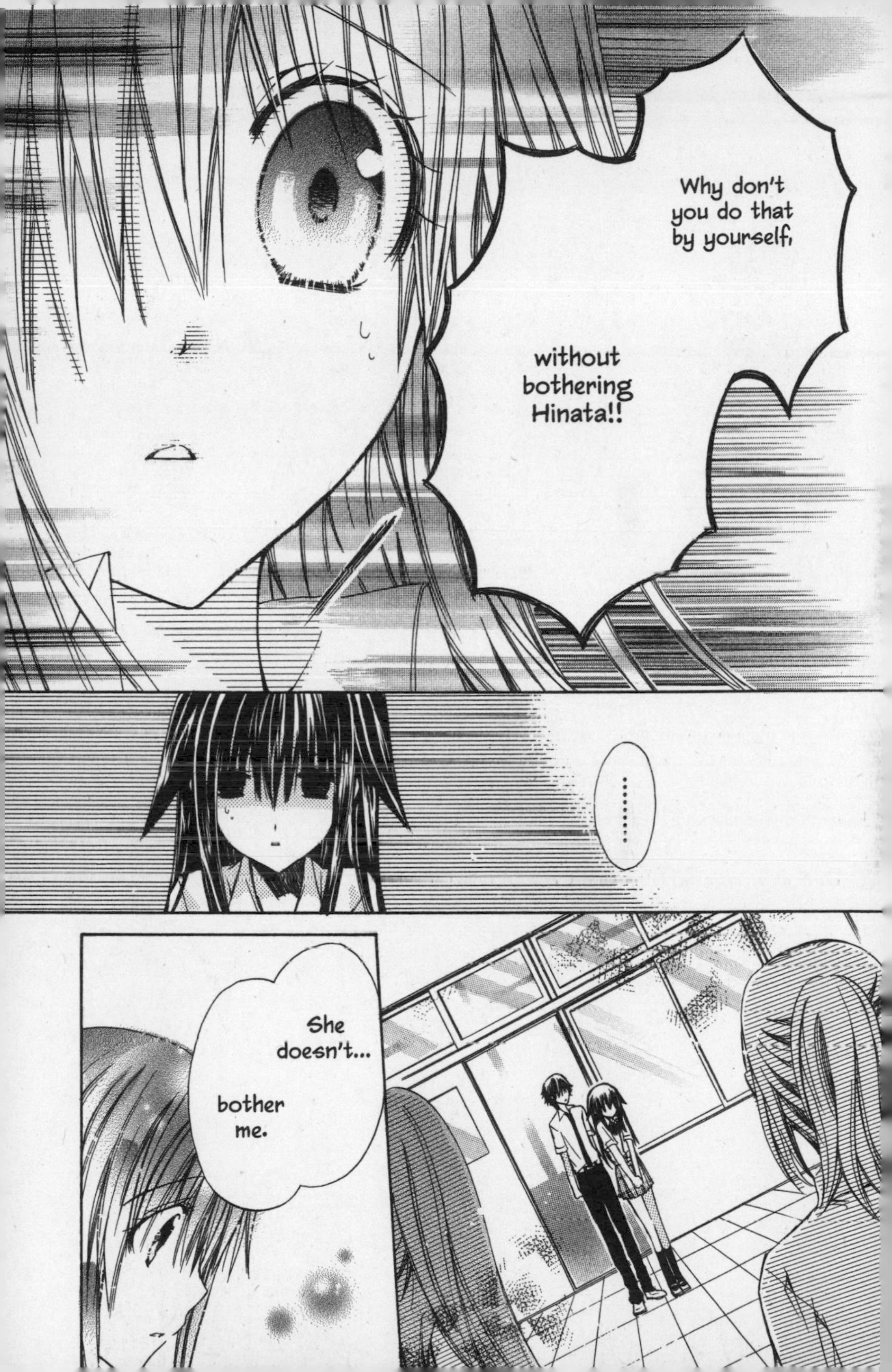
Why don't you do that by yourself,
without bothering Hinata!!
......!
She doesn't...
bother me.

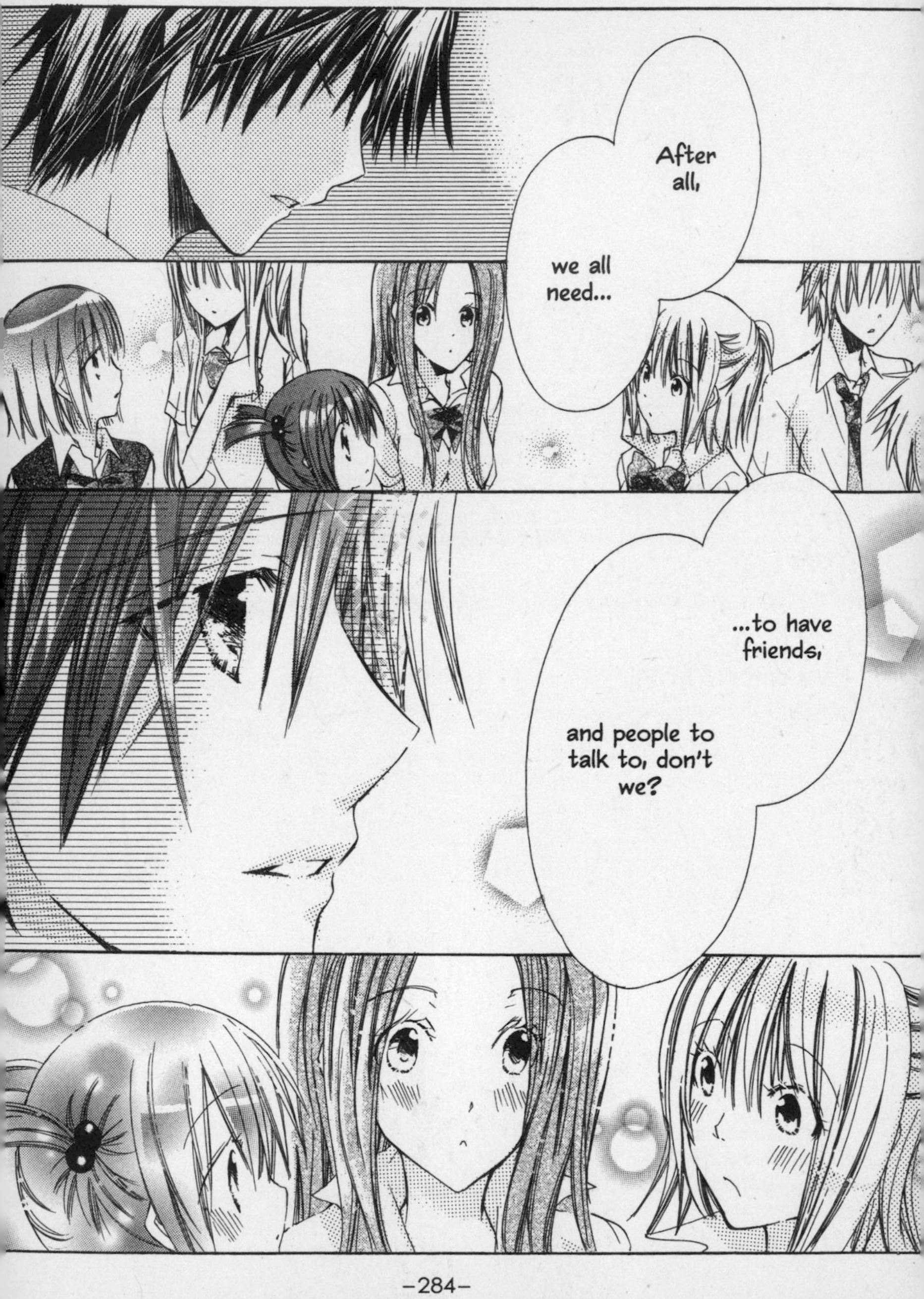
After all,
we all need...
...to have friends,
and people to talk to, don't we?

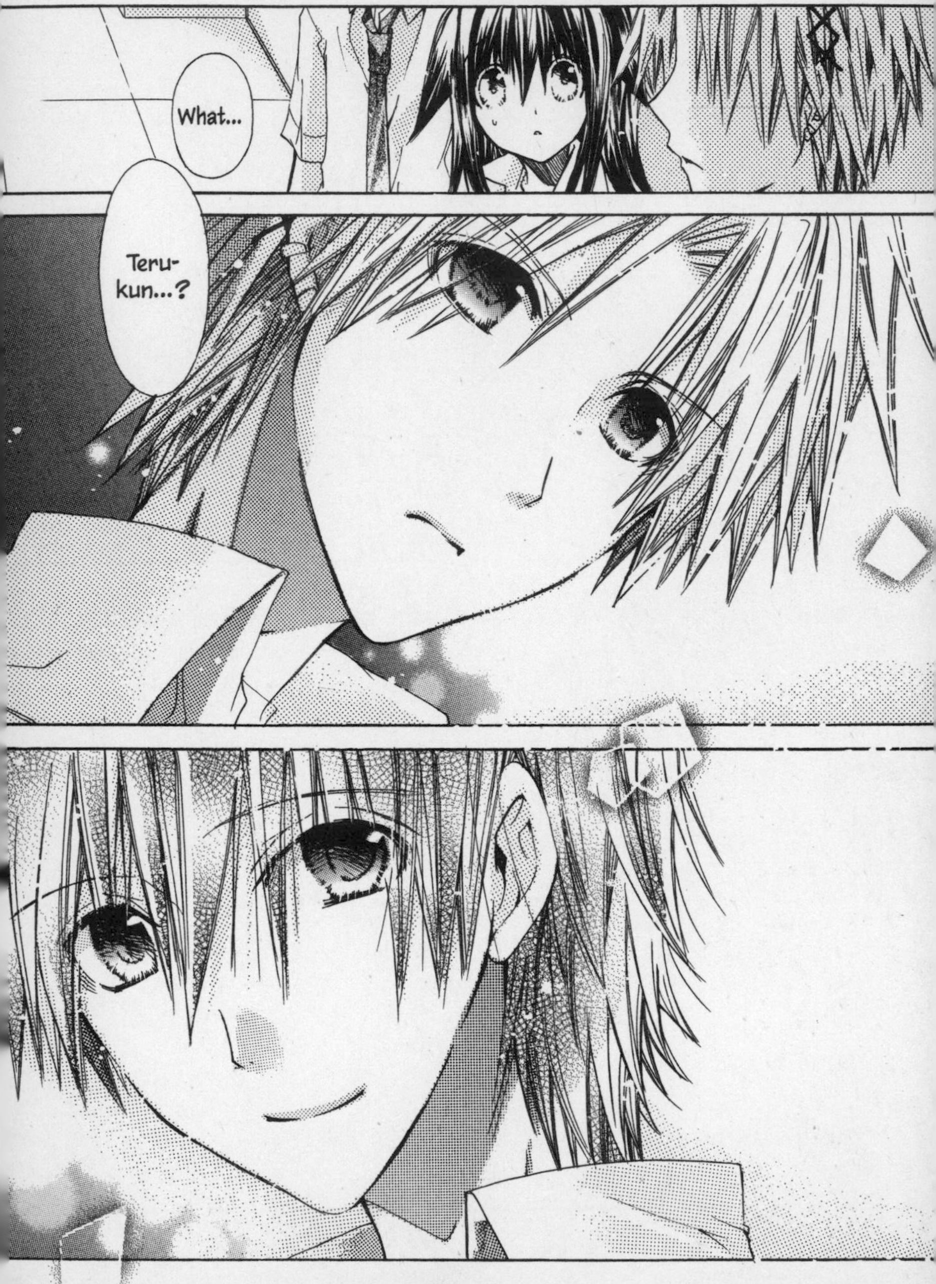
What...
Teru-kun...?

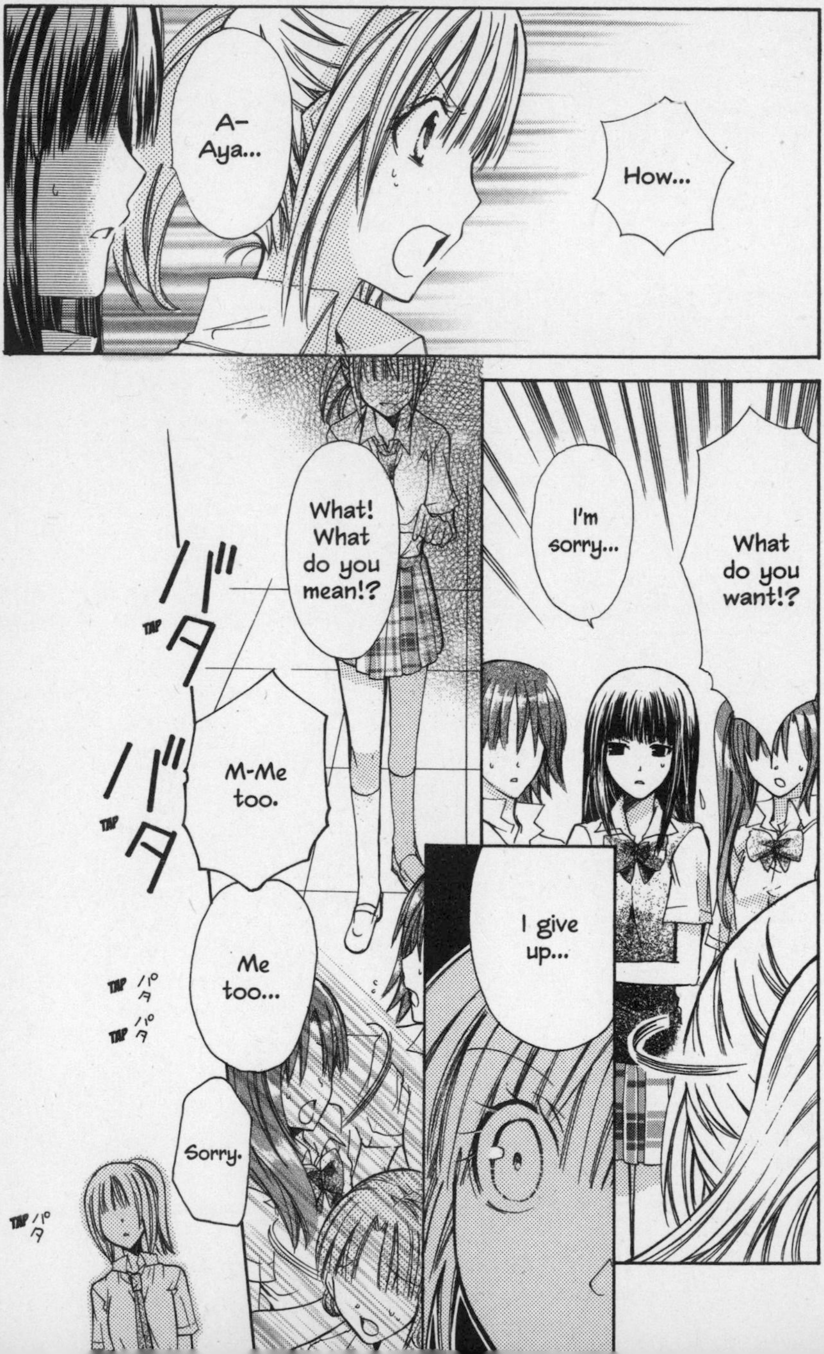
How...
A-Aya...
What do you want!?
I'm sorry...
I give up...
What! What do you mean!?
バタ TAP
バタ TAP
M-Me too.
Me too...
パタ TAP
パタ TAP
Sorry.
パタ TAP

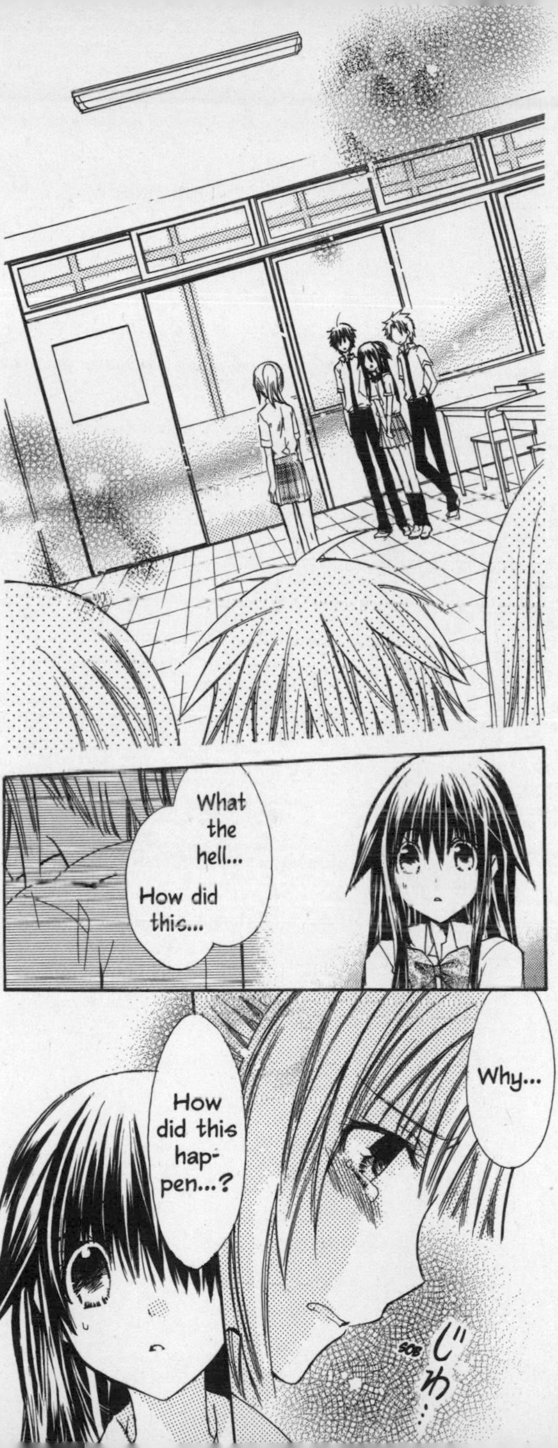
What the hell...
How did this...
Why...
How did this hap-pen...?
SOB

Since You Demanded

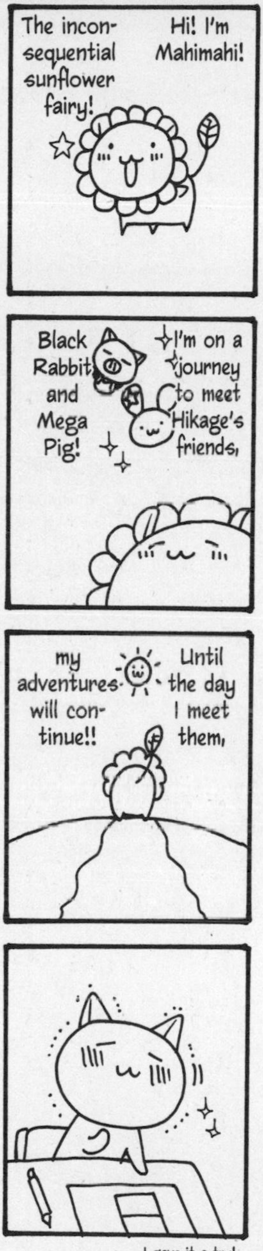
Hi! I'm Mahimahi!
The incon-sequential sunflower fairy!
I'm on a journey to meet Hikage's friends,
Black Rabbit and Mega Pig!
Until the day I meet them,
my adventures will con-tinue!!
I gave it a try!

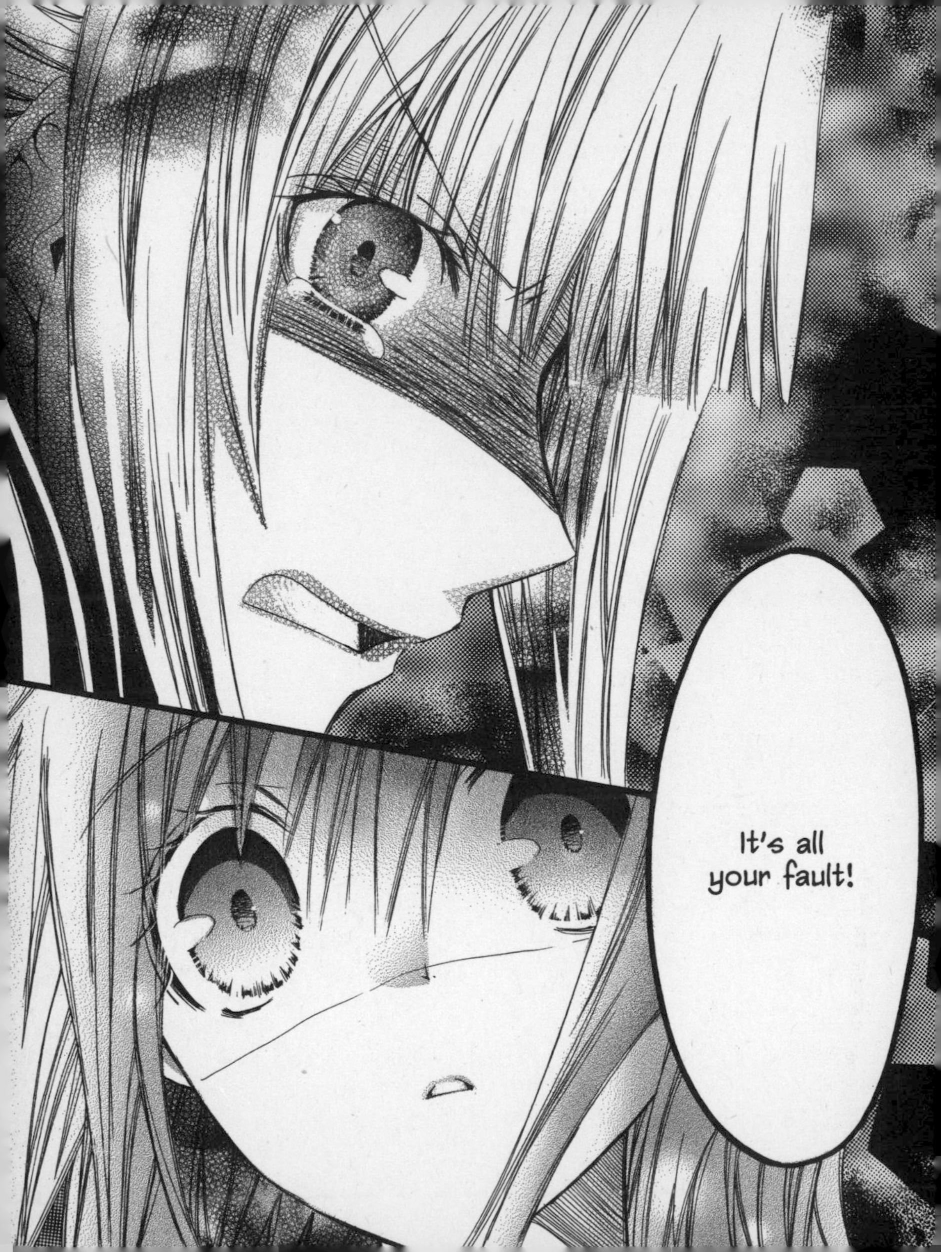
It's all your fault!

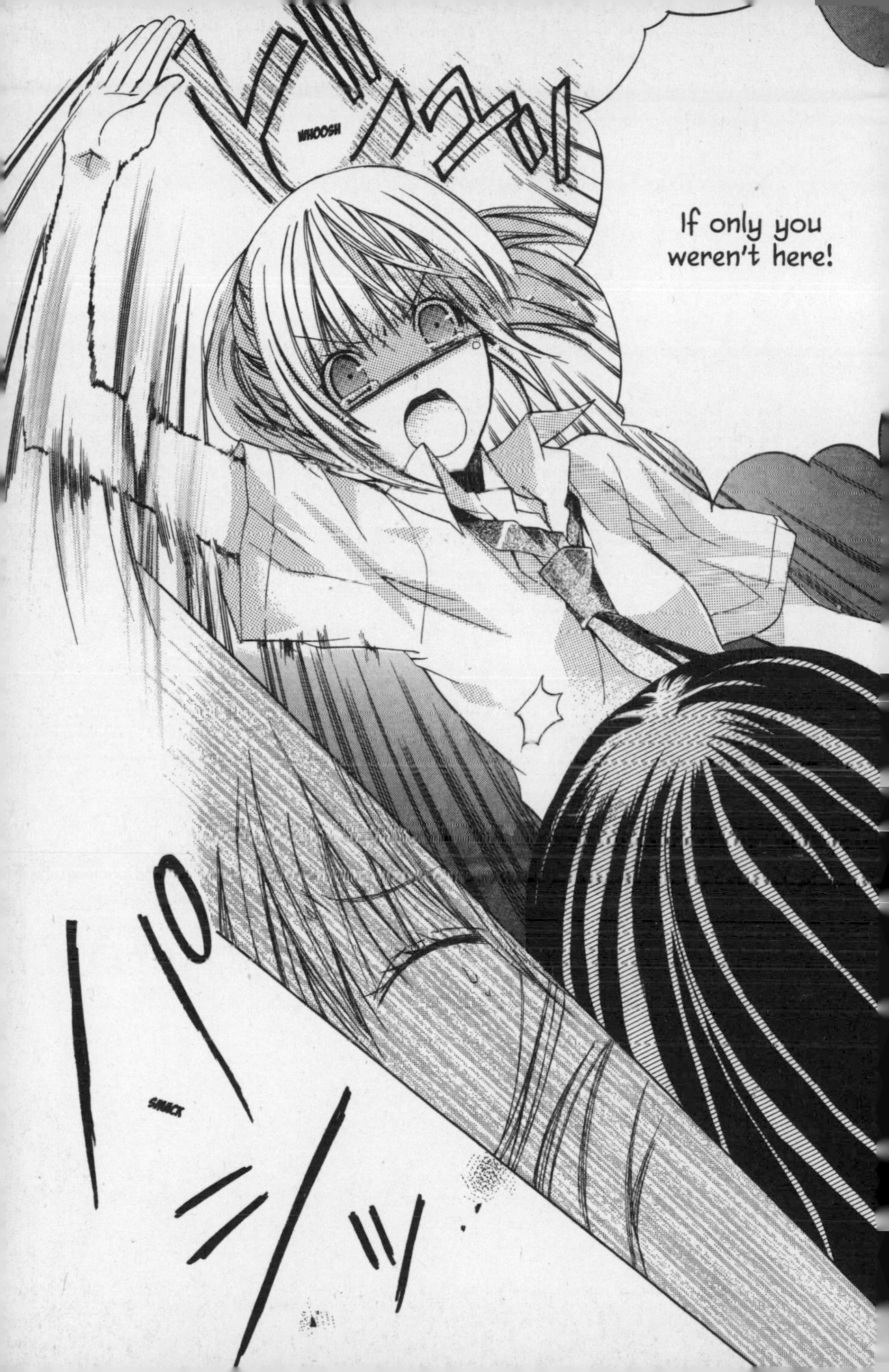
If only you weren't here!
WHOOSH
SMACK

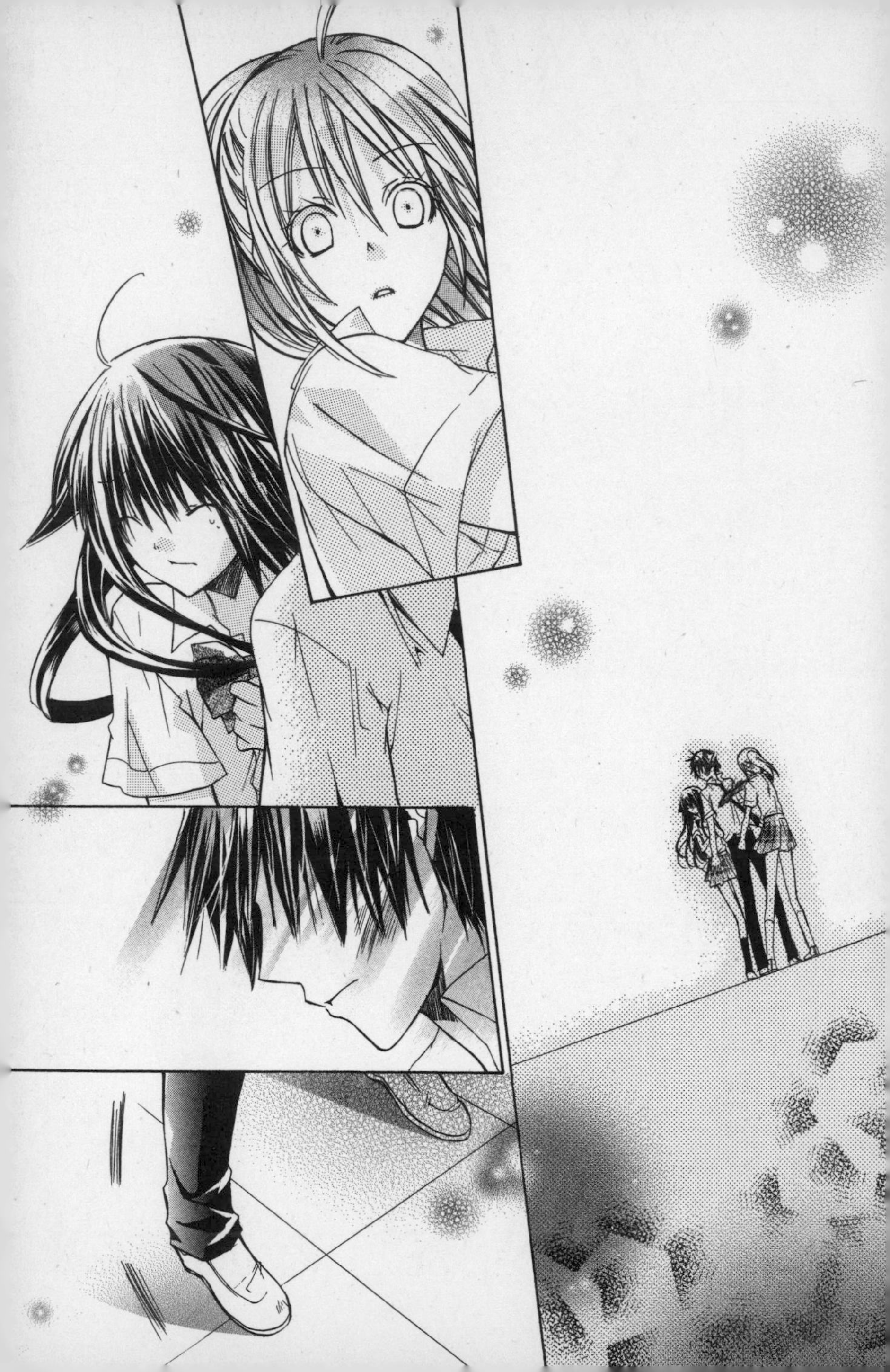

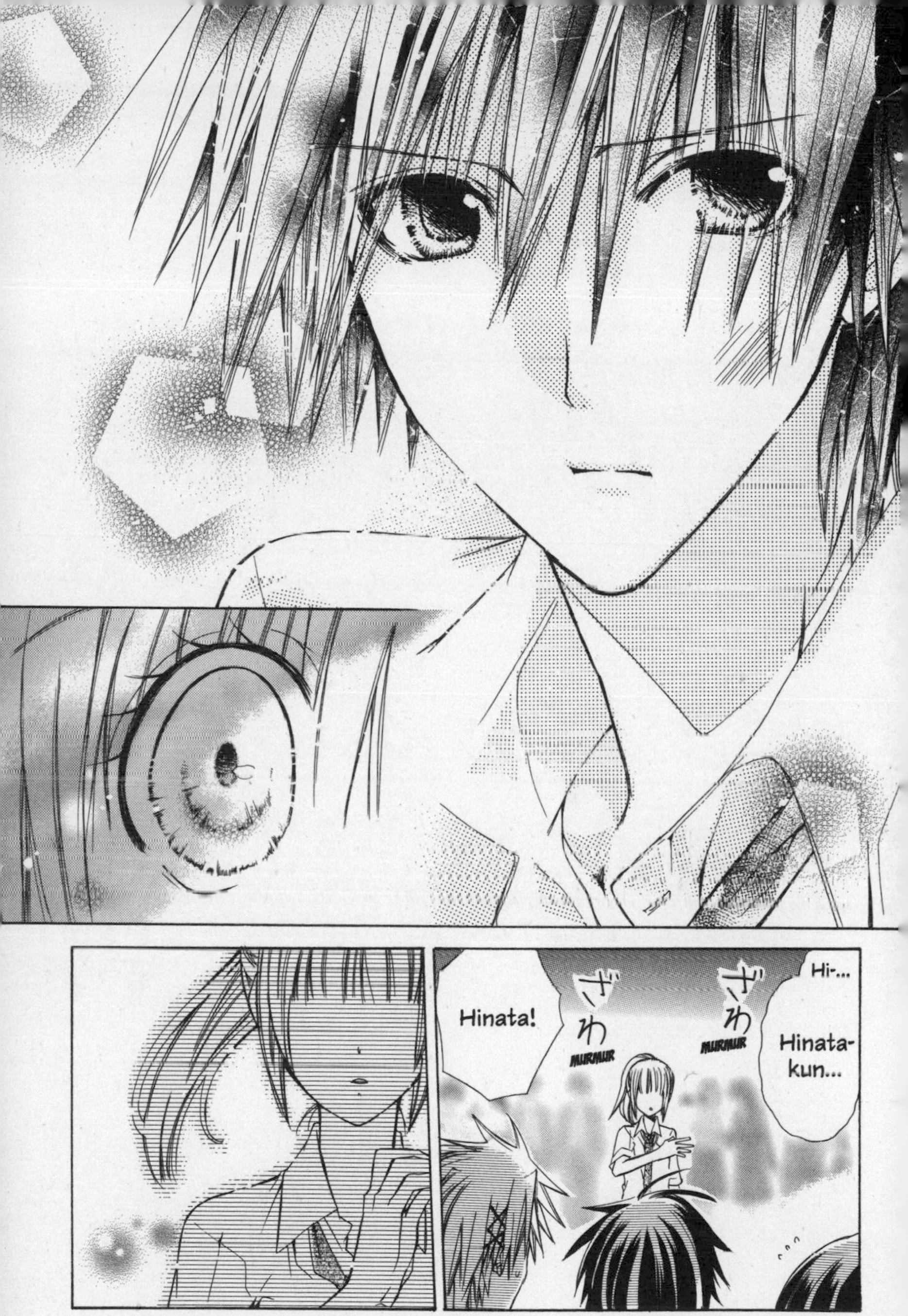
Hi-... Hinata-kun...
ざわ
MURMUR
ざわ
MURMUR
Hinata!

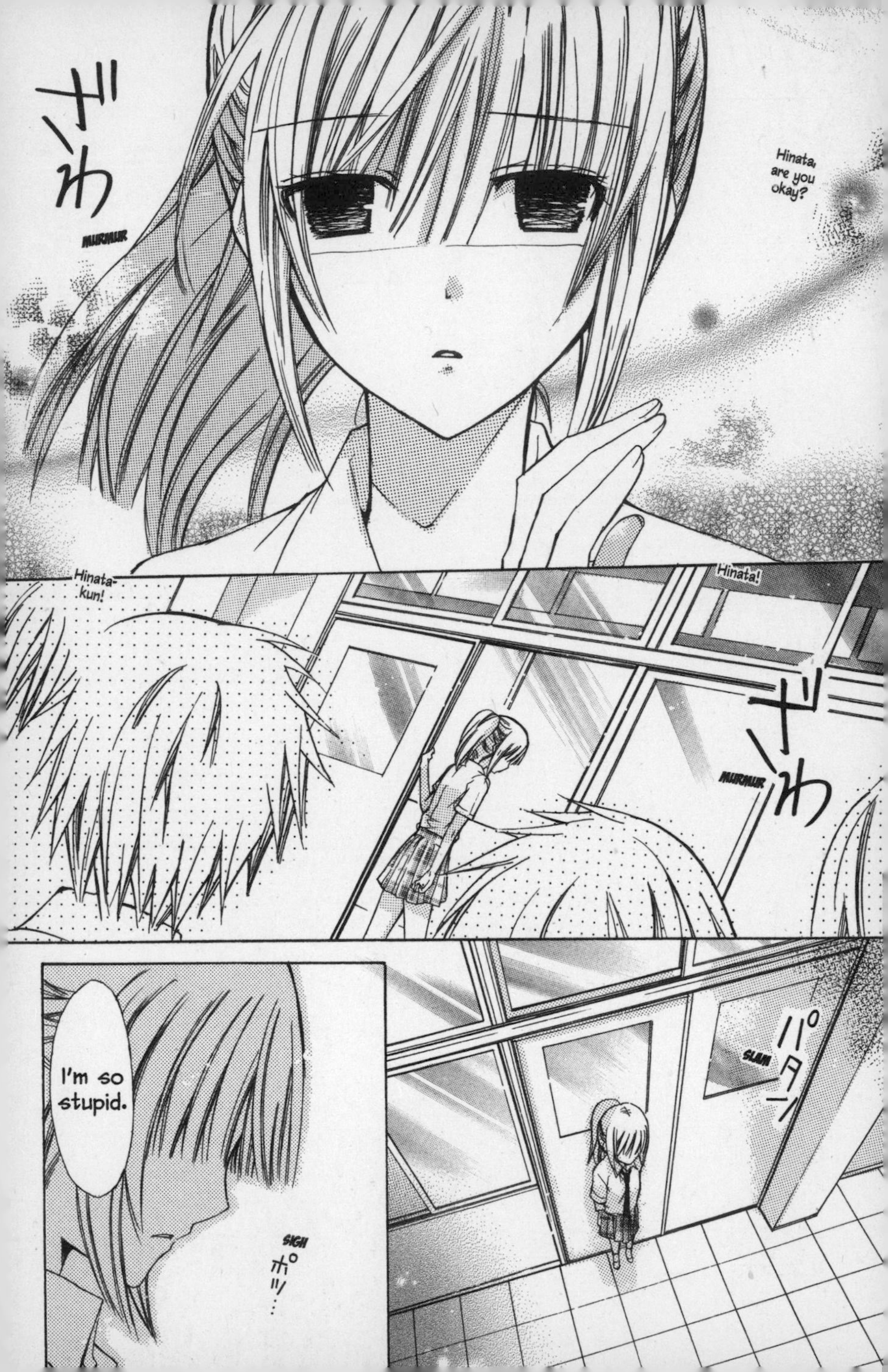
Hinata, are you okay?
ざわ
MURMUR
Hinata!
ざわ
MURMUR
Hinata-kun!
パタン
SLAM
I'm so stupid.
SIGH
ポツ…

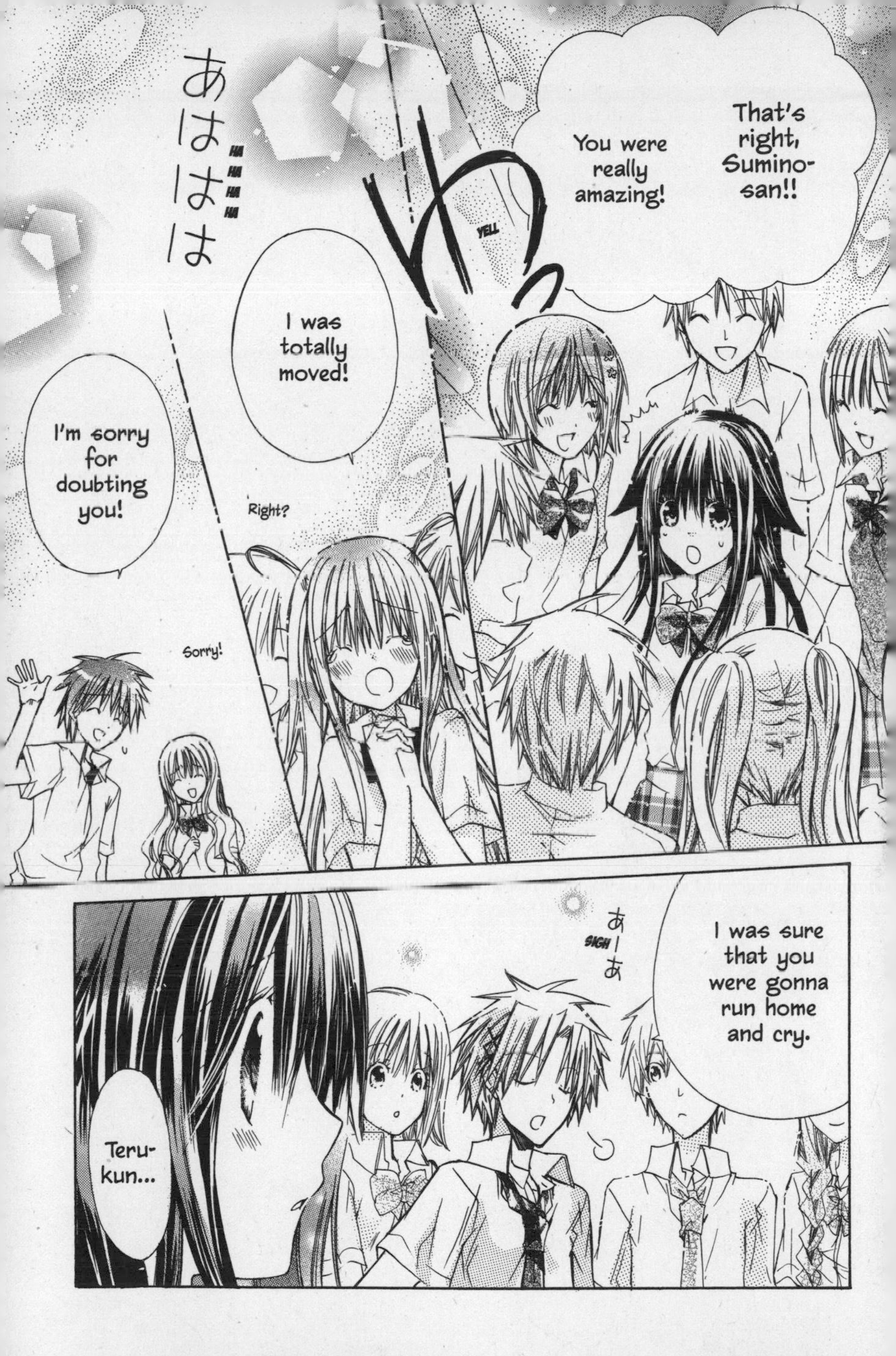
That's right, Sumino-san!!
You were really amazing!
YELL
わっ
I was totally moved!
Right?
あはは
HA HA HA HA
I'm sorry for doubting you!
Sorry!
あーあ
SIGH
I was sure that you were gonna run home and cry.
Teru-kun...

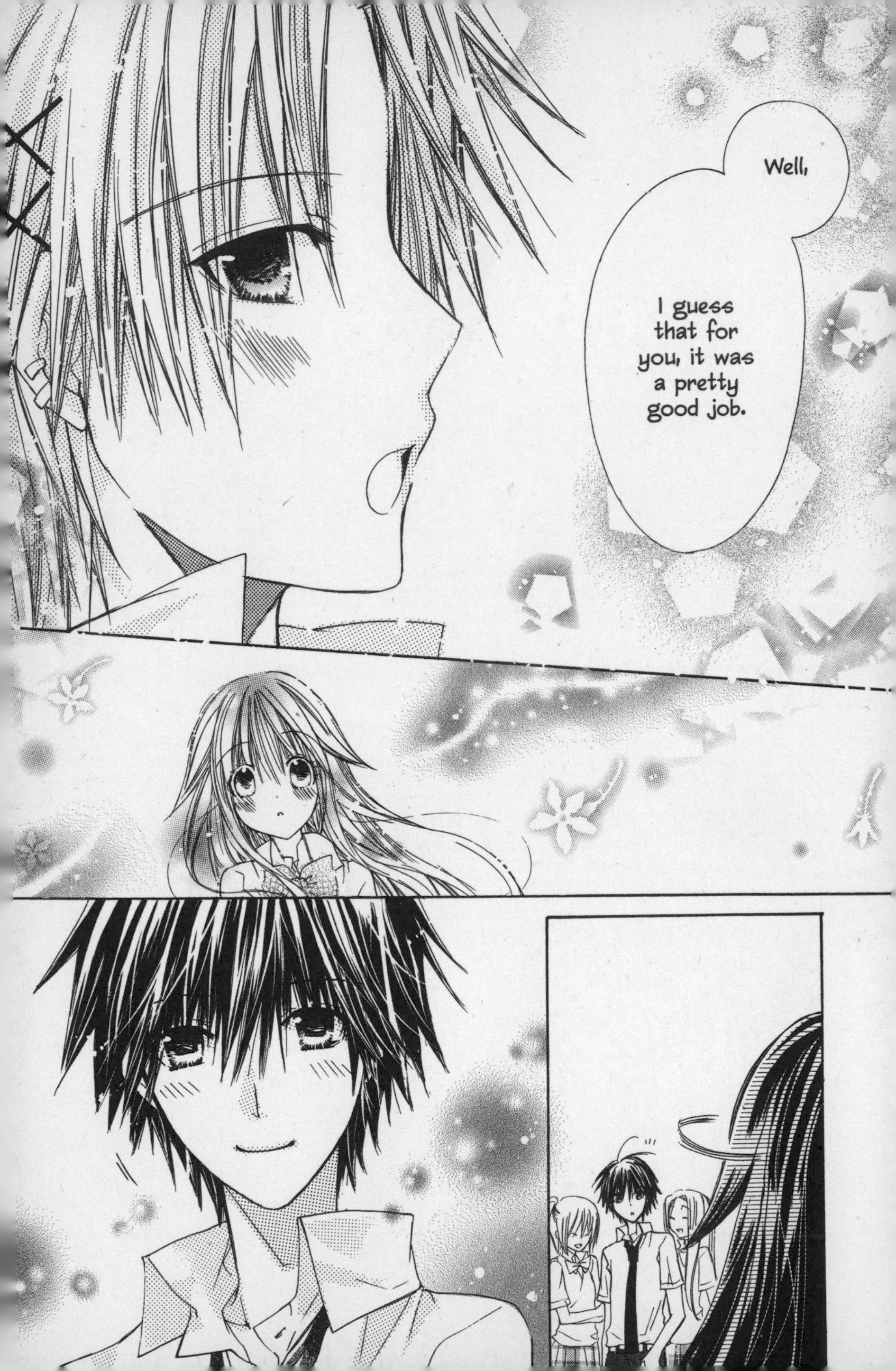
Well,
I guess that for you, it was a pretty good job.

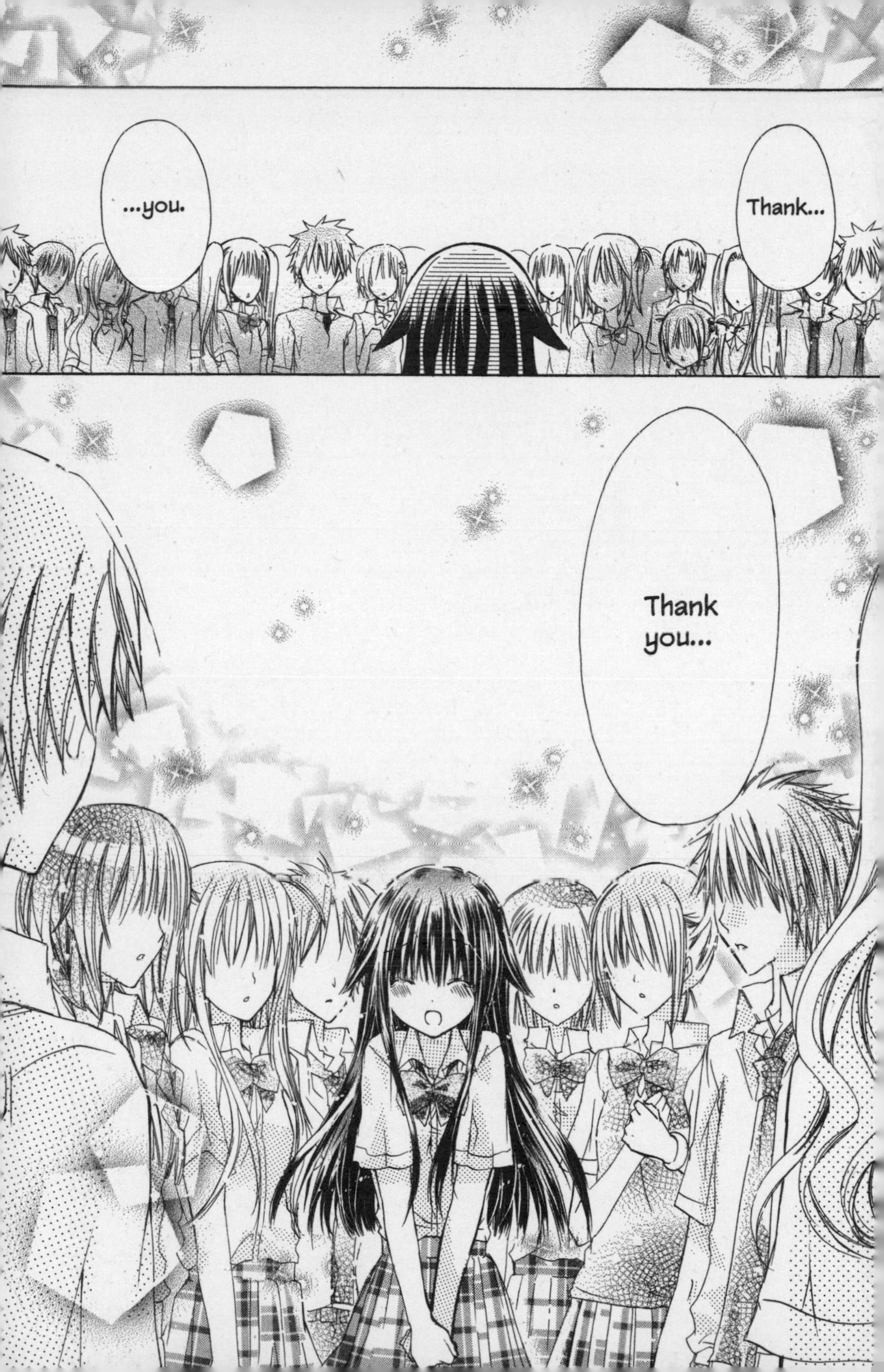
Thank...
...you.
Thank you...

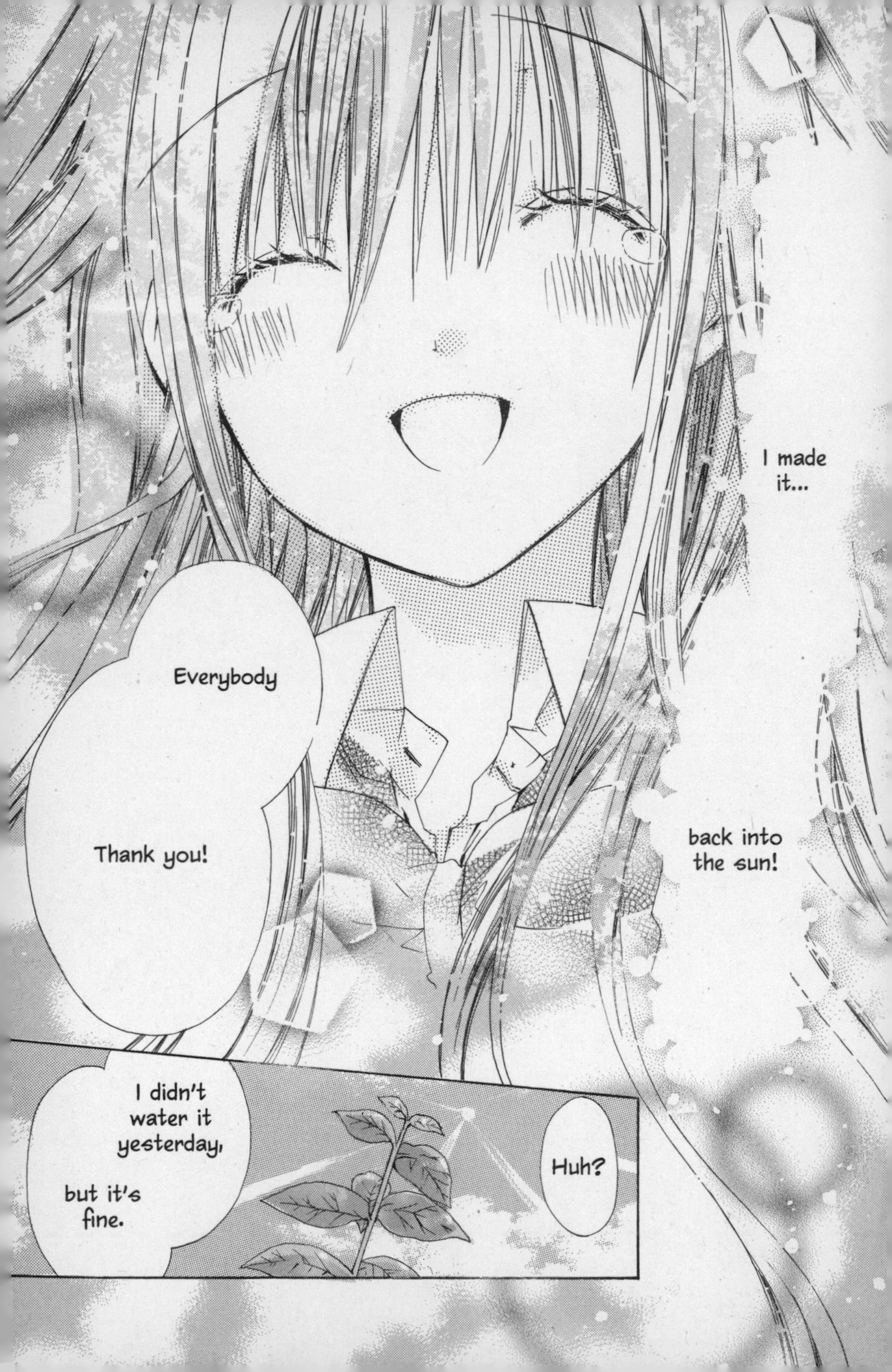
I made it...
back into the sun!
Everybody
Thank you!
Huh?
I didn't water it yesterday,
but it's fine.

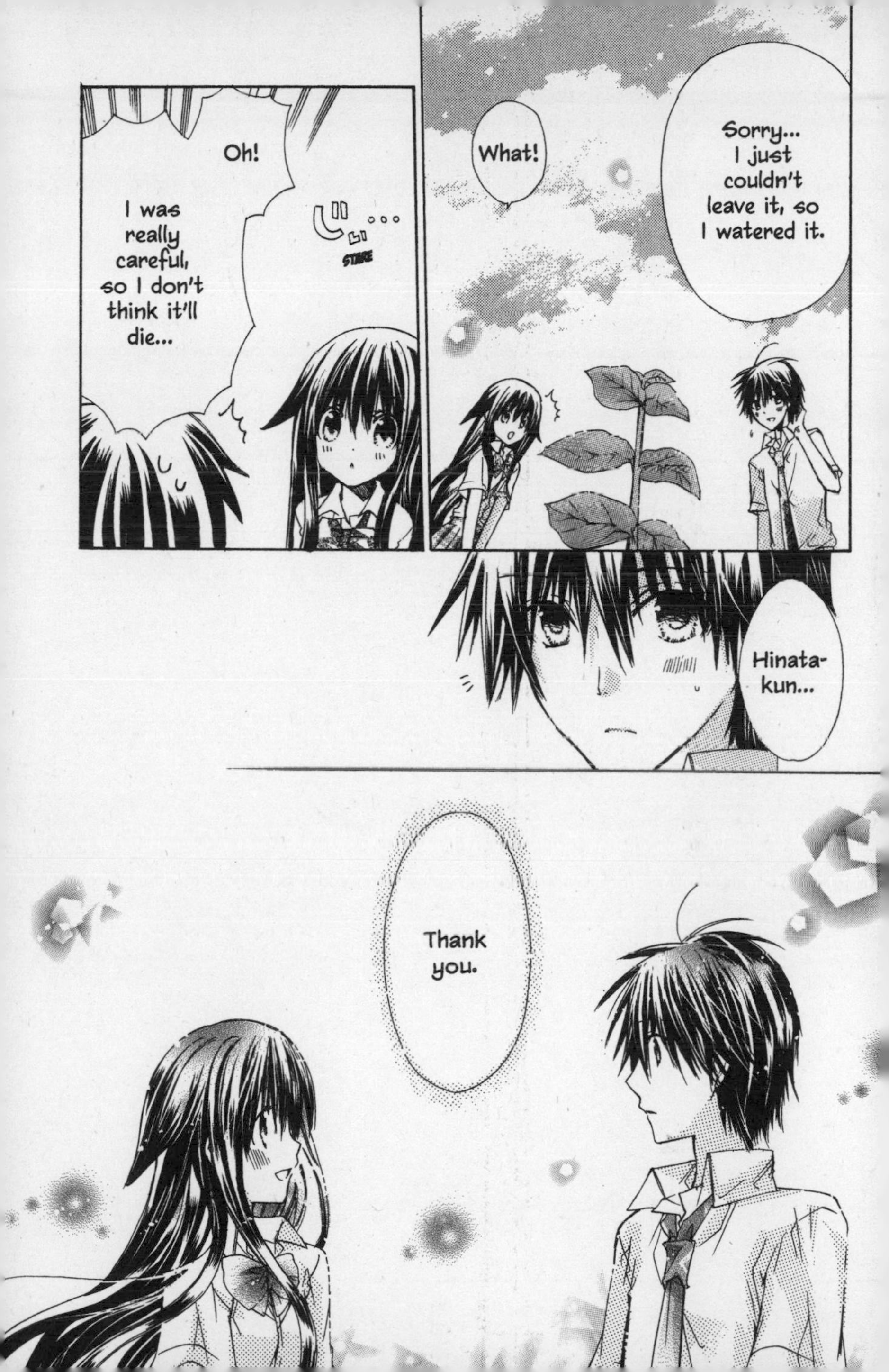
Sorry... I just couldn't leave it, so I watered it.
What!
Oh!
I was really careful, so I don't think it'll die...
STARE
Hinata-kun...
Thank you.

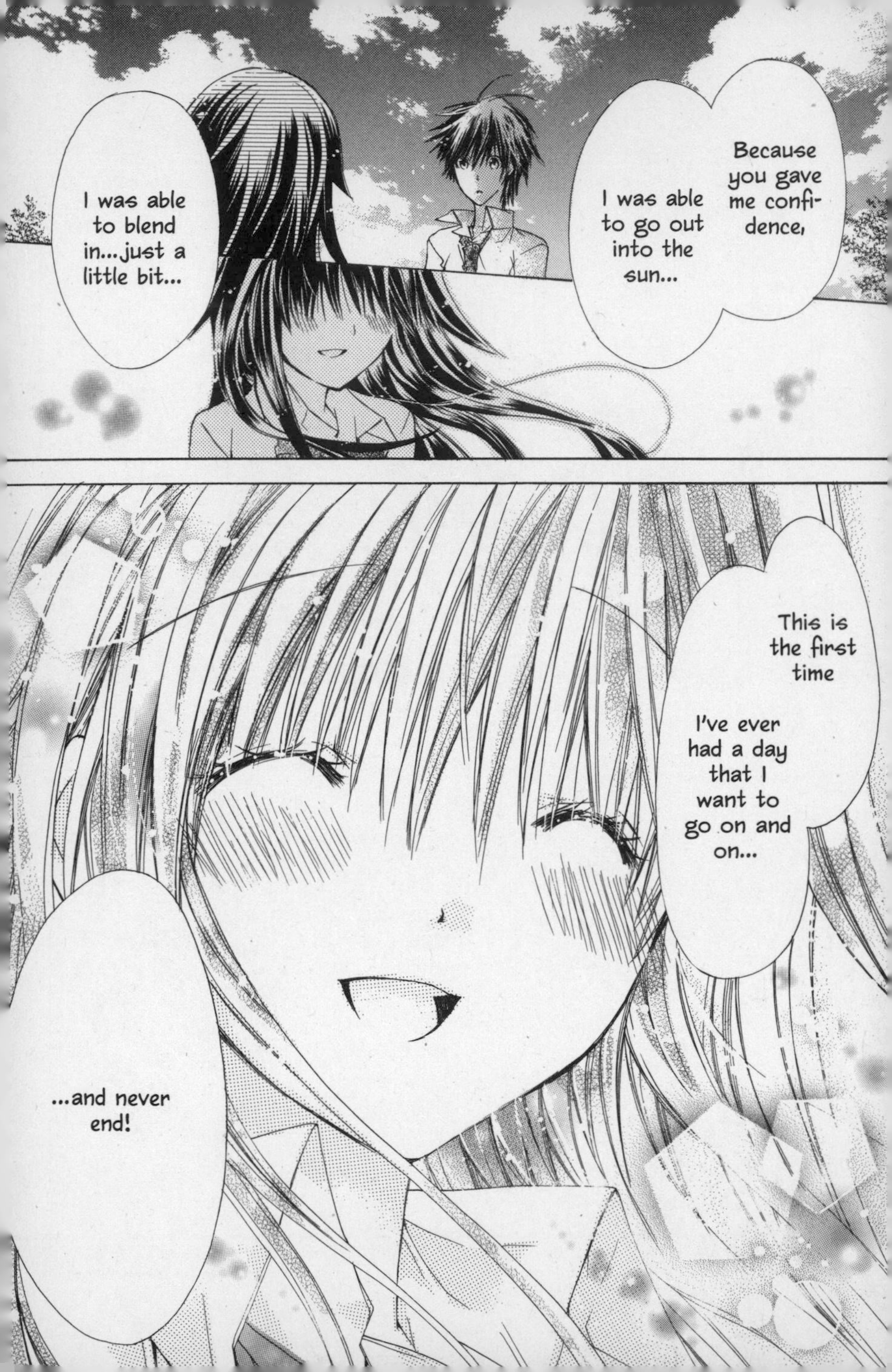
Because you gave me confi- dence,
I was able to go out into the sun...
I was able to blend in...just a little bit...
This is the first time
I've ever had a day that I want to go on and on...
...and never end!

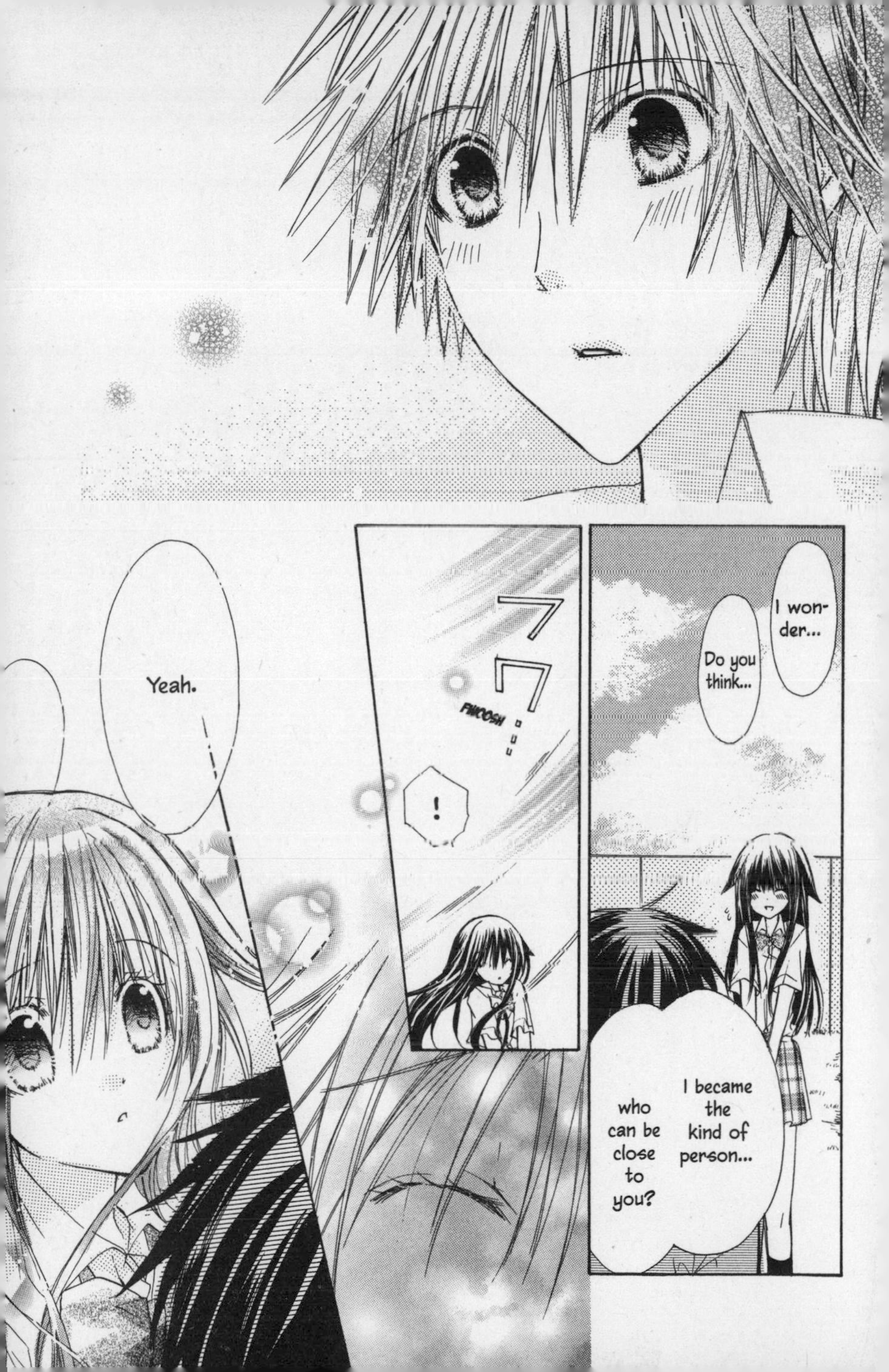
I won-der...
Do you think...
I became the kind of person...
who can be close to you?
FWOOSH
!
Yeah.

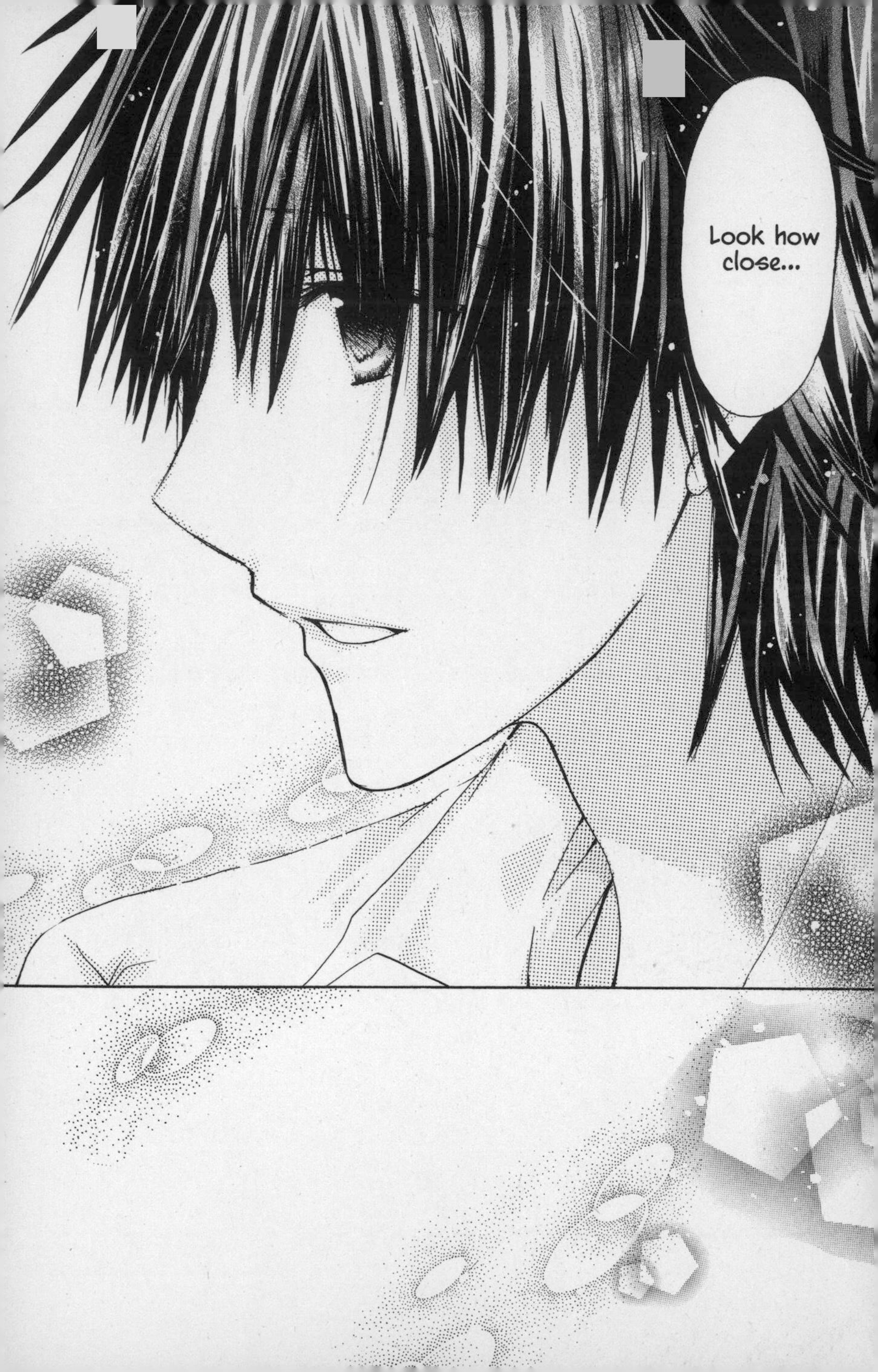
Look how close...

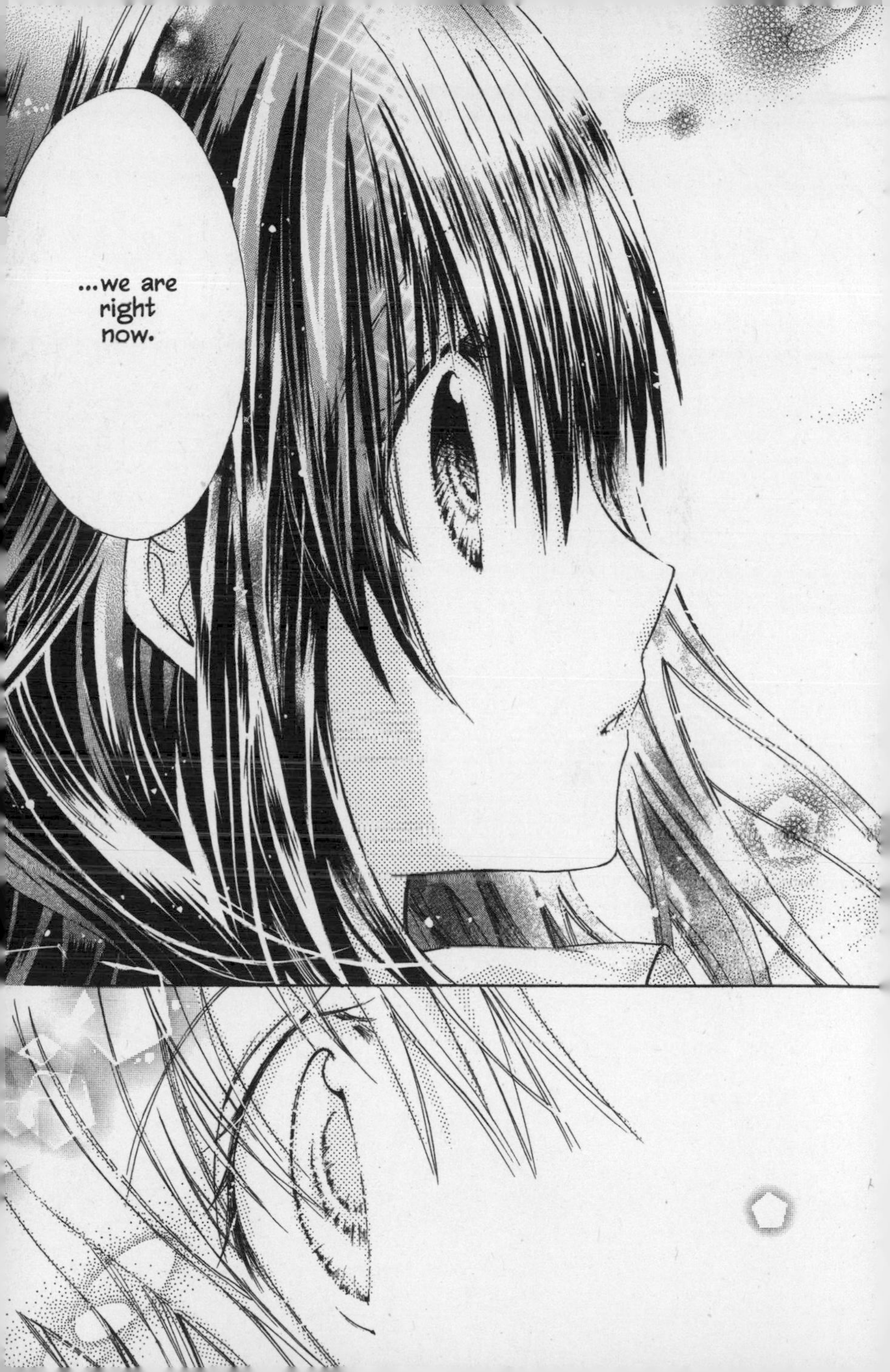
...we are right now.

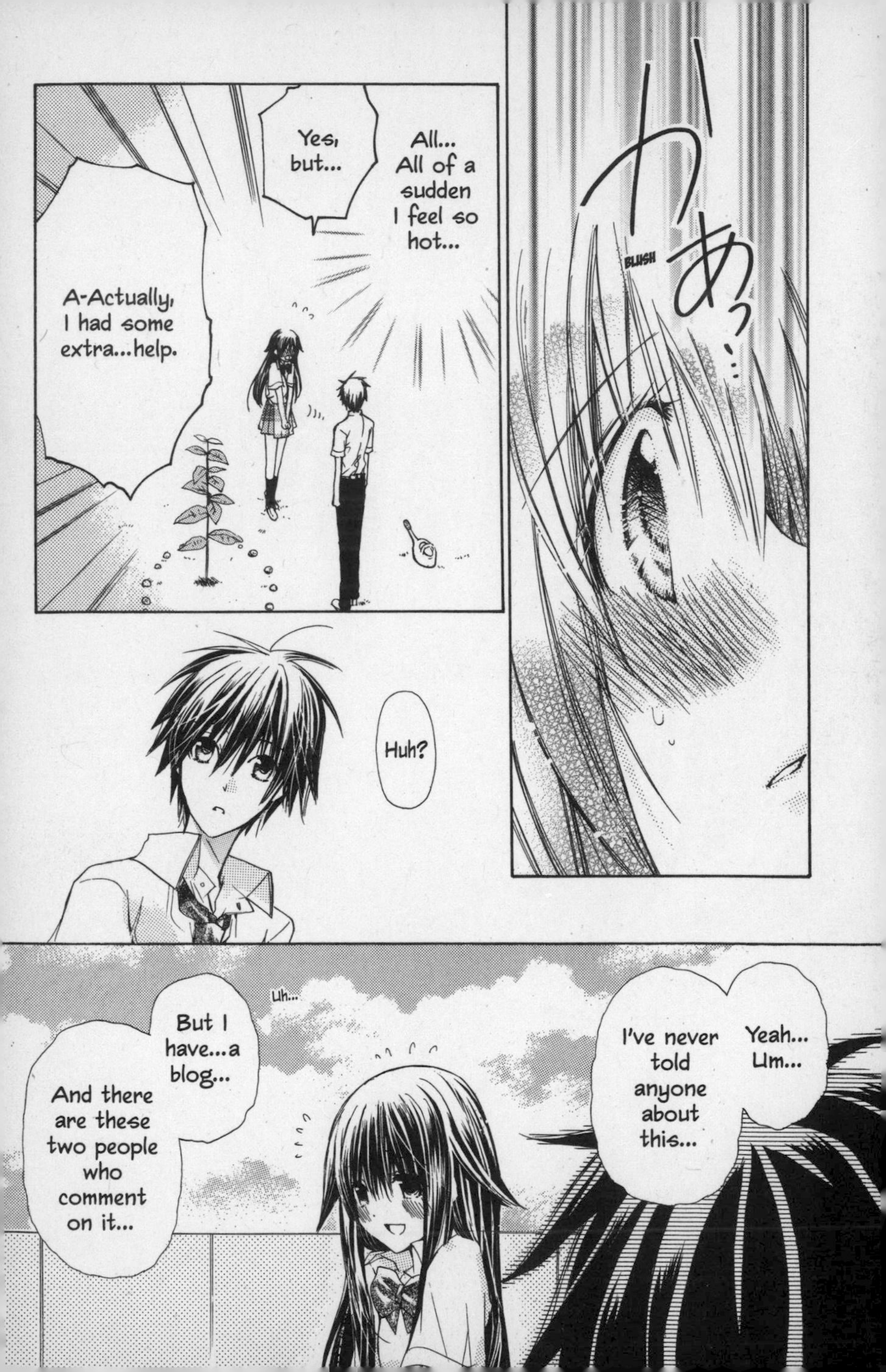
BLUSH
あっ…
All... All of a sudden I feel so hot...
Yes, but...
A-Actually, I had some extra...help.
Huh?
Yeah... Um...
I've never told anyone about this...
Uh...
But I have...a blog...
And there are these two people who comment on it...

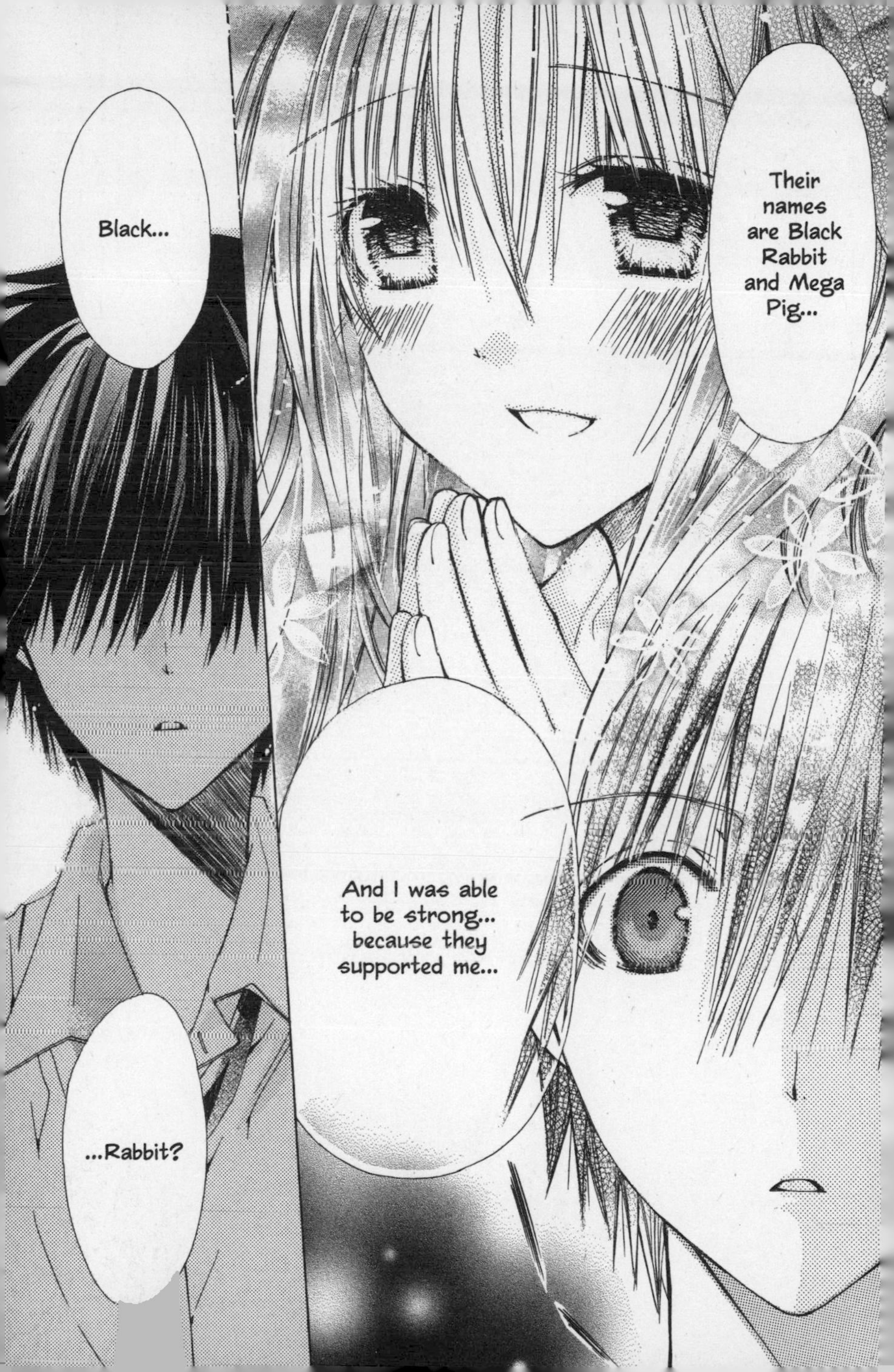
Their names are Black Rabbit and Mega Pig...
And I was able to be strong... because they supported me...
Black...
...Rabbit?

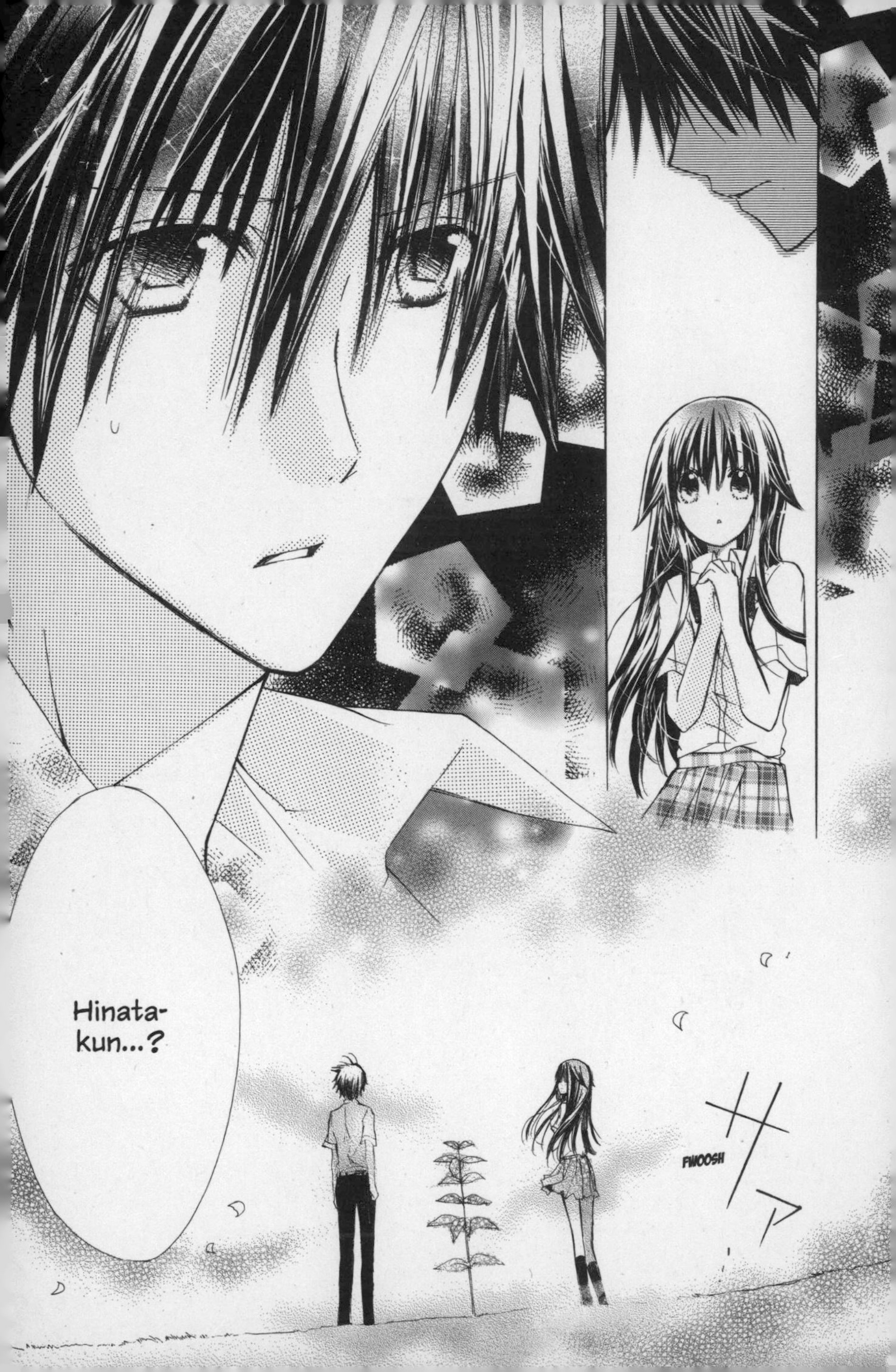
Hinata-kun...?
FWOOSH
サァ

Hi, everyone!

While it's not quite Hikage-level, I remember that I had a
homeroom teacher who called me "Endō-san" and a cram-school
teacher who called me "Mae-chan" by mistake.

There's something about being called by the wrong name that
goes beyond sad...it's more agonizing.

PROFILE
Born May 23
Gemini
Blood Type B

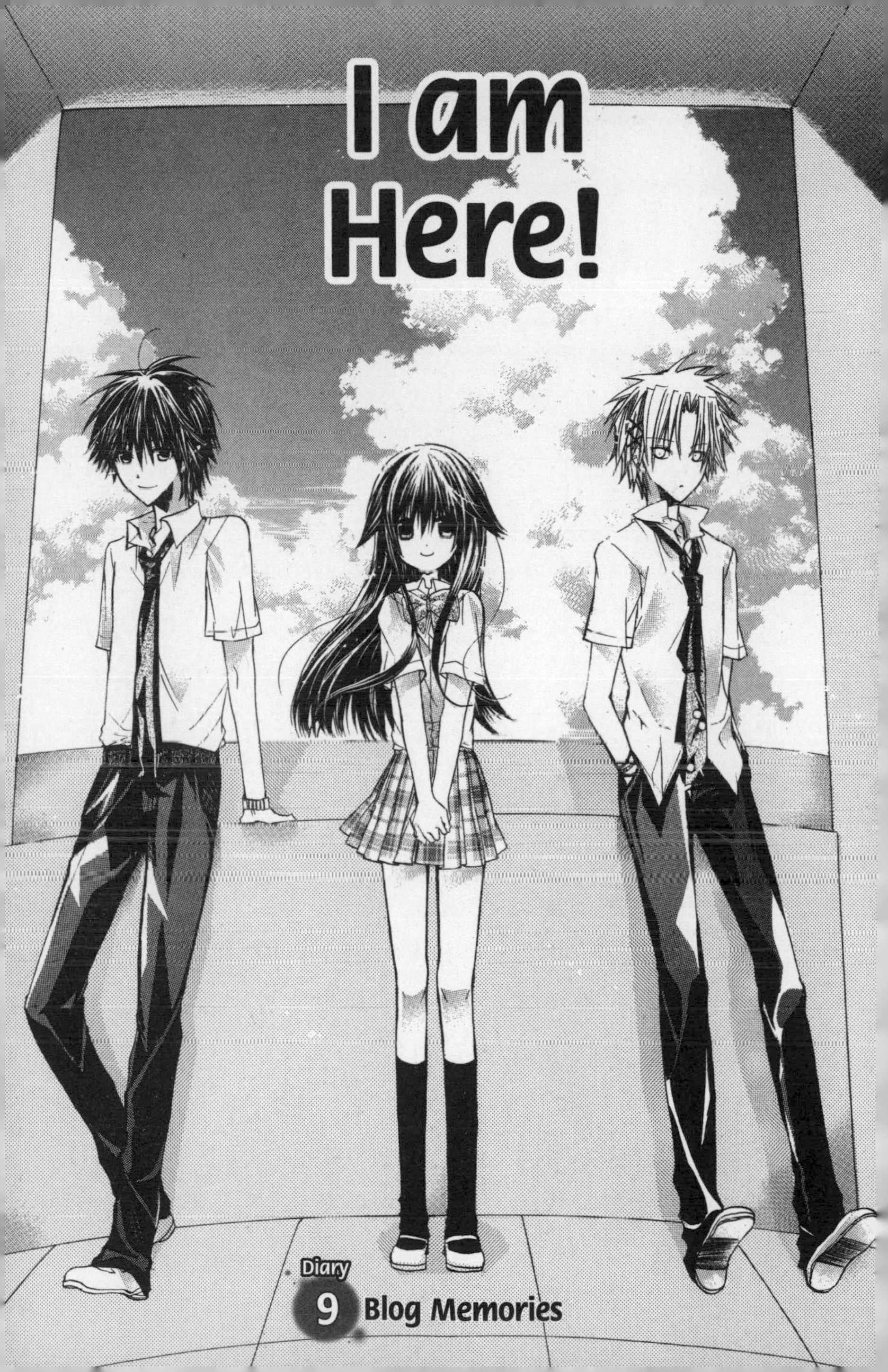
I am Here!
Diary 9 Blog Memories

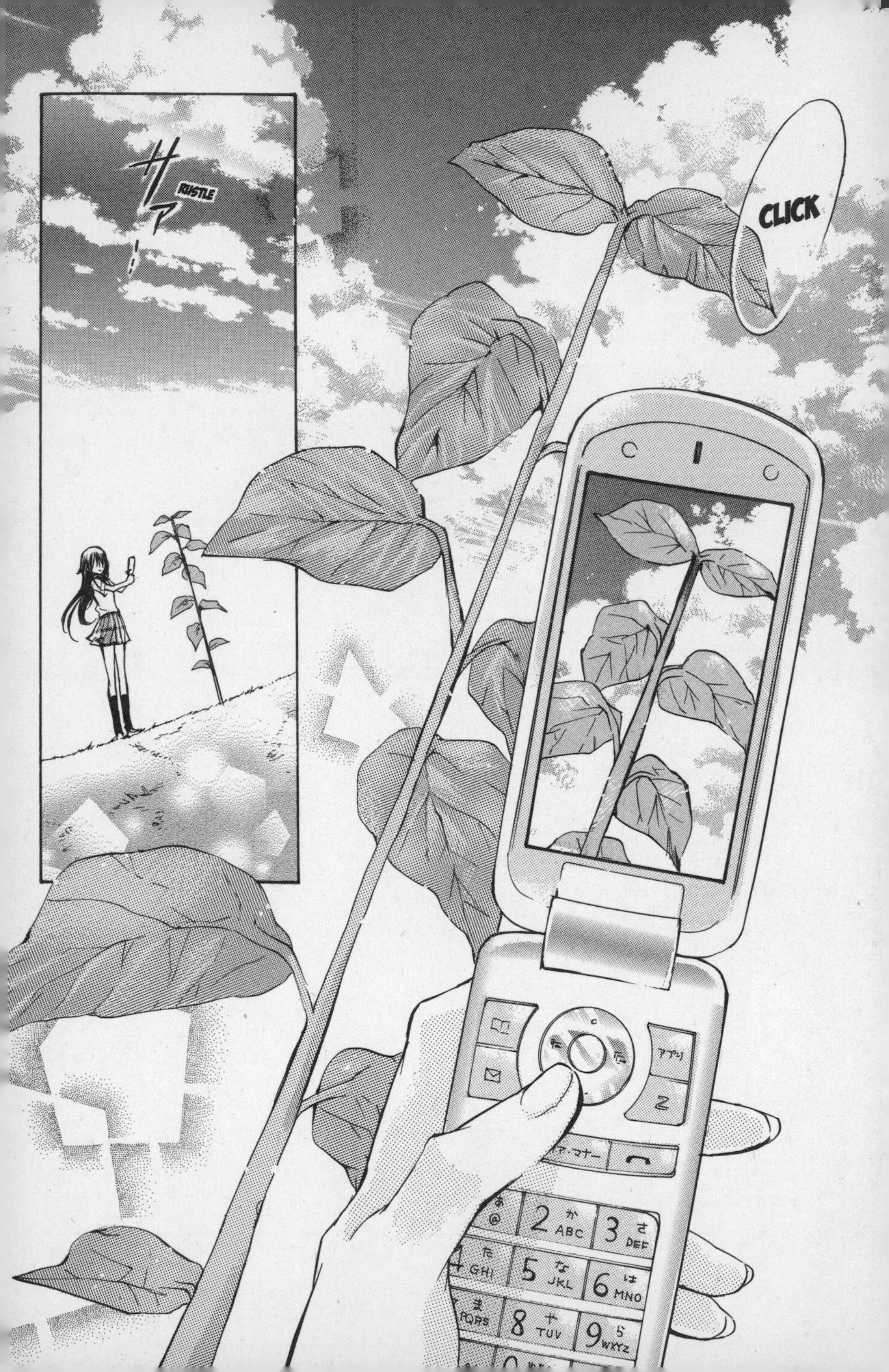
CLICK
サァ
RUSTLE

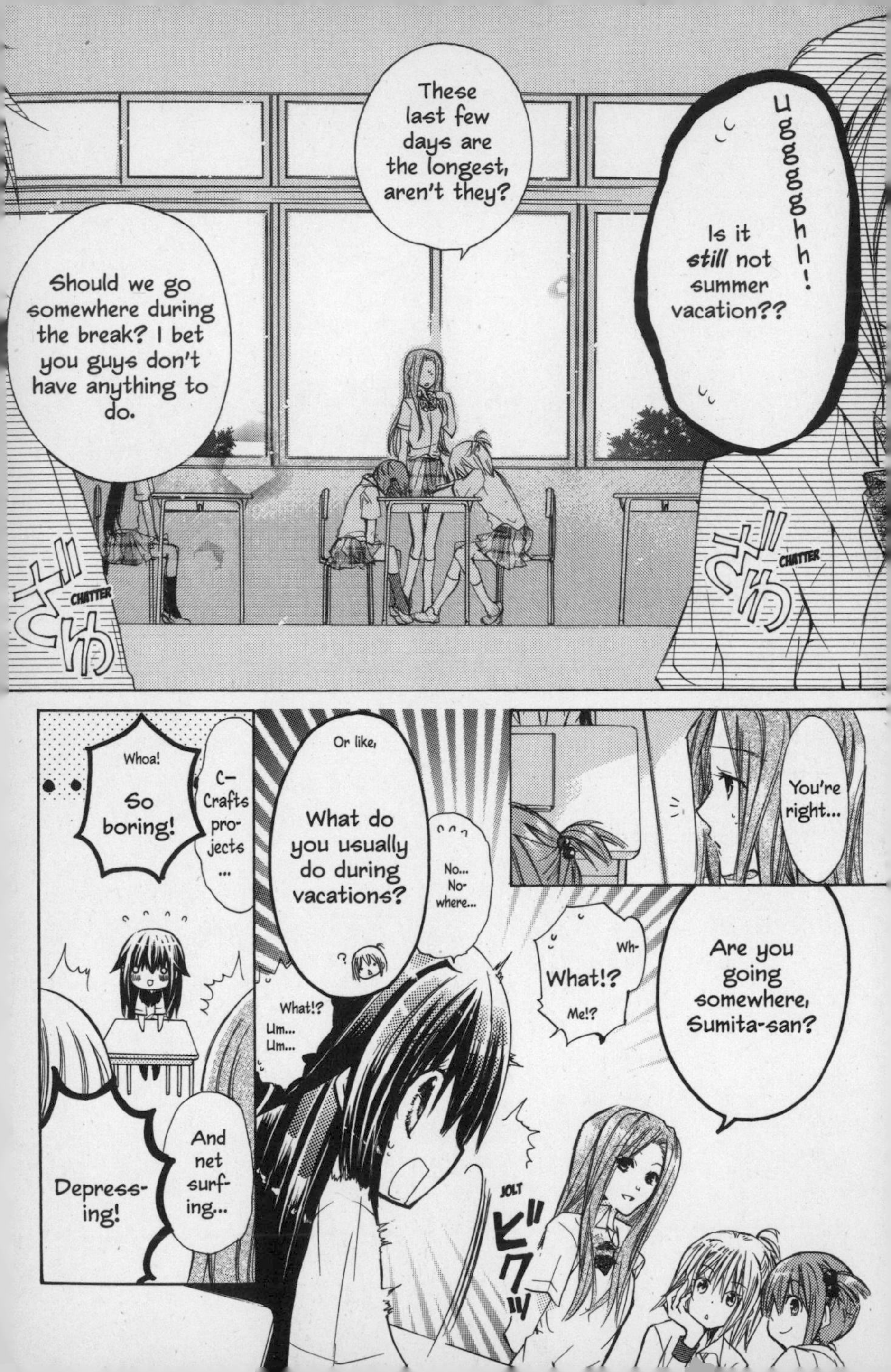
Ugggghhh!
Is it still not summer vacation??
These last few days are the longest, aren't they?
Should we go somewhere during the break? I bet you guys don't have anything to do.
CHATTER
CHATTER
You're right...
Are you going somewhere, Sumita-san?
Wh- What!? Me!?
JOLT
Or like, What do you usually do during vacations?
No... No-where...
What!? Um... Um...
C-Crafts projects...
Whoa! So boring!
And net surfing...
Depress-ing!

While they still get my name wrong, my classmates sometimes talk to me now.

You'll never make friends like that!!

Just call me Arisa! ♡

Tanaka-san!

...let's go to the fireworks show!

In that case...

It's right after vacation starts!

Yeah! You'll remember it forever!

What? What was that?

I wonder what's up?

Class 3 is excited about something!

Whoa!

What!? If Teru and Hinata are going, we want to go too!

Maybe I'll go...

Me too!

In that case, I'm going too!

Oh ...

?

ひそ
WHISPER

Is she still clinging all over him?

...That's the girl who was with Hinata in that picture...

ひそ

ひそ
WHISPER

...

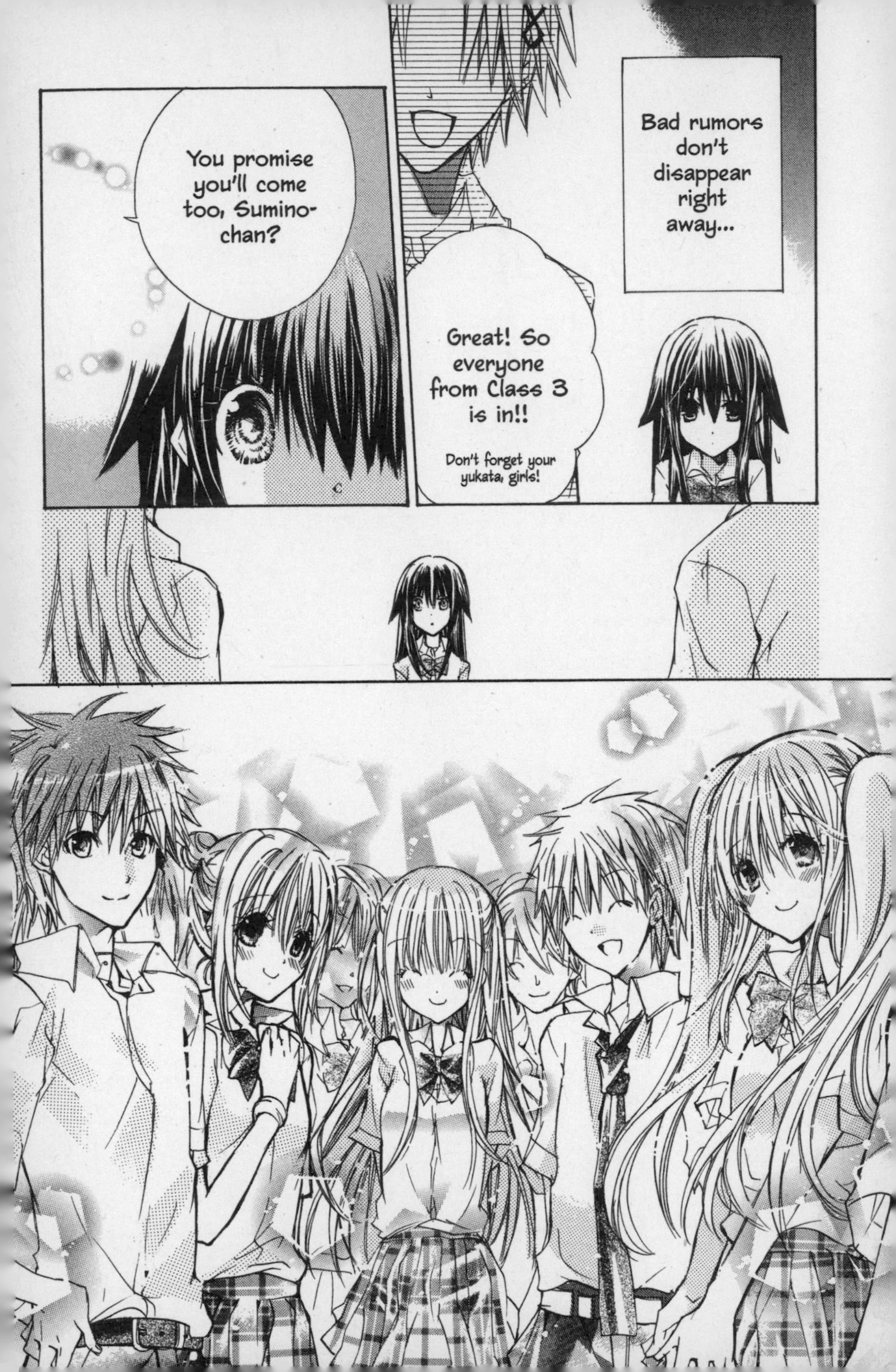
Bad rumors don't disappear right away...
Great! So everyone from Class 3 is in!!
Don't forget your yukata, girls!
You promise you'll come too, Sumino-chan?

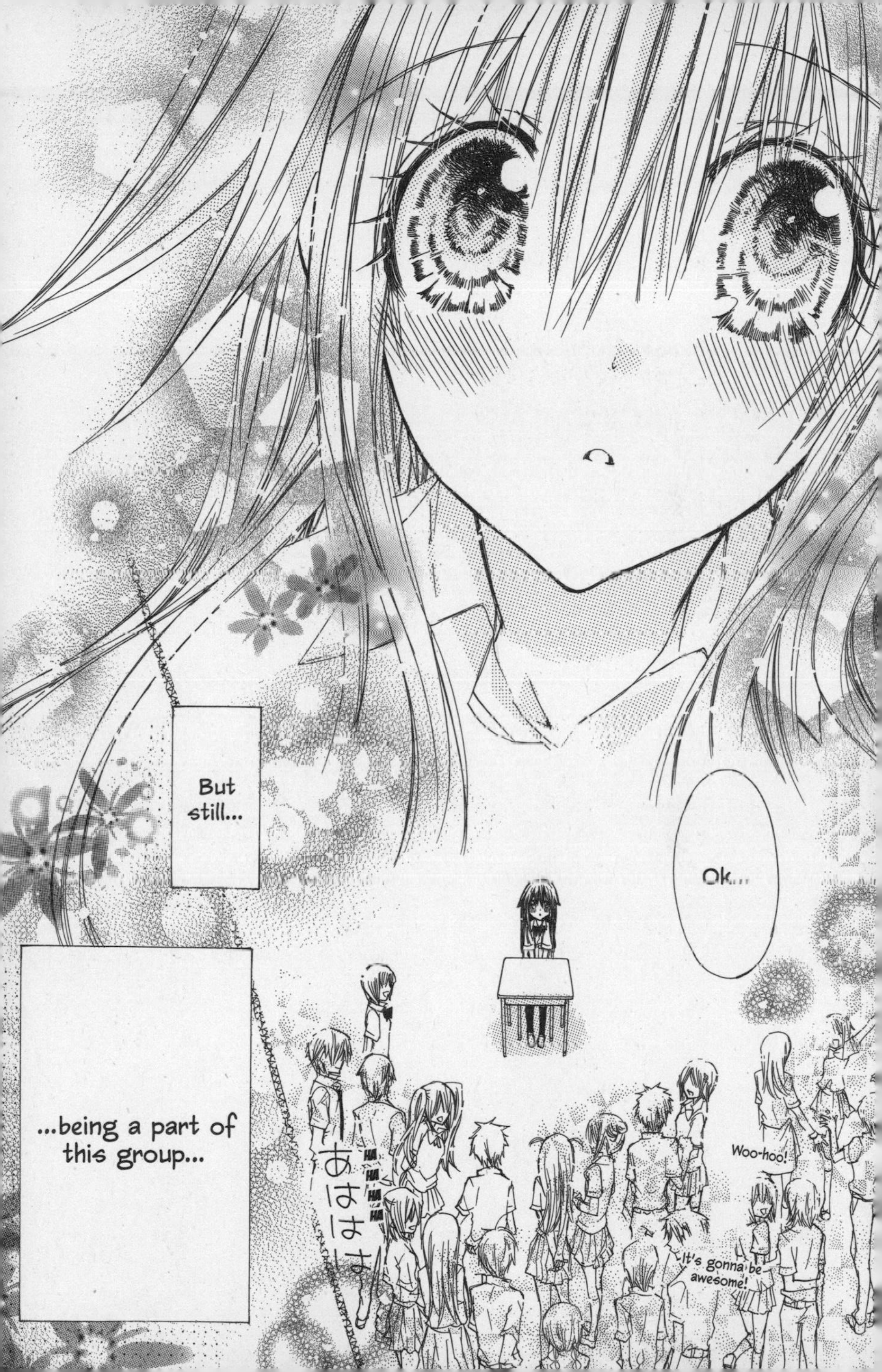
Ok...
But still...
Woo-hoo!
It's gonna be awesome!
HA HA HA HA
...being a part of this group...

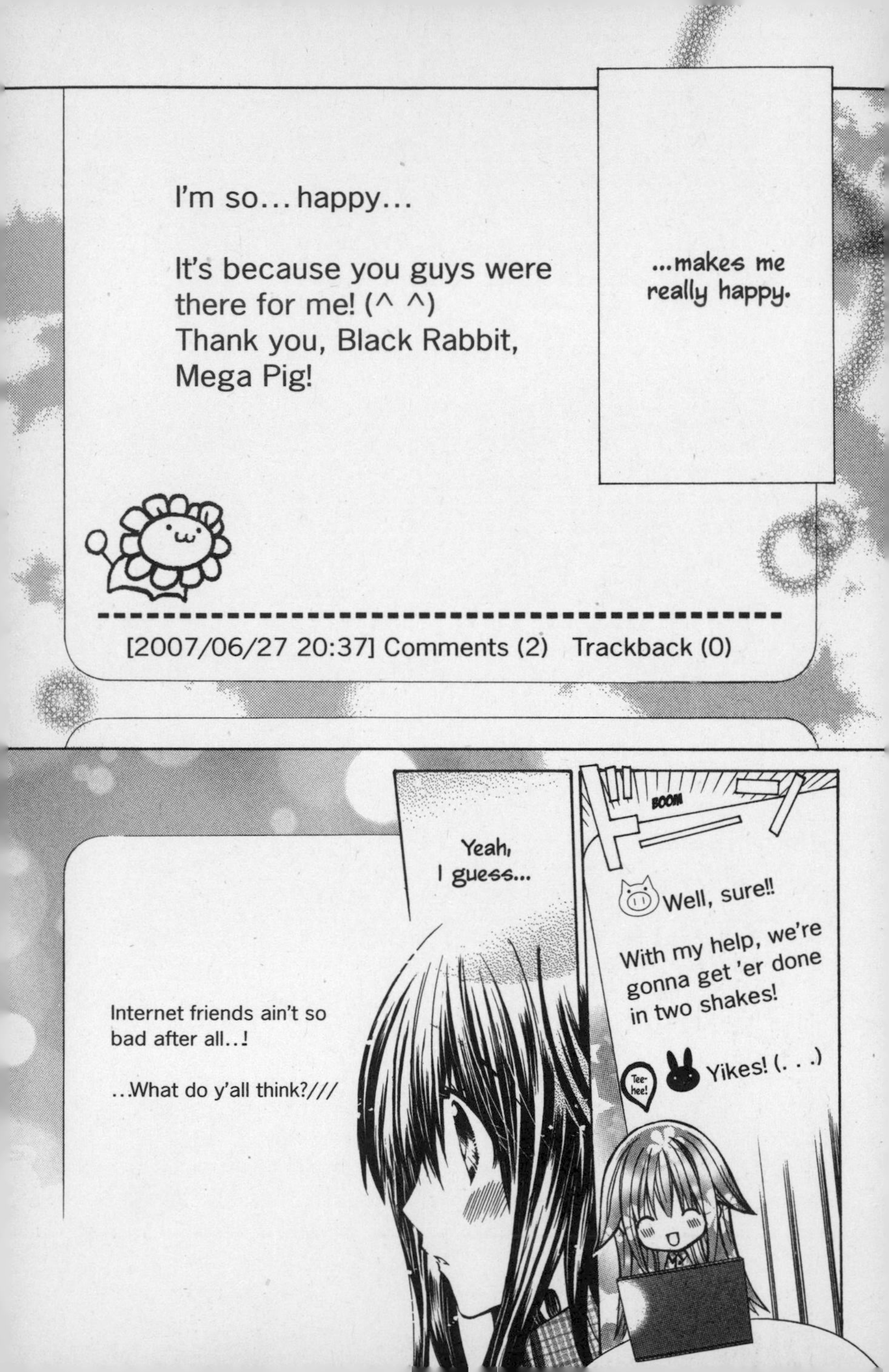
...makes me really happy.
I'm so... happy...
It's because you guys were there for me! (^ ^)
Thank you, Black Rabbit, Mega Pig!
[2007/06/27 20:37] Comments (2) Trackback (0)
BOOM
Well, sure!!
With my help, we're gonna get 'er done in two shakes!
Tee-hee!
Yikes! (. . .)
Yeah, I guess...
Internet friends ain't so bad after all..!
..What do y'all think?///

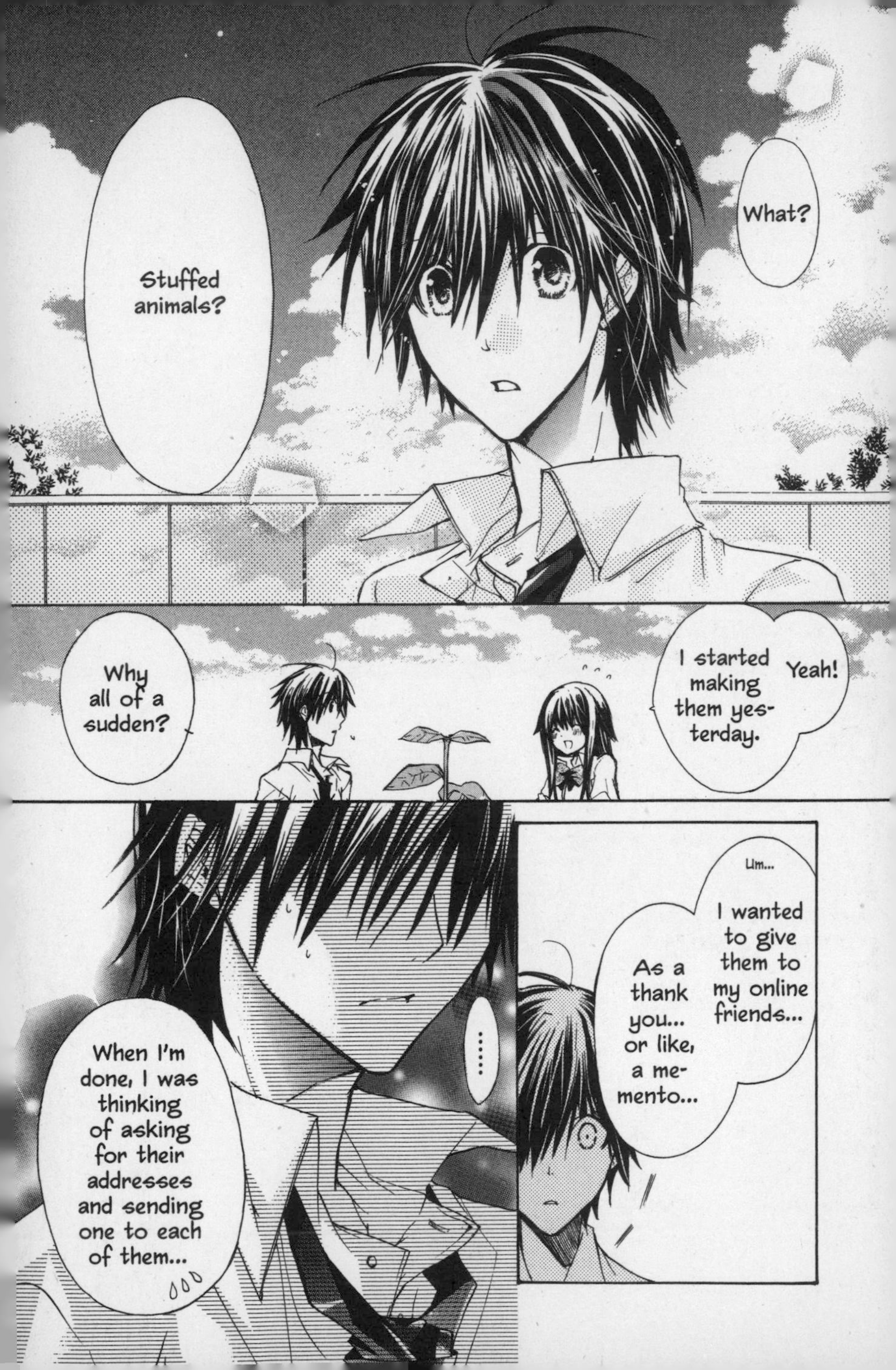
What?
Stuffed animals?
Yeah!
I started making them yes-terday.
Why all of a sudden?
Um...
I wanted to give them to my online friends...
As a thank you... or like, a memento...
......
When I'm done, I was thinking of asking for their addresses and sending one to each of them...

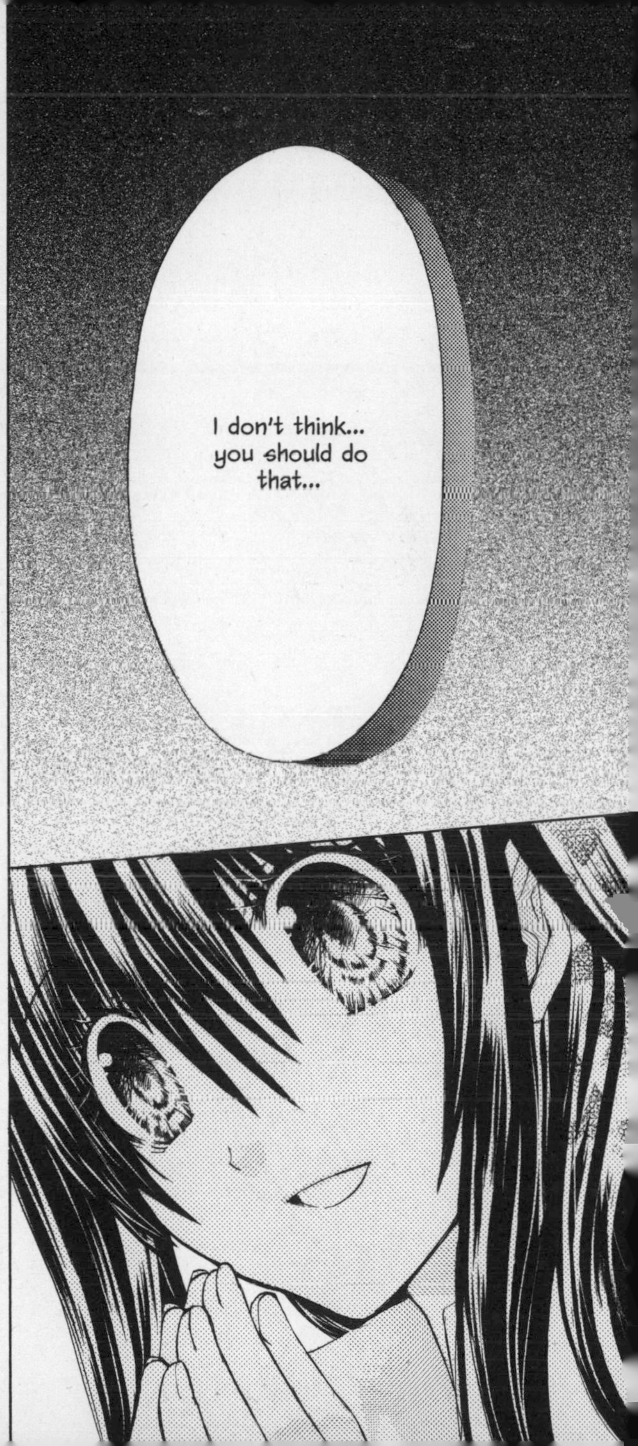
I don't think... you should do that...

The Adventures of Mahimahi 2

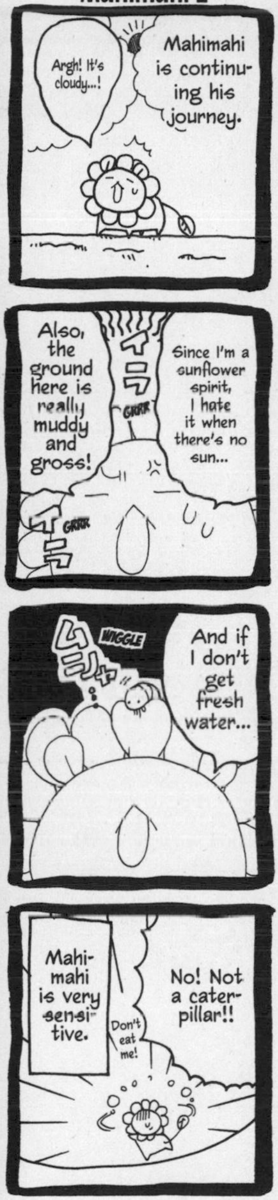
Mahimahi is continuing his journey.
Argh! It's cloudy...!
Since I'm a sunflower spirit, I hate it when there's no sun...
Also, the ground here is really muddy and gross!
GRRR
GRRR
And if I don't get fresh water...
WIGGLE
No! Not a caterpillar!!
Don't eat me!
Mahimahi is very sensitive.

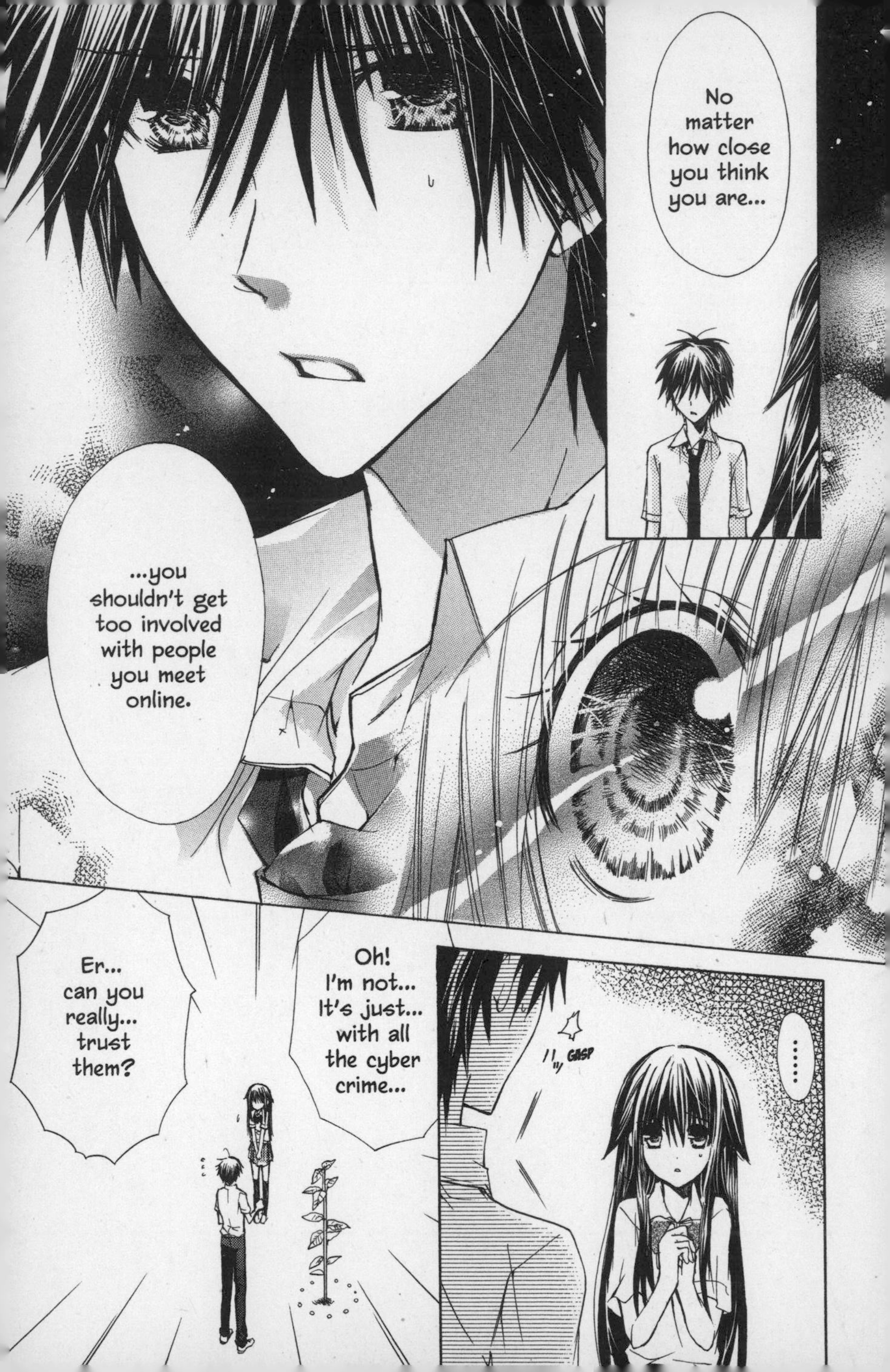
No matter how close you think you are...
...you shouldn't get too involved with people you meet online.
......
GASP
Oh! I'm not... It's just... with all the cyber crime...
Er... can you really... trust them?

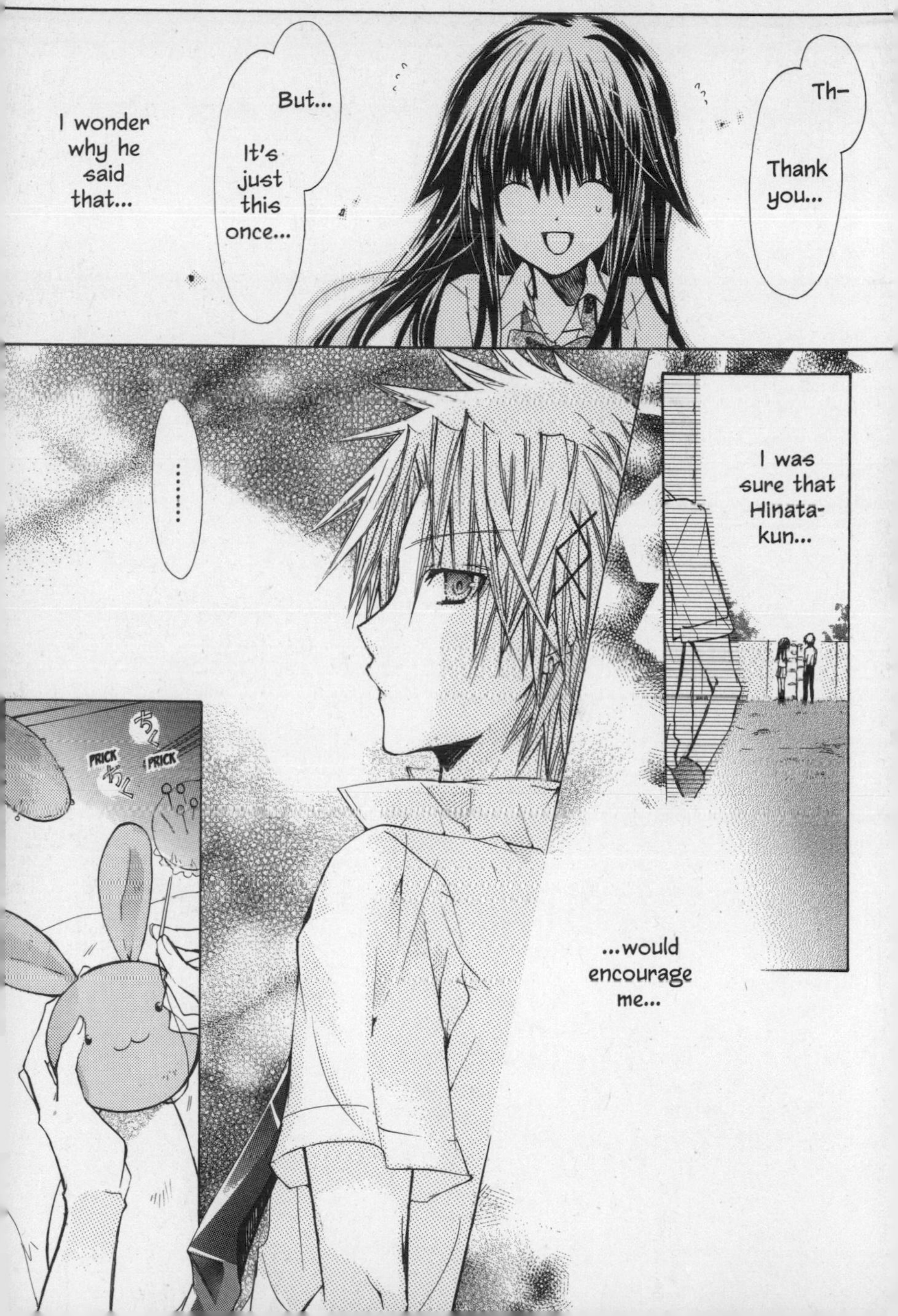
Th- Thank you...
But... It's just this once...
I wonder why he said that...
I was sure that Hinata-kun...
...would encourage me...
......
PRICK
PRICK

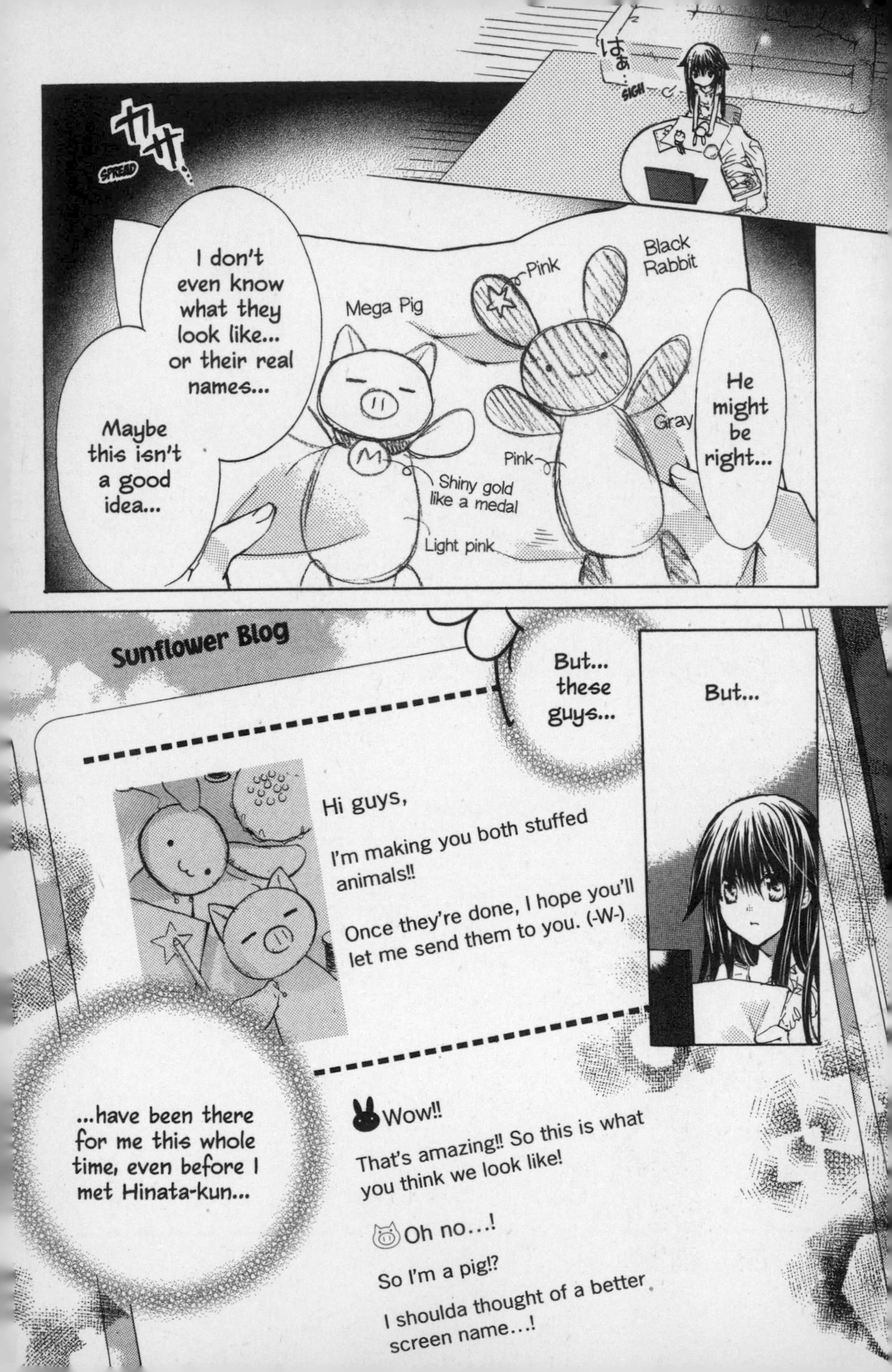
はぁ…
SIGH
カサ…
SPREAD
He might be right...
Black Rabbit
Pink
Gray
Pink
Mega Pig
Shiny gold like a medal
Light pink
I don't even know what they look like... or their real names...
Maybe this isn't a good idea...
But...
But... these guys...
Sunflower Blog
Hi guys,
I'm making you both stuffed animals!!
Once they're done, I hope you'll let me send them to you. (-W-)
Wow!!
That's amazing!! So this is what you think we look like!
Oh no…!
So I'm a pig!?
I shoulda thought of a better screen name…!
...have been there for me this whole time, even before I met Hinata-kun...

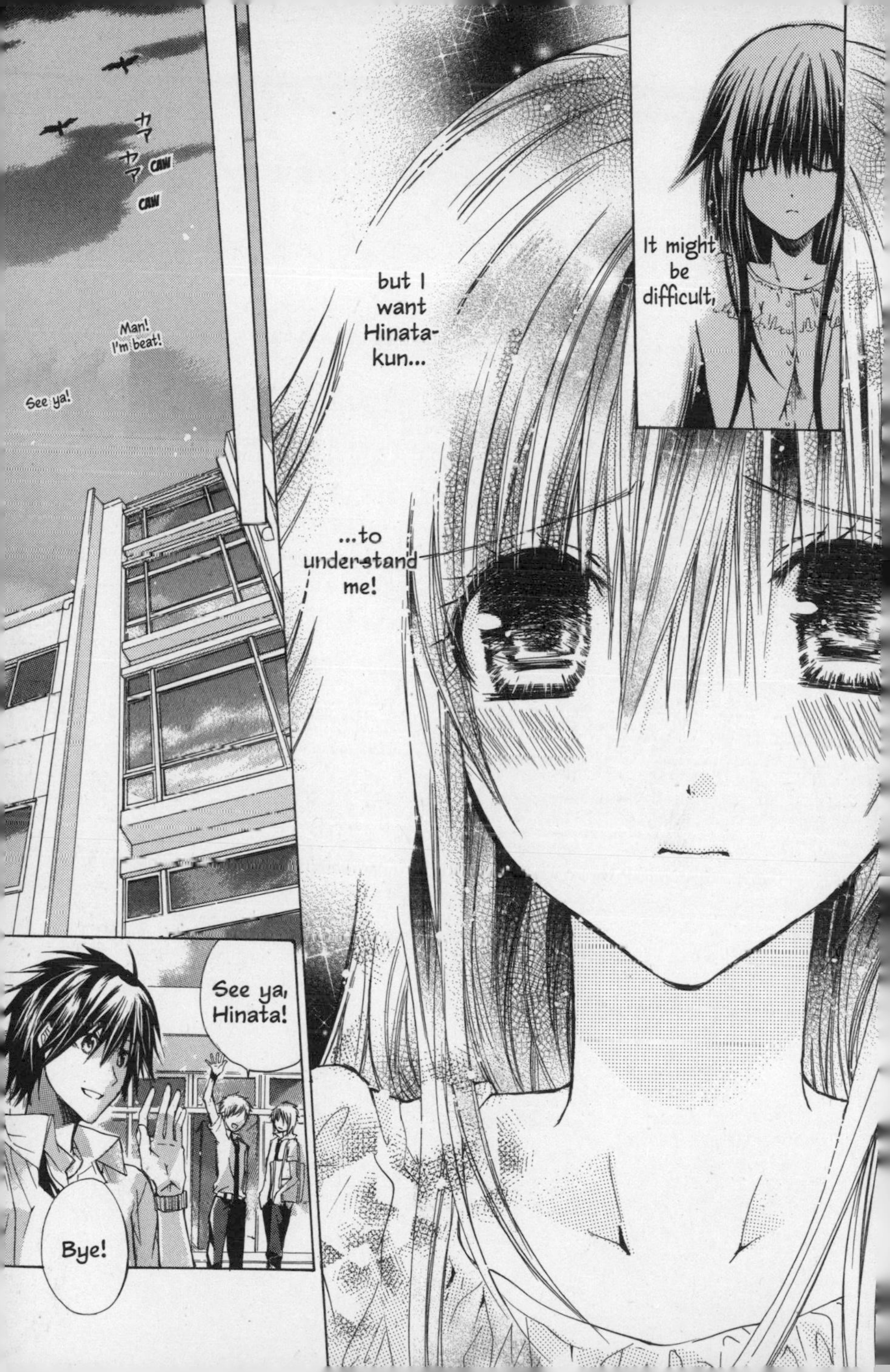
It might be difficult,
but I want Hinata-kun...
...to understand me!
カァ カァ
CAW
CAW
Man! I'm beat!
See ya!
See ya, Hinata!
Bye!

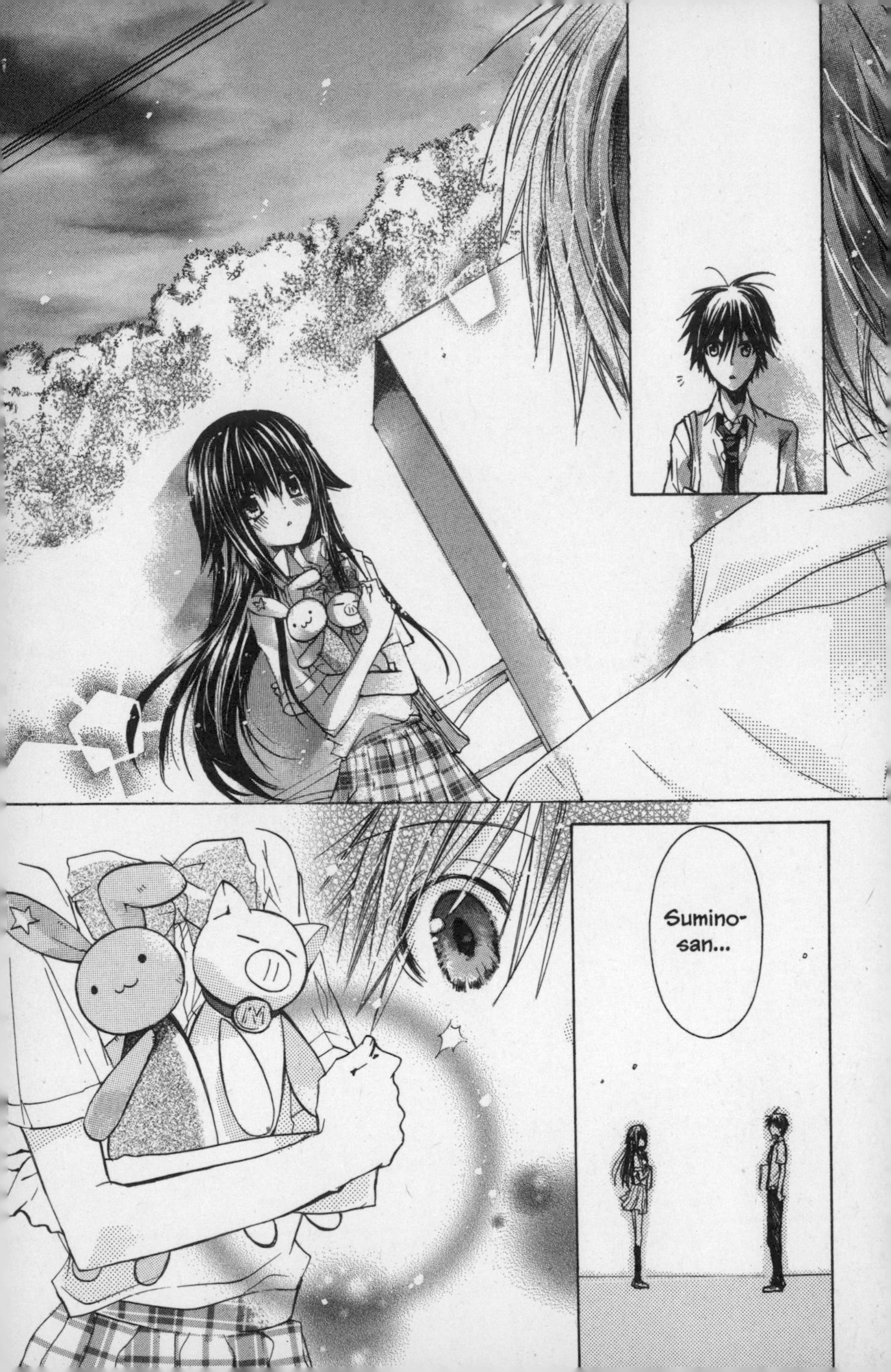
Sumino-san...

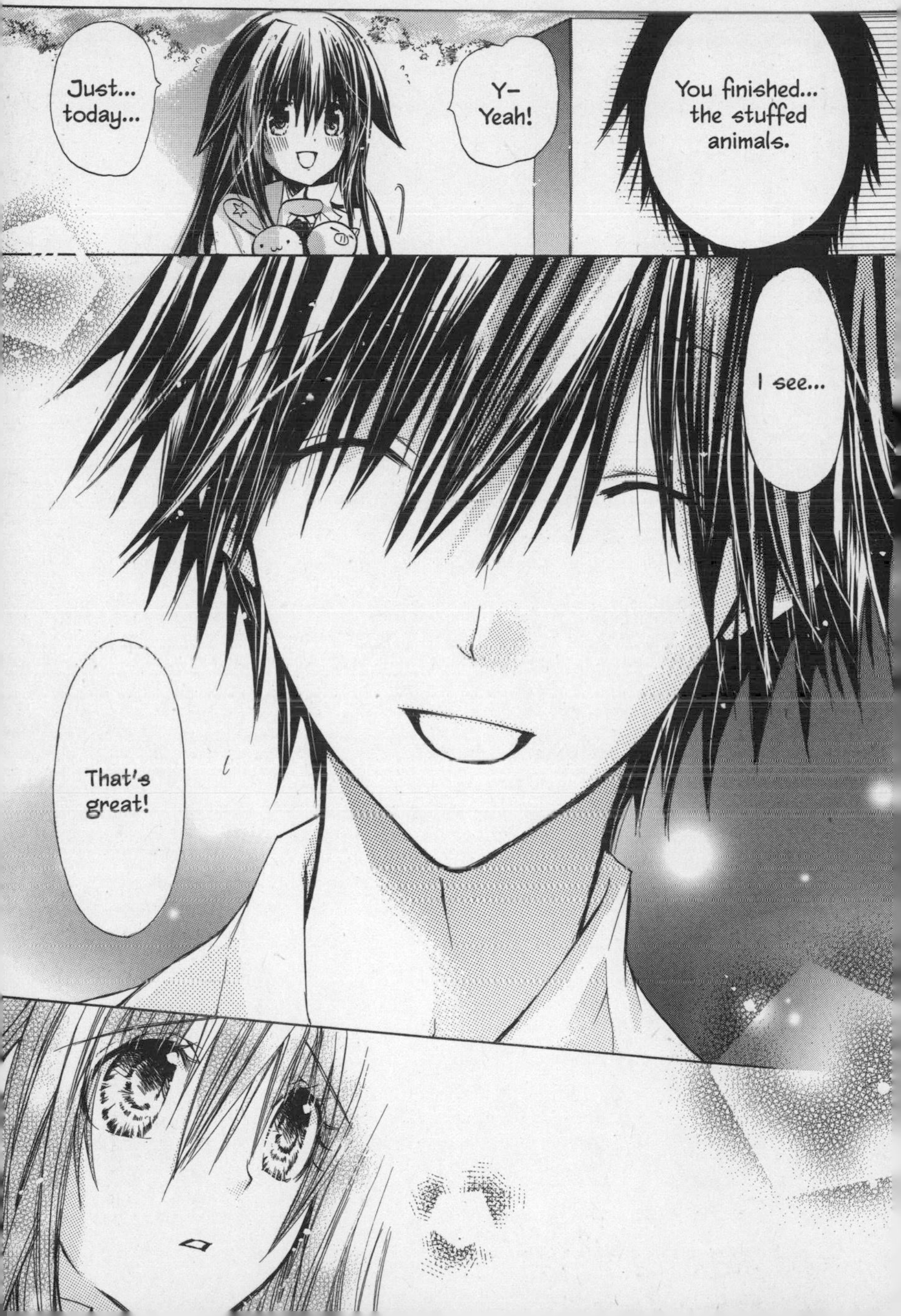
You finished... the stuffed animals.
Y-Yeah!
Just... today...
I see...
That's great!

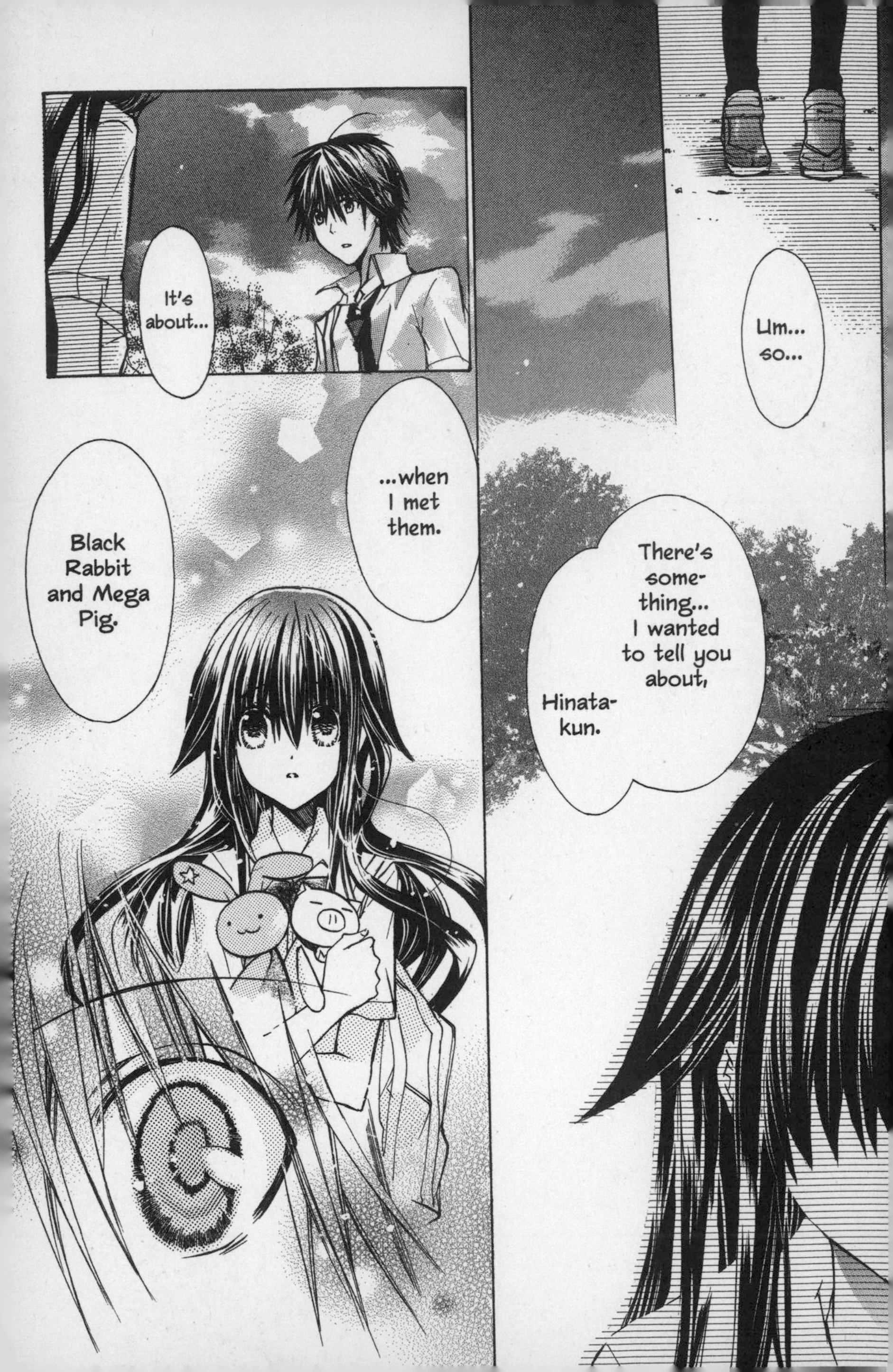
Um... so...
There's some-thing... I wanted to tell you about, Hinata-kun.
It's about...
...when I met them.
Black Rabbit and Mega Pig.

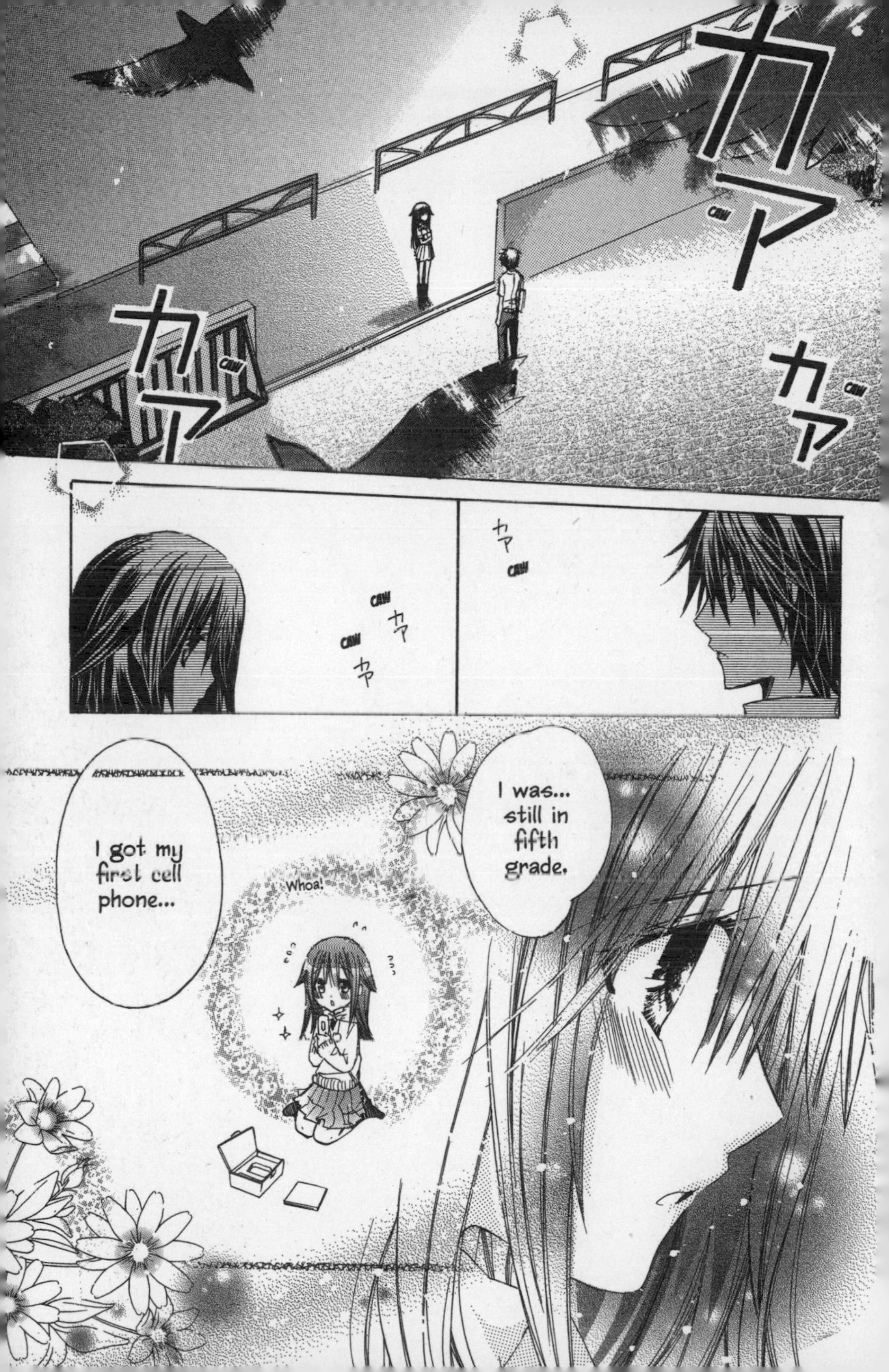
カアー
CAW
カア
CAW
カア
CAW
カア
CAW
CAW
カア
CAW
カ
I was... still in fifth grade.
I got my first cell phone...
Whoa!

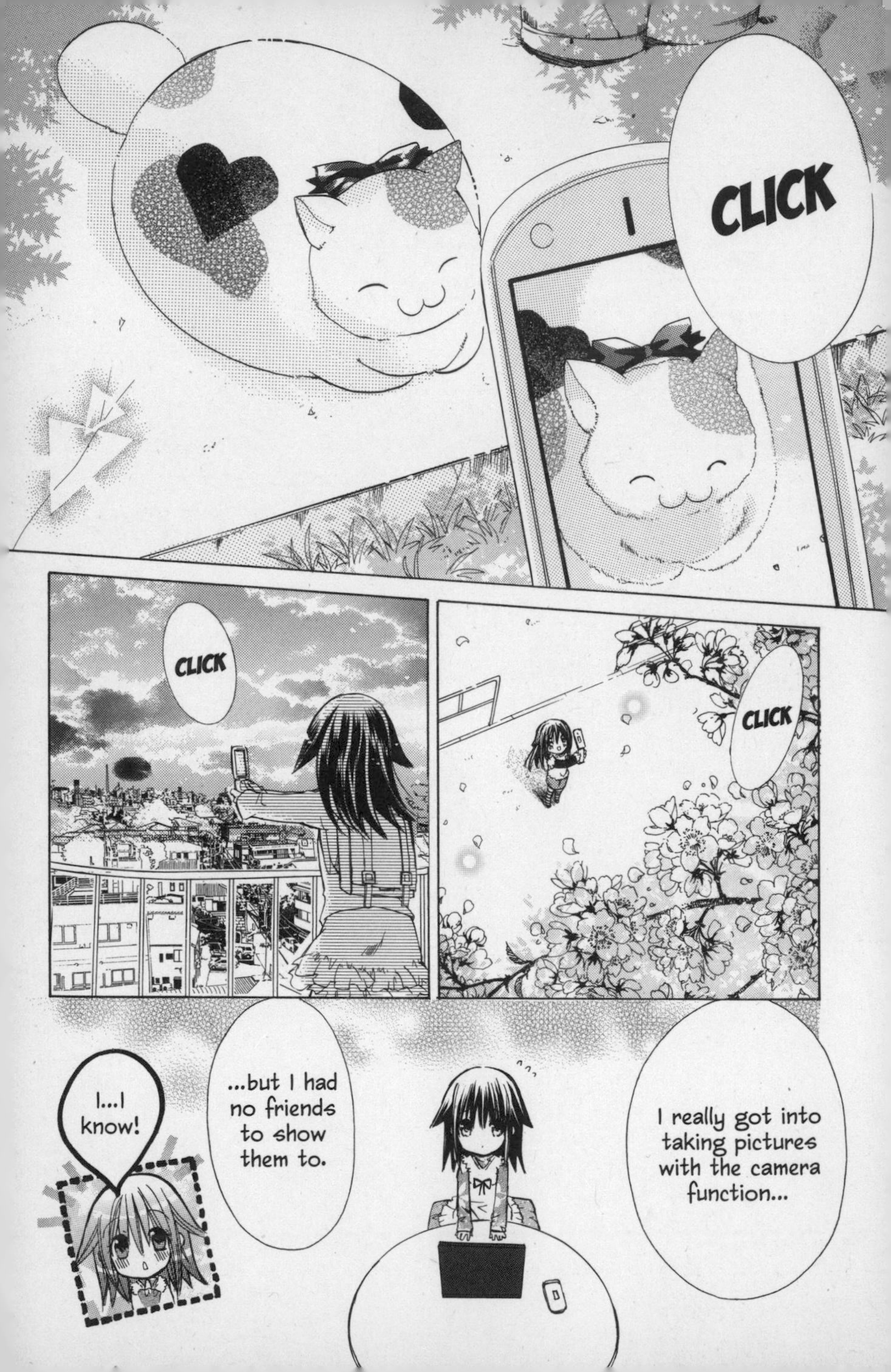
CLICK
CLICK
CLICK
I really got into taking pictures with the camera function...
...but I had no friends to show them to.
I...I know!

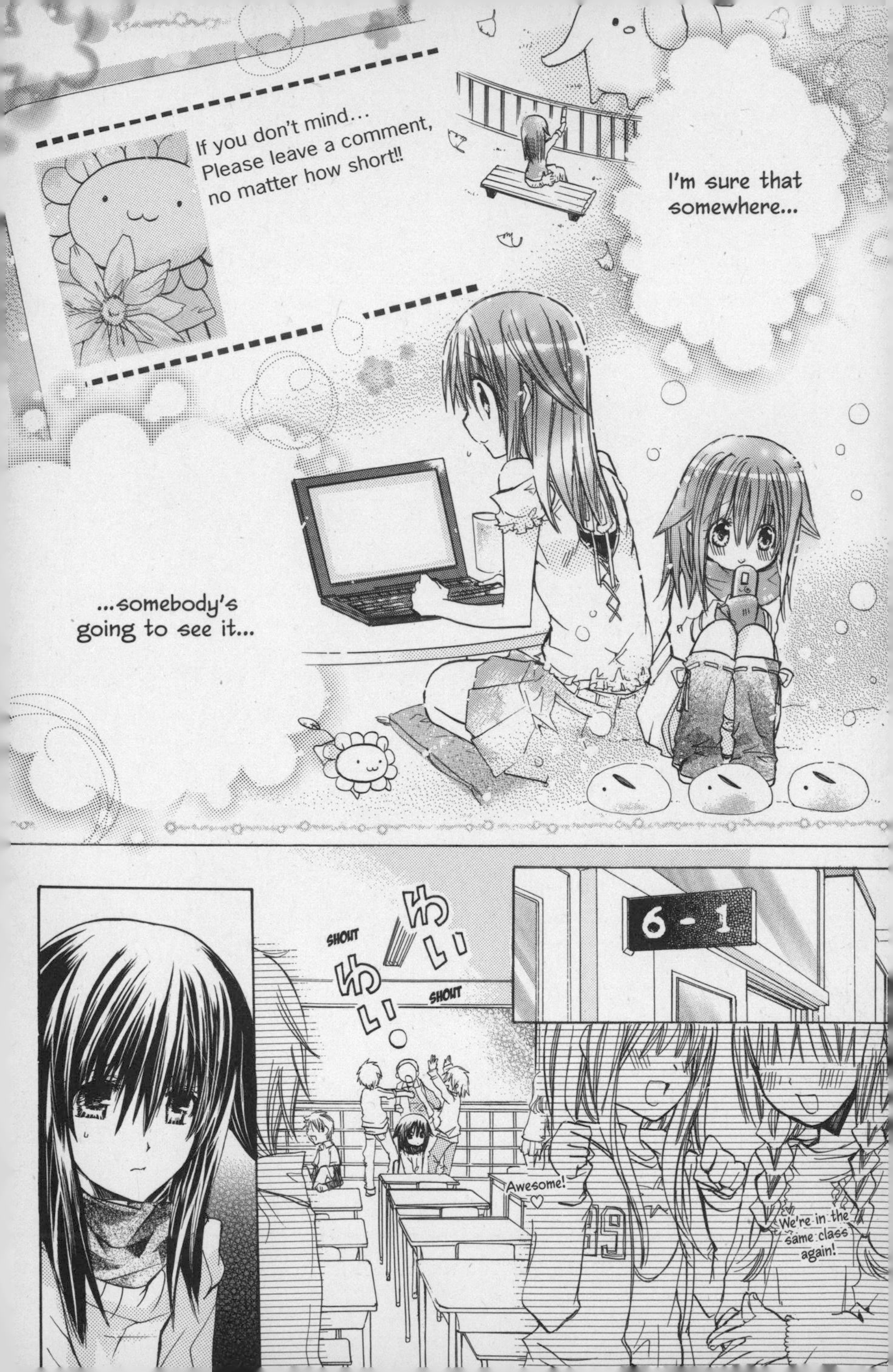
I'm sure that somewhere...
If you don't mind...
Please leave a comment,
no matter how short!!
...somebody's going to see it...
6-1
We're in the same class again!
Awesome! ♥
SHOUT
わい
わい
SHOUT

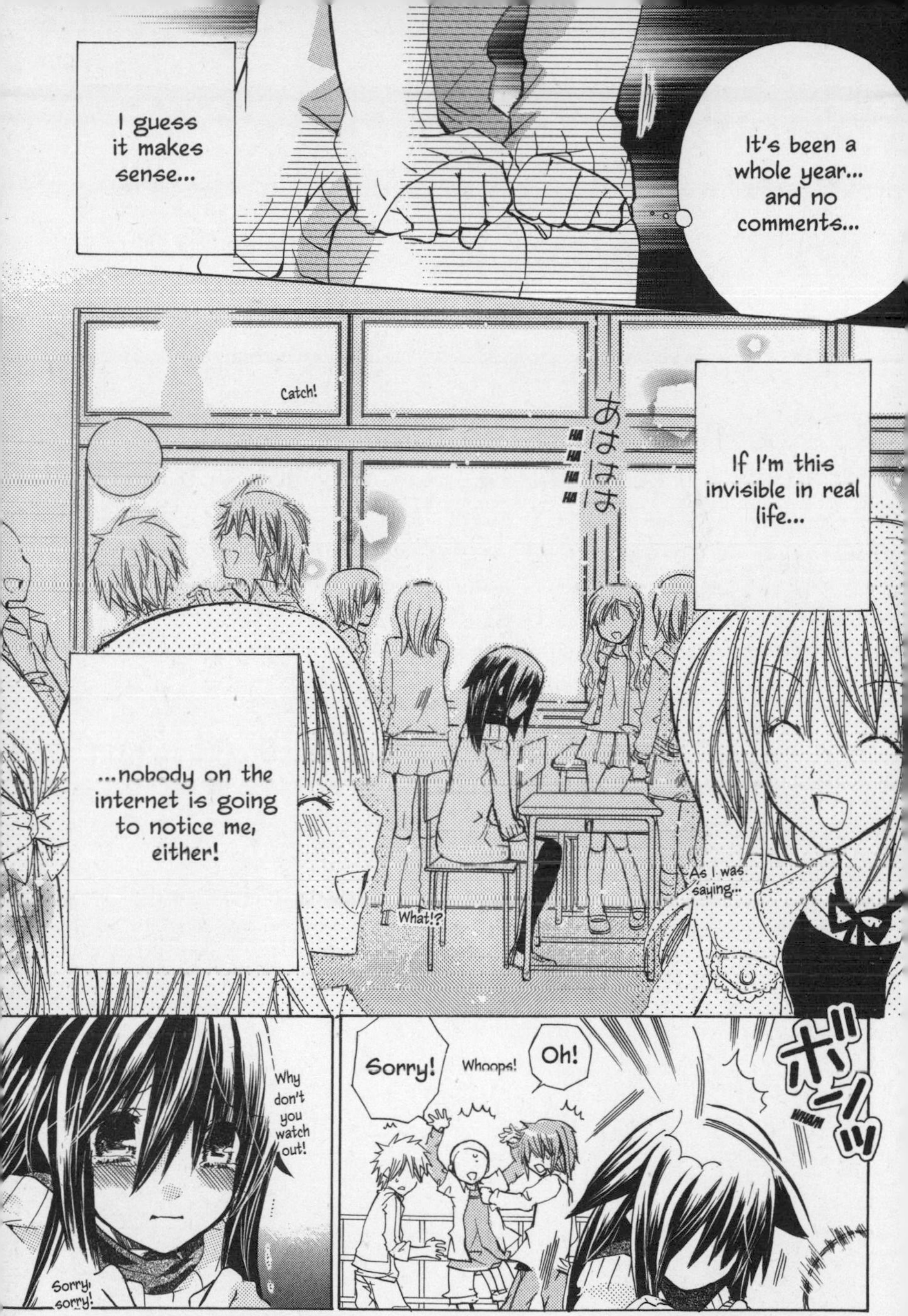
It's been a whole year... and no comments...
I guess it makes sense...
If I'm this invisible in real life...
あははは
HA HA HA HA
Catch!
As I was saying...
What!?
...nobody on the internet is going to notice me, either!
WHAM
Oh!
Whoops!
Sorry!
Why don't you watch out!
Sorry, sorry!

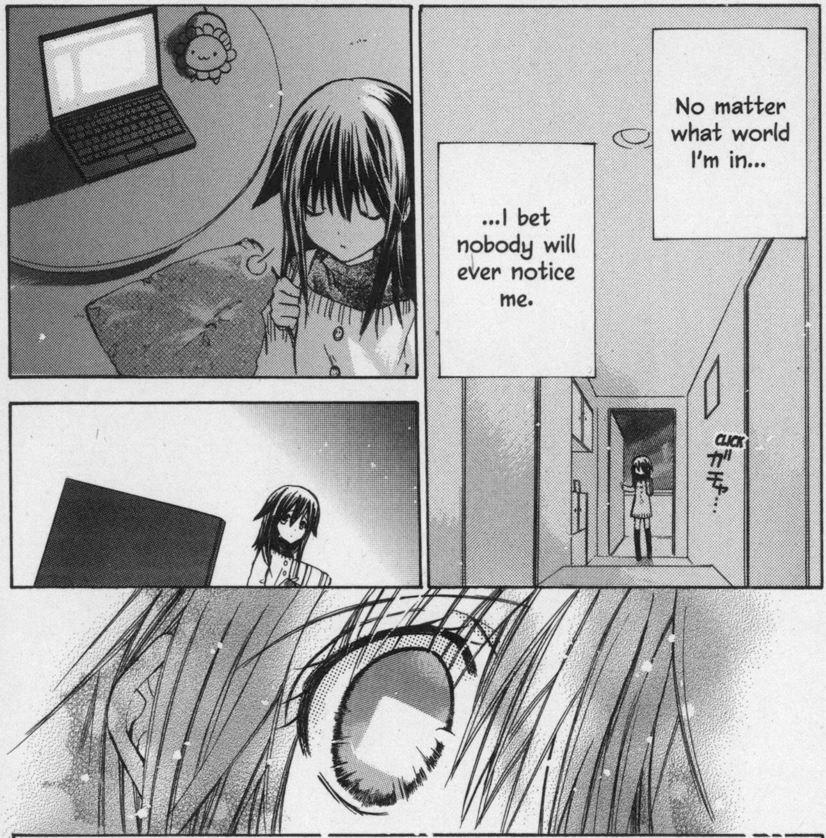
No matter what world I'm in...
...I bet nobody will ever notice me.
CLICK
ガチャ...

Comment (1)

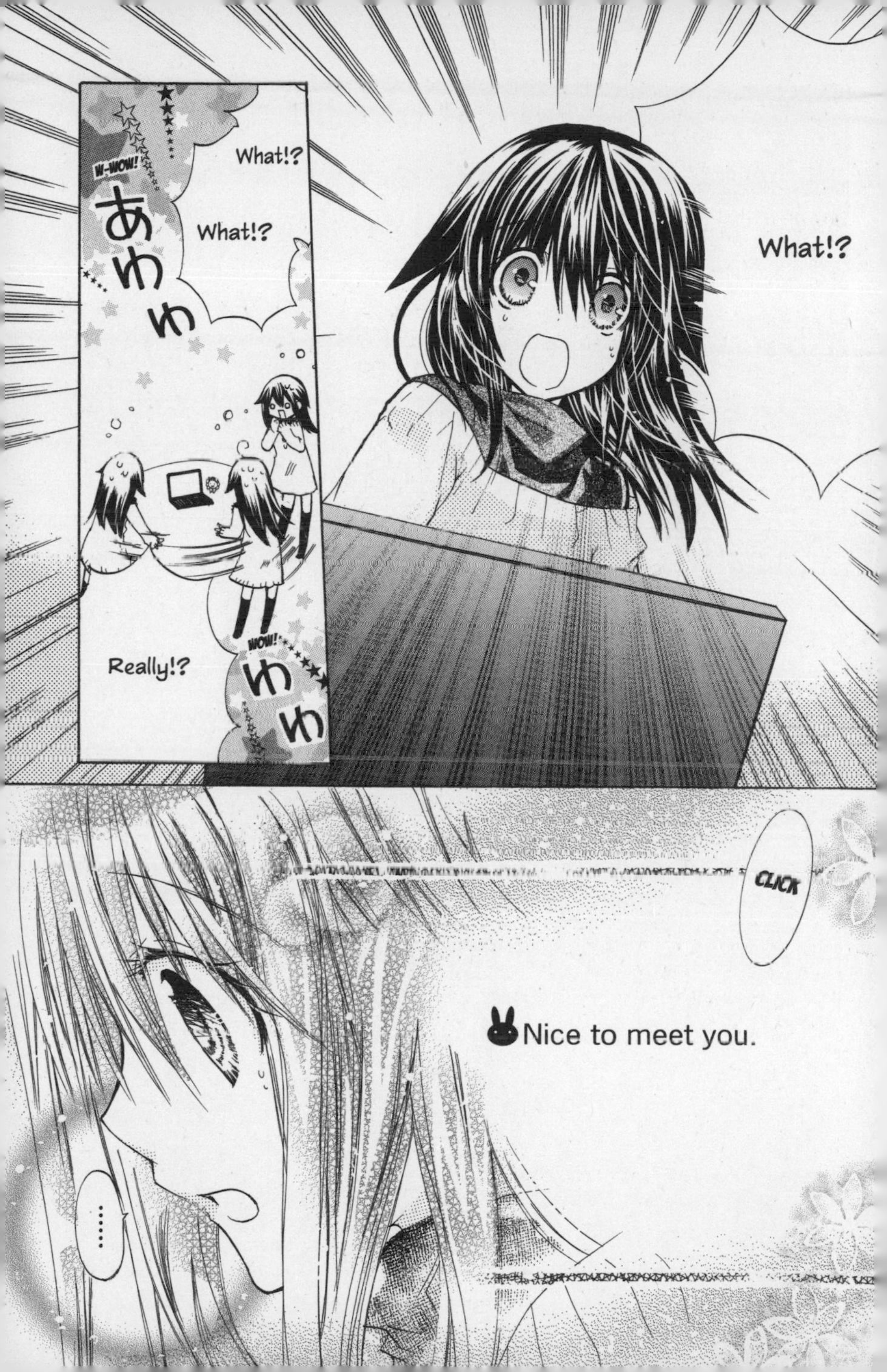
What!?
W-WOW!
あゎゎ
What!?
What!?
WOW!
ゎゎ
Really!?
CLICK
Nice to meet you.
......

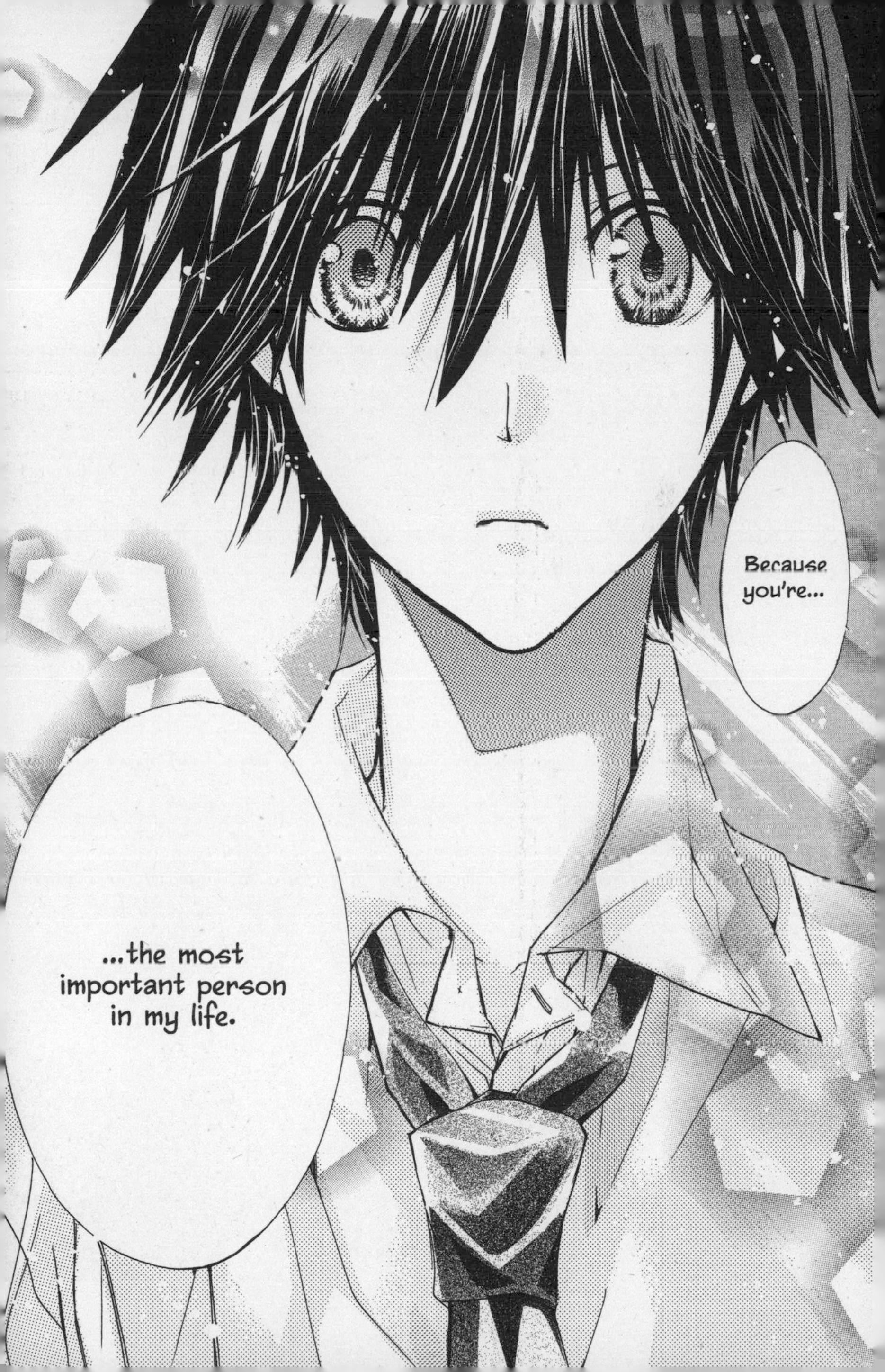
Because you're...
...the most important person in my life.

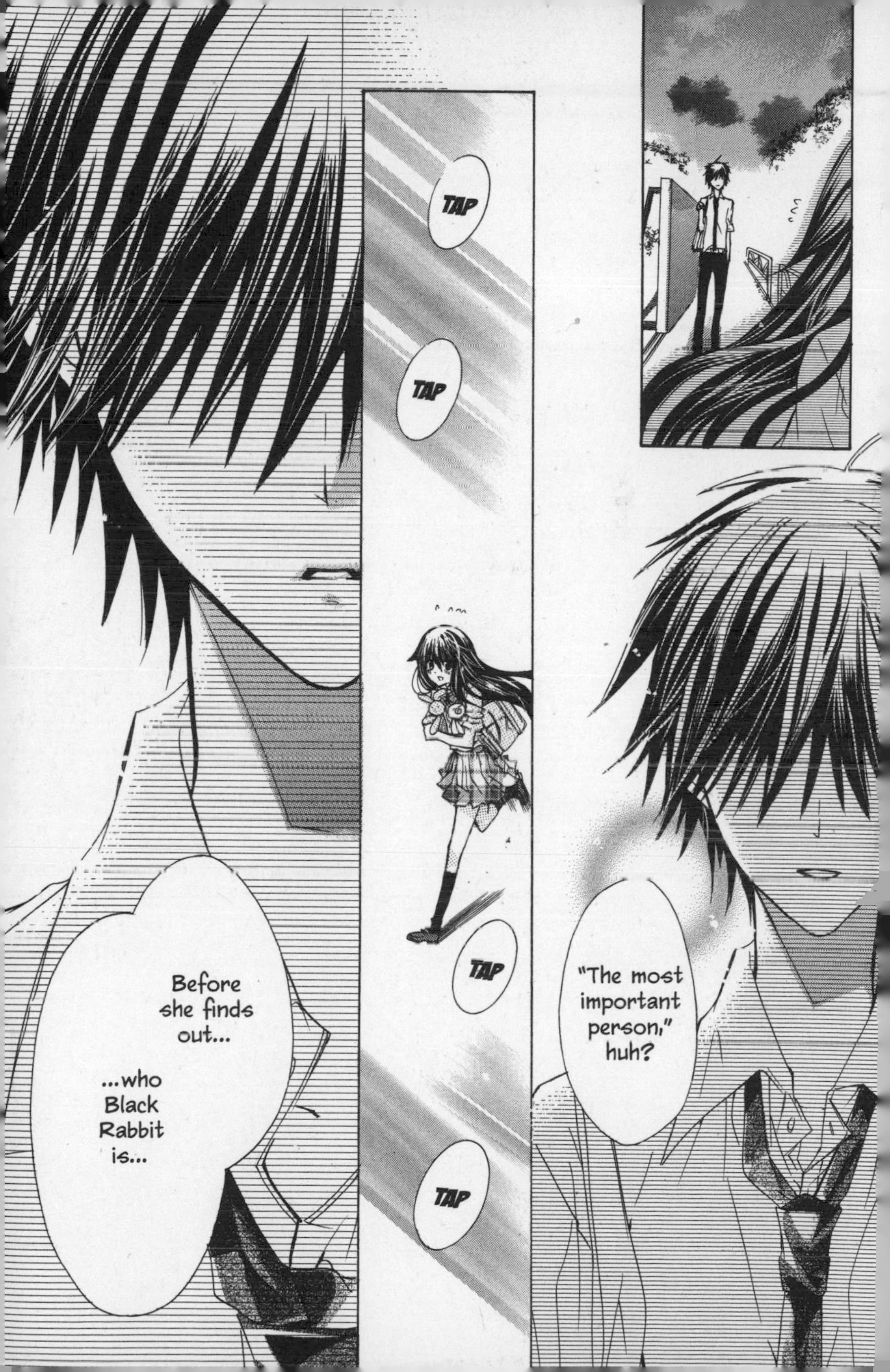
"The most important person," huh?
TAP
TAP
TAP
TAP
Before she finds out...
...who Black Rabbit is...

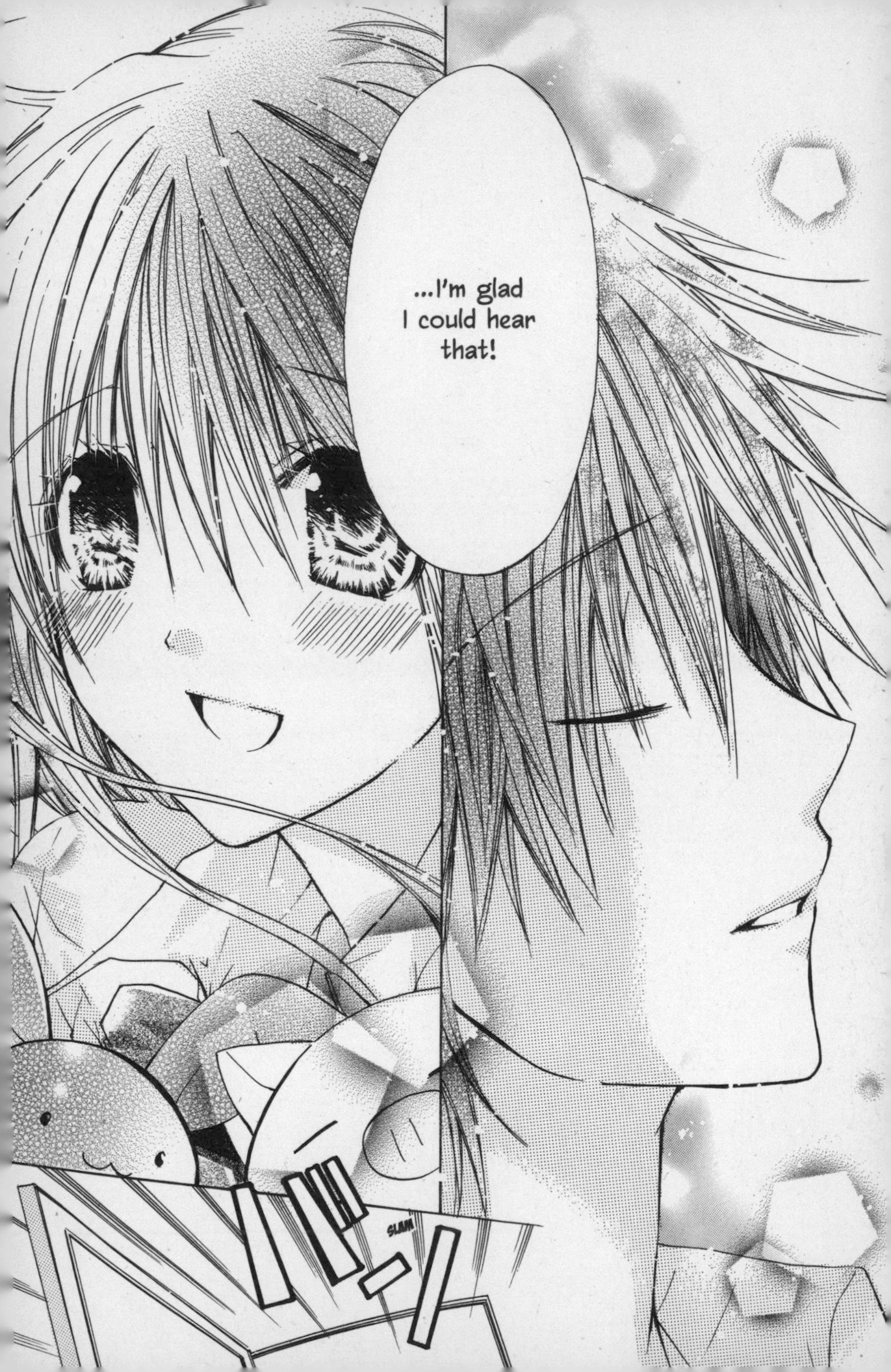
...I'm glad I could hear that!
SLAM

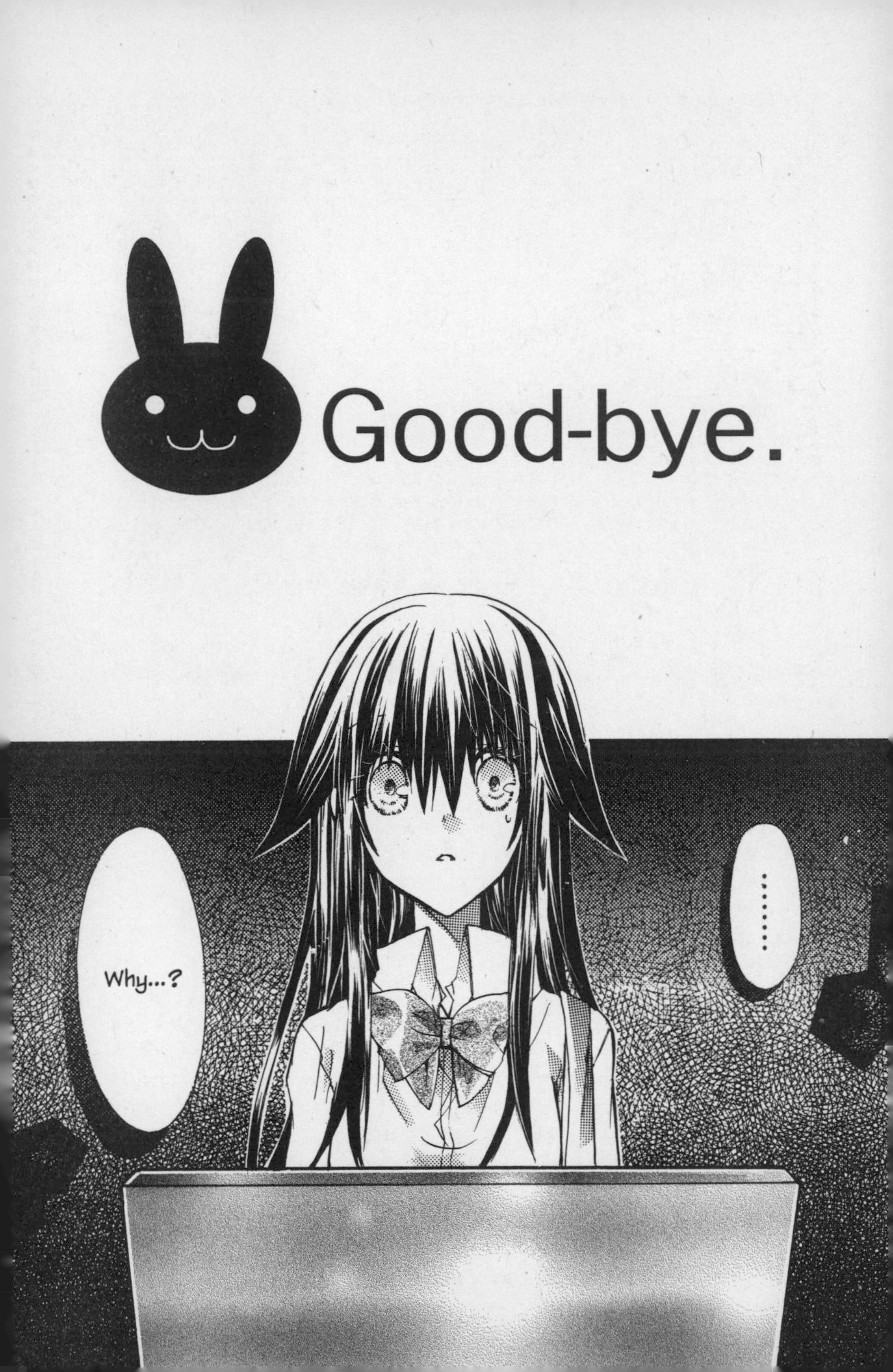
Good-bye.
......
Why...?

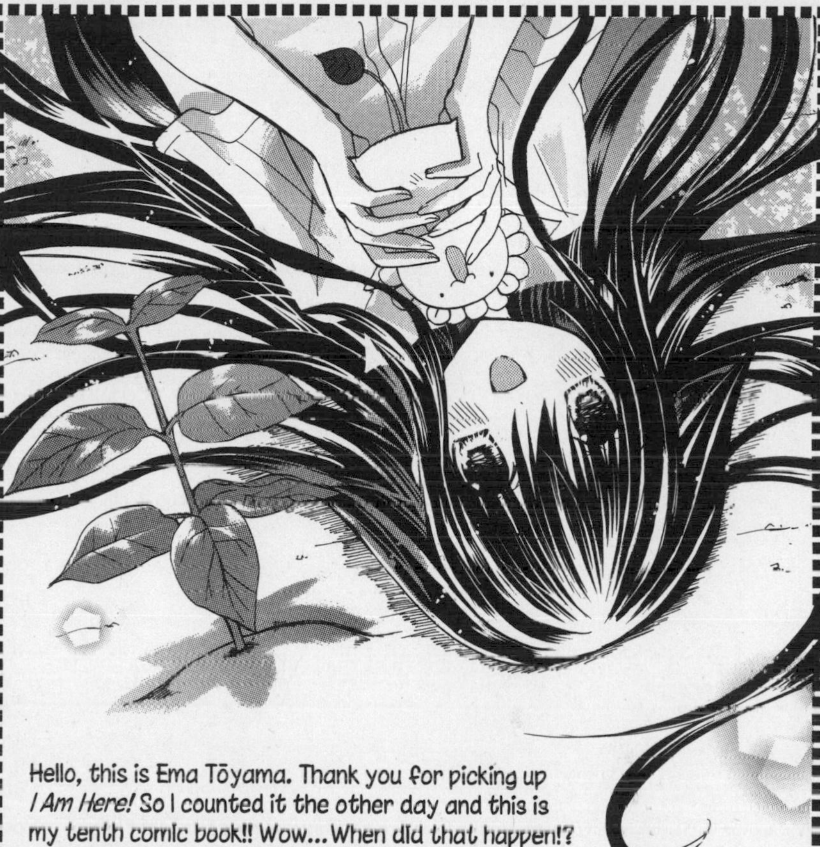

Hello, this is Ema Tōyama. Thank you for picking up *I Am Here!* So I counted it the other day and this is my tenth comic book!! Wow...When did that happen!? When I'm drawing manga, one year just flies by. I'm getting old so quickly!! At first my mother was helping out, and now I have assistants...I used to be able to pull all-nighters, but now I need six hours of sleep (it's called aging).... Thinking about it makes me emotional. I'm looking forward to all the changes in the future as I work, so I hope you'll stick with me! :P It's been a year since I started drawing *I Am Here!*, but it's still summer in the story... Some mangas don't have fall and winter. Errr... The next volume is still summer, too. I hope you keep reading! See you!

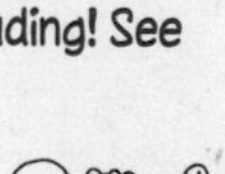

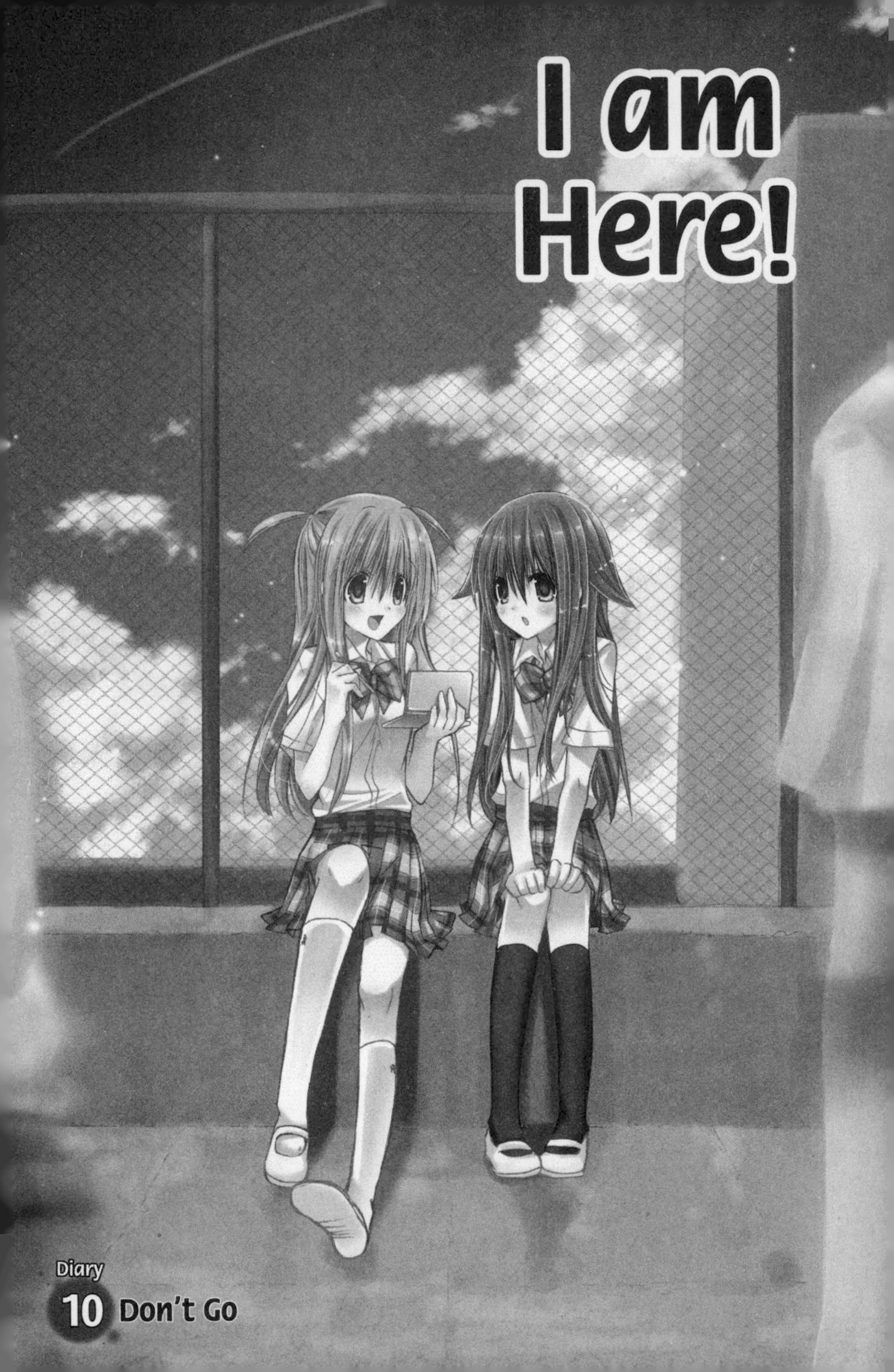
I am Here!
Diary
10 Don't Go

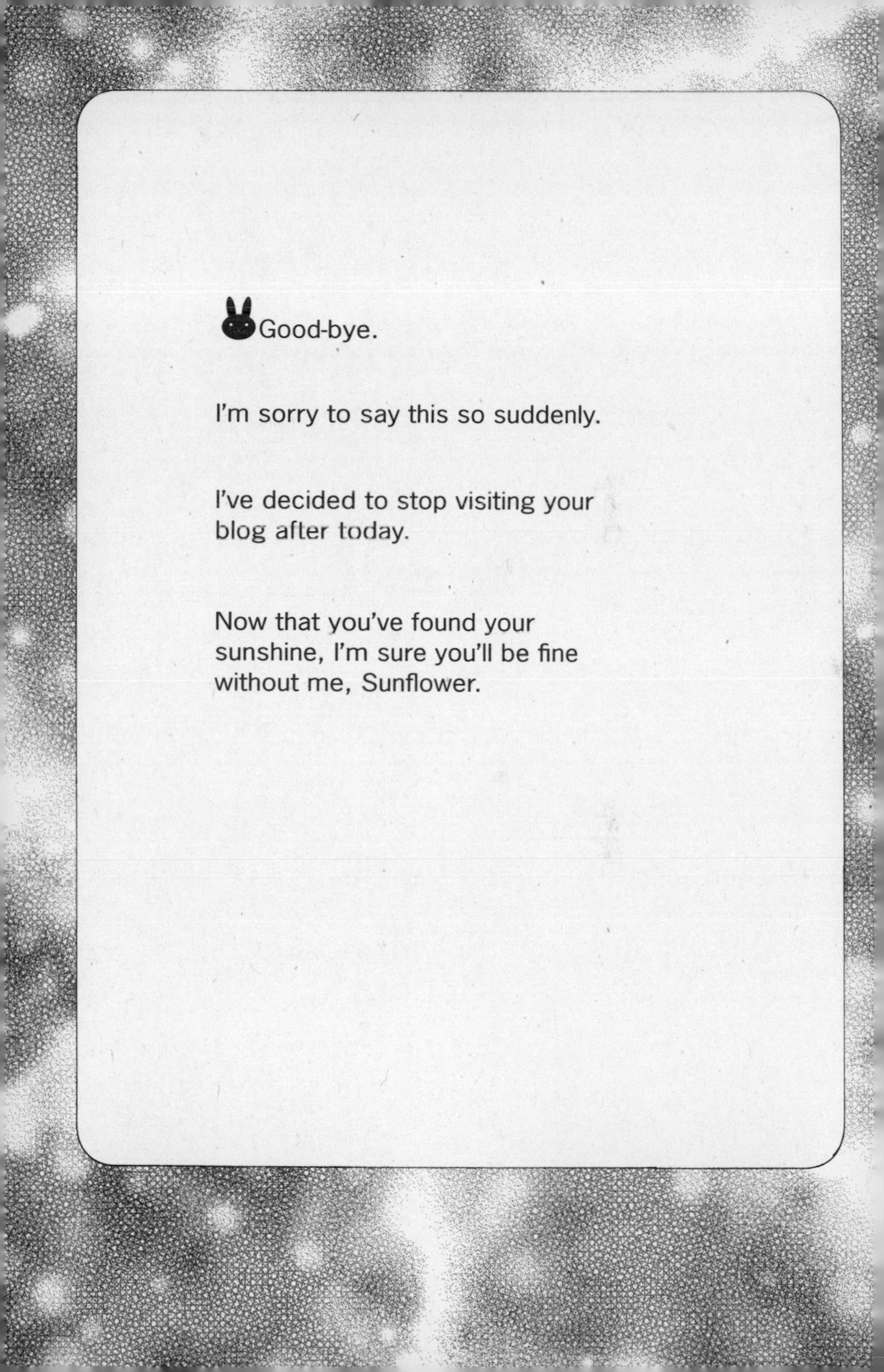
Good-bye.
I'm sorry to say this so suddenly.
I've decided to stop visiting your blog after today.
Now that you've found your sunshine, I'm sure you'll be fine without me, Sunflower.

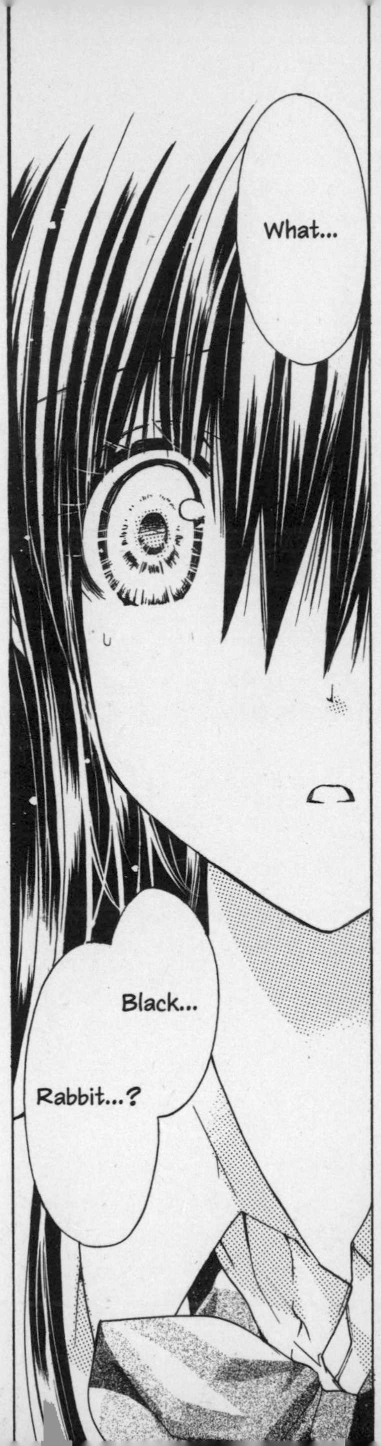
What...
Black... Rabbit...?

I had so much fun spending time with you and Mega Pig.

Even if we're apart,

my heart will always
be with you.

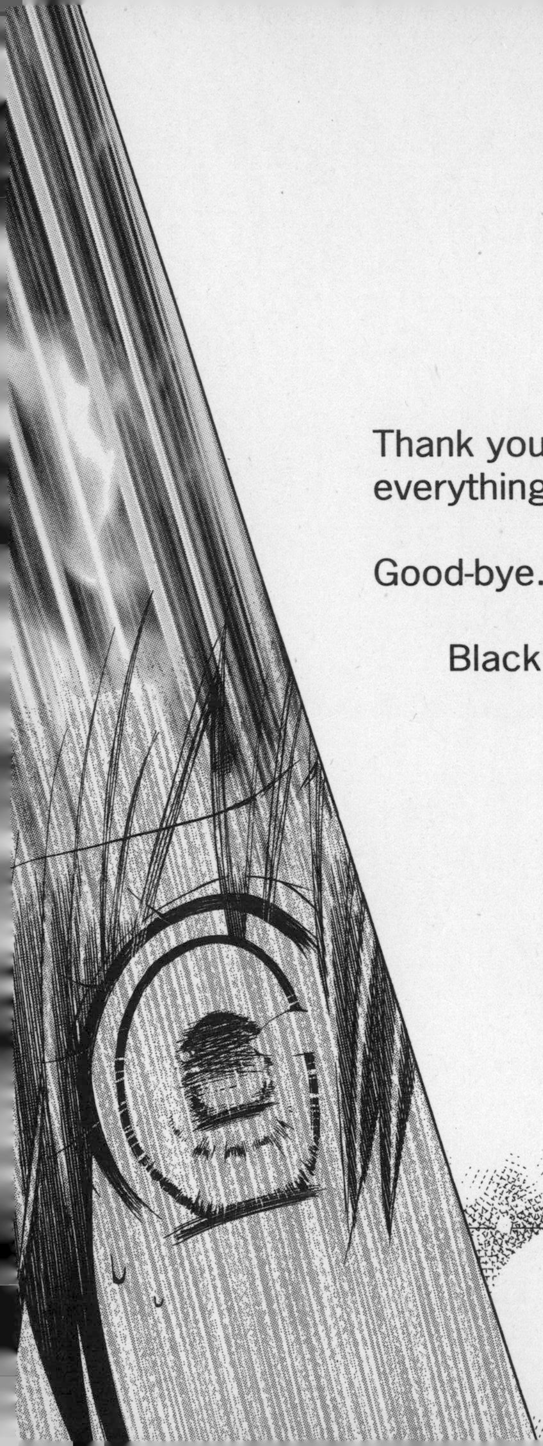

Thank you for
everything.

Good-bye.

Black Rabbit

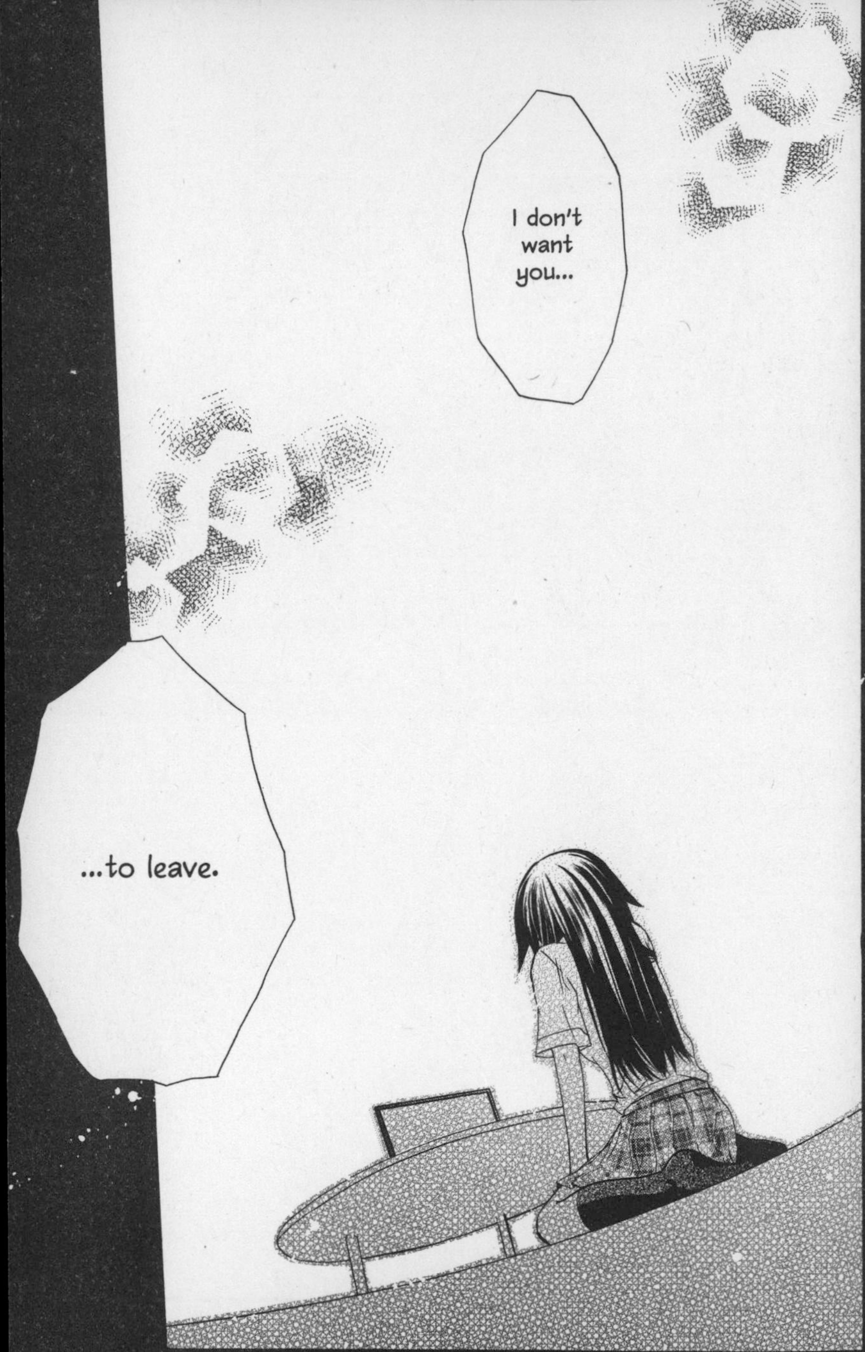
I don't want you...
...to leave.

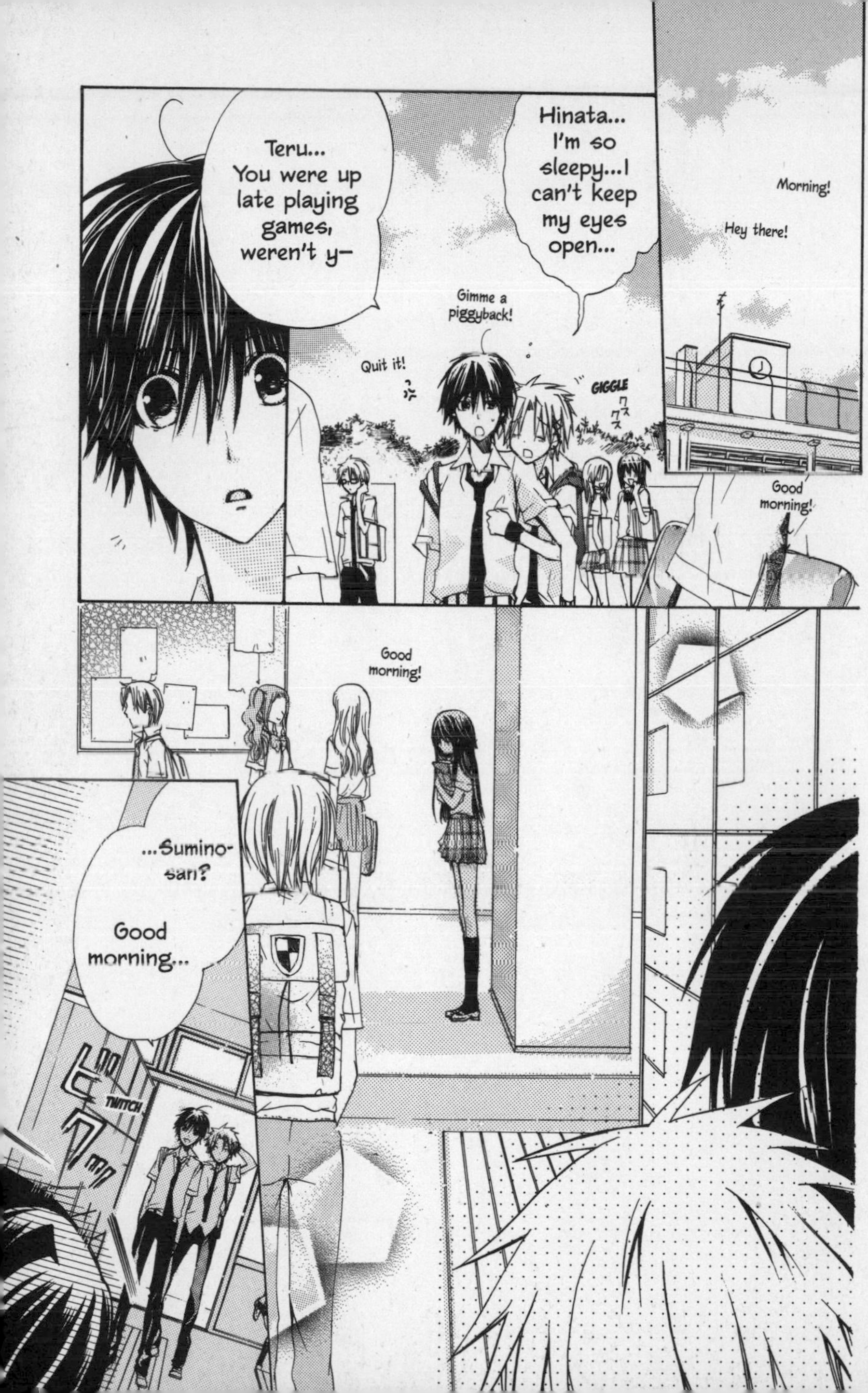
Morning!
Hey there!
Good morning!
Hinata... I'm so sleepy...I can't keep my eyes open...
Gimme a piggyback!
GIGGLE
Quit it!
Teru... You were up late playing games, weren't y–
Good morning!
...Sumino-san?
Good morning...
TWITCH

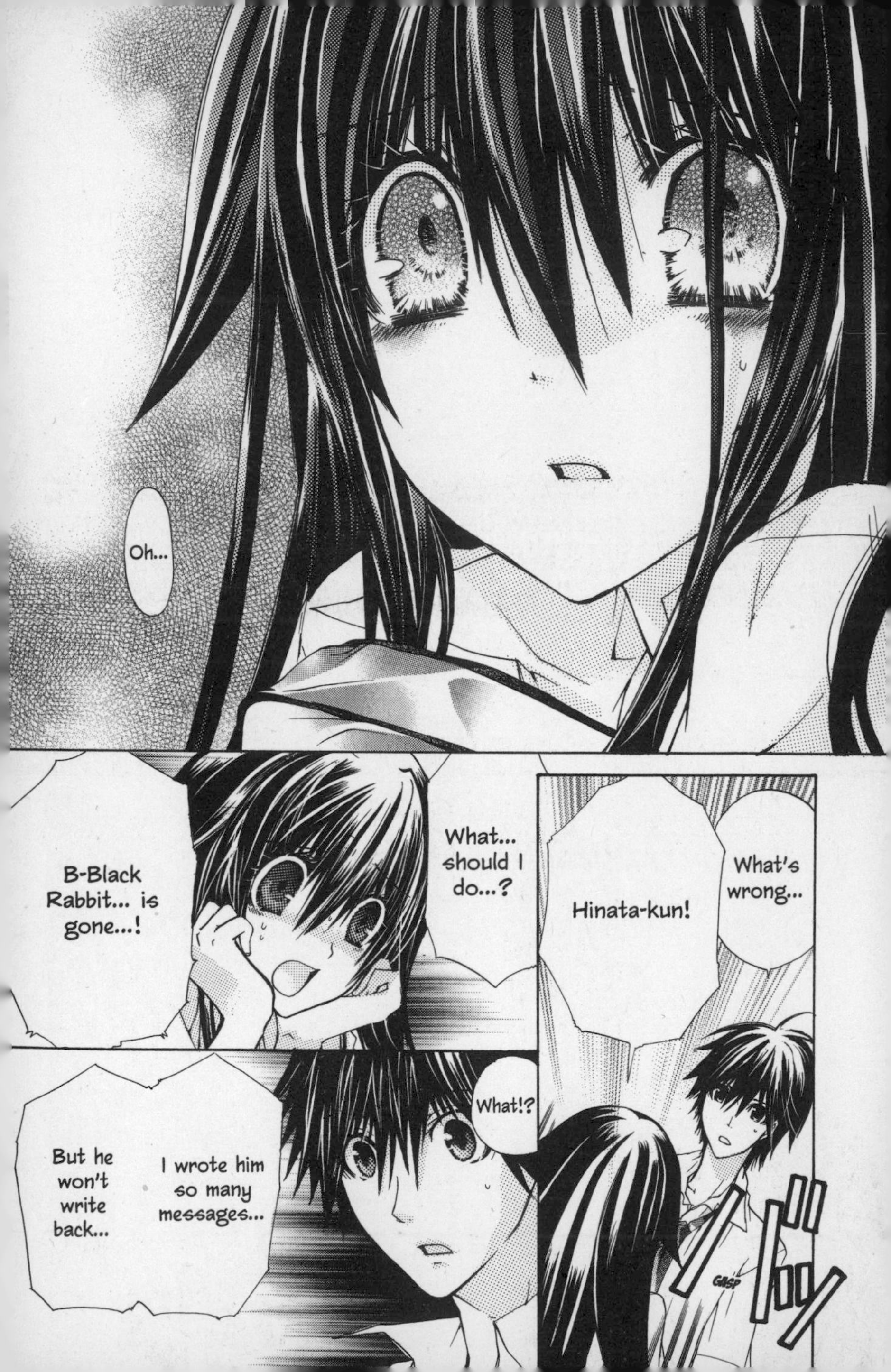
Oh...
What's wrong...
Hinata-kun!
GASP
What... should I do...?
B-Black Rabbit... is gone...!
What!?
I wrote him so many messages...
But he won't write back...

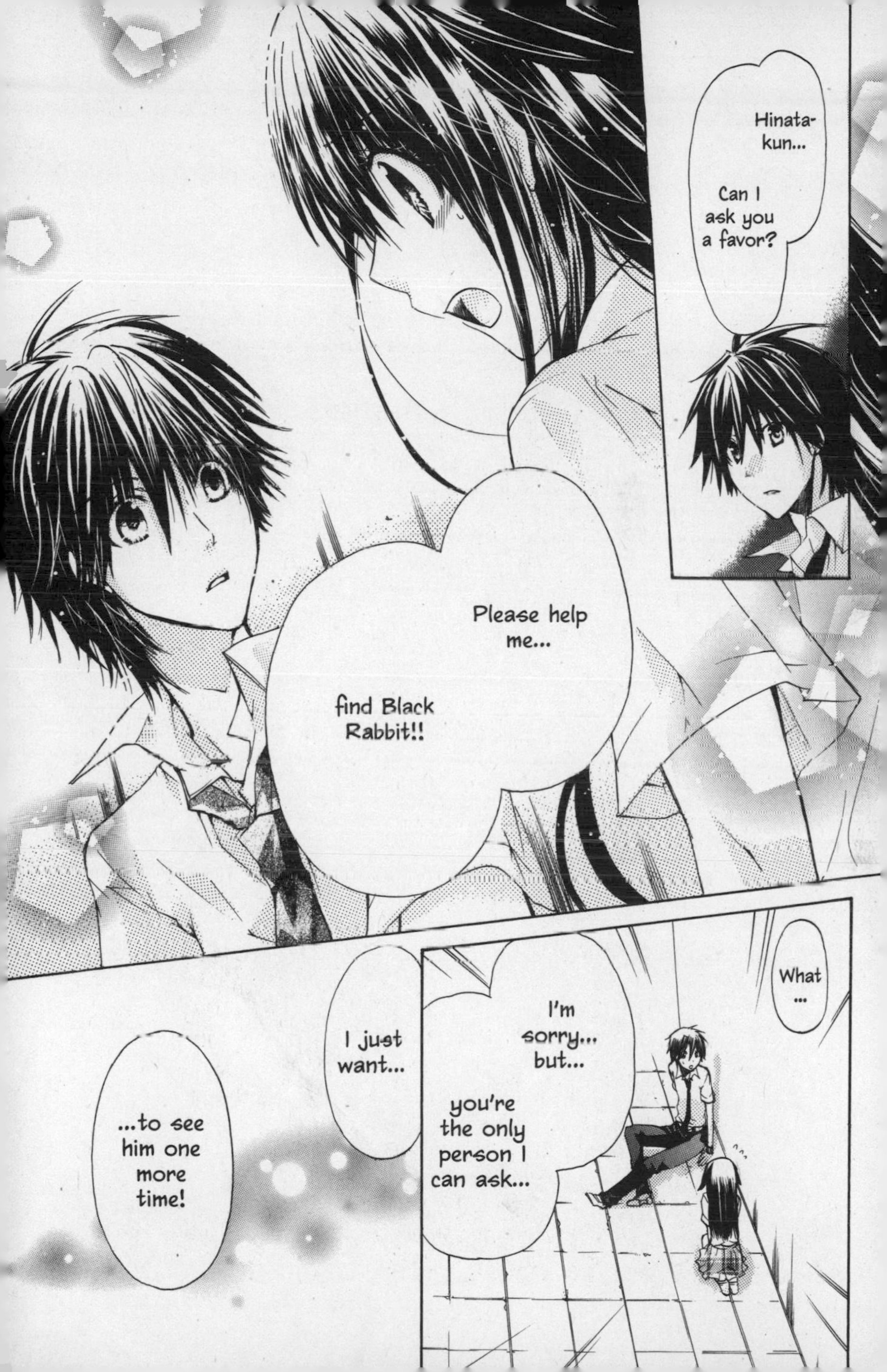
Hinata-kun... Can I ask you a favor?
Please help me... find Black Rabbit!!
What...
I'm sorry... but... you're the only person I can ask...
I just want...
...to see him one more time!

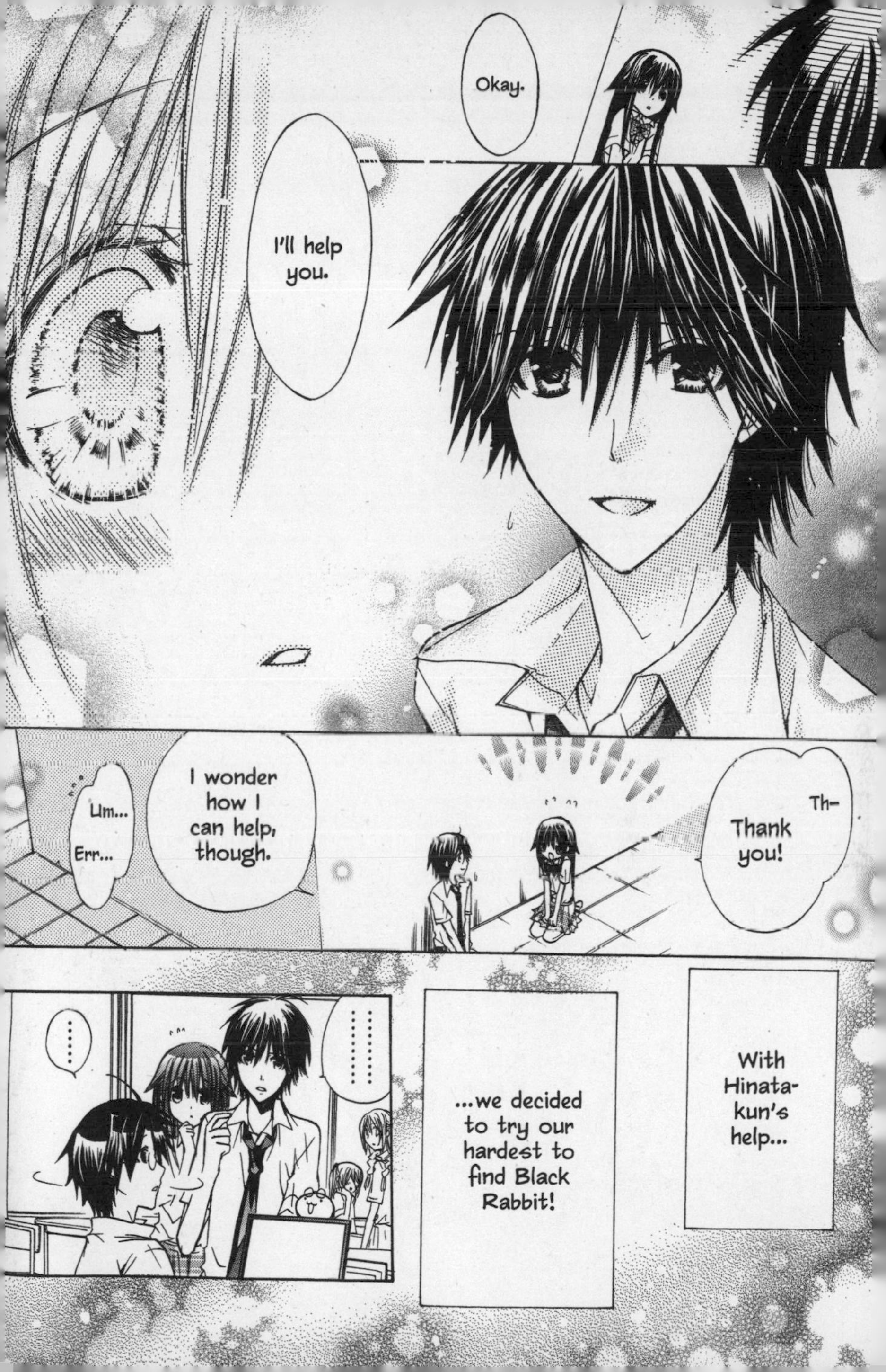
Okay.
I'll help you.
Th- Thank you!
I wonder how I can help, though.
Um... Err...
With Hinata-kun's help...
...we decided to try our hardest to find Black Rabbit!
......
.....

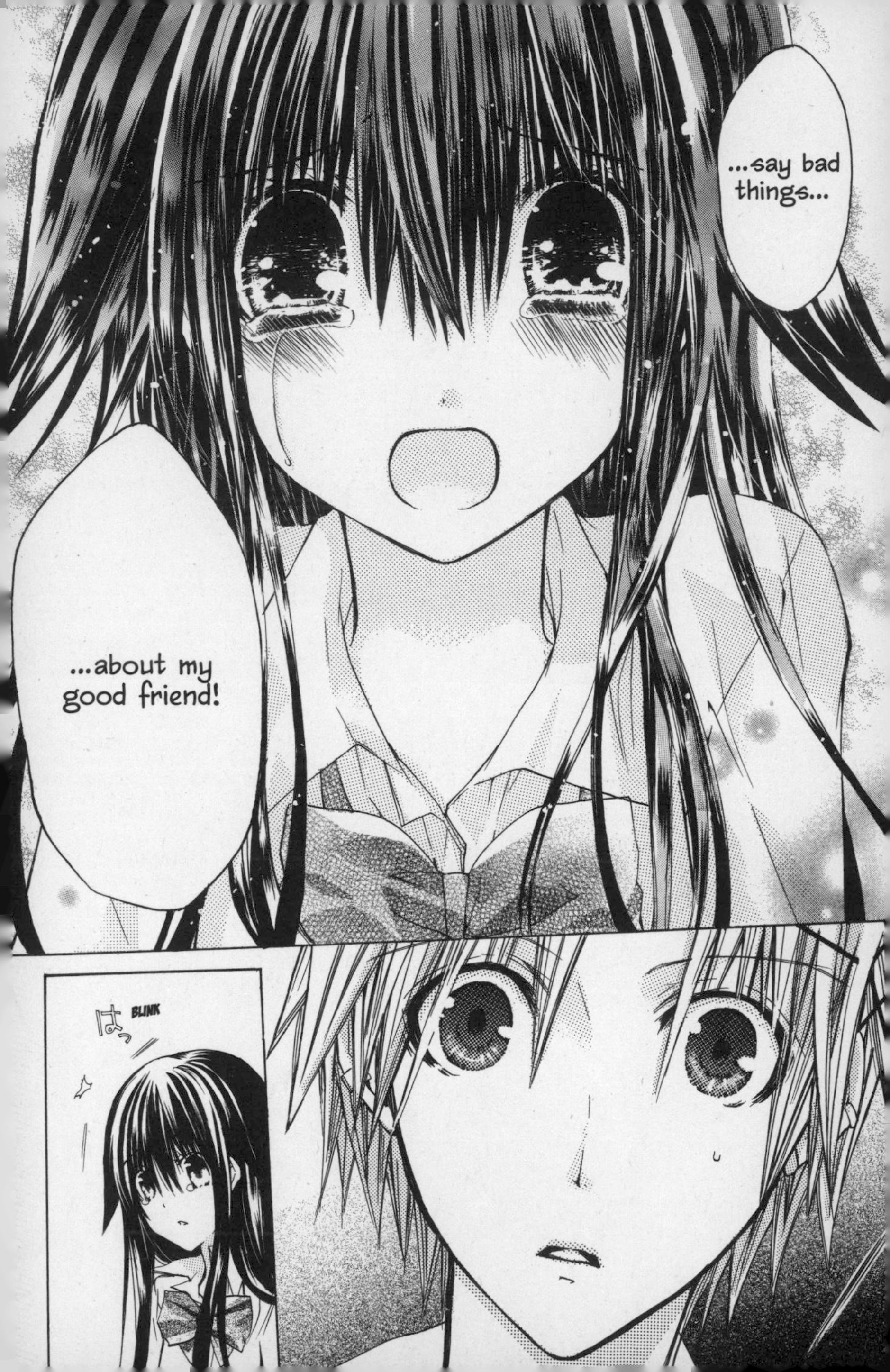
...say bad things...
...about my good friend!
はっ
BLINK

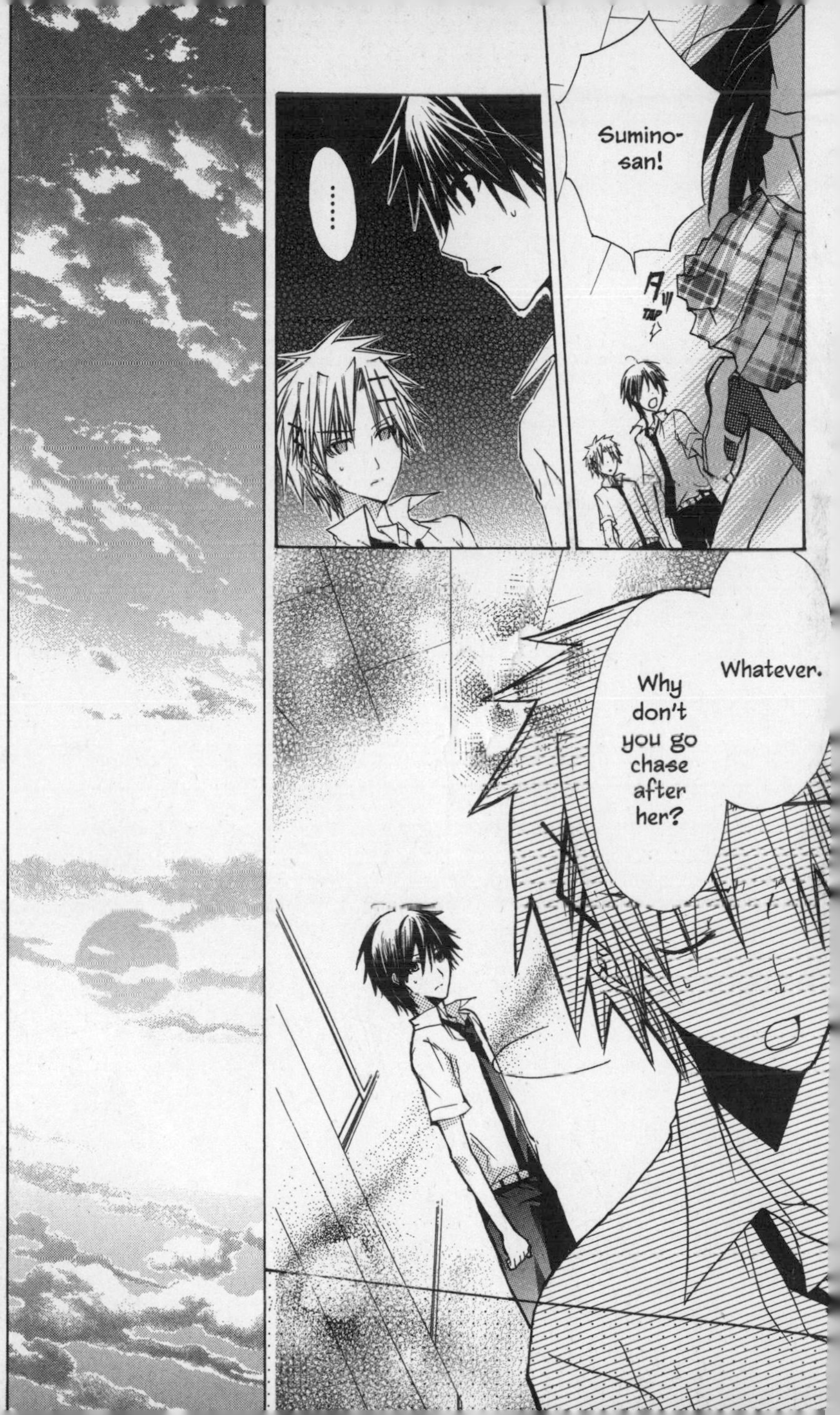
Sumino-san!
TAP
......
Whatever.
Why don't you go chase after her?

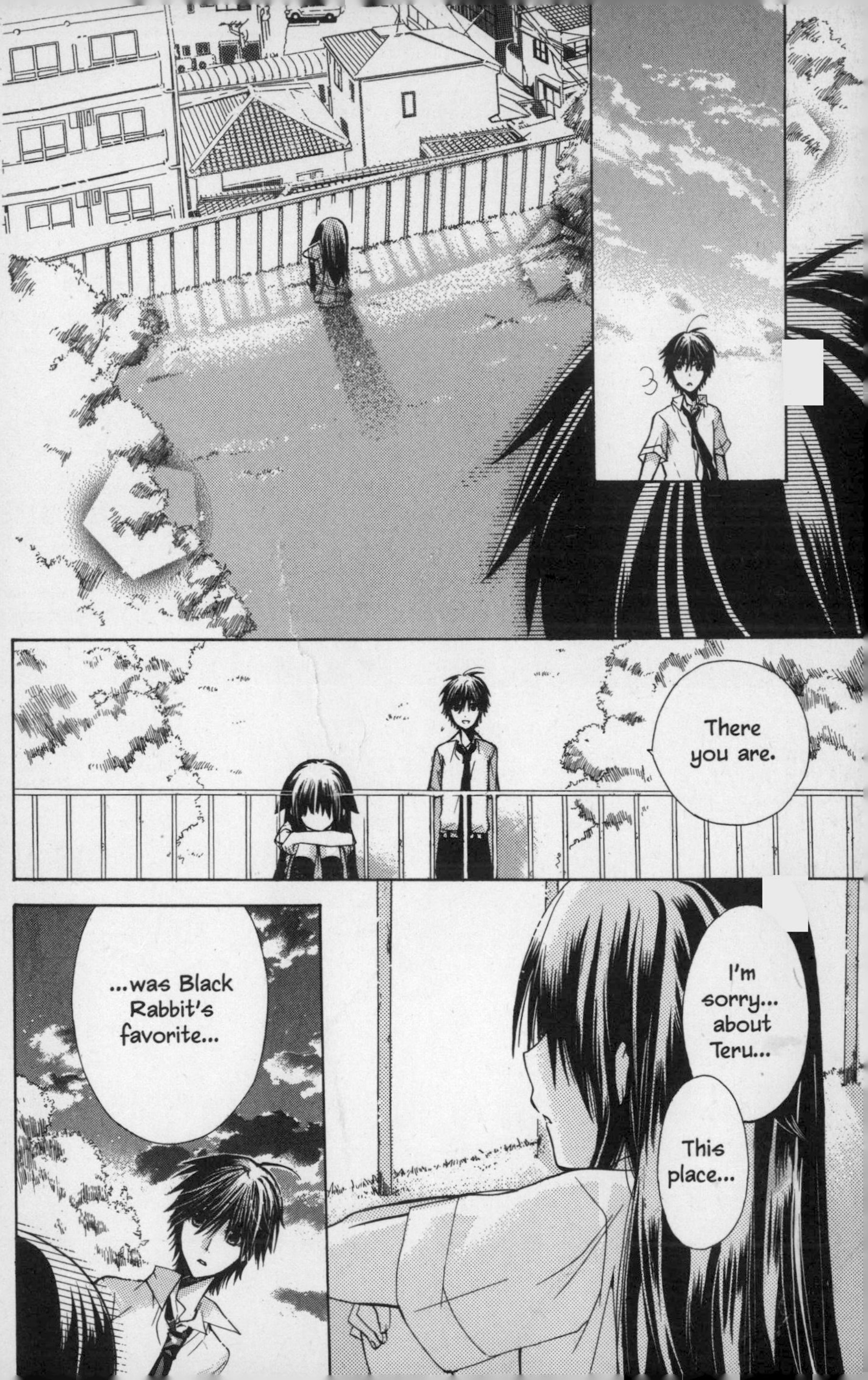
There you are.
I'm sorry... about Teru...
This place...
...was Black Rabbit's favorite...

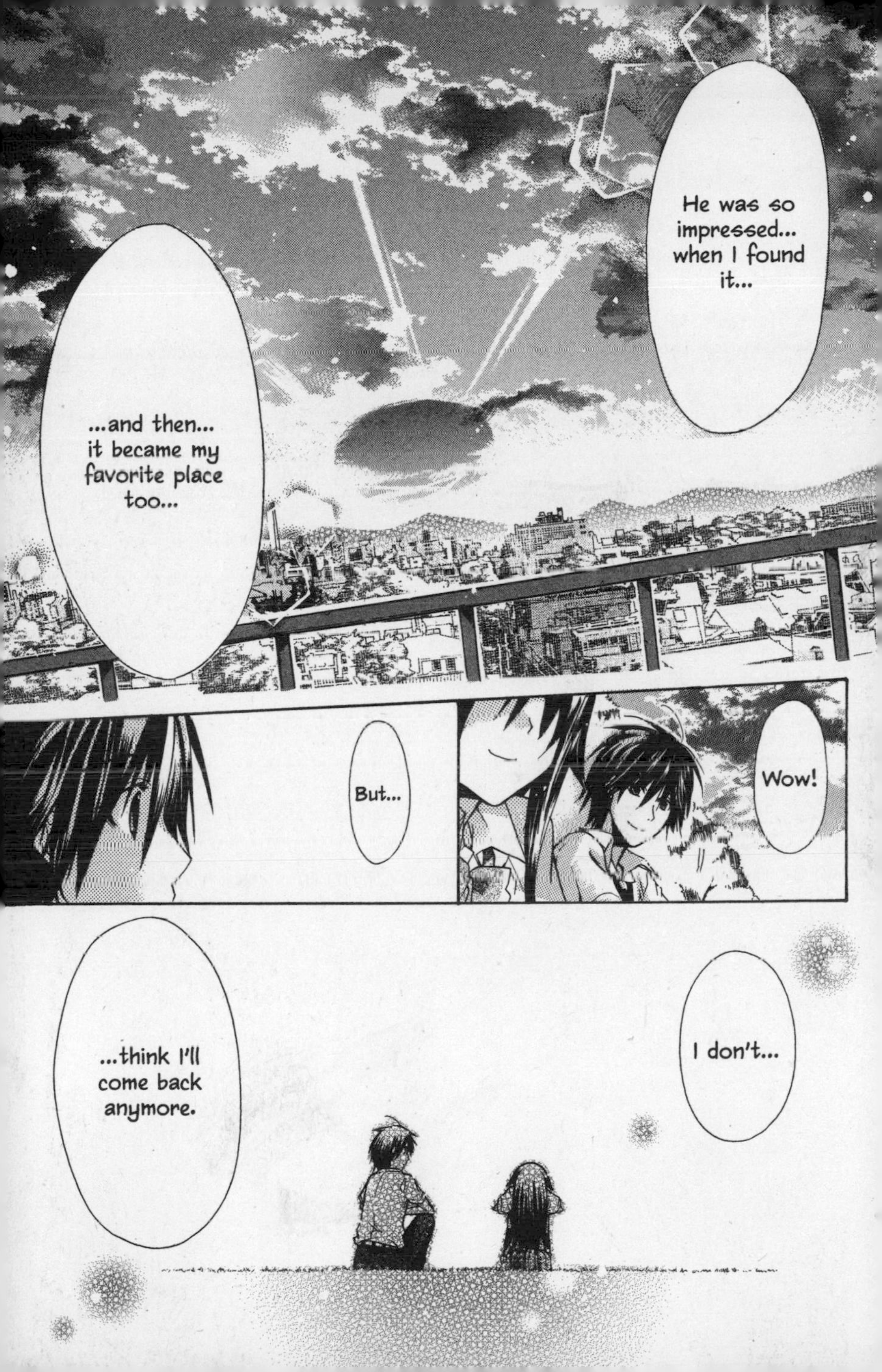
He was so impressed... when I found it...
...and then... it became my favorite place too...
Wow!
But...
I don't...
...think I'll come back anymore.

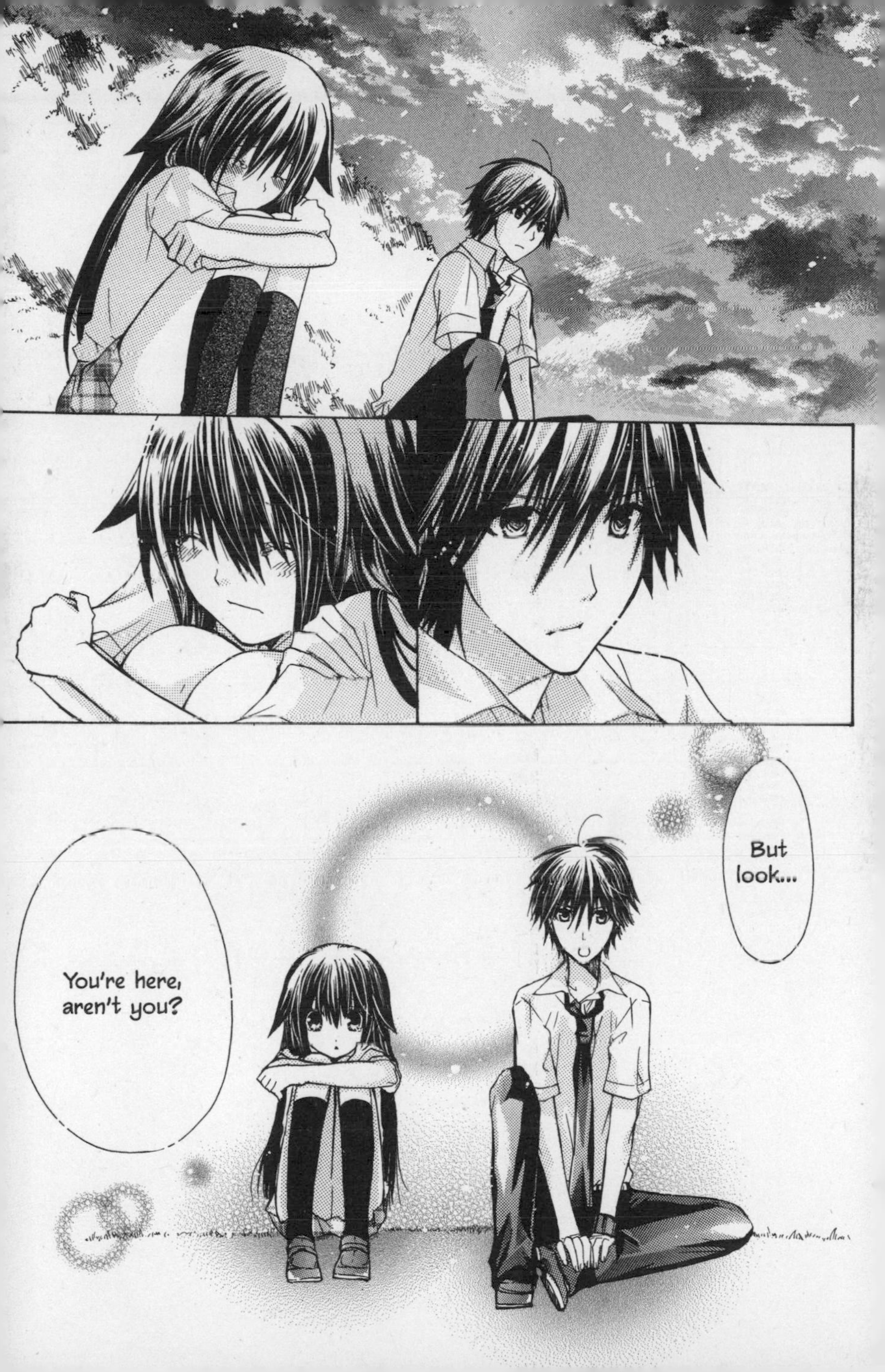
But look...
You're here, aren't you?

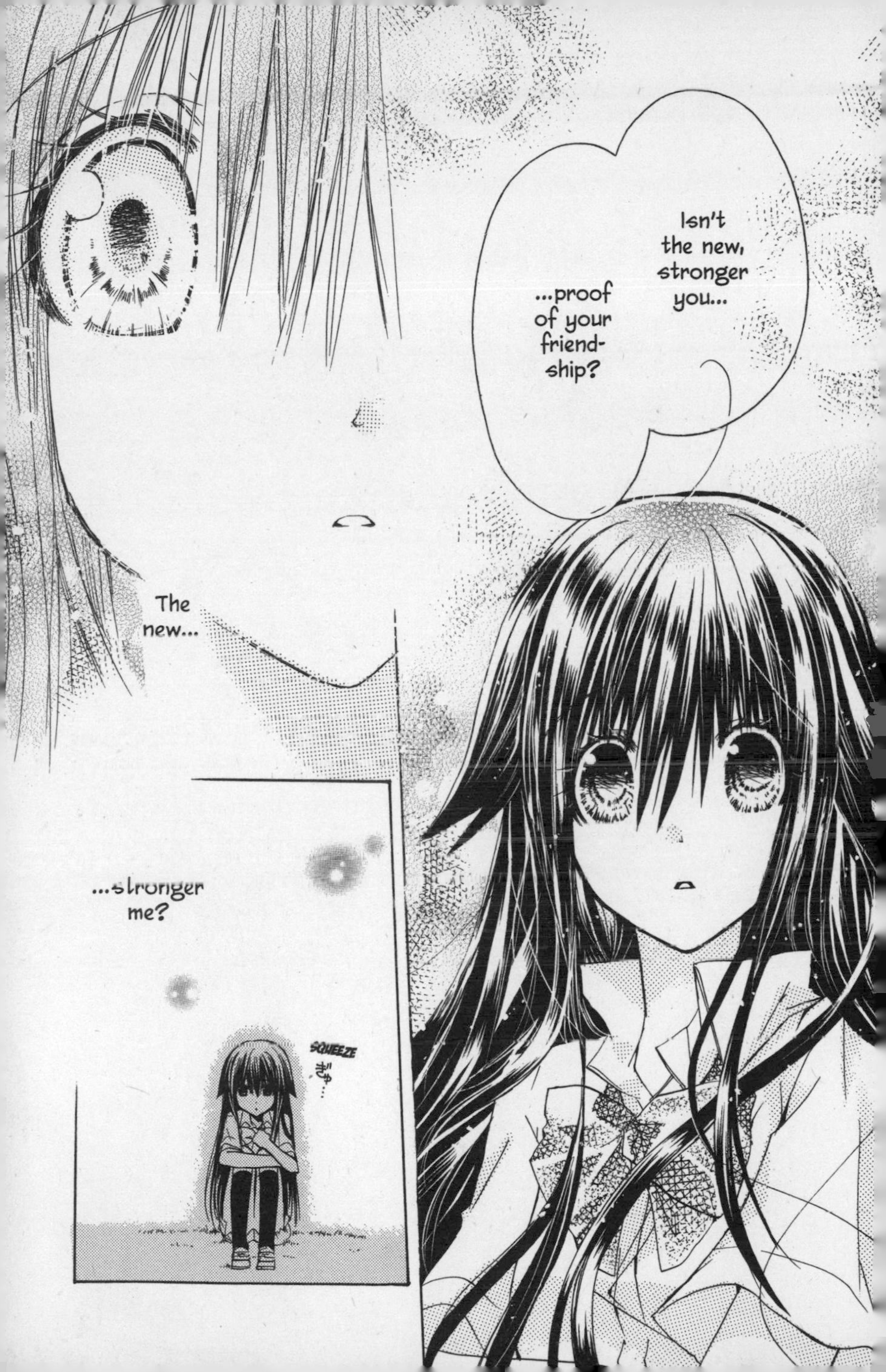
Isn't the new, stronger you... ...proof of your friend-ship?
The new...
...stronger me?
SQUEEZE
ぎゅ…

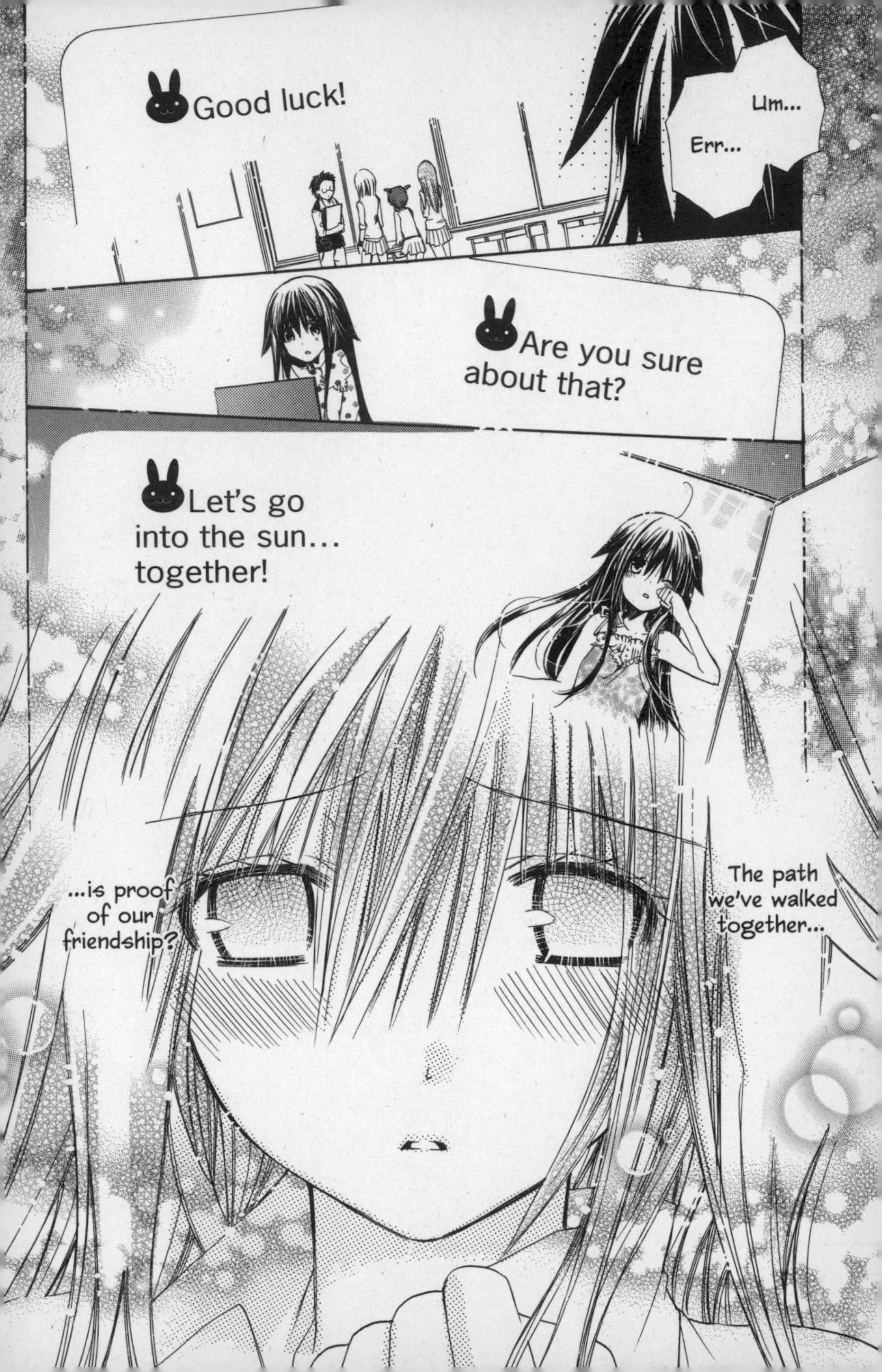
Um...
Err...
Good luck!
Are you sure about that?
Let's go into the sun... together!
The path we've walked together...
...is proof of our friendship?

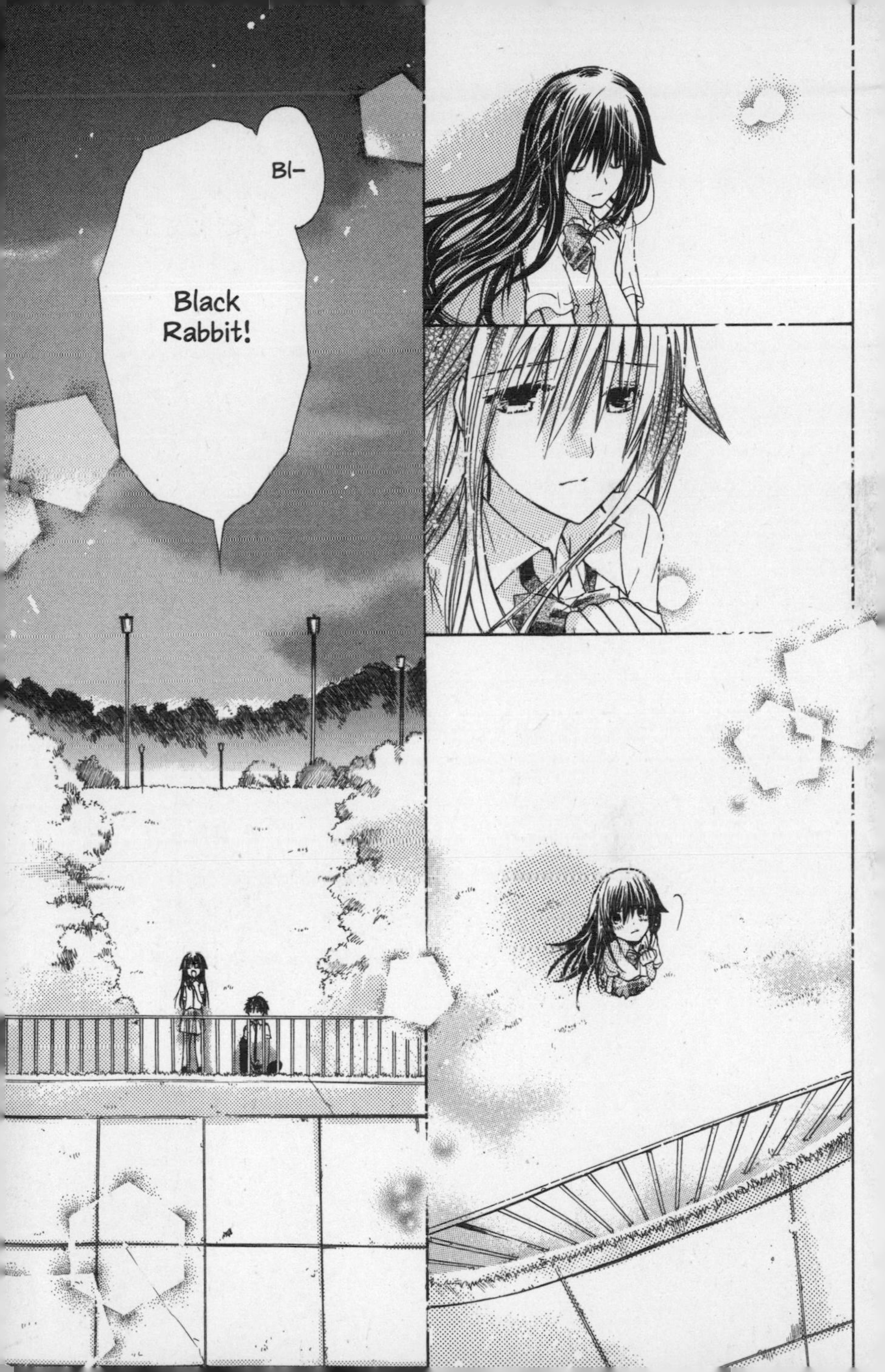
Bl-
Black Rabbit!

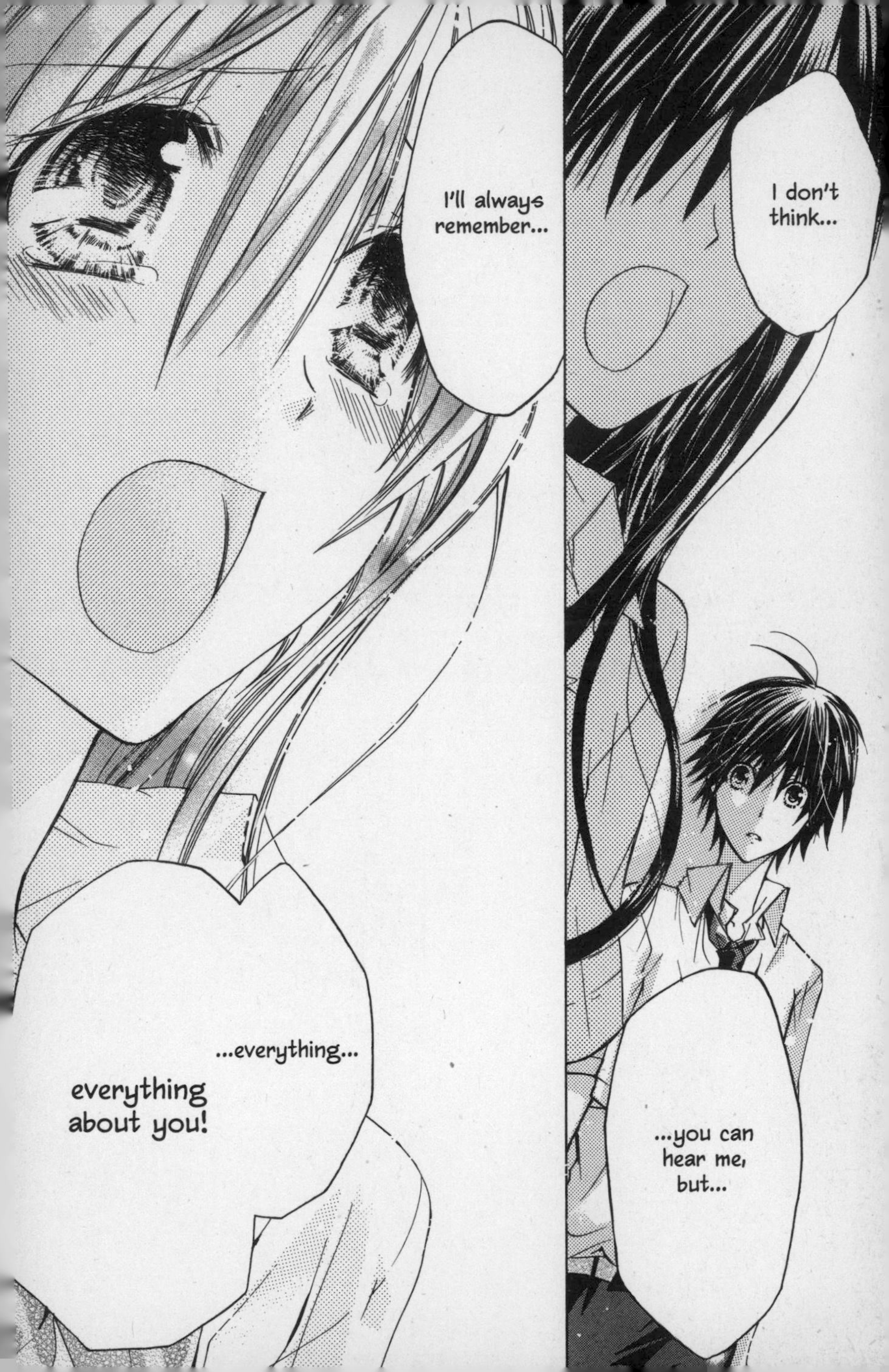
I don't think...
...you can hear me, but...
I'll always remember...
...everything...
everything about you!

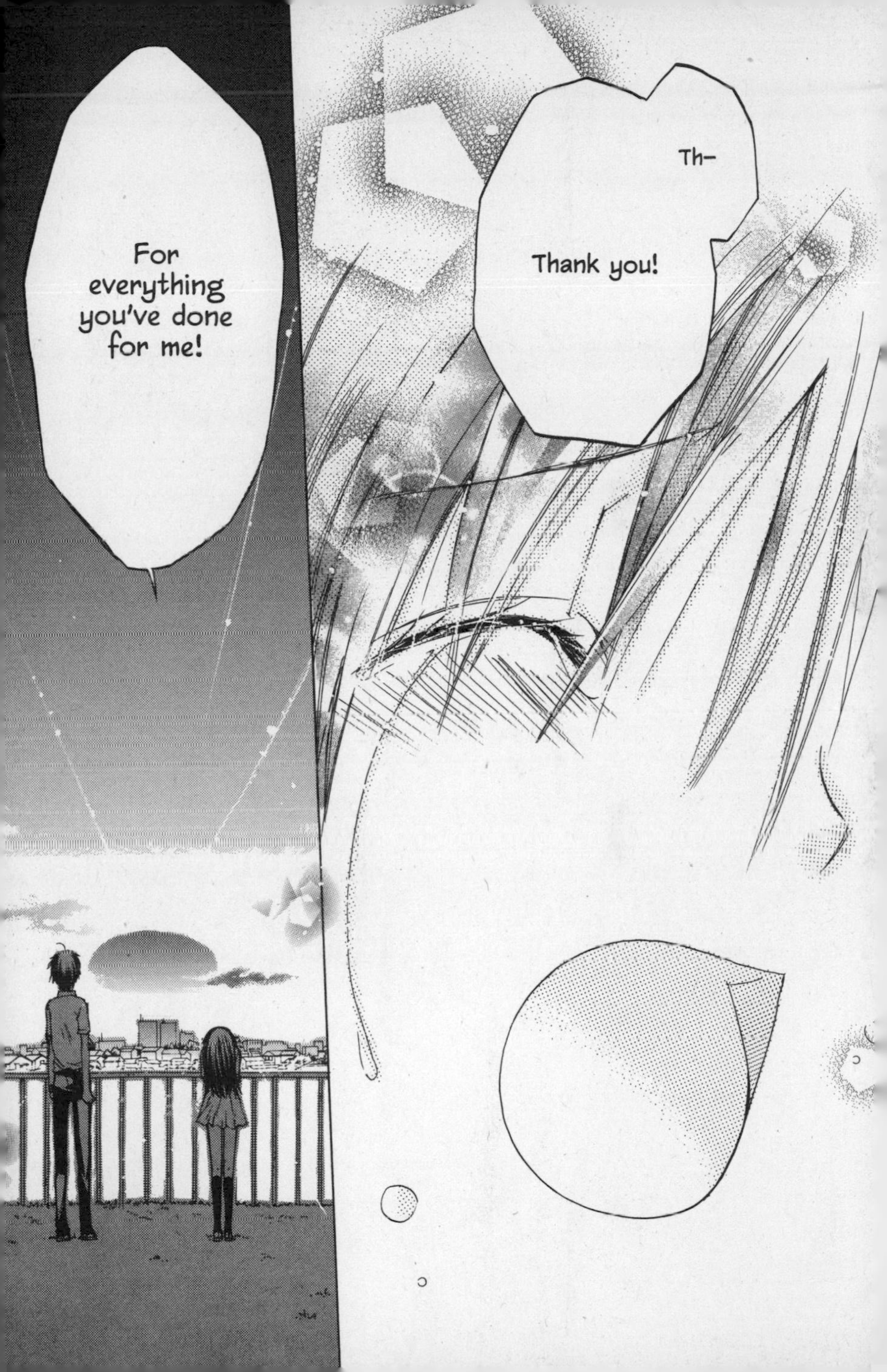
Th-
Thank you!
For everything you've done for me!

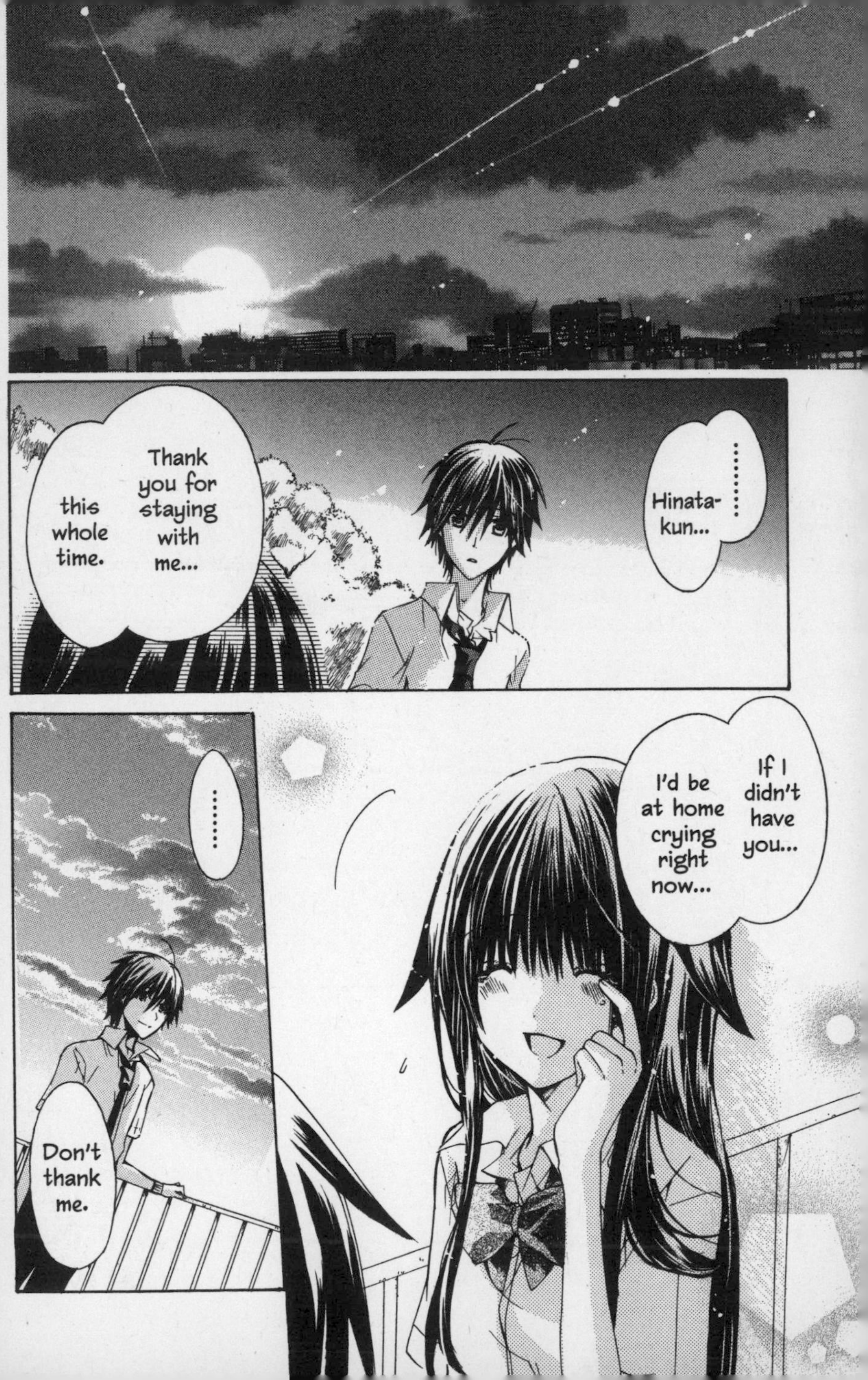

......
Hinata-kun...
Thank you for staying with me... this whole time.
If I didn't have you... I'd be at home crying right now...
......
Don't thank me.

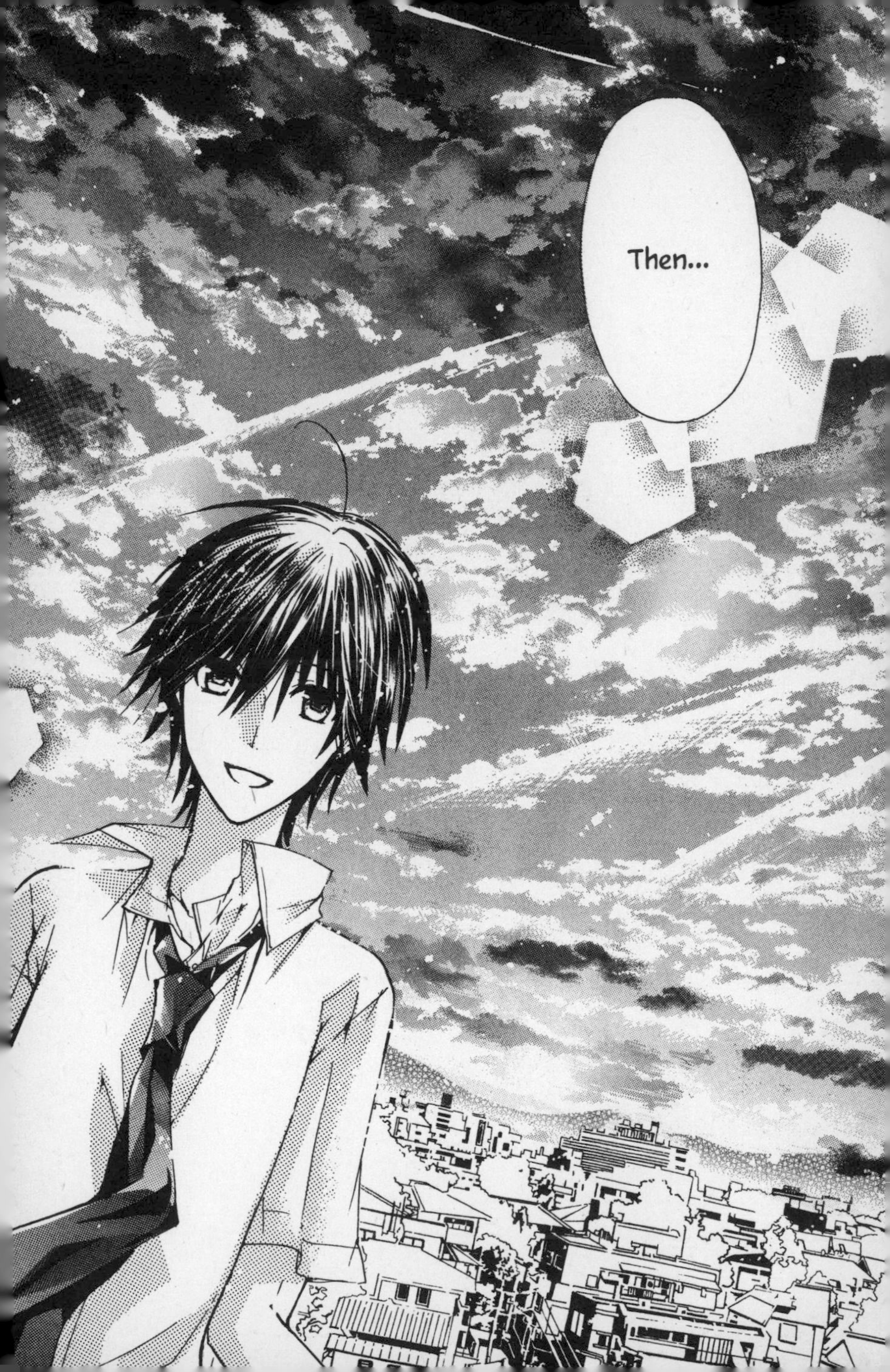
Then...

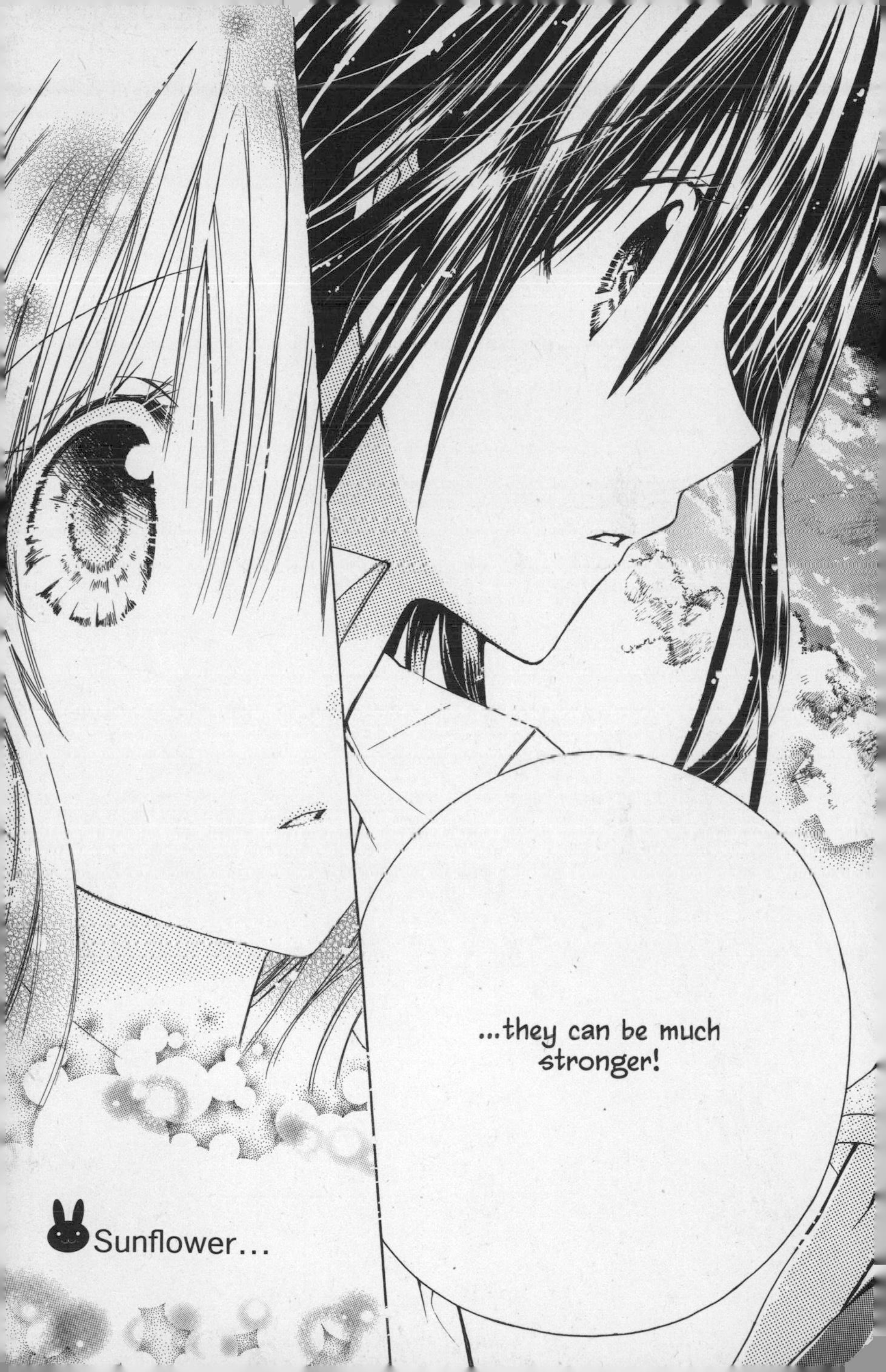
...they can be much stronger!
Sunflower...

People are weak
on their own,

but when they have friends to
lean on,

and friends who are important to
them,

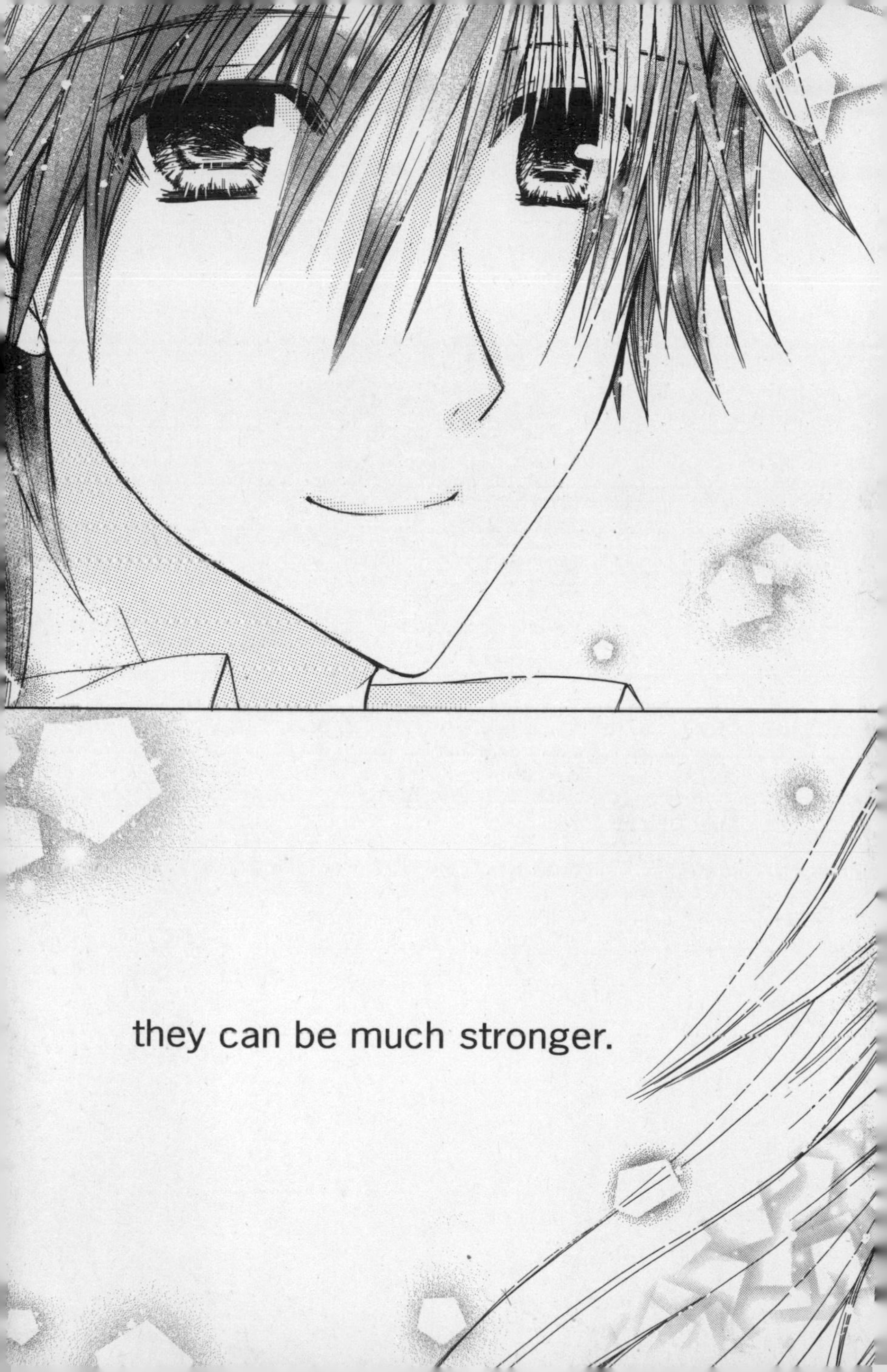
they can be much stronger.

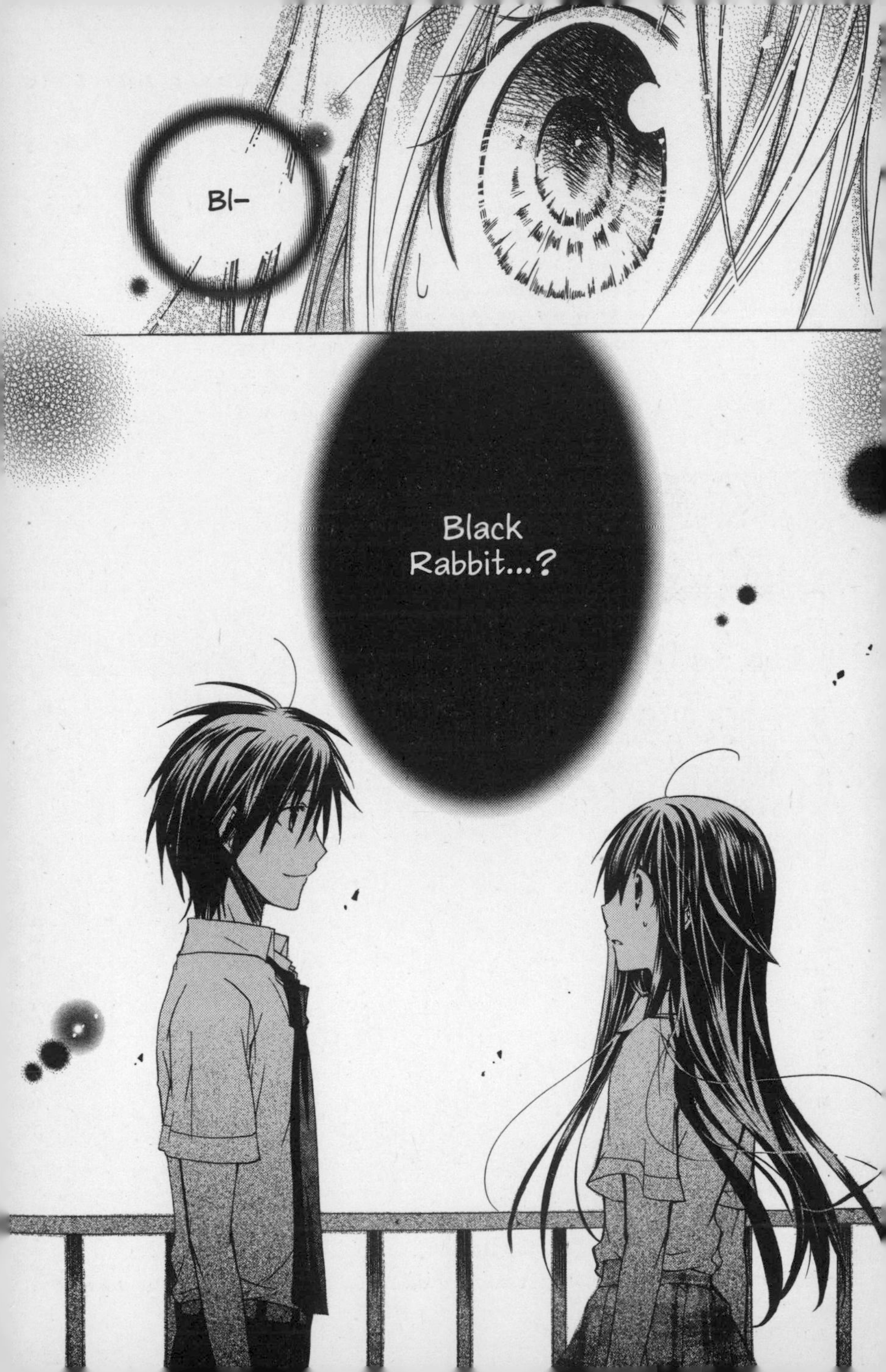
Bl-
Black Rabbit...?

Hello, this is Ema Tōyama. Thank you so much for reading *I Am Here!* How did you like it? This was my first manga with almost no funny scenes, and each episode was really hard for me to draw. But it also helped me learn how much fun it is to construct a story! Thank you to the Nakayoshi Editorial Department for making it possible for me to make this manga, to my editor who made it with me, and to everyone who read it! I hope to see you again in the next volume. See you!

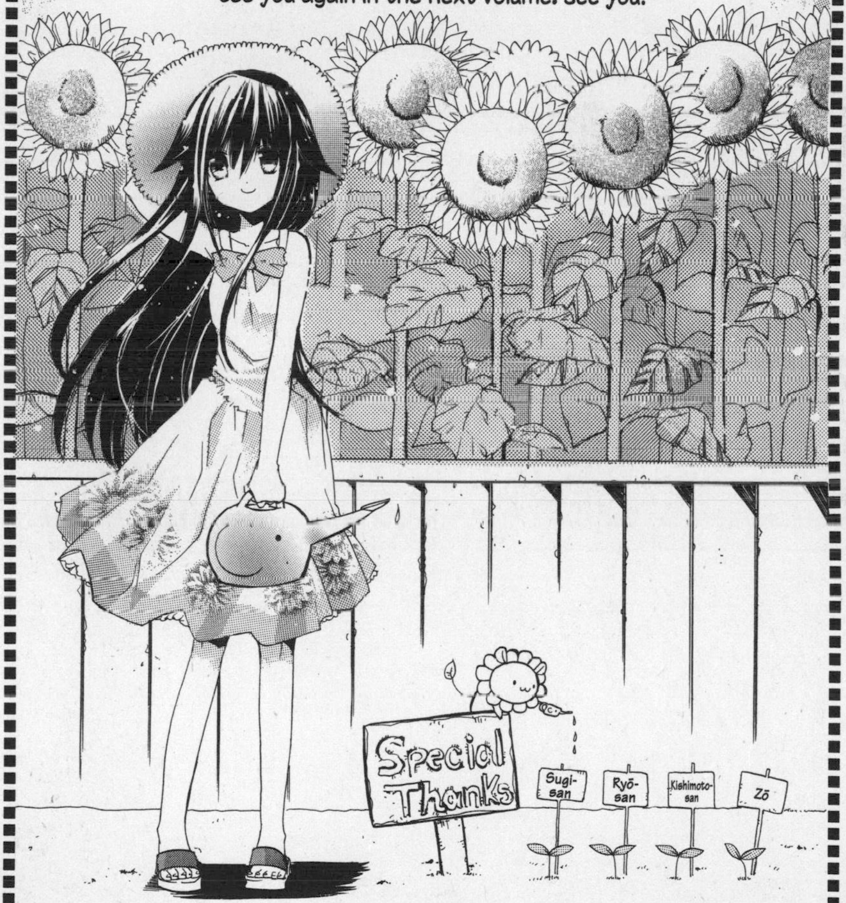
Special Thanks
Sugi-san
Ryō-san
Kishimoto-san
Zō

END

Please enjoy the following *I Am Here Extra!* ♪
It's a story from before Hinata finds Hikage.

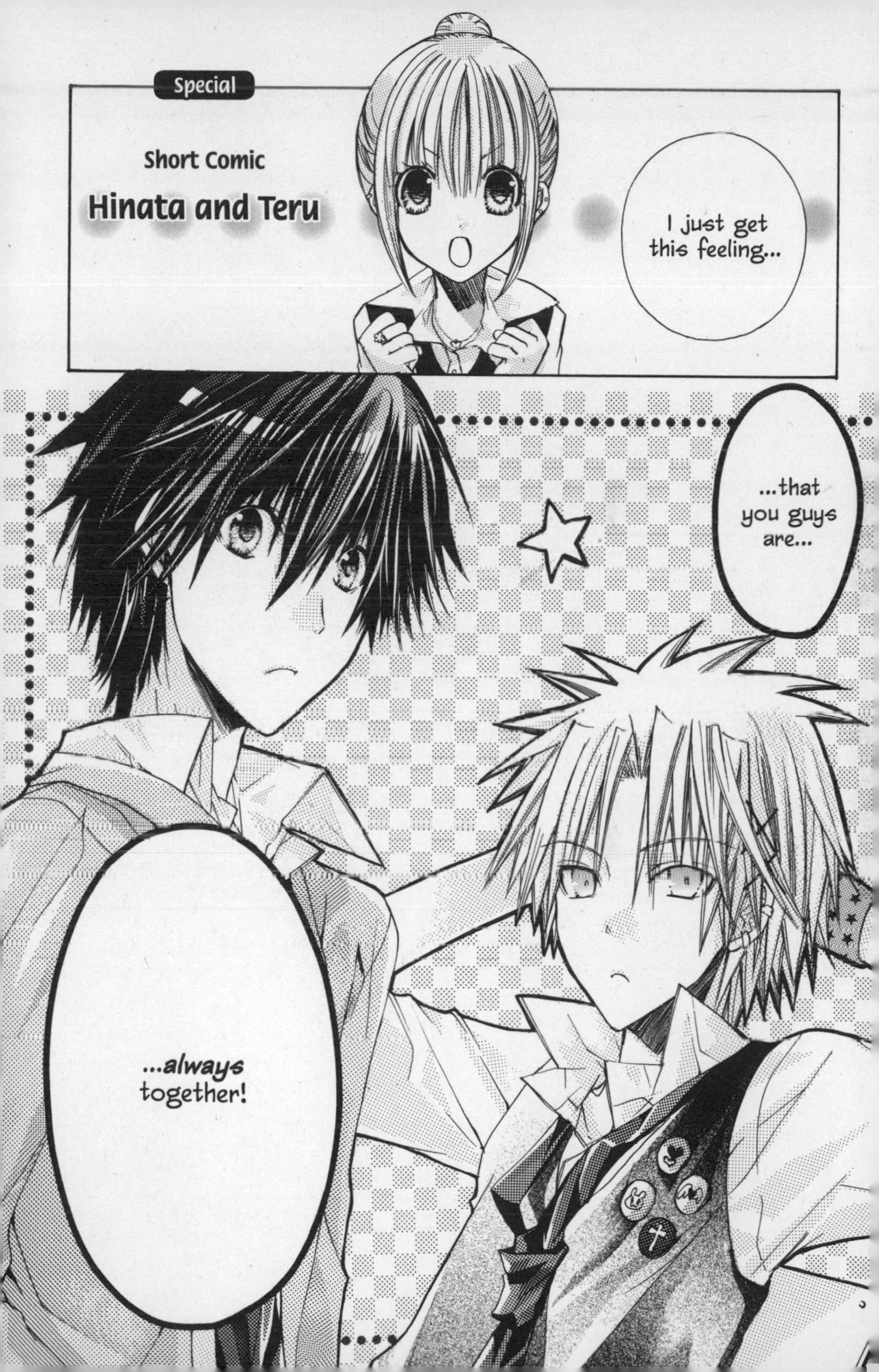
Special
Short Comic
Hinata and Teru
I just get this feeling...
...that you guys are...
...always together!

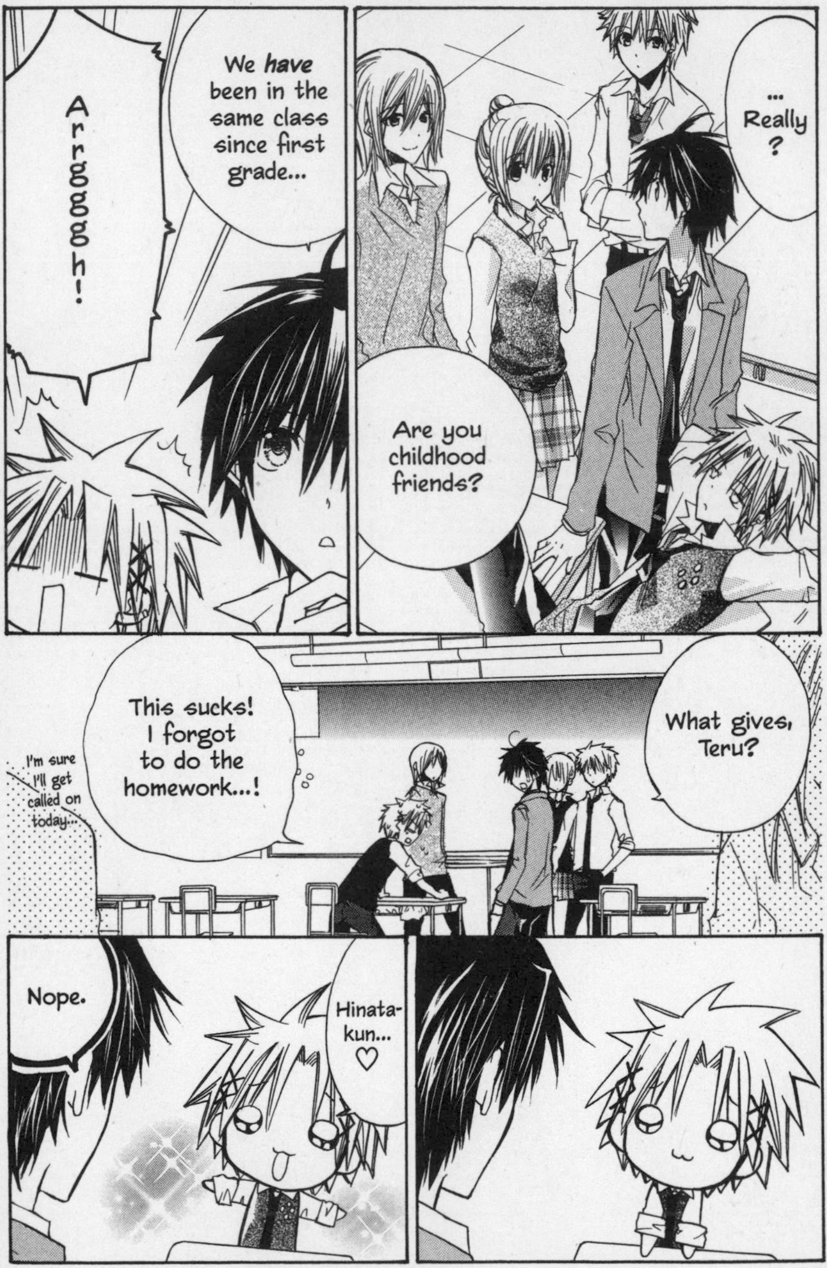
... Really?
Are you childhood friends?
We *have* been in the same class since first grade...
Arrgggh!
What gives, Teru?
This sucks! I forgot to do the homework...!
I'm sure I'll get called on today...
Hinata-kun... ♡
Nope.

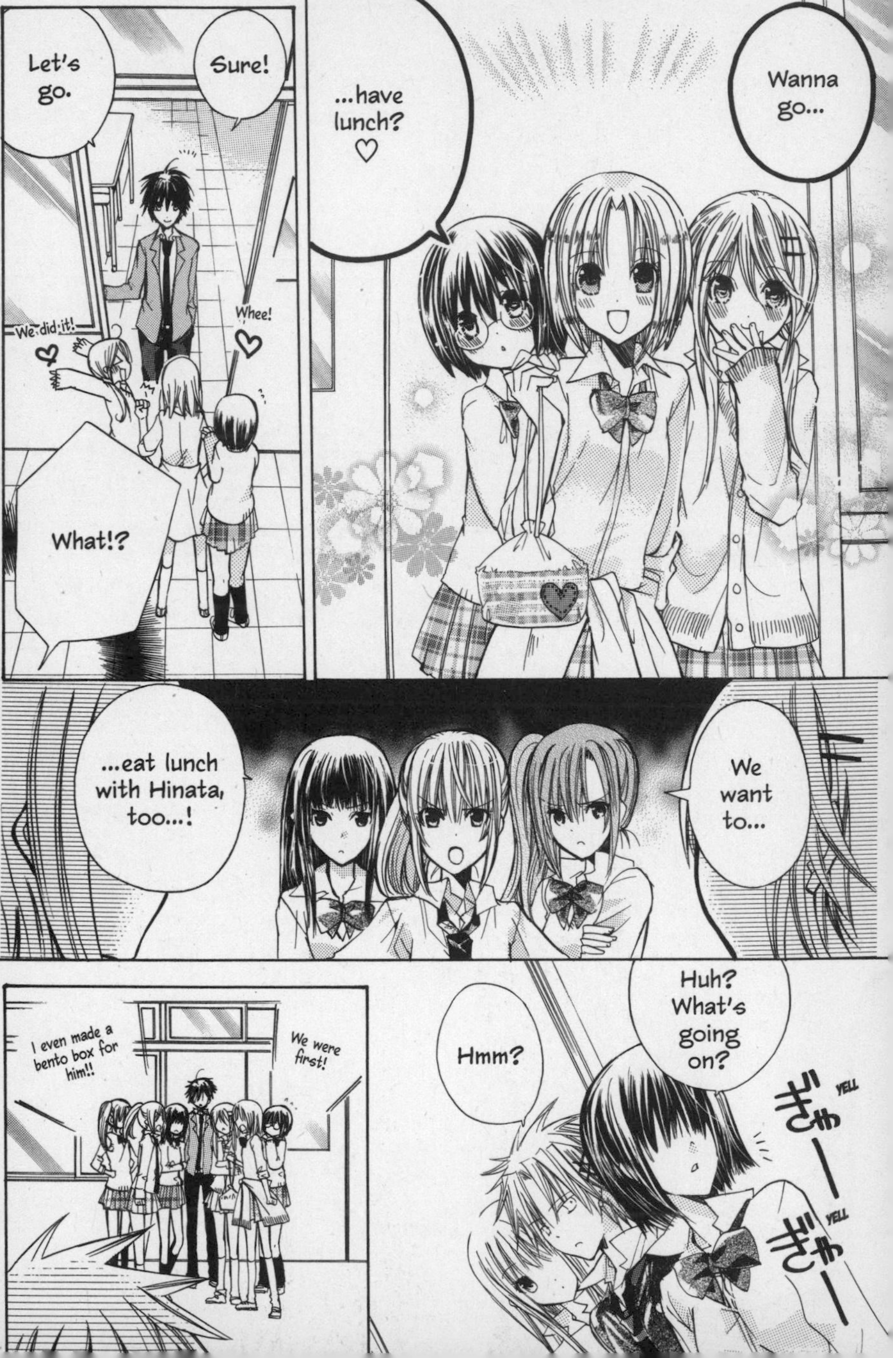

Wanna go...
...have lunch? ♡
Let's go.
Sure!
Whee! ♡
We did it! ♡
What!?
We want to...
...eat lunch with Hinata, too...!
Huh? What's going on?
Hmm?
ぎゃー YELL
ぎゃー YELL
We were first!
I even made a bento box for him!!

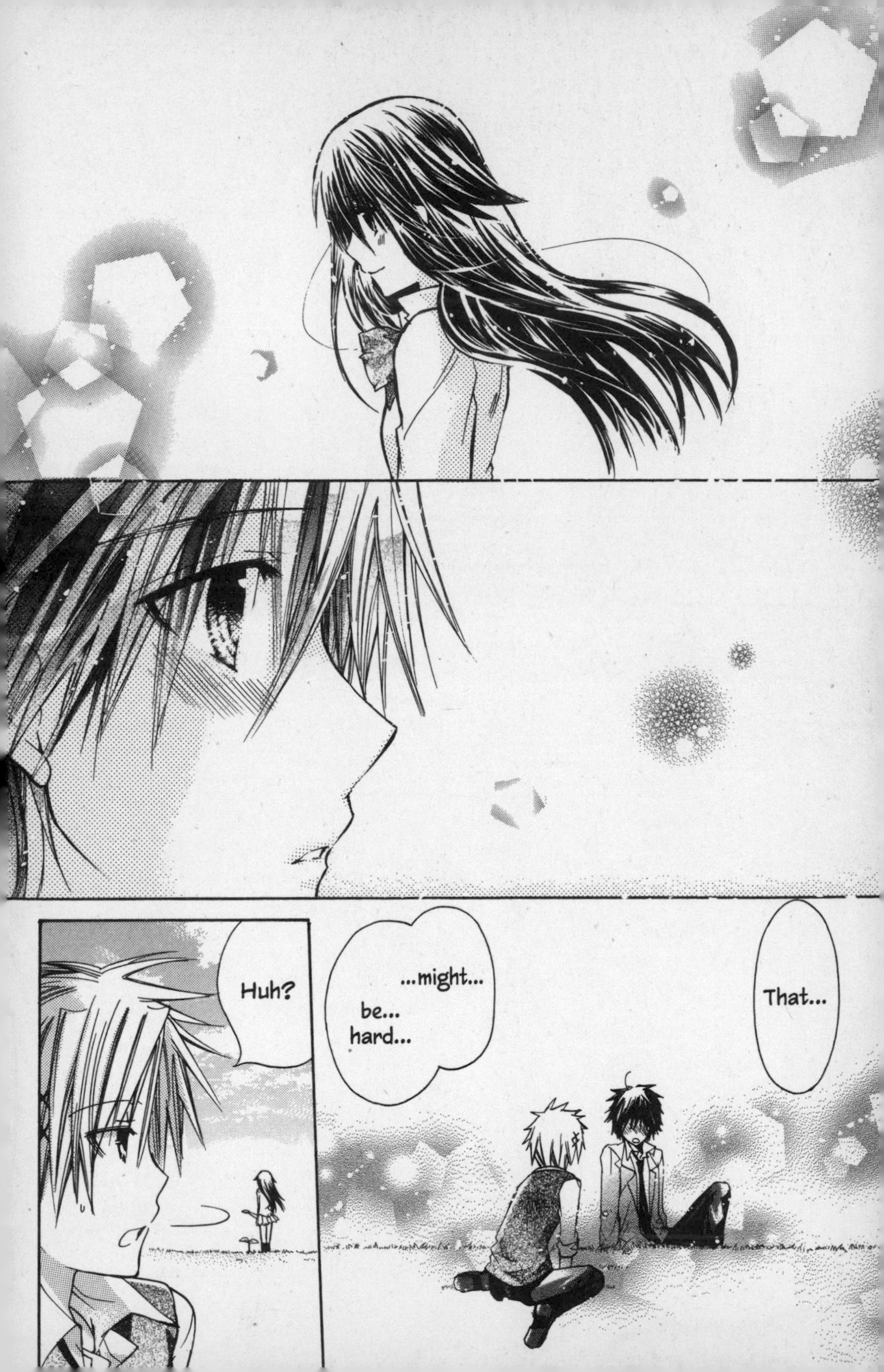

That...
...might... be... hard...
Huh?

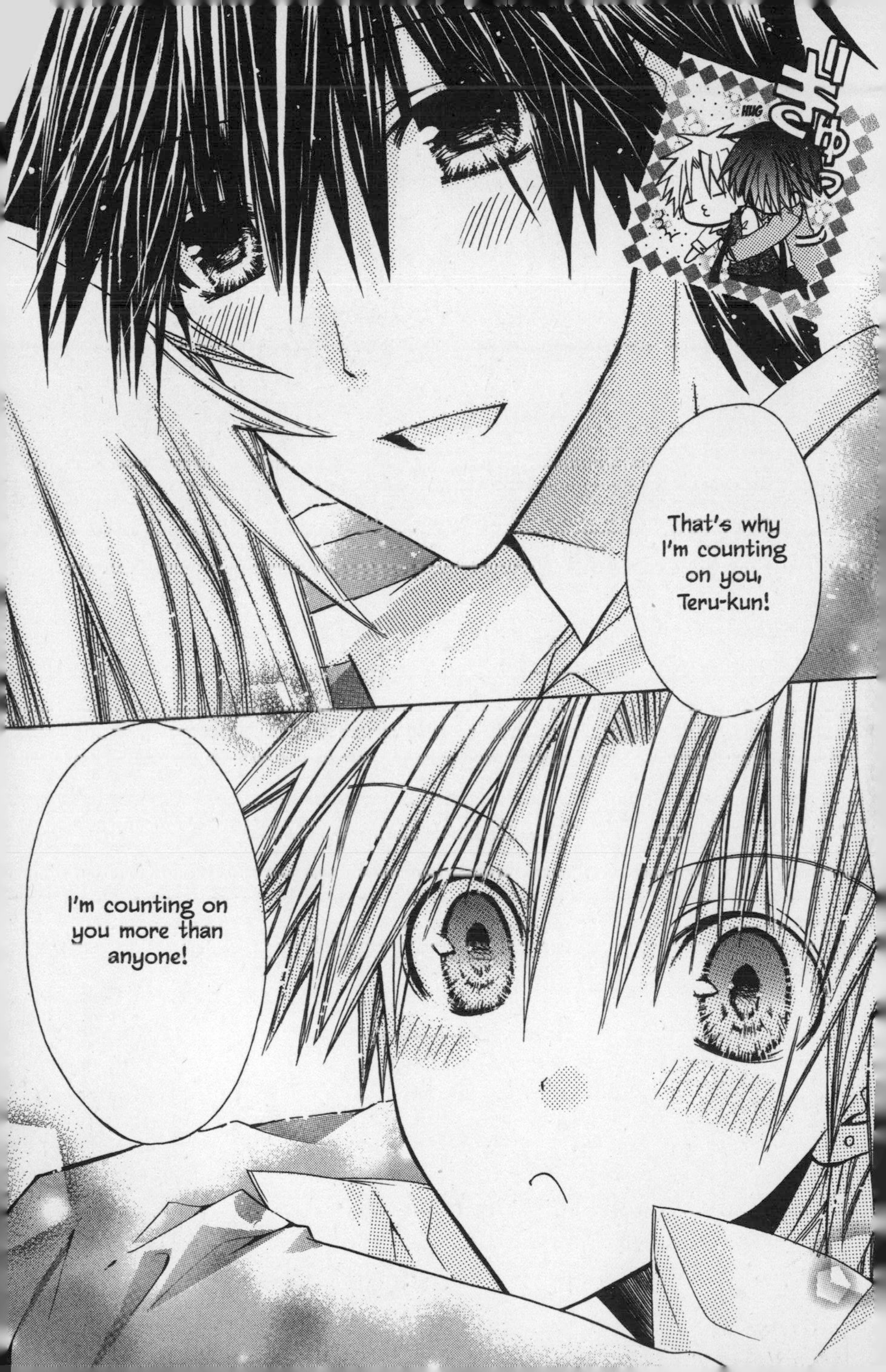
HUG
That's why I'm counting on you, Teru-kun!
I'm counting on you more than anyone!

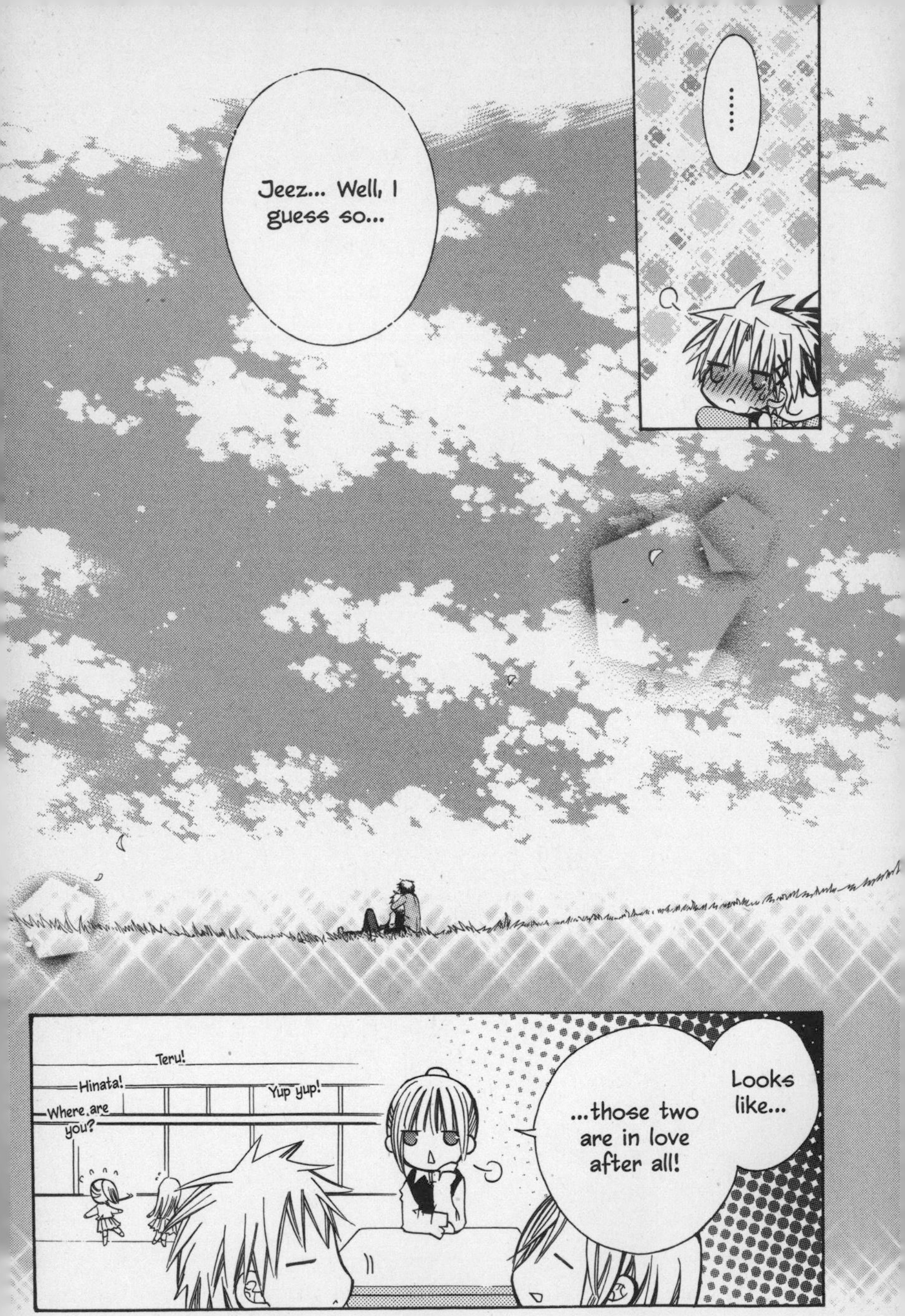
......
Jeez... Well, I guess so...
Looks like...
...those two are in love after all!
Yup yup!
Teru!
Hinata!
Where are you?

END

Hello, this is Ema Tōyama! Thank you for reading *I Am Here!* That was the longest special comic I've ever drawn, so I hope you enjoyed it! It feels like I had to draw a lot of scary-looking faces in this volume. Ha ha...I never thought that I would make a comic about bullying. But none of the elements were forced, and I think that they were all necessary for the story.

Ema Tōyama, January 2008.

Hikage from the Special

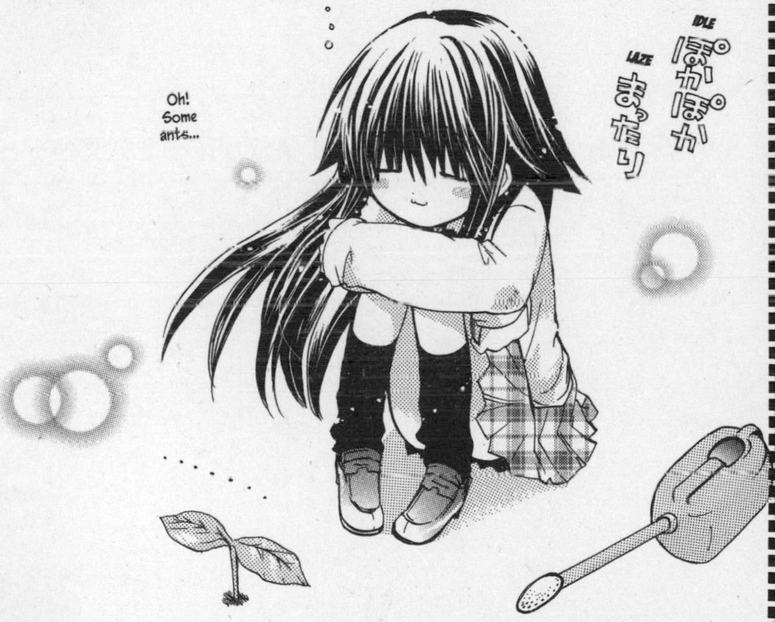

IDLE
ぽかぽか
LAZE
まったり
Oh! Some ants...

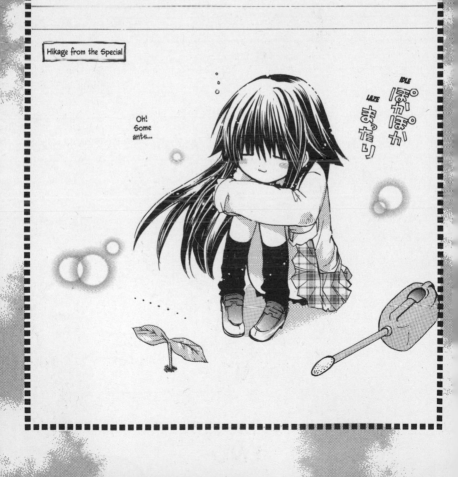

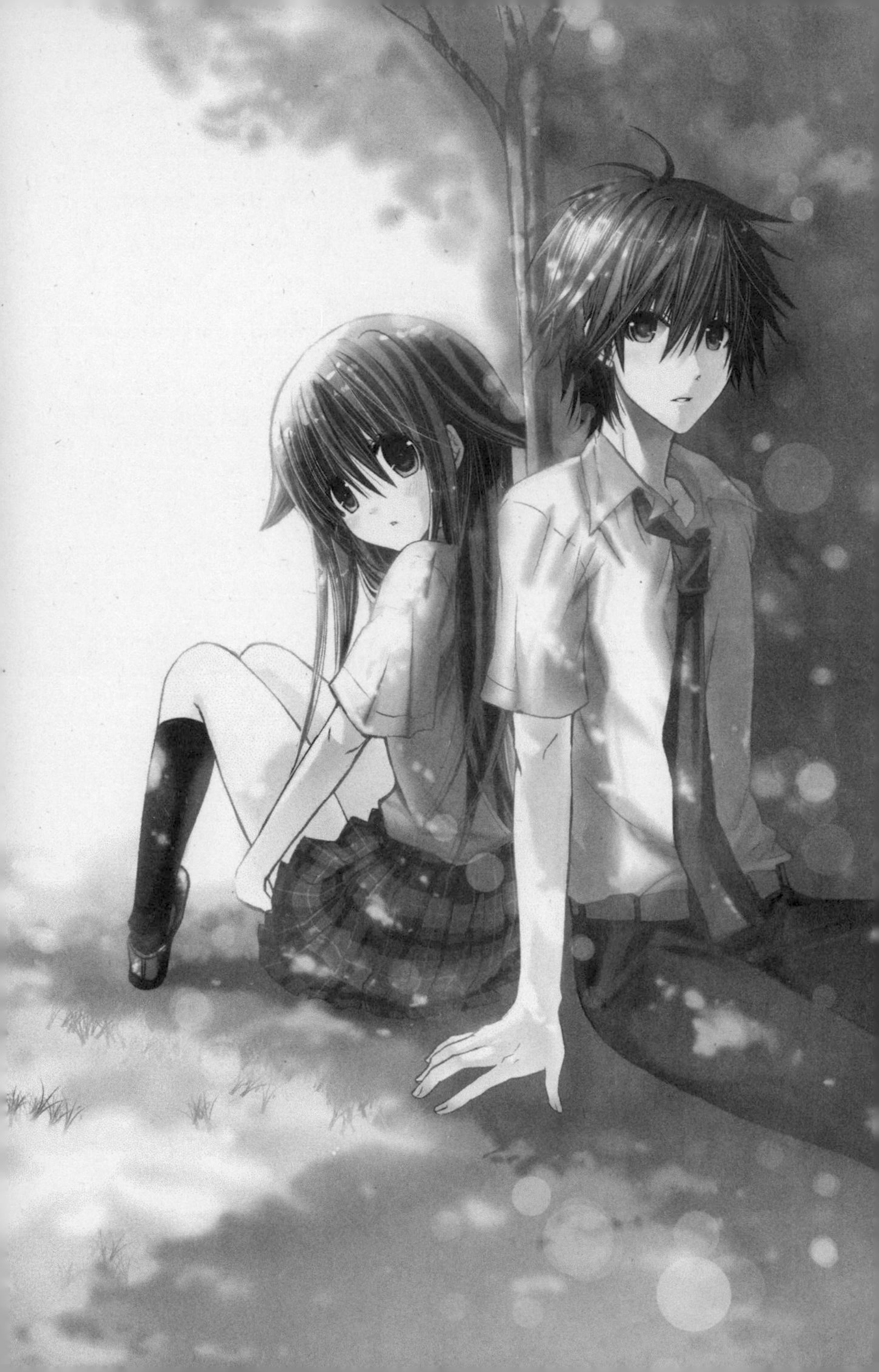

Translation Notes

Japanese is a tricky language for most Westerners, and translation is often more art than science. For your edification and reading pleasure, here are notes on some of the places where we could have gone in a different direction with our translation of the work, or where a Japanese cultural reference is used

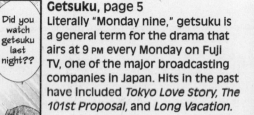

Getsuku, page 5

Literally "Monday nine," getsuku is a general term for the drama that airs at 9 PM every Monday on Fuji TV, one of the major broadcasting companies in Japan. Hits in the past have included *Tokyo Love Story*, *The 101st Proposal*, and *Long Vacation*.

Yukata, page 312

A *yukata* is a summer kimono usually made of cotton. People wearing *yukata* are a common sight in Japan at fireworks displays, *bon-odori* festivals, and other summer events.

Bento Box, page 393

A bento box is a single-portion takeout or home-packed meal common in Japanese cuisine. Commonly consisting of rice, fish or meat, and one or more pickled or cooked vegetable, it is common in manga for girls to make bento for boys that they like.

BY TOMOKO HAYAKAWA

It's a beautiful, expansive mansion, and four handsome, fifteen-year-old friends are allowed to live in it for free! But there is one condition—within three years the young men must take the owner's niece and transform her into a proper lady befitting the palace in which they all live! How hard can it be?

Enter Sunako Nakahara, the horror-movie-loving, pock-faced, frizzy-haired, fashion-illiterate hermit who has a tendency to break into explosive nosebleeds whenever she sees anyone attractive. This project is going to take far more than our four heroes ever expected; it needs a miracle!

Ages: 16 +

Special extras in each volume! Read them all!

VISIT WWW.KODANSHACOMICS.COM TO:

- View release date calendars for upcoming volumes
- Find out the latest about new Kodansha Comics series

SHUGO CHARA!

PEACH-PIT
CREATORS OF *DEARS* AND *ROZEN MAIDEN*

Everybody at Seiyo Elementary thinks that stylish and supercool Amu has it all. But nobody knows the real Amu, a shy girl who wishes she had the courage to truly be herself. Changing Amu's life is going to take more than wishes and dreams—it's going to take a little magic! One morning, Amu finds a surprise in her bed: three strange little eggs. Each egg contains a Guardian Character, an angel-like being who can give her the power to be someone new. With the help of her Guardian Characters, Amu is about to discover that her true self is even more amazing than she ever dreamed.

Special extras in each volume! Read them all!

VISIT WWW.KODANSHACOMICS.COM TO:

- View release date calendars for upcoming volumes
- Find out the latest about new Kodansha Comics series

KC
KODANSHA
COMICS

The Pretty Guardians are back!

Kodansha Comics is proud to present *Sailor Moon* with all new translations.

For more information, go to **www.kodanshacomics.com**